The Complete Book Of V·F·L Finals

From 1897 To The Present

The Complete Book Of V.F.L Finals

From 1897 To The Present

The Five Mile Press

Graeme Atkinson

THE FIVE MILE PRESS
379 Smith Street
Fitzroy Victoria 3065 Australia

First published 1973
Reprinted 1981, 1983
This edition published 1989

Cover design by Geoff Hocking
Cover photograph courtesy *The Herald* Melbourne, from the 1988 grand final

Typeset by Meredith Typesetters, Melbourne
Printed in Australia by The Book Printer

National Library of Australia
Cataloguing-in-Publication data

Atkinson, Graeme.
The complete book of VFL finals.

Rev. & expanded ed.
ISBN 0 86788 191 X.
1. Australian football – Matches. I. Atkinson, Graeme. Book of Australian rules finals. II. Title. III. Title: The book of Australian rules finals.

796.33'6'0994

Preface

In the sixteen years since this book was first published, readers have been kind enough to write to me and point out inaccuracies which, after they have been researched, have been incorporated. I invite readers again to write to me should they spot something wrong, or can tell me something interesting that I may have missed. There is, in fact, a strong interest in football history now that was not apparent when this book first came out and no club worth its salt would now be without its club historian.

This activity is pleasing, for sixteen years ago there were a mere two or three people who had such interests and they were, of course, of great help to me. The 'doyen' of football historians, Mr. Norm Sowdon, continues to provide invaluable assistance whilst the contributions of the late Mr. Cec. Mullin were similarly gratefully received. As well, I thank most sincerely my wife Karen for her typing and our four boys Brook, Jarrod, Brant and Joel for all their help.

There were, particularly for the period 1897-1910, many conflicting reports in the newspapers of the day concerning team placements, goalkickers etc., and I am pleased that the *Complete Book of VFL Finals* now seems to be the accepted record of the continuing battle for the coveted VFL premiership, a battle which, I trust, will forever continue.

I hope that this book will be a valuable reference for commentators, students of the game, and for the fan who has a 20 cent bet riding on the information herein.

Graeme Atkinson Melbourne March 1989.

Preface

[illegible]

[illegible]

[illegible]

[illegible]

Acknowledgements

The Author wishes to thank the editorial staff of the *Sun*, the *Herald*, the *Sporting Globe* and the *Age* for their valuable assistance in compiling this work. Thanks are also due to Mr. Norm. Sowden and the late Cec. Mullen.

Acknowledgements

The Author wishes to thank the editorial staff of the *Sun*, the *Herald*, the *Sporting Globe* and the *Age* for their valuable assistance in compiling this work. Thanks also — to [illegible], Norm. Sowden and the late Geo. Mullen.

Introduction

A history of the Victorian Football League's final series is the history of the struggle of a relatively obscure and minor football competition to become a great and dynamic athletic force.

From the time a handful of renegade clubs broke away from the Victorian Football Association to form their own competition, the League has grown in power and prestige until it now stands among the great sporting bodies of the world. The story of how this precocious youngster was conceived in disgruntled factionism quite properly belongs in a history of the game itself. But the phenomenal growth of an offspring to proportions well in excess of its parent can be traced, step by step and year by year, through the support and interest of the public in the end of the season fixtures, the finals.

There is something paradoxical about a game that describes itself as 'Australian' football and has as its controlling body the Australian 'National' Football Council and yet has as the ultimate goal for aspiring players a place in a VFL premiership team. It is reminiscent of the story of the young child whose father played international rugby. On being informed of the fact by the proud parent, the child pondered for a moment and then asked rather ingenuously, 'Gee, Dad, is that as good as playing for Carlton?'

Indeed. Is it as good as playing for Carlton? Fanatical prejudice in sport is not necessarily confined to international contests: as an impartial observer of an intensely partisan Australian Rules crowd would remark. Paradoxical or not (and one must remember that geographical boundaries do not necessarily dictate a footy fan's allegiance) there is a charisma about VFL football that is impossible to deny—or ignore. Melbourne may be the only place in the world that declares a public holiday for a horse race (no doubt were the grand final to be played on a weekday it would be honoured in similar fashion) but it is also the only place in the world where people are prepared to queue up for days in the rain and mud for the privilege of watching a contest between two teams in whom they had no interest four weeks previously, and who were, in fact, more than likely the objects of deadly enmity.

The facts speak for themselves. Each year there are fears expressed about falling attendances and the inroads other codes are making into the football scene. This may be so: but any sport that can muster a crowd of 100,000 to watch the grand final of an inter-club competition has a reasonable assurance of continuing success.

1897

At the end of the first VFL season, Geelong (after losing their first three games) headed the ladder with eleven wins, three losses, followed by Essendon, Melbourne and Collingwood, the latter being in the finals for the first of a record fifteen consecutive seasons.

The League's system of playing the finals in 1897 was for each of the first four teams to play each other once. The side with the best record in these three games would be then entitled to the premiership.

In the first of these second round games, Collingwood narrowly beat Melbourne in probably the finest game of the season, and Essendon staged a tremendous finish to beat Geelong. Collingwood showed vastly improved form, although Melbourne was sadly depleted through injuries. Geelong, leading by three goals in the last term, were unable to stop an Essendon comback in which Collins and Cleghorn reduced the deficit to six points before an error by Henry Young let Colin Campbell in for the equalising goal. Soon after, the Essendon men scored again to seal the game.

The following week, Essendon played brilliantly to account for Collingwood, kicking five goals five to three points in the last term. The same day at Fitzroy, Geelong finished the stronger to down Melbourne; a goal by James at the end winning the game for them.

Finally, on the third Saturday, Essendon one goal eight beat Melbourne eight points in the lowest scoring game on record, and became the first premier team, having beaten all the other finalists. In the other match, Geelong, by virtue of a brilliant first quarter burst of five goals two to nil, had just enough in hand to beat the tenacious Magpies by four points. This game, however, had no bearing on the result of the premiership, as it still left Geelong a game behind Essendon. Had Melbourne beaten Essendon though, a play-off game between Geelong and Essendon would have been required.

The Melbourne—Essendon game was extremely interesting. Melbourne hit the post on no fewer than three occasions but Essendon, too, had some bad luck when a goal by Waugh at the close of the second term was disallowed on the grounds that the bell had sounded before the kick had been taken. Edgar Croft was the Essendon hero, as it was he who scored the only goal of the game. Somewhat lucky, it came after Forbes (Essendon) had a ridiculously easy shot from only a slight distance out, and most of the players of both sides had returned to their positions in anticipation of a goal. Croft hadn't, however, and when a shocking miskick by Forbes slewed into the pocket, he was there to mark and kick his match-winning goal.

RESULTS

AUGUST 21 — FIRST ROUND FINALS

	1st	2nd	3rd	Final	
Essendon	0 . 2	1 . 4	1 . 4	5 . 5	(35)
Geelong	1 . 5	1 . 6	2 . 10	3 . 11	(29)

Geelong CG — Umpire Crapp
Attendance 5,000 — Gate £110

	1st	2nd	3rd	Final	
Collingwood	1 . 4	5 . 5	6 . 8	7 . 9	(51)
Melbourne	1 . 1	2 . 2	4 . 5	7 . 5	(47)

MCG — Umpire McCoy
Attendance 7,000 — Gate £174

BEST —	(Ess)	Forbes, Kearney, Vautin, Barry, Croft, T. Collins
	(Geel)	Sime, Pannam, Smith, Strickland, Leach, Gregory, Hailwood
	(Col)	McGuire, Burns, McCallum, Conway, Pontin, Brockwell
	(Melb)	McGinis, Wardill, Robinson, Moysey, Herring, Lewis, Leith
GOALS —	(Ess)	T. Collins (2), Campbell, Cleghorn, Wright
	(Geel)	Leith (4), Young, Geddes, McGinis
	(Col)	James, Quinn, White
	(Melb)	Dowell (2), Condon, Kay, J. F. Leach, T. Lee, McDonald

AUGUST 28 — SECOND ROUND FINALS

	1st	2nd	3rd	Final	
Essendon	1 . 1	2 . 8	4 . 11	9 . 16	(70)
Collingwood	1 . 2	2 . 2	4 . 3	4 . 6	(30)

MCG — Umpire McCoy
Attendance 8,000 — Gate £135

	1st	2nd	3rd	Final	
Geelong	0 . 3	2 . 8	4 . 9	5 . 16	(46)
Melbourne	3 . 2	4 . 4	5 . 6	5 . 7	(37)

FFG — Umpire Crapp
Attendance 4,000 — Gate £41

BEST —	(Ess)	Forbes, Cleghorn, Barry, Kearney, O'Loughlin
	(Col)	Calleson, Smith, Dowdell, Strickland, Sime
	(Geel)	Rankin, J. McShane, Young, Flynn, Burns, Pontin
	(Melb)	Moysey, Herring, McLeod, Healing, Sutton, F. Sheahan
GOALS —	(Ess)	Waugh (4), Gavin (2), Croft, Cochrane, Cleghorn
	(Col)	Calleson (2), Pannam, Tulloch
	(Geel)	James (2), Parkin, White, Young
	(Melb)	Moysey (2), McGinis, Steele, Young

SEPTEMBER 4 — THIRD ROUND FINALS

	1st	2nd	3rd	Final	
Essendon	0 . 1	0 . 4	1 . 6	1 . 8	(14)
Melbourne	0 . 3	0 . 4	0 . 6	0 . 8	(8)

SMCG — Umpire Hood
Attendance 3,800 — Gate £87

1897-1898

	1st	2nd	3rd	Final	
Geelong	5 . 2	7 . 2	8 4	8 . 4	(52)
Collingwood	0 . 0	2 6	3 7	6 . 12	(48)

EMCG — Umpire McCoy

Attendance 3,000 — Gate £95

BEST —	(Ess)	Forbes, Sykes, Cleghorn, Officer, Anderson, Barry, Wright
	(Melb)	McGinis, Lewis, Strachan, Wood, Herring, Wardill, Moodie, Hughes
	(Geel)	Rankin, Parkin, J. McShane, Young, McCallum, Conway, Flynn, Burns
	(Col)	Condon, Hailwood, Gregory, O'Brien, Calleson, Sime, Strickland
GOALS —	(Ess)	Croft
	(Melb)	—
	(Geel)	James (2), Quinn (2), White (2), Jas. McShane, Thompson
	(Col)	Condon (2), Kay, J. F. Leach, Smith, Stranger

FINALS TEAMS

The Essendon team in the final three matches came from the following players— 'Gus' Kearney, Ned Officer, J. Anderson, Tod Collins, Hugh Gavin, Colin Campbell, G. Cochrane, H. T. Wright, A. Cleghorn, George Vautin, Ted Kinnear, 'Tracker' Forbes, Norman Waugh, E. Croft, Pat O'Loughlin, 'Son' Barry, G. Martin, A. Sykes, J. M. Groves, G. Stuckey (Capt), G. Hastings, and D. Ferguson.

Note that in 1897–8, teams comprised twenty players (two extra followers).

Colin Campbell's only games for the season were in the three finals, as were G. Cochrane's. D. Ferguson's game in the second final was the only game he ever played for Essendon.*

Geelong players who participated in the three finals matches included— Peter Burns, C. Coles, J. Flynn (later Carlton skipper), E. Holligan, E. James, James McShane, Joe McShane, J. Parkin, A. Pontin, A. Quinn, E. W. Rankin (father of Cliff, who coached Geelong's first premiership team). A. Thompson, F. White, H. Young, S. L. Brockwell, J. Conway (Capt), E. G. Greeves (father of the first Brownlow Medallist), A. McCallum, Henry McShane, S. T. Maguire, A. Pincott.

Greeves' two games in the last two finals were his only games of the year.

1898

Deciding that their system of playing the finals was not entirely satisfactory, the VFL in 1898 came up with a new system that was little better. The eight teams played fourteen normal rounds (in which Essendon finished on top with eleven wins), then played three more rounds in two sections. That is, Section 'A' comprised the four teams who had finished first, third, fifth ,and seventh and Section 'B' comprised the other four teams who had finished second, fourth, sixth and eighth, each team playing the other three teams in their section, for leadership of that section. At the end of this, leader of section 'A' (which proved to be Fitzroy) met leader of section 'B' (Collingwood) in a play-off. Fitzroy, with a goal to Potter right at the end, won this and were then matched against Essendon, who had finished on top in the home and away games, but second to Fitzroy in the section 'A' contests. It was felt that the team finishing on top in the home and away games should receive another chance if it failed to win in its section contests, otherwise the first fourteen games would count virtually for nothing. The team which headed the home and home ladder was designated the minor premiers.

The grand final match between Fitzroy and Essendon was nearly not played. At that time the MCG was not the ground it is now and finals matches were spread around several different grounds; venues usually being agreed on by delegates of the opposing clubs. However, on this occasion Fitzroy would not take the risk of tossing for a ground and so the choice devolved upon the VFL. Both clubs had definite dislikes—Essendon refused to play at Collingwood, and Fitzroy refused to play at South Melbourne. The St. Kilda ground was suggested by the Fitzroy delegates to which Essendon's delegates replied that they would forfeit the game rather than play on that sub-standard surface. In fact, as late as the Friday night before the game, Essendon officials were still debating and questioning players on whether to participate. Finally, late that night, Essendon agreed to play at St. Kilda—and it later transpired that in actual fact they would have preferred to play at Fitzroy—their opponents' home ground!

At any rate, it all made little difference. Fitzroy won the toss, jumped into an early lead and held it all day to win by fifteen points. Star of the Fitzroy side was the Reverend S. S. Reid at half back. A year later he was dead—the first league footballer to die in the Boer War.

Umpire Keenan set a record in the first final when he umpired a second round game in his first season as a senior umpire.

RESULTS

SEPTEMBER 17 — FIRST PLAY OFF

	1st	2nd	3rd	Final	
Fitzroy	0 . 3	1 . 5	1 . 8	2 . 10	(22)
Collingwood	1 . 2	1 . 4	1 . 4	1 . 5	(11)

FCG — Umpire Keenan
Attendance 13,120 — Gate not available

BEST — (Fitz) M. Grace, Potter, Descrimes, McSpeerin, Noonan, Robinson, Fontaine, Sharp, J. Dalton
(Col) J. F. Leach, Pannam, Condon, Fell, Dowdell, Proudfoot
GOALS — (Fitz) Potter, Fontaine
(Col) Gillard

SEPTEMBER 24 — GRAND FINAL

	1st	2nd	3rd	Final	
Fitzroy	2 . 5	4 . 5	5 . 6	5 . 8	(38)
Essendon	1 . 0	3 . 1	3 . 2	3 . 5	(23)

		St.KCG Attendance 16,538	Umpire Crapp Gate not available
BEST	— (Fitz)	M. Grace, Reid, Drohan, Hickey, Potter, Sloan, Descrimes, McSpeerin, J. Grace.	
	(Ess)	Forbes, Stuckey, Jackson, Cleghorn, Hastings, Gavin, Officer, Kearney	
GOALS	— (Fitz)	J. Grace (2), M. Grace, McDougall, McSpeerin	
	(Ess)	T. Collins (2), Moore	

GRAND FINAL TEAMS

Fitzroy	B	Reid	Power	Nolan
	HB	Sloan (c)	Hickey	J. Dalton
	C	Drohan	Clarke	Robinson
	HF	Kiernan	A. Sharpe	W. Dalton
	F	Fontaine	J. Grace	McDougall
	Ruck	M. Grace	McSperrin	Potter
		Descrimes	Noonan	
Essendon	B	Kinnear	E. Officer	Gavin
	HB	Stuckey (c)	Anderson	Vautin
	C	Groves	Wright	Gray
	HF	T. Collins	Campbell	Hastings
	F	Tenbrink	Moore	Kearney
	Ruck	Forbes	Cleghorn	O'Loughlin
		Jackson	Barry	

1899

For the first time, VFL teams comprised only eighteen players instead of twenty, two ruckmen being dropped. At this stage, too, there were no reserves—in fact it was 1930 before even one was allowed. If players were lost through injury a side was naturally severely handicapped, although players who had gone off injured could return to the game at any time.

The finals system was the same as the previous season, Fitzroy with eleven wins and three losses finishing on top and also winning the contest in section 'A'. In section 'B' South Melbourne, who had finished sixth in the first round, suddenly found form and won their section honours. Thus the play-off (only the one was needed, as Fitzroy were minor premiers and section leaders) was between Fitzroy and South. This took place at St. Kilda, mainly because that ground's trustees demanded only ten per cent of the gate, compared to a demand for thirty-three and a third per cent at East Melbourne. The game was a thriller, but played in bad conditions. It rained for eleven hours before the game and only 4,800 attended. Fitzroy fielded their best side while South missed Purdy, and had Fraser, Jeanerett and Pleass obviously unfit. Bryce came in for only his second VFL game. South's failure to score more than one point against the wind plus several bad misses with it in the third quarter, did not help them and they went down in a heart-stopping finish by one point. Billy McSpeerin of Fitzroy scored what proved to be the winning goal fifteen minutes into the last quarter. This left South still with time to get up but Lampe kicked badly for a behind and then just before the bell kicked even more poorly and completely failed to score. Fitzroy, however, on the day and on the year's performances were a better side and they would probably have been unlucky to lose as two 'posters' were included in their score. Fitzroy kept three sides goalless during the year, equalling the record set by South Melbourne in 1897.

RESULTS

SEPTEMBER 16 — PLAY OFF AND GRAND FINAL

	1st	2nd	3rd	Final	
Fitzroy	0 . 1	2 . 4	2 . 6	3 . 9	(27)
South Melbourne	2 . 3	2 . 3	3 . 7	3 . 8	(26)

St.KCG
Attendance 4,823

Umpire Crapp
Gate not available

BEST —	(Fitz)	Hickey, Clarke, Deas, Jenkins, McEwen, Drohan, Robinson, Sloan
	(S. Melb)	Howson, Trimm, Davidson, Garbutt, Lampe, Pleass
GOALS —	(Fitz)	McSpeerin, M. Grace, Fontaine
	(S. Melb)	H. Lampe (2), Colgan

FINAL TEAMS

Fitzroy	B	McEwen	G. Moriarty	Jenkins
	HB	Deas	Hickey	Sloan (c)
	C	Drohan	Clarke	Robinson
	HF	Descrimes	Fontaine	W. Dalton
	F	McDougall	J. Grace	Cleary
	Ruck	M. Grace	Potter	McSpeerin *
South Melbourne	B	F. O'Hara	Adamson (c)	Armstrong
	HB	Trimm	Goding	Davidson
	C	J. O'Hara	Windley	Herb Howson
	HF	James	Lampe	Jeanerett
	F	Fraser	Colgan	Henley
	Ruck	Pleass	Garbutt	Bryce

One of South's ruckmen in this game was later to become more famous as a cricketer—Warwick Armstrong, captain of the great Australian teams of the early 1920's.

*C. Kiernan was selected but failed to turn up.

1900

The first year of the new century was a momentous one for the Melbourne club, who annexed their first VFL pennant after finishing only sixth on the ladder at the end of the home and home games. In fact, even including the finals, the premier team won only ten games in the whole season. But they found form at the right time and when the VFL's section system of playing for the premiership gave them their chance, they certainly seized it.

Fitzroy, eleven wins, three losses, actually finished atop the first round ladder, but only second to Essendon in section 'A'. In section 'B' Melbourne took top place on percentage from Collingwood and Geelong, mainly due to an enormous score against St. Kilda who had finished last on the home and home ladder and had only recently completed the remarkable record of losing forty-eight successive games. Melbourne and Essendon met in the first play-off final, with Fitzroy having the right to challenge the winner. Both sides had players out through injury or disqualification, but the changes did not really weaken either side. Jackson, Essendon, was carried off early in the first quarter with a ricked knee, leaving them a man short, and Melbourne raced on three goals before Essendon could score one. But the second quarter was a reversal of the first, with Melbourne able to score only a point. Essendon squandered several opportunities and their only goal of the quarter came from a free to Scott.

A high class third quarter in which Melbourne increased their score by three goals and Essendon by two was highlighted by a controversial kick by Essendon's Fred Hiskins. His shot was paid as a behind although most spectators behind the goals thought it was a six pointer. As Essendon eventually lost by only two points the decision was a vital one. Even more disheartening to the Don supporters was a mistake by George Stuckey. The Essendon captain ran right into goal unopposed and calmly tapped the ball through for a behind—he had mistaken the behind post for the goal post! The last quarter of the game was tremendously exciting as Essendon threw away chance after chance, scoring only one goal (to Fitzpatrick) from eight scoring shots. Melbourne's only goal, from a free to McGinis, was enough to enable them to hold the lead and win the game.

Melbourne (as challengers) met Fitzroy (minor premiers) in the final game of the season to decide the 1900 premiership. Melbourne had both wingmen, Sowden and E. Gardner, out injured for the big game, and omitted Strahan. In came Hay, C. Gardner and Ryan. Fitzroy, on the other hand, had almost a full list to choose from, with the exception of Fontaine (broken leg). They omitted Jack Deas and W. Dalton and brought in two stars in Jim Sharp and McSpeerin.

Wardill (Melbourne) won the toss, and kicked with a slight breeze. Lou Barker immediately eluded two Redleg defenders to notch first blood for Fitzroy, but Tim Ryan answered for Melbourne who led at the first change by fifteen points to ten.

The second term was rather a negative one, as the Melbourne rucks endeavoured to bog down the Fitzroy attacks, by forcing the ball continually out of bounds. So successful was this tactic that the Maroons could manage only one major—from a strong mark by Mick Grace—for the quarter. At the half-way mark, Melbourne still led by two points, and they increased this lead with a brilliant third term which netted them two goals three to nothing and, as it turned out, won them the game. With a long lead, Melbourne again adopted their second quarter tactics of keeping the ball as close to the boundary line as possible. Although they scored only two points themselves in the last term, they held Fitzroy to one goal five, which was sufficient to give them a four point win and the pennant. It was a shock defeat for the confident Fitzroy, who were aiming for a 'hat-trick' of premierships. In fact, anticipating victory, they had previously arranged for their carriages, decorated in maroon and blue and inscribed 'Fitzroy—Premiers 1900', to be waiting at the ground to race them to their premiership dance.

RESULTS

SEPTEMBER 15 — PLAY OFF

	1st	2nd	3rd	Final	
Melbourne	3 . 0	3 . 1	6 . 3	7 . 3	(45)
Essendon	1 . 1	2 . 5	4 . 6	5 . 13	(43)

SMCG — Umpire Crapp
Attendance 16,000 — Gate £300

BEST — (Melb) Wardill, Sowden, Young, Cumberland, Moodie, McGinis, Langley, Parkin, Herring
(Ess) Stuckey, Gavin, Thurgood, Collins, Barry, Martin, Griffith, Anderson, Officer, Kinnear

GOALS — (Melb) Wardill (3), McGinis (2), Leith, Cumberland
(Ess) Scott (2), Hiskins, Thurgood, Fitzpatrick

SEPTEMBER 22 — GRAND FINAL

	1st	2nd	3rd	Final	
Melbourne	2 . 3	2 . 5	4 . 8	4 . 10	(34)
Fitzroy	1 . 4	2 . 7	2 . 7	3 . 12	(30)

EMCG — Umpire Crapp
Attendance 20,181 — Gate £516

BEST — (Melb) McGinis, Moodie, Cumberland, Wardill, Purse, Langley, Parkin
(Fitz) M. Grace, Clarke, Robinson, Drohan, Moriarty, Hickey, Jenkins

GOALS — (Melb) Geddes, Ryan, Leith, Wardill
(Fitz) M. Grace (2), L. Barker

FINAL TEAMS

Melbourne				
	B	Herring	Scholl	L. Rippon
	HB	Parkin	Purse	McClelland
	C	C. Gardner	Young	H. Hay
	HF	Lewis	Leith	Langley
	F	Wardill (c)	Geddes	Ryan
	Ruck	Moodie	Cumberland	McGinis

1900-1901

Fitzroy	B	McEwen	Moriarty	Jenkins
	HB	J. Sharp	Sloan (c)	Hickey
	C	Drohan	Clarke	Robinson
	HF	Beauchamp	McDougall	L. Barker
	F	Descrimes	Brosnan	Kiernan
	Ruck	M. Grace	Potter	McSpeerin

1901

At the end of the 1901 home and away round, Geelong sat well clear on top of the ladder and looked to have an undeniable chance of winning their first VFL flag. But, as had happened before and has happened many times since, the favourtie crashed and it was Essendon (third) who gained the honours. But it must be admitted that Essendon, when they had the mighty Albert Thurgood in their line-up and in form, took a power of beating. Probably one of the best half-dozen footballers ever, Thurgood first played with Essendon in 1892, kicking fifty-six goals from centre-half-forward and ruck besides playing in defence. Before Thurgood came on the scene only once in the whole of Australia had a player kicked fifty goals in a season, and Thurgood followed up his feat with sixty-three and sixty-three in his next two seasons before going to Western Australia. There, amongst other feats, he once booted fifteen goals in one match—this in an era where five goals for an entire team was an excellent score! Standing six foot and weighing twelve stone ten pounds, Thurgood could run even time over 100 yards, was a brilliant mark and a tremendous kick, being credited with four kicks of over 100 yards!

When he returned from the West, Thurgood was for a long time out of form. But he came good again in 1901 and although he played only a few games that season, he was the dominating player in most of them. He had an accurate forward in Hiskins ahead of him in goals and with these two, Essendon's forward line was such a prolific scorer that the Dons became the first VFL team to kick over 1000 points in a season. They headed their section ladder and met Fitzroy in the first play-off.

The Fitzroy men had finished only sixth on the home and home ladder but as had happened with Melbourne the previous season they had come good at the vital time and headed their section. Essendon, however, just held on to eliminate them by one point in the play-off, due almost entirely to the play of Thurgood. He kicked five of the teams six goals (three from more than fifty yards), and shepherded for Larkin to score the other, and then as if that wasn't enough, he played at centre-half-back when Essendon kicked against the wind.

All in all it was probably one of the most brilliant individual displays in the history of the finals but the victory had one sour note when Fitzroy supporters claimed that Thurgood's first goal—a snap—had actually hit the post but been allowed as a goal. From reports at the time it appears that this was in fact true—and but for a goal umpire's error, Essendon would then and there have been eliminated from the contest for the premiership of 1901. But of course, they weren't and the following Saturday they met Collingwood in the grand final. The Woodsmen had beaten Geelong in their play-off and eliminated them under the VFL's new rule (in force for the first time this season) that the teams finishing second in their sections should also play-off and that the home and home round leaders (in this case Geelong) should have no further chance if they lost after failing to head their section. (This rule caused such discontent that the VFL changed it after only the one season).

Grand final day was fine and suited speedy Essendon who ran right away from Collingwood to win convincingly by four goals, although they had Kennedy and Peppard out and three others not completely fit. The Magpies missed their champion centre-half-back Monohan, who had been omitted because of lack of form, but he might have been the man to hold Thurgood in the aerial duels. As it turned out, the mighty Don forward kicked three goals, one from eighty-six yards out, which was more than the entire Collingwood score and he and Hugh Gavin were the best two men afield. In addition, Wright in the centre more than broke even with Fred Leach, the best centreman in the League in those years, and with these three winners down the goal-to-goal line, Essendon 'walked in'. Collingwood, in fact, did not kick a goal until the third quarter. But they had Proudfoot injured in the first quarter and Boyack also injured later, and these two were virtual passengers during the game.

RESULTS

AUGUST 31 — FIRST PLAY OFF

	1st	2nd	3rd	Final	
Essendon	0 . 1	3 . 2	5 . 7	6 . 10	(46)
Fitzroy	2 . 4	2 . 6	3 . 8	6 . 9	(45)

Victoria Park — Umpire Crapp
Attendance 15,000 — Gate £340

BEST —	(Ess)	Thurgood, Stuckey, Griffith, Gavin, Kinnear, Wright, Hiskins
	(Fitz)	Fontaine, Moriarty, Sloan, Drohan, Smith, Kiernan, Brosnan
GOALS —	(Ess)	Thurgood (5), Larkin
	(Fitz)	Brosnan (2), J. Sharp (2), A. Sharpe (2)

AUGUST 31 — SECOND PLAY OFF

	1st	2nd	3rd	Final	
Collingwood	2 . 3	3 . 5	5 . 8	6 . 9	(45)
Geelong	0 . 2	1 . 3	3 . 4	3 . 6	(24)

EMCG — Umpire Gibson
Attendance 10,000 — Gate £240

BEST —	(Col)	J. F. Leach, Hyman, Dow, Dummett, Hailwood, Tulloch, Martin, Rowell
	(Geel)	Young, O'Loughlin, Bowey, Flynn, Burns, McKeegan, Donaghy, Holligan
GOALS —	(Col)	Smith (2), Bryce, Morgan, Rowell, Tulloch
	(Geel)	Bennion, E. Rankin, Woods

1901-1902

SEPTEMBER 7 — GRAND FINAL

	1st	2nd	3rd	Final	
Essendon	3 . 0	5 . 2	5 . 4	6 . 7	(43)
Collingwood	0 . 1	0 . 3	2 . 3	2 . 4	(16)

SMCG — Umpire Crapp

Attendance 30,000 — Gate £639

BEST —	(Ess)	Gavin, Thurgood, Wright, Griffith, McKenzie, Kinnear
	(Col)	Morgan, Hailwood, Fell, Pannam, J. F. Leach, Boyack, Farrell
GOALS —	(Ess)	Thurgood (3), Kinnear, Martin, McKenzie
	(Col)	Bryce (2)

GRAND FINAL TEAMS

Essendon	B	Mann	Anderson	M. Collins
	HB	Barry	Gavin	T. Collins
	C	Hastings	Wright	Vollugi
	HF	Hiskins	Thurgood	Larkin
	F	Martin	Kinnear	Stuckey * (c)
	Ruck	Robinson	McKenzie	Griffith
Collingwood	B	Dow	Proudfoot (c)	Dummett
	HB	Hyman	Tulloch	McCulloch
	C	Pannam	J. Leach	Martin **
	HF	Bryce	Rowell	A. Leach
	F	Farrell	Smith	Morgan
	Ruck	Fell	Hailwood	Boyack

* George Stuckey, Essendon's captain, was a unique sportsman in that he captained football premiership sides, played interstate cricket for Victoria—and won a Stawell Gift!

** Killed in World War I.

1902

A new style game gave Collingwood the pennant in 1902. Previously the game was mostly mark and kick but the perfecting of the previously almost unknown stab-kick by Collingwood led to a faster play-on style, where the ball was carried rapidly from player to player as each got clear and made position for the pass. Collingwood players had experimented with the new kick during a mid-season tour of Tasmania and when they returned to Melbourne on the Saturday morning of a match with Geelong and had trouble regaining their land legs, they realised that the new kick could be the secret weapon to defeat Geelong. And in fact it was. The small Magpies ran rings around Geelong and began a triumphant march to their first League premiership. They finished atop the ladder with twelve wins and two losses, won all three of their section matches, and were drawn to contest Fitzroy in the first of the semi-finals. In that match, to general surpirse Fitzroy proved too strong and held on to win by three goals— beating Collingwood at their own short game which most clubs were by this time using. Collingwood, however, as minor premiers, had a second chance. In the other semi-final played on the same day, Essendon nine goals seven eliminated Melbourne seven goals nine, but the Demons (or Redlegs as they were then known) had three of their best men out injured.

The two winners then met for the right to play Collingwood and before 24,110 people and after a hard-fought game Essendon defeated Fitzroy by an unconvincing eleven points, but it cost them two good players in Vollugi and Baxter, the latter suffering injuries which put him out of the grand final, and the former injuries which hampered him in that game. For the grand final Essendon brought in O'Loughlin for Baxter (injured) Monohan (injured previous match) was unable to take his place in Collingwood's side and Incoll replaced him.

The grand final, the first ever at the MCG, was attended by 35,202 people—only three times previously had such a crowd witnessed a football game in Australia—the record was 37,200, Essendon versus South Melbourne in 1891. Essendon, wearing white knicks (the first time these had been worn in any final) matched Collingwood for the first half, and were only a point behind at half-time. They could have even been ahead but for effective tactics by Collingwood in having two men on Essendon's Thurgood at all times. With Monohan out of the side, the regular centreman, McCormack, took on the job of minding Thurgood in the first half and did the task manfully. But at half-time Collingwood switched Fred Leach to centre-half-back on the Essendon champion, with instructions to try to spoil at all times, and so well did Leach play that Thurgood faded right out of the game. Collingwood added six goals four to one goal two in the last half to win, easing up by thirty-three points and became the first of a long line of Collingwood VFL premiership teams. It may be noted that 'rumour has it that the test cricket games were still in progress, when Collingwood began their preparations for the (1902) season's battles.'

RESULTS

SEPTEMBER 6 — FIRST SEMI-FINAL

	1st	2nd	3rd	Final	
Fitzroy	2 . 3	5 . 5	8 . 9	9 . 10	(64)
Collingwood	0 . 5	1 . 7	2 . 8	6 . 12	(48)

MCG — Umpire Gibson
Attendance 13,000 — Gate not available

BEST — (Fitz) McSpeerin, R. Smith, Sharpe, Brosnan, Trotter, G. Moriarty
(Col) Tulloch, Rush, E. Lockwood, J. F. Leach, Hailwood, Fell, Condon, Monohan (till injured)

GOALS — (Fitz) McSpeerin (3), Brosnan (2), Naismith (2), Trotter, Milne
(Col) E. Lockwood (3), Rowell (2), Monohan

SEPTEMBER 6 — SECOND SEMI-FINAL

	1st	2nd	3rd	Final	
Essendon	2 . 2	3 . 5	5 . 7	9 . 7	(61)
Melbourne	3 . 3	6 . 4	6 . 8	7 . 9	(51)

1902

	Carlton CG	Umpire Crapp
	Attendance 8,000	Gate not available

BEST —	(Ess)	Martin, Gavin, McKenzie, Griffith, Thurgood, Kennedy, Larkin
	(Melb)	Langley, Moodie, Anderson, Hocking, Leith, Sowden
GOALS —	(Ess)	Thurgood (3), McKenzie (2), Larkin (2), Holligan, Geggie
	(Melb)	Ryan (3), Leith (2), Rainey, Langley

SEPTEMBER 13 — PRELIMINARY FINAL

	1st	2nd	3rd	Final	
Essendon	2 . 5	4 . 5	6 . 7	6 . 9	(45)
Fitzroy	1 . 2	3 . 7	3 . 8	4 . 10	(34)
	MCG		Umpire Crapp		
	Attendance 26,000		Gate £600		

BEST —	(Ess)	Anderson, Kennedy, Gavin, Thurgood, Vollugi, Hastings, Baxter
	(Fitz)	Barker, A. B. Sharp, R. Smith, Beauchamp, Brosnan, J. Sharp
GOALS —	(Ess)	Thurgood (2), Hiskins (2), Martin, Hutchens
	(Fitz)	Wilkinson, Milne, Barker, Trotter

SEPTEMBER 20 — GRAND FINAL

	1st	2nd	3rd	Final	
Collingwood	1 . 2	3 . 2	5 . 5	9 . 6	(60)
Essendon	1 . 3	2 . 7	3 . 7	3 . 9	(27)
	MCG		Umpire Crapp		
	Attendance 35,202 (record)		Gate £891		

BEST —	(Col)	Hailwood, Pannam, Allan, J. F. Leach, McCormack, Rush, Fell, Condon, Tulloch, Rowell, E. Lockwood
	(Ess)	McKenzie, Hutchens, Anderson, Hastings, Gavin, Mann, Kinnear, Larkin, Wright, Thurgood
GOALS —	(Col)	E. Lockwood (3), Rowell (3), Pears, J. Allan, Angus
	(Ess)	Hiskins, P. O'Loughlin, Thurgood

GRAND FINAL TEAMS

Collingwood	B	G. Lockwood	Proudfoot	Fell
	HB	Rush	J. F. Leach	Dummett
	C	Pannam	C. McCormack	Allen
	HF	Incoll	Rowell	Angus
	F	Pears	E. Lockwood	A. Leach
	Ruck	Hailwood	Tulloch (c)	Condon
Essendon	B	F. Mann	Geggie	Robinson
	HB	Anderson	Gavin (c)	Hastings
	C	Kennedy	Wright	Vollugi
	HF	Hiskins	Thurgood	Hutchens
	F	Larkin	Kinnear	O'Loughlin
	Ruck	Martin	McKenzie	Griffith

Collingwood's premier side included no fewer than seven first-year players. The grand final was the fifth in succession umpired by Ivo. Crapp.

1903

Essendon (second in 1902) slumped to sixth in 1903 and Collingwood and Fitzroy were 'streets' ahead of the other teams in standings on the home and home ladder, Collingwood losing only two games and Fitzroy three. The VFL decided to abandon the 'section' system of finals and instead first team met third in a play-off and second met fourth. As usual, the minor premiers if they lost, had the right to challenge. Carlton, under the coaching of ex-Fitzroy champion, Jack Worrall, leapt into the Four for the first time and other clubs began to investigate the idea of appointing coaches. Until Worrall took over at Carlton, captains and vice-captains usually supervised training often haphazardly—and coaches were almost unknown.

Worrall's iron discipline was to bring a rich reward in later years, and even in 1903 Carlton went within one kick of downing Collingwood in their semi-final. Inexperience in the last term cost them the game after they had led by seven points at the change, despite having three stars in Roland, Leeds and Topping, all unable to play. Collingwood rushed on two quick goals to snatch the lead in the last quarter, then Sullivan had an angle shot right on the final bell which missed, and left Collingwood winning by four points. In the other semi-final on the same day, Fitzroy annihilated Geelong to win by fifty-two points, a record margin for a final, and it looked to be Fitzroy's premiership there for the asking. Collingwood, however, had other ideas.

Before 32,363 people in the grand final, on an extremely hot day, they struggled to a four point lead at three-quarter time and then added a goal in the last term to leave them seemingly safe. But Fitzroy came with a dash at the last. Milne goaled and the difference was three points. Then Beauchamp in the centre passed to Trotter who found Brosnan thirty yards out as the bell rang. Brosnan, Fitzroy's captain, lined up for the most vital kick of his career—and missed the goal by inches. It was Fitzroy's second easy miss of the quarter, and it gave Collingwood their second successive premiership. Their success was not over popular, however, as many veiled rumours had been circulating that some players at Collingwood were actually paid to play!

RESULTS

SEPTEMBER 5 — FIRST SEMI-FINAL

	1st	2nd	3rd	Final
Collingwood	0 . 1	2 . 2	2 . 2	4 . 3 (27)
Carlton	1 . 3	1 . 3	3 . 3	3 . 5 (23)

		FCG	Umpire Crapp
		Attendance 16,600	Gate £228

BEST —	(Col)	Angus, Incoll, A. Leach, McCormack, Drohan, Fell
	(Carl)	Walton, Ross, Opie, Trimm, Bruce, Ford, H. McShane
GOALS —	(Col)	Incoll (2), Angus, E. Lockwood
	(Carl)	M. Crowe, B. Lithgow, A. Snell

SEPTEMBER 5 — SECOND SEMI-FINAL

	1st	2nd	3rd	Final	
Fitzroy	2 . 5	5 . 9	7 . 12	11 . 15	(81)
Geelong	0 . 2	0 . 2	3 . 3	4 . 5	(29)

MCG — Umpire Gibson
Attendance 15,000 — Gate £184

BEST —	(Fitz)	Trotter, Beauchamp, Jenkins, Fontaine, Millis, Clarke, M. Shea, McSpeerin
	(Geel)	Rankin, Quinton, Newling, Mesley, Bowley, Holligan
GOALS —	(Fitz)	Brophy (3), Trotter (2), McSpeerin (2), Brosnan, Kiernan, Milne, Millis
	(Geel)	Woods (2), A. McKenzie, Rankin

SEPTEMBER 12 — GRAND FINAL

	1st	2nd	3rd	Final	
Collingwood	2 . 3	3 . 4	3 . 6	4 . 7	(31)
Fitzroy	2 . 2	2 . 5	2 . 8	3 . 11	(29)

MCG — Umpire Gibson
Attendance 32,363 — Gate £838

BEST —	(Coll)	Pannam, McCormack, Monohan, Proudfoot, Fell, Rowell, Addison, Drohan, Condon.
	(Fitz)	Trotter (BOG), Beauchamp, McSpeerin, Milne, Barker, Walker,
GOALS —	(Coll)	Addison (2), Condon, E. Lockwood.
	(Fitz)	Milne, Mills, McSpeerin.

GRAND FINAL TEAMS

Collingwood	B	G. Lockwood	Proudfoot	Dummett
	HB	Fell	Monohan	Rush
	C	Pannam	McCormack	Drohan
	HF	E. Lockwood	Rowell	Tulloch (c)
	F	A. Leach	Addison	Pears
	Ruck	Incoll	Angus	Condon
Fitzroy	B	A. Sharp	Jenkins	L. Barker
	HB	W. Naismith	J. Sharp	Fontaine
	C	Clarke	Beauchamp	Brophy
	HF	A. Wilkinson	Brosnan (c)	Kiernan
	F	Trotter	Millis	A. B. Sharpe
	Ruck	Walker	Milne	McSpeerin

E. Holligan (Geelong) figured in a unique record when he appeared in the first semi-final with Geelong. He had appeared in the previous two seasons with Geelong (1901) and Essendon (1902), before returning to Geelong in 1903, and in each of the three seasons appeared in a final game.

1904

When Fitzroy opened their campaign for the 1904 premiership by beating Carlton by ninety-four points, critics never for a moment thought that five months later the same two sides would meet in the grand final. But they did, and it was the continuation of a rise to the dizzy heights for the Blues, for although they didn't win, they were later to have revenge with three flags in a row. Collingwood and Fitzroy, as in the previous season, appeared to have an edge on all the other sides early in 1904, but Collingwood slumped so badly—even losing to St. Kilda—that Carlton, coached by the rigid diciplinarian Jack Worrall, took their place as main contenders for the flag. Coaching Worrall style was at this stage still unpopular at Carlton despite the success he had in 1903 and players almost queued up to put in for clearances. But few got them and by the end of that season most of them were probably quite happy that they hadn't.

The new finals system which had eliminated the section contest matched Carlton (second) and Essendon (fourth) in the first semi-final. Despite a scoreless first quarter, and only two points in the last, the Blues held on to beat the Dons by three points, before 16,000 people. A miss by McKenzie in the last minute lost the game for Essendon. In the second semi-final, played on the same day, a far larger crowd saw Fitzroy (first) beat Collingwood (third) by eleven points, partly due to the play of Brosnan and Trotter who contributed three goals each to the Fitzroy score. At the other end E. Lockwood (Collingwood), hit the post on three occasions. The stage was set for Fitzroy and Carlton to meet on the MCG the following week for premiership honours.

A strong north-west wind favoured Carlton in the first term but Fitzroy outscored them kicking against it. Carlton fought back, however, and they too did better against the breeze and in fact went to a one point lead at half time, three goals three to three goals two. The third term was their undoing, however, as they put up five successive behinds to Fitzroy's two goals from two shots. This spurred Fitzroy, and the Blues were powerless to stop the Fitzroy run in the last quarter when they rushed on four goals to win the match by exactly that margin.

RESULTS

SEPTEMBER 10 — FIRST SEMI-FINAL

	1st	2nd	3rd	Final	
Carlton	0 . 0	4 . 4	6 . 5	6 . 7	(43)
Essendon	1 . 2	4 . 3	6 . 3	6 . 4	(40)

	Victoria Park	Umpire Crapp
	Attendance 16,000	Gate not available

BEST — (Carl) Leeds, Boyle, Kennedy, Bruce, Topping, Elliott, Roland, Flynn, Snell, H. McShane
(Ess) McDonald, F. Robinson, McKenzie, Busbridge, Barker, Gavin, Legge, Anderson
GOALS — (Carl) Snell (2), Topping (2), Grace, Prescott
(Ess) G. Barker (3), McKenzie (2), Madden

SEPTEMBER 10 — SECOND SEMI-FINAL

	1st	2nd	3rd	Final	
Fitzroy	3 . 3	5 . 4	8 . 6	9 . 7	(61)
Collingwood	2 . 1	2 . 4	5 . 7	7 . 8	(50)

MCG	Umpire Gibson
Attendance 25,000	Gate not available

BEST — (Fitz) McSpeerin, Brosnan, Trotter, Milne, Walker, J. Sharp
(Col) Pannam, Incoll, Angus, Monohan, Dummett, Green
GOALS — (Fitz) Trotter (3), Brosnan (3), Walker, J. McDonough, Milne
(Col) E. Lockwood (2), Pannam (2), A. Leach, Pears, Monohan

SEPTEMBER 17 — GRAND FINAL

	1st	2nd	3rd	Final	
Fitzroy	3 . 1	3 . 2	5 . 2	9 . 7	(61)
Carlton	1 . 1	3 . 3	3 . 7	5 . 7	(37)

MCG	Umpire Crapp
Attendance 32,688	Gate £1,100

BEST — (Fitz) J. Sharp, Johnson, Millis, Clarke, Fontaine, Brosnan, Milne, Walker, McSpeerin, Trotter
(Carl) Elliott, Snell, Topping, Flynn, Trimm, Roland, Leeds, Kennedy, Boyle
GOALS — (Fitz) Brosnan (2), E. Kneen (2), Millis, McDonough, Trotter, Sheehan, Walker
(Carl) Bruce, Grace, Prescott, Snell, Topping

GRAND FINAL TEAMS

Fitzroy	B	A. Sharpe	Fontaine	W. Naismith
	HB	Jenkins	J. Sharp	Johnson
	C	Bartlett	Clarke	Millis
	HF	Kneen	Brosnan (c)	L. Barker
	F	McDonough	Sheehan	Trotter
	Ruck	Milne	Walker	McSpeerin
Carlton	B	Payne	Hince	Walton
	HB	Leeds	Trimm	Roland
	C	Bruce	Boyle	Kennedy
	HF	H. McShane	M. Grace	J. McShane (c)
	F	Marchbank	Topping	Prescott
	Ruck	Flynn	Elliott	Snell
	Coach	J. Worrall		

1905

Collingwood, always a power, came back to top the home and home ladder in 1905 with fifteen wins and two losses, two and a half games ahead of Fitzroy (second) and six games ahead of Essendon (fourth). Carlton (third) recruited fantastically well and five new names included 'Mallee' Johnson, Frank Caine, Rod McGregor, Charlie Hammond, and Norman Clark, all of whom were to become champions.

The two semi-finals resulted in great victories to Fitzroy (who more than doubled Essendon's score) and Carlton (who also more than doubled Collingwood's score in a real boil-over). Percy Trotter, the brilliant Fitzroy rover, kicked six goals in a match-winning performance against Essendon which was a record for any finals match.

The following week, the two winners met with honours going easily to Fitzroy, who ran right away in the second half to win by over four goals. This meant that they were matched against Collingwood (who had been minor premiers) in the grand final. Collingwood, despite their humiliating loss to Carlton in their semi, were equal in favouritism with Fitzroy, but no match in ability as it proved.

The Maroons won the toss, and a slugging first quarter produced a total of only four behinds, three to the Maroons, and an equally hard second term saw the scores level at one goal three each when the interval came. On the resumption, Trotter banged home a goal for Fitzroy from far out. This sparked Fitzroy and after three near misses Brosnan and L. Barker added further goals, before Pears replied on the Bell with a shot that left Collingwood fourteen points down. Both sides had injuries by then—Condon for Collingwood and J. Sharp for Fitzroy. Then a scrambly but hard fought final term resulted in only one point being scored (by Collingwood) which left Fitzroy victors by thirteen points, their second successive flag and their fourth in the nine years of the VFL. When one bears in mind that they lost two other premierships by less than a goal in those years, then they must stand as one of the greatest sides in the long history of the VFL.

RESULTS

SEPTEMBER 16 — FIRST SEMI-FINAL

	1st	2nd	3rd	Final	
Fitzroy	5 . 1	8 . 2	12 . 4	12 . 7	(79)
Essendon	0 . 2	2 . 8	4 . 8	4 . 12	(36)

	Carlton CG Attendance 14,000	Umpire Crapp Gate not available

BEST — (Fitz) Trotter, G. Barker, J. Sharp, Walker, Beauchamp, Bailes, Millis, Johnson
(Ess) McKenzie, McDonald, Madden, Phipps, Shea, Baxter, Callan, Barry, Davis
GOALS — (Fitz) Trotter (6), Brosnan (2), Fontaine, Johnson, Millis, L. Sharp
(Ess) G. Barker, Blackmore, McKenzie, Smith

SEPTEMBER 16 — SECOND SEMI-FINAL

	1st	2nd	3rd	Final	
Carlton	4 . 3	5 . 5	8 . 7	11 . 10	(76)
Collingwood	0 . 1	0 . 3	2 . 4	4 . 6	(30)
	MCG Attendance 14,000		Umpire Norden Gate not available		

BEST — (Carl) Roland, Caine, Grace, Parke, McNeil, Flynn, Elliott, Hammond
(Col) Dummett, Green, McHale, Rush, Fraser, Pears, Angus, Gibb
GOALS — (Carl) J. Kennedy (2), Roland (2), Topping (2), Caine, M. Grace, Elliott, Flynn, G. Johnson
(Col) Condon, Green, Nash, Stancliffe

Umpire Norden, in this match, became the first umpire to have charge of a final in his first VFL season.

SEPTEMBER 23 — PRELIMINARY FINAL

	1st	2nd	3rd	Final	
Fitzroy	3 . 2	5 . 3	8 . 6	11 . 6	(72)
Carlton	3 . 4	4 . 6	6 . 7	6 . 9	(45)
	MCG Attendance 30,000		Umpire Crapp Gate not available		

BEST — (Fitz) J. Johnson, Sheehan, Trotter, Milne, J. Sharp, Jenkins, Naismith, L. Barker, Beauchamp, Walker, Millis
(Carl) Flynn, Johnson, Hammond, Snell, McGregor, Boyle, Grace, Roland, Elliott
GOALS — (Fitz) Wilkinson (2), Trotter (2), Johnson (2), Milne (2), Brosnan, Millis, Walker
(Carl) M. Grace (2), Elliott, McGregor, Roland, Snell

SEPTEMBER 30 — GRAND FINAL

	1st	2nd	3rd	Final	
Fitzroy	0 . 3	1 . 3	4 . 6	4 . 6	(30)
Collingwood	0 . 1	1 . 3	2 . 4	2 . 5	(17)
	MCG Attendance 30,000		Umpire Crapp Gate £1,061		

BEST — (Fitz) Bailes (B.O.G.), Beauchamp, Jenkins, Moriarty, Sheehan, Naismith, Milne, Walker, Millis
(Col) Dummett, Pears, Strachan, Rush, Monohan, Green, Gibb, Nash, Drohan
GOALS — (Fitz) L. Barker, Brosnan, Trotter, Millis
(Col) Nash, Pears

GRAND FINAL TEAMS

Fitzroy	B	W. Naismith	Moriarty	L. Barker
	HB	Jenkins	J. Sharp	Sheehan
	C	G. Barker	Beauchamp	Bailes
	HF	Brosnan (c)	Fontaine	Johnson
	F	Wilkinson	McDonough	Trotter
	Ruck	Milne	Walker	Millis
Collingwood	B	Fell	Proudfoot	Dummett
	HB	Rush	Monohan	Fraser
	C	Green	McHale	Gibb
	HF	Pannam (c)	Nash	Pears
	F	Angus	Drohan	Incoll
	Ruck	A. Leach	Strachan	Condon
	Coach	R. Condon		

1906

With a side that old timers still reckon to be the best ever to wear the Carlton colours, the Blues stormed to their first VFL premiership in 1906. Coach Jack Worrall's policy of iron discipline, his weeding out of players and shuffling of positions since 1902, finally paid dividends—and it didn't stop there, either, for Carlton went on to play in four more grand finals in succession.

Carlton in 1906 won sixteen out of their nineteen matches, the three losses being to Essendon, Fitzroy and South Melbourne. Their season's score of 187 goals 207 behinds, against their opponents' 116 goals 166 behinds was a fair indication of their superiority over the season's play. Mick Grace, full-forward, became the first league forward to kick fifty goals in a season, while Frank Caine scored thirty-seven and George Topping twenty-five. Carlton, of course, topped the home and home ladder with fourteen wins out of seventeen games followed by Fitzroy (thirteen wins) with Collingwood third and Essendon fourth.

In the semi-finals, Carlton, finishing strongly, proved too good for Collingwood, and Fitzroy easily accounted for Essendon. The latter match was notable for the break-down of Albert Thurgood (Essendon) who, after kicking the first goal of the day, had to leave the ground, and then announced his retirement. The semi-finals left Carlton and Fitzroy to play-off for the premiership and they met on the MCG on September 22 before a then record crowd for Australia of 44,437. Both sides were at their top, although Carlton had Gotz unavailable through injury. His replacement H. Parke, who had not played since the 1905 finals, broke down at training and also was ruled out, and finally Beck came into the side.

In the match, Carlton ran up seven goals four to one goal seven by half-time and then added a further eight goals in the second half to coast home by fifteen goals four to six goals nine. In actual fact Carlton went from four goals four to fifteen goals four with eleven successive goals, which was yet another record, and they never looked in the slightest danger, although Fitzroy drew to within fourteen points in the third quarter. A mark to Mick Grace in the last quarter which gave him his fiftieth goal for the season, was about the only interest after three quarter time. One goal scored by Caine of Carlton was later measured at eighty-three yards.

RESULTS

SEPTEMBER 15 — FIRST SEMI-FINAL

	1st	2nd	3rd	Final	
Carlton	5 . 1	6 . 3	6 . 8	9 . 10	(64)
Collingwood	2 . 1	4 . 3	7 . 5	8 . 6	(54)

Fitzroy CG — Umpire Wregg
Attendance 15,000 — Gate not available

BEST — (Carl) Flynn, Jinks, Elliott, Johnson, Hammond, Gotz, McGregor, Bruce
(Col) Nash, Hyman, McHale, Rowell, Lee, A. Leach, Incoll, Condon (till injured)
GOALS — (Carl) Topping (2), Grace (2), Jinks (2), Bruce, McGregor, Marchbank
(Col) Lee (4), Rowell (2), Pannam, Angus

SEPTEMBER 15 — SECOND SEMI-FINAL

	1st	2nd	3rd	Final	
Fitzroy	2 . 4	5 . 5	8 . 9	10 . 12	(72)
Essendon	2 . 2	3 . 2	4 . 6	5 . 6	(36)

MCG — Umpire Tulloch
Attendance 8,500 — Gate not available

BEST — (Fitz) Milne, Walker, Millis, C. Naismith, Smith, Fontaine, Beauchamp, Moriarty
(Ess) McKenzie, Belcher, Davis, Sewart, Madden, Griffith, Shea, George
GOALS — (Fitz) C. Naismith (3), Trotter (3), Millis (2), Bailes, Walker
(Ess) Cameron, J. Fogarty, Hiskins, McKenzie, Thurgood

SEPTEMBER 22 — GRAND FINAL

	1st	2nd	3rd	Final	
Carlton	3 . 2	7 . 4	9 . 4	15 . 4	(94)
Fitzroy	1 . 6	1 . 7	6 . 8	6 . 9	(45)

MCG — Umpire Wregg
Attendance 44,437 — Gate £1,368

BEST — (Carl) Payne, Beck, Clark, Gillespie, Bruce, McGregor, Kennedy, Grace, Caine, Jinks, Elliott, Lang
(Fitz) L. Barker, Jenkins, Sharp, Abbott, Kneen, Bailes, Beauchamp, Johnson, Fontaine, Walker, Milne, Millis
GOALS — (Carl) Grace (3), Caine (3), Elliott (2), Little (2), Topping (2), Marchbank, Hammond, Topping
(Fitz) Brosnan, Fontaine, Millis, Naismith, Walker, Trotter

1906-1907

GRAND FINAL TEAMS

Carlton	B	Clark	Doug Gillespie	Beck
	HB	Payne	Johnson	Hammond
	C	Bruce	McGregor	Kennedy
	HF	Caine	Marchbank	M. Grace
	F	Lang	Topping	Little
	Ruck	Flynn (c)	Jinks	Elliott
	Coach	J. Worrall		
Fitzroy	B	Abbott	Moriarty	Johnson
	HB	L. Barker	J. Sharp	Sheehan
	C	Bailes	Beauchamp	Kneen
	HF	Fontaine	Brosnan	R. Smith
	F	Millis	C. Naismith	Jenkins (c)
	Ruck	Walker	Milne	Trotter

1907

Carlton stayed atop the ladder in 1907 but they were joined by two newcomers in South Melbourne (second) and St. Kilda (third), the latter making the finals for the first time. The old reliable, Collingwood made up the Four. Once again the VFL reverted to a section system, but at the end of it the four finalists were unchanged. Thus, South met Collingwood in the first semi-final—and proved far too good winning by nearly six goals. Collingwood was very disappointing, but South played together like a team and leapt to equal favouritism for the flag.

In the second semi, Carlton made mincemeat of St. Kilda, but it cost them their star centre-man Rod McGregor who broke his nose in the last five minutes of the game and was forced to miss the grand final. Carlton and South met the following week in the greatest finals clash since the formation of the VFL. South, building up since 1905, had at last arrived and had Carlton not been on the scene they would undoubtably have won the flag, as they were a great side with many champions. But then, so was Carlton.

Neither side was at top strength. Franks (disqualified), Goddard (injured), Maine (injured) and Gent missing for South, and McGregor (injured) and Elliott and Marchbank (disqualified) being out for Carlton. Before 45,000 people, both sides turned on a great game. Carlton struggled to a seven point lead at half time and increased this to fifteen points at the final change. South fought back magnificently and four times in that hectic final term they reduced the deficit to two points. But Carlton were equal to the occasion and added three more behinds to win their second successive flag by five points. Hughie Callan, later to lose his life in World War I, played a great game for South after being best on the ground in their semi-final win over Collingwood.

'Lardie' Tulloch, umpire in the grand final, set a unique record as he had previously captained two premiership sides whilst a player. Collingwood [1902-03.])

RESULTS

SEPTEMBER 7 — FIRST SEMI-FINAL

	1st	2nd	3rd	Final	
South Melbourne	3 . 3	4 . 7	7 . 7	12 . 10	(82)
Collingwood	0 . 2	2 . 5	3 . 10	6 . 12	(48)

MCG — Umpire Coombes
Attendance 25,000 — Gate not available

BEST — (S. Melb) Callan, Ricketts, Cameron, Drane, Wade, Kerr, Moxham
(Col) Gibb, Pannam, Angus, Leach, Ryan, Lee, Baxter, Diggle, O'Donoghue

GOALS — (S. Melb) Mortimer (4), Kerr (4), Belcher, Callan, Casey, Cameron
(Col) Lee (2), Angus, Baxter, A. Leach, Pannam

SEPTEMBER 14 — SECOND SEMI-FINAL

	1st	2nd	3rd	Final	
Carlton	4 . 2	9 . 5	11 . 8	13 . 13	(91)
St. Kilda	1 . 0	2 . 2	3 . 8	4 . 11	(35)

MCG — Umpire Wregg
Attendance 26,100 — Gate not available

BEST — (Carl) Johnson, Hammond, Jinks, Bruce, Flynn, Harris, Payne, Gotz, Lang, Topping
(St. K) McNamara, Cumberland, J. Wells, Morrisey, Barwick, Feehan, C. Bent, Scott

GOALS — (Carl) M. Grace (4), Harris (3), Topping (2), Caine, Kelly, Hammond, Lang
(St. K) McNamara (3), Cowell

SEPTEMBER 21 — GRAND FINAL

	1st	2nd	3rd	Final	
Carlton	1 . 4	4 . 6	6 . 10	6 . 14	(50)
South Melbourne	1 . 3	3 . 5	4 . 7	6 . 9	(45)

MCG — Umpire Tulloch
Attendance 45,477 — Gate £1,471

BEST — (Carl) Johnson, Flynn, Gotz, Kelly, Ingleman, Bruce, Jinks, Hammond, Beck, Payne, Lang, Caine
(S. Melb) Callan, Ricketts, Drane, Casey, Woods, Wilson, Atkins, Lampe, Strang, Belcher

GOALS — (Carl) Topping (3), Lang, Jinks, Kelly
(S. Melb) Strang (3), Mortimer (2), Casey

The Essendon football team—premiers 1897

Fitzroy, training for the grand final, season 1899

To attain this means very hard work and strict attention to diet and abstemiousness. Footballers train twice a week, and when once in condition this suffices to keep them so for the season.

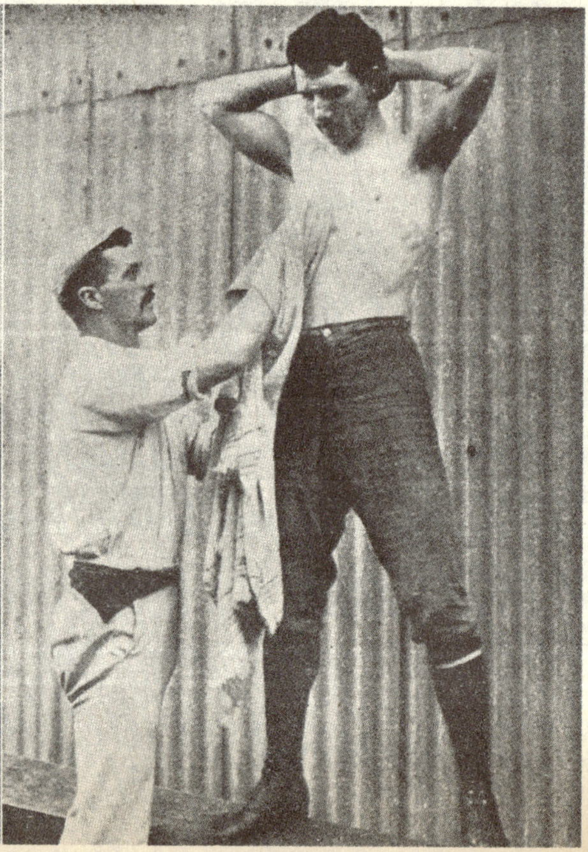

Captains Wardill (Melbourne) and Sloan (Fitzroy) 1900.

On the road to the ground—MCG circa 1897

Semi-final—Carlton V Collingwood on the Fitzroy ground. September 5, 1903.

Grand final 1904—Fitzroy V Carlton—G. Brosnan (Fitzroy captain) marks.

Fitzroy V Collingwood grand final 1903.

Grand final 1903—Fitzroy V Collingwood.

Grand final 1907, Carlton V South Melbourne on the M.C.G., 21st September.

Ruck duel grand final 1905—Fitzroy V Collingwood

Grand final 1906—Carlton V Fitzroy

Collingwood V South Melbourne first semi-final 1907

D. Smith (Essendon) hand passing. Collingwood V Essendon semi-final 1908

A special tram, direct to the football circa 1909

W. E. Busbridge (Essendon). Outstanding player on the field in the grand final of season 1908.

1909 first semi-final at the MCG. Carlton beat Essendon by thirty-six points

South Melbourne on their way to their first premiership—South Melbourne V Carlton 1909—Charlie Ricketts, South's coach, is all smiles on the extreme left of the picture.

GRAND FINAL TEAMS

Carlton	B	Clark	Doug Gillespie	Beck
	HB	Gotz	Flynn (c)	Payne
	C	Bruce	Ingleman	Kennedy
	HF	Jinks	Kelly	Cainé
	F	M. Grace	Topping	Harris
	Ruck	G. Johnson	Hammond	Lang
	Coach	J. Worrall		
South Melbourne	B	Lampe	Dolphin (c)	Wilson
	HB	Woods	Atkins	G. Anderson
	C	Moxham	Wade	Drane
	HF	Casey	Strang	W. Kerr
	F	Callan *	Mortimer	A. Kerr
	Ruck	Belcher	Cameron	Ricketts

* Killed in World War I.

1908

Two new teams in Richmond (from the VFA) and Melbourne University (newly formed) were admitted to the VFL in 1908, bringing the number of teams up to ten. Neither new team was immediately successful in the League ranks, Richmond taking until 1919 to reach the finals for the first time, while University in fact never made the four and eventually disbanded in 1915.

Essendon, last in 1907, raided the VFA clubs and obtained star players in W. Davis, M. Londerigan, Parkinson, Johnson from North Melbourne, and L. Armstrong, Ryan, Minto, Gregory, Heaphy, Farnsworth and Harrison from West Melbourne. These and their few established stars welded Essendon into a power again and when they gave Carlton their only beating of the season at home on July 11, critics claimed they were the best Essendon side yet to play in the League ranks. But Carlton at that stage were at the height of their powers and went through the home and home series with only that one reverse debited against them. Essendon were second, followed by St. Kilda—third for the second season in a row—and Collingwood who had sneaked in after a cut-throat clash with South Melbourne in the last game. After one season the League had dispensed with the section system. The first semi, in which Essendon eliminated Collingwood, was a good hard game, though rather rough at times, and in fact everyone was surprised that there were no reports. Essendon held a half-time lead due only to their centreline superiority but after the interval they had winners all over the ground.*

* A new rule was introduced in this game in which the ball was bounced in a five-yard clear space in the centre and no player could come within two yards until the ball touched the ground.

The second semi-final became a farce when the ground was flooded soon after the start by a torrential downpour. Carlton already had four goals (all to Vin Gardiner) on the board and although good football was impossible they kept adding to their total to win effortlessly by nearly ten goals. The luckless Saints were, in fact, unable to score even one goal in the first three quarters.

Carlton were the hottest favourites for years when the grand final was played the following week. They had seventeen players with grand finals experience—their opponents, Essendon, had two. In addition, Essendon had five regulars unable to play. To fill the gaps they brought in two country players who had one game each and a college boy who had not played League at all. A raking wind blew down the MCG and spoilt the game completely as a spectacle. Some critics described it as the most mediocre final seen for years, and said it was Carlton's worst display for the season. It probably was, but nobody could deny that the defensive display by both sides in the last half was excellent; although Carlton was later criticised for hugging the boundary and continually forcing play into the southern pocket at the Richmond end. It seems that these tactics were regarded as unsporting.

The Blues, opening up a lead of three goals by half-time, were kept to one point in the second half, but their own defence limited the Dons to one goal four and that was good enough to win the game with a score of five goals five to three goals eight. The Dons came close with four near misses in the vital last quarter, but not close enough to stop Carlton becoming the first team to win three successive League pennants.

RESULTS

SEPTEMBER 12 — FIRST SEMI-FINAL

	1st	2nd	3rd	Final	
Essendon	2 . 2	3 . 7	5 . 11	9 . 14	(68)
Collingwood	2 . 1	3 . 2	3 . 2	5 . 3	(33)

MCG — Umpire Coombes
Attendance 28,856 — Gate £1,000

BEST — (Ess) Griffith, Busbridge, Johnson, M. Shea, Davis, Sewart, Minto, P. Shea, Londerigan, Belcher
(Col) Baxter, Nash, Heatley, Rowell, O'Donoghue, Sadler, McHale, A. Leach, Angus, Strachan, Lee, Daykin, Pannam

GOALS — (Ess) Farnsworth (3), D. Smith (2), Minto (2), Busbridge, Belcher
(Col) Lee (4), Pannam

SEPTEMBER 19 — SECOND SEMI-FINAL

	1st	2nd	3rd	Final	
Carlton	4 . 1	8 . 7	8 . 10	12 . 12	(84)
St. Kilda	0 . 3	0 . 4	0 . 5	3 . 8	(26)

MCG — Umpire Coombes
Attendance 25,531 — Gate £676

BEST — (Carl) Payne, Clark, Beck, McGregor, Bruce, Kennedy, Johnson, Hammond, Elliott, Flynn
(St. K) W. Stewart, J. Stewart, Feehan, H. Bant, Dangerfield, Barwick, Scott, Morrissey

GOALS — (Carl) Gardiner (4), Elliott (2), Kelly, Lang, Gotz, Topping, Kennedy, Ford
(St. K) Lever, M. Grace, Cowell

1908-1909

SEPTEMBER 26 — GRAND FINAL

	1st	2nd	3rd	Final	
Carlton	2 . 3	5 . 4	5 . 5	5 . 5	(35)
Essendon	1 . 1	2 . 4	3 . 5	3 . 8	(26)

MCG Umpire Elder
Attendance 50,261 (record) Gate £1,791

BEST — (Carl) Hammond, Lang, Payne, Clark, Elliott, Johnson, Bruce, Beck, Ford, Flynn
(Ess) Busbridge (B.O.G.), Griffith, Martin, Daykin, Bowe, Johnson, Sewart, Davis

GOALS — (Carl) Elliott, Gotz, Kelly, Kennedy, Marchbank
(Ess) Legge, Martin, P. Shea

GRAND FINAL TEAMS

Carlton	B	Clark	Beck	Ford
	HB	Flynn	Payne	Jinks
	C	Bruce	McGregor	Kennedy
	HF	Lang	Marchbank	Gotz
	F	H. Kelly	Gardiner	Topping
	Ruck	Johnson	Hammond	Elliott (c)
	Coach	J. Worrall		

This was the first premiership side not containing a single first year player.

Essendon	B	Bowe	Griffith (c)	Daykin
	HB	M. Shea	Busbridge	Johnson
	C	Davis	Sewart	Minto
	HF	P. Shea	D. Smith	Prout
	F	Heaphy	Farnsworth	Legge
	Ruck	Belcher	Martin	Cameron

1909

Three of the final four sides remained the same in 1909—Carlton (second), Collingwood (third) and Essendon (fourth). South moved up to take first place on percenages while St. Kilda fell from third to last, with only two wins. Carlton had struck trouble early in the season with a blow-up between players and the coach, Jack Worrall. Eventually things reached such a stage that Worrall, under pressure, resigned as coach and the captain, Fred Elliott, took over. Under him the Blues reached their fourth grand final in as many seasons.

1909

Meeting Essendon in the first semi-final Carlton proved too strong all over the field and went away to a convincing six goal win despite an early injury to Fred Jinks which immobilised him for the rest of the day. An interesting sidelight on the match was the performance of Bill Payne, the Carlton defender, who took the field despite medical advice that his eyes were so badly infected that he risked his sight if he received a bump on them. He was one of the Blues' best. For the Dons, little Ernie Cameron received a broken jaw. Three seasons later, also in a final, Cameron was to go down in a pack with a broken leg.

Collingwood continued their dismal run of finals failures when they went down to South in the second semi by twenty-one points. South went away and sealed the game in about five minutes soon after half time, when they added four goals (three to Mortimer) and two behinds. Perhaps Collingwood should have used the oxygen which was available in their rooms at half time. Oxygen was not then in general use and only one player—Shorten—availed himself of it.

In an extremely rough final, Carlton edged out the minor premiers, South Melbourne, by twenty-one points. Each side had a player out injured, while South's Caldwell got himself reported and missed the grand final. A feature of the game, which old-timers still remembered for years afterwards, was the magnificent kicking-in of South's full-back, Bill Dolphin, who, unfortunately, was unable to play in the grand final.

South tried different tactics in the grand final. Having come off second best in a clash of brawn in the final, they decided to head for the open spaces. With their blistering pace they avoided becoming bogged down in the crushes. The grand final consequently, was fast and open and tremendously exciting. The Southerners gained a slender lead after half time and held onto it even when Carlton charged forward time and time again in the last five minutes to the cheering voices and stomping feet of 38,000 spectators. But every attack was turned by the resolute South backmen Thomas, Grimshaw, Scobie, Deas and Pentland and South held on to win the flag by two points. This was the first of South's three pennants—the other two were in 1918 and 1933.

RESULTS

SEPTEMBER 11 — FIRST SEMI-FINAL

	1st	2nd	3rd	Final	
Carlton	4 . 1	7 . 4	12 . 7	14 . 8	(92)
Essendon	3 . 1	5 . 1	6 . 2	9 . 2	(56)

MCG — Umpire Elder
Attendance 40,000 — Gate £1,430

BEST — (Carl) Lang, Johnson, Gotz, Hammond, Baquie, Ford, Bruce
(Ess) Busbridge, Belcher, Ryan, Davis, Sewart, Daykin, Cameron

GOALS — (Carl) Caine (3), Elliott (2), Kelly (2), Topping (2), Bruce, Gotz, Jinks, Marchbank, Johnson
(Ess) P. Shea (3), Prout (2), A. Armstrong (2), Beckley, Martin

SEPTEMBER 18 — SECOND SEMI-FINAL

	1st	2nd	3rd	Final	
South Melbourne	3 . 4	3 . 4	9 . 7	10 . 8	(68)
Collingwood	0 . 1	3 . 6	4 . 6	6 . 11	(47)

MCG — Umpire Elder
Attendance 35,000 — Gate £1,050

BEST —	(S. Melb)	Kerr, Ricketts, Franks, Belcher, Caldwell, Bower, Thomas, Scobie, Pentland, Deas
	(Col)	T. & J. Baxter, McHale, Vernon, Angus, Ryan, Hughes, Wilson, Gibb
GOALS —	(S. Melb)	Mortimer (3), Cameron (2), Franks (2), Kerr, Gough, Casey
	(Col)	Lee (3), Hughes, Ryan, Vernon

SEPTEMBER 25 — PRELIMINARY FINAL

	1st	2nd	3rd	Final	
Carlton	2 . 0	5 . 5	7 . 7	10 . 9	(69)
South Melbourne	3 . 3	4 . 3	6 . 4	7 . 5	(47)

MCG **Umpire Elder**
Attendance 45,000 **Gate £1,500**

BEST —	(Carl)	Lang, Baquie, Johnson, Payne, Marchbank, Gotz, Jinks, McGregor
	(S. Melb)	Thomas, Bower, Franks, Belcher, Kerr, Barry, Pentland, Scobie, Grimshaw
GOALS —	(Carl)	Caine (4), Marchbank (2), Topping, Baquie, Lang, Elliot
	(S. Melb)	Gough (3), Belcher, Mortimer, Bower, Franks

OCTOBER 2 — GRAND FINAL

	1st	2nd	3rd	Final	
South Melbourne	0 . 5	2 . 9	4 . 12	4 . 14	(38)
Carlton	0 . 5	2 . 9	3 . 11	4 . 12	(36)

MCG **Umpire Elder**
Attendance 36,700 **Gate £1,200**

BEST —	(S. Melb)	Franks, Thomas, Cameron, Kerr, Scobie, Mortimer, Pentland, Wade, Grimshaw
	(Carl)	McGregor, Jinks, Payne, Ford, Lang, Marchbank, Hammond
GOALS —	(S. Melb)	Ricketts, Mortimer, Franks, Gough
	(Carl)	Topping (2), Kelly, Baquie

GRAND FINAL TEAMS

South Melbourne	B	Pentland	Scobie	Wade
	HB	Hiskins	Thomas	Grimshaw
	C	Drane	Bower	Moxham
	HF	Cameron	Deas	Barry
	F	Kerr	Mortimer	Gough
	Ruck	Franks	Belcher	Ricketts (c)
	Coach	C. Ricketts		
Carlton	B	Clark	Doug Gillespie	Marchbank
	HB	Gotz	Payne	Ford
	C	Bruce	McGregor	Kennedy
	HF	Caine	Kelly	Jinks
	F	Elliott (c)	Topping	Baquie
	Ruck	Johnson	Hammond	Lang
	Coach	F. Elliott		

Both grand final coaches were in their first year in that capacity. The only other time both coaches in a grand final have been first-year coaches was in 1933—J. Bissett (South Melbourne) and W. Schmidt (Richmond).

1910

South were able to maintain their position as one of the leading teams in the home and home games in 1910, and eventually they finished third, just ahead of Essendon, with Carlton (fifteen wins, three losses) and Collingwood (thirteen wins, five losses) filling first and second places respectively. Carlton, did remarkably well to finish on top, as in another internal upheaval at the start of the season, a reform group took control and champions in Fred Jinks, Charlie Hammond, 'Mallee' Johnson, Harvey Kelly, Frank Caine, Les Beck, and Ted Kennedy all left the club. Rod McGregor also wished to leave, but later changed his mind. The loss of stars such as these would normally have been disastrous but there was an enormous amount of talent at Princes Park at that time.

The first semi saw Collingwood easily eliminate Essendon from the premiership fight, the muddy conditions suiting the Magpies. Dick Lee, with six goals equalled the scoring record for a final.

The following week came the season's biggest sensation. Just one hour before the start of the second semi, Carlton selectors removed the names of three of their top players from the team sheet. No reasons were given, but it soon became known that the players concerned had been offered bribes to 'play dead'. One or two of the team grumbled and were inclined to rebel but after being spoken to privately by various committeemen they decided to play. To fill the gaps Carlton's ex-captain Jim Flynn turned out, and two reliable reserves in Goddard and Harris also stripped. Most spectators soon knew what was afoot, and when the teams came out Carlton received a thunderous ovation, while South, whom the crowd suspected of doing the bribing (they hadn't), were met with silence. This continued right through the match and South, naturally resenting it, went in hard, often with elbows and fists, and the game became a fiery one. Carlton threw away their chances with innacurate shooting for goal—two goals eleven in the first half—and South won well, easing up.

Inquiries after the match by both Carlton and the VFL found that one of the three players dropped was innocent of the charges and he was back in the side for the next match. But the other two, after a searching investigation by the VFL, were each suspended for five years. (One of them in fact actually served the suspension, then returned to play two more seasons with the Blues.)

Again the crowd was anti-South when the final was played the following week. In perfect conditions, the Magpies slowly but surely wore South down, and sealed the game early in the last term when four onslaughts on goal yielded a behind and three goals to Gilchrist (two) and Angus. South replied through Deas and Hiskins, but time ran out on the Southerners, and the bell went with them trailing by ten points.

On grand final day, 42,577 people rolled up to see the game, played on a hot and windy October 1, 1910. And what a game it turned out to be! Collingwood were brilliant in the first quarter but in the second they went defensive—even putting star goal-kicker Dick Lee on the backline—and this nearly cost them the game. Except for their inaccuracy Carlton must have passed Collingwood's score, but even so the Magpies held a good lead at half time. Early in the third term, both sides were carrying injured men—D. Ryan and Scaddan for the Magpies were both out of action, while for Carlton, Rod McGregor and Arch Wilson (both with injured knees) were virtually useless. Carlton played their best football in this quarter, but once again their forwards let them down. Tempers, which had been frayed since half-time, finally exploded in the last quarter. Fists began to fly and eventually a free fight broke out in front of the old Harrison stand. Team mates rushing in to separate combatants were felled like logs and before the game was re-started Baquie and Sheehan (Carlton) and Baxter and Shorten (Collingwood) had been reported. Old-timers say the fight would have been going still except for the quick thinking of umpire Jack Elder who, all else having failed, eventually blew his whistle and bounced the ball, leaving players to decide whether to concentrate on the game or the fight. Clashes continued until the game's end; but in between fisticuffs Collingwood held their grip on the game and finally won it by nine goals seven to six goals eleven; their third VFL pennant.

When the four reported players appeared before the tribunal, their sentences were harsh. Players Sheehan and Shorten went out for all of 1911 and half of 1912, and players Baquie and Baxter were put out for all of 1911.

Baxter's sentence was later quashed on appeal to the VFL.

RESULTS

SEPTEMBER 10 — FIRST SEMI-FINAL

	1st	2nd	3rd	Final	
Collingwood	3 . 4	5 . 7	9 . 9	14 . 11	(95)
Essendon	1 . 1	1 . 3	2 . 6	5 . 7	(37)

MCG — Umpire Elder

Attendance 24,000 — Gate £676

BEST —	(Col)	McHale, Scaddan, Shorten, Lee, Baxter, Ryan, Angus, Sadler, Norris
	(Ess)	Belcher, White, Anderson, Baring, Ogden, Prout, Busbridge
GOALS —	(Col)	Lee (6), Gilchrist (4), Wilson, Ryan, McHale, Hughes
	(Ess)	P. Shea (2), Belcher, Martin, McLeod

SEPTEMBER 17 — SECOND SEMI-FINAL

	1st	2nd	3rd	Final	
South Melbourne	2 . 1	5 . 2	7 . 5	10 . 5	(65)
Carlton	1 . 4	2 . 11	5 . 12	6 . 17	(53)

MCG — Umpire Elder

Attendance 42,000 — Gate £1,500

1910

BEST — (S. Melb) Belcher, Prince, Kerr, Grimshaw, Thomas, Dolphin, Barry, Bower
(Carl) Marchbank, Payne, Elliott, McCluskey, Clancy, McGregor, Jamieson

GOALS — (S. Melb) Carpenter (4), Mortimer (2), Cameron, Deas, A. Hiskins, Kerr
(Carl) Gotz (2), Gardiner, Elliott, Marchbank, McDonald

SEPTEMBER 24 — PRELIMINARY FINAL

	1st	2nd	3rd	Final	
Collingwood	2 . 1	4 . 3	5 . 6	8 . 7	(55)
South Melbourne	1 2	3 4	4 7	6 8	(44)

MCG — Umpire Elder
Attendance 43,000 — Gate £1,530

BEST — (Col) McHale, McIvor, Wilson, Baxter, Vernon, Shorten, Rowell, Angus, Ryan, Daykin, Lee
(S. Melb) Prince, Bower, Thomas, Grimshaw, Punshon, Dolphin, Mortimer, Kerr

GOALS — (Col) Lee (3), Angus (3), Gilchrist (2)
(S. Melb) A. Hiskins (3), Mortimer (2), Deas

OCTOBER 1 — GRAND FINAL

	1st	2nd	3rd	Final	
Collingwood	4 3	5 3	8 5	9 . 7	(61)
Carlton	1 2	2 6	4 9	6 11	(47)

MCG — Umpire Elder
Attendance 42,577 — Gate £1,420

BEST — (Col) Lee (B.O.G.), Scadden, Shorten, McIvor, McHale, Rowell, Vernon, Baxter, Hughes
(Carl) Payne, Clark, Harris, Elliott, Marchbank, Baquie, McDonald, McGregor

GOALS — (Col) Lee (4), Vernon, Angus, Daykin, Gibb, Gilchrist
(Carl) McGregor (2), Baquie, Gardiner, Marchbank, Wells

GRAND FINAL TEAMS

Collingwood	B	Sadler	Rowell	Norris
	HB	Scaddan,	Shorten	McIvor
	C	Gibb	McHale	Oliver
	HF	Angus (c)	Hughes	Vernon
	F	Gilchrist	Lee	Wilson
	Ruck	Ryan	Daykin	T. Baxter
	Coach	G. Angus		
Carlton	B	Harris	Doug Gillespie	Goddard
	HB	McCluskey*	Payne	Clark
	C	Jamieson	McGregor	Clancy
	HF	Sheehan	Marchbank	Baquie
	F	McDonald	Gardiner	Wilson
	Ruck	Wells	Gotz	Elliott (c)
	Coach	F. Elliott		

* Killed in World War I.

1911

The most notable and far-reaching decision made by the League delegates in 1911 was the one, carried by sixteen votes to four, that enabled League clubs to openly pay players. Previously all players were supposedly amateurs; but most clubs had been paying good sums to their top players for many years, and disguising these sums in various ways in their annual financial balances. Now for the first time all this was brought into the open.

Essendon, now under the astute coaching of the ex-Carlton mentor, Jack Worrall, bounded up the ladder in 1911 to finish on top after the home and home round, with fifteen wins and a draw in eighteen games. South were two games back in second place with Carlton and Collingwood completing the Four.

Collingwood and South met in the first semi, and the Magpies, although missing captain George Angus, went away to an easy victory, with thirty-four points to spare. This put the 1909 premiers once again out of the race and when the following week Essendon, with a tremendous last quarter, proved too strong for Carlton, the stage was set for an Essendon-Collingwood grand final. The Dons suffered setbacks before this match when Alan Belcher and White were unable to take their places in the side and their ace forward, Martin, was unavailable (suspended on a charge of which he was later proven innocent).

Rain fell at intervals for most of the day. Essendon were all over Collingwood in the first term and but for Rowell's fine play at full back for Collingwood and their own bad play in front of goals, Essendon would have sealed the game then and there. Lee scored Collingwood's first goal right on quarter time, and that was their only goal until the third quarter. Collingwood swapped Lee and Rowell at half-time and this move brought them within three points at the last change. Goals by Walker and Shea (Essendon) were answered by one from Baxter (Collingwood) with four minutes to go. Baxter had another chance but kicked into the man on the mark (for the second time that quarter) and Essendon held a six point lead when the final bell went. Tom Baxter's play in that vital last term, when he twice kicked into the man on the mark, got behinds from two easy chances, and completely missed another easy chance, was inquired into by his club, and he was later cleared to St. Kilda.

RESULTS

SEPTEMBER 9 — FIRST SEMI-FINAL

	1st	2nd	3rd	Final	
Collingwood	1 . 4	3 . 7	8 . 10	11 . 11	(77)
South Melbourne	1 . 2	2 . 7	3 . 10	6 . 11	(47)

	MCG	Umpire Elder	
	Attendance 43,575	Gate £1,625	

BEST — (Col) Rowell, McHale, McIvor, Hughes, Gibb, Sharp, Green, Gilchrist, Ryan, Baxter, Wilson
(S. Melb) Scobie, Prince, Milne, Carpenter, Deas, Walsh, Grimshaw, Thomas
GOALS — (Col) Baxter (3), Lee (2), Gilchrist (2), Anderson, Hughes, Ryan, Rowell
(S. Melb) Belcher (3), Ricketts (2), Deas

SEPTEMBER 16 — SECOND SEMI-FINAL

	1st	2nd	3rd	Final	
Essendon	2 . 1	3 . 4	4 . 9	9 . 15	(69)
Carlton	2 . 6	4 . 7	5 . 11	6 . 12	(48)

MCG — Umpire Elder
Attendance 40,669 — Gate £1,398

BEST — (Ess) Belcher, Armstrong, Chalmers, Baring, Bowe, Sewart, O'Shea
(Carl) Valentine, Bruce, McGregor, Clancy, Clark, Dick, Wells, Wilson, McDonald, Harris, Payne
GOALS — (Ess) Belcher (2), Shea (2), Walker (2), Kirby (2), L. Armstrong
(Carl) Gardiner (3), Dick, McDonald, Valentine

SEPTEMBER 23 — GRAND FINAL

	1st	2nd	3rd	Final	
Essendon	2 . 4	3 . 9	3 . 11	5 . 11	(41)
Collingwood	1 . 1	1 . 5	3 . 8	4 . 11	(35)

MCG — Umpire Elder
Attendance 43,905 — Gate £1,583-18-9

BEST — (Ess) Busbridge, Bowe, Baring, Walker, Shea, Armstrong, Cameron, Ogden, Smith
(Col) Sharp, Wilson, McHale, Rowell, Sadler, Ryan, Hughes, Baxter, Vernon, Gibb
GOALS — (Ess) Shea, Baring, Kirby, McLeod, Walker
(Col) Rowell, Minogue, Baxter, Lee

GRAND FINAL TEAMS

Essendon	B	Hazel	Griffith	Hanley
	HB	Monteith	Busbridge	Bowe
	C	Chalmers	Sewart	O'Shea
	HF	P. Shea	L. Armstrong	Ogden
	F	Kirby	Smith (c)	Walker
	Ruck	Baring	McLeod	Cameron
	Coach	J. Worrall		
Collingwood	B	Thomas	Rowell	Rowan
	HB	J. Green	Sharp	McIvor
	C	Sadler	McHale	Gibb
	HF	Anderson	Minogue	Wilson
	F	Gilchrist	Lee (c)	Vernon
	Ruck	Hughes	Ryan	Baxter
	Coach	G. Angus		

1912

For the first time numbers were worn on the back of players' jerseys in 1912. This and the listing of names and numbers in a new publication, called the 'Football Record', made it much easier to identify individual players. The experiments with numbering had been tried a few times before, first in the 1911 final between Essendon and Carlton, and also in the grand final. In the former match Essendon had small red numbers under their sash and Carlton wore small white numbers. As a matter of interest, the first man to run onto a VFL ground wearing a number was Dave Smith* (Essendon) wearing number thirteen in that same match, and first goal of the game was kicked by Vin Gardiner (Carlton) also a bearer of number thirteen.

In 1912 the VFL also introduced paid officials called 'stewards' whose job it was to report any rough play that might or might not have been seen by the umpires. It was an excellent attempt to clean up the game which had become extraordinarily dirty. But for several reasons the idea was not a success and stewards were dispensed with after only a few seasons.

South Melbourne and Carlton (both fourteen wins) emerged as top teams of the 1912 home and home round, with Essendon and Geelong making up the Four. Surprise of the year was the form of Collingwood, who slumped to seventh—their first time out of the Four since the VFL began.

A confident Geelong came up to the MCG for the first semi-final and received a hiding at the hands of Carlton. But the Pivotonians had only themselves to blame—from two more scoring shots than Carlton, they kicked an attrocious four goals nineteen while the Blues ran up ten goals eleven. Geelong's score included one goal nine in the second quarter.

History was made in the second semi when the opposing captains were brothers! Alan Belcher led Essendon, and his younger brother Vic captained SouthMelbourne. Alan's team won the day on this occasion as Essendon ran up seven goals twelve to South's six goals six in a tough, hard game. Kirby's goal for the Dons late in the third term won the game, as neither side goaled again.

The Dons repeated the dose over Carlton the following week, although this time the winning margin was only four points. For disobeying his captain's orders on the field, and for other incidents, the Carlton committee suspended Rod McGregor for twelve months. Essendon lost winger Fred O'Shea (leg) and star rover Ernie Cameron (broken ankle) in the latter part of the game. This left them severely handi-

* Smith, Essendon's captain, was unable to play in 1912—he was touring England with the Australian XI cricketers.

capped for the grand final, as their champion centre-half-back Billy Busbridge was also unable to play. South on the other hand had only Grimshaw out injured, and dropped Bower and Tandy, for Ricketts, Mullaly and Mortimer.

Scoring was even in a fumbling first quarter in which players of both sides showed over-anxiousness. Russich, from an acute angle, scored the first goal for South, but Frank Caine equalised. When the teams crossed over, the Dons led by one goal four to one goal three, and both sides had hit the post once, V. Belcher for South and Kirby for Essendon.

L. Armstrong gained another poster for Essendon early in the second term, but Ogden, dominating around the ground, continually drove them forward and goals came from Kirby and Ogden himself. But for poor shooting for goal, Essendon would have held a longer lead at three quarter time, as they had only four goals from eighteen scoring shots up till then. Just as the last quarter started, Russich (South Melbourne) hurt his knee and was of little use, but despite this, South attacked ferociously and Charge goaled to give them heart. But when Baring (Essendon) made a great dash from the centre and single handedly eluded several South backmen to score a great goal, the result was no longer in doubt. V. Belcher added the fourth goal for South soon after, but all interest had gone out of the game as Essendon had no intention of losing their grip on their second successive premiership.

RESULTS

SEPTEMBER 7 — FIRST SEMI-FINAL

	1st	2nd	3rd	Final	
Carlton	3 . 3	3 . 7	5 . 8	10 . 11	(71)
Geelong	2 . 4	3 . 13	3 . 15	4 . 19	(43)

MCG — Umpire Elder
Attendance 40,000 — Gate £1,540

BEST — (Carl) McGregor, Barningham, Gardiner, Wilson, Marchbank, Valentine, Green
(Geel) Slater, Heinz (till injured), Marsham, Martin, Grigg, W. Eason, Freeman, Scown

GOALS — (Carl) Green (4), Gardiner (3), Clancy (2), Wells
(Geel) Martin (2), Grigg, Healey

SEPTEMBER 14 — SECOND SEMI-FINAL

	1st	2nd	3rd	Final	
Essendon	2 . 3	4 . 5	7 . 7	7 . 12	(54)
South Melbourne	1 . 1	3 . 1	6 . 2	6 . 6	(42)

MCG — Umpire Elder
Attendance 34,160 — Gate £1,261

BEST — (Ess) Cameron, Shea, White, O'Brien, Sewart, Bowe, Hanley, Chalmers
(S. Melb) Scobie, Milne, Prince, Saltau, Thomas, Bower, Charge, R. Deas

GOALS — (Ess) Kirby (3), Caine (2), Baring, Cameron
(S. Melb) Carpenter (4), Charge, Franks

SEPTEMBER 21 — PRELIMINARY FINAL

	1st	2nd	3rd	Final	
Essendon	1 . 2	3 . 4	6 . 6	7 . 10	(52)
Carlton	0 . 5	1 . 7	4 . 10	6 . 12	(48)

	MCG Attendance 47,356	Umpire Elder Gate £1,790	

BEST — (Ess) Cameron, Baring, Ogden, Bowe, Sewart, White, McLeod, Belcher
(Carl) Haughton, Dick, McDonald, Mills, Gillespie, Moran, Wells, Wilson, Green

GOALS — (Ess) Baring (3), Kirby (2), P. Shea, O'Shea
(Carl) Moran (2), Valentine (2), Baquie, Gardiner

SEPTEMBER 28 — GRAND FINAL

	1st	2nd	3rd	Final	
Essendon	1 . 4	3 . 9	4 . 14	5 . 17	(47)
South Melbourne	1 . 3	2 . 4	2 . 6	4 . 9	(33)

MCG — Umpire Elder
Attendance 54,463 — Gate £1,952

BEST — (Ess) Baring, Sewart, Ogden, Bowe, Caine, Armstrong, Chalmers, Shea, Belcher
(S. Melb) Milne, Scobie, Saltau, Prince, Mortimer, Thomas, Caldwell, Franks

GOALS — (Ess) Caine, Kirby, Baring, Ogden, Walker
(S. Melb) Belcher, Casey, Franks, Russich

GRAND FINAL TEAMS

Essendon	B	O'Brien	Griffith	McLeod
	HB	White	Hanley *	Bowe
	C	Chalmers	Sewart	Kirkwood
	HF	Kirby	Caine	P. Shea
	F	Martin	L. Armstrong	Walker
	Ruck	A. Belcher (c)	Baring	Ogden
	Coach	F. Worrall		
South Melbourne	B	Saltau	R. Deas	Sloss
	HB	Scobie	Thomas	Walsh
	C	Prince	Mullaly	Caldwell
	HF	V. Belcher	Franks	Carpenter
	F	Casey	Mortimer	Russich
	Ruck	Milne *	Charge	Ricketts (c)
	Coach	C. Ricketts		

An interesting comparison between training methods of now and 75 years ago is seen in the report of the training of both clubs on the Thursday evening before the grand final.

Essendon did mainly short, sharp sprints and long and half distance passing. Work was over soon after 6.00 p.m. and at 7.00 p.m. the team met at Hookers Cafe for dinner.

South Melbourne did lots of sprints but concentrated mainly on ball handling, low passing, etc. Then kicking from the angle, followed by gym work and a session on the punching bag. They too finished working out before dark.

* Both killed in World War I.

1913

For over fifty years old-time St. Kilda supporters always thought nostalgically of season 1913, the year their team reached their first grand final. And there were many who always maintained that with an ounce of luck and a little more experience their team would have won the premiership.

Lucky to make the finals (they finished fourth, four points ahead of Geelong, who thrashed them in the last game), they teamed brilliantly to down South in the first semi, helped by six goals from full-forward Ernie Sellars, which equalled the finals record. Then, after Fitzroy (who finished first, with sixteen wins and two losses) eliminated Collingwood (third) from the fight after a brilliant third quarter burst of five goals, the Saints met Fitzroy in the final. Had Fitzroy won, Fitzroy would have been premiers. Had they lost, then as minor premiers they would still have the right of challenge to another match. And as it turned out, they did lose. After an even battle up to half-time, St. Kilda added five goals six to Fitzroy's one goal three in the last half for their most important win since the formation of the club in 1873. It meant that they had only to down Fitzroy again the following week and the premiership was theirs. Their semi-final win was a triumph of team-work as, lacking the stars that Fitzroy could field, they had to rely on each man to play his part and not let the side down.

For the grand final on the following Saturday, St. Kilda lined up unchanged. Fitzroy, on the other hand, made two alterations, both of them compulsory— Willoughby (suspended) and Bamford (injured) out, and McLennan and Harrison in.

A massive crowd of 59,479 paid £2304 at the gates (both of these figures setting new records), but they must have been initially disappointed with St Kilda's weak display. Fitzroy had three goals up by quarter time to the one solitary behind scored by the Saints. They added another goal and twice hit the post in the second term so that at half-time the scoreboard made miserable reading for St. Kilda supporters— Fitzroy four goals eight to St. Kilda five points.

Alex Millhouse put the first St. Kilda goal on the board half-way through the third term, but it seemed as if Fitzroy had the match in their keeping. At 'orange-time' they held what seemed an unbeatable twenty-five point lead, but within minutes of the start of the last quarter St. Kilda belatedly came good. After Toohey and Buist had missed for Fitzroy, Ernie Sellers accepted a pass from Lynch to notch St. Kilda's second goal. Then Schmidt to Baird resulted in another, and the crowd began to come to life. Johnson (Fitzroy) floored Morrisey (St. Kilda) and the resultant free kick brought still another St. Kilda goal. Minutes later Morrisey marked a few yards out and goaled again. Finally, another attack produced a behind and Fitzroy were stunned to find their lead had been cut to a single point. And here the Saints lost the game. Seeing victory within their grasp, they panicked slightly and several bad mistakes in hand-balling instead of kicking cost them dearly. Then a free to Fitzroy at full-back led to the ball being swiftly relayed downfield to Martin, who goaled with a long place kick. Shaw added another as the bell rang, taking Fitzroy home safely to a thirteen point victory, and their fifth VFL flag.

RESULTS

SEPTEMBER 6 — FIRST SEMI-FINAL

	1st	2nd	3rd	Final	
St. Kilda	3 . 4	5 . 5	8 . 9	12 . 12	(84)
South Melbourne	0 . 6	2 . 9	3 . 13	6 . 15	(51)

MCG — Umpire Elder
Attendance 40,178 — Gate £1,373

BEST — (St. K) Sellars, Lever, Schmidt, Eicke, Cumberland, Woodcock, Millhouse, Collins, Morrissey
(S. Melb) Sloss, A. Hiskins, Thomas, Bower, Prince, H. Kelly, Charge, Franks

GOALS — (St. K) Sellars (6), Morrissey (3), Collins, Jory, Schmidt
(S. Melb) Belcher, Franks, Deas, S. Hiskins, Kelly, Mortimer

SEPTEMBER 13 — SECOND SEMI-FINAL

	1st	2nd	3rd	Final	
Fitzroy	1 . 1	4 . 5	9 . 11	11 . 14	(80)
Collingwood	2 . 2	2 . 5	3 . 6	6 . 7	(43)

MCG — Umpire Elder
Attendance 43,164 — Gate £1,588

BEST — (Fitz) Holden, Freake, Parratt, P. Heron, Heaney, Willoughby, Shaw, Cooper, Bamford
(Col) Mutch, Laxton, Minogue, Gibb, McHale, Green, Seddon, Hughes, Wilson

GOALS — (Fitz) Freake (3), Shaw (2), Heaney, Holden, Martin, Norris, Toohey, Parratt
(Col) Fielding, Lee, Laxton, Seddon, Rush, Wilson

SEPTEMBER 20 — PRELIMINARY FINAL

	1st	2nd	3rd	Final	
St. Kilda	4 . 2	5 . 4	7 . 8	10 . 10	(70)
Fitzroy	1 . 2	5 . 6	5 . 8	6 . 9	(45)

MCG — Umpire Elder
Attendance 54,747 (record) — Gate £2,104 (record)

BEST — (St. K) Schmidt, Eicke, Dangerfield, Lever, Lynch, Jory, Cazaly, Cumberland
(Fitz) P. Heron, Shaw, Parratt, Lethbridge, Willoughby, Norris, Johnson, Holden, Lenne

GOALS — (St. K) Cazaly (3), Morrisey (3), Cumberland, Jory, Schmidt, Collins
(Fitz) Freake (3), Parratt, Shaw, Toohey

SEPTEMBER 27 — GRAND FINAL

	1st	2nd	3rd	Final	
Fitzroy	3 . 6	4 . 8	5 . 11	7 . 14	(56)
St. Kilda	0 . 1	0 . 5	1 . 10	5 . 13	(43)

MCG — Umpire Elder*

Attendance 59,479 (record) — Gate £2,304-4-3 (record)

BEST —	(Fitz)	Holden, McLennan, Parratt, Johnson, Cooper, Shaw, Lethbridge, Heaney, Toohey
	(St. K)	Eicke, Woodcock, Schmidt, Ellis, Bowden, Cumberland, Baird, Collins
GOALS —	(Fitz)	Shaw (2), Freake, Norris, Toohey, Parratt, Martin,
	(St. K)	Morrisey (2), Millhouse, Sellars, Baird

GRAND FINAL TEAMS

Fitzroy	B	Lethbridge	Lenne	Harrison**
	HB	Bamford	Johnson	Cooper**
	C	Buist	McLennan	Holden
	HF	Parratt	Heaney	Toohey
	F	Martin	Freake	Shaw
	Ruck	Walker (c)	Norris	P. Heron
	Coach	P. Parratt		
St. Kilda	B	Hattam	Lever (c)	Harris
	HB	Eicke	Dangerfield	Ellis
	C	Collins	Schmidt	Bowden
	HF	Cazaly	Lynch	Jory
	F	Baird	Sellars	Morrisey
	Ruck	Cumberland	Woodcock	Millhouse
	Coach	G. Sparrow		

*This was Jack Elder's sixth successive grand final as umpire.
** Killed in World War I.

1914

A most remarkable performance was put up by Carlton in this the fiftieth year of the Club's life, and the last season of play before war swept the World.

Introducing new blood liberally into their side, the Blues stunned the experts by going from success to success and winning the premiership with a side that contained no fewer than nine first-year players. The belief that team building must extend over several years before results could be expected was thus shown to be completely false.

Starting slowly, but finishing strongly, they topped the ladder with thirteen wins, three losses and two draws. South, back in the Four again, finished second, followed by Fitzroy and Geelong, the latter a game ahead of Collingwood who missed the finals for the second time in three seasons. St. Kilda, after their great effort in 1913, slumped to seventh.

Geelong held a slight lead at three-quarter time in a low scoring first semi-final, but the fast finishing South Melbourne flashed away in the last term to sneak home by six points. Then a mediocre second semi saw Carlton win well by nine goals eight to Fitzroy's five goals twelve. There was little attractive play by either side, but Fitzroy were particularly disappointing as most of their work was done by half a dozen men only. Carlton's team-work was much superior.

In showery weather the heavy Blues paced it with South until half-time in the final. But it was a different tale in the second half as South, adapting better to the conditions, went on to an excellent win. Carlton struggled to add only one point to their score in the final fifty minutes.

This defeat left Carlton as minor premiers still in the position of being able to challenge South to another game: and so a grand final became necessary. The affects of the War on football attendances showed in the crowd figures for that day—only 30,427 people went along to the match, a drop of nearly fifty per cent on the 1913 figure. They saw an excellent game. South fielded an unchanged side, while Carlton omitted Stan McKenzie and Frank Triplett, replacing them with Alf Baud and George Calwell. South began with the breeze, but scoring was even for the first term. The wind then shifted diagonally across the ground, and Carlton made better use of it than their opponents, running up a twenty-one point lead by half-time.

The red and whites came back with a vengeance in the third term. They seemed to be everywhere, but their forwards let them down badly, kicking one goal six while the backline held Carlton scoreless. Then selfishness and unsteadiness in the last literally threw the game away. They should have gone well ahead, but still trailed by a goal when, with a minute to go, Caldwell (South) kicked high to Bollard in the goal-square. Jamieson (Carlton) leapt straight into Bollard's back, and the ball was rushed away. Had the free been awarded, Bollard could hardly have missed, and the game, despite all South's fumbling, poor kicking, and selfishness, would have been a draw—the first in finals history—but of course, the free was not awarded, and Carlton took out the 1914 pennant by the narrow margin of six points.

Their nine first year players in the premiership team was a record. Previous best—seven by Collingwood in 1902, and six by Carlton in 1906. Umpire Harry Rawle equalled the record of Arthur Norden (1905) by umpiring a final in his first season. In addition, he shares with seven others the record of officiating in all finals in a season. Rawle's effort was remarkable as he umpired only the last two home and home games, then the finals. What is more amazing is that he never became a regular umpire, never umpired another final, and retired in 1924 after only 21 VFL games.

RESULTS

SEPTEMBER 5 — FIRST SEMI-FINAL

	1st	2nd	3rd	Final	
South Melbourne	1 . 7	1 . 9	2 . 12	5 . 14	(44)
Geelong	0 . 2	2 . 4	4 . 6	5 . 7	(37)

MCG — Umpire Rawle
Attendance 24,846 — Gate £1,242

BEST	—	(S. Melb)	Belcher (B.O.G.), Caldwell, O'Donoghue, Charge, Bollard, Russich, Hair, Prince, Tandy
		(Geel)	Gray, Dalton, A. Rankin, Johns, W. Eason, James, Grigg
GOALS	—	(S. Melb)	Freeman (2), Russich, Morgan, Caldwell
		(Geel)	Grigg, A. Eason, Heinz, Johns, Martini

SEPTEMBER 12 — SECOND SEMI-FINAL

	1st	2nd	3rd	Final	
Carlton	3 . 3	5 . 3	8 . 6	9 . 8	(62)
Fitzroy	1 . 1	3 . 4	3 . 5	5 . 12	(42)

MCG — Umpire Rawle
Attendance 28,194 — Gate £1,281

BEST	—	(Carl)	Hammond, Lowe, Brown, O'Brien, Morris, McDonald, Jamieson, Challis, Dick
		(Fitz)	Cooper (B.O.G.), McLennan, Parratt, Willoughby, Holden, Bamford, Buist, Millen, Norris
GOALS	—	(Carl)	Cook (3), Lowe (2), Haughton, Green, Morris, Daykin
		(Fitz)	Heaney (3), Toohey, Jones

SEPTEMBER 19 — PRELIMINARY FINAL

	1st	2nd	3rd	Final	
South Melbourne	1 . 4	3 . 6	4 . 12	5 . 13	(43)
Carlton	0 . 1	3 . 5	3 . 6	3 . 6	(24)

MCG — Umpire Rawle
Attendance 20,229 — Gate £863

BEST	—	(S. Melb)	Charge (B.O.G.), Prince, Tandy, Russich, Sloss, Caldwell, Hair, Deas, Belcher, Freeman
		(Carl)	Burleigh, Jamieson, O'Brien, McDonald, Leehane, Green, Haughton
GOALS	—	(S. Melb)	Freeman (2), Tandy, Charge, Kelly
		(Carl)	McKenzie, Green, Cook

SEPTEMBER 26 — GRAND FINAL

	1st	2nd	3rd	Final	
Carlton	2 . 3	5 . 8	5 . 8	6 . 9	(45)
South Melbourne	2 . 5	2 . 5	3 . 11	4 . 15	(39)

MCG — Umpire Rawle
Attendance 30,427 — Gate £1,491

BEST	—	(Carl)	Dick, O'Brien, Brown, Lowe, Haughton, Leehane, Jamieson, Daykin, McGregor
		(S. Melb)	Sloss (B.O.G.), Prince, Charge, Kelly, Belcher, Hair, Caldwell Deas, Morgan
GOALS	—	(Carl)	Brown, Burleigh, Cook, Fisher, Green, Morris
		(S. Melb)	Sloss, Freeman, Charge, Mullaly

GRAND FINAL TEAMS

Carlton	B	O'Brien	Jamieson	McDonald
	HB	Leehane	Dick (c)	Haughton
	C	Baud	McGregor	Brown
	HF	Lowe	Cook	Daykin
	F	Fisher	Green	Burleigh
	Ruck	Calwell	Hammond	Morris
	Coach	N. Clark		

South Melbourne	B	Saltau	R. Deas	Rademacher
	HB	S. Hiskins	Kelly	Belcher (c)
	C	Tandy	Bollard	Prince
	HF	Sloss*	O'Donoghue	Russich
	F	Mullaly	Freeman*	Morgan
	Ruck	Charge	Hair	Caldwell
	Coach	V. Belcher		

* Both killed in World War I.

1915

With World War I raging, public interest in football was at a low ebb. Attendances were halved, and most of the League clubs fell heavily into debt. Newspapers thundered that all sport should be discontinued, but football came under fire more than any other. The pressure was such that in July, a meeting of VFL delegates discussed terminating the season. Six clubs voted to do so, and four voted against, but as a three-quarter majority was needed the motion lapsed. And so, in a season of trial and tribulation, the following clubs battled their way into the finals:—
Collingwood (fourteen wins, two losses), Carlton (thirteen wins, two losses and a tie), Fitzroy (eleven wins, four losses and a tie), and Melbourne, after an absence of fifteen years (nine wins, seven losses). The Demons just sneaked in when South (fourth) lost to Collingwood in the last game.

The first semi-final was considered a certainty for Carlton, but Melbourne sprang the surprise of the season by going within an ace of winning the match. They actually led at three-quarter time, but then Carlton's greater strength prevailed and goals to Gardiner (two), Valentine and Green took them on to a hard-fought victory.

A wet ball and slippery ground in the second semi suited Fitzroy better than Collingwood, when it really should have been the other way around; for Collingwood were a much more skilful side than their opponents. But so badly did Collingwood play in the second half that they were able to add only four points to their half-time score and lost by nearly six goals.

A tremendous struggle took place in the preliminary final. A real trial of strength in which neither side would give an inch until late in the last term when after getting to within four points, Fitzroy folded and Carlton whipped on two quick goals to seal the game. One of the goals kicked by Fitzroy's T. Heaney during the game was later measured at seventy-eight yards.

The grand final, in which Carlton met Collingwood (minor premiers), was said by

Jack Worrall, in the *Australasian* to be 'a glorious contest—one of the grandest that has ever been seen in the finals'. Collingwood sprang a surprise by bringing the veteran Ted Rowell in for his first game of the season while Carlton had their skipper Billy Dick out. He'd earlier been disqualified until the end of the season, and Alf Baud had taken over as captain. The grand final proved to be Baud's fifty-fourth and last game. Wounded in France the following year, the twenty-two year old was forced to retire.

Collingwood lined up with two players (Rowan and Seddon) who had just finished a ten mile route march with the AIF at Broadmeadows and only arrived at the ground in the nick of time. Holding a slight edge in the rucks and winning in defence and across the centre, Carlton led well at half-time. Collingwood then struck back and were well on top until the last ten minutes and at one stage were even in front. The turning point came when Morris (Carlton) broke away towards goal and his opponent Clancy fell and cut his lip badly, forcing him to leave the field for a short time. While he was off, Carlton slammed on five goals including three to Harry Burleigh, to win easing up.

RESULTS

AUGUST 28 — FIRST SEMI-FINAL

	1st	2nd	3rd	Final	
Carlton	2 . 1	4 . 9	7 . 10	11 . 12	(78)
Melbourne	3 . 5	4 . 5	8 . 7	10 . 7	(67)

MCG — Umpire Elder
Attendance 14,413 — Gate £382

BEST — (Carl) Valentine (B.O.G.), McGregor, Baud, Challis, Gardiner, Hammond
(Mel) Allen, Hassett, George, Brake, Evans, Walker, Lilley, Johnston
GOALS — (Carl) Gardiner (5), Green (3), Burleigh (2), Valentine
(Mel) Brereton (2), J. McKenzie, Elston, Gibb, Huntington, Allan, McQuade, Hassett, W. McKenzie

SEPTEMBER 4 — SECOND SEMI-FINAL

	1st	2nd	3rd	Final	
Fitzroy	1 . 8	3 . 9	7 . 12	9 . 16	(70)
Collingwood	1 . 3	4 . 8	4 . 10	4 . 12	(36)

MCG — Umpire Elder
Attendance 25,938 — Gate £877

BEST — (Fitz) McLennan, Lethbridge, Shaw, Fergie, Millen, Lowrie, Stone, Norris, Toohey
(Col) Anderson, Sadler, Reynolds, Laxton, Green, Mortimer, Clancy
GOALS — (Fitz) Heaney (2), Buist, Freake, Fergie, Lowrie, Norris, Shaw, Toohey
(Col) Curtis (2), Lee (2)

SEPTEMBER 11 — PRELIMINARY FINAL

	1st	2nd	3rd	Final	
Carlton	3 . 3	3 . 8	5 . 12	6 . 18	(54)
Fitzroy	1 . 2	4 . 5	4 . 6	5 . 8	(38)

MCG — Umpire Elder
Attendance 30,630 — Gate £1,049

1915-1916

BEST —	(Carl)	Robinson, O'Brien, McDonald, Challis, Gardiner
	(Fitz)	Norris, Heaney, Johnson, Lethbridge, Toohey
GOALS —	(Carl)	Gardiner (2), Green (2), Sharpe, Fisher
	(Fitz)	Toohey (3), Heaney, Parratt

SEPTEMBER 18 — GRAND FINAL

	1st	2nd	3rd	Final	
Carlton	2 . 5	6 . 6	6 . 8	11 . 12	(78)
Collingwood	3 . 0	4 . 2	5 . 9	6 . 9	(45)

MCG — **Umpire Norden**

Attendance 39,211 — **Gate £1,470**

BEST —	(Carl)	McDonald, Challis, Brown, Burleigh, Daykin, McGregor, Baud, Valentine, Robinson, Morris
	(Col)	Hughes, Anderson, Dobrigh, Rowell, Laxton, Rowan, Clancy, Sadler, Mutch, Minogue
GOALS —	(Carl)	Burleigh (4), Gardiner (3), Hammond (2), Green, Daykin
	(Col)	Lee (3), Dobrigh, Seddon, Hughes

GRAND FINAL TEAMS

Carlton	B	O'Brien	Jamieson	A. McDonald
	HB	Baud (c)	Robinson	Brown
	C	Morris	McGregor	Challis*
	HF	Burleigh	Daykin	Fisher
	F	Green	Gardiner	Sharp
	Ruck	Hammond	Haughton	Valentine
	Coach	N. Clark		
Collingwood	B	Mutch	Rowell	Mortimer
	HB	Green	Minogue (c)	Anderson
	C	Clancy	McHale	Sadler
	HF	Rowan*	Seddon	Laxton
	F	Curtis	Lee	Dobrigh
	Ruck	Hughes	Reynolds	Wilson
	Coach	J. McHale		

T. Clancy, on the wing for Collingwood, played in the grand final of 1910 for Carlton against Collingwood.

* Killed in World War I.

1916

1916 was most certainly a unique season. For one thing, only four teams competed, and for another the premiership was won by a team which had been victorious in only two home and home games.

1916

The season began with great difficulty when, due to the demands of the World War, Melbourne, Essendon, St. Kilda, Geelong and South Melbourne all found themselves unable to field sides, and this left only Carlton, Collingwood, Richmond and Fitzroy to compete. The VFL, faced with this problem, ruled that all clubs had to play, but, naturally, the distressed clubs could not comply.

So, the season went on, despite incessant pressure on the VFL to abandon football. It was felt that men should not stay at home and play sport when a war was being fought. With only the four teams, each side had to play the others three times to complete the first round of matches. Obviously, this soon became monotonous and crowds fell by more than sixty percent. Clearances were waived, and players received only out-of-pocket expenses. At the end of the home and home round, Carlton (ten wins, two losses), Collingwood (six wins, five losses and a draw) and Richmond (five wins and seven losses) finished well ahead of Fitzroy (two wins and a draw).

Fitzroy met the Magpies in the first semi, and, kicking with the wind, it took them twenty minutes to score their first goal. By half-time they trailed by nine points. But in the third term, they found the form that had eluded them for most of the season, and sweeping the Magpie defence aside, they booted four goals two to four points. Then, by withstanding a solid Collingwood fight-back in the last quarter they ran out winners by a goal. A result that came as a complete surprise to every critic.

Appearing in their first VFL finals match, Richmond put up an excellent fight against a strong Carlton team. Battling on in the second half, after trailing at one stage by four goals, they actually hit the front in the last term. A goal by Gardiner put Carlton back in the lead, but almost immediately Harley and then Alessio replied for the yellow and blacks. A series of attacks by Carlton whittled the Richmond lead to two points with only a couple of minutes to go, and then a pass from Gardiner found Valentine who goaled to again put Carlton ahead. Richmond had just one more chance and mulled it—Bayliss marked dead in front and missed.

The toll of the war was graphically shown in this and the following semi-final. Richmond players appeared in black arm-bands, worn in memory of Bill Nolan, their great follower, whose death in France had just been announced. In the preliminary final, it was Carlton's turn to wear black bands. News of the death of Sgt. George Challis, one of their best players in the 1915 finals, had just been released. He too, had been killed in France.

A weakened Carlton (with McGregor and O'Brien both out ill) met Fitzroy in the final. Both sides were not at their best early, and injuries quickly upset them. In the first term Sharp (Carlton) broke his collarbone and early in the second, Jamieson (Carlton) fractured his arm in a collision. Thus, Carlton was forced to play with sixteen men. On Fitzroy's side, Lethbridge (follower) was crippled early, but although not much use, he stayed on the field. In the latter stages the game became very rough and the stewards worked overtime cautioning players. Fitzroy, three points down at the final change, looked as though they were about to throw their chances away with poor forward play early in the last quarter, but they finally got on target and a burst of four goals to Carlton's none gave them the game, and put them into the 1916 grand final.

Carlton, as minor premiers, had another chance in the grand final. Both sides were nowhere near pre-war strength, and even had some of their top 1916 players out. For Fitzroy, Lethbridge, Toohey and Freake were all unable to participate and Lal McLennan (ex-captain) came out of retirement for the match. Carlton had their champion Rod McGregor still out, and Calwell and Morris came in for their first games of the season. Kicking with a light breeze to the Railway end, Fitzroy got off to a good start with O'Dee, Moore and Parratt all goaling early and they outplayed Carlton in the second term to lead by five goals at half-time. At this stage their teamwork was better, and their marking and play-on game was far superior. In the third term, a classic long punt goal on the run by G. Holden (Fitzroy) followed by another goal to Heaney forced Carlton's captain Billy Dick to move himself from defence to centre-half-forward to try and lift the side, and curb Fitzroy skipper Wal. Johnson, who had been starring. Dick immediately came under notice with two long drop kick goals but his team trailed by twenty-seven points at three-quarter time. Carlton came with a run early in the last quarter. Fisher and Dick goaled and Lang missed from right in front. Then Fitzroy steadied and goals to Jenkin and Parratt put the issue beyond all doubt. The 1916 'No-Hopers' had won the premiership!

RESULTS

AUGUST 12 — FIRST SEMI-FINAL

	1st	2nd	3rd	Final	
Fitzroy	1 . 3	2 . 6	6 . 8	9 . 9	(63)
Collingwood	2 . 1	4 . 3	4 . 7	8 . 9	(57)

MCG — Umpire Norden
Attendance 9,638 — Gate £183

BEST — (Fitz) Johnson (B.O.G.), Lethbridge, Buist, Millen, Heaney
(Col) Wilson, Drummond, Brown, Hughes, Jose, Oram, Curtis, McCarthy, Dobrigh

GOALS — (Fitz) Jenkins (3), Heaney (2), Lowrie, Lethbridge, Moore, Parratt
(Col) W. H. Lee (2), Hughes (2), Curtis (2), Wraith, P. Wilson

AUGUST 19 — SECOND SEMI-FINAL

	1st	2nd	3rd	Final	
Carlton	4 . 2	7 . 5	8 . 8	10 . 15	(75)
Richmond	3 . 3	4 . 6	7 . 9	10 . 12	(72)

MCG — Umpire Elder
Attendance 11,683 — Gate £226

BEST — (Carl) Dick, Hammond, McDonald, Daykin, Valentine, Canet, Brown, Sharp
(Rich) Alessio, Herbert, Moffatt, Hede, Bettles, Thomas, Bayliss

GOALS — (Carl) Gardiner (4), Hammond (3), Fisher (2), Valentine
(Rich) Alessio (4), Harley (4), Hall (2)

AUGUST 26 — PRELIMINARY FINAL

	1st	2nd	3rd	Final	
Fitzroy	1 . 1	3 . 6	5 . 7	9 . 11	(65)
Carlton	2 . 5	4 . 6	5 . 10	5 . 12	(42)

MCG — Umpire Elder
Attendance 15,557 — Gate £323

BEST — (Fitz) Shaw, Lenne, Millen, Bamford, Buist, Norris, Holden
(Carl) Valentine, Fisher, Haughton, Daykin, Hammond, Shortill, Gardiner

GOALS — (Fitz) Heaney (5), Parratt, Jenkin, Moore, Lethbridge
(Carl) Gardiner (3), Daykin, Fisher

1916-1917

SEPTEMBER 2 — GRAND FINAL

	1st	2nd	3rd	Final	
Fitzroy	4 . 6	8 . 8	10 . 11	12 . 13	(85)
Carlton	2 . 0	4 . 2	6 . 8	8 . 8	(56)

MCG — Umpire Norden
Attendance 20,953 — Gate £503

BEST —	(Fitz)	Millen (B.O.G.), Johnson, Shaw, Norris, McLennan, Buist, Heaney, Parratt
	(Carl)	Morris, Daykin, Brown, Dick, Hammond, Fisher
GOALS —	(Fitz)	Heaney (3), Parratt (3), O'Dee (2), Jenkin, Moore, Holden, Lowrie
	(Carl)	Dick (3), Fisher (2), Lang, Gardiner, Haughton

GRAND FINAL TEAMS

Fitzroy	B	R. King	Lenne	Bamford
	HB	E. McDonald	Johnson (c)	McLennan
	C	Buist	Holden	Millen
	HF	O'Dee	Heaney	Parratt
	F	Lowrie	Jenkin	Purcell
	Ruck	Norris	Moore	Shaw
	Coach	P. Parratt		
Carlton	B	A. McDonald	Leehane	Greaves
	HB	O'Brien	Dick (c)	Robinson
	C	Brown	Morris	Kiely
	HF	Fisher	Shorthill	Daykin
	F	Calwell	Gardiner	Lang
	Ruck	Haughton	Hammond	Valentine
	Coach	N. Clark		

E. McDonald, who appeared for Fitzroy in this game, was later better known as the opening bowler for Australia in the great Test Teams of the early 1920's.

1917

Once again a restricted season (fifteen games only, plus finals) saw attendances at a low level, although up a bit on the 1916 figures. South Melbourne and Geelong re-entered the competition, and the former was able to gain a place in the finals. Collingwood headed the list at the conclusion of the home and home round with ten wins and a draw in fifteen games, followed by Carlton (nine wins and a draw), South (nine wins), and Fitzroy (eight wins and a draw).

1917

Fitzroy surprisingly eliminated Carlton in the first semi-final. Starting off with the wind, they put on two quick goals but Carlton, through Shortill, Hammond and Dick, added three goals straight against the wind. After that quarter, Fitzroy got off target and climaxed their efforts in the last quarter with a lamentable one goal six and numerous out of bounds, or kicks into the man on the mark. But even so, they were always a jump ahead of Carlton and eventually ran out winners by nine points. It was a fiery game and four players were reported.

Collingwood scored one of their best finals wins to date in their second semi-final victory over South, thirteen goals seventeen to three goals seventeen. The game was played in bad weather, but Collingwood made very few mistakes. Up until half-time, the game was quite even, but in a tremendous third term Collingwood, sparked by Curtis, took South apart. Curtis kicked four goals and Laxton three of the eight goals four added by the Magpies in the quarter, and the Magpies' score was the biggest ever in one quarter of a finals match to that time. That burst sealed the game for Collingwood, who won easing up.

The Fitzroy-Collingwood final was one of the best and most exciting second round matches for years. After an even first three quarters which saw the scores showing one point the difference, both teams threw themselves into the fray in the last. Rattray (Fitzroy) found Parratt for a lovely goal, but Curtis (Collingwood) quickly replied. Then Heaney (Fitzroy) hit the post with a long shot, and Laxton (Collingwood) twice missed. Reynolds (Collingwood) was on target with his shot, but a quick Fitzroy fight-back saw Rattray goal to level the scores, and Freake steal the game right on the bell when he took the ball on his own and ran right into an open goal to post the winning score.

Collingwood, as minor premiers, were entitled to a further match (the grand final), against Fitzroy. For the first time in the finals series, the Magpies had the services of their brilliant goal-kicker Dick Lee, although he was still carrying an injured knee. To play him, the Magpies took a risk and left out one of their best forwards, the fast and clever Wraith. McHale also came in, taking the place of Colechin. Fitzroy brought in Byrne and Lowrie and left out Jim Atkinson (injured) and Lambert.

The Magpies established their superiority in a hard slugging first half on the rain-softened MCG. Inspired by a gift from their old player 'Doc' Seddon (serving with the Army in France), of a horseshoe made from a German shell and nails from a German plane, and inscribed 'France to C.F.C. Good Luck from Doc, 1917' the Magpies put on three goals eight to Fitzroy's two goals two by half-time, but should have led by more. Only poor shooting for goal spoilt their good play. Despite the efforts of Bamford (Fitzroy), the Magpies went further ahead in the third quarter, although still kicking poorly. It was a case of the failure of the brilliant Heaney for Fitzroy meaning the failure of the side. He was completely out of form—as also was Toohey—and without his fine play the Fitzroy forward line lost a lot of drive. Collingwood were untroubled to fight off a late challenge and take out the 1917 premiership by thirty-five points.

RESULTS

SEPTEMBER 1 — FIRST SEMI-FINAL

	1st	2nd	3rd	Final	
Fitzroy	2 . 4	4 . 9	5 . 11	6 . 17	(53)
Carlton	3 . 0	3 . 1	4 . 6	6 . 8	(44)

MCG — Umpire Norden

Attendance 14,946 — Gate £324

BEST —	(Fitz)	Toohey, Parratt, Millen, R. King, Holden, McDonald, Freake
	(Carl)	Downs, Fisher, O'Brien, Hammond, Dick, Daykin, Canet, McGregor
GOALS —	(Fitz)	Freake (3), Millen, Parratt, McDonald
	(Carl)	Dick (3), Valentine, Shortill, Hammond

SEPTEMBER 8 — SECOND SEMI-FINAL

	1st	2nd	3rd	Final	
Collingwood	2 . 4	3 . 9	11 . 13	13 . 17	(95)
South Melbourne	0 . 2	2 . 5	2 . 6	3 . 17	(35)

MCG — **Umpire Norden**
Attendance 16,643 — **Gate £378**

BEST —	(Col)	Drummond (B.O.G.), Curtis, Wilson, Anderson, Brown, Laxton, McCarthy
	(S. Melb)	Belcher, Rademacher, Howell, Boyce, Deas, Payne, Hair
GOALS —	(Col)	Curtis (4), Laxton (4), Hughes (2), Dobrigh, Lumsden, Wraith
	(S. Melb)	Deas, Payne, Robertson

SEPTEMBER 15 — PRELIMINARY FINAL

	1st	2nd	3rd	Final	
Fitzroy	1 . 4	3 . 6	5 . 7	8 . 10	(58)
Collingwood	2 . 1	4 . 3	5 . 6	7 . 10	(52)

MCG — **Umpire Norden**
Attendance 22,786 — **Gate £577**

BEST —	(Fitz)	Heaney, Toohey, McDonald, Holden, Parratt, Millen, Lethbridge
	(Col)	Curtis, Wilson, Anderson, Green, Mutch, Pannam, McCarthy, Wraith
GOALS —	(Fitz)	Freake (3), Parratt (3), Moore, Rattray
	(Col)	Curtis (5), Wraith, Reynolds

SEPTEMBER 22 — GRAND FINAL

	1st	2nd	3rd	Final	
Collingwood	2 . 6	3 . 8	6 . 14	9 . 20	(74)
Fitzroy	1 . 0	2 . 2	3 . 4	5 . 9	(39)

MCG — **Umpire Norden**
Attendance 28,385 — **Gate £773**

BEST —	(Col)	P. Wilson (B.O.G.), Pannam, Anderson, Drummond, Dobrigh, Saunders, Hughes, Mutch, McCarthy, Green, Brown, R. Lee, Curtis
	(Fitz)	Bamford, Millen, Parratt, McDonald, Lenne, Norris, King, Keller, Rattray, Moore
GOALS —	(Col)	W. H. Lee (4), Curtis (3), Dobrigh, Hughes
	(Fitz)	Norris, Freake, Parratt, Rattray, Toohey

GRAND FINAL TEAMS

Collingwood	B	McHale	Saunders	Mutch
	HB	Anderson	Brown	Green
	C	Drummond	P. Wilson (c)	Pannam
	HF	Dobrigh	Curtis	C. Lee
	F	McCarthy	W. H. Lee	Lumsden
	Ruck	Hughes	Reynolds	Laxton
	Coach	J. McHale		

1917-1918

Fitzroy	B	W. Byrne	Lenne	Bamford
	HB	Lethbridge	Toohey	R. King
	C	Millen	Holden (c)	Keller
	HF	Parratt	Heaney	Rattray
	F	Wigraft	Freake	Lowrie
	Ruck	Moore	Norris	E. McDonald
	Coach	G. Holden		

1918

With the worst years of the World War past, football returned almost to normal in 1918. Essendon and St. Kilda rejoined the League, leaving only Melbourne an absentee. South Melbourne, a brilliant team, went through the first round of fourteen games with only one defeat, at the hands of St. Kilda, by five points, on King's Birthday. Had South won that game, they would have been the first team to go through the season undefeated. (In fact, no team has ever accomplished this feat, although Collingwood in 1929 won all their home and home games but lost the second semi-final. Collingwood in that season, Carlton in 1908, South in 1918 and Essendon in 1950 are the only teams to go through a season with only one defeat). Collingwood finished second on the 1918 ladder with ten wins, followed by Carlton with eight wins, and St. Kilda—with many of their 1913 team plus the great Dave McNamara back—eight wins.

Collingwood, just a shade stronger over the closing stages of the first semi ran St. Kilda down in the last quarter to turn a seven point deficit into a nine point win. The scores were twice equal, and twice the difference was a point only, but two behinds and a goal in the last minutes made the game safe for the Magpies.

A tremendous downpour which flooded the MCG caused the postponement of the second semi-final, the first postponement of a finals match in VFL history. The following week, however, a crowd of over 35,000—biggest since 1914—saw South just beat Carlton in a grand game with a heart-stopping finish. Looking steadier throughout, South led by seven points at three-quarter time. But within minutes of the start of the last quarter, the Blues had levelled the scores. Then O'Halloran (South Melbourne) goaled, Carlton replied with a behind, and South, through Doherty, added another goal. Furnell goaled to reduce the deficit to five points before Woolley (Carlton) kicked out of bounds from the angle. O'Halloran (South Melbourne) turned a hot Carlton attack right on the bell.

Winners of the two semi-finals matches, Collingwood and South, met in the final with South (minor premiers) having the right of challenge if defeated. The game was played in ideal weather, although a chill wind blew up the ground. South kicked with the wind, but missed a couple of easy shots and were outscored by the Magpies, who went further ahead in the second quarter when South were held scoreless. But it was Collingwood's turn to squander chances and they added only one goal six from numerous shots. After a very even third quarter, the teams went for lemons with Collingwood holding a twelve point lead and coming home with what remained of the wind. South were kicking to the end at which they had not even scored a point in the second quarter. Vic Belcher went into the ruck for South, and immediately got them going. Ryan goaled, and Howell added a point to reduce their deficit to a goal. Belcher, in everything, got South forward again, and Ryan added another goal to level the scores. Lee (Collingwood) had a shot but Belcher saved. Next, a passage of play in which no South player got near the ball saw Lumsden (Collingwood) add a point, and the Magpies were ahead with minutes to go. Then a brilliant effort by Tandy drove the ball forward for South, for Ryan to put the ball within a yard of goal. There Laird dashed in and booted it through off the ground. With sixty seconds left for play, the ball was bounced and a struggle for possession on South's half-forward line was ended by the sounding of the bell. South Melbourne had won their second VFL pennant by the narrow margin of five points.

RESULTS

AUGUST 17 — FIRST SEMI-FINAL

	1st	2nd	3rd	Final	
Collingwood	2 . 5	4 . 6	5 . 11	7 . 16	(58)
St. Kilda	2 . 1	6 . 5	7 . 6	7 . 7	(49)

MCG **Umpire Elder**
Attendance 29,191 **Gate £729**

BEST —	**(Col)**	Hughes, P. Wilson, Twomey, McCarthy, Reynolds, Saunders, Brown, Wraith, Walton
	(St. K)	Maloney, Collins, Boyd, Eicke, James, Turnbull, Cazaly, Ostberg, Lang, Dangerfield
GOALS —	**(Col)**	Wraith (3), W. Lee (2), Lumsden, Hughes
	(St. K)	Boyd (2), McNamara (2), Schmidt, Turnbull, Berry

AUGUST 24

Game postponed due to bad weather.

AUGUST 31 — SECOND SEMI-FINAL

	1st	2nd	3rd	Final	
South Melbourne	3 . 3	4 . 3	6 . 8	8 . 10	(58)
Carlton	2 . 3	4 . 6	5 . 7	7 . 11	(53)

MCG **Umpire Norden**
Attendance 35,855 **Gate £1,103**

BEST —	**(S. Melb)**	Howell, Robertson, Tandy, Wood, Daly, Belcher, Turner, Caldwell, Barber
	(Carl)	Daykin, Downs, O'Brien, McDonald, Furnell, Woolley, Valentine, Fisher
GOALS —	**(S. Melb)**	Robertson (2), Doherty (2), Barber (2), Hynes, O'Halloran
	(Carl)	Downs (2), Furnell (2), Daykin, Valentine, Woolley

1918-1919

SEPTEMBER 7 — GRAND FINAL

	1st	2nd	3rd	Final
South Melbourne	2 . 5	2 . 5	6 . 6	9 . 8 (62)
Collingwood	3 . 3	4 . 9	7 . 12	7 . 15 (57)

MCG — Umpire Elder
Attendance 39,168 — Gate £1,175

BEST — (S. Melb) O'Halloran, Howell, Turner, O'Donoghue, Rademacher, C. Laird, Ryan, Tandy, Wood
(Col) Hughes (B.O.G.), Walton, Saunders, Pannam, P. Wilson, Twomey, W. Lee, Lumsden, Laxton

GOALS — (S. Melb) Ryan (3), C. Laird (3), Robertson (2), Barber
(Col) W. Lee (3), Lumsden (2), Laxton, Hughes

GRAND FINAL TEAMS

South Melbourne	B	Graham	Turner	V. Belcher
	HB	Rademacher	O'Donoghue	Daly
	C	Tandy	Hynes	Wood
	HF	Caldwell (c)	O'Halloran	Robertson
	F	Barber	Ryan	C. Laird
	Ruck	Howell	Skehan	Doherty
	Coach	H. Howson		
Collingwood	B	Sheehy	Saunders	Mutch
	HB	Colechin	McCarthy	Brown
	C	Pannam	P. Wilson (c)	Twomey
	HF	Wraith	Walton	Green
	F	Lumsden	W. Lee	Dobrigh
	Ruck	Hughes	Reynolds	Laxton
	Coach	J. McHale		

1919

With Melbourne back in the VFL in 1919 (although they failed to win a game), the League was back to pre-war strength. With the war over, crowds were on the increase again and harassed club treasurers heaved sighs of relief. Half way through 1919, things were back to normal.

The main innovation in 1919 was the introduction of the League Second Eighteens, the premiership of which competition was won by Collingwood.

In the senior competition, the Magpies were again to the fore, finishing on top of the ladder with thirteen wins and three defeats in the sixteen games. South Melbourne carried on their good form of 1918 to finish second on the ladder with twelve wins, followed by Carlton and Richmond, both ten wins, and who sneaked in by two premiership points from Fitzroy, a team with a better percentage than either of them.

Richmond, appearing in their first VFL final (if one omits the farcical 1916 season) met South Melbourne before 45,318 people at the MCG in the first semi-final. Overcoming their early over-eagerness, the Tigers built up a handy lead by three quarter time, and then sealed the game with two quick goals early in the last quarter. South, it must be admitted, were severely handicapped by the absence through injury of Harold Robertson (an elder brother of Austin Robertson senior), who earlier in the season had kicked a League record score of fourteen goals in a match against St. Kilda. One of South's best players in this match, Skehan, later transferred to Williamstown (VFA) and died after being injured in a collision between players in a match in 1923, one of the very few deaths through injury which have occurred in senior football.

Helped by the poor forward work of Carlton, Collingwood had the second semi-final sewn up when they led by forty-three points at three-quarter time. The Blues made a fighting come-back with three goals in the first eight minutes of the last term, and cut the Collingwood lead to eighteen points with half the quarter gone. Then the Magpie back-line steadied and they had three goals to spare at the final bell.

Richmond scored the first and last goals of the preliminary final, and in between played excellent football to defeat the redoubtable Collingwood. They were never headed and ran the Magpies off their feet in the latter stages to win by nearly five goals.

Collingwood, as minor premiers, were entitled to a re-match (the grand final) the following Saturday. They made only two changes to personnel but several positional ones, which strengthened the team. Richmond, on the other hand, made no changes, although they were still without star players in Bobby Carew (broken ankle) and captain 'Son' Thomas (broken leg) both of whom had also missed the preliminary final.

Collingwood won the toss and within a minute had two behinds and another near miss to their credit. But it was Richmond who eventually scored the first goal, from the boot of George Bayliss. Dick Lee replied for Collingwood, but the great forward was off target in this quarter, and four of Collingwood's five behinds in the term came from his boot. The tables were turned in a thrilling second quarter when Richmond added three goals five to the Magpies four goals straight, and the difference at half time was a mere four points in Collingwood's favour. Richmond's giving away of costly free kicks in front of goal in the third term negated their good play in other positions, and they entered the last quarter trailing by sixteen points. Collingwood quickly wrapped up the 1919 premiership by adding goals through Seddon, Lumsden and Laxton and were untroubled to hold their lead for the last fifteen minutes of the game.

RESULTS

SEPTEMBER 20 — FIRST SEMI-FINAL

	1st	2nd	3rd	Final	
Richmond	3 . 3	6 . 3	8 . 11	10 . 13	(73)
South Melbourne	2 . 0	5 . 3	7 . 4	9 . 5	(59)

MCG — Umpire Elder

Attendance 45,318 — Gate £2,414

BEST —	(Rich)	Hall, Don, Herbert, James, Carew, Hede, Hislop, Huggard, Bayliss, Parkinson
	(S. Melb)	Turner, Lugg, Brereton, Caldwell, Rademacher, O'Halloran, Sampson, Tandy
GOALS —	(Rich)	Herbert (3), Bayliss (3), Don (2), Smith (2)
	(S. Melb)	Lugg (3), Brereton (3), Doherty, (2) C. Laird

SEPTEMBER 27 — SECOND SEMI-FINAL

	1st	2nd	3rd	Final	
Collingwood	4 . 7	6 . 7	9 . 9	9 . 10	(64)
Carlton	0 . 2	2 . 6	2 . 8	6 . 10	(46)

MCG **Umpire Norden**
Attendance 47,336 **Gate £2,465**

BEST —	(Col)	Mutch, Colechin, McCarthy, Twomey, Hughes, Walton, Curtis, W. Lee, Seddon
	(Carl)	McGregor, Downs, Fisher, McDonald, Johnson, Brown, Haughton, Martin, Prince
GOALS —	(Col)	W. Lee (4), Wraith (2), Seddon (2), Walton
	(Carl)	Daykin (3), Furnell (2), Leehane

OCTOBER 4 — PRELIMINARY FINAL

	1st	2nd	3rd	Final	
Richmond	3 . 4	5 . 7	7 . 10	10 . 14	(74)
Collingwood	2 . 2	4 . 4	6 . 6	6 . 9	(45)

MCG **Umpire Elder**
Attendance 51,000 **Gate £2,678**

BEST —	(Rich)	Huggard, Parkinson, Hislop, Thorp, Bayliss, Smith, Herbert, Moffatt, James, Don, Hall
	(Col)	Twomey, Walton, Mutch, McCarthy, Laxton, Pannam, Drummond, Hughes
GOALS —	(Rich)	Bayliss (3), Don (2), Smith (2), James, Maybury, Hall
	(Col)	R. Lee (2), Wraith (2), Lumsden, Laxton

OCTOBER 11 — GRAND FINAL

	1st	2nd	3rd	Final	
Collingwood	1 . 5	5 . 5	8 . 8	11 . 12	(78)
Richmond	1 . 2	4 . 7	5 . 10	7 . 11	(53)

MCG **Umpire Elder**
Attendance 45,413 **Gate £2,194**

BEST —	(Col)	McCarthy, Hughes, Pannam, Curtis, E. Wilson, Colechin, Seddon, Walton, Laxton
	(Rich)	Hislop, Smith, Harley, Herbert, James, Hede, Hughes, Parkinson
GOALS —	(Col)	W. Lee (3), Seddon (2), Hughes, Curtis, Walton, Twomey, Laxton, Lumsden
	(Rich)	Bayliss (2), Don (2), James (2), Harley

Collingwood	**B**	Haysom	Saunders	Sheehy
	HB	Mutch	Walton	Colechin
	C	Drummond	Pannam	Twomey
	HF	E. Wilson	Curtis	Seddon
	F	Reynolds	W. Lee	Lumsden
	Ruck	Hughes	McCarthy (c)	Laxton
	Coach	J. McHale		

Richmond	B	Bettles	Thorp	Abbott
	HB	Huggard	M. Hislop	Parkinson
	C	S. Morris	Hughes	Hede
	HF	Maybury (c)	Bayliss	Harley
	F	Smith	James	Don
	Ruck	Herbert	Moffatt	Hall
	Coach	N. Clark		

1920

Richmond, led by ex-Collingwood champion Danny Minogue, were the glamour side of 1920. They went through the home and home games with fourteen wins and two defeats, as did Fitzroy (fifth in 1919). Making up the final Four were Carlton and Collingwood, each with ten wins.

Collingwood eliminated Fitzroy in a low-scoring first semi on the rain-soaked MCG. After leading at half-time by one goal seven to one goal four the Magpies combined better in a fiery second half and held Fitzroy to one goal one while adding three goals ten themselves. Of interest was the fact that young Collingwood centre-half-forward Gordon Coventry scored his first of a record 112 goals in finals matches in this game. His last goal of that 112 was scored seventeen years later in 1937.

A record crowd of 62,200 attended the Carlton-Richmond second semi-final. The Blues, with star rover Lyle Downs out suspended, caused a stir by introducing a country lad in Maurie Beasy for his first game. But Beasy vindicated the selectors' judgement with a good game and eventually went on to be elected Blues' captain. In a tough rugged game on another mud-heap, the heavier Blues ran to a four goals four to one goal two lead by half-time, but Richmond fought back with good scouting to convert their deficit to a one point lead at the last change. But that was as far as they could go, and the Blues added three goals five to nil to win quite easily, the main interest in the last quarter was when umpire Jack Elder had to stop the game while police moved the crowd back from the boundary line.

The preliminary final was a different story. On a ground still wet from previous heavy rain, the pacy Collingwood team jumped Carlton early and held their lead all day. Carlton's rucks floundered, while the Magpie little men ran riot all over the ground in a brilliant team display. Carlton's only good patch was in the last quarter when, with Collingwood relaxing slightly, the Blues added four goals four to one goal one. But the victory cost Collingwood dearly—Bill Twomey senior and Ernie Wilson were injured, and 'Doc' Seddon was reported and missed the grand final.

Wilson and Twomey played with their injuries, but skipper Dick Lee, another injured player for the Magpies, could not front up. The sensation of the week prior to the grand final, however, was the suspension of George Ogilvie's permit by the VFL. Ogilvie, one of Richmond's star recruits, and one of their best players in the second semi, had his permit withdrawn when it was found he was actually bound to Essendon, and he was unable to appear in the grand final. The Tigers had a further setback when the top goal-kicker of the season, George Bayliss, was also unable to play due to injury. His replacement was W. James (Kyabram), for his first VFL game—and, in fact, the only one he ever played for Richmond.

Richmond won the toss in perfect conditions. The pace was tremendously fast, with Richmond generally leading to the ball, and holding Collingwood scoreless when they were kicking with a slight breeze in the second term, Richmond gained a strong grip on the game. Evidence of how hard it was to get goals was shown when an exciting struggle involving 12 players five yards from the Collingwood goal failed to gain any score at all. This was the fate of most Richmond attacks—they should have held a far bigger half-time lead than their nine points. An early goal to Harley (Richmond) in the third term and another by Donald Don were both answered by Collingwood's G. Coventry, who was having an excellent match, but Richmond retained their nine point lead at three-quarter time. Both sides attacked feverishly for minor scores early in the last quarter, before Don and R. Weatherill added goals in quick succession for the Tigers. Misses by Wilson and Drummond were followed by a goal to Sheehy for Collingwood, but Richmond always had Collingwood's measure. Don missed three times in succession before W. James, running in from the wing, goaled to make the game safe beyond all doubt. Just on the bell, G. Coventry got his third goal for Collingwood, but the result was already on the board, the Tigers' first VFL pennant.

RESULTS

SEPTEMBER 11 — FIRST SEMI-FINAL

	1st	2nd	3rd	Final	
Collingwood	1 . 2	1 . 7	3 . 9	4 . 17	(41)
Fitzroy	1 . 2	1 . 4	2 . 5	3 . 5	(23)

MCG — Umpire Elder

Attendance 40,000 — Gate £1,950

BEST —	(Col)	Drummond, Twomey, Dobrigh, Lumsden, Brown, Laxton
	(Fitz)	Sherry, Molan, Gale, Wigraft, Fergie, Parratt, Lenne, Taylor
GOALS —	(Col)	W. Lee, G. Coventry, Seddon, Lumsden
	(Fitz)	Freake, Fergie, McGrath

SEPTEMBER 18 — SECOND SEMI-FINAL

	1st	2nd	3rd	Final	
Carlton	2 . 3	4 . 4	4 . 5	7 . 11	(53)
Richmond	1 . 2	1 . 2	4 . 6	4 . 6	(30)

MCG — Umpire Elder

Attendance 62,220 — Gate £3,228

BEST —	(Carl)	Greenhill, Johnson, O'Brien, Martin, Chandler, Bickford, Canet, Boromeo, Beasy, Green
	(Rich)	Thorp, Parkinson, Taylor, Smith, Ogilvie, Harley, James, Moffatt, Herbert, Hall
GOALS —	(Carl)	Daykin (2), Bickford (2), McLatchie, Carter, Martin
	(Rich)	Harley (2), Bayliss, James

1920

SEPTEMBER 25 — PRELIMINARY FINAL

	1st	2nd	3rd	Final	
Collingwood	5 . 5	9 . 8	11 . 10	12 . 11	(83)
Carlton	1 . 2	4 . 5	4 . 7	8 . 11	(59)

MCG — Umpire Elder
Attendance 57,764 — Gate £2,864

BEST —	(Col)	McCarthy, Pannam, Drummond, P. Wilson, Brown, Tyson, Sheehy, Saunders
	(Carl)	O'Brien, McKenzie, Canet, Bickford, Hiskins, McLatchie
GOALS —	(Col)	G. Coventry (5), P. Wilson (3), Lumsden (2), Pannam, Laxton
	(Carl)	Clover (3), Fisher (2), Daykin, McLatchie, Wittman

OCTOBER 2 — GRAND FINAL

	1st	2nd	3rd	Final	
Richmond	1 . 2	2 . 5	4 . 7	7 . 10	(52)
Collingwood	1 . 2	1 . 2	3 . 4	5 . 5	(35)

MCG — Umpire Elder
Attendance 53,908 — Gate £2,550

BEST —	(Rich)	Hislop, H. James, Hall, Moffatt, Herbert, Smith, Hughes, Hede
	(Col)	Brown, Dobrigh, Saunders, Drummond, McCarthy, Pannam, Rowe, Tyson, G. Coventry, Hughes
GOALS —	(Rich)	Don (2), H. James, W. James, Harley, Hall, R. Weatherill
	(Col)	G. Coventry (3), Lumsden, Sheehy

GRAND FINAL TEAMS

Richmond	B	Hede	Thorp	Taylor
	HB	Parkinson	M. Hislop	Smith
	C	S. Morris	F. Hughes	Carew
	HF	Don	R. Weatherill	Harley
	F	H. James	Minogue (c)	W. James
	Ruck	Herbert	Moffatt	Hall
	Coach	D. Minogue		
Collingwood	B	Dobrigh	Saunders	Colechin
	HB	Brown	Rowe	Tyson
	C	Drummond	Pannam	Twomey
	HF	E. Wilson	G. Coventry	Sheehy
	F	Lumsden (c)	Curtis	P. Wilson
	Ruck	Hughes	McCarthy	Laxton
	Coach	J. McHale		

1921

Carrying on their form of 1920, Richmond gained second place on the 1921 home and home ladder. But the improver of the year was undoubtedly Carlton. With height, weight and pace the dark blues closely resembled their great teams of 1906-7-8, and must be counted one of the best teams not to have won the premiership. They lost only one of sixteen home and home games (Richmond lost four) but failed against the Tigers in two of the hardest fought finals matches in VFL history.

Richmond met Geelong (fourth with nine wins, seven losses) in the first semi-final, and annihilated them. Kicking six goals four to Geelong's attrocious eleven points in the last quarter, the Tigers won handsomely by sixteen goals nineteen to six goals eighteen. Cliff Rankin was the main offender in Geelong's total of eighteen behinds. No fewer than ten of them came from his boot, including six in the last quarter. An interesting name in the Geelong team was Dick Grigg—he had been in their 1914 finals side and had played only one game between then and his appearance in the finals seven seasons later.

Carlton had Collingwood on toast at half-time in the second semi (the Magpies had finished third with nine wins, seven losses). Leading at that stage by five goals six to one goal seven, the Blues were shocked by a Magpie third quarter fight back which gave them five goals (four to Dick Lee) and cut their deficit to only four points. But the Blues greater strength gained them the day and in a slogging last quarter they went ahead to win by a couple of goals. Their champion Horrie Clover—who earlier in the season had kicked thirteen goals in a match from centre-half-forward—was a casualty, however, and was forced to miss the following week's final.

In that particular final Carlton and Richmond clashed, and the result was one of the most amazing second round matches in VFL history. For fifty minutes, conditions were ideal and in a rugged but cleanly played first half, Richmond ran up a lead of five goals six to Carlton's two goals ten. Then, a tremendous hail-storm hit the MCG at half-time, and when the players came out to resume the game, the ground was awash with a white coat of hail, water, and mud. In places the arena was inches under water. In impossible conditions, the Blues slipped and skidded forward and within minutes had succeeded in levelling the scores. Then a behind post was knocked clean out of the ground, and had to be replaced—another unique incident in a unique match. With heavy rain falling and lightning flashing, the two teams matched each other goal for goal. Duncan (Carlton), missed a sitter, but Fisher's lucky goal put Carlton three points ahead at the last change. Fisher had marked as the bell went, and took his kick as the players walked off. His shot fell about fifteen yards short, and skidded through for a goal between four Richmond defenders.

The final quarter was also fought out in pouring rain. Richmond put on two quick goals early in the term and held out the battling Blues for the remainder of the game to eventually win by eight points.

This, of course, meant a grand final match, for Carlton had been minor premiers. 43,122 people rolled up for the big match and were astounded to see Carlton win the toss—and kick against the wind. But the move paid off early, for with Clover marking brilliantly despite the steady rain, Carlton went to a lead of three goals four to one goal three by half-time, a lead that would have been greater but for the resolute play of the rock-like Richmond backline. In the third quarter, Carlton's long-game slipped, the Richmond big men came into their own in the muddy conditions, and the Tigers whittled the Carlton lead to two points at the final change. Immediately the last quarter began, Richmond, through Hughie James, scored a vital goal to give them the lead. Carlton replied and battled to a two point lead with eight minutes left for play. Then Richmond's Norm Turnbull marked and kicked truly from thirty yards out—a goal which, as it turned out, won the match for his side. Black with mud, the two sides fought out those last eight minutes, the Tigers standing up to the fiercest sustained onslaught on the goals that Carlton could produce. In the last minute, with the score unaltered, the ball flew towards Carlton's Alec Duncan, not far from goal. It looked a certain mark until Richmond's vice-captain Max Hislop brilliantly hurled himself into the path of the ball and saved the 1921 Premiership for the Richmond Football Club.

As a result of an incident behind the play when Greenhill (Carlton) was knocked unconscious, a Richmond player was disqualified for eight weeks. No report was made, but action was taken when the matter was raised at a VFL meeting six weeks later.

RESULTS

SEPTEMBER 24 — FIRST SEMI-FINAL

	1st	2nd	3rd	Final	
Richmond	2 . 3	6 . 8	10 . 15	16 . 19	(115)
Geelong	3 . 2	4 . 4	6 . 7	6 . 18	(54)

MCG — Umpire McMurray

Attendance 41,649 — Gate £2,271

BEST — (Rich) Thorp, M. Hislop, Smith, Hughes, Minogue, M. Morris, Don, R. Weatherill, Turnbull

(Geel) Sharland, Hagger, Johns, Smith, Craven, Gross, Kroger, Murrell, Peck

GOALS — (Rich) Bayliss (5), R. Weatherill (2), James (2), M. Morris (2), Don (2), Hughes (2), Minogue

(Geel) C. Rankin (2), Mathieson (2), Sharland, Hagger

OCTOBER 1 — SECOND SEMI-FINAL

	1st	2nd	3rd	Final	
Carlton	2 . 0	5 . 6	7 . 7	9 . 11	(65)
Collingwood	1 . 3	1 . 7	6 . 9	7 . 10	(52)

MCG — Umpire Elder

Attendance 37,813 — Gate £1,682

1921

BEST —	(Carl)	O'Brien, Blackman, Chandler, Hiskins, Clover, Raleigh, McLatchie
	(Col)	Twomey, McCarthy, Buck, Hammond, Tyson, Murphy, Rowe, Lee ,Sheehy
GOALS —	(Carl)	Clover (4), McLatchie (2), Toole, Hiskins, Chandler
	(Col)	W. Lee (4), G. Coventry, Curtis, Rowe

OCTOBER 8 — PRELIMINARY FINAL

	1st	2nd	3rd	Final	
Richmond	4 . 2	5 . 5	8 . 5	10 . 7	(67)
Carlton	1 . 4	2 . 10	7 . 14	7 . 17	(59)

MCG — **Umpire McMurray**
Attendance 42,866 — **Gate £1,967**

BEST —	(Rich)	Hall, Herbert, James, McIntosh, Smith, Minogue, Carew, Hughes, Bayliss, Thorp, Hislop
	(Carl)	Hiskins, Boromeo, Blackman, Fisher, McLatchie, Raleigh, Duncan, Stevenson, O'Brien
GOALS —	(Rich)	M. Morris (2), Bayliss (2), Herbert (2), Don, Hall, Minogue, H. James
	(Carl)	Daykin (2), Fisher, Martin, Green, Bickford, McLatchie

OCTOBER 15 — GRAND FINAL

	1st	2nd	3rd	Final	
Richmond	1 . 2	1 . 3	3 . 4	5 . 6	(36)
Carlton	2 . 2	3 . 4	3 . 6	4 . 8	(32)

MCG — **Umpire McMurray**
Attendance 43,122 — **Gate £2,016**

BEST —	(Rich)	Hislop, Smith, Taylor, McIntosh, James, Minogue, Hughes, Hall, G. Weatherill
	(Carl)	Boromeo (B.O.G.), McLatchie, O'Brien, Fisher, Jamieson, Greenhill, Hiskins
GOALS —	(Rich)	Bayliss (2), M. Morris, H. James, Turnbull
	(Carl)	Duncan, McLatchie, Boromeo, Stephenson

GRAND FINAL TEAMS

Richmond*	B	G. Weatherill	Thorp	Taylor
	HB	McIntosh	M. Hislop	Smith
	C	Harley	M. Morris	Carew
	HF	Don	R. Weatherill	Turnbull
	F	Herbert	Bayliss	Hall
	Ruck	Minogue (c)	H. James	Hughes
	Coach	D. Minogue		
Carlton	B	Toole	Jamieson	McKenzie
	HB	Raleigh	O'Brien	Greenhill
	C	Stephenson	Blackman	Chandler
	HF	Duncan	Clover	Boromeo
	F	Daykin	Green (c)	Fisher
	Ruck	Martin	R. Hiskins	McLatchie
	Coach	N. Clark		

* The Richmond team was unchanged throughout the finals series.

1922

The top four teams of 1922 stood out to such an extent that the fifth team (Richmond, 1921 premiers) finished twelve premiership points behind the fourth (Carlton, 1921 runners-up). The other three places were filled by Collingwood (twelve wins, four losses), Essendon (ten wins, five losses and a draw—this after finishing last in 1921 with only three wins), and Fitzroy (also ten wins, five losses and a draw).

Just on 64,000 people saw the first semi-final between Essendon and Carlton, but the match was rather disappointing. Carlton particularly were unimpressive, but both sides passed inaccurately, and fumbled in the air and on the ground. Blows were exchanged several times as Carlton struggled to a nine point lead by three-quarter time but were powerless to stop Essendon chipping away at their lead in the last term. Finally, Essendon's Jack Moriarty (later a Fitzroy champion) was paid a doubtful mark and kicked the winning goal.

Fitzroy, with sheer strength, blasted their way through Collingwood in the second semi-final. The Maroons, known then as the 'Men' or 'The Man's Team' were not over-endowed with skill, but made up for this with muscle-power and weight, steam-rolling their way through the opposition in most games. They did this to perfection in this semi-final, and with the heavy conditions helping them and hindering the skilful Magpies, they held on to win the match by the narrow margin of four points, when Cheswass (Collingwood) missed a fairly easy goal right at the end.

Meeting Essendon in the final, the Maroons played the same game, this time wearing their opposition down to the extent that they could add only two points to Fitzroy's five goals two in the last quarter, after leading for most of the day.

The 1922 grand final (played as late as October 14) was a great match. Amongst its unique features was the fact that all the boundary and goal umpires were ex-players of the competing sides—J. Monohan and E. Jenkins (ex Collingwood and Fitzroy respectively) were in goal, and W. Naismith and H. McKay (both Fitzroy) ran the boundary. Another feature was that it was the last game of three of the principals of the match—Dick Lee (Collingwood), Chris Lethbridge (Fitzroy's captain) and Jack Elder, the field umpire (after 295 League games—including an unequalled record of thirty-nine finals matches).

After an even first half, in which both sides missed easy shots, Fitzroy sealed the game with a brilliant third quarter burst which netted them six goals. They began with a goal to Freake five seconds after the start of the second half. Freake quickly got another, and Fergie added the third after six minutes play. Collingwood fought back well, but scoring was even for the rest of the match, and the Maroons eventually proved victorious by thirteen points. Collingwood, however, threw the game away in the last term, kicking two goals seven, some of the misses being very easy shots. Dick Lee finished his VFL career with his side's last goal of the game—his 708th in League football and fiftieth in finals matches (both records—since broken).

RESULTS

SEPTEMBER 23 — FIRST SEMI-FINAL

	1st	2nd	3rd	Final	
Essendon	1 . 0	3 . 3	3 . 5	5 . 9	(39)
Carlton	2 . 4	2 . 5	4 . 8	4 . 10	(34)

MCG — Umpire Elder
Attendance 64,148 — Gate £3,248

BEST — (Ess) Fitzmaurice, Laing, Stockdale, Hardy, Jenkins, Beckton, Barker, Watt
(Carl) O'Brien, Johnson, Boromeo, Bolt, McLatchie, Hiskins, Pritchard
GOALS — (Ess) Jenkins (2), Watt, Maher, Moriarty
(Carl) Clover (2), Pritchard, McLatchie

SEPTEMBER 30 — SECOND SEMI-FINAL

	1st	2nd	3rd	Final	
Fitzroy	2 . 3	2 . 7	6 . 8	6 . 10	(46)
Collingwood	3 . 0	4 . 7	4 . 8	5 . 12	(42)

MCG — Umpire Elder
Attendance 43,405 — Gate £1,905

BEST — (Fitz) Corrigan, Freake, Rattray, Atkinson, Lethbridge, Elliott, Collins, Sherry
(Col) Twomey (B.O.G.), Brown, G. Coventry, L. Murphy, Pannam, Wescott, Webb, Sheehy
GOALS — (Fitz) Freake (5), Gale
(Col) Webb (2), E. Wilson, G. Coventry, L. Murphy

OCTOBER 7 — PRELIMINARY FINAL

	1st	2nd	3rd	Final	
Fitzroy	0 . 3	3 . 4	4 . 12	9 . 14	(68)
Essendon	1 . 2	3 . 5	6 . 6	6 . 9	(45)

MCG — Umpire Elder
Attendance 50,021 — Gate £2,261

BEST — (Fitz) Molan, Gale, Rattray, Lethbridge, Elliott, Atkinson
(Ess) Fitzmaurice, Beckton, Laing, Hardy, Garden, Donaldson, Stockdale
GOALS — (Fitz) Wigraft (3), Freake (2), Parratt, Fergie, Corrigan, McCracken
(Ess) Stockdale (5), McCarthy

OCTOBER 14 — GRAND FINAL

	1st	2nd	3rd	Final	
Fitzroy	2 . 5	3 . 6	9 . 10	11 . 13	(79)
Collingwood	2 . 3	4 . 5	7 . 7	9 . 14	(68)

1922-1923

		MCG Attendance 50,054	Umpire Elder Gate £2,221
BEST	— (Fitz)	Taylor (B.O.G.), Fergie, Atkinson, Molan, Jenkin, Wigraft, McCracken, Parratt	
	(Col)	Drummond, Wescott, Baker, Tyson, S. & G. Coventry, Brown, Lee	
GOALS	— (Fitz)	Freake (4), Parratt (3), Fergie, McCracken, Wigraft, F. Williams	
	(Col)	G. Coventry (3), S. Coventry (2), W. Lee (2), E. Baker, Drummond	

GRAND FINAL TEAMS

Fitzroy	B	Atkinson	Jenkin	Taylor
	HB	Lethbridge (c)	Molan	Elliott
	C	Sherry	Corrigan	F. Williams
	HF	Parratt	Donnellan	Rattray
	F	Wigraft	Freake	Gale
	Ruck	McCracken	Collins	Fergie
	Coaches	V. Belcher, J. Worrall		
Collingwood	B	E. Wilson	Saunders	L. Murphy
	HB	Tyson	Brown	Twomey
	C	Drummond (c)	Pannam	Wescott
	HF	Cheswass,	S. Coventry	G. Coventry
	F	Cock	W.H. Lee	E. Baker
	Ruck	Rowe	Sheehy	Webb
	Coach	J. McHale		

1923

Essendon, under the coaching of the ex-North Melbourne (VFA) star Syd Barker, continued their climb up the ladder in 1923, finishing on top with thirteen wins and three losses in the home and home round, two games clear of Fitzroy (Second), and four clear of South Melbourne (Third) (up from last in 1922). Geelong, also with nine wins and seven losses, scraped into the Four by two premiership points from Collingwood. This was the era of the now-famous Essendon 'Mosquito Fleet', so named because of the number of little men in the line-up—amongst others Charlie Hardy five feet one inch, Rowley Watt five feet three inches, George Shorten five feet five inches, Jack Garden five feet five inches, Jim Sullivan (vice-captain) five feet six inches, Vince Irwin five feet six inches and Frank Maher five feet six inches. But it should not be forgotten that the side also contained six, six footers—more than most sides of that time, although Tom Fitzmaurice at only six feet two-and-a-half inches was the tallest. Average height of the side was, in fact, five feet nine inches.

1923

There was a sensation before the first semi-final when Geelong dropped their captain, Bert Rankin. His brother, Cliff, was appointed captain in his stead, but refused to play as he considered his brother poorly treated. Alf McCarter then took over the captaincy, and in a spiteful and vicious game, the demoralized Geelong men were thrashed by Fitzroy who booted eight goals three in a magnificent third term effort.

The game was so vicious that the press demanded an inquiry, although there had been no reports. The *Argus* said—'The incidents of last Saturday may cost Fitzroy the football premiership, for while the forthcoming inquiry may not result in any disqualifications, the attention directed to the methods of last Saturday's game will have such a steadying effect that there may not be the same force and determination in Fitzroy's play as there has been in the past. These are their assets, and without them Fitzroy is not a strong side'. These proved to be prophetic words.

South Melbourne, spear-headed by the goal-kicking of Ted Johnson (with a record equalling seven goals) played a fine last quarter to beat the favourites, Essendon, by three goals in the second semi. But they were no match for the Maroons the following week. Fitzroy in that match led by seven goals seven to four goals four at half time, but then could manage only six behinds to South's two goals two in a dreary last half which became a battle of the defences. It was one of the dullest games of football seen for years. Fitzroy never looked like losing and South never looked like winning.

The grand final was postponed the following week due to the ground being water-logged, although the day turned out to be fine. This was only the second time a finals match had been postponed.

When the match did take place the following week, Essendon, who had had only one match in six weeks, sprung the surprise of the season by selecting George Rawle, the thirty-three year old coach of Essendon Juniors, for his first League game. Rawle did not let his side down. He played well and gained a place in the 1924 premiership team as well.

Essendon began the match with a goal to Stockdale early in the first term, his sixty-seventh for the year and a new VFL record. But Fitzroy stuck with them and in fact led by a point at half time, although this was due mainly to Essendon's attrocious goal-kicking—four goals ten for the half.

In the third, McCarthy and Maher added goals for Essendon, who kept Fitzroy goalless. Then the excitement began in the last term. Stockdale missed, and, Fergie (Fitzroy) passed to Carter for a goal to reduce Essendon's lead to five points. The game see-sawed until, with nine minutes to go, Essendon still led by four points. Then Hardy (Essendon) brilliantly passed to Maher, who dodged the pack and goaled. Baring turned another Fitzroy attack before Shorten (Essendon) goaled on the run to seal the game.

Alex Mutch, ex-Collingwood player, equalled records with his performances in his first year as a senior umpire. He equalled the records of Norden (1905) and Rawle (1914) by officiating at a final in his first season, and the record of Tulloch (also ex-Collingwood) as the only ex-League players to umpire a grand final. (Ellingsen equalled the first of these records in 1931—curiously enough he was also an ex-player having appeared with Richmond and Geelong.) Mutch's performance was the more amazing as he umpired only seven home and home games during the season.

1923

RESULTS

SEPTEMBER 22 — FIRST SEMI-FINAL

	1st	2nd	3rd	Final	
Fitzroy	3 . 6	5 . 9	13 . 12	14 . 13	(97)
Geelong	1 . 2	2 . 8	5 . 9	8 . 14	(62)

MCG — Umpire McMurray
Attendance 56,240 — Gate £869

BEST — (Fitz) Fergie, Cockram, Freake, Williams, Tarbotton, Dickens, McCracken, Bryant
(Geel) Hagger, Greeves, McCarter, Dunstan, Mathieson, Stevenson, Keane, Pink

GOALS — (Fitz) Freake (5), Fergie (2), Parratt (2), Bryant, Cockram, McCracken, Carter, Rattray
(Geel) Hagger (4), Fleming (2), Keane, Mathieson

SEPTEMBER 29 — SECOND SEMI-FINAL

	1st	2nd	3rd	Final	
South Melbourne	1 . 2	4 . 7	6 . 10	10 . 14	(74)
Essendon	2 . 5	5 . 5	7 . 8	8 . 9	(57)

MCG — Umpire Mutch
Attendance 55,617 — Gate £2,621

BEST — (S. Melb) Johnson, Tandy, Robertson, Mathews, Condon, Hynes, A. Hiskins, P. Scanlon
(Ess) Donaldson, Watt, Shorten, Maher, Farrell Hunter (till injured), Beckton

GOALS — (S. Melb) Johnson (7), Tandy, Ross, Robertson
(Ess) Stockdale (2), Maher (2), McCarthy (2), Watt, Shorten

OCTOBER 6 — PRELIMINARY FINAL

	1st	2nd	3rd	Final	
Fitzroy	4 . 4	7 . 7	7 . 11	7 . 13	(55)
South Melbourne	0 . 4	4 . 5	5 . 6	6 . 7	(43)

MCG — Umpire Mutch
Attendance 55,039 — Gate £2,461

BEST — (Fitz) Collins, Jenkin, Wigraft, Atkinson, Tarbotton, Fergie, Corrigan, Dickens
(S. Melb) Brown, Tandy, O'Connell, P. Scanlon, A. Hiskins, F. Laird, Hynes

GOALS — (Fitz) Freake (2), Fergie, Parratt, Cockram, Byrant, Carter
(S. Melb) Johnson (2), Cazaly (2), Mathews, Alexander

OCTOBER 13

Postponed for one week due to rain.

OCTOBER 20 — GRAND FINAL

	1st	2nd	3rd	Final	
Essendon	3 . 2	4 . 10	6 . 13	8 . 15	(63)
Fitzroy	3 . 3	5 . 5	5 . 9	6 . 10	(46)

MCG — Umpire Mutch
Attendance 46,566 — Gate £1,912

BEST —	(Ess)	Shorten, McCarthy, Fitzmaurice, Maher, Garden, May, Watt, Hardy
	(Fitz)	Collins, Bryant, Carter, Wigraft, Fergie, Tarbotton, Atkinson, Freake
GOALS —	(Ess)	Stockdale (2), McCarthy (2), Maher (2), Jenkins, Shorten
	(Fitz)	Freake (4), Rattray, Carter

GRAND FINAL TEAMS

Essendon	B	Irwin	Baring	Donaldson
	HB	J. Harrison	Fitzmaurice	Laing
	C	Garden	May	Watt
	HF	Jenkins	McCarthy	Shorten
	F	Barker (c)	Stockdale	Hardy
	Ruck	Beckton	Rawle	Maher
	Coach	S. Barker		
Fitzroy	B	Atkinson	Jenkin	Wigraft
	HB	Tarbotton	Molan	Elliott
	C	Dickens	Corrigan	Sherry
	HF	Parratt	Cockram	Rattray (c)
	F	Bryant	Freake	Carter
	Ruck	McCracken	Collins	Fergie
	Coach	V. Belcher		

1924

After a very spiteful season, Essendon again topped the home and home ladder with eleven wins, four losses and a tie, ahead of South Melbourne (eleven wins, five losses), and Fitzroy and Richmond (both ten wins, six losses).

The VFL made a foolish decision to change the finals system in 1924, and revert to the old system whereby the top four teams played each other and the premier team was decided on the results of those matches. This led to the ludicrous situation where Essendon was defeated by Richmond in the last final but still won the premiership on percentage. The system was a farce, and was never repeated. In addition, the public was not interested and gate takings for the six finals amounted to only £6,433, compared with £7,862 for four matches in 1923.

Anyway, Essendon won the flag on percentage, despite the thrashing by Richmond at South Melbourne in the last game. It was their second successive flag, but they were a very unhappy team. After their loss to Richmond, players exchanged blows in the rooms. Then, following a team dinner at Carlyon's Hotel, the side returned to Essendon where fists flew once more.

The following week, Essendon met Footscray (VFA premiers) in a charity match for 'the Championship of Victoria'. Footscray won nine goals ten to four goals twelve, and again fists flew in the Essendon rooms after the game, when it was alleged that some of the Dons had 'played dead'. In fact, one of the Essendon champions refused ever to appear with the side again, and in 1925 turned out with another League team (where he played in his third successive premiership side).

RESULTS

SEPTEMBER 13 — FIRST PLAY-OFF

	1st	2nd	3rd	Final	
Richmond	3 . 0	5 . 1	12 . 2	13 . 7	(85)
South Melbourne	2 . 0	7 . 1	7 . 2	9 . 3	(57)

ERR — Umpire McMurray
Attendance 22,300 — Gate £830

BEST — (Rich) Valentine, McCaskill, McIntosh, Harrison, Thorp, Hislop, McIsaac, Barnett
(S. Melb) McDonald, J. Scanlan, Hando, Cazaly, Alexander, Fleiter
GOALS — (Rich) Hayes (5), Millar (2), M. Morris (2), Minogue, Barnett, Rudolph, E. Taylor
(S. Melb) Johnson (3), Cazaly (2), Brown, Tandy, Alexander, Allison

SEPTEMBER 13 — SECOND PLAY-OFF

	1st	2nd	3rd	Final	
Essendon	0 . 2	4 . 6	4 . 10	8 . 10	(58)
Fitzroy	0 . 1	1 . 3	1 . 5	2 . 6	(18)

MCG — Umpire Wickham
Attendance 45,000 — Gate £1,885

BEST — (Ess) Donaldson, Laing, Maher, Hunter, McCarthy, Shorten, Fitzmaurice
(Fitz) Atkinson, Adams, Jenkin, Collins, Williams, Wigraft
GOALS — (Ess) Jenkins (3), Maher (2), Fitzmaurice, McCarthy, Stockdale
(Fitz) McCracken, Wigraft

SEPTEMBER 20 — THIRD PLAY-OFF

	1st	2nd	3rd	Final	
Fitzroy	3 . 2	4 . 5	5 . 8	11 . 10	(76)
Richmond	2 . 4	6 . 5	7 . 7	8 . 8	(56)

Princes Oval — Umpire McKinnon
Attendance 26,000 — Gate £1,150

BEST — (Fitz) Batchelor, Corrigan, Bryant, Wigraft, Gale, Rattray, Atkinson, Adams
(Rich) Rudolph, McIsaac, Smith, M. Hislop, Spain, Empey, Morris, Hall
GOALS — (Fitz) Moriarty (3), Freake (2), Chapman (2), Molan, Donnellan, McCracken, Williams
(Rich) M. Morris (4), Bourke, Millar, McIsaac, Rudolph

SEPTEMBER 20 — FOURTH PLAY-OFF

	1st	2nd	3rd	Final	
Essendon	2 . 3	6 . 4	7 . 7	10 . 12	(72)
South Melbourne	1 . 3	2 . 4	3 . 9	4 . 15	(39)

	MCG Attendance 35,400	Umpire McMurray Gate £1,373

BEST — (Ess) Maher, Shorten, Watt, Sullivan, Farrell, Fitzmaurice
(S. Melb) Woodfield, Condon, C. McDonald, R. McDonald, J. Scanlan, Hando
GOALS — (Ess) Jenkins (4), Maher (2), Shorten (2), Hunter, McCarthy
(S. Melb) Nicholls, Johnson, Cazaly, Ross

SEPTEMBER 27 — FIFTH PLAY-OFF

	1st	2nd	3rd	Final	
Richmond	4 . 2	5 . 7	7 . 8	9 . 13	(67)
Essendon	1 . 4	2 . 8	6 . 9	6 . 11	(47)

SMCG — Umpire Wickham
Attendance 25,000 — Gate £773

BEST — (Rich) J. Smith, Hayes, Empey, McCaskill, Morris
(Ess) Fitzmaurice, Beckton, Laing, Hardy
GOALS — (Rich) Hayes (3), Empey (2), Barnett, Millar, M. Morris, Rudolph
(Ess) Hardy (2), Beckton (2), Stockdale (2)

SEPTEMBER 27 — SIXTH PLAY-OFF

	1st	2nd	3rd	Final	
South Melbourne	4 . 1	8 . 3	10 . 5	13 . 8	(86)
Fitzroy	4 . 2	5 . 5	8 . 11	10 . 13	(73)

MCG — Umpire McMurray
Attendance 17,500 — Gate £422

BEST — (S. Melb) J. Scanlon, Woodfield, Harris, Cazaly, Tandy, P. Scanlon
(Fitz) Atkinson, Wigraft, Bryant, Gale, Chapman, Moriarty, Jenkin, Corrigan
GOALS — (S. Melb) Johnson (4), J. Harris (3), O'Connell (2), Brown, Cazaly, Miller, Tandy
(Fitz) Moriarty (4), Freake (2), Chapman (2), Bryant, Gale

SECOND ROUND LADDER

Team	P	W	L	For	Agst	Pts	P/C
Essendon	3	2	1	177	124	8	142.7
Richmond	3	2	1	208	180	8	115.5
Fitzroy	3	1	2	167	200	4	83.5
South Melbourne	3	1	2	182	230	4	79.1

FINALS TEAMS

Essendon's team in the final three matches included:—Donaldson, Baring, Gregory, Laing, Fitzmaurice, Farrell, Garden, May, Sullivan, Rowley Watt, McCarthy, Shorten, Hunter, Jenkins, Stockdale, Barker (c), Rawle, Maher, Beckton, Hardy.
Coach—S. Q. Barker

Richmond's team in the final three matches included:— Harrison, Thorp, Taylor, J. Smith, M. Hislop, Spain, McCaskill, McIntosh, Valentine, Empey, Rudolph, Millar, Bourke, M. Morris, Barnett, Minogue (c), McIsaac, Hayes, G. Hislop, Hall, Reid, Karthaus.
Coach — D. Minogue

1925

After twenty-eight frustrating years in the League, Geelong finally won their first League pennant in 1925. Captained and coached by Cliff Rankin, they lost the first game of the season, won twelve more in succession and finished on top of the home and home ladder with fifteen wins and two losses. Essendon (thirteen wins, four losses) were second, and Melbourne, appearing in the finals for the first time since 1915, were third with twelve wins, four losses and a draw. Collingwood (twelve wins, five losses), scraped into the Four by one per cent from Fitzroy.

Three new teams joined the League in 1925, all from the Association, and all had a tough introduction to League football, Footscray taking until 1938 to reach the finals for the first time, North Melbourne taking until 1945, and Hawthorn until 1957. North, although winners of a string of VFA premierships, are still the only club that has not won a VFL flag.

Collingwood met Essendon in the first semi-final, which began at a fast pace with nine goals kicked (five to Essendon, four to Collingwood) in the first quarter. Essendon aided by three quick goals to Vince Irwin in the third quarter, led by two points at the last change, and maintained this lead until three minutes before the end of the game. Then Hunter and Harrison, Essendon defenders, hurled themselves at Collingwood's Gordon Coventry, setting him up for a 'sandwich'. But they missed Coventry, collided, and the unguarded Collingwood man slammed the ball through for a goal. Minutes later he marked for another, and Collingwood had won by ten points.

Melbourne had three goals six on the board before Geelong had scored in the second semi-final, but thereafter the scoring was fairly even. Geelong's Lloyd Hagger equalled the semi-final record by kicking seven goals, but the Cats went down by thirteen goals eight to fourteen goals seventeen.

The final saw Collingwood assert their superiority in the second half, after Melbourne had Taylor and Dunbar hampered by injuries, and Harold Davie carried off, and go on to a crushing thirty-seven point win. Melbourne were held goalless in the last half, and but for a great individual effort by Ivor Warne-Smith in defence—nine marks in eleven minutes at one stage—would have lost by much more.

A record 64,288 people attended the grand final. Geelong were on top from the start, when Cliff Rankin had two goals on the board within the first nine minutes, but they won the game with four goals against the wind in the second quarter. The game, which had begun to get willing after Wilson (Collingwood) was flattened early, got out of hand in the third quarter with several fiery clashes. A goal to Stevenson (Geelong) right on the bell gave Geelong a commanding ten goals thirteen to six goals twelve lead at three-quarter time. Then Collingwood fought back. Webb fumbled a couple of chances before Chesswas snapped a behind, then a goal, and Stainsby added another goal to reduce the Collingwood deficit to twelve points with only six minutes of the last quarter gone. The unfortunate Gordon Coventry (who was held goalless by Johns, the only time this happened to Coventry in a grand final) kicked out of bounds, an easy chance. Geelong added four behinds, while Collingwood twice missed, Lawn's shot going close enough to hit the post for the Magpies third poster. Tyson then goaled, and Geelong's lead was cut to only eight points. Hagger and Rayson added behinds for Geelong, and then with three minutes to go, F. Murphy (Collingwood) forwarded from the wing where Ferguson (Geelong) slipped as he ran in to contest the mark with three Collingwood men. Flat on his back, Ferguson marked to break up the Magpie attack. The bell rang soon after and the flag was Geelong's!

The Cats received a tumultuous welcome when they arrived back at Geelong station at 8.00 p.m. that night. 5,000 people met the train, which blew its whistle all the way into North Geelong, the signal being taken up by every engine and fire-bell in the yard. 200 detonators were exploded, the band struck up, and the 3,000 cars at the station added to the tumult with blasting horns. Captain Cliff Rankin was chaired to the Town Hall (the others of the team were driven), where Mayor C. Ritchie met and congratulated the Geelong heroes.

Tom Fitzmaurice equalled a unique record by appearing with two different premiership teams in two successive years, Essendon in 1923-24 and Geelong in 1925. This feat had previously been accomplished by J. Martin Essendon 1912, and Fitzroy 1913.

RESULTS

SEPTEMBER 19 — FIRST SEMI-FINAL

	1st	2nd	3rd	Final	
Collingwood	4 . 1	7 . 4	9 . 4	12 . 6	(78)
Essendon	5 . 2	6 . 2	9 . 6	10 . 8	(68)

MCG — Umpire McMurray

Attendance 59,905 — Gate £2,964

BEST — (Col) F. Murphy, G. Coventry, Dibbs, E. Wilson, Beasley, Tyson, S. Coventry, Baker, Harris, Webb, Stainsby

(Ess) Campbell, Harrison, Hunter, Donaldson, Farrell, Stockdale, May, Simpson, Garden, Irwin

GOALS — (Col) G. Coventry (5), Stainsby (2), F. Murphy, Webb, S. Coventry, Lawn, Milburn

(Ess) Maher (4), Irwin (4), Quinn, G. Shorten

SEPTEMBER 26 — SECOND SEMI-FINAL

	1st	2nd	3rd	Final	
Melbourne	3 . 9	8 . 10	13 . 13	14 . 17	(101)
Geelong	1 . 1	5 . 2	9 . 5	13 . 8	(86)

MCG — Umpire McMurray

Attendance 51,256 — Gate £2,570

BEST — (Melb) Wittman, Taylor, Haines, Corbett, Deane, Chadwick, Lilley, Collins, Coy, Tulloh, Warne-Smith

(Geel) Warren, Greeves, Hall, Chambers, Heagney, Hagger, Johns

GOALS —	(Melb)	Tulloh (5), Wittman (3), Haines (2), Davie (2), Mollison, Taylor
	(Geel)	Hagger (7), C. Rankin (4), Fleming, Jones

OCTOBER 3 — PRELIMINARY FINAL

	1st	2nd	3rd	Final	
Collingwood	1 . 3	4 . 8	5 . 9	8 . 15	(63)
Melbourne	2 . 2	3 . 4	3 . 5	3 . 8	(26)

MCG — Umpire McMurray
Attendance 49,833 — Gate £2,423

BEST —	(Col)	S. Coventry, E. Wilson, Dibbs, Beasley, Shanahan, Makeham, Chesswas, Milburn, Wescott
	(Melb)	Warne-Smith (B.O.G.), Corbett, Thomas, Streeter, Lilley, Haines, Taylor, Collins
GOALS —	(Col)	G. Coventry (5), Harris, Stainsby, Tyson
	(Melb)	Corbett, Tulloh, Taylor

OCTOBER 10 — GRAND FINAL

	1st	2nd	3rd	Final	
Geelong	3 . 2	7 . 8	10 . 13	10 . 19	(79)
Collingwood	2 . 5	4 . 9	6 . 12	9 . 15	(69)

MCG — Umpire McMurray
Attendance 64,288 (record) — Gate £3,132

BEST —	(Geel)	Chambers, Johns, C. Rankin, Rayson, Leahy, Warren, Hudd, Greeves (till injured)
	(Col)	S. Coventry, Webb, Stainsby, Milburn, Chesswas, Dibbs, F. Murphy
GOALS —	(Geel)	C. Rankin (5), Hagger, Heagney, Chambers, Hall, Stevenson
	(Col)	F. Murphy (2), Stainsby (2), Webb (2), Baker, Chesswas, Tyson

GRAND FINAL TEAMS

Geelong	B	Smith	Johns	Ferguson
	HB	Hudd	Fitzmaurice	Leahy
	C	Stevenson	Greeves	Williams
	HF	Rayson	Todd	Chambers
	F	C. Rankin (c)	Hagger	Hall
	Ruck	Fleming	Heagney	Warren
	Coach	C. Rankin		
Collingwood	B	Beasley	Dibbs	Shanahan
	HB	Tyson (c)	Makeham	E. Wilson
	C	Milburn	Chesswas	Wescott
	HF	Harris	F. Murphy	Lawn
	F	Stainsby	G. Coventry	A. Baker
	Ruck	S. Coventry	L. Murphy	Webb
	Coach	J. McHale		

1926

Collingwood and Geelong, 1925 grand finalists, were oustanding teams in the home and home games in 1926, both finishing with fifteen wins and three losses, although Collingwood won top position by virtue of a better percentage. Melbourne (fourteen wins) and Essendon (twelve wins) filled the other two spots in the final Four, Essendon sneaking in on percentage from South Melbourne.

Essendon eliminated Geelong in the first semi when, by kicking six goals six to one goal four in the last quarter, including four goals in the first five minutes they piled up a record finals score of seventeen goals fifteen. It was a good win by Essendon as Geelong were very hot favourites.

The Magpies went down to defeat in a slugging second semi-final. Leading by eight goals eight to four goals ten at half-time, the Magpies looked to have the game won, but after sending Col Deane into the ruck at half-time, Melbourne got moving. In twenty minutes of scintillating football, the Redlegs made an amazing recovery to add eight goals one to their score and lead by twelve goals twelve to nine goals twelve at three-quarter time. Starting the last, Moyes and Taylor both hit the post for Melbourne, and Collingwood's score crept up until with only eight minutes left, they trailed by only nine points. At that critical stage, Bob Johnson kicked a vital goal for Melbourne which sealed the game, amidst scenes of unprecedented enthusiasm.

The preliminary final also produced its sensations. It was played in a high wind on a dry, unpleasant day, and Melbourne led at half-time by three goals four to two goals seven. They were however, faced with the predicament of playing the second half without their champion centre-man, Bob Corbett. Corbett had been viciously 'king-hit' from behind while leaving the ground at the interval, and suffered a broken jaw. Replacements were not permitted for injured players until 1930. The uneven struggle went on until the last few minutes when, with Melbourne holding a slender lead of a few points, a figure with head swathed in bandages ran onto the field. It was the injured Corbett who had made his way unnoticed from the dressing room to try and help his side. Alhough he was barely conscious and was not able to gain a kick, his presence on the field inspired his team-mates, who lifted themselves and in a do-or-die effort, held on to win by three points.

A side result of the Corbett 'incident'—although it took until 1930 to be introduced—was the VFL's decision to allow a reserve to be named who could replace another player during a game.

1926

To replace the injured Corbett in the grand final, Melbourne brought in a 'first-gamer', F. S. 'Pop' Vine from Old Melburnians. Melbourne won the toss, and had a goal on the board to Johnson within one minute. Taylor, and Johnson (twice) added further goals and Melbourne led by four goals five to one goal one at the first change. Johnson continued to dominate play for Melbourne, but Collingwood came back well to add five goals three in the second quarter and the game was evenly poised at half-time.

Collingwood moved Syd Coventry on Johnson at half-time and Beveridge, who had been playing brilliantly in the centre, went to the half-forward flank. Melbourne astutely moved the focus of their attacks from Johnson to Moyes to Duff and back again until the Collingwood defenders were completely befuddled. Moyes added three goals in quick succession, answered by only a single goal from Harry Collier. Wittman added another goal for Melbourne, and then with Warne-Smith coming good in the centre, the Redlegs peppered the big sticks for further goals to Vine, Duff and Johnson, to have an unbeatable lead at three-quarter time. The last term was a repetition of the first three, the only interest for Collingwood being when Gordon Coventry marked and kicked his eighty-third goal of the season to set a new VFL record. Melbourne added another three goals eight to set a new finals record score and Bob Johnson took his tally for the match to six goals seven—as Melbourne romped home to their first VFL pennant for twenty-six years.

RESULTS

SEPTEMBER 18 — FIRST SEMI-FINAL

	1st	2nd	3rd	Final	
Essendon	5 . 5	7 . 7	11 . 9	17 . 15	(117)
Geelong	2 . 3	7 . 5	9 . 6	10 . 10	(70)

MCG — Umpire Netherton
Attendance 50,662 — Gate £2,721

BEST —	(Ess)	May, Donaldson, Garden, Rowley Watt, Maher, Vosti, Shorten, Quinn
	(Geel)	Fitzmaurice, Chambers, Williams, Todd, Greeves, Warren, Jones
GOALS —	(Ess)	Vosti (5), Beckton (4), Maher (3), Garden (2), Hammond, E. Shorten, Watt
	(Geel)	C. Rankin (2), Rayson (2), Chambers (2), Jones (2), Fitzmaurice, Warren

SEPTEMBER 25 — SECOND SEMI-FINAL

	1st	2nd	3rd	Final	
Melbourne	2 . 7	4 . 10	12 . 12	13 . 17	(95)
Collingwood	3 . 2	8 . 8	9 . 12	12 . 12	(84)

MCG — Umpire McMurray
Attendance 44,286 — Gate £2,165

BEST —	(Melb)	Deane, Wittman, Corbett, Collins, Streeter, Coy, Thomas, Tymms
	(Col)	Dibbs, Harris, Libbis, Beveridge, Beasley, Clayden, A. Collier, Poulter
GOALS —	(Melb)	Moyes (5), Duff (2), Wittman (2), Abernethy, Deane, Johnson, Collins
	(Col)	H. Collier (3), G. Coventry (3), Libbis (2), Tyson, Poulter, Harris, Chesswas

1926

OCTOBER 2 — PRELIMINARY FINAL

	1st	2nd	3rd	Final
Melbourne	1 . 1	3 . 4	5 . 5	6 . 6 (42)
Essendon	1 . 6	3 . 7	4 . 8	5 . 9 (39)

MCG — Umpire Netherton
Attendance 49,319 — Gate £2,411

BEST — (Melb) Streeter, Abernethy, Tymms, Collins, Corbett, Davidson, Deane
(Ess) Gregory, Hunter, Campbell, Rowley Watt, Maher, Quinn, Vosti

GOALS — (Melb) Duff (3), Johnson (2), Davidson
(Ess) Vosti (4), Maher

OCTOBER 9 — GRAND FINAL

	1st	2nd	3rd	Final
Melbourne	4 . 5	7 . 7	14 . 9	17 . 17 (119)
Collingwood	1 . 1	6 . 4	7 . 6	9 . 8 (62)

MCG — Umpire McMurray
Attendance 59,362 — Gate £3,007

BEST — (Melb) Johnson, Wittman, Moyes, Streeter, Abernethy, Warne-Smith, White, Davidson, Chadwick, Duff
(Col) S. Coventry, H. Collier, Harris, Beasley, Shanahan, Wescott, Wilson, Beveridge

GOALS — (Melb) Johnson (6), Moyes (3), Wittman (3), Duff (2), Taylor, Vine, Deane
(Col) H. Collier (3), G. Coventry (2), Makeham, A. Collier, A. Baker, Libbis

GRAND FINAL TEAMS

Melbourne	B	Streeter	Coy	Abernethy
	HB	Tymms	H. Dunbar	Thomas
	C	Taylor	Warne-Smith	Collins
	HF	Wittman	Johnson	Davidson
	F	Vine	Duff	Moyes
	Ruck	Chadwick (c)	C. Deane	White
	Coach	A. Chadwick		
Collingwood	B	Wescott	Beasley	Poulter
	HB	E. Wilson	A. Collier	Shanahan
	C	Harris	Beveridge	Milburn
	HF	A. Baker	F. Murphy	Chesswas
	F	Tyson (c)	G. Coventry	H. Collier
	Ruck	S. Coventry	Makeham	Libbis
	Coach	J. McHale		

1927

After their great 1926 flag, Melbourne slipped down the list to fifth in 1927, one game out of the Four, after being equal first after ten games. Collingwood, with the record-breaking Gordon Coventry at full-forward, finished on top of the list with fifteen wins, three losses. Richmond were next, a game behind, followed by Geelong (same number of wins as Richmond but inferior percentage), and Carlton thirteen wins.

Carlton and Richmond met in the first semi-final, and blood flowed. Bad feeling dated back to their previous clash two weeks before, in which five men were knocked out and four, two from each side, reported. Richmond, kicking with the breeze in the first quarter, took a grip on the semi-final with four quick goals, but Carlton, playing the long game, fought back well to lead at half-time. Then Richmond also switched to the long game, and went to a nine point lead at three-quarter time. Two quick goals to Vallence at the start of the last term put Carlton back on top, and then the game fluctuated crazily as Hayes (Richmond) and Downs (Carlton) goaled in turn. Then the Blues made the mistake of dropping into the short game around the flanks. Richmond's near misses levelled the scores, and just on the bell the ball was hit out to Weidner, whose left-foot drop-kick sailed through for a goal to win the game for the Tigers.

A merciless Collingwood, with seven goals from Gordon Coventry, thrashed Geelong in the second semi-final, the Pivotonians having only two goals four on the board at three-quarter time. Collingwood handled the mud and rain far better then their opponents, only relaxing late in the last quarter to let Geelong in for four quick goals.

Collingwood then met Richmond in the final, having a second chance (as minor premiers) if they lost. But they didn't need two chances. On one of the most shocking days for football which it would be possible to imagine, they slipped and slid their way to their sixth League flag. There was rain all Friday night preceding the game, and continuous rain all Saturday. The MCG was completely waterlogged, with one wing under water, and the day was bitterly cold.

Geddes (Richmond) won the toss, and kicked to the Richmond end, favoured by a strong breeze. The Tigers hoped to get a few quick goals on the board before the ball became too wet, but in blinding rain, Collingwood's great skipper Syd Coventry was impassable in defence. By driving the ball continually to the Stand wing, Collingwood held Richmond to four points and this virtually won the game. In the second, the rain increased as Collingwood forced the ball forward with soccer kicks, one of which Gordon Coventry hugged to his chest and punted the first goal. Some ten minutes later, the same player scored again with a left foot snap, which, considering the conditions, gave Collingwood an almost unbeatable lead. Both goals came from mistakes by Richmond backmen who defended to Collingwoods attacking flank.

The remainder of the game was a fierce scramble, in the mud and slush with Fincher finally scoring Richmond's only goal in the last quarter. But although Richmond did most of the attacking, Collingwood were in no danger of defeat and most of the meagre 34,551 crowd were glad when the bell went to mercifully end the match with the scores showing Collingwood two goals thirteen, Richmond one goal seven.

G. Coventry's two goals took his total for the season to ninety-seven, a new VFL record.

RESULTS

SEPTEMBER 17 — FIRST SEMI-FINAL

	1st	2nd	3rd	Final	
Richmond	4 . 3	6 . 6	10 . 7	12 . 10	(82)
Carlton	2 . 2	7 . 7	8 . 10	11 . 10	(76)

MCG — Umpire McMurray
Attendance 63,590 — Gate £3,434

BEST — (Rich) Harris, Lilburne, O'Halloran, Geddes, O'Brien, Gallagher, Baggott, Bentley
(Carl) Beasy, Downs, Duncan, Kelleher, Donoghue, Brewis, Clover, Johnson

GOALS — (Rich) J. McCormack (4), Baggott (3), Weidner (2), Bentley, Fincher, Hayes
(Carl) Downs (4), Clover (3), Vallence (2), Davey, Carter

SEPTEMBER 24 — SECOND SEMI-FINAL

	1st	2nd	3rd	Final	
Collingwood	5 . 6	9 . 10	13 . 15	16 . 18	(114)
Geelong	1 . 0	1 . 2	2 . 4	7 . 6	(48)

MCG — Umpire Coffey
Attendance 40,595 — Gate £2,200

BEST — (Col) S. Coventry, G. Coventry, H. Collier, Chesswas, Harris, Rumney, Makeham, Dibbs, A. Collier
(Geel) Hickey, Coghlan, Baker, Williams, Hall

GOALS — (Col) G. Coventry (7), H. Collier (4), F. Murphy (2), Rowe, Libbis, Harris
(Geel) C. Rankin (2), Jerram, Hall, Chambers, E. Baker, Todd

OCTOBER 1 — GRAND FINAL

	1st	2nd	3rd	Final	
Collingwood	0 . 1	2 . 6	2 . 9	2 . 13	(25)
Richmond	0 . 4	0 . 4	0 . 7	1 . 7	(13)

MCG — Umpire McMurray
Attendance 34,551 — £1,779 Gate

BEST — (Col) S. Coventry, Makeham, F. Murphy, Beveridge, Rowe, H. Collier
(Rich) B. McCormack, Geddes, Hayes, Fincher, Harris, Rudolph, O'Halloran

GOALS — (Col) G. Coventry (2)
(Rich) Fincher

GRAND FINAL TEAMS

Collingwood	B	Wescott	Dibbs	Poulter
	HB	E. Wilson	Clayden	A. Collier
	C	Chesswas	Beveridge	Milburn
	HF	F. Murphy	Makeham	Harris
	F	Rumney	G. Coventry	H. Collier
	Ruck	S. Coventry (c)	Rowe	Libbis
	Coach	J. McHale		
Richmond	B	Harris	Powell	McIsaac
	HB	Lilburne	Bentley	B. McCormack
	C	O'Brien	Gallagher	Geddes (c)
	HF	Weidner	Rudolph	Jamieson
	F	Robinson	J. McCormack	Fincher
	Ruck	O'Halloran	O'Neill	Hayes
	Coach	F. V. Hughes		

1928

Collingwood and Richmond again finished first and second in 1928, with fifteen wins and fourteen wins respectively. Melbourne (also fourteen wins) jumped up to third, while fourth place was a real scramble between Essendon, St. Kilda, and Carlton (all eleven wins) with the latter finally scraping in on percentage, by point one per cent from Essendon.

A new record crowd of 66,381 saw a spiteful first semi-final between Carlton and Richmond. One player on either side was reported, but many more were lucky to escape. Lumbering Carlton could not pace it with the Tigers who went right away in the second half to equal the first semi-final scoring record—seventeen goals fifteen. Young Jack Titus, with six goals, was a Tiger star. These were the first of his total of sixty-seven goals in finals matches for Richmond. T. Downs (Carlton) was suspended for twelve weeks, and A. Geddes (Richmond) for eight weeks from incidents in this match.

Collingwood had to 'fall over' to lose the second semi-final against Melbourne, and, while they didn't actually lose, they were extremely lucky not to. Leading by nine goals eight to four goals eight at three-quarter time, they stopped to a walk as Melbourne, inspired by the brilliance of Warne-Smith, slammed on five goals to nothing in the last quarter.

Played on a hard ground, in a blustery and warm westerly wind, Collingwood was far too strong for three-quarters. Then, just on the three-quarter time bell, a shot by

Collingwood's Bruce Andrew went through for a behind which was disallowed. This was important in view of what happened later—many people, including Andrew himself, believed the kick was well on its way before the bell sounded. In the last, Syd Coventry ordered Collingwood to defend, which turned out to be a mistake. Melbourne, inspired by the brilliant Warne-Smith, went forward for Bob Johnson to mark and punt a long goal. Then Taylor, quiet all day, flashed a pass to Johnson for another, and Deane booted a third from half-forward. Melbourne had kicked three vital goals in six minutes. Soon after, McConville got their fourth, and when Collingwood went forward, G. Coventry foolishly short-passed and the Melbourne defenders swept the ball away. Murphy (Collingwood) took a clean mark which was disallowed before McConville (Melbourne), tearing through three packs, put a towering punt through to equal the scores seconds before the bell and bring up the first tie in a semi-final.

In the replay, an amazing last quarter in which Melbourne scored six goals two and Collingwood five goals one saw the Magpies just hold on to win by four points. McConville nearly repeated his previous week's effort, his flying shot from the pack with seconds to go scoring only a point instead of the goal which would have won the game. Surprisingly, in view of the previous week's drawn game, only 42,175 people came along to see the replay.

Meeting Richmond in the final, Collingwood won easily to take their second successive pennant, a grand final not being necessary.

There was scrambly play in the first quarter, with defences of both sides on top, A. Collier (Collingwood) and J. Murdoch (Richmond) being the dominating figures. Collingwood put up two early goals through L. Murphy (from fifty-five yards out) and G. Coventry. Syd Coventry made quick changes with his followers, and in all used six in the first half, saving Percy Rowe for the last two quarters. Forwards began to get on top in the second quarter and the game opened out into a classical display of the football skills. O'Halloran and Weidner marked and goaled for the Tigers, and then G. Coventry broke loose for Collingwood and kicked three goals with three successive shots. Titus, very quiet, kicked the Tigers' third, Harris and G. Coventry replied for Collingwood and Goding kicked Richmond's fourth so that the scores at half-time were Collingwood seven goals eight, Richmond four goals five. Richmond made their big effort in the third term. Titus marked and goaled, but after ten minutes attacking Murphy replied for Collingwood after a mark, and G. Coventry snapped his sixth. Empey (Richmond) with some clever play got in a long shot which eluded a group of players and bounced through. Minutes later a chain of passes ended with the same player goaling once again, and Richmond were still well in it at the final change. Makeham opened the last term with a Magpie goal, but O'Halloran, after a 'screamer' in the goal-square, replied for the Tigers. Richmond were beginning to press Collingwood, but G. Coventry marked in a pack and goaled to ease the pressure. Collingwood missed a couple of 'sitters' before Richmond's Weidner goaled with a great left foot snap which just cleared the pack and left Richmond only fifteen points down. But that was the end of it, as in the remaining twelve minutes Collingwood added two goals six to nothing. Both goals were scored by G. Coventry, making his total for the match nine—a new finals record. He was too tall and strong for Richmond's skipper, the great Donald Don, at full back, but he had the excellent assistance of Percy Rowe who took all the Richmond backs could throw at him in order to give Coventry a clear run to the ball. The worth of these tactics was reflected in Coventry's nine magnificient goals, and the Magpies' seventh VFL flag.

1928

RESULTS

SEPTEMBER 8 — FIRST SEMI-FINAL

	1st	2nd	3rd	Final	
Richmond	6 . 2	11 . 8	13 . 11	17 . 15	(117)
Carlton	3 . 0	6 . 4	7 . 7	9 . 10	(64)

MCG — Umpire McMurray
Attendance 66,381 — Gate £3,402

BEST — (Rich) Harris, Lilburne, Judkins, Titus, Don, Bissett, Murdoch, McCormack
(Carl) Clover, Gough, Kelly, Martyn, Gilby, Brewis, Vallence

GOALS — (Rich) Titus (6), Empey (3), Lilburne (2), Weidner (2), Baggott, Fincher, Rudolph, O'Halloran
(Carl) Gough (4), Clover (3), Vallence, Dunn

SEPTEMBER 15 — SECOND SEMI-FINAL

	1st	2nd	3rd	Final	
Melbourne	3 . 1	3 . 4	4 . 8	9 . 8	(62)
Collingwood	4 . 5	5 . 5	9 . 8	9 . 8	(62)

MCG — Umpire McMurray
Attendance 41,423 — Gate £1,958

BEST — (Melb) Collins, Thomas, Barnes, Chadwick, Warne-Smith, Usher, Deane
(Col) Beveridge, Dibbs, Rumney, S. Coventry, Clayden, Andrew H. Collier

GOALS — (Melb) Johnson (4), McConville (2), Davidson, Wittman, Deane
(Col) Makeham (3), G. Coventry (2), F. Murphy (2), H. Collier, Libbis

SEPTEMBER 22 — SECOND SEMI-FINAL REPLAY

	1st	2nd	3rd	Final	
Collingwood	2 . 2	3 . 3	5 . 7	10 . 8	(68)
Melbourne	1 . 4	1 . 6	3 . 8	9 . 10	(64)

MCG — Umpire McMurray
Attendance 42,175 — Gate £2,009

BEST — (Col) S. Coventry, Libbis, Makeham, Harris, H. & A. Collier, L. Murphy, Beveridge, Rumney
(Melb) Tymms (B.O.G.), Warne-Smith, Chadwick, Usher, Thomas, McConville, Johnson

GOALS — (Col) Libbis (3), Makeham (2), H. Collier (2), A. Collier, Harris, Beveridge
(Melb) Johnson (5), Wittman, White, Vine, Deane

SEPTEMBER 29 — GRAND FINAL

	1st	2nd	3rd	Final	
Collingwood	2 . 4	7 . 8	9 . 11	13 . 18	(96)
Richmond	0 . 3	4 . 5	7 . 7	9 . 9	(63)

MCG — Umpire McMurray
Attendance 50,026 — Gate £2,533

BEST — (Col) A. Collier, G. Coventry, F. Murphy, S. Coventry, H. Collier, Rumney, Libbis, Rowe
(Rich) O'Halloran, Murdoch, Watson, B. McCormack, Harris, Lilburne, Fincher

1928-1929

GOALS — (Col) G. Coventry (9), L. Murphy (2), Harris, Makeham
(Rich) Weidner (2), Titus (2), O'Halloran (2), Empey (2), Goding

GRAND FINAL TEAMS

Collingwood	B	Rumney	Dibbs	Lauder
	HB	A. Collier	Clayden	Makeham
	C	McLeod	Beveridge	Andrew
	HF	Harris	F. Murphy	Chesswas
	F	Rowe	G. Coventry	H. Collier
	Ruck	S. Coventry (c)	L. Murphy	Libbis
	Coach	J. McHale		
Richmond	B	Harris	Don (c)	Bissett
	HB	Murdoch	Foster	B. McCormack
	C	Judkins	Gallagher	Watson
	HF	Weidner	Rudolph	Baggott
	F	Empey	Titus	Goding
	Ruck	O'Halloran	Lilburne	Fincher
	Coach	F. V. Hughes		

1929

Records fell by the wayside before the brilliant football of the 1929 Collingwood team. They went right through the eighteen home and home games without suffering a defeat, the only time a side has ever accomplished this feat, and including their semi-finals wins of 1928, won twenty consecutive games, another record. They became the first team to kick more than 2000 points in a season—2058 to be exact—and full-forward Gordon Coventry became the first man in League history to kick 100 goals in a season. He finished the season with a mammoth total of 124—including a record sixteen in one game. In addition, the Magpies equalled their 1927 record of providing the top goalkicker and Brownlow Medallist, as well as winning the premiership.

Naturally, the Magpies topped the ladder with seventy-two premiership points (yet another record)*, followed by Carlton (fifteen wins), Richmond (twelve wins and a tie) and St. Kilda (twelve wins). The Saints only just sneaked in by two premiership points from Melbourne whose drawn game against Footscray cost them dearly.

Injury riddled St. Kilda—Carr, Sanneman, and Ludlow were all out—met Carlton in the first semi-final. The Blues had their top goal-kicker, Vallence, out, but otherwise were at full-strength. The Saints looked to have a second to none chance of victory

* Until beaten by Hawthorn in a 22 game season in 1971; the record, shared by several clubs, now stands at 76 points (19 wins) in a season.

when they slowly pegged Carlton back after the Blues had jumped away to an early lead. But early in the last quarter a violent dust storm hit the ground and almost obscured players. This upset St. Kilda more than Carlton and the Blues booted four quick goals while the Saints looked on. St. Kilda rallied in the last ten minutes to reduce the leeway to eight points, but then ran out of time. They were unlucky to lose a ruckman and wingman injured at a vital stage of the game. Horrie Clover almost single-handedly won the game for the Blues, booting five goals himself and beating three opponents, but St. Kilda's Fred Phillips was the star of the match, playing the best game of his career.

The second semi-final, expected to be a mere formality for Collingwood, provided the upset of the season. The mighty Magpies, unbeaten in eighteen games, met a rugged and determined Richmond team who played them side by side, stuck like shadows, and applied liberal doses of vigour to upset the talented Magpies. The crowd roared when Syd Coventry and George Clayden, two of the Collingwood big-guns, were flattened (Basil McCormick was reported for striking Clayden and missed the grand final). The Magpie machine crumbled under pressure and 51,000 fans stared in disbelief when the half-time scoreboard showed Richmond nine goals seven to Collingwood two goals eight, and fifty minutes later Richmond eighteen goals fifteen to Collingwood eight goals thirteen. It was an incredible loss of form by Collingwood, but as minor premiers, they still had another chance at the premiership.

Carlton met Richmond in the preliminary final in a clash of muscle. Certainly both sides did not lack skill, but neither did they lack brawny big men who were quite willing to trade bumps (and blows) for their side. One player on each team was reported as the Tigers struggled to a ten point lead at half time, after a sudden storm had lashed the ground and soaked the oval late in the second term. This caused Carlton to lose its aerial superiority, but they fought back well to lead by four points at three-quarter time, and thirteen points with ten minutes to go. Then they made a tactical error by trying to break through for more goals instead of closing up the game and holding their lead. This suited the Tigers who punched holes in the harassed Carlton defence, and Jack Titus scored the winning goal for Richmond, right on the bell.

This meant a further Richmond—Collingwood clash in the grand final. It was anticipated that the Magpies—despite their drubbing at the hands of the Tigers in the second semi—would take a lot of beating, and one anonymous fan (or bookmaker) must have thought so, for he tried hard to put them off their game by posting death-threat letters to eleven prominent players before the grand final. All were received in the Collingwood rooms, and wisely withheld by officials until after the game. After Syd Coventry won the toss and kicked with the breeze, Collingwood, with three changes from their beaten semi-final side, never looked like losing. They piled up a match winning six goals three in the first quarter, and went on to an easy win eleven goals thirteen to seven goals eight, despite receiving only thirty-four free kicks to Richmond's sixty-one.

For once the Magpies' ace goal-kicker, G. Coventry, was subdued but pocket forward 'Tubby' Edmonds came to the party with five match-winning goals. The Magpies thus won their third successive flag, to equal the record of Carlton's great 1906-7-8 teams.

1929

RESULTS

SEPTEMBER 7 — FIRST SEMI-FINAL

	1st	2nd	3rd	Final	
Carlton	4 . 5	5 . 5	8 . 8	12 : 9	(81)
St. Kilda	0 . 1	4 . 4	7 . 6	11 . 7	(73)

MCG — Umpire R. Scott
Attendance 58,481 — Gate £3,036

BEST — (Carl) Clover, Kelly, Davey, C. Martyn, Gill, Brew, Williams
(St. K) Phillips (B.O.G.), Cubbins, Neill, Bence, Mason, Roberts, Scott
GOALS — (Carl) Clover (5), Green (3), Brew, Collins, Downs, Dunn
(St. K) Mason (2), Neill (2), Outram (2), Scott (2), Mohr (2), Morden

SEPTEMBER 14 — SECOND SEMI-FINAL

	1st	2nd	3rd	Final	
Richmond	4 . 2	9 . 7	12 . 8	18 . 15	(123)
Collingwood	2 . 5	2 . 8	6 . 13	8 . 13	(61)

MCG — Umpire R. Scott
Attendance 51,069 — Gate £2,485

BEST — (Rich) Hunter, Sheahan, Dunne, Murdoch, Bentley, O'Halloran, Baggott, Titus
(Col) Libbis, Clayden, Wescott, Dibbs, Harris, H. Collier
GOALS — (Rich) Titus (5), Baggott (5), Hunter (5), Dunne, Weidner, Ryan
(Col) G. Coventry (4), Libbis (3), Clayden

SEPTEMBER 21 — PRELIMINARY FINAL

	1st	2nd	3rd	Final	
Richmond	4 . 1	8 . 6	11 . 6	15 . 7	(97)
Carlton	6 . 1	7 . 2	12 . 4	14 . 7	(91)

MCG — Umpire R. Scott
Attendance 60,750 — Gate £3,127

BEST — (Rich) Hunter, Fincher, Harris, Murdoch, Dunne, Sheahan, Heifner, Baggott
(Col) Davey, Downs, Brew, C. Martyn, Parsons, Gilby, Clover, Doyle
GOALS — (Rich) Titus (4), Hunter (3), Weidner (3), Baggott (2), Fincher, Heifner, O'Halloran
(Col) Clover (5), Green (2), Vallence (2), Dunn (2), Collins (2), Doyle

SEPTEMBER 28 — GRAND FINAL

	1st	2nd	3rd	Final	
Collingwood	6 . 3	7 . 6	9 . 6	11 . 13	(79)
Richmond	2 . 0	3 . 3	5 . 5	7 . 8	(50)

MCG — Umpire R. Scott
Attendance 63,336 — Gate £3,227

BEST — (Col) Libbis (B.O.G.), Wescott, S. Coventry, Aherne, Clayden, Dibbs, A. Collier, Edmonds
(Rich) Murdoch, Bentley, Geddes, Watson, Empey, Weidner, Harris
GOALS — (Col) Edmonds (5), G. Coventry (2), H. Collier, Libbis, F. Murphy, L. Murphy
(Rich) Baggott (2), Weidner (2), Geddes, O'Halloran, Lilburne

1929-1930

GRAND FINAL TEAMS

Collingwood	B	Wescott	Dibbs	Clayden
	HB	Lauder	A. Collier	Rumney
	C	Chesswas	Beveridge	Bowyer
	HF	F. Murphy	L. Murphy	Makeham
	F	Edmonds	G. Coventry	H. Collier
	Ruck	S. Coventry (c)	Aherne	Libbis
	Coach	J. McHale		
Richmond	B	Heifner	Benton	Harris
	HB	Dunne	Murdoch	Sheahan
	C	Geddes	Lilburne (c)	Watson
	HF	Empey	O'Halloran	Weidner
	F	Fincher	Baggott	Titus
	Ruck	Bentley	Ryan	Hunter
	Coach	F. V. Hughes		

1930

A new innovation, and one that was long overdue, was the introduction in 1930 of a reserve, known as the nineteenth man, who could replace a player leaving the ground due to injury or lack of form. At first only one reserve was allowed but in 1946 a second was introduced.

Collingwood continued their triumphant progress in 1930, kicking a new record of 2190 points for the season, winning their fourth successive premiership (a feat never equalled in the League, although Essendon had done it in the old VFA competition in 1891-2-3-4), and kicking a record thirteen scores of 100 points or more during the season. (Beaten by Melbourne Football Club in 1939.) Again the Magpies finished on top, winning fifteen games and losing three. Carlton, with thirteen wins in their first fourteen games, had looked certain to take top place, but losses in two of the last four games saw them relegated to second, Collingwood gaining top place only after the last game. Richmond, Geelong and Melbourne, all with eleven wins, filled the next three spots on the ladder, the percentage figures between Geelong and Melbourne, however, being quite considerable. Melbourne only needed to beat Hawthorn in the last game to make the finals, and as Hawthorn were third last, and had never beaten Melbourne, the result was deemed a foregone conclusion. But the Hawthorn team combined brilliantly to down the Redlegs twelve goals eighteen to ten goals seventeen, putting Melbourne out of the final Four and Geelong in.

Carlton took the field against Geelong in the first semi with a team greatly weakened by injury and suspension. Captain Ray Brew decided to play, although suffering torn rib muscles, but he had to be replaced at half time. Geelong attacked with first use of the wind but Carlton played excellently to kick three goals one to two points in a good first quarter. Then the Blues proceeded to throw away the game with an attrocious one goal thirteen with the wind in the second term. Had even half of these shots been on target, the Blues would have held a huge half-time lead, but as it was their innacuracy kept Geelong in the game and the Pivotonians booted seven goals two in the third quarter to win easing up. Carlton finished the game with an attrocious score of eight goals twenty-one. Jack Collins was the Geelong hero with four great goals in the Geelong third quarter comeback.

In a bone-crushing second semi-final played in the wet, old rivals Richmond and Collingwood met once again. Scoring in the first term was almost even, Collingwood taking fourteen minutes to hoist their first goal although kicking with a strong wind. Then the Tigers showed how to use the wind, by booting seven goals straight at one stage, and leading by almost four goals at the interval. Then the Magpies staged a revival and with eight goals two to a goal in the third quarter, looked likely winners, especially as Richmond had lost star defender Basil McCormack injured. Twenty-eight points down half way through the last term, however, the Tigers scored four goals in seven minutes before their pocket forward, Maurie Hunter, who had already scored five goals, pulled his shot for a behind and the Magpies scraped in by three points, fourteen goals ten to fourteen goals seven. This brought Collingwood and Geelong together in the final—as in the previous three seasons, Collingwood (minor premiers) had the right to a further game if defeated. And defeated they were as the underdogs, Geelong, ran to a thirty-seven point half-time lead, and then withstood a Collingwood fight-back in the second half to win by twenty-six points. Geelong's win was all the more meritorious as Baker, their star rover, was carried off injured early in the third quarter. During the game Gordon Coventry broke ex-Collingwood champion Dick Lee's VFL record of 708 goals in a career. Lee had taken from 1906-22 to kick his goals—Coventry had taken only twelve seasons, from 1920.

Collingwood, exercising their right of challenge, met Geelong in the grand final. The day was cloudy and sultry, but the turf was good, and a light south-east breeze prevailed. Geelong had Baker out injured, but Clayden and L. Murphy, although both very sore, turned out for Collingwood. The Magpies famous coach Jock McHale was not at the match, being confined to bed with the flu. This seemed to affect the Magpies, and Geelong played superior football in a high standard first half. Collingwood tended to play the man too much, and in the second term crowded the game to their own disadvantage, as they were then unable to open out with their famous short game. But for some shocking misses in front of goal, Geelong would have led by ten goals at half-time.

Magpie old-timer Bob Rush gave the dispirited Magpies a stirring half-time talk, and the team went out inspired, despite the loss of L. Murphy (shoulder). In the wind and rain, the Magpies lifted their game to great heights. G. Coventry, kicked a single, then his brother helped him to Collingwood's fourth goal. Makeham, beating Hickey, snapped another and H. Collier yet another to reduce the Geelong lead to a point after five minutes of the second half. Play livened up as Coghlan (Geelong) spread-eagled several Magpies, but Libbis snapped a point to equal the scores, and G. Coventry goaled to give Collingwood the lead just as drizzling rain began again. Clever play by Bruce Andrew led to another Collingwood goal, scored by Beveridge. F. Murphy added a behind and Makeham snapped another goal, Collingwood's sixth for the quarter.

Metherell got Geelong's first score of the term—a behind—which was replied to by Makeham. G. Coventry snapped Collingwood's tenth goal, and, as the rain stopped and the wind switched to favour Collingwood, he kicked yet another with a great shot from a long way out. Collingwood's dazzling third quarter had given them a thirty-two point lead at the last change. Geelong knew they were beaten, and Collingwood was content to just hold the lead. Scoring was almost even during a tight last term, but G. Coventry kicked his seventh goal for the game to establish a grand final record that, though since equalled, has yet to be broken.

This was the fourth successive Magpie premiership, and ended the Magpies' golden era. What a galaxy of talent they had put into the field in those four glorious years, during which they had played eighty-two games, won seventy of them, tied one, and lost only eleven. Names that are still remembered even today, nearly half a century later—the Coventry brothers, Syd (1927 Brownlow Medallist) and champion goal-kicker Gordon, the Collier brothers, Albert (1929 Brownlow Medallist) and Harry (runner-up in 1930), Charlie Dibbs, great full back, Harold Rumney, Percy Bowyer, George Clayden, Jack Beveridge, Bob Makeham, the Murphy brothers, Frank and Len, 'Tubby' Edmonds, Billy Libbis, Leo Wescott, Percy Rowe, Joe Poulter, Ernie Wilson, Harold Chesswas, Alf Lauder, Bruce Andrew and 'Jiggy' Harris. These and other lesser names gave the football public countless hours of enjoyment watching football as played by one of the greatest of all football teams—the Mighty Magpies of 1927-28-29-30!

RESULTS

SEPTEMBER 20 — FIRST SEMI-FINAL

	1st	2nd	3rd	Final	
Geelong	0 . 2	3 . 5	10 . 7	13 . 11	(89)
Carlton	3 . 1	4 . 14	7 . 16	8 . 21	(69)

MCG — Umpire Scott
Attendance 47,985 — Gate £2,315

BEST — (Geel) Collins, Todd, Carney, Rayson, Coghlan, Kuhlken, Baker, Troughton, Llewelyn
(Carl) Gill, Davey, C. Martyn, Clarke, Gilby, Arthur
GOALS — (Geel) Collins (4), Kuhlken (3), Llewellyn (2), Evans, Baker, Rayson, L. Hardiman
(Carl) Vallence (2), Allen (2), Clarke, Clover, Doyle, Green

SEPTEMBER 27 — SECOND SEMI-FINAL

	1st	2nd	3rd	Final	
Collingwood	2 . 3	5 . 5	13 . 7	14 . 10	(94)
Richmond	2 . 1	9 . 3	10 . 3	14 . 7	(91)

MCG — Umpire Scott
Attendance 40,218 — Gate £1,836

BEST — (Col) S. Coventry, H. Collier, Libbis, Beveridge, F. & L. Murphy, Rumney, Dibbs, Clayden
(Rich) Hunter, Foster, Fincher, O'Neill, Bolger, Judkins, Titus, Baggott, Sheahan
GOALS — (Col) Libbis (4), G. Coventry (3), H. Collier (3), Edmonds, F. Murphy, Barr, Makeham
(Rich) Hunter (5), Titus (3), Weidner (3), Benton (2), Foster

1930

OCTOBER 4 — PRELIMINARY FINAL

	1st	2nd	3rd	Final	
Geelong	4 . 7	8 . 12	9 . 14	12 . 19	(91)
Collingwood	0 . 1	3 . 5	7 . 7	9 . 11	(65)

MCG | **Umpire Scott**
Attendance 42,495 | **Gate £1,984**

BEST —	**(Geel)**	Coghlan, Baker, Carney, Collins, Williams, Evans
	(Col)	Lauder, Dibbs, Rumney, Beveridge, S. & G. Coventry, L. & F. Murphy, H. Collier
GOALS —	**(Geel)**	Kuhlken (3), Llewellyn (2), L. Hardiman (2), Troughton (2), Rayson, Evans, Baker
	(Col)	G. Coventry (4), F. Murphy (2), Gibbs, Bird, Makeham

OCTOBER 11 — GRAND FINAL

	1st	2nd	3rd	Final	
Collingwood	3 . 2	3 . 7	11 . 13	14 . 16	(100)
Geelong	2 . 5	6 . 10	6 . 11	9 . 16	(70)

MCG | **Umpire Scott**
Attendance 45,022 | **Gate £2,061**

BEST —	**(Col)**	Makeham, G. Coventry, F. Murphy, Clayden, Andrew, H. Collier, S. Coventry, Chesswas
	(Geel)	Troughton, Llewellyn, Evans, Mockridge, Carney, Todd, H. Hardiman
GOALS —	**(Col)**	G. Coventry (7), Makeham (2), L. Murphy, H. Collier, Beveridge, Edmonds, Froude
	(Geel)	Troughton (3), Llewellyn (2), Kuhlken, Rayson, Williams, L. Hardiman

GRAND FINAL TEAMS

Collingwood	**B**	Lauder	Dibbs	Bowyer
	HB	Rumney	A. Collier	Clayden
	C	Andrew	Beveridge	Chesswas
	HF	Makeham	F. Murphy	Aldag
	F	Edmonds	G. Coventry	H. Collier
	Ruck	S. Coventry (c)	L. Murphy	Libbis
	Nineteenth	Froude	**Coach** J. McHale	
Geelong	**B**	Lamb	Todd	Mockridge
	HB	Coghlan (c)	Hickey	McDonald
	C	Keppel	Williams	Carney
	HF	Rayson	Collins	L. Hardiman
	F	Llewellyn	Kuhlken	Troughton
	Ruck	H. Hardiman	Evans	L. Metherell
	Nineteenth	Lancaster*	**Coach** A. Coghlan	

*Killed in World War II.

1931

In 1931, for the first time since 1925, the VFL altered their system of playing the finals. Known as the Page system of finals, after the man who recommended it, it remained unaltered until the introduction of the final Five in 1972. Fourth played the third team in the first semi (loser eliminated), second versus first in the second semi (winner advanced to grand final, loser met the winner of the first semi in a preliminary final) and, finally, the winner of the preliminary final met the winner of the second semi in the grand final.

Geelong carried on their good form of 1930 in 1931, finishing atop the League ladder with fifteen wins and three losses. Richmond, still a power, finished second with the same number of wins. Carlton, Collingwood and Footscray staged a tremendous fight for the last two places, the latter finally missing out by fourteen per cent, although all three sides had forty-eight premiership points.

Carlton, in a murderous mood, met fierce rivals Collingwood in the first semi-final. Bad feeling went back to the last meeting between the clubs, when the Magpies convincingly drubbed the Blues. After the match, the rumour went around that Carlton had 'thrown in the towel', and Carlton, rightly or wrongly, blamed the Collingwood men for the report. They went into the semi-final determined to tear the Magpie team to shreds. Certainly they were helped by Collingwood's injuries—L. Murphy (flu) was unable to take the field, H. Collier went off in the second term, Tatham was carried off later, Edmonds and F. Murphy were lame and Syd Coventry was useless through injury throughout the last quarter—but Carlton played premiership football.

After the Magpies won the toss, Collingwood put four behinds on the board before Vallence marked and kicked his and Carlton's first goal. He got his second before the quarter ended, and at quarter-time Carlton led three goals one to one goal seven. Half-nearted Collingwood attacks were easily repulsed by the Carlton backs as they moved the ball with blistering speed down the ground in the second term. Carlton added five goals straight to Collingwood's two points, and Vallence scored three of the goals to have five by half-time.

Mass positional changes by the Magpies did not bring the desired result, and third quarter scoring was exactly even, Carlton having a thirty-four point lead at the last change.

Then came the deluge, as the magnificent Blues ground Collingwood, premiers

Preliminary final 1910—South Melbourne V Collingwood

The grand final of 1910. Collingwood beat Carlton in a fiery clash

Members' Reserve and Grand Stand, 1910.

Essendon V Collingwood grand final 1911. The first time numbers were worn by players in a grand final.

Action from the 1926 semi-final. Abernethy (Melbourne) kicks a goal in spite of the efforts of Poulter and Dibbs (Collingwood). *Sun photo.*

First semi-final, Collingwood V Essendon, 1925. Frank Maher scores the first goal for the Dons. *Herald & Weekly Times photo*

Collingwood captain Syd. Coventry chaired from the ground after he led the Magpies to their third successive premiership in 1929. *Herald & Weekly Times photo*

A strong mark to Hillis (South Melbourne) over Collingwood champion Gordon Coventry in the 1935 grand final. *Herald & Weekly Times photo*

Geelong's defence blankets Collingwood's attack 1937. Hardiman and Hore backed up by Hickey keep Coventry from the ball.
Herald & Weekly Times photo

Geelong V Collingwood grand final 1937. Todd (No 27) flies as L. Hardiman attempts to spoil. *Herald & Weekly Times photo*

Jim Park (Carlton) arrives too late to stop Albert Collier from getting his kick away in the 1938 grand final. *Herald & Weekly Times photo*

Ron Todd (Collingwood) punt kicks his third goal in the 1939 grand final against Melbourne. *Herald & Weekly Times photo*

Richmond V Melbourne second semi-final 1940. Players are (L-R) Priestley (Richmond) N. Smith (Melbourne) Harris
(Richmond) [illegible]

Geelong players could still laugh although miles behind. Semi-final V Carlton 1912

Carlton's Gardiner. Leading goalkicker 1911

Dave Smith, Essendon's captain 1911.

Supporters 1911

J. Kirby (Essendon) looks for an opening. Grand final 1912.

'oohey (Fitzroy) marks against his St. Kilda opponents in the grand final of 1913

Nearly half-time and only five points on the board to the Saints. 1913 grand final

The Fitzroy V South Melbourne final of 1923. Fitzroy won by two goals and advanced to the grand final. Fitzroy's 'Goldie' Collins marks strongly over a team-mate. *Herald & Weekly Times photo*

for four consecutive seasons, into the MCG turf. They added a total of nine goals seven to Collingwood's one goal one for the quarter and of that total full-forward Harry Vallence kicked six goals to make his total for the match eleven, a record which still stands. The Blues set three other records in the match—their score of twenty goals ten was then the highest finals score ever recorded. Their nine goals seven was the highest last quarter score in finals, and their eighty-eight point winning margin was a finals record.* The Blues at one stage scored eleven goals straight and, just for the record, Vallence scored eleven goals four from sixteen shots, while at the other end Collingwood's star full-forward, Gordon Coventry, scored three points.

Richmond had a long list of players out for their clash with Geelong—Bentley (injured), and O'Neill, O'Halloran and Baggott all out ill, and in the first quarter of the match Weidner had to be replaced—but they surprised the critics with a fighting win, kicking seven goals to three after half-time.

Underdogs Carlton surprised the pacy Geelong in a thrilling preliminary final. Kicking with the wind, the Blues booted seven goals five to nil in the first term, and it seemed impossible that a side with such a lead could lose. But Geelong came back so brilliantly that when their turn with the wind came, they converted a forty-seven point deficit into a three point lead by half-time, booting a magnificent eight goals nine to one point for the quarter. Geelong seemed to have won the game in the third quarter with a cleverly executed offensive-defence that limited Carlton to two goals five, while Geelong themselves scored two goals one. But the dark Blues were not quite finished and, in a stirring finish, harassed Geelong to the extent that they scored six behinds in a row in the last ten minutes of the last quarter. But it was to no avail as, with two and a half minutes to go, Geelong centre-half-forward Jack Collins marked and goaled to settle the issue. Carlton had scored seven of their eleven goals for the match in the first quarter, and Geelong eight of their eleven in the second.

Geelong and Richmond met for the first time in a grand final the following week.

Geelong, kicking with the breeze, was quickly into attack and L. Hardiman marked and goaled. After some see-sawing play, Titus replied for Richmond, but the Geelong defence was generally on top, with Hickey and Todd the stars. Greeves, giving Geelong great drive from the centre, forwarded for Baker to kick their second.

Goals to L. Hardiman and Titus began the second term, as they had the first. Richmond came back, but Hunter and Bissett, twice, missed. Finally the brilliant G. Strang took a glorious high mark and goaled to put the Tigers two points ahead. Another goal to Twyford (Richmond) followed, before Geelong recovered and a thirty-yard dash and goal to Troughton restored the balance. Then, the Blue and Whites came in a rush—Metherell got another, Moloney snapped an 'impossible' goal, and then he and Collins missed as the half-time siren sounded.

The second half began with a great seventy-yard punt goal by Metherell (Geelong), but Ford quickly equalised for Richmond. Geelong, receiving great drive from their rucks, kept coming forward, and although they missed several easy shots, Collins and Baker both goaled and Geelong had a huge lead at the last change.

D. Strang, with a goal off the ground, raised Richmond's hopes as the last term began, but Metherell took the pressure off with a six-pointer for Geelong. Good defence by O'Neill turned back several more Geelong rushes, but Geelong were in no danger of defeat and a last minute Richmond goal to D. Strang made no difference to the result.

*** Highest last quarter score now 11.3 by Essendon 1985 grand final. Largest winning margin now 133 points by Essendon 1984.**

RESULTS

SEPTEMBER 19 — FIRST SEMI-FINAL

	1st	2nd	3rd	Final	
Carlton	3 . 1	8 . 1	11 . 3	20 . 10	(130)
Collingwood	1 . 7	1 . 9	4 . 11	5 . 12	(42)

MCG — Umpire Ellingsen
Attendance 52,140 — Gate £2,495

BEST — (Carl) Vallence, Arthur, Gill, Clarke, Clover, Davey, Crisp, Gilby, Green
(Col) Wescott, Bowyer, Beveridge, F. Murphy, Tatham, Rumney, Makeham

GOALS — (Carl) Vallence (11), Arthur (3), Crisp (2), Clarke (2), Davey, Kelly
(Col) Froude, Harris, Tatham, Makeham, Bowyer

SEPTEMBER 26 — SECOND SEMI-FINAL

	1st	2nd	3rd	Final	
Richmond	5 . 0	8 . 6	12 . 8	15 . 9	(99)
Geelong	5 . 2	7 . 2	9 . 3	10 . 6	(66)

MCG — Umpire Scott
Attendance 49,056 — Gate £2,507

BEST — (Rich) Bissett, McCormack, Foster, Hunter, Titus, Dunne, Dyer, Geddes
(Geel) Troughton (B.O.G.), Hickey, Carney, Walker, Todd, Lamb, McDonald

GOALS — (Rich) Titus (4), D. Strang (3), Dyer (3), Hunter (3), Ford, Foster
(Geel) Troughton (3), Rayson (2), Evans (2), L. Hardiman, Maloney, Quinn

OCTOBER 3 — PRELIMINARY FINAL

	1st	2nd	3rd	Final	
Geelong	0 . 0	8 . 9	10 . 10	11 . 17	(83)
Carlton	7 . 5	8 . 6	10 . 11	11 . 11	(77)

MCG — Umpire Scott
Attendance 36,653 — Gate £1,766*

BEST — (Geel) Greeves, Hickey, Todd, Lamb, Carney, Metherell, Coghlan, Evans, Collins
(Carl) Davey, Huxtable, Morrissey, Kelly, Crisp, Vallence

GOALS — (Geel) Maloney (4), Evans (3), Coghlan, Metherell, Quinn, Rayson
(Carl) Vallence (3), Davey (2), Doyle, Kelly, Morrissey, Crisp, Arthur, Crowe

OCTOBER 10 — GRAND FINAL

	1st	2nd	3rd	Final	
Geelong	2 . 3	5 . 6	8 . 11	9 . 14	(68)
Richmond	1 . 2	4 . 5	5 . 5	7 . 6	(48)

MCG — Umpire Scott
Attendance 60,712 — Gate £3,110

BEST — (Geel) Carney, Hickey, Todd, McDonald, Lamb, Williams, H. Hardiman. Collins
(Rich) Geddes, O'Neill, G. Strang, Foster, Zschech, Ford

GOALS — (Geel) Metherell (2), Baker (2), L. Hardiman (2), Troughton, Collins, Moloney
(Rich) D. Strang (3), Titus (2), Ford, Twyford

* Plus £1,000 rain insurance.

GRAND FINAL TEAMS

Geelong	B	Lamb	Todd	H. Hardiman
	HB	Williams	Hickey	McDonald
	C	Carney	Greeves	Walker
	HF	L. Hardiman	Collins	Troughton
	F	Moloney	Evans	Quinn
	Ruck	Coghlan	L. Metherell	Baker (c)
	Nineteenth	Mockridge	Coach C. Clymo	
Richmond	B	O'Neill	Murdoch	Heifner
	HB	McCormack	Dunne	Bolger
	C	Geddes	Zschech	Judkins
	HF	Titus	G. Strang	Twyford
	F	Dyer	D. Strang	Ford
	Ruck	Bissett	Foster	Hunter (c)
	Nineteenth	O'Halloran	Coach F. V. Hughes	

1932

Carlton and Richmond, deadly rivals, topped the 1932 home and home ladder, with fifteen wins, and fourteen wins and a draw respectively. Collingwood (fourteen wins), and South Melbourne (thirteen wins) made up the Four with the 1931 premiers, Geelong, finishing six premiership points away in fifth place. (This despite 109 goals from George Moloney, the first man to kick 100 goals for a team finishing outside the Four.)

South Melbourne, with their famous 'Foreign Legion' side taking shape, met Collingwood in the first semi-final. The 'Bloods' (as they were then known) had won their first ten games, but then illness and injury played havoc with the team's performance. They went into the finals in a bad slump, and with their two best followers, Diggins and Reville, out with broken bones. In the first fourteen minutes of the game the Magpies played like men possessed, and rattled up seven goals two behinds before South had scored. Finally, Robertson posted South's first goal but G. Coventry answered immediately and the Magpies led at quarter-time by eight goals five to one goal one, a record first quarter score by any team in the finals.

This, of course, sealed the game, although South fought back as well as they were able. But key players were obviously unfit, and Collingwood were quick to exploit the weaknesses. South's best quarter was the last, in which they kicked three goals three to nil in the first eleven minutes, but the burst petered out and Collingwood hit back with goals to G. Coventry (two) and H. Collier to seal the issue.

The second semi-final was highlighted by brilliant aerial displays by Richmond's Strang brothers, with twenty-seven marks between them. After Carlton jumped to a long lead in the first quarter, Richmond fought back to trail by only two goals at the final change. Then came a sensation as they repeatedly ripped through the rugged Blues' defence in a stunning last quarter. Kicking three goals five to nil in the first eight minutes, the Tigers took the lead for the first time in the game, and went on with the business to kick five more goals in succession before Mick Crisp got two goals late in the game for the Blues. Hunter actually kicked four goals, D. Strang three, and Anderson (nineteenth man) one in that tumultuous last quarter burst by the Tigers, which won the game.

The preliminary final between Carlton and Collingwood was a boil-over, and an almost exact repetition of the previous season's first semi-final. Carlton drubbed Collingwood, and in the process kicked the highest score in a finals game, the first century in a preliminary final, the highest by any team against the Magpies, and the record one quarter score in any final (ten goals seven in the third). In addition, full-forward Harry Vallence equalled his own finals record with eleven goals.

The game did not look as though it would be the massacre it turned out to be when the Magpies led by a goal at the first change, with Gordon Coventry having kicked four magnificent goals for the black and whites. In the second term, however, Carlton got some system going and Vallence, who earlier had been well held by Dibbs and forced to roam far afield for his kicks, started to dominate in the air. From his efforts for the quarter, he booted five lovely goals, missed several others, and passed to Crisp for yet another goal. Yet, even though Vallence was excelling on the forward line for Carlton, the Magpies did their share of attacking and but for inaccuracy could have held their early lead.

Mick Crisp started Carlton's amazing third quarter burst when he drop-kicked an impossible angle goal. Edmonds and L. Murphy replied for Collingwood before Vallence booted his eighth, ninth, and tenth goals with majors to Johnson (Carlton) and H. Collier (Collingwood) sandwiched in between. Carlton were now playing unbeatable football, and in quick succession Cooper, Shea, Green (two) and Crisp raised Carlton's total at the last change to twenty-one goals. They had kicked ten goals seven for the term.

Collingwood made several positional changes at the last break, but to no avail. After the thrills of the previous fifty minutes the spectators were disappointed when the Blues were able to add only a further two goals six to Collingwood's five behinds. But they saw Vallence kick his eleventh goal, and Crisp throw away chances of four certain goals while endeavouring to pass to Vallence for the record twelfth. But the Blues champion was off-target and he finished the game with eleven goals nine from twenty-three shots, sixteen of which were from marks. This is still the most scoring shots by any player in a finals match.

The victorious Blues made only one change for the grand final, and that was compulsory, the injured Green being replaced by Egan. Richmond, the underdogs, also made one change. Geddes, who had been injured, came in to the side and Benton went out. The Tigers missed their young ruck star, Jack Dyer, who had been sidelined for several weeks through injury.

Perce Bentley (Richmond) won the toss, and kicked to the end which seemed to be against the breeze. It was, however, an even quarter, with Hunter, Doug Strang and Heifner goaling for Richmond and Vallence and Clarke for Carlton.

Richmond's chances of success depended on their containing the Carlton half-forward line and depriving Vallence of scoring chances, so the Tigers were bumping hard and often. Shea in particular looked very sore and Crisp was being held well in check. However, Cooper found the dangerous Vallence who goaled, and shortly after he added another. Carlton now held control across the centre and Shea goaled, but Richmond were not to be denied and posted six pointers from Martin, Titus, D. Strang, and G. Strang, to give them a handy fifteen-point lead at half-time.

Players were throwing themselves at the ball and at each other with ruthless determination as the second half began. Carlton swapped half-forward flanks and the move brought a goal to Crisp, but the Richmond backs then took over again. After play had swung up and down the field several times D. Strang goaled for Richmond, and Clarke, after Martyn had taken a tremendous mark, replied for Carlton. Another even quarter ended with punches flying and umpire Scott talking to three offenders.

A do-or-die last quarter effort saw the two forward lines come into the game for the first time. Zschech found Bentley for a goal to give Richmond a thirteen-point lead, but Clarke, roving superbly for Carlton, put his team into attack where Vallence goaled for Carlton from a free. Soon after, Johnson made a great run, nearly the length of the ground, before passing to Vallence, who goaled again. Richmond were rattled, but came back with a chain of passes which was topped off by O'Halloran goaling. Vallence kicked the Blues tenth goal and, minutes later, another shot by him was sharked in the goal-square and put through by Street, to give the Blues a five-point lead. Immediately D. Strang restored the lead to the Tigers, and Street snatched it back for Carlton, the two goals sending the crowd into a frenzy of excitement. With five minutes remaining, and Carlton leading by four points, a Carlton backman dropped a mark almost in the goal-square, and in the struggle that followed Anderson, Richmond's nineteenth man, picked up and goaled. Carlton seemed to falter, and Titus slammed through another and Geddes hit the post right on the bell to give the Tigers a well earned, and certainly hard earned, premiership flag.

RESULTS

SEPTEMBER 10 — FIRST SEMI-FINAL

	1st	2nd	3rd	Final	
Collingwood	8 . 5	12 . 8	14 . 11	17 . 12	(114)
South Melbourne	1 . 1	5 . 7	7 . 13	12 . 16	(88)

MCG — Umpire Scott

Attendance 51,209 — Gate £2,531

BEST — (Col) S. Coventry, Clayden, Edmonds, Dibbs, L. Murphy, H. Collier, Ross, Harris

(S. Melb) Brain, Leonard, Faul, Robertson, McKay, Pratt, Beard, McLaughlin

GOALS — (Col) G. Coventry (5), Edmonds (3), H. Collier (3), Clayden (2), L. Murphy (2), Libbis (2)

(S. Melb) Leonard (3), Pratt (3), Robertson (2), Brain, L. Thomas, Meitzcke, Hearn

SEPTEMBER 17 — SECOND SEMI-FINAL

	1st	2nd	3rd	Final	
Richmond	1 . 4	5 . 8	10 . 11	18 . 16	(124)
Carlton	5 . 4	6 . 9	12 . 12	14 . 15	(99)

MCG — Umpire Scott

Attendance 63,326 — Gate £3,340

1932

BEST —	(Rich)	Zschech (B.O.G.), Baggott, Murdoch, McCormack, Bolger, O'Halloran, O'Neill, D. & G. Strang
	(Carl)	Kelly, Street, Bullen, Davey, Mackie, Clarke, Vallence, Shea, Cooper
GOALS —	(Rich)	D. Strang (7), Hunter (6), G. Strang, Titus, Martin, O'Halloran, Anderson
	(Carl)	Vallence (4), Crisp (3), Bullen (2), Shea (2), Green, Clarke, Davey

SEPTEMBER 24 — PRELIMINARY FINAL

	1st	2nd	3rd	Final	
Carlton	4 . 3	11 . 6	21 . 13	23 . 19	(157)
Collingwood	5 . 3	8 . 10	11 . 11	11 . 16	(82)

MCG — Umpire McMurray
Attendance 46,447 — Gate £2,197

BEST —	(Carl)	Vallence, C. Martyn, Oprey, Johnson, Mackie, Cooper, Crisp, Shea, Bullen
	(Col)	S. Coventry, H. Collier, G. Coventry, Clayden, Andrew, L. Murphy Rumney
GOALS —	(Carl)	Vallence (11), Crisp (4), Green (3), Johnson (2), Shea (2), Cooper
	(Col)	G. Coventry (6), H. Collier (2), Libbis, Edmonds, L. Murphy

OCTOBER 1 — GRAND FINAL

	1st	2nd	3rd	Final	
Richmond	3 . 3	7 . 9	8 . 12	13 . 14	(92)
Carlton	2 . 3	5 . 6	7 . 11	12 . 11	(83)

MCG — Umpire Scott
Attendance 69,724 — Gate £3,633 (both records)

BEST —	(Rich)	G. Strang, McCormack, O'Neill, Baggott, Bolger, Titus, Martin
	(Carl)	Mackie, C. Martyn, Oprey, Huxtable, Johnson, Egan, Crowe
GOALS —	(Rich)	D. Strang (4), Titus (2), Hunter, Heifner, Martin, G. Strang, Anderson, Bentley, O'Halloran
	(Carl)	Vallence (5), Shea (2), Clarke (2), Bullen (2), Crisp

GRAND FINAL TEAMS

Richmond	B	Bolger	Sheahan	O'Neill
	HB	Baggott	Murdoch	McCormack
	C	Judkins	Zschech	Geddes
	HF	Twyford	G. Strang	Titus
	F	Heifner	D. Strang	Hunter
	Ruck	Bentley (c)	O'Halloran	Martin
	Nineteenth	Anderson	Coach F. V. Hughes	
Carlton	B	Crowe	Gill	Street
	HB	Huxtable	Mackie	Gilby
	C	Kelly	C. Martyn (c)	Oprey
	HF	Shea	Egan	Crisp
	F	Bullen	Vallence	Cooper
	Ruck	Davey	Johnson	Clarke
	Nineteenth	Young	Coach D. Minogue	

1933

Halfway through season 1933, South Melbourne, known to the sporting public as the 'Foreign Legion' because of the number of interstate players in their ranks, were eighth on the premiership ladder with only four wins. But, as was inevitable with such a galaxy of talent, they finally struck form and won their last nine games to finish second, only two games behind 1932 premiers Richmond. The other finalists were Carlton (thirteen wins) and Geelong (twelve wins) with Collingwood dropping down to an unaccustomed sixth position, their first time out of the finals since 1924. Fitzroy, a chopping block for most of the 1930's, finished fifth, only two points behind Geelong, although with an inferior percentage.

The first semi was a poor exhibition of football. Both sides, to quote one critic, 'appeared so eager and anxious they fell over themselves'. Marks were fumbled and kicks slurred as Carlton, although playing poorly, battled to a three-goal lead by half-time, due mainly to their first quarter burst of six goals two. But Geelong fought their way back into the game, reduced their deficit to five points at the final change, and drew level at nine goals ten each halfway through the last quarter. For a while it looked as though Carlton might win, but, playing with more pace and more direct methods on the forward line, Geelong broke away from the tiring Blues in the last ten minutes to add three goals which won the game.

When Richmond, playing with great vigour and an equal amount of skill, led by six goals at half-time, it looked as if the 1933 second semi-final was all over. After a reasonably even first quarter, the Tigers had broken away to kick six goals two to one goal four in the second, mainly through the agency of Hunter (three goals), D. Strang (two) and Titus who were in brilliant form up forward. But South fought back, doggedly at first, then excitingly. They outscored Richmond in the third term to draw within twenty-six points at the last change. Then, in a scintillating last quarter, Pratt sparked off a South burst which produced three quick goals to himself, Bertram and Reville. Then, despite good defence by Richmond, O'Meara (South Melbourne) goaled and South had cut Richmond's twenty-six-point lead to a single point. D. Strang gave the Tigers relief with a hard-earned goal, but O'Meara scored again for South. Then Bowe picked out Brain and the South rover goaled to give his side the lead for the first time in the game. The Tigers' resistance collapsed as Brain, again, and Reville added further goals to take South into the grand final.

Richmond battled it out with Geelong the following week. The Tigers won the toss, kicked with the wind, and booted four goals straight in the first term, another in the second, and headed Geelong at half-time. The latter from numerous chances, and the majority of the play having kicked their opportunities away with an atrocious three goals ten, including seven behinds in a row. The Geelong men found the target in the second half, but by then the damage was done. Immediately play resumed after half-time Geelong bombarded the goals and were rewarded with majors to Selwood (two), Moloney, and Quinn to take them to a twenty-three-point lead. But Richmond staged a strong comeback, and blows were exchanged which resulted in three reports (one of which put the Tigers' ace forward Doug Strang out of the grand final). The last quarter was all Richmond, despite the fact that they had Hunter and Baggott injured, when Doug Strang broke loose with four fine goals. Even so, the game could still have gone either way before Jack Dyer's goal for the Tigers at a vital stage sealed the issue.

A record crowd of 75,754 turned out to see Richmond clash with South Melbourne in the grand final. Richmond had four key players out through injury or suspension, considerably weakening their side. South had two stars in Hillis and Austin Robertson out, but they were replaced by players of equal ability in Hec McKay and Herbie Mathews. South began well, having four behinds on the board before Richmond went forward, and towards the end of the quarter kicking three quick goals to Diggins, Pratt and Thomas, to have a good lead at the first change. It was a battle of the back-lines from then on, and goals were hard to get. Thomas, out-pointing Richmond's star centreman, Zschech, was giving South a ton of drive, and Nash was out-pointing G. Strang at centre-half-back. Ironically, it was Strang and another losing Tiger player in Farmer who scored Richmond's only two goals till half-time. South during the quarter added goals through Reville, Brain and Pratt to lead by twenty-eight points at the long interval.

Richmond attacked determinedly at the commencement of the third term, and but for the fantastic play of Laurie Nash at centre-half-back for South, would have considerably narrowed the lead. Nash, however, turned back four successive attacks and then combined well with Reville and O'Meara to enable Diggins to snap South's seventh goal. This took a lot of steam out of the Tigers but Dyer forced them forward again only to see Nash, then Austin, in the way once more. When they did get up forward, Richmond's goal kicking was very poor; Farmer finally got their third goal only to see Brain reply for South from a free. South had a big lead of thirty-nine points at the last change, but Richmond came back with a goal in the first minutes of the last quarter. Pratt replied for South with his 109th goal of the season, which made him top goalkicker of the league, one goal ahead of Collingwood's Gordon Coventry. That was the only interest in the last term, as it became apparent very early that Richmond were not going to get up. In the last minutes Mathews snapped a point, Reville hit the post (South's third) and Pratt kicked the final point which gave South a forty-two-point lead at the siren. It was their first flag since 1918, and their third and last to date.

RESULTS

SEPTEMBER 9 — FIRST SEMI-FINAL

	1st	2nd	3rd	Final	
Geelong	2 . 2	5 . 6	7 . 10	12 . 12	(84)
Carlton	6 . 2	8 . 6	8 . 9	10 . 11	(71)

MCG — Umpire Ellingsen

Attendance 40,225 — Gate £1,893

BEST — (Geel) Troughton (B.O.G.), Carney, L. Hardiman, Moloney, Evans, Quinn, Selwood
(Carl) Clarke, Shea, Davey, Vallence, Crisp, Leffanue, Gilby, Mackie
GOALS — (Geel) Moloney (4), Troughton (3), L. Metherell (2), Evans, Selwood, L. Hardiman
(Carl) Davey (3), Vallence (2), Crisp (2), Leffanue, Clarke, Shea

SEPTEMBER 16 — SECOND SEMI-FINAL

	1st	2nd	3rd	Final	
South Melbourne	2 . 1	3 . 5	6 . 9	14 . 11	(95)
Richmond	3 . 4	9 . 6	10 . 11	11 . 11	(77)

MCG — Umpire McMurray
Attendance 49,303 — Gate £2,434

BEST — (S. Melb) McLaughlin, Clarke, Austin, Brain, Faul, McKay, Bowe, Bertram
(Rich) Baggott, O'Neill, O'Halloran, Bolger, Murdoch, Martin, Zschech, Geddes
GOALS — (S. Melb) Pratt (4), Reville (3), O'Meara (2), Brain (2), Diggins, Clarke, Bertram
(Rich) D. Strang (4), Hunter (3), Titus (2), O'Halloran, Martin

SEPTEMBER 23 — PRELIMINARY FINAL

	1st	2nd	3rd	Final	
Richmond	4 . 0	5 . 0	7 . 3	13 . 5	(83)
Geelong	1 . 3	3 . 10	8 . 11	10 . 14	(74)

MCG — Umpire Blackburn
Attendance 48,125 — Gate £2,273

BEST — (Rich) Baggott, Bolger, O'Neill, McCormack, Zschech, Geddes, Titus, Dyer
(Geel) Coles, Todd, McDonald, Williams, Walker, Kuhlken, Collins, Quinn
GOALS — (Rich) D. Strang (4), Titus (3), McConchie (2), Hunter, G. Strang, O'Halloran, Dyer
(Geel) Selwood (3), L. Metherell, (2) Moloney (2), Quinn, H. Hardiman, Evans

SEPTEMBER 30 — GRAND FINAL

	1st	2nd	3rd	Final	
South Melbourne	3 . 5	6 . 7	8 . 12	9 . 17	(71)
Richmond	0 . 2	2 . 3	3 3	4 . 5	(29)

MCG — Umpire Scott
Attendance 75,754 (record) — Gate £4,020

BEST — (S. Melb) Nash, Diggins, Austin, Mathews, Thomas, Bowe, Reville, Clarke, Bissett
(Rich) O'Neill, Martin, Zschech, Murdoch, Dyer, Geddes, McCormack
GOALS — (S. Melb) Pratt (3), Diggins (2), Brain (2), Reville, Thomas
(Rich) Farmer (2), G. Strang, Martin

1933-1934

GRAND FINAL TEAMS

South Melbourne	B	McKenzie	McKay	Austin
	HB	Faul	Nash	McLaughlin
	C	Bowe	Thomas	Clarke
	HF	O'Meara	Diggins	Reville
	F	Bertram	Pratt	Mathews
	Ruck	Bissett (c)	Kelleher	Brain
	Nineteenth	Beard	Coach J. J. Bissett	
Richmond	B	Bolger	Sheahan	O'Neill
	HB	Stenhouse	Murdoch	McCormack
	C	Geddes	Zschech	Judkins
	HF	Farmer	O'Halloran	Baggott
	F	Dyer	Titus	Foster
	Ruck	Bentley (c)	G. Strang	Martin
	Nineteenth	Anderson	Coach W. Schmidt	

1934

Carrying on their goal-scoring form of 1933, South Melbourne booted a new VFL record of 2187 points in the eighteen home and home games of 1934. They carried this record to 2462 in the finals, during which their two ace forwards, Bob Pratt and Laurie Nash, took their goal-kicking tallies to 150 and forty-nine respectively.

Among South's records in 1934 were: nine scores of twenty goals, including five in succession; sixty-six goals in seven successive games by full-forward Bob Pratt, and a total of 150 for the season; and thirteen scores of 100 points or more (equalling Collingwood's 1929 record—since broken).

However, despite such mammoth scoring, South with fourteen wins could finish only third on the league ladder behind Richmond (fifteen wins) and Geelong (fourteen wins and a draw). Making up the Four was Collingwood with thirteen wins and a drawn game against Geelong. It was a season of massive scoring by all clubs, with seven of the twelve sides averaging eighty-five points a game, but, rather surprisingly, the scoring in the finals was not exceptionally high.

South and Collingwood met in the first semi-final, the latter being handicapped by the loss of Charlie Dibbs through injury, necessitating the inclusion of K. Asling for only his fifth VFL game. The Magpies got away to a good start in the early part of the game, kicking five goals three to one goal three in the first quarter. South, however, fought back in the next two quarters, but were aided by Collingwood's atrocious kicking in an amazing third term. The Magpies, from numerous shots, kicked ten successive behinds to allow South to draw level at the last change, and that cost them the game as South, with a goal from Pratt with almost the last kick of the day, eventually won by three points. Collingwood, in the last half, kicked three goals fifteen to South's six goals four, which tells the story of their loss. It was a poor send-off for Collingwood's great skipper Syd Coventry, only man to lead his side to four successive league premierships, and who was playing his last VFL game.

On a wet ground in the second semi-final, Geelong proved hopeless in the last half after putting up a good show in the first. Immediately play resumed after the break, Harris goaled for the Tigers. Moloney replied for Geelong, but Titus got another for the Tigers from a mark and this started a Richmond run in which they added eight goals six in a quarter and a half while Geelong did not even score. Kicking fourteen goals ten to two goals four after half-time, the Tigers went away to an easy win and, in fact, kicked a record finals score of nineteen goals twenty in doing so.

Rain again spoiled the following week's preliminary final, the attendance slumping to 30,401 following on the 35,000 who attended the second semi-final. Again Geelong proved themselves to be no mud runners. With Pratt and Nash in brilliant form in the drizzling rain, South had the game sewn up at three-quarter-time when they led by nearly six goals, an imposing lead in the conditions. In the last term, Pratt two, Nash, Reville and Bertram added further goals for South, who also kicked nine behinds, taking them to fifteen goals eighteen as against Geelong's miserable seven goals six.

For a change, sunshine bathed the MCG for the grand final between South Melbourne and Richmond. A brilliant beginning saw both sides playing scintillating football. Richmond did all the early scoring with a classic long drop kick goal from Zschech, and snap goals from Harris and Murdoch, before Nash finally accepted a pass from Thomas and booted South's first. Soon after came a South burst in which they added three goals—from Brain, O'Meara and Nash—in three minutes. A feature was that Pratt, needing only two goals for his 150 for the season, had so far been limited to one behind. The Richmond defence, playing fair but hard had two men minding South's trump whenever he went near the ball, but South continued to look for him and ignore the loose man created by these tactics. In fact, this continued throughout the game, and contributed in no small measure to South's loss.

In the second quarter play see-sawed for ten minutes before Titus goaled for Richmond and Pratt took a screamer to kick his first for South. Titus, from an impossible angle goaled again, Richmond's sixth, and Martin and Harris added further goals in quick succession. Titus, after a most amazing mark, added yet another before Bertram finally snapped South's sixth. But Titus was in brilliant form for the Tigers, and soon after added still another goal, giving him a total of four goals three from eight marks by half-time. He was proving to be of more value at the full-forward position for the Tigers than Pratt was for South.

The Tigers sealed the 1934 premiership in the twenty-five minutes of the third quarter. After several attacks which yielded only minor scores, O'Halloran goaled, this being followed by further goals from Baxter (snap), Martin (snap), O'Halloran (mark), Titus (mark) and Harris (snap) while South struggled to score six points for the term.

Facing a three-quarter-time deficit of ten goals, South failed to make much headway, Bentley increasing the Tigers' lead after several South attacks had moved their score up by only three behinds, one of which was Nash's sixth miss for the game. Finally, Nash broke the drought for South and then went berserk to add three more goals in very short time; however, it was obvious that South were much too far behind to win the game, despite Nash's burst. The only other interest of the last term was Pratt's second goal, his 150th of the season, and several violent flare-ups which resulted in three players being reported. The crowd was drifting away as the siren proclaimed Richmond the VFL Premiers of 1934.

RESULTS

SEPTEMBER 22 — FIRST SEMI-FINAL

	1st	2nd	3rd	Final	
South Melbourne	1 . 3	5 . 8	7 . 10	11 . 12	(78)
Collingwood	5 . 3	6 . 6	6 . 16	9 . 21	(75)

MCG — Umpire McMurray
Attendance 52,022 — Gate £2,605

BEST — (S. Melb) Faul, Mathews, Brain, Pratt, McKay, Richards, McLaughlin, Kelleher
(Col) Whelan, Regan, Carmody, Fraser, Froude, Rumney, A. & H. Collier

GOALS — (S. Melb) Pratt (4), Reville (3), Brain (2), Davies, Kelleher
(Col) G. Coventry (5), Riley (2), Doherty, H. Collier

SEPTEMBER 29 — SECOND SEMI-FINAL

	1st	2nd	3rd	Final	
Richmond	3 . 5	5 . 10	11 . 15	19 . 20	(134)
Geelong	1 . 4	5 . 4	6 . 6	7 . 8	(50)

MCG — Umpire R. Scott
Attendance 35,934 — Gate £1,661*

BEST — (Rich) Martin, Titus, Baggott, Judkins, Bentley, O'Halloran, McCormack, Foster
(Geel) McGregor, Hickey, Evans, L. Metherell, Quinn, J. Metherell, Troughton, Coles

GOALS — (Rich) Titus (5), Harris (4), Bentley (3), Martin (2), O'Halloran (2), Baxter, Dyer, Murdoch
(Geel) Quinn (2), Everett, L. Hardiman, J. Metherell, L. Metherell, Moloney

OCTOBER 6 — PRELIMINARY FINAL

	1st	2nd	3rd	Final	
South Melbourne	4 . 2	6 . 6	10 . 9	15 . 18	(108)
Geelong	2 . 2	4 . 4	5 . 5	7 . 6	(48)

MCG — Umpire R. Scott
Attendance 30,401 — Gate £1,413*

BEST — (S. Melb) Mathews, Bissett, Richards, McKay, Faul, McKenzie, Pratt, Thomas
(Geel) Hickey, Coles, McDonald, Carney, Quinn, J. Metherell, Collins

GOALS — (S. Melb) Pratt (6), Nash (4), Bertram (4), Reville
(Geel) Troughton (2), Moloney (2), Quinn (2), Collins

* Plus £1,000 rain insurance.

OCTOBER 13 — GRAND FINAL

	1st	2nd	3rd	Final	
Richmond	4 . 4	10 . 8	16 . 11	19 . 14	(128)
South Melbourne	4 . 3	6 . 5	6 . 11	12 . 17	(89)

MCG — Umpire R. Scott
Attendance 65,335 — Gate £3,495

BEST — (Rich) Titus, O'Neill, Baggott, Bolger, McCormack, Sheahan, G. Strang, Martin
(S. Melb) Pratt, Reville, Austin, Nash, McLaughlin, McKenzie, McKay, Faul, Richards

GOALS — (Rich) Titus (6), O'Halloran (3), Harris (3), Bentley (2), Martin (2), Baxter, Murdoch, Zschech
(S. Melb) Nash (6), Pratt (2), Brain, Diggins, O'Meara, Bertram

GRAND FINAL TEAMS

Richmond	B	Bolger	Sheahan	O'Neill
	HB	Baggott	G. Strang	McCormack
	C	Judkins	Zschech	Geddes
	HF	O'Halloran	Baxter	Murdoch
	F	Harris	Titus	Foster
	Ruck	Bentley (c)	Dyer	Martin
	Nineteenth	Edmonds	Coach P. Bentley	
South Melbourne	B	McKay	Austin	McKenzie
	HB	McLaughlin	Richards	Faul
	C	Mathews	L. Thomas	Clarke
	HF	Reville	Nash	O'Meara
	F	Diggins	Pratt	Bertram
	Ruck	Bissett (c)	Kelleher	Brain
	Nineteenth	Harris	Coach J. J. Bissett	

Between editions, a letter from Jack Baggott, one of the Richmond champions of this era, pointed out that 1934 was the Centenary year of the City of Melbourne and the Richmond team was awarded special, inscribed medallions by the Melbourne City Council for winning the Centenary premiership. As Jack added, it will be 2034 before another team can equal Richmond's feat.

1935

After showing promise the previous season, Geelong slumped from third to ninth, but the other 1934 finalists retained their places. South (sixteen wins, two losses) finished first, Collingwood (fourteen wins, two draws, two losses) second, Carlton (fourteen wins, three losses and a draw) were third, and Richmond (twelve wins, six losses) fourth. Missing out by only four points due to a loss to Collingwood in the last round was St. Kilda, having their best season since 1929.

1935

Hot favourites Carlton caused a shock when they went down to Richmond in the first semi-final. Both teams, however, gave clever scientific exhibitions, quite the reverse of the crashing, brawling tactics usually adopted when these sides met in second round games.

Carlton, perhaps, were expecting softening-up tactics in the first quarter, but the Tigers kept the game open and rushed on seven goals five to two goals four. This was a heavy leeway to make up in a semi-final, and the Blues after another quarter of trying in vain to reduce the deficit, still trailed by thirty-one points at half-time. They had only themselves to blame, however, as several of their seven behinds during the term should have been goals. Richmond's tactics were interesting. Their ace forward, Jack Titus, made long leads downfield, and Edmonds, on the forward flank, lured Huxtable, the star Carlton backman, out to the boundary. Thus, in the open space created, Richmond's resting rovers, Harris and Martin, became focal points of attack.

Though still trying hard, Carlton slipped further behind in the third term, mainly due to their failure to direct their attacks wide of the Tigers' great centre-half-back Gordon Strang. Strang, having a day out, turned seven promising Carlton drives and some of the zip disappeared from the Blues' attacks. Later, however, they were able to add five goals in a belated last quarter burst, but the Tigers' lead was far too big and they won quite easily by twenty-one points. Gordon Strang, in a brilliant aerial display, pulled down no fewer than twenty-one marks.

In a 'clash of the year' second semi-final, Collingwood and South were neck-and-neck after the first fifty minutes. Then, with their attack revolving around Pratt, South broke through in the third term with a burst of six goals two to Collingwood's four goals six. This gave them a lead of fourteen points at three-quarter time, and the Magpies pulled out all stops in a desperate attempt to bridge the gap in the final term. But South's defence, equal to the occasion—leading them was Hillis, who turned four attacks single-handedly—held Collingwood to only two goals, and South were untroubled to win by twenty-one points, the same margin as had decided the previous week's semi-final.

Richmond, installed by the critics as hot favourites to win the preliminary final, went into the game full of confidence. However, it was confidence which was soon knocked out of them by the never-say-die Collingwood team. With their little men, in particular, in dominant form the Magpies kicked five goals two in the first term, whilst Richmond, from two more scoring shots, put up three goals six. The Tigers fought back to lead by three points at the half-time interval, but that ended the resistance as they were able to add only another three goals four in the remaining fifty minutes of the game, whilst Collingwood played brilliant football to kick eight goals five and enter their first grand final since 1930.

There was a sensation on the Friday night before the grand final when South's star full-forward, Bob Pratt, was knocked down and injured by a truck. The injury put him out of the big game, and he was replaced by Herbie Mathews (who was later to win a Brownlow Medal). South made only one other change and Collingwood made two including the recall of the veteran Charlie Dibbs for his 216th and last game with the club. It is interesting, in comparing heights of players of different eras, to note that Dibbs, Collingwood's full-back in this game, was five feet nine and a half inches. Tallest on the field was Collingwood's nineteen-year-old Phonse Kyne, at six feet two inches, and of the thirty-eight players who took the field that day, only eight were six-footers.

South Melbourne won the toss, and were soon on top. Leading to the ball and winning in the air, South quickly had two goals on the board. Moore outmarked Dibbs for the first, and Robertson, breaking away at tremendous pace, found Nash for the second. South bombarded the goals but could increase their score to only two goals four before Pannam goaled for the Magpies from an acute angle on the boundary. Sustained good play by Fraser (ruck) and Whelan (centre) got Collingwood back on even terms for the remainder of the first term.

Hillis twice turned Collingwood out as the second quarter commenced, but G. Coventry snapped a goal over his head to spur the Magpies on. South, however, came back and Davies brilliantly outmarked Ross, and goaled. As a change came over the game, Regan (Collingwood) began to get on top of Nash, with Rumney another sterling defender. Hitherto, South had kicked wide to the flanks, but now that Collingwood, and particularly Fraser, were asserting themselves, the Magpies went straight down the ground and South followed suit. This resulted in players of both teams converging on the centre and, in the congested play, tempers quickly became frayed. Kyne snapped a clever goal for Collingwood, who now trailed by only four points. Two great dashes by Reid (South Melbourne) opened up play but no score resulted, and Collingwood hit back to add two goals two and take the lead at the interval.

A poster to Morgan and a goal to G. Coventry increased that lead when the third term began. Diggins and Bissett missed sitters for South before clever handball between Mathews, O'Meara and Kelleher resulted in the latter goaling. Soon after, Austin's dashing defence again got the ball to Kelleher, who sent it on to Reid to Mathews to Moore for another. Rumney, Regan and Froude held off what threatened to become a rush of goals. But that was the end of it for South. Bissett, their great captain, was helped off the ground at three-quarter time and Diggins took over as skipper. South made several positional changes, but all to no avail as Collingwood added three goals to one to easily take out the 1935 premiership.

RESULTS

SEPTEMBER 14 — FIRST SEMI-FINAL

	1st	2nd	3rd	Final	
Richmond	7 . 5	11 . 6	16 . 9	19 . 11	(125)
Carlton	2 . 4	5 . 11	9 . 16	14 . 20	(104)

MCG — Umpire Blackburn
Attendance 49,759 — Gate £2,524

BEST —	(Rich)	G. Strang, Martin, Harris, Symons, Heifner, O'Neill, Bolger, Sheahan
	(Carl)	Francis, Gill, Shea, Clarke, R. Cooper, Davey, Crisp
GOALS —	(Rich)	Harris (6), Titus (5), Martin (3), Zschech, Symons, Heifner, Edmonds, Bentley
	(Carl)	Vallence (4), Crisp (4), Clarke (3), R. Cooper (2), Pollock

SEPTEMBER 21 — SECOND SEMI-FINAL

	1st	2nd	3rd	Final	
South Melbourne	3 . 4	6 . 7	12 . 9	15 . 14	(104)
Collingwood	3 . 2	5 . 7	9 . 13	11 . 17	(83)

MCG — Umpire McMurray
Attendance 53,766 — Gate £2,720

BEST —	(S. Melb)	Hillis, McKenzie, Reid, O'Meara, Bissett, Nash
	(Col)	Rumney, A. Collier, H. Collier, Bowyer, Fraser, Regan, Kyne
GOALS —	(S. Melb)	Pratt (6), Nash (3), Moore (3), Brain (2), Kelleher
	(Col)	G. Coventry (3), Todd (3), H. Collier (2), A. Collier, Knight, Kyne

SEPTEMBER 28 — PRELIMINARY FINAL

	1st	2nd	3rd	Final	
Collingwood	5 2	6 5	10 8	14 10	(94)
Richmond	3 6	6 8	7 10	9 12	(66)

MCG — Umpire Blackburn
Attendance 46,181 — Gate £2,253

BEST —	(Col)	Regan, Bowyer, A. Collier, Dibbs, Kyne, Riley, Doherty, Whelan
	(Rich)	Guinane, Bolger, G. Strang, Symons, Martin
GOALS —	(Col)	G. Coventry (4), Pannam (3), Bowyer (2), Kyne (2), Knight, H. Collier, Riley
	(Rich)	Harris (2), Martin (2), Dyer, Foster, Heifner, Titus, Symons

OCTOBER 5 — GRAND FINAL

	1st	2nd	3rd	Final	
Collingwood	1 3	6 6	8 10	11 12	(78)
South Melbourne	3 6	4 8	6 10	7 16	(58)

MCG — Umpire Scott*
Attendance 54,154 — Gate £2,912

BEST —	(Col)	H. Collier, A. Collier, Kyne, Regan, Rumney, Froude, Whelan, Carmody, Doherty
	(S. Melb)	Clarke, Austin, Hillis, McKenzie, Diggins, Kelleher, Bissett, Robertson
GOALS —	(Col)	G. Coventry (4), Kyne (2), Pannam (2), H. Collier, A. Collier, Stackpole
	(S. Melb)	Davies (2), Moore (2), Nash, Kelleher, McEachern

GRAND FINAL TEAMS

Collingwood	B	Rumney	Dibbs	Ross
	HB	Woods	Regan	Froude
	C	Morgan	Whelan	Carmody
	HF	Riley	Kyne	Doherty
	F	Pannam	G. Coventry	Fraser
	Ruck	A. Collier	Bowyer	H. Collier (c)
	Nineteenth	Stackpole	Coach J. McHale	
South Melbourne	B	Austin	Hillis	Humphries
	HB	McKenzie	Richards	Faul
	C	Clarke	Mathews	Reid
	HF	O'Meara	Nash	Robertson
	F	Kelleher	Moore	Davies
	Ruck	Bissett (c)	Diggins	Brain
	Nineteenth	McEachern	Coach J. J. Bissett	

* This was umpire Bob Scott's seventh successive grand final. He had officiated in 1929-30-31-32-33-34, and broke the previous record.

1936

Both 1935 grand finalists began excellently in 1936, Collingwood winning their first nine games before losing to South and South themselves winning their first eight games. The Magpies actually commenced the season with five successive scores of 100 points, and topped the century no less than thirteen times in all games, thus equalling the VFL record. (Shared by themselves in 1929, and South Melbourne in 1934.)* Even scoring on that scale was insufficient, however, to put them on top of the ladder; South Melbourne with sixteen wins and two losses gained that honour. Collingwood (second) had fifteen wins, while Carlton (third) and Melbourne (fourth) both finished with twelve wins, one game ahead of Geelong.

Disaster overtook the Magpies just before the finals when their champion goal-kicker, Gordon Coventry, was suspended for eight weeks after a clash with Richmond's Joe Murdoch. It was a severe sentence, and shocked the entire football world, especially as Coventry had been provoked, and it was the first time in seventeen VFL seasons that he had even been spoken to by an umpire. Public demonstrations and even an expression of regret by the Speaker of the Legislative Assembly failed to move the Tribunal, and Coventry's sentence was allowed to stand, putting him out of the finals. Disappointed and upset, Coventry then announced his retirement.**

Melbourne caused the sensation of the season by downing the red-hot favourite, Carlton, in the first semi-final. Brilliant work by Wartman (wing) sparked Melbourne to a fine first-quarter burst of five goals and, winning in the ruck, they went to a twenty-two point lead at half-time. Carlton, however, always gave the impression that they would at any moment unleash a tremendous burst of goals which would crush the Redlegs. It looked as if this was about to happen in the third term, when Cooper, Clarke and Carney rose to great heights and had the Blues continually in attack. But easy shots were missed, and the Blues totalled three goals seven for the term to trail by nineteen points at three-quarter time. Then a brilliant burst of three goals in three minutes at the start of the last term by Carlton had Melbourne on the run, but again the Blues faltered and they threw away the game with five behinds and three out-of-bounds in the time-on period, nearly all from easy shots. The Redlegs, kicking straighter, just held on to win by nine points, fourteen goals thirteen to eleven goals twenty-two. They would almost certainly have lost, but for the magnificent display of Wartman on the wing and the brilliance of Mueller at centre-half-back.

Collingwood and South met in the second semi-final, and both were inaccurate early, scoring only eight goals from twenty-nine scoring shots between them by

* Since broken several times, currently the record is held by Carlton with 22 such scores in 1979.

** He was persuaded to re-appear in 1937—and headed the VFL goalkicking.

half-time. South made a courageous third quarter comeback, however, with six goals three to a point, converting a twenty-five point deficit into a handy lead. Thomas, who had come on at half-time in place of Diggins (broken jaw) was the star of the South recovery. Collingwood wiped off South's lead within minutes of the start of the last term when Doherty and Knight goaled. The game then see-sawed for some time, with South gaining a one point lead with only a few minutes to go, but again the Magpies were equal to the occasion and goals to Kyne and Stackpole sealed the issue.

Laurie Nash's dominance over Melbourne's Jack Mueller, plus South's uncanny accuracy, decided the result of the preliminary final. South, aided by eight successive goals from the start of play until just after half-time, had a score of eleven goals one on the board at three-quarter-time, while the Redlegs, from seven more shots, had seven goals twelve and trailed by thirteen points. South had paralyzed the opposition with a burst of five goals (of which Pratt scored three) in nine minutes at the start of the second term. The last quarter, however, saw South misplace their 'true-boots' and rattle up two goals ten, but they still easily beat the tiring Redlegs by twenty-six points and entered their fourth successive grand final.

The grand final saw the Magpies open brilliantly with a goal to Knight one minute after the first bounce. Another to Todd and a flurry of misses followed—it was all Collingwood at this stage, but Nash finally snapped first goal for South, and the pacy Robertson* got the second. Goals to either side towards the end of an interesting first term put the Magpies into the lead by two points.

The brilliant Todd, who was adequately replacing Coventry at full-forward, struck a bad patch in the second term, booting four behinds. But between misses, he got two badly needed goals, and with Pannam, was proving a menace around goals for the hotly-pressed South defence. Collingwood had a grip on the game at half-time, having kicked four goals ten from many chances during the term, while South could manage only two goals three. But, as they had done in the second semi-final, South fought back well in the third quarter. After Todd had goaled for the Magpies, South took over and were constantly in attack for the rest of the term. Only the sterling defence of Regan, Fraser and Ross saved the Magpies from having their lead cut to even less than the seven points by which they led at three-quarter-time.

Immediately the last term began, South's Dineen drove to Johnson in the goal-square for a major which made the difference a single point. Todd booted a behind for the Magpies, and then Pannam gave them breathing space with a goal, his fourth, and soon after another, his fifth. Pratt twice missed for South who about now had a bad series of misses. When they finally broke through for a goal, Collingwood immediately replied and were able to hold their eleven point lead until the final bell. Great performances up forward by Pannam (thirty-two kicks and five goals) and Todd (four goals ten from sixteen shots), and Jack Ross' dogged tagging of Laurie Nash, were decisive factors in the Magpies' win.

*Robertson was the ex-world professional sprint champion.

RESULTS

SEPTEMBER 12 — FIRST SEMI-FINAL

	1st	2nd	3rd	Final	
Melbourne	5 . 4	9 . 7	12 . 11	14 . 13	(97)
Carlton	2 . 4	5 . 9	8 . 16	11 . 22	(88)

MCG — Umpire Blackburn

Attendance 54,693 — Gate £2,725

BEST —	(Melb)	Wartman, Mueller, Taylor, L. Jones, Lewis, Fisher, Ogden, Roberts
	(Carl)	Carney, R. Cooper, Hale, G. Mackie, Shea, Clarke, Green, Dunn, Mutimer
GOALS —	(Melb)	Baggott (3), Glass (3), Jones (3), Reiffel (2), Taylor (2), Wartman
	(Carl)	Vallence (3), Clarke (3), Cooper (2), Anderson, Shea, Wrout

SEPTEMBER 19 — SECOND SEMI-FINAL

	1st	2nd	3rd	Final	
Collingwood	1 . 7	6 . 11	6 . 12	12 . 18	(90)
South Melbourne	1 . 6	2 . 10	8 . 13	10 . 17	(77)

MCG **Umpire Blackburn**
Attendance 55,623 **Gate £2,761**

BEST —	(Col)	Whelan, Pannam, Morgan, H. Collier, Woods, Froude, Bowyer, Kyne
	(S. Melb)	Austin, Reid, Nash, Richards, Evans, Thomas
GOALS —	(Col)	Kyne (3), Knight (3), Doherty (2), Pannam (2), Riley, Stackpole
	(S. Melb)	Nash (4), Evans (2), Johnson, Pratt, Mullane, Robertson

SEPTEMBER 26 — PRELIMINARY FINAL

	1st	2nd	3rd	Final	
South Melbourne	2 . 0	7 . 0	11 . 1	13 . 11	(89)
Melbourne	1 . 4	3 . 8	7 . 12	8 . 15	(63)

MCG **Umpire Blackburn**
Attendance 50,758 **Gate £2,483**

BEST —	(S. Melb)	Graham, Mathews, Bissett, Dineen, Pratt, Nash, Robertson, Richards, Cleary
	(Melb)	Fischer, Wartman, LaFontaine, Ogden, Lewis, Muller, Reiffel, Jones, Furniss
GOALS —	(S. Melb)	Pratt (5), Moore (2), Dineen (2), Nash (2), Thomas, Robertson
	(Melb)	Glass (3), Reiffel, Lewis, Taylor, Jones, Baggott

OCTOBER 3 — GRAND FINAL

	1st	2nd	3rd	Final	
Collingwood	3 . 6	7 . 16	8 . 19	11 . 23	(89)
South Melbourne	3 . 4	5 . 7	8 . 12	10 . 18	(78)

MCG **Umpire Blackburn**
Attendance 74,091 **Gate £4,008**

BEST —	(Col)	Pannam, Whelan, Carmody, Kyne, Todd, Fraser, Doherty, Ross, Regan
	(S. Melb)	Robertson, Cleary, Hillis, Richards, Nash, Evans, Moore
GOALS —	(Col)	Pannam (5), Todd (4), Knight, Kyne
	(S. Melb)	Pratt (3), Johnson (2), Moore (2), Nash, Robertson, Evans

GRAND FINAL TEAMS

Collingwood	B	Crowe	Regan	Woods
	HB	Fraser	Ross	Froude
	C	Morgan	Whelan	Carmody
	HF	Riley	Kyne	Doherty
	F	Knight	Todd	Pannam
	Ruck	A. Collier	Bowyer	H. Collier (c)
	Nineteenth	Stackpole	**Coach** J. McHale	

1936-1937

South Melbourne	B	Richards	Hillis	Austin
	HB	Cleary	Graham	Faul
	C	Reid	Thomas*	Mathews
	HF	Dineen	Nash	Evans
	F	Johnson	Pratt	Moore
	Ruck	Bissett (c)	Kelleher	Robertson
	Nineteenth	Pettiona	Coach J. Bissett	

* Killed in World War II.

1937

The falling off in form of South Melbourne (who slumped to ninth with only six wins) and the rise of Geelong (top with fifteen wins) were features of 1937. Melbourne continued to display the promise they had shown in 1936, and opened the season with eight successive wins, which put them well on the way to eventually finishing second to Geelong with an equal number of wins. Collingwood (thirteen wins) was third, and Richmond, after a thrilling five point victory over Hawthorn in the last game, scraped into the final Four by two points from Carlton.

Richmond looked a better side than Collingwood in the first semi-final, but made the mistake of trying to imitate the Magpies' short game. Collingwood emerged with a three-goal lead after a congested first half, and increased this to four at the last change. When the Tigers badly needed goals their forwards, with the exception of Titus, fell down. When Rumney in the back pocket held Harris, Richmond's other main goal-scorer, the Tigers were out of business and the Magpies were untroubled to boot six goals in the last term and win quite easily by eight goals.

The second semi-final, one week later, saw Geelong down Melbourne by a bare two goals after the highest scoring finals match in League history. Geelong scored nineteen goals eleven, Melbourne sixteen goals seventeen. The Cats got away to a good start, with five goals to two in the first term, and adequately answered Melbourne's brilliant seven goals seven in the second quarter with a burst of six goals two themselves. Melbourne's score would have been higher if Mueller had kicked accurately. Geelong started the third term with three goals to Melbourne's one before a Melbourne re-shuffle enabled them to draw to within fourteen points. But Geelong steadied, and paced it with Melbourne in a high-scoring last term in which both sides scored six goals. The Redlegs were unable to bridge the gap. Jack Metherell, with eight goals for the Cats, was the main difference between victory and defeat.

Melbourne again failed in the preliminary final against Collingwood. After a very even first half, at the end of which Collingwood led by a point, the Melbourne resistance crumbled. A heavy shower at half-time suited the Magpies and they had three bursts of two goals in two minutes during the third term, always just as Melbourne seemed to be catching up. Adding ten goals seven to one goal seven for the second half, the Magpies won convincingly.

The stage was set for what old-timers still argue was the greatest grand final of all time. A record crowd of 88,540 crowded into the MCG and spilled out over the boundary line. Both sides fielded their strongest teams, and both were superbly fit.

H. Collier (Collingwood) won the toss, and the Magpies kicked with a slight breeze. Inspired by the dazzling marking of Todd at centre-half-forward and the brilliant display of Regan at full-back, 88,000 fans urged their teams on as the Magpies ran to a three goal lead at the first change. At the break, Geelong made several matchwinning moves. L. Hardiman, a flop at full-forward and in the ruck, moved to centre-half-back onto the brilliant Todd. Ruckman Jack Evans went to full-forward, Selwood went from centre-half-back to centre-half-forward, and Abbott from centre-half-forward to the ruck. All four moves paid off, as each player eventually contributed to victory. Collingwood, however, did most of the attacking for the first few minutes of the second term, but missed several reasonably easily chances before Kyne goaled. Geelong were quick to respond with majors to Coles, Evans and Metherell. Todd (Collingwood) and Coles and Evans (Geelong) added further goals before the term ended with the Cats trailing by five points.

Soon after the start of the third term, Evans goaled for Geelong, but Fothergill quickly replied for Collingwood. Quick goals to Metherell and Coles restored the Geelong lead, and the Cats bombarded the goals. However, several bad misses were their only reward, although Evans managed to kick accurately for a major which was quickly answered by Coventry for Collingwood, and the same player added another just before the bell. Right on time, A. Collier took a fine mark and place-kicked a behind to level the scores.

As soon as the last term began, Slack picked out Metherell who brilliantly twisted and turned before snapping an excellent goal for Geelong. Soon after, Hore and Metherell combined to get the ball to Abbott for another major. Both sides had a succession of behinds, including the third 'poster' of the game, before Wills ran into an open goal to score and increase the Geelong lead to twenty points. Moments later Abbott and Evans added further goals to seal the result. Pannam (Collingwood) kicked his side's twelfth goal, but Hickey immediately began a drive that ended with Metherell kicking Geelong's eighteenth as they cruised to a decisive victory.

The game had everything—it featured magnificent high marking, long kicking and rugged bumping, but it was entirely free from malice. In addition, it was seen by the largest crowd ever to watch a football match in Australia—88,540 fans, some of whom sat six deep inside the boundary on the actual playing area. Critics were unanimous in declaring it to be the greatest of all grand finals.

The game was the last played by Collingwood's great forward Gordon Coventry—his three goals brought his League total to 1,299 and his total in finals alone to 112 (both records).

RESULTS

SEPTEMBER 4 — FIRST SEMI-FINAL

	1st	2nd	3rd	Final	
Collingwood	4 . 3	7 . 5	12 . 8	18 . 12	(120)
Richmond	2 . 2	4 . 5	8 . 8	10 . 9	(69)

MCG — Umpire Blackburn
Attendance 41,663 — Gate £2,521

BEST —	(Col)	Whelan, Fothergill, Boyall, Regan, Ross, H. Collier, Woods, Todd, G. Coventry
	(Rich)	Guinane, Bolger, Dyer, Bentley, Bates, Titus, Martin, Sleeth, Henderson
GOALS —	(Col)	Coventry (6), Pannam (3), Knight (3), Fothergill (2), Doherty (2), Todd (2)
	(Rich)	Titus (4), Henderson (2), Sleeth, Symons, Bentley, Harris

SEPTEMBER 11 — SECOND SEMI-FINAL

	1st	2nd	3rd	Final	
Geelong	5 . 3	11 . 5	13 . 9	19 . 11	(125)
Melbourne	2 . 2	9 . 9	10 . 13	16 . 17	(113)

MCG — Umpire Batt
Attendance 47,730 — Gate £2,808

BEST —	(Geel)	Quinn, Muller, Metherell, Glenister, Evans, Dougherty, Arklay
	(Melb)	Buckley, Mueller, Baggott, Beames, Long, G. Jones, Kinnear, Lewis
GOALS —	(Geel)	J. Metherell (8), Dougherty (4), Quinn (2) L. Hardiman, (2), Glenister, Abbott, Evans
	(Melb)	Mueller (4), Beames (4), Smith (2), Baggott (2), Reiffel, Truscott, Lewis, LaFontaine

SEPTEMBER 18 — PRELIMINARY FINAL

	1st	2nd	3rd	Final	
Collingwood	5 . 2	6 . 4	12 . 6	16 . 11	(107)
Melbourne	2 . 2	6 . 3	7 . 7	7 . 10	(52)

MCG — Umpire Batt
Attendance 55,615 — Gate £3,296

BEST —	(Col)	Bowyer, H. Collier, Regan, Rumney, G. Coventry, Todd, Carmody, Dowling, Doherty, Fothergill, Pannam
	(Melb)	Truscott (B.O.G.), Chandler, Roberts, Baggott, Penberthy, Fischer, Beames
GOALS —	(Col)	Coventry (7), Fothergill (3), Pannam (3), Doherty (2), Todd
	(Melb)	LaFontaine (2), Baggott (2), Lock, L. Jones, Smith

SEPTEMBER 25 — GRAND FINAL

	1st	2nd	3rd	Final	
Geelong	3 . 3	8 . 5	12 . 8	18 . 14	(122)
Collingwood	6 . 3	8 . 10	11 . 14	12 . 18	(90)

MCG — Umpire Batt
Attendance 88,540 — Gate £5,961

BEST —	(Geel)	Quinn, Muller, L. Hardiman, H. Hardiman, J. Metherell, Coles, Everett, Evans, Sellwood
	(Col)	Froude, Regan, Ross, Todd, A. Collier, Woods, Dowling, Carmody, Whelan
GOALS —	(Geel)	Evans (6), J. Metherell (4), Coles (4), Abbott (2), Sellwood, Wills
	(Col)	Todd (4), Coventry (3), Pannam (2), Doherty, Kyne, Fothergill

GRAND FINAL TEAMS

Geelong	B	Hore	Hickey (c)	Everett
	HB	Grant	Sellwood	Arklay
	C	Slack	Hawking	Muller
	HF	Wills	Abbott	Coles
	F	Dougherty	L. Hardiman	J. Metherell
	Ruck	Evans	H. Hardiman	Quinn
	Nineteenth	Mahon	**Coach** R. Hickey	
Collingwood	B	Woods	Regan	Rumney
	HB	Froude	Boyall	Ross
	C	Dowling	Whelan	Carmody
	HF	Fothergill	Todd	Doherty
	F	Pannam	G. Coventry	Kyne
	Ruck	A. Collier	Bowyer	H. Collier (c)
	Nineteenth	L. Murphy	**Coach** J. McHale	

1938

Season 1938 saw probably the highest standard of play that football had yet attained. All teams gave the fans week after week of thrills, with astonishing form reversals, close-fought finishes, and some classic textbook football.

Carlton provided the success story of the season. Under the coaching of ex-South Melbourne star Brighton Diggins, they headed the first round ladder with fourteen wins in eighteen games. Geelong, continuing their form of 1937, were second with thirteen wins, followed by Footscray (making their first appearance in the finals) also thirteen wins. Filling fourth place was the redoubtable Collingwood (twelve wins, one game ahead of Melbourne).

The overawed Bulldogs met the Magpies in the first semi, and were convincingly defeated. Collingwood began with a burst of six goals one in the first term, and held on in the second as Footscray peppered the goals. Inaccuracy cost the Bulldogs dearly, and they had three goals nine for the term to trail at half time by eight points. Both sides made changes at half-time, and MacRae (Footscray) with two quick goals, put the Bulldogs ahead. Just as quickly, Pannam replied for Collingwood and this precipitated a Magpie burst of six goals in as many minutes to leave Footscray reeling. This magnificent effort converted a Magpie deficit of three points into a three-quarter time lead of thirty-three points, and, handicapped by injuries in the last term, Footscray were powerless to stop Collingwood increasing that lead and going on to a big win.

Carlton, although successful in the second semi, were discounted by the critics as a possible premiership side. They did not, in fact, play well, but the form of Geelong was even worse.

After an even first quarter, Carlton hammered the goals for five goals two in the second, but Geelong, with five successive behinds towards the end of the term, should have been much closer than they were. Geelong's inaccuracy continued—half way through the third term they had kicked four points to Carlton's three goals two, before Quinn broke the sequence with a goal, but further misses followed. From halfway through the second quarter, the Geelong forwards had booted a lamentable one goal thirteen.

The Cats hit back in the last term, however, with two goals within minutes of the start, but Baxter and Vallence were quick to reply for Carlton, and the game petered out into a tame finish with the Blues well ahead.

The Collingwood-Geelong final was yet another one-horse race. Collingwood began with five goals straight in the first term, and another five goals in the second, after they had begun the quarter with four behinds in succession. Geelong were again plagued by inaccuracy—one goal six in the first term which could easily have been six goals one—and five goals nine on the board at half-time. However, following several positional changes at the interval, they hit back, with quick goals to Coles (two) and Selwood. The brilliant Collingwood pair, Todd (his eighth goal) and Fothergill replied but another goal to Selwood brought Geelong to within thirteen points. It was as close as they got—Pannam goaled twice within minutes of the start of the last term and then Todd booted his ninth, tenth and eleventh goals for the Magpies, who increased their lead from eighteen to fifty-five points in nine minutes. Towards the finish, Clyde Helmer (later to lose his life in the War) goaled twice for Geelong but it was too late. Ron Todd's eleven goals equalled the finals goalkicking record of Harry Vallence in 1931 and 1932.

The largest crowd ever to see a football match in Australia—96,834—crowded into the MCG for the 1938 grand final, a game in which tactics played a large part in Carlton's ultimate victory. It was known that Magpie skipper Albert Collier was carrying a leg injury into the game, and to ensure that he was kept on the field and not replaced by a fit player, the Blues were instructed not to bump him and to keep clear of him as much as possible. Eventually, Collier became something of a liability to the Magpies and finished the game limping badly in the forward pocket, while the nineteenth man sat watching from the bench.

Carlton's forward flankers, Schmidt and Vallence (his last game) were told to play wide, and allow the Blues to attack through Jack Wrout at centre-half-forward. At full-forward, Ken Baxter was told to play from the square and so deprive Regan of the run he needed for his screaming marks. Jack Hale stuck like a shadow to Fothergill, and likewise, when Pannam roved, Mick Price took on the task of shadowing him. In addition, Carlton swung Jim Park onto Todd during the game, and Park effectively held the Magpie champion.

It was a fierce 'big-man's' type of grand final. There was no score for a long time as each side softened the other up, but finally Todd goaled twice from frees, goals which were answered for Carlton by Price and Crisp. The teams changed ends with Carlton leading by a point, but Fothergill, freed by Hale, levelled the scores within minutes. Then came several more misses by both sides—Carlton three behinds in a row, and Collingwood two behinds—before Doherty goaled for the Magpies. But a brilliant burst of four goals—to Wrout, Baxter, Green and Wrout, in the last five minutes of the quarter gave the Blues a half-time lead of twenty points. Immediately the third term began, some brilliant team-work by the Magpies led to a goal by Knight, and with two lone and accurate attacks, the Magpies reduced the Blues lead to nine points. The veteran Diggins, however, steadied Carlton who came back strongly to go to a seventeen point lead at the last change.

The final term began excitingly as both teams matched each other kick for kick. In quick succession, Fothergill (Collingwood), Schmidt (Carlton), Pannam (Collingwood) and Fothergill (again) goaled and once more Collingwood trailed by only nine points. Goals to Wrout (Carlton) and Fothergill (Collingwood) followed and play see-sawed for ten hectic minutes before Todd's goal made the difference only four points, and it was anybody's game.

Again Carlton rose to the occasion—Hale flew high above the pack to mark brilliantly and goal. When soon after, Wrout found Baxter for another, the game was all over and the VFL premiership had come to Princes Park for the first time in twenty-three years.

RESULTS

SEPTEMBER 3 — FIRST SEMI-FINAL

	1st	2nd	3rd	Final	
Collingwood	6 . 1	9 . 1	16 . 5	18 . 9	(117)
Footscray	3 . 2	6 . 11	9 . 14	10 . 16	(76)

MCG Umpire Blackburn
Attendance 67,566 (record) Gate £4,500

BEST — (Col) Fothergill (B.O.G.), Regan, Pannam, Whelan, Kyne, Boyall, A. Collier
(Foots) Spargo, Greenham, MacRae, Miller, Standfield, Ware, Hickey, Evans

GOALS — (Col) Fothergill (6), Pannam (5), Todd (4), Williams, Doherty, Kyne
(Foots) MacRae (5), Morrison (2), Palmer, Luke, Evans

SEPTEMBER 10 SECOND SEMI-FINAL

	1st	2nd	3rd	Final	
Carlton	2 . 5	7 . 7	11 . 9	16 . 17	(113)
Geelong	2 . 3	5 . 10	6 . 18	10 . 21	(81)

MCG Umpire Blackburn
Attendance 65,332 (record) Gate £4,229

BEST — (Carl) Carney, Francis, Crisp, Wrout, Baxter, Price, Hale, Diggins
(Geel) Glenister, Arklay, Everett, Abbott, Mahon, Dougherty, Dyer

GOALS — (Carl) Baxter (8), Price (3), Vallence (2), Wrout, Hollingshead, Schmidt
(Geel) Glenister (4), Coles (2), Helmer (2), Slack, Quinn

SEPTEMBER 17 — PRELIMINARY FINAL

	1st	2nd	3rd	Final	
Collingwood	5 . 0	10 . 5	15 . 7	21 . 9	(135)
Geelong	1 . 6	5 . 9	11 . 13	14 . 14	(98)

MCG Umpire Blackburn
Attendance 60,971 (record) Gate £3,872

BEST — (Col) Todd, Fothergill, Ross, Boyall, Froude, Dowling, Pannam
(Geel) Selwood, Helmer, Mahon, Hawking, Abbott, Everett, Grant

GOALS — (Col) Todd (11), Fothergill (5), Pannam (2), Knight, Doherty, Collier
(Geel) Helmer (6), Selwood (4), Coles (3), Dougherty

1938-1939

SEPTEMBER 24 — GRAND FINAL

	1st	2nd	3rd	Final	
Carlton	3 . 2	7 . 6	11 . 9	15 . 10	(100)
Collingwood	3 . 1	4 . 4	8 . 5	13 . 7	(85)

MCG — Umpire Blackburn
Attendance 96,834 (record) — Gate £6,778

BEST —	(Carl)	Hale (B.O.G.), Wrout, Crisp, Diggins, Green, Gill, Park, Anderson, Francis
	(Col)	Whelan, Balfour, Williams, Doherty, Froude, Fothergill, Boyall, Morgan
GOALS —	(Carl)	Wrout (4), Baxter (3), Schmidt (2), Hale (2), Price, Crisp, Vallence, Green
	(Col)	Fothergill (4), Todd (3), Pannam (2), Doherty (2), Knight, Kyne

GRAND FINAL TEAMS

Carlton	B	McIntyre	Gill	Park*
	HB	Chitty	Francis	Anderson
	C	Bob Green	Crisp	Carney
	HF	Vallence	Wrout	Schmidt
	F	McLean	Baxter	Price
	Ruck	Diggins (c)	Hollingshead	Hale
	Nineteenth	McInnes	Coach B. J. Diggins	
Collingwood	B	Balfour	Regan	Woods
	HB	Ross	Boyall	Froude
	C	Dowling	Whelan	Morgan
	HF	Doherty	Hocking	Kyne
	F	Knight	Todd	Pannam
	Ruck	A. Collier (c)	Williams	Fothergill
	Nineteenth	Carmody	Coach J. J. McHale	

* Killed in World War II.

1939

Melbourne, after missing the Four in 1938, bounced back to actually top the League ladder in 1939, and shatter several records in the process. In winning fifteen of their eighteen games, they kicked fifteen 100 point scores (breaking Collingwood's record of thirteen), and nine of these were scored in succession, breaking Geelong's 1935 record of seven in a row. It was, however, a season of exceptionally high-scoring by all the bigger teams—helped as they were by the re-introduction of the boundary throw-in.* This enabled those side with big ruckmen to continually get the ball clear of the packs, or for backs to force the ball out if they were in trouble in the hope that the rucks could again get the ball clear on the throw-in.

Collingwood (second) won fifteen out of their eighteen games, and equalled their old VFL record of thirteen century scores. Behind them on the ladder came Richmond and St. Kilda (first finals appearance since 1929), both with thirteen wins. Carlton, a game behind, filled fifth position after making a desperate attempt to reach the Four with a late run of six successive wins, but a loss to Richmond at Punt Road put paid to their chances.

In a lack-lustre first semi-final, the Saints were yards faster than a sluggish Richmond, and with Fountain and Garvin unexpectedly beating Bentley and Dyer in the ruck, they went to a lead of almost six goals at the last change. Richmond made some drastic changes at three-quarter time, Bentley going into the ruck, Harris to the forward pocket and Titus to a half-forward-flank, but, although Titus kicked a couple of quick goals, the Saints had no intention of relaxing and two snap goals by Killegrew put them out of any danger of defeat.

The second-semi was highlighted by a brilliant Melbourne comeback in the third quarter, when they booted five goals two to two goals four after trailing by thirteen points at half-time. Collingwood had cleverly nullified Melbourne's pace and high-marking early, but there was no doubt after half-time as to which was the better side. With Wartman, Jones and Mueller dominant in their respective positions, the Demons booted another five goals in the last term and won easing up. Todd's 100th goal of the season was the feature of the last half.

In probably the best finals game since the memorable 1937 grand final, Collingwood the following week convincingly defeated St. Kilda in the preliminary final. The Magpies unexpectedly matched the Saints in pace and all-round ability, and in addition they had a brilliant spearhead in Ron Todd, who took some unforgettable marks while kicking eleven goals four from sixteen shots. After an even first quarter, the Magpies were generally on top, although St. Kilda pressed them closely until three-quarter time. A last quarter burst of six goals three, in which Todd was outstanding, sealed the result of the game, Collingwood winning quite easily by almost five goals. Todd's eleven goals equalled the VFL finals record shared by himself (1938) and Vallence (Carlton—1931-32).

The grand final, the last before the world was plunged into another war, saw the Magpies get away to a good start. They were quickly into attack, and Knight was freed close in to bring up first goal. Immediately, Melbourne swung Mueller into the ruck, and put Kimberley full-back, and they went forward with good handball between L. Jones, Anderson and Truscott to enable Beames to run in and goal. Just as quickly, Todd had an answering goal on the board for Collingwood. Then A. Collier took the ball from a bounce, and handballed to Fothergill for another. A Baggott-Smith handpass let Rodda in to goal for the Redlegs, but again the dangerous Todd provided the equaliser for Collingwood. Short passes from Baggott to Smith to Beames saw the latter goal, but Knight to Todd, and then a glorious drop-kick by McRae brought up fifth and sixth goals for Collingwood, who then had a three goal lead at the first change.

Immediately the second term began, Ball (Melbourne) missed a sitter, but made up for it by goaling from a lucky free. Then came a sensation Umpire Coward went down in a pack and while he was on the ground a series of passes from Wartman to Truscott

* Since 1925, a free kick had been awarded for kicking out of bounds, even if the ball bounced over the line.

to Beames saw the latter goal; but it was disallowed as the umpire was unable to give the all-clear. After a five minute delay, Coward was assisted off with a dislocated elbow and Umpire Blackburn took over. L. Jones goaled from an angle for Melbourne, and Smith followed a moment later with another which gave the Redlegs a three point lead. Todd marked, but was pushed over and a scrimmage started, out of which came a Todd handpass to Fothergill, and a Collingwood goal. Then Todd, proving a headache to the Melbourne defenders, added another himself. Melbourne came with a run towards the end of the term, and in quick succession put up six-pointers to LaFontaine, Wartman, and Truscott, which left them trailing by four points at half-time.

The Redlegs continued to apply the pressure with three more goals within ten minutes of the start of the third term. It was obvious now that Collingwood was slowing down, although they managed to break even on the scoreboard for the remainder of the quarter, which was highlighted by a magnificent seventy yard goal by Todd. But it was only a matter of time before Melbourne got away, and, with the Magpies left with only sixteen men in the last term, the Redlegs added goals to Beames, Rodda and Jones, which started a burst of six goals eight to Collingwood's one goal two. By kicking eleven goals twelve to the Magpies' four goals five in the last half, the Redlegs posted a new grand final record score of twenty-one goals twenty-two and won their first premiership since 1926.

RESULTS

SEPTEMBER 9 — FIRST SEMI-FINAL

	1st	2nd	3rd	Final	
St. Kilda	3 . 2	5 . 7	8 . 9	10 . 12	(72)
Richmond	1 . 2	2 . 4	3 . 4	6 . 6	(42)

MCG — Umpire E. Coward
Attendance 51,411 — Gate £3,403

BEST — (St. K) Rayment, Maslen, Kelly, Fountain, Williamson, Garvin, Sawley
(Rich) Crane, Bawden, Guinane, Cotter, Edwards, Martin, Titus

GOALS — (St. K) Killegrew (3), Clarke (2), Vontom (2), Coles, Walker, Weiss
(Rich) Titus (3), O'Donnell, McDonald, Dyer

SEPTEMBER 16 — SECOND SEMI-FINAL

	1st	2nd	3rd	Final	
Melbourne	3 . 4	5 . 9	10 . 11	15 . 14	(104)
Collingwood	3 . 3	7 . 10	9 . 14	12 . 18	(90)

MCG — Umpire Coward
Attendance 54,466 — Gate £3,339

BEST — (Melb) Wartman, Mueller, Jones, Beames, Smith, Maher, Kingston
(Col) Whelan, H. Collier, Fothergill, Woods, Knight, A. Collier, Todd

GOALS — (Melb) Mueller (4), Smith (3), Beames (3), Barassi (2), Truscott, Ball, Jones
(Col) Todd (6), Fothergill (2), Balfour, Knight, Powell, J. Murphy

1939

SEPTEMBER 23 — PRELIMINARY FINAL

	1st	2nd	3rd	Final	
Collingwood	6 . 1	11 . 6	14 . 11	20 . 14	(134)
St. Kilda	6 . 4	9 . 7	13 . 9	15 . 15	(105)

MCG — **Umpire Blackburn**
Attendance 66,484 (record) — **Gate £4,291**

BEST — (Col) Campbell, Doherty, Todd, Regan, Williams
(St. K) Lowry, Garvin, Vontom, Killegrew, Mohr, Rayment, Hoppen

GOALS — (Col) Todd (11), Doherty (4), Fothergill (3), Knight, Kyne
(St. K) Mohr (4), Regnier (3), Vontom (3), Weiss, Fountain, Killegrew, Garvin, Kelly

SEPTEMBER 30 — GRAND FINAL

	1st	2nd	3rd	Final	
Melbourne	3 . 5	10 . 10	15 . 14	21 . 22	(148)
Collingwood	6 . 5	10 . 6	13 . 9	14 . 11	(95)

MCG — **Umpires Coward, Blackburn**
Attendance 78,110 — **Gate £5,194**

BEST — (Melb) Roberts, Beames, Anderson, Wartman, Truscott, Smith, Mueller
(Col) Regan, Todd, Knight, H. Collier, Kyne, Ross, Hocking

GOALS — (Melb) Beames (4), Rodda (4), L. Jones (3), Ball (2), Mueller (2), Truscott (2), Smith, Wartman, LaFontaine, Baggott
(Col) Todd (6), Fothergill (3), Knight (2), Balfour, MacRae, Doherty

GRAND FINAL TEAMS

Melbourne	**B**	R. Emselle	J. Mueller	R. Fischer
	HB	R. Hingston	G. Jones	F. Roberts
	C	R. Wartman	A. LaFontaine (c)	S. Anderson
	HF	L. Jones	R. Baggott	K. Truscott
	F	H. Ball	N. Smith	A. Rodda
	Ruck	J. Furness	R. Kimberley	P. Beames
	Nineteenth	S. O'Keefe	**Coach** F. V. Hughes	
Collingwood	**B**	J. Murphy	J. Regan	G. Hocking
	HB	J. Ross	A. Williams	D. Balfour
	C	P. Fricker	M. Whelan	N. Campbell
	HF	C. McRae	A. Kyne	V. Doherty
	F	D. Fothergill	R. Todd	J. Knight
	Ruck	A. Collier	B. Woods	H. Collier (c)
	Nineteenth	J. Green	**Coach** J. McHale	

1940

In one of the roughest seasons since the 1920's—forty-seven players were reported—Melbourne again emerged as the top dog of the League winning fourteen games and kicking a record sixteen scores of over 100 points. Richmond and Essendon, each with twelve wins, took second and third positions, with Geelong a game behind and Carlton (ten wins) occupying fifth place. 1939 Runners-up Collingwood, fell back to eighth position, but they had lost their champion full-forward, Ron Todd, who crossed to Williamstown (VFA) without a clearance in the season's biggest sensation.

Despite a choppy wind which blew throughout the day, the long kicking, high marking Essendon began brilliantly in the first semi-final against Geelong. Winning hands down in the ruck and with Buttsworth dominant at centre-half-back, the Dons played magnificently after Bryce got first goal, and they quickly had five goals on the board to Geelong's one. The Pivotonians increased their score by two goals towards the end of the term, and added two more early in the second, but Essendon then put on a paralyzing burst of six goals. Geelong played right into their opponents' hands by fiddling about trying to go around the flanks instead of straight down the centre.

Geelong began the third term with several positional changes, but Reynolds goaled for the Dons. Helmer (Geelong) replied and Geelong finally started to get on top, but woeful kicking for goal cost them dearly and they kicked three goals eight for the term to trail by four clear goals at the final change. This was more than enough for Essendon, who were untroubled to hold off a determined Geelong bid in the last quarter and win well.

Melbourne began the second semi with two goals in as many minutes, but it was a first quarter of errors. Ball (Melbourne) missed from two yards out, Titus (Richmond) hit the post (although a poor kick-off let Harris in for a goal), Bentley (Richmond) fumbled while running into an open goal (but again a mistake was retrieved as Titus picked up and goaled) and a mulled handball by Dyer (Richmond) was intercepted by Mueller who goaled for Melbourne.

In the second, a brilliant dash by Waldron led to a Tiger goal, and another quick major to Bawden started a burst of Richmond goals. Then, just before half-time, came a sensation as Richmond's Jack Dyer heavily crashed Norm Smith of Melbourne. The half-conscious Smith collapsed at half-time, and had to be replaced by Truscott, but the bump led to bitter demonstrations against Dyer from the Melbourne fans for the remainder of the game.

Truscott made his presence felt with a fine goal immediately play resumed. Then McDonald replied for the Tigers, who booted four more before Mueller marked a few yards out just before the bell and kicked Melbourne's eleventh. It took fourteen minutes of the last quarter for another goal to be scored, when Titus and Harris got majors in quick succession for Richmond. Baggott sank two equalisers, before Truscott goaled right on the bell to reduce the Tigers' winning margin to six points.

In a very hard-fought final, Melbourne, finishing with sixteen men, held out Essendon to win by five points. Both teams battled it out in a last term rain storm after an even first three quarters.

Reynold's goal grabbed the lead for Essendon as soon as the last term began, but Rodda quickly regained it for Melbourne. Then, a series of injuries forced Melbourne to swing Harold Ball, a spare ruckman, to full-back and the move proved to be a matchwinning one. With the ground a quagmire, and players finding it difficult to take even chest marks, Ball thrilled the crowd with brilliant finger-tip marking, dragging down screamer after screamer on the last line of defence. In all, he pulled down fifteen marks in an amazing last quarter. Right at the end, a goal to Exelby gave the Dons a three point lead, and in a tense finish further goals to Baggott (Melbourne), Beames (Melbourne) and Bryce (Essendon) left Melbourne clinging to their slender lead.

A point of interest in this game was that one of Essendon's goals, credited to Bryce, was actually kicked off the ground by Melbourne back-pocket, Emselle. As players of both sides were black with mud at the time, the goal umpire's mistake was understandable.

Melbourne, hit by injuries, were unable to name their grand final side until just before the start of the game. Fischer, Lock and Baxter were unable to play, Dowsing was omitted, and O'Keefe, Fanning, Truscott and Roberts came in. The ground was sodden, and another heavy downpour fell just as the game began.

From the bounce, Baggott was freed and found Smith for the first Melbourne goal. Crane and Harris quickly replied for the Tigers, who were getting the best of the free kicks—Melbourne were tending to play the man. Good shepherding by Smith let Beames in to goal, and with persistence, Melbourne finally broke through for several more, although missing other easy shots. At the quarter time change, Wartman (Melbourne) limped off, and was replaced by Barassi. Melbourne, applying the pressure, booted two quick goals, both from frees, and as Richmond became ragged, the Redlegs crashed on four more goals to lead by forty-five points at half-time.

Posters to both sides—Melbourne two, Richmond one—had the crowd groaning in the third term, but two goals by Norm Smith gave Melbourne an almost unbeatable lead at three-quarter-time. Richmond resorted to wholesale positional changes, and gained belated success when Bentley passed to Titus for a goal (his 100th of the season) and Harris added another soon after. However, Melbourne were not to be denied, and great defence by Mueller and Ball got the ball to Baggott, whose screw-pass found Smith for the Redleg full-forward's seventh goal.* Soon after Baggott added another himself, and the game was all over. Richmond rattled on several quick goals towards the end, but had no chance of overhauling Melbourne's lead.

The Redlegs' instructions for the game were interesting—O'Keefe was told to shadow Richmond's matchwinner, Jack Dyer, all day, and Melbourne were to keep the ball away from Dyer whenever possible. Mueller was never to be in the ruck at the same time as the Tiger champion. Kevin O'Neill (Richmond) was to be kept on

* Some critics still claim Smith actually kicked eight goals—a grand final record—but one was wrongly credited to Ron Baggott.

the wrong foot as much as possible. Full-forward Norm Smith, normally a brilliant lead, was told to play shoulder to shoulder with Richmond's George Smeaton, and a man would always be running past anticipating Smeaton's usual tactics of punching the ball down when contesting with Smith. By following these tactics, and their easy adaptation to the wet conditions, Melbourne won the premiership.

RESULTS

SEPTEMBER 7 — FIRST SEMI-FINAL

	1st	2nd	3rd	Final	
Essendon	5 . 4	11 . 10	12 . 11	13 . 14	(92)
Geelong	3 . 2	5 . 3	8 . 11	10 . 14	(74)

MCG — Umpire Hawkins
Attendance 44,257 — Gate £2,661

BEST — (Ess) Buttsworth, Green, Plummer, Torney, H. Lambert, Caesar
(Geel) Dean, Arklay, J. Lynch, Glenister, Harwood, Gneil, Everett, Taylor

GOALS — (Ess) Bryce (4), T. Reynolds (3), R. Reynolds (2), Griggs (2), Bushby, Exelby
(Geel) Arklay (3), N. Glenister (2), Dougherty, Harwood, Grant, Lynch, Helmer

SEPTEMBER 14 — SECOND SEMI-FINAL

	1st	2nd	3rd	Final	
Richmond	4 . 3	9 . 7	13 . 8	16 . 11	(107)
Melbourne	4 . 4	6 . 8	11 . 17	14 . 17	(101)

MCG — Umpire Coward
Attendance 54,763 — Gate £3,555

BEST — (Rich) Harris, Quinn, Waldron, Edwards, Dyer, O'Neill
(Melb) Gibb, Ball, LaFontaine, Truscott, Emselle, Mueller

GOALS — (Rich) Titus (5), Harris (5), Quinn (2), McDonald, Priestley, Bawden, Waldron
(Melb) Baggott (4), Truscott (4), Mueller (2), Dowsing, Gibb, Smith, Beames

SEPTEMBER 21 — PRELIMINARY FINAL

	1st	2nd	3rd	Final	
Melbourne	4 . 7	8 . 11	9 . 16	12 . 18	(90)
Essendon	3 . 4	8 . 8	9 . 11	12 . 13	(85)

MCG — Umpire Coward
Attendance 47,348 — Gate £2,811

BEST — (Melb) Fischer, Ball, Emselle, Baggott, Smith, Rodda
(Ess) R. Reynolds, Bryce, Griggs, Torney, H. Lambert, C. Lambert

GOALS — (Melb) Smith (3), Rodda (3), Mueller (2), Baggott (2), LaFontaine, Beames
(Ess) Bryce (4), Watts (3), Exelby (2), R. Reynolds, Griggs, C. Lambert

SEPTEMBER 28 — GRAND FINAL

	1st	2nd	3rd	Final	
Melbourne	4 . 8	10 . 11	13 . 15	15 . 17	(107)
Richmond	3 . 0	4 . 2	5 . 4	10 . 8	(68)

MCG — Umpire Coward

Attendance 69,061 — Gate £4,528*

BEST — (Melb) Baggott, Beames, LaFontaine, Mueller, Ball, Smith
(Rich) McDonald, Harris, Titus, Dyer, Edwards, Cotter

GOALS — (Melb) Smith (7), Baggott (2), Beames (2), O'Keefe (2), Truscott, Fanning
(Rich) Harris (5), Titus (3), Crane, Bawden

GRAND FINAL TEAMS

Melbourne	B	R. Emselle	F. Roberts	H. Ball
	HB	C. McLean	G. Jones	R. Hingston
	C	R. Wartman	A. LaFontaine (c)	S. Anderson
	HF	K. Truscott	R. Baggott	M. Gibb
	F	F. Fanning	N. Smith	A. Rodda
	Ruck	J. Mueller	S. O'Keefe	P. Beames
	Nineteenth	R. Barassi	Coach F. V. Hughes	
Richmond	B	K. O'Neill	G. Smeaton	J. Symons
	HB	R. Steele	I. Hull	J. Cotter
	C	A. McDonald	B. Waldron	B. Edwards
	HF	R. Martin	J. Crane	L. Smith
	F	R. Bawden	J. Titus	R. Harris
	Ruck	P. Bentley	J. Dyer (c)	J. Quinn
	Nineteenth	L. Merrett	Coach P. Bentley	

* Plus £1,000 rain insurance.

1941

Carlton, fifth in 1940, did much better in 1941 and actually finished on top of the ladder, winning fourteen games and losing four. They were only slightly ahead of Melbourne on percentage but beat the Redlegs twice in the home and home games. Third place was also decided on percentage as the first three teams all had fourteen wins. Richmond filled this position, less than one per cent behind Melbourne, and Essendon (thirteen wins) were fourth.

The influence of the war was now more marked than in 1940, and attendances fell drastically, averaging around 66,000 for each week of the home and home games. Most clubs were in difficulties financially, but the worst was yet to come.

Hot favourites Richmond fell in a heap in an amazing reversal of form in the first semi-final. Essendon, passing with great accuracy and using handball to devastating effect, booted eight goals one in the opening quarter and never looked back. They were always able to create a loose man, and with four of their forwards kicking eighteen goals between them, they ran up a total of twenty-one goals nine to Richmond's eleven goals fifteen and notched an effortless win. Essendon, in the end, could do nothing wrong, and even miskicks found a team-mate, whilst many of the Richmond big-names were sadly out of form. Despite this, however, they got to within nine points of Essendon early in the third quarter.

Melbourne, with Baggott and Smith luring Carlton's defenders well downfield to leave the high-marking Mueller lurking in the goal-square, were untroubled to defeat Carlton in the second semi-final. The Blues had proved too good when the sides had met in the last home and home game a fortnight before but the Redlegs had learned their lesson. On a heavy ground, Carlton frittered away early chances, and then had to look on helplessly as Melbourne booted seven goals five in a brilliant first quarter and led by more than five goals at half-time. Carlton fought back well in the third term, but in the closing stages Baggott, Mueller and Beames all goaled for Melbourne, goals that were answered by only a lone major from Carlton's Cooper just before the bell.

Wholesale changes by Carlton at three-quarter-time, including the move of Chitty from full-back to the ruck, worked wonders for the Blues. After three near misses, McInnes, Gill and Mann all goaled, before Wrout missed a sitter which would have made things interesting had he kicked it. That was the end of Carlton's effort, however, for goals to Mueller and Baggott (two) put Melbourne out of danger, two last-minute Carlton goals coming far too late.

An interesting preliminary final, played in a swirling, tricky wind, saw Carlton make far too many errors to hope to beat the pacy Essendon. The Blues got the first major of the game, but after that goals were few and far between, as for the next three quarters the Blues could add only another three goals twelve to Essendon's twelve goals two.

The only time Carlton looked a threat was early in the third term, when they went in very determinedly, but easy Essendon goals by Cassin and Bryce took the heart out of them. Mass changes for the last quarter brought Carlton a belated five goals, but Essendon had slowed down and were taking it easy in anticipation of the following week's grand final.

Melbourne, sadly depleted of players—Ball, Furniss, Truscott, Barassi (killed in action), G. Jones, Maher and Atkins were all in the Services, and Murnane, Fanning, Rodda and Baxter out injured—delayed the naming of their grand final side until the last minute. Essendon lined up at almost full strength.

A blustery north wind, an overcast sky, and a high temperature prevailed as the game began. Essendon, with a goal to Abbott within seconds of the first bounce, began well but then fell into errors through over-anxiousness. Some of their kicking was atrocious and Melbourne were quick to capitalise. Also, Melbourne was surprisingly winning in the ruck and goals came from Dullard, Beames (two), Mueller (two) and Wartman before the quarter ended. Essendon's poor form was again no match for Melbourne's brilliance in the next quarter, and the score-board at half-time made sorry reading for the Don's supporters—Melbourne eleven goals nine, Essendon two goals six.

Belatedly, the Dons came good after half-time. T. Reynolds and Bryce goaled soon after the resumption, but Daly (a brilliant angle goal) and O'Keefe replied for Melbourne, who led by nine goals one. However, with Lane providing plenty of drive at centre-half-forward, Essendon got further goals from Bryce and Regan, and actually outscored Melbourne during the quarter.

A high-scoring final twenty-five minutes saw Essendon right on top for the only time during the game, scoring seven goals eight from numerous shots, but their defence was not equal to the occasion and Melbourne were able to almost match this with five goals of their own. Those five goals were more than enough to win the game, and Melbourne were quite untroubled to take the 1941 pennant by the clear margin of twenty-nine points. It is curious to note that the Demons received only twenty free kicks during the game as opposed to Essendon's fifty-two.

Melbourne's S. 'Pop' Heal, a Western Australian serving with the Navy, set a unique record when he appeared with West Perth in the W.A. grand final the following week. As both Melbourne and West Perth won their respective premierships, Heal's record was a perfect one.

This, their third successive flag, ended the first Melbourne 'Golden Era'. During the three years 1939-40-41 the Redlegs had played sixty-one games, winning forty-nine and losing only twelve. In those sixty-one games, they had kicked scores of over 100 points forty-six times (an amazing scoring rate), but in those same three seasons their opponents had averaged eighty-four, ninety-two and ninety-four points per game against them. In 1942, following the retirement of their great coach 'Checker' Hughes and the demands of the war, the great Melbourne side fell to eighth place.

In mentioning those great days of Melbourne, it should be remembered that four of the members of those premiership teams did not return from the war—Ron Barassi, Harold Ball, Syd Anderson and the immortal 'Bluey' Truscott all paid the supreme sacrifice.

RESULTS

SEPTEMBER 6 — FIRST SEMI-FINAL

	1st	2nd	3rd	Final	
Essendon	8 . 1	10 . 7	13 . 8	21 . 9	(135)
Richmond	2 . 4	7 . 7	8 . 11	11 . 15	(81)

MCG — Umpire Hawkins
Attendance 57,741 — Gate £4,853

BEST — (Ess) Griggs (B.O.G.), Bryce, Coward, Lambert, Buttsworth, Torney, Lane, Abbott, Plummer

(Rich) Bawden, Symons, Edwards, Merrett, Steel, Nagle, O'Connell, Dyer, Laird-Smith

GOALS — (Ess) T. Reynolds (5), Lane (5), Griggs (4), Bryce (4), Cassin (2), Abbott

(Rich) Titus (3), Harris (2), Randall (2), Merrett, O'Connell, Bawden, Dyer

SEPTEMBER 13 — SECOND SEMI-FINAL

	1st	2nd	3rd	Final	
Melbourne	7 . 5	9 . 8	13 . 11	16 . 13	(109)
Carlton	2 . 2	4 . 5	6 . 9	11 . 16	(82)

MCG — Umpire Coward
Attendance 59,435 — Gate £4,830

1941

BEST	—	(Melb)	Mueller, Baggott, LaFontaine, Heal, Gibb, Anderson
		(Carl)	Chitty (B.O.G.), K. Baxter, Bailey, McIntyre
GOALS	—	(Melb)	Baggott (6), Mueller (5), Gibb (2), Beames (2), Smith
		(Carl)	Mann (3), Mooring (2), Gill (2), McInnes (2), Cooper, Wrout

SEPTEMBER 20 — PRELIMINARY FINAL

	1st	2nd	3rd	Final	
Essendon	2 . 6	6 . 8	12 . 12	13 . 15	(93)
Carlton	2 . 2	2 . 6	4 . 12	9 . 14	(68)

MCG — Umpire Bride
Attendance 65,105 — Gate £5,379 (record)

BEST	—	(Ess)	Cassin, Torney, R. Reynolds, Bryce, Buttsworth, Ruddell, Coward
		(Carl)	Baxter (B.O.G.), Anderson, McIntyre, Mann, Cooper, Brown, Mooring
GOALS	—	(Ess)	Cassin (6), Lane (3), R. Reynolds (2), Bryce, Griggs
		(Carl)	Schmidt (2), Mann (2), Wrout (2), Crisp, Cooper, Savage

SEPTEMBER 27 — GRAND FINAL

	1st	2nd	3rd	Final	
Melbourne	6 . 6	11 . 9	14 . 11	19 . 13	(127)
Essendon	1 . 1	2 . 6	6 . 12	13 . 20	(98)

MCG — Umpire Hawkins
Attendance 79,687 — Gate £6,507

BEST	—	(Melb)	Lock, Heal, Mueller, Beames, Dullard, LaFontaine, E. Cordner, Emselle
		(Ess)	Coward, Buttsworth, Abbott, R. Reynolds, H. Lambert
GOALS	—	(Melb)	Beames (6), Smith (3), Mueller (3), Wartman (2), Daly, Dullard, O'Keefe, Anderson, Gibb
		(Ess)	T. Reynolds (3), R. Reynolds (2), Bryce (2), Abbott, Lane, Regan, Cassin, Exelby, Torney

GRAND FINAL TEAMS

Melbourne	B	R. Emselle	S. McGrath	S. O'Keefe
	HB	C. McLean	E. Cordner	W. Lock
	C	S. Heal	A. LaFontaine (c)	S. Anderson*
	HF	R. Wartman	R. Baggott	M. Gibb
	F	A. Dullard	N. Smith	G. Daly
	Ruck	Don Cordner	J. Mueller	P. Beames
	Nineteenth	W. Lewis	Coach F. V. Hughes	
Essendon	B	Plummer	Ruddell	Green
	HB	Flanagan	Buttsworth	Hird
	C	Coward	H. Lambert	Caesar
	HF	Lane	Griggs	Exelby
	F	Bryce	T. Reynolds	Cassin
	Ruck	Torney	Abbott	R. Reynolds (c)
	Nineteenth	Regan*	Coach R. S. Reynolds	

* Killed in World War II.

1942

The influence of the World War through the years of 1942-43 was considerable. Not only were clubs struggling to field teams, often having to use second-class players, but attendances fell by sixty per cent. Totals of 112,000 at a normal pre-war round now stabilised at around 30,000 to 35,000. War-time travel restrictions forced Geelong to withdraw from the League, and the VFA competition was forced to disband in its entirety. The League suspended the Brownlow Medal and all interstate games.

To add to difficulties, several grounds were taken over for essential services. The MCG, St. Kilda, South Melbourne and Footscray grounds became service camps or depots. Footscray played at Yarraville, Melbourne at Richmond, St. Kilda at Prahran and South Melbourne at Carlton.

With only eleven teams competing, the season's programme extended over sixteen weeks, some teams having two byes, others one.

Essendon with twelve wins, three losses and one bye finished atop the League ladder, followed by Richmond (eleven wins, four losses and a bye), South Melbourne (eleven wins, four losses and one bye) and Footscray (ten wins, four losses and two byes). Missing the Four by six per cent was an unlucky Carlton. After a bad start, they won their last eight games, including fifty-three point victories over both Essendon and Richmond in the last three games. Never before had a team won its last eight games and failed to make the finals.

South Melbourne defeated an extraordinarily inaccurate Footscray in the first semi-final at Princes Oval. After an even first quarter, during which both sides missed easy shots, Footscray bombarded the goals during the second term but were rewarded with a heart-breaking two goals ten. When Lin White (South Melbourne) kicked four goals in a brilliant third quarter, and Footscray continued to miss easy shots—they hit the post no fewer than five times during the game—the writing was on the wall. South added four goals in the last term to win easily, Footscray finishing with an atrocious seven goals twenty-two, of which Norman Ware kicked three goals fourteen.

Richmond, who had scored ninety-nine goals in the first four games of the season, including a League record score of thirty goals nineteen against Melbourne, were too strong for Essendon in the second semi-final. The game generally was below standard, with both sides kicking poorly and fumbling frequently. After a low-scoring first half, Richmond added five goals through the clever play of Titus and Harris in the third quarter, and were untroubled to hold their lead for the remainder of the game.

1942

The preliminary final was noteworthy for the brilliant goalkicking display given by Lin White (South Melbourne) and for the fact that it was the first time that Essendon had won at Princes Oval since May 9, 1925.

The South Melbourne team was selected only ten minutes before the first bounce, but this didn't seem to affect them and they outscored Essendon in a fine first quarter, with Lindsay White at full-forward booting their entire first quarter score of four goals four. After a high-scoring second term, the teams were separated by only five points at half-time. The Dons grabbed the lead immediately play resumed, but White grabbed it back with a sixty-yard drop-kick goal. Then a collision between two South team-mates unsettled the Bloods, and Essendon raced on six quick goals to have a firm grip on the game at three-quarter-time. Wally Buttsworth, who had been dominant at centre-half-back for Essendon, moved to full-back on White as the last term began. Leehane and R. Reynolds goaled for Essendon but White, after three brilliant marks, goaled three times to give South a chance. But then they cracked, and Essendon rushed on two more goals to put the issue beyond doubt.

Forty-nine thousand fans, the largest crowd of the season, watched the 1942 grand final. Richmond, hot favourites, announced their team only minutes before the start. Reilly (seconds) and Morris came in, Hill and Ablett went out. Essendon lined up unchanged.

Richmond kicked with a slight breeze, but Essendon did all the early attacking for two behinds before the Tigers' first forward move resulted in a goal to Merrett. Essendon's consistent attacks yielded six successive behinds before Exelby got their first goal. Harris (Richmond) and Lane (Essendon) added further goals to end an even first quarter.

Immediately play resumed, a goal was scored by Richmond, but Essendon replied with three majors within minutes and, as Richmond panicked, launched an all-out blitz on the goals which produced another three goals and gave them a convincing half-time lead. The Tigers, after looking the better side in the first term, had failed to pick up the loose men, kicked poorly, and neglected to back up. Essendon, but for inaccuracy, would have led by ten goals.

The start of the third term saw Bawden, Symonds and Randall miss easy chances for Richmond, but Essendon still had loose men creating havoc, and goals came to Lane (three), Dearle and Cassin, to which Richmond could reply with only a belated goal to Dyer. A melee broke out after one of Lane's goals, and numbers were taken. Soon after another scuffle broke out in front of the Heatley Stand, and players went down like nine-pins. Just on three-quarter-time, with some players losing control of themselves, Essendon goaled again to increase their lead to ten goals, and the break gave players a chance to cool their tempers.

Relentlessly, the Dons ground Richmond into the dirt with three goals within minutes of the commencement of the last quarter. Titus kicked his first of the day for Richmond, who started to play better, and in a rush made their score look a bit more respectable. But Essendon were coasting, for it was obvious well before the bell that they had won their seventh League premiership.

Six players—four Richmond, two Essendon—were reported during the game. Richmond's George Smeaton did not mind copping a suspension—he served it whilst overseas with the AIF.

1942

RESULTS

AUGUST 29 — FIRST SEMI-FINAL

	1st	2nd	3rd	Final	
South Melbourne	1 . 4	3 . 5	9 . 9	13 . 13	(91)
Footscray	1 . 4	3 . 14	5 . 18	7 . 22	(64)

Princes Oval — Umpire Hawkins
Attendance 25,000 — Gate £2,300

BEST — (S. Melb) King, Bywater, Williams, Traynor, White, Graham, Chinn
(Foots) Ware, Ellis, Palmer, Thoms, Olliver, Morrison, Sampson
GOALS — (S. Melb) White (4), Chinn (4), Collard (2), Traynor (2), King
(Foots) Ware (3), G. Tribe, Palmer, Dougherty, Sampson

SEPTEMBER 5 — SECOND SEMI-FINAL

	1st	2nd	3rd	Final	
Richmond	2 . 3	3 . 5	9 . 10	11 . 12	(78)
Essendon	2 . 1	3 . 2	6 . 5	8 . 8	(56)

Princes Oval — Umpire Hawkins
Attendance 32,000 — Gate £2,768

BEST — (Rich) Dyer, Harris, Guinane, Waldron, Steele, Randall, Sullivan, Titus
(Ess) Buttsworth, Coward, Lane, R. Reynolds, Ruddell, Dearle, Leehane
GOALS — (Rich) Harris (5), Titus (3), Dyer (2), Bawden
(Ess) T. Reynolds (5), Lane (2), Bryce

SEPTEMBER 12 — PRELIMINARY FINAL

	1st	2nd	3rd	Final	
Essendon	2 . 4	8 . 6	15 . 9	19 . 10	(124)
South Melbourne	4 . 4	9 . 5	10 . 11	14 . 12	(96)

Princes Oval — Umpire Hawkins
Attendance 26,000 — Gate £2,405

BEST — (Ess) Buttsworth, Coward, Flanagan, Torney, Cassin, Abbott, Bushby, Lane
(S. Melb) White, Williams, Cleary, Hacker, Harwood, Castles
GOALS — (Ess) Leehane (4), Lane (4), T. Reynolds (4), R. Reynolds (2), Hutchison (2), Dearle, Cassin, Abbott
(S. Melb) White (9), Castles (2), Bennison, Graham, Traynor

SEPTEMBER 19 — GRAND FINAL

	1st	2nd	3rd	Final	
Essendon	2 . 6	8 . 14	14 . 16	19 . 18	(132)
Richmond	2 . 4	4 . 4	5 . 10	11 . 13	(79)

Princes Oval — Umpire Hawkins
Attendance 49,000 — Gate £4,640

BEST — (Ess) R. Reynolds (B.O.G.), Dearle, Coward, Abbott, Buttsworth, Flanagan, Torney, Lane
(Rich) Merrett, Steele, Guinane, Edwards, Morris, Hay, Scott
GOALS — (Ess) Lane (6), R. Reynolds (4), Cassin (3), Exelby (2), Dearle (2), Abbott, T. Reynolds
(Rich) Harris (3), Dyer (2), Titus (2), Merrett, D. Martin, Randall, Hay

GRAND FINAL TEAMS

Essendon	**B**	D. Plummer	C. Ruddell	P. Bushby
	HB	R. Flanagan	W. Buttsworth	A. Hird
	C	Caesar	L. Dearle	E. Coward
	HF	W. Hutchison	G. Lane	G. Abbott
	F	T. Reynolds	E. Leehane	P. Exelby
	Ruck	H. Torney	J. Cassin	R. Reynolds (c)
	Nineteenth	S. Silk	**Coach** R. Reynolds	

Richmond	**B**	D. Guinane	G. Smeaton	Reilly
	HB	R. Steele	Sullivan	Scott
	C	Edwards	B. Waldron	L. Merrett
	HF	Randall	Symons	Hay
	F	R. Bawden	J. Titus	Burge
	Ruck	J. Dyer (c)	W. Morris	R. Harris
	Nineteenth	D. Martin	**Coach** J. Dyer	

1943

With the war still curtailing sport, only sixteen home and home rounds were played. The lowest club, St. Kilda, was eliminated from the competition after eleven rounds, and transport difficulties still prevented Geelong from fielding a team. This meant that each side received a bye until St. Kilda was eliminated. Richmond, Essendon and Fitzroy all won ten of their fifteen games and finished in that order on the ladder. Carlton with nine wins took fourth place on percentage from Hawthorn, having their best season since joining the VFL. Had the Hawks downed North in the last game instead of losing by a point, they would have displaced Carlton from the Four. One goal eight from thirteen shots in the last quarter against North, however, did not help Hawthorn's cause.

Carlton and Fitzroy, both with many servicemen in their ranks, met in the first semi-final. Carlton, hit hard by injury but playing on their own ground, looked like giving Fitzroy a run when both sides were level at three goals two each halfway through the opening quarter. But then Fitzroy started to get away, taking charge in the latter half of the first term and in the second term to lead by twenty-nine points at half-time.

Carlton began the second half aggressively, but Fitzroy's defence was too strong. When their rucks began to control the game, the result was a foregone conclusion. Stawell Gift winner Jack Grant, at full-forward for the Maroons, capped off their attacking moves and they went on to an effortless fifty-one point win.

Essendon, after winning the toss in the second semi-final, had three goals on the board within the first three minutes. Then rain began to fall and continued for two and a half quarters, but the Dons shattered the belief that they were not a wet weather side. Fighting back late in the second term after Richmond had kicked four quick goals, the Dons held a four-point lead at half-time.

In a desperate third term, the Tigers drew level with four successive behinds before Coward and Rawle goaled for Essendon. Taking the initiative, the Dons came forward again, for Dick Reynolds to goal and Dearle to hit the post. Two more quick goals and they had added five goals four while Richmond had not scored. Then the Tigers hit back with two sorely needed goals right at the end of the term.

As the last quarter began, Harris boosted the Richmond hopes with two quick goals, but Tom Reynolds goaled for Essendon to virtually seal the game and both sides played out time before a dwindling crowd.

Fitzroy jumped Richmond in the first quarter of the preliminary final, kicking five goals one to two goals three. But the Tigers fought their way back into the game, although kicking atrociously in front of goal, and a string of missed shots in the second term took them up to three goals seven behind Fitzroy's five goals one. Then Fitzroy went away again and led by fifteen points at half-time.

The second half was a reversal of form by Richmond. With Waldron burning in the centre, they went forward for Cahill to goal. Miller replied for the Maroons, and then Quinn twice goaled for the Tigers. Pressing their attacks, Richmond levelled the scores at half-time.

Continuous attacks in the last quarter at length brought goals to Broadstock and Cahill of Richmond, and two more goals in quick succession put the Tigers ahead by twenty-three points. This was almost the final margin, with Richmond going on to the grand final.

Both teams were unchanged when they lined up the following week. Dyer won the toss for the Tigers, and Harris immediately hit the post and then goaled from a free. It was the start of what was to be an auspicious day for Harris. Excelling in the air and displaying superior pace, Richmond forwarded again for goals to Bawden and Harris to give them a flying lead of three goals two to nil.

Tom Reynolds marked for Essendon's first goal, but Richmond were more systematic and quickly replied with Harris hand-balling to Broadstock who kicked their fourth. Essendon steadied and at length hit their straps to reduce the Tigers' lead to ten points at quarter-time.

Winning across the centre in the second term, Richmond continued to drive forward but staunch defence by the Dons kept them out. Suddenly Essendon slipped into top gear and broke away for two quick goals to take the lead. Richmond, however, regained it through Harris and led by eight points when the half-time break came.

Gaining more drive from their ruck and with some smart work on the wings, the Dons in five glorious minutes at the start of the third quarter booted three goals, including Tom Reynolds' fourth and fifth. The edge was now wearing off the Tigers' speed and the Dons were pacing it with them. They goaled through Harris only to see Tom Reynolds outmark Dyer and reply for Essendon. A Tiger rally finally brought Harris' fifth goal but they trailed by five points at the last change.

Play became spiteful as Richmond attempted to bridge the gap. Two behinds which should have been goals were followed by a Dyer mark and goal which gave his team the lead. Harris electrified the crowd with a magnificent long drop-kick goal, his sixth, and then with a rush Dyer and Harris both goaled again. Harris' seventh goal made him top goal-kicker for the year—his total of sixty-three beating Fred Fanning of Melbourne by one. Broadstock, who had been a dominant player for the Tigers, made the bad mistake of twice taking the ball to the wrong flank, errors which allowed Lane and Torney in for goals. Tom Reynolds kicked his seventh to reduce the Tiger lead to six points and, almost on time, Betson (Essendon) had the chance to win the game for his side. However, his kick got too much height and not enough distance, and was punched through for a behind by the hard-worked Tiger defence. The bell went with 'Captain Blood's' Richmond men five points ahead —but the Tigers were to wait twenty-four years for another flag.

RESULTS

SEPTEMBER 4 — FIRST SEMI-FINAL

	1st	2nd	3rd	Final	
Fitzroy	5 . 3	7 . 9	12 . 10	13 . 16	(94)
Carlton	3 . 2	3 . 4	4 . 9	5 . 13	(43)

Princes Oval — Umpire Hawkins
Attendance 39,874 — Gate £3,570

BEST — (Fitz) Hughson, Dawson, Brown, Hilliard, Monaghan, Dyring, M. Hearn, Grant, Hoskins
(Carl) Gneill, Savage, Chitty, Price, Tuohill, Fitzgibbon, Howell, Clark

GOALS — (Fitz) Grant (5), Dawson (3), Spokes (2), Dyring (2), Brown
(Carl) Wrout (2), Bennett (2), Price

SEPTEMBER 11 — SECOND SEMI-FINAL

	1st	2nd	3rd	Final	
Essendon	4 . 1	6 . 6	12 . 14	13 . 16	(94)
Richmond	1 . 3	5 . 8	7 . 12	9 . 17	(71)

Princes Oval — Umpire Hawkins
Attendance 24,100 — Gate £2,180

BEST — (Ess) R. Reynolds, Dearle, Ruddell, Coward, Plummer, Rawle, Hutchison, Exelby, Torney
(Rich) Dyer, Kemp, Waldron, Scott, Steele, Maguire, Bawden, Brennan

GOALS — (Ess) Rawle (4), R. Reynolds (2), T. Reynolds (2), Dearle (2), Hutchison, Cassin, Coward
(Rich) Bawden (2), Harris (2), Quinn (2), Randall, Ablett, Brannan

SEPTEMBER 18 — PRELIMINARY FINAL

	1st	2nd	3rd	Final	
Richmond	2 . 3	3 . 8	7 . 9	12 . 14	(86)
Fitzroy	5 . 1	6 . 5	7 . 9	8 . 13	(61)

Princes Oval — Umpire Hawkins
Attendance 27,335 — Gate £2,495

BEST — (Rich) Durham, Scott, Kemp, Merrett, Cahill, Dyer, Steele, Oppy, Broadstock
(Fitz) Hughson, Hearn, Wright, Hallahan, Hoskins, Dyring, Denning, Monaghan, Grant

GOALS — (Rich) Cahill (3), Broadstock (2), Quinn (2), Harris (2), Merrett, Oppy, Bawden
(Fitz) Grant (3), Spokes, Ruthven, Wright, Miller, B. Clay

1943-1944

SEPTEMBER 25 — GRAND FINAL

	1st	2nd	3rd	Final
Richmond	4 . 2	6 . 5	8 . 8	12 . 14 (86)
Essendon	2 . 4	4 . 9	8 . 13	11 . 15 (81)
	Princes Oval		Umpire Hawkins	
	Attendance 42,100		Gate £3,510	

BEST —	(Rich)	Dyer, Harris, Perkins, Merrett, Broadstock, Bawden, Oppy
	(Ess)	Lane, Ruddell; Cassin, Buttsworth, Coward, R. & T. Reynolds
GOALS —	(Rich)	Harris (7), Dyer (3), Bawden, Broadstock
	(Ess)	T. Reynolds (7), Torney (2), Rawle, Lane

GRAND FINAL TEAMS

Richmond	B	Scott	Durham	Steele
	HB	Hunt	Maguire	Perkins
	C	Merrett	Waldron	Edwards
	HF	Quinn	Broadstock	Randall
	F	Cahill	Bawden	Harris
	Ruck	Dyer (c)	Kemp	Oppy
	Nineteenth	Ablett	Coach J. Dyer	
Essendon	B	Plummer	Ruddell	Bushby
	HB	Cockburn	Buttsworth	Hird
	C	Hutchison	Gardiner	Coward
	HF	Dearle	Lane	Abbott
	F	T. Reynolds	Cassin	Rawle
	Ruck	Torney	Betson	R. Reynolds (c)
	Nineteenth	Langley*	Coach R. S. Reynolds	

* Gil Langley was later better known as the Australian XI wicket-keeper.

1944

With the easing of war-time travel restrictions, Geelong was able to re-enter the VFL competition, bringing the number of teams again to twelve and allowing eighteen rounds to be played.

The final Four comprised Richmond (thirteen wins, four losses and a tie), Fitzroy (ditto), Essendon (twelve wins, four losses, two ties) and Footscray (twelve wins, five losses, one tie). Carlton, who had been on top at the end of June, were an unlucky fifth. In the Four by two points before the last game against Footscray, they would still have made the finals even if the last game had been drawn. But with the last kick of the match and the scores equal, Footscray's Harry Hickey booted a behind from fifty yards out to allow his side to win by one point and take Carlton's position in the final Four.

The Footscray-Essendon first semi-final was played on a wet ground after rain on Friday night and Saturday morning. Footscray appeared 'stage-struck' and fumbled badly in a poor first term. Both sides scored only one goal each during the quarter, but even at that stage Essendon looked likely winners.

The second and third terms saw remarkable reversals of fortunes—in the second Essendon combined brilliantly and were far too fast for their opponents in kicking six goals three to nil. But the third saw Footscray on top, and they kicked six goals three while holding the Dons to one goal. The match was thus evenly poised at three-quarter-time, with Essendon only eight points ahead. In an exciting start to the last term R. Reynolds brilliantly goaled for Essendon, to which Footscray quickly replied. Then the tough Footscray defence limited Essendon to eight behinds in a row before Reynolds goaled again ten minutes before the end. The Dons then added three more in quick succession and ran out the easiest of winners.

Richmond quickly had two goals to a point within minutes of the start of the second semi-final, but Fitzroy came back strongly to lead by eight points at quarter-time. The Tigers suffered a severe setback when their champion rover, Dick Harris, had to be replaced in the first quarter, the injury ending his VFL career. Later in the game Broadstock was also hurt and his injury kept him out of the grand final.

After a battling second term, with scoring even for most of the twenty-five minutes, Fitzroy scored three goals in the last three minutes to have a strong grip on the game at half-time. Then a strong Richmond third quarter fight-back brought them five goals and they trailed by only four points at the last change. Fitzroy gained breathing space when Wright dashed in and goaled as soon as the last term began. But after a disputed mark between Hughson (Fitzroy) and Bawden (Richmond), Bawden grabbed the ball and goaled, and the umpire allowed the score. The game was still swinging when Price found Wright for another Fitzroy goal which sealed the game.

Richmond sprung a surprise by moving Jack Dyer to full-forward in the opening minutes of the preliminary final. The move was a startling success—Dyer booted four goals himself and helped in three more in Richmond's first quarter burst of eight goals two to Essendon's five behinds. The Dons surprisingly left Lane, inexperienced at full-back, to mind him until Buttsworth took over in the second quarter, but by then the damage was done. Reynolds and Hutchison, with quick goals, started an Essendon run of five goals two in the second term, but even this good effort still left them five goals behind at half-time and eight down at three-quarter-time. Dyer, with nine goals in three quarters, had been the difference between the two sides. Powell and Bushby (two) goaled for the Dons early in the last quarter, forcing Dyer to come on to the ball. Randall (Richmond) and Reynolds (Essendon) goaled for their respective sides, but the Richmond lead was too great for Essendon to overtake.

The conditions for the grand final were the worst of the series. The temperature—eighty-six degrees in the shade—was the hottest on record in the finals, and a strong north wind blew down the ground to the St. Kilda end.

There was a rather scrambly start but Fitzroy, through Sier, soon had the first goal on the board. Dyer immediately went to full-forward for the Tigers, hoping for a repeat of his nine-goal effort from that position the previous week, but it was not to be. Towards the end of the quarter Richmond got goals through Wilson and Burge, and the latter added another against the breeze in the first minute of the second quarter. Fitzroy bounced back quickly and kicked five successive behinds before two brilliant dashes by Calverley saw Ruthven goal, and Calverley himself add another.

Goals came quickly as the third term began—Stackpole (Fitzroy), Dyer (Richmond) and Randall (Richmond) all kicked truly, and the game was even again. Symonds snapped Fitzroy's sixth goal just before three-quarter-time.

Richmond made wholesale positional changes at the break, but these did not pay off as Sier (Fitzroy) immediately outmarked Smeaton (for one of the few occasions during the game) and goaled. Randall (Richmond) snapped one in reply but Dyer, from the angle, and K. Cook both missed.

There was little in it as the game drew to its conclusion—Stackpole kicked Fitzroy's eighth goal, then both teams had a succession of misses before Richmond goaled through Wilson. This left the issue still in doubt, but Sier, with a fine left-foot snap, kicked accurately and the bell went soon after to herald Fitzroy's first premiership for twenty-two years.

RESULTS

SEPTEMBER 9 — FIRST SEMI-FINAL

	1st	2nd	3rd	Final	
Essendon	1 . 3	7 . 6	8 . 6	14 . 17	(101)
Footscray	1 . 1	1 . 1	7 . 4	8 . 4	(52)

St.KCG — Umpire Hawkins

Attendance 24,542 — Gate £2,074

BEST — (Ess) R. Reynolds, Tonkes, Griggs, Coward, Buttsworth, Hird, Betson, Powell., Smith

(Foots) A. McTaggart (B.O.G.), Hickey, Miller, Ryan, McCankie, Grove, T. Tribe, G. Tribe

GOALS — (Ess) R. Reynolds (4), Dearle (3), Smith (3), Powell (2), Abbott, Griggs

(Foots) W. McTaggart (3), Grove (2), Wood, Ryan, Collins

SEPTEMBER 16 — SECOND SEMI-FINAL

	1st	2nd	3rd	Final	
Fitzroy	3 . 5	7 . 10	9 . 12	11 . 15	(81)
Richmond	2 . 3	4 . 3	9 . 8	10 . 10	(70)

St.KCG — Umpire Hawkins

Attendance 32,000 — Gate £3,121

BEST — (Fitz) B. Clay, B. Calverley, Hearn, Wright, Hillard, Hosking, Stackpole, Hughson

(Rich) Burge, Merrett, Broadstock, Dyer, F. Cook, Smeaton, Oppy, Morris, Maguire

GOALS — (Fitz) Stockpole (5), Wright (2), Price (2), Symons, Sier

(Rich) Burge (3), Broadstock (3), F. Cook, Dyer, Randall, Bawden

1944

SEPTEMBER 23 — PRELIMINARY FINAL

	1st	2nd	3rd	Final	
Richmond	8 . 2	10 . 5	15 . 9	16 . 12	(108)
Essendon	0 . 5	5 . 7	7 . 9	12 . 15	(87)

St.KCG — Umpire Hawkins
Attendance 38,000 — Gate £4,220

BEST — (Rich) Dyer, Merrett, Waldron, Burge, Smeaton, Wilson, F. Cook, Jones, Edwards, Randall
(Ess) R. Reynolds, Lane, Hutchison, Powell, Hird, Smith, Griggs

GOALS — (Rich) Dyer (9), Burge (3), Randall (2), Bawden, Wilson
(Ess) R. Reynolds (3), Powell (3), Bushby (3), Hutchison, Smith, McIvor

SEPTEMBER 30 — GRAND FINAL

	1st	2nd	3rd	Final	
Fitzroy	1 . 2	4 . 8	6 . 10	9 12	(66)
Richmond	2 2	3 . 2	5 . 5	7 9	(51)

St.KCG — Umpire Hawkins
Attendance 43,000 — Gate £4,430

BEST — (Fitz) Calverley, Hillard, Price, Hughson, Hearn, Clay
(Rich) Smeaton, Oppy, Perkins, Maguire, Edwards, Wilson

GOALS — (Fitz) Sier (3), Stackpole (2), Calverley, Symons, Wright, Ruthven
(Rich) Wilson (3), Randall (2), Burge, Dyer

GRAND FINAL TEAMS

Fitzroy	B	Denning	Hughson (c)	Fields
	HB	Bickerton	Hilliard	O'Bryan
	C	Jarvis	Hoskins	B. Calverley
	HF	Dawson	Wright	Price
	F	Hearn	Sier	Stackpole
	Ruck	B. Clay	Symons	Ruthven
	Nineteenth	Murray	Coach F. Hughson*	
Richmond	B	Oppy	Smeaton	Priestly
	HB	Waldron	Maguire	Perkins
	C	Merrett	F. Cook	Edwards
	HF	Mooney	Randall	Jones
	F	Bawden	Scott	Burge
	Ruck	Dyer (c)	Morris	Wilson
	Nineteenth	K. Cook	Coach J. Dyer*	

* This was the last occasion (to date) in which both grand final teams had been led by playing coaches.

1945

Ask a Carlton supporter—young or old—what was 'the Bloodbath', and the chances are good that you will quickly be informed that this was the 1945 grand final, in which Carlton, by defeating South Melbourne, won their seventh League premiership. The game has passed into history as one of the roughest, toughest and bloodiest of all VFL football finals and, mainly for that reason, it will not quickly be forgotten.

Four new teams comprised the final Four in 1945, the first time that all finalists had been different from the four finalists of the previous season. South Melbourne (sixteen wins, four losses) were on top of the ladder, followed by Collingwood (in the Four for the first time since 1939) fifteen wins, with North Melbourne (first time in the finals) and Carlton, both with thirteen wins, finishing third and fourth. Footscray (fifth) just missed out, losing to Carlton in the last game, although they would still have got in on percentage if Essendon had beaten North the same day. (North won by a goal, and Carlton went into the final Four.) The Blues would have been unfortunate, however, to miss the finals, after coming from the bottom after four games, and ninth after eleven, to win eight of the last nine home and home games.

North Melbourne, after waiting twenty years to appear in the finals, threw away their chances of victory in the first semi-final with some atrocious kicking for goal—twenty behinds (four posters) from twenty-eight scoring shots. Carlton, however, always looked the better side, and North were forced to make no fewer than eleven positional changes in an attempt to get into the game. The match itself was one of the most disappointing finals for years—North had scored only one goal twelve at half-time and two goals thirteen (10 goals behind) at the last change. Carlton's half-forward flanker, Lance Collins, booted four goals in the first term and eight for the match to seal the game for the Blues well before North belatedly came good with six last-quarter goals, three of them from rover Bill Findlay.

Another disappointing final, the second semi, saw South Melbourne, favoured with every advantage in height, weight, marking and kicking ability, plus winning rucks, play into Collingwood's hands by adopting the short-passing game, and the Magpies were actually able to lead at half-time. South's best quarter was the third when, with Jack Graham dominant in the aerial duels, they kicked eight goals to Collingwood's five. Displaying great pace, using effective handball and passing accurately, South at one stage kicked six goals to Collingwood's one in fifteen minutes.

When Moore and Newman goaled for the Magpies halfway through the last term, South's lead was reduced to a mere five points, but a goal to Nash four minutes from the end sealed the result in South Melbourne's favour.

A vicious preliminary final—many participants still regard it as even more of a bloodbath than the grand final—saw Carlton defeat Collingwood by ten points. In a fiery first quarter, Collingwood kicked five goals two to Carlton's solitary goal, but tempers really flared in the second term. Price and Baxter goaled early for the Blues, and soon players were openly punching and kicking. Carlton, however, threw away many scoring chances and still trailed at half-time. Continuing to use vigour instead of skill in the third quarter, Carlton enabled the Magpies to boot four quick goals to their own two. After a further punch-up, Fothergill goaled again for Collingwood, who then led by twenty-eight points at three-quarter-time, and increased this when Hustler goaled immediately the last term began. A fierce melee, with boots being used liberally, interrupted proceedings for some minutes before Collins, who had been beaten all day, goaled for the Blues. Goals from McLean, Savage, Collins and Baxter reduced the Collingwood lead to two points, and two further goals to Collins gave Carlton a win by ten points. In a fantastic last quarter someback, they had kicked seven goals three in nineteen minutes. Bob Chitty, Blues' skipper, took his place in the side despite an accident at work in which he sliced off the top of one of his fingers. Playing with a special guard over the injury, Chitty was one of the Blues' best.

South, promised twenty pounds a man for a win, certainly had incentive in the grand final, although the game was played at Princes Oval, Carlton's home ground. The biggest crowd the famous old ground had ever seen (62,986 people) crammed into Princes Oval on grand final day and the gates had to be shut at 2.45 p.m.

Play was fast and vigorous from the start. Kicking with the wind, Carlton could manage only one goal in the first fifteen minutes and soon had Lance Collins, their previous week's matchwinner, limping around the flank. The Blues looked decidedly unimpressive, and their first quarter netted only two goals four to South's five behinds.

Ten minutes into the second term, Smith and Nash respectively snapped South's first two goals. A goal to each side followed before things started to happen. The game, which had been scrambly and a trifle fiery early, now erupted into violence—Bob Chitty floored South's Ron Clegg, and McLean (Carlton) somersaulted Danckert (South Melbourne) to the turf after a scrimmage. A slanging match followed and Umpire Spokes wisely held the ball until peace prevailed. A minute or so later, South's Billy Williams was crashed by Chitty, and players pushed and shoved while he was revived to take his kick. Then Price goaled for Carlton, and as the ball was returned to the centre, Ken Hands was knocked unconscious at Carlton's full-forward position; 63,000 fans screamed for blood as players converged on each other, throwing fists and boots. Only the half-time bell broke up the melee, and the unconscious Hands was carried to the dressing room while South, as a team, were booed from the arena, trailing Carlton by two points. Rain fell during the interval, further increasing the chances of fisticuffs, for mud and fights seem to go together in football.

Both sides had their reserves on, so Hands returned to the game in the second half, although suffering severe concussion. He immediately took a fine mark, and goaled. Savage followed with another, and it was evident that the rain was interfering with South's brilliant short-passing game. Carlton added three more goals to have a good twenty-three point lead at the last change.

The last term began with another clash—Bob Chitty was dropped—and players, trainers, ambulance men and officials converged angrily. Police eventually moved in to break up the melee and the groggy Chitty trotted to the forward pocket—where he promptly goaled. Heavy rain was falling as Carlton's Jim Mooring and South's Ron Clegg were both flattened. Wines, with a long-distance goal, scored for the Blues, who now had a big lead.

After another clash, in which players, umpires, trainers, spectators and police all intermingled, Goal Umpire Whyte chased South's Ted Whitfield up the ground to take his number, but Whitfield wasn't having any of it, and eventually pulled his jersey up over his head to hide his number. Two police seized an overcoated man and hurried him off the field to the officials' seats beside the arena—it was stormy Carlton winger Fred Fitzgibbon, already under suspension after the preliminary final, who had rushed onto the ground to join the fight.

Play resumed, and Hands, after marking in the goal-square, was pushed heavily. Umpires rushed in to report South full-back Jim Cleary. A Carlton player intervened, and it was on again: bottles showered the players and police. When they were cleared off, Hands had his shot and missed. When the bell rang soon after, the happy Carlton fans chaired their battered players from the arena, and the umpires, with a heavy police escort, retired to their rooms for two hours of writing reports.

After severe newspaper condemnation of the events of Saturday, no fewer than ten reported players appeared before the Tribunal the following Tuesday night.

Ted Whitfield (South Melbourne) was suspended for the whole of season 1946 for his part in numerous incidents.

Jack Williams (South Melbourne) went out for eight weeks for adopting a fighting attitude to the umpire and to Carlton's Rod McLean, and for another four weeks for abusing the Goal Umpire.

South captain, Herbie Mathews, was severely reprimanded for throwing the ball away after a free was given against him.

Keith Smith (South Melbourne) was found not guilty of striking Jim Mooring (Carlton).

Ken Hands (Carlton) was found not guilty of jumping into the back of Ron Clegg.

Don Grossman (South Melbourne) went out for eight weeks for striking Mooring in the last quarter.

Bob Chitty (Carlton) was suspended for eight weeks for elbowing South's Billy Williams.

South's Jim Cleary also received eight weeks for striking Hands, after the Carlton player had marked. Another charge against him was not sustained.

Ron Savage (Carlton)—eight weeks for striking Don Grossman.

Fred Fitzgibbon (Carlton)—already serving three weeks suspension—received another four for running onto the field and joining in one of the numerous brawls.

RESULTS

SEPTEMBER 8 — FIRST SEMI-FINAL

	1st	2nd	3rd	Final	
Carlton	5 . 3	8 . 4	13 . 7	14 . 10	(94)
North Melbourne	0 . 4	1 . 12	2 . 13	8 . 20	(68)

Princes Oval
Attendance 54,846

Umpire Spokes
Gate £4,744

BEST — (Carl) Collins, Savage, Deacon, Wines, Chitty, Turner
(N. Melb) Crane, Findlay, Quinn, Condon, Fairweather, Malone

GOALS — (Carl) Collins (8), Turner (2), Hands, Price, McLean, Baxter
(N. Melb) Findlay (4), Roulent (2), Condon, Quinn

SEPTEMBER 15 — SECOND SEMI-FINAL

	1st	2nd	3rd	Final	
South Melbourne	2 . 1	3 . 5	11 . 8	13 . 10	(88)
Collingwood	1 . 2	4 . 7	9 . 10	11 . 11	(77)

Princes Oval — Umpire Sawyer
Attendance 46,224 — Gate £5,122

BEST — (S. Melb) Graham, Cleary, Castles, Grossman, Clegg, K. Smith
(Col) Utting, Williams, Holten, Wallis, Murphy, Mears

GOALS — (S. Melb) Castles (4), Nash (4), Clegg, Williams, King, Smith, Blumfield
(Col) Fothergill (2), L. Richards (2), Moore (2), Holten (2), Burns, Newman, Mears

SEPTEMBER 22 — PRELIMINARY FINAL

	1st	2nd	3rd	Final	
Carlton	1 . 0	4 . 7	6 . 9	13 . 12	(90)
Collingwood	5 . 2	6 . 4	11 . 7	12 . 8	(80)

Princes Oval — Umpire Sawyer
Attendance 41,305 — Gate £4,738

BEST — (Carl) Brown, Clark, Chitty, Baird, Savage, McLean, Collins, Sanger
(Col) Williams (B.O.G.), Wallis, W. Twomey, Holten, L. Richards, Newman, Murphy

GOALS — (Carl) Collins (4), Baxter (3), Savage (2), Price, Hands, McLean, Mooring
(Col) L. Richards (3), Newman (2), Fothergill (2), Hustler (2), Dalkin, Murphy, Holten

SEPTEMBER 29 — GRAND FINAL

	1st	2nd	3rd	Final	
Carlton	2 . 4	7 . 5	12 . 9	15 . 13	(103)
South Melbourne	0 . 5	6 . 9	8 . 10	10 . 15	(75)

Princes Oval — Umpire Spokes
Attendance 62,986 — Gate £5,467

BEST — (Carl) Brown, Sanger, K. Baxter, Chitty, Wines, McLean, Deacon
(S. Melb) Castles, Smith, Dempsey, King, Grossman, Graham

GOALS — (Carl) Hands (3), Price (3), Mooring (2), Baxter (2), Bennett, Chitty, Wines, McLean, Savage
(S. Melb) Castles (3), Nash (2), Smith (2), Linden (2), Richards

GRAND FINAL TEAMS

Carlton	B	Sanger	Brown	Baird
	HB	Chitty (c)	Deacon	Clark
	C	Turner	Wines	Williams
	HF	Collins	Hands	Way
	F	McLean	K. Baxter	Mooring
	Ruck	Savage	Bennett	Price
	Nineteenth	McInnes	**Coach** P. Bentley	
South Melbourne	B	Grossman	Cleary	Kelly
	HB	Matlock	J. Williams	Danckert
	C	Whitfield	Mathews (c)	King
	HF	Castles	Clegg	Smith
	F	Linden	Nash	W. Williams
	Ruck	Graham	Dempsey	R. Richards
	Nineteenth	Hartridge	**Coach** W. Adams	

1946

The surprise of 1946 was the poor form of the previous season's finalists, of whom Collingwood was the only team to again make the final Four. Carlton slipped from premiers to sixth and South Melbourne from second to seventh (after losing their first four games), the first time such a fate had ever befallen either of the previous season's grand finalists (an unwanted record which was beaten by Collingwood in 1959) and North Melbourne fell from fourth to ninth.

Essendon was the surprise packet of the season, winning fifteen of their nineteen home and home games and finishing first. Collingwood (second) won thirteen games and lost six, whilst Footscray, after looking 'the goods' in winning their first nine games, slumped badly to lose six of their last ten and just hold on to third place. Next came Melbourne, who emulated Carlton's 1945 effort by coming from ninth with three wins to win ten of their last eleven games and take fourth place.

All the finals were played at the MCG, which had by now been vacated by the Army. The day of the first semi-final was fine and dry, and the large crowd was treated to a grand exhibition as Melbourne battled to a four-goal lead over Footscray by half-time. The Bulldogs fought back in an exciting third term with a six-goal burst which actually took them to a one-point lead, and the stage was set for a stirring final quarter, and one of the most sensational finishes in finals history. The last term was a typical hard-fought issue, and going into time-on, the Bulldogs led by seven points, with Arthur Olliver having just missed an easy shot, thirty yards out and right in front. Olliver's kick curled off line, and went out of bounds in the forward pocket. Melbourne's Fred Fanning had been thrown onto the ball, and from his mighty knock-out, Melbourne raced upfield to start a paralysing burst of four goals one in the last four minutes of the game. Norm Smith got the first goal, followed by three more from Jim Mitchell, Len Dockett and Ernie O'Rourke which left the crowd completely dumbfounded. It was an amazing win to Melbourne, bordering on the unbelievable, and a game which the Bulldogs were unlucky to lose.

The crowd again got their money's worth the following week when Essendon and Collingwood played a draw in the secomd semi-final. Collingwood, as had Footscray the previous week, looked to have the game won when, in control of the rucks and winning handsomely across the centre, they led by ten goals thirteen to seven goals seven halfway through the third term. Hutchison's brilliant roving, and a tightening of their defence, led to an Essendon revival, but they were still sixteen points down at three-quarter-time. However, Essendon was not to be denied, and quickly wiped off the deficit with three goals in five minutes. The crowd was at fever pitch as the game then see-sawed amazingly—the lead changing no fewer than five times, and twice being equal before, with time-on being played, behinds to Dick Reynolds and Jack Cassin made the game a tie.

The replay gave promise of being a repeat performance when, after three quarters of slugging wet-weather football, scores were equal at forty-nine points each. But, at that stage, good judges predicted that Essendon's big man-power would finally wear down the Magpies as it had the previous week; and so it proved. Essendon added two quick goals through Harper and Equid, and the Magpies slowed to a walk. But, although their pace slackened, their courage and determination did not, and Essendon had to fight all the way to finally win by nineteen points.

Going into action for the third successive Saturday, the leg-weary Magpies dictated play for three quarters in the preliminary final against Melbourne. They led by twenty-three points at quarter-time, twenty points at half-time and twenty-three at three-quarter-time. In the process, the Magpies unearthed a new star in Neil Mann, who came on as reserve in place of Jack Green (ankle) at half-time. Young Mann immediately came under notice with a brilliant left-foot snap shot goal from deep on the boundary. Then he went on to boot three more of the Magpies' five goals for the term, and the game looked all over at the last change. Even as late as halfway through the final term, when Mann added another goal—his fifth—it looked like a case of how far Collingwood. But then the Magpies' resistance collapsed, and Melbourne veteran Jack Mueller took control in the air to boot four goals in the last twenty minutes. Melbourne added no less than seven goals one for the quarter to convincingly win the game and eliminate Collingwood from the 1946 finals.

The grand final was a game of sensations. Fanning lined up for Melbourne in the ruck instead of centre-half-forward and his tap at the first bounce went to Dockett, who got the ball to Dullard for a goal after six seconds of play. Minutes later, Fanning marked and drove through a long punt, and then Mueller picked up in front and snapped truly. Dominating the air, Melbourne led by four goals to nothing when Fanning, dominant, hit out to Rodda for another. After ten minutes, Essendon struggled forward for Brittingham to goal, and Lane to add another shortly after. Then came an absolute deluge of goals—to O'Rourke (Melbourne), Mueller (Melbourne), Reynolds (Essendon) and Mueller (Melbourne) and a great first term ended with fifteen goals and five behinds on the board—eight goals three to Melbourne and seven goals two to Essendon. Both sides had dominant forwards, Mueller for Melbourne, after Fanning had faded after his great start, and Lane for Essendon, who was now on top of Ted Cordner at centre-half-forward.

The shaken defences of both sides tightened up somewhat in the second term, and while the play lacked the spectacle of the first term, it was nonetheless enthralling as the Demons battled to a half-time lead of three points.

No one was prepared for the events of the third quarter. Essendon attacked for behinds to Hutchison and Reynolds which levelled the scores for the fourth time. Then followed three more behinds before Brittingham goaled—his sixty-fourth of the season, making him top VFL goal-kicker. Essendon were well on top now, with Lane taking apart his second opponent (Dullard) and McClure dominating the ruck. In quick succession, McClure, Equid and Hutchison all goaled for the Dons before Dullard, now up forward, answered for the Demons sixteen minutes into the quarter. Essendon, with pace to burn and using intelligent hand and foot passing, made it look easy as Lane, Rawle, Reynolds and Cassin added goals. Then Lane snapped his sixth goal, Brittingham put through another from fifty yards out, on the boundary, and the Dons added another goal on the bell to make their total for the term an amazing eleven goals eight, a still unequalled finals record, and ranking high amongst the best in a quarter of any game. That, of course, was the end of the game as far as Melbourne's chances of winning were concerned. Trailing by ten goals, they brought on both reserves and moved Fanning to full-forward, but to no avail. Brittingham immediately goaled from a few yards out and the Dons were content to hold their mammoth lead. After twenty-one minutes, Dullard goaled for Melbourne, but Lane snapped a reply from an acute angle, on his left foot, to equal the then goal-kicking record for the VFL grand final, seven goals.

The fans who had drifted away missed only a brief melee in front of the Essendon goal as the Dons went on to win the 1946 flag and commence a golden era during which they were to play in six successive grand finals and win three premierships.

RESULTS

SEPTEMBER 7 — FIRST SEMI-FINAL

	1st	2nd	3rd	Final	
Melbourne	2 . 8	10 . 13	12 . 15	17 . 18	(120)
Footscray	4 . 4	7 . 7	13 . 10	15 . 12	(102)

MCG — Umpire Spokes
Attendance 61,277 — Gate £6,774

BEST — (Melb) McGrath, Mueller, McLean, E. Cordner, Lock, Rodda, Dockett, Smith, Mitchell
(Foots) Olliver, Rees, Miller, McLaren, Sutton, Moncrieff, Wearmouth, Laffey

GOALS — (Melb) Mueller (4), Mitchell (3), O'Rourke (3), Rodda (3), Smith (3), Dockett
(Foots) Ware (4), Olliver (3), Hickey (2), Thoms (2), Laffey (2), Fountain, Wood

SEPTEMBER 14 — SECOND SEMI-FINAL

	1st	2nd	3rd	Final	
Essendon	5 . 2	6 . 5	9 . 11	14 . 16	(100)
Collingwood	3 . 6	7 . 12	11 . 15	13 . 22	(100)

MCG — Umpire Bride
Attendance 77,370 — Gate £8,477

BEST — (Ess) Hutchison, Lane, Brittingham, Ruddell, Hassell, Buttsworth, H. Lambert
(Col) Holten, Lambert, Richards, Murphy, Kyne, Whelan, Wallis, Fitzgerald

GOALS — (Ess) Lane (4), Hutchison (3), Brittingham (3), Cassin, Jones, Pearson, Hassell
(Col) L. Richards (4), Fitzgerald (3), Lambert (3), Murphy (2), Rose

SEPTEMBER 21 — SECOND SEMI-FINAL REPLAY

	1st	2nd	3rd	Final	
Essendon	2 . 4	4 . 8	6 . 13	10 . 16	(76)
Collingwood	3 . 5	6 . 5	7 . 7	8 . 9	(57)

MCG — Umpire Bride
Attendance 64,903 — Gate £6,670

BEST —	(Ess)	Ruddell, Buttsworth, Reynolds, Harper, Hassell, H. Lambert, Lane
	(Col)	Murphy, Kyne, Hocking, Richards, Rose, Holten, Green
GOALS —	(Ess)	Lane (3), Hutchison, Reynolds, Pearson, Brittingham, Equid, Harper, Rawle
	(Col)	Pimm (4), Rose (2), Hocking, Lambert

SEPTEMBER 28 — PRELIMINARY FINAL

	1st	2nd	3rd	Final	
Melbourne	2 . 3	5 . 9	9 . 13	16 . 17	(113)
Collingwood	5 . 8	8 . 11	13 . 12	14 . 16	(100)

MCG — Umpire Bride
Attendance 59,444 — Gate £5,810

BEST —	(Melb)	Mueller, Mitchell, Dockett, McGrath, McLean, Lock, Stabb, Dullard
	(Col)	Richards, Kyne, Murphy, Ryan, Burns, Mann, Utting, Whelan
GOALS —	(Melb)	Mueller (8), O'Rourke (3), Mitchell (2), Smith, Dullard, Rodda
	(Col)	Mann (5), Lambert (2), Pimm (2), Holten, P. Ryan, Kyne, L. Richards, Fitzgerald

OCTOBER 5 — GRAND FINAL

	1st	2nd	3rd	Final	
Essendon	7 . 2	9 . 7	20 . 15	22 . 18	(150)
Melbourne	8 . 3	10 . 4	11 . 5	13 . 9	(87)

MCG — Umpire Bride
Attendance 73,743 — Gate £7,402

BEST —	(Ess)	Lane (B.O.G.), Hutchison, Buttsworth, Ruddell, Bushby, H. Lambert, Reynolds, Pearson
	(Melb)	Mueller, Rodda, McGrath, Bickford, Mitchell, Dullard
GOALS —	(Ess)	Lane (7), Brittingham (4), Hutchison (3), Reynolds (3), McClure (2), Equid, Rawle, Cassin
	(Melb)	Mueller (6), Dullard (3), Fanning, Rodda, O'Rourke, Bowman

GRAND FINAL TEAMS

Essendon	B	Gardiner	Ruddell	Bushby
	HB	Tonkes	Buttsworth	H. Lambert
	C	Hassell	Pearson	Harper
	HF	Equid	Lane	R. Reynolds (c)
	F	McClure	Brittingham	Rawle
	Ruck	Abbott	Cassin	Hutchison
	Reserves	Jones,	C. Lambert	
	Coach	R. S. Reynolds		
Melbourne	B	Deans	McGrath	Don Cordner
	HB	C. McLean	E. Cordner	Lock
	C	Bickford	Dockett	Stabb
	HF	Bowman	Fanning	Mitchell
	F	Dullard	Smith (c)	O'Rourke
	Ruck	Mueller	Rule	Rodda
	Reserves	F. Kennedy,	Byfield	
	Coach	F. V. Hughes		

1947

In a surprise announcement at the beginning of the 1947 season, Carlton Football Club stunned supporters and opponents alike by announcing that ex-Western Australian star, Ern Henfry, would captain the team. Henfry had played only two VFL games, both with Carlton whilst on leave from the RAAF in 1944, but in his first year proved to be an inspirational leader, and under his guidance the Dark Blues took their second premiership within three seasons.

For the first time, nineteen home and home games were played. Carlton (fifteen wins, four losses) headed the ladder, followed by Essendon (fourteen wins, five losses), Fitzroy (thirteen wins) and Richmond (twelve wins). Two points out of the Four and with a better percentage than the Tigers came Collingwood. Two points further back again were Melbourne (also with a better percentage than Richmond) and Geelong. Two goals in time-on by Essendon in the last game cost the Magpies the match and a position in the finals.

In ideal conditions, Fitzroy and Richmond met in the first semi-final. There was a great deal of fumbling, but both sides goaled early in the term before Richmond star Max Oppy limped from the field. Loss of Oppy upset the Tigers considerably, although they were able to cover his loss for a time, and trailed by only one point at half-time. Slipping further behind at the last change, the Tigers let Johnstone (Fitzroy) in for a goal early in the last term when one of their backman made a bad error. That goal virtually sealed the result of the match, and Fitzroy, with their tails up, added five more goals before the game ended with them well ahead.

An exciting second semi-final saw Essendon commence with the aid of a strong wind and kick three goals eight to a point in the first term. The Essendon forwards were hopelessly inaccurate, but the brilliance of Brownlow Medallist Bert Deacon and full-back Olly Grieve for Carlton kept them under constant pressure.

Getting their turn with the wind, Carlton—with Davies giving great drive from the ruck—booted a match-winning seven goals four in the second quarter. When Bert Deacon limped off injured in the third term, it seemed as if Carlton were to be badly handicapped, but Hands (twentieth man) began to dominate up forward and the Blues wisely directed their attacks through him. In addition, Carlton ran two rovers and this move created no little confusion amongst the Essendon defenders. In the last, several bad errors by the Dons let Carlton in—Howell and Hands (two) both goaled and this gave the Blues a lead which their opponents were unable to overtake.

The game, though not unduly rough, featured some bad injuries—Leehane (broken collarbone) and Harper (concussion) were both off before three-quarter-time for Essendon and Carlton's Deacon (leg) and Mooring (broken hand) also had to be replaced.

After an even battle for three quarters, Essendon finished the stronger and had two goals to spare over Fitzroy at the conclusion of the preliminary final.

Earlier, fine play by Lane at centre-half-forward had helped Essendon to five goals four in the first quarter, but when that player went off with broken ribs early in the second, Fitzroy, with rucks and rovers getting on top, slowly began to bridge the gap. Then, they too received a set-back when Chanter dislocated his shoulder and also had to be replaced, but despite this they were able to wipe off their deficit and go to a one-point lead at three-quarter-time.

Moving Jones from centre-half-forward into the ruck gave Essendon a big boost in the last quarter. After several misses, the Don's broke through when a Fitzroy backman kicked across goal—Harper nipped in and scored, and this spurred the Dons to a six-goal burst which made the game safe and put them into the grand final.

The injury-hit Dons, with several stars out, recalled Seconds captain Jack Cassin for the grand final. Carlton brought Hands in to the side in place of the injured Mooring.

A crowd of 85,815 saw Essendon do almost a repeat of the second semi-final when they kicked three goals seven in the first quarter, with Brittingham (four misses) the main offender. Carlton, on the other hand, were deadly accurate, and after Turner got their first, they added three more in succession to trail by only a point at quarter-time, although the Dons had taken six more scoring shots.

The same pattern continued in the following quarter. With amazing precision, the Blues took their score to eight goals at half-time, whilst the battling Dons, from many more shots, had only eight goals eleven—Brittingham, Jones and Hutchison were the main offenders in front of goal, but the entire Essendon forward line was poor, although the side had many winners further up the field.

By three-quarter-time the story was the same—Carlton ten goals four, Essendon ten goals fifteen. Then, with ten minutes of the game to go and Essendon twelve points ahead, the Blues came to life. Suddenly, Howell came good in the ruck, Hands (down all day) began to pick up kicks and Baxter (coming on in place of Deacon, whose injured leg had badly hampered him) went into the ruck a fresh man, and did well. The Blues began to hammer the Essendon defence, and finally Davies outmanoeuvered Ruddell to goal, leaving Carlton only a straight kick behind. Howell marked over the pack to start another attack, but the brilliant Buttsworth saved for Essendon—his twenty-fifth mark. Ern Henfry, dominating the centre for Carlton, continually had his side into attack. A shot by Hands was marked in the goal-square by Essendon full-back Ruddell, before Carlton had a string of heart-stopping near misses. In quick succession, Davies marked and missed from fifteen yards out, and Baxter and Hands had shots which just failed to make the distance. Finally, with just forty-four seconds to go, Baxter came through hard in the ruck, the ball went to ground and Carlton half-forward flanker Fred Stafford, momentarily unguarded, picked up and put a left foot snap right through the centre from twenty-five yards out. There was barely time for the game to be restarted when the bell went to proclaim a Carlton premiership—won by the narrow margin of one point, the closest margin since Collingwood beat Fitzroy in 1903.

RESULTS

SEPTEMBER 6 — FIRST SEMI-FINAL

	1st	2nd	3rd	Final	
Fitzroy	2 . 0	7 . 1	10 . 4	16 . 7	(103)
Richmond	2 . 3	6 . 6	8 . 8	11 . 9	(75)

MCG **Umpire Sawyer**
Attendance 82,570 **Gate £7,027**

BEST — (Fitz) Denning, Monaghan, Nicholls, Chanter, Jarvis, Hart, McLaughlin
(Rich) Burge, Durham, F. Cook, Currie, Wright, Stokes, Wilson, Morris
GOALS — (Fitz) E. Hart (3), Monaghan (3), Ruthven (2), Johnstone (2), Toohey, Curcio, Clay, Coates, McLaughlin, Sier
(Rich) Taylor (3), Wilson (3), Currie (2), Fraser (2), Mooney

SEPTEMBER 13 — SECOND SEMI-FINAL

	1st	2nd	3rd	Final	
Carlton	0 . 1	7 . 5	9 . 11	14 . 15	(99)
Essendon	3 . 8	6 . 12	10 . 14	11 . 17	(83)

MCG **Umpire Spokes**
Attendance 75,475 **Gate £7,979**

BEST — (Carl) Davies, Grieve, Bennett, Howell, Stafford, Turner, Deacon (till injured)
(Ess) Rawle, Reynolds, Jones, Hassell, H. Lambert, McClure, Leehane
GOALS — (Carl) Turner (4), Davies (3), Baird (3), Hands (2), Stafford, Mooring
(Ess) R. Reynolds (2), Brittingham (2), Jones (2), Leehane, Hutchison, Rawle, Lane, Tate

SEPTEMBER 20 — PRELIMINARY FINAL

	1st	2nd	3rd	Final	
Essendon	5 . 4	9 . 7	10 . 8	16 . 13	(109)
Fitzroy	3 . 1	6 . 7	10 . 9	14 . 12	(96)

MCG **Umpire Spokes**
Attendance 55,648 **Gate £5,521**

BEST — (Ess) Jones (B.O.G.), Reynolds, McDonald, Buttsworth, Brittingham, Bushby, Ruddell, Hassell
(Fitz) Denning, Coates, Ruthven, Jarvis, Curcio, Hoskins, Miller, Nicholls, Monaghan
GOALS — (Ess) Brittingham (4), R. Reynolds (4), Hutchison (2), Jones (2), Lane (2), Harper, Tate
(Fitz) Coates (5), E. Hart (5), Ruthven (2), Price (2)

SEPTEMBER 27 — GRAND FINAL

	1st	2nd	3rd	Final	
Carlton	4 . 0	8 . 0	10 . 4	13 . 8	(86)
Essendon	3 . 7	8 . 11	10 . 15	11 . 19	(85)

MCG **Umpire Sawyer**
Attendance 85,815 **Gate £9,142**

BEST — (Carl) Henfry, Davies, Bennett, Clark, Howell, Grieve, Stafford, Green
(Ess) Buttsworth (B.O.G.), Hutchison, McClure, Jones, Reynolds, Bradley
GOALS — (Carl) Davies (4), Baird (3), Turner (2), Stafford, Howell, Garby, Henfry
(Ess) Hutchison (4), Brittingham (2), R. Reynolds (2), Goodingham, Rawle, Cassin

1947-1948

GRAND FINAL TEAMS

Carlton	B	Richie Green	Grieve	Bailey
	HB	Brown	Deacon	Clark
	C	Williams	Henfry (c)	Fitzgibbon
	HF	Stafford	Hands	Garby
	F	Davies	Baird	Turner
	Ruck	Howell	Bennett	Conley
	Reserves	Baxter	Greenshields	
	Coach	P. Bentley		
Essendon	B	Gardiner	Ruddell	McClure
	HB	Allanson	Buttsworth	McDonald
	C	Bradley	H. Lambert	Hassell
	HF	R. Reynolds (c)	Jones	Harper
	F	Goodingham	Brittingham	Rawle
	Ruck	Bushby	Cassin	Hutchison
	Reserves	Tate	Newton	
	Coach	R. Reynolds		

1948

As had also happened after their 1945 premiership, the Blues slumped down the ladder and finished sixth in 1948, well behind Essendon (sixteen wins, two losses and a tie), Melbourne and Collingwood (each thirteen wins) and Footscray (twelve wins). Two points outside of the Four, with a vastly superior percentage to Footscray's and with the highest scoring attack in the League, came Richmond whose drawn game with Essendon cost them that vital fourth place, although a five-point loss to Carlton in the last game actually put them out. They were the League's unlucky side —they had beaten Essendon once and tied once and also defeated Melbourne, Collingwood and Footscray (twice). Footscray, who had to win the last game to get in if Richmond lost, trailed North Melbourne by two points at three-quarter-time, but kicked eleven goals seven in the last term to win easily. Melbourne, fifth with four games to go, got into the Four the following week and, by beating Collingwood in the last game, displaced that team from second position. Fitzroy, on top after eleven games, plummeted to seventh with eight successive losses.

Meeting Footscray in the first semi-final, Collingwood booted three goals eight from numerous chances in the first term, while the more methodical Bulldogs kicked four goals three. Bob Rose, with one goal four of Collingwood's total, was the main offender. Then the positions were reversed. From halfway through the second term until early in the third, six consecutive Footscray shots went astray, although two by Robb went close enough to hit the post. However Footscray, despite these misses, increased their lead to seventeen points before the crunch came—injured Magpie centreman Bill Twomey, who had limped to the forward pocket just before half-time, began to drag down some glorious marks. He was quickly switched to the spearhead, his brother Pat went to the centre, and both became match-winners. In fifty minutes, Bill booted eight goals one from full-forward, and Pat took Bulldog's star Harry Hickey right out of the game while the Magpies added eleven goals six to four goals three to win quite easily.

Melbourne turned on their worst display of the year in the second semi-final. Only resolute defence by McGrath and Deans in the first half stopped Essendon having a mammoth lead, but after an improved third quarter effort, Melbourne could score only a meagre two points in the last. Although they held the Dons to one goal four, this was nowhere near good enough for them to hope to win. Leehane, who defeated three successive Melbourne opponents during the course of the game, gave supporters an indication of how much Essendon had missed him when injury forced him out of the previous season's grand final.

Jack Mueller, thirty-four-year old coach of Melbourne Seconds, came back into the senior line-up for the preliminary final against Collingwood. The Magpies started the game brilliantly, with three goals in as many minutes, but then Mueller started to come into the play. Collingwood foolishly tried to swap bumps with the physically stronger Melbourne and by half-time they had run out of steam. Melbourne, slipping easily into the long-kicking game and with their attacks capped off by Mueller (forward pocket) and Smith (full-forward), booted seven goals in the second term, eight in the third and six more in the last while Collingwood struggled. Of this, Mueller (after kicking three behinds from his first three shots) kicked seven goals in the second and third terms, and a further one goal one in the last. Norm Smith, always active, finished with six goals three and the Melbourne score of twenty-five goals sixteen set a new finals record.

The Melbourne selectors sprang a surprise when they announced their grand final team. Taking up the centre-half-back position was Denis Cordner, brother of captain Don, who had played only one previous game with the Demons, in 1943. Denis, however, was no raw recruit but a top-notch Amateurs star, and he certainly earned his place with good performances in the two finals in which he played.

Essendon took almost half the second quarter of the grand final to score their first goal, through Hutchison. At half-time, after numerous chances had been frittered away, they had a match-losing two goals fifteen on the board, two points behind Melbourne's four goals five. Slightly improved forward work brought Essendon four goals in the third quarter, and gave them a twelve-point lead at the last change, but they again lapsed into inaccuracy in the last with one goal six and four out-of-bounds when just one straight kick would have won them the game. Goals to Mueller and Dullard for Melbourne in the dying stages equalled the scores before, in the last sixty seconds of play, Smith (Melbourne) marked forty-five yards out and played on. His shot drifted across goal and out. Seconds later, the same player grabbed the ball at a boundary throw-in, but team-mate Don Cordner knocked it from his hands. Following on, Smith was about to pick up a few feet from the goal line when he slipped and Essendon full-back Ruddell swept the ball clear. The siren sounded with the match still tied—the first tie ever in a grand final—Essendon seven goals twenty-seven, Melbourne ten goals nine. Responsibility for Essendon's lamentable scoring—one of the most inaccurate forward efforts ever—was equally shared by several players; one had four behinds, and five others kicked three behinds each.

Essendon had two setbacks prior to the grand final replay; both Buttsworth and H. Lambert had to drop out through injury. Melbourne, on the other hand, made only one change, McKenzie coming in on the half-forward flank. The game was poorly attended, partly due to the wet conditions, but Melbourne proved their superiority from the outset. Halfway through the first term, they had four goals two on the board to Essendon's three points, forcing Essendon skipper Dick Reynolds to go into the ruck. There, Melbourne's McLean dogged his every step, and held the triple-Brownlow Medallist to an average game. The Demons, with Mueller again in superb form, led from start to finish and ran out the easiest of winners by the clear margin of thirty-nine points. Melbourne's two veterans, Mueller (twenty goals in three matches) and Smith (who helped in almost as many) contributed in no small measure to the Demons' sixth VFL flag.

RESULTS

SEPTEMBER 11 — FIRST SEMI-FINAL

	1st	2nd	3rd	Final	
Collingwood	3 . 8	6 . 11	12 . 14	17 . 17	(119)
Footscray	4 . 3	8 . 9	9 . 9	12 . 12	(84)

MCG — Umpire Spokes
Attendance 71,514 — Gate £5,976

BEST — (Col) Rose, W. & P. Twomey, Nolan, Kyne, Green, Richards, Holten
(Foots) Sutton, Ryan, Bryden, Webb, McDonnell, Hickey

GOALS — (Col) W. Twomey (8), Fitzgerald (2), Richards (2), Rose (2), Holten Kyne, Moore
(Foots) Ryan (4), Webb (2), Laffey, Hickey, Robb, Wood, Reid, Isaac

SEPTEMBER 18 — SECOND SEMI-FINAL

	1st	2nd	3rd	Final	
Essendon	3 . 2	8 . 9	12 . 12	13 . 16	(94)
Melbourne	3 . 2	4 . 3	8 . 8	8 . 10	(58)

MCG — Umpire Sawyer
Attendance 72,394 — Gate £5,602

BEST — (Ess) Leehane, H. Lambert, McDonald, Harper, Bigelow, May, Jones, Rawle
(Melb) McGrath, Deans, Cordner, Dullard, Bickford, Dockett

GOALS — (Ess) Bigelow (4), Reynolds (3), Leehane, Brittingham, Hutchison, Bradley, Syme, Rawle
(Melb) Dullard (3), Craddock (3), Smith, McKenzie

SEPTEMBER 25 — PRELIMINARY FINAL

	1st	2nd	3rd	Final	
Melbourne	4 . 6	11 . 13	19 . 15	25 . 16	(166)
Collingwood	6 . 2	8 . 5	11 . 8	15 . 11	(101)

MCG — Umpire McMurray
Attendance 63,500 — Gate £4,874

BEST — (Melb) Mueller, Dullard, McGrath, Smith, Arnold, Cordner
(Col) Healey, L. Richards, Rose, Denney, Hocking, Kyne, W. Twomey

GOALS —	(Melb)	Mueller (8), Smith (6), McKenzie (2), Craddock (2), Rodda (2), Dullard, Arnold, McMahon, McGrath, Bowman
	(Col)	Rose (4), W. Twomey (3), McIntyre (2), Kyne (2), P. Twomey, L. Richards, Hocking, Fitzgerald

OCTOBER 2 — GRAND FINAL

	1st	2nd	3rd	Final	
Melbourne	3 . 0	4 . 5	6 . 8	10 . 9	(69)
Essendon	0 . 6	2 . 15	6 . 20	7 . 27	(69)

MCG — **Umpire McMurray**
Attendance 85,658 — **Gate £8,897**

BEST —	(Melb)	Rodda, Smith, Collins, Mueller, Bickford, McGrath, Denis Cordner
	(Ess)	Reynolds, McClure, McDonald, H. & C. Lambert Leehane
GOALS —	(Melb)	Mueller (6), Smith, Craddock, Arnold, Dullard
	(Ess)	Hutchison (2), Brittingham (2), Rawle, Bigelow, Bradley

OCTOBER 9 — GRAND FINAL REPLAY

	1st	2nd	3rd	Final	
Melbourne	6 . 2	9 . 3	11 . 6	13 . 11	(89)
Essendon	0 . 3	5 . 5	6 . 6	7 . 8	(50)

MCG — **Umpire McMurray**
Attendance 52,226 — **Gate £4,475**

BEST —	(Melb)	Smith (B.O.G.), Mueller, McGrath, Spittle, Bickford, Arnold
	(Ess)	McDonald, Bushby, Hassell, McClure, Syme, C. Lambert
GOALS —	(Melb)	Mueller (6), Arnold (2), Rodda (2), Smith, Dullard, McMahen
	(Ess)	Brittingham (2), Syme (2), Reynolds, Hutchison, Jones

GRAND FINAL TEAMS

Melbourne	B	Deans	McGrath	Rule
	HB	Collins	Denis Cordner	McLean
	C	Dockett	Bickford	Spittle
	HF	McMahen,	Arnold	McKenzie
	F	Mueller	Smith	Craddock
	Ruck	Don Cordner (c)	Dullard	Rodda
	Reserves	Bowman	Jackson	
	Coach	F. V. Hughes		
Essendon	B	C. Lambert	Ruddell	McClure
	HB	Gardiner	May	McDonald
	C	Bradley	Harper	Hassell
	HF	Jones	Leehane	Reynolds (c)
	F	Equid	Brittingham	Rawle
	Ruck	Syme	Bushby	Hutchison
	Reserves	Fisher	McEwin	
	Coach	R. S. Reynolds		

1949

The arrival on the football scene of a new star in John Coleman gave Essendon what they had lacked for the previous couple of seasons—a full forward who could kick goals. Had a player like Coleman been at the spearhead in Essendon's 1947-48 sides, it is more than likely that those sides would have won the premiership.

Despite the goalkicking feats of the young Coleman, however, Essendon in 1949 lost six of their first ten games and were eighth on the ladder. Later, though, they won their last eight games to sneak into fourth place.

On the other hand Carlton, after having won eight of their first nine games, slumped to lose five of their last ten, and eventually they finished second to North Melbourne (thirteen wins, five losses). This was the first time since their entry into the VFL that North had headed the ladder.

The final member of the 1949 final Four was Collingwood (twelve wins, six losses). A defeat at the hands of St. Kilda in the last game relegated the Magpies from second to third position. One game out of the Four in fifth place was Richmond.

Essendon proved far superior to Collingwood in the first semi-final. Despite the wet conditions, Collingwood's defence did a good job early, crowding Coleman whenever the ball came forward. The Dons, however, switched their attacks through others of their talented forward line. In the second term, the Collingwood defence lapsed and Coleman took a series of spectacular marks. He and Reynolds dominated the quarter as the Dons booted seven goals two to two goals one and went to a commanding lead at half-time. The remainder of the match was all Essendon—Collingwood were able to score only four more goals for the day as Essendon piled up another nine goals thirteen to win effortlessly. Coleman's six goals made his season's total ninety-one, and gave him an outside chance of notching 100 in his first season.

The second semi-final was an exciting affair. North proved superior in the first half, but Carlton fought back well after the interval, winning so well down the goal-to-goal line that North were forced to play the flanks. Drawing to within six points at three-quarter-time, Carlton hit their straps in the last term. Aided by some deadly passing from Henfry, and spectacular marking by Howell (first game for nine weeks), the Blues booted six goals three to North's three goals three and won by twelve points. The win was better than it looked on the scoreboard, especially as North had thrashed Carlton by fifty-six points just a fortnight earlier.

Some fiery incidents took place in the preliminary final. Essendon, with North's

McCorkell holding Coleman, struggled to a twelve-point lead by three-quarter-time, after kicking only one goal five from their first six shots in the second quarter.

The last term was North's best—immediately it began they mounted some fanatical attacks which yielded only behinds before Spencer broke through for a goal which left them only three points down. Coleman missed a sitter, but Tate made no mistake. Essendon now led by eleven points—and then came the incident of the series. A high kick came down to the North forward line where Spencer (North Melbourne) flew high to take a screamer over McClure (Essendon). A goal seemed certain until Umpire McMurray intervened, took the ball from Spencer and handed it to McClure. The umpire was of the opinion that Spencer had pushed McClure out with his foot while flying for the mark—Spencer, however, claimed that, as he had his eye on the ball and took the mark, a free was not justified. The incident certainly upset North, for although Condon goaled minutes after, they panicked slightly and a forty-yard goal by Leehane and a snap by Reynolds sealed the game for Essendon. Had Spencer been paid his mark, and goaled, North after Condon's goal would have been a point ahead, and may have held on to win the game.

When the gates opened at the MCG on grand final day, 1949, there were already 20,000 people waiting to gain admittance. Conditions were perfect for football. As thousands more fans streamed into the ground, the gates had to be closed, and by the time the two teams ran out, hundreds of people were sitting around the boundary line inside the oval.

The game began with no beg pardons. In one scrimmage three Essendon men punched into Carlton's Ken Hands, and elbows and forearms were much in evidence. McClure (Essendon) was knocked out, but the Dons went into attack where Hutchison broke clear for Essendon's first goal and then clashed with Carlton rover Mooring. Henfry (Carlton) went down in a tremendous 'sandwich' which took a lot out of him—he did not get back into the game until late in the day. Howell, after a great mark, goaled for the Blues, but Coleman rose high to mark and reply for the Dons, who led at the first change by five points. The star players on each side had methodically been singled out and roughed up, with the exception of Coleman, who Grieve was beating on sheer ability.

By half-time, Essendon were well on their way to winning the premiership. With every Don's backman concentrating on Howell, Carlton's centre-half-forward, the Blues persisted in trying to play through him. He was forced to kick hurriedly every time he managed to gain possession, but all of the Carlton forwards were under similar pressure. From eleven shots, they added only six points for the term, while Essendon kicked four goals four, including Coleman's ninety-sixth goal of the year, which came up just before half-time.

The further the game went, the further ahead went the Dons. They started the third quarter with goals to Reynolds and Rawle and were continually in attack. McClure, despite vigorous attention, was proving a match-winner for Essendon. Towards the end of the term, Garby kicked Carlton's third goal, but McEwin replied for Essendon who ran wild in the last few minutes. By three-quarter-time, they had an unbeatable fifty-seven point lead, and were able to turn their attention to helping Coleman score the four goals required for his century.

Rawle goaled for the Dons immediately the last term began and Syme added another soon after. With half the quarter gone, Coleman soared high to mark and kick his ninety-seventh and then added number ninety-eight after a nice handball from Leenhane. The Dons twice muffed chances as they tried to find Coleman, and Carlton rushed forward for B. Baxter to goal.

Now Leehane, after marking near goal, unselfishly turned back upfield and slammed a beautiful pass into Coleman's chest. After a tension-filled few seconds, the Essendon full-forward guided goal number ninety-nine straight through the centre. Time was running out, but Reynolds flashed a glorious pass to the fast leading Coleman, giving him the chance he wanted. As he lined up the vital kick, Carlton's Bert Deacon ran down to Coleman and tried to steady him with words of encouragement. But the Essendon star had no intention of missing out on being the first League player to kick 100 goals in his first season—amid thunderous acclaim, he booted the memorable goal to raise the century and the happy crowd chaired him from the ground when the siren sounded soon after.

RESULTS

SEPTEMBER 3 — FIRST SEMI-FINAL

	1st	2nd	3rd	Final	
Essendon	4 . 1	11 . 3	15 . 9	20 . 16	(136)
Collingwood	2 . 0	4 . 1	6 . 4	8 . 6	(54)

MCG — Umpire J. McMurray Jnr.
Attendance 67,702 — Gate £6,901

BEST — (Ess) R. Reynolds, McClure, H. Lambert, Coleman, May, Hutchison, Jones
(Col) Hams, Hamilton, Rose, Green, Healey, R. Richards, Utting

GOALS — (Ess) Coleman (6), R. Reynolds (4), Jones (3), Hutchison (3), Syme (2), Leehane, McEwin
(Col) Pimm (3), Thompson (2), Stevens, Rose, R. Richards

SEPTEMBER 10 — SECOND SEMI-FINAL

	1st	2nd	3rd	Final	
Carlton	3 . 5	5 . 9	9 . 10	15 . 13	(103)
North Melbourne	2 . 3	7 . 3	11 . 4	14 . 7	(91)

MCG — Umpire Sawyer
Attendance 70,856 — Gate £8,889

BEST — (Carl) Henfry, K. Baxter, Hands, Baird, Clark, Davies, Turner, Howell
(N. Melb) Francis, Brooker, L. Reeves, Marchesi, McKenzie, Malone, Spencer

GOALS — (Carl) K. Baxter (7), Howell (3), Brokenshire (2), Mooring, Conley, Turner
(N. Melb) Spencer (6), Brooker (2), Foote (2), Dynon, Marchesi, Radloff, Robb

SEPTEMBER 17 — PRELIMINARY FINAL

	1st	2nd	3rd	Final	
Essendon	3 . 2	6 . 8	8 . 10	11 . 12	(78)
North Melbourne	2 . 1	4 . 1	7 . 4	9 . 7	(61)

MCG — Umpire J. McMurray Jnr.
Attendance 69,281 — Gate £6,931

BEST — (Ess) McClure, R. Reynolds, Gardiner, Hutchison, McDonald, Brittingham, Lambert, Leehane
(N. Melb) Jarrard, J. Reeves, McCorkell, Marchesi, Foote, Dynon, Francis

GOALS — (Ess) R. Reynolds (4), Coleman (3), Syme (2), Leehane, Tate
(N. Melb) Condon (3), Spencer (2), Dynon, Foote, Radloff, Marchesi

Jack Dyer (Richmond) dashes forward to kick one of his nine goals in the 1944 preliminary final against Essendon. *Herald & Weekly Times photo*

Grand final, St. Kilda Cricket Ground, 1944.

McClure (Essendon) marks against Carlton—grand final 1949. *Herald & Weekly Times photo*

Essendon V North Melbourne—grand final 1950. This shows how the crowd encroached on the playing area. *Herald & Weekly Times photo*

Essendon captain Dick Reynolds chaired off the ground after winning the 1950 flag. It was his 319th and last game. Although he came out of retirement for the 1951 grand final. *Herald & Weekly Times photo*

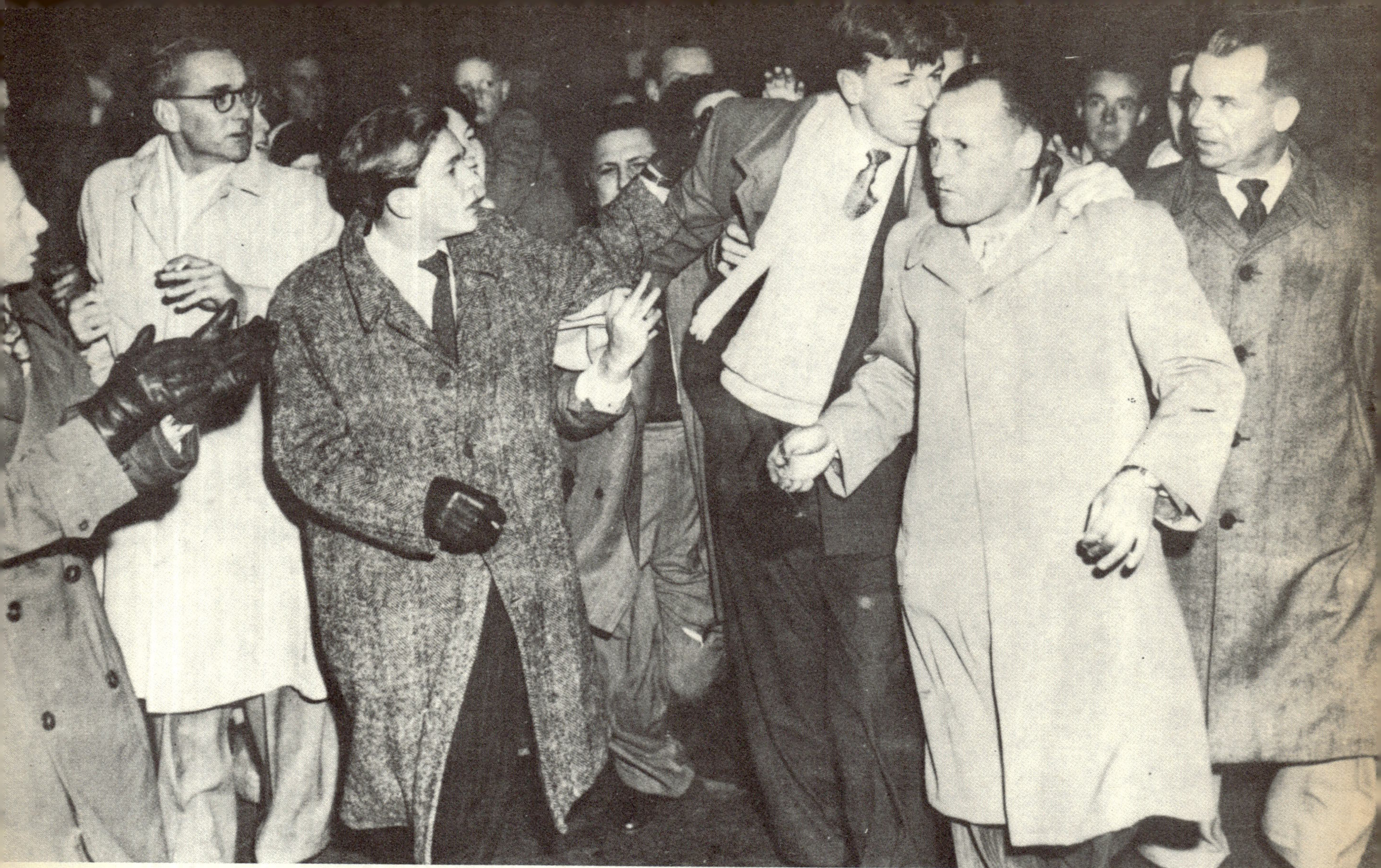

John Coleman leaving Harrison House after the last game of 1951. His four week suspension probably cost Essendon their third successive premiership. *Herald & Weekly Times photo*

Footscray full-forward Jack Collins creates an excellent how-to-do-it picture as he eludes Ken Christie (Melbourne) and steers through one of his seven goals—Grand final 1954.

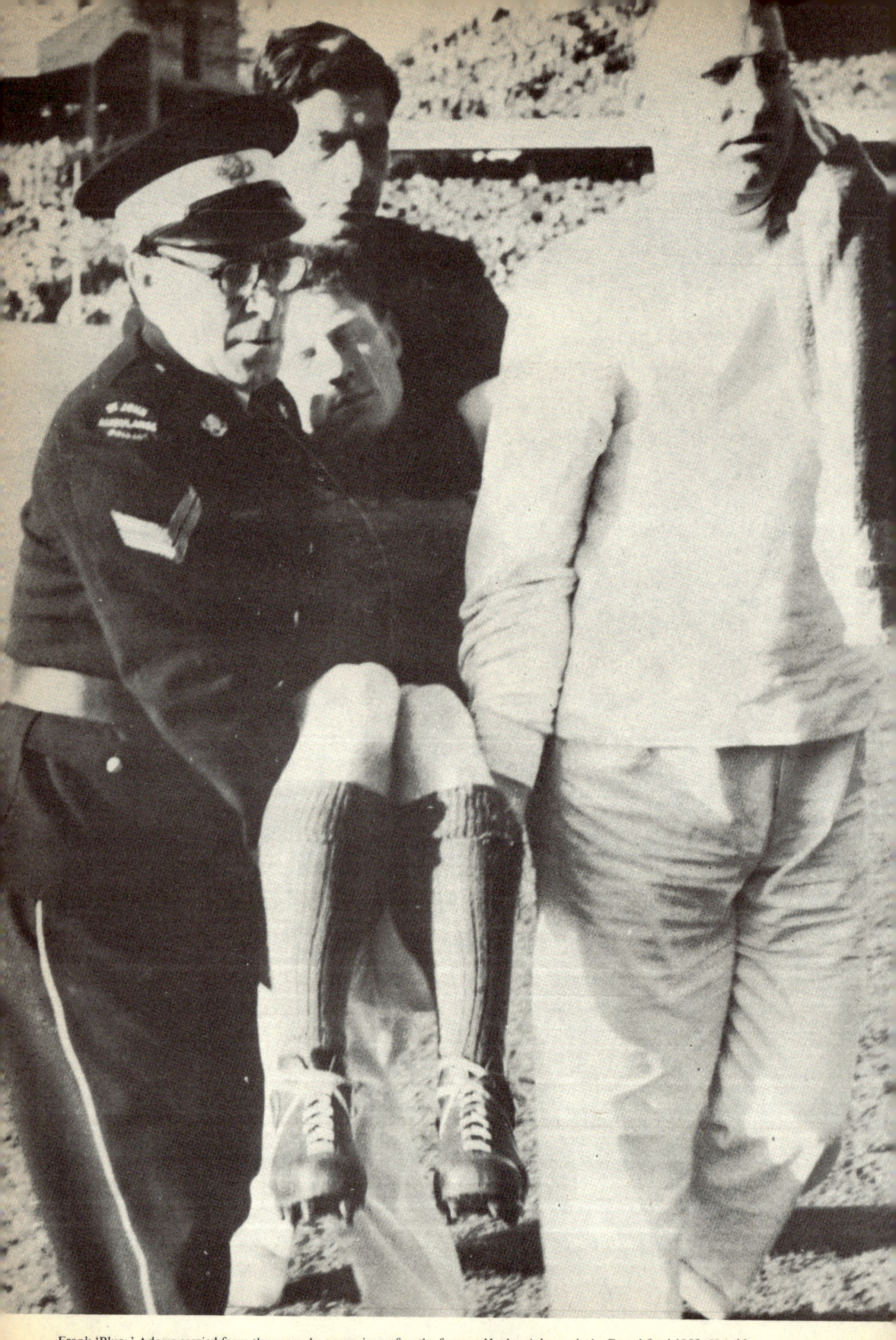

Frank 'Bluey' Adams carried from the ground unconscious after the famous Healey-Adams clash. Grand final 1955. *Herald & Weekly Times photo*

Barassi kicks for goal, second semi-final 1956.

Grim determination by Barassi as he goals on the run despite a strong tackle by Suter—grand final 1957.

A fiery clash in the 1958 grand final, with combatants being separated by umpire Alan Nash.

A Collingwood player goes down in the 1958 grand final. The Melbourne players are Mithen, Bob Johnson and Dixon
Herald & Weekly Times photo

Ray Gabelich (Collingwood) goals after one of the most memorable incidents of any finals series—his amazing 70-yard run from the half-forward flank—grand final, Collingwood V Melbourne 1964. *Age photo*

The Somerville incident—preliminary final 1965. Somerville had just been felled behind the play ten minutes after the opening bounce. *Age photo*

Ian Stewart (St. Kilda) outmarks Collingwood's Ray Gabelich as Mynott (St. Kilda) looks on—grand final 1966. *Herald-Sun photo*

Bob Murray (St. Kilda) marks brilliantly—grand final 1966. *Herald-Sun photo*

SEPTEMBER 24 — GRAND FINAL

	1st	2nd	3rd	Final
Essendon	3 . 3	7 . 7	12 . 15	18 . 17 (125)
Carlton	2 . 4	2 . 10	3 . 12	6 . 16 (52)
	MCG		Umpire J. McMurray Jnr.	
	Attendance 90,453		Gate £9,050	

BEST —	(Ess)	McClure, May, Hutchison, McDonald, Brittingham, McConnell
	(Carl)	Deacon, Grieve, Green, Clark, Howell, Henfry
GOALS —	(Ess)	Coleman (6), Rawle (3), Hutchison (2), Syme (2), McEwin (2), Jones, Leehane, R. Reynolds
	(Carl)	Howell, Turner, Garby, B. Baxter, K. Baxter, Hands

GRAND FINAL TEAMS

Essendon	B	Thaw	Brittingham	May
	HB	McDonald	McConnell	Gardiner
	C	Fisher	H. Lambert	Bradley
	HF	Jones	Leehane	McEwin
	F	R. Reynolds (c)	Coleman	Rawle
	Ruck	McClure	Syme	Hutchison
	Reserves	Lane	Hassell	
	Coach	R. S. Reynolds		
Carlton	B	Richie Green	Grieve	Davies
	HB	Clark	Deacon	Baird
	C	Williams	Henfry (c)	Hodgson
	HF	Conley	Howell	Garby
	F	Brokenshire	K. Baxter	Turner
	Ruck	Hands	Bateman	Mooring
	Reserves	B. Baxter	Stafford	
	Coach	P. Bentley		

1950

Essendon reached the peak of their form in 1950. Aided by another century of goals from Coleman, they went through eighteen home and home games with only one defeat. No League team has yet gone through a complete season without a loss, although Collingwood in 1929 won all their home and home games, before losing the second semi-final. Carlton (1908) and South Melbourne (1918) are the only other teams, besides Collingwood and Essendon, to lose only one game in a season.

Naturally, the 1950 Dons were on top of the ladder, followed by North Melbourne (thirteen wins, five losses), Melbourne (twelve wins, six losses) and Geelong (ten wins, eight losses). Fitzroy (fifth) and Richmond (sixth) were also on ten wins, but both had percentages much inferior to Geelong.

In the first semi-final, played in the wet, Melbourne never recovered from the setback of a first quarter collision between team-mates Geoff Collins and Shane McGrath. Collins broke his jaw, and his loss left a gap in the Demon defence. Geelong, with Flanagan and Goninon dominating on the forward line, went right away from the opposition after half-time, to exactly double Melbourne's score by the end of the game.

There was an early surprise in the second semi-final when Les Foote won the toss for North and kicked against the wind. In a violent and fiery start, Essendon piled up five goals five to three points by quarter-time, but North fought back excellently to bridge the gap and trail by only eight points at three-quarter-time. Heavy rain began in the last term as North stormed forward. The Essendon lead was cut to three points, before Marchesi goaled and Spencer booted a behind for North to lead by five points with ten minutes to go. The desperate Coleman dived full-length over the shoulders of two North backmen to grab an incredible mark, but his shot was astray. In a frantic finish, Coleman went down in a pack and was kicked heavily in the head, and Reynolds was knocked unconscious as he fell while attempting to mark. Thirty seconds remained when North full-back McCorkell punched the ball back into play instead of letting it go out of bounds. The dangerous Coleman swooped on the ball and passed accurately to McEwin in the goal-square. McEwin's goal put the Dons three points ahead and won the game. Coleman, with four goals, had played excellently considering that he had suffered a broken finger against St. Kilda in the last home and home game. The finger had been in plaster until the morning of the second semi-final, but after further knocks in that game, more fractures were sustained and the finger was back in plaster until the grand final. The Essendon camp kept news of the injury as quiet as possible.

The unlucky North had to battle hard to beat Geelong in the preliminary final. Again Foote won the toss and kicked against the wind, and again the opposition got away to a flying start, Geelong in this instance kicking seven goals three to a goal in the first term. Despite shocking inaccuracy, North fought back well in the second quarter, but their third term, when they slammed on six goals three against the breeze, was by far their best of the game. From two points down at three-quarter-time, they launched a virtually non-stop onslaught on goals in the last term, with Foote the leading light in most attacks. Geelong slowed to a walk, and North's four last-quarter goals enabled them to complete a remarkable victory.

For the grand final, Essendon made only one change from the side which won the second semi-final. North relied on the same side which had defeated Geelong.

Winning the toss and kicking with the wind, Essendon swept North aside with a burst of seven goals in the first term. Their first attack brought a goal, when Reynolds found Coleman whose fifty-yard punt beat the backs and bounced through. Reynolds added Essendon's second within five minutes of the start. Punches were thrown as Essendon drove forward again for Reynolds to kick his second. Coleman went down heavily and was in the hands of the trainers for some time. He was evidently shaken up, as he promptly missed two sitters before Snell added Essendon's fourth. Two Essendon mistakes let North in for their first two goals, and scoring thereafter was fairly even. The spirit of the game was indicated when an Essendon boot was pushed into the ribs of North's Tim Robb as he lay on the ground after marking, and by the end of the first term there had been three reports.

After a low-scoring second term—only one goal, by North's Spencer, was scored—North had succeeded in reducing the Essendon lead to thirteen points. Both sides missed easy shots, but Coleman's miss from ten yards out was the most glaring. The knocks which the Don's full-forward had been receiving were certainly having an effect—he had missed several chances in the first half.

During the interval, the wind changed to favour North, but heavy rain negated this advantage. Coleman, after again being flattened, came back to goal for Essendon. Other goals followed to Mogg (North Melbourne), Hutchison (Essendon) and Spencer (North Melbourne), making the difference fourteen points. After a melee on the member's wing in which Harper was flattened, Coleman marked well out and kicked Essendon's tenth. After more fighting and a fair amount of fumbling, the teams went to the three-quarter-time break with Essendon twenty points ahead.

In a bone-crushing finish, Essendon had to hold on as North roughed them up in the last quarter. Reynolds was flattened with a punch to the head, Harper ran into a hook to the jaw, McEwin was on the receiving end of a haymaker, and Leehane went down before a vicious charge. The punch which Harper received led to Essendon's first goal of the term. McCorkell (North Melbourne) took a clean mark, was hit heavily by Harper, and spun around and laid the Essendon man out (and was reported). Harper goaled from the free. Coleman scored another to make the game safe for the Dons, and Syme got yet another just on the bell as North Melbourne, outclassed, slowed to a walk. Essendon cruised home by thirty-eight points.

RESULTS

SEPTEMBER 2 — FIRST SEMI-FINAL

	1st	2nd	3rd	Final	
Geelong	1 . 1	4 . 5	8 . 6	13 . 10	(88)
Melbourne	2 . 2	3 . 2	5 . 4	6 . 8	(44)

MCG — Umpire McMurray
Attendance 54,817 — Gate £5,407

BEST — (Geel) Flanagan (B.O.G.), Davis, Turner, Tate, Scott, Morrison, Fitzgerald
(Melb) Bickford, Arnold, Denis Cordner, Don Cordner, Woods, Rodda

GOALS — (Geel) Goninon (6), Flanagan (2), Tate (2), Lynch (2), Tresize
(Melb) Denis Cordner (3), Mueller (2), Rule

SEPTEMBER 9 — SECOND SEMI-FINAL

	1st	2nd	3rd	Final	
Essendon	5 . 5	6 . 8	9 . 11	11 . 14	(80)
North Melbourne	0 . 3	5 . 7	8 . 9	11 . 11	(77)

MCG — Umpire Jamieson
Attendance 75,433 — Gate £7,755

BEST — (Ess) McDonald, McClure, Jones, Syme, May, McConnell
(N. Melb) Foote, Robb, L. Reeves, Brooker, Marchesi, Ryan

GOALS — (Ess) Coleman (4), Reynolds (2), Hutchison (2), McEwin (2), Syme
(N. Melb) Robb (3), Spencer (2), Marchesi (2), Condon (2), Hedley, Dynon

1950

SEPTEMBER 16 — PRELIMINARY FINAL

	1st	2nd	3rd	Final	
North Melbourne	1 . 0	4 . 8	10 . 11	14 . 16	(100)
Geelong	7 . 3	8 . 4	11 . 7	12 . 11	(83)

MCG — Umpire J. McMurray Jnr.
Attendance 73,539 — Gate £7,556

BEST — (N. Melb) Foote (B.O.G.), Marchesi, Robb, Dynon, J. & L. Reeves, Jeeves, Spencer, McKenzie
(Geel) Fitzgerald, Flanagan, Turner, Hyde, Morrow, Lynch, Renfrey

GOALS — (N. Melb) Spencer (5), Marchesi (3), Robb (3), Dynon, Thornton, Condon
(Geel) Flanagan (3), Lynch (3), Goninon (2), Condon (2), Tate, Tresize

SEPTEMBER 23 — GRAND FINAL

	1st	2nd	3rd	Final	
Essendon	7 . 3	7 . 6	10 . 11	13 . 14	(92)
North Melbourne	4 . 0	5 . 5	7 . 9	7 . 12	(54)

MCG — Umpire J. McMurray Jnr.
Attendance 87,601 — Gate £8,708

BEST — (Ess) McDonald (B.O.G.), Reynolds, May, McClure, Syme, Gardiner
(N. Melb) Foote, Robb, Dynon, Jarrard, Brooker, McCorkell

GOALS — (Ess) Coleman (4), Reynolds (2), Syme (2), Hutchison, McEwin, Dale, Harper, Snell
(N. Melb) Spencer (3), Robb (2), Dynon, Brooker

GRAND FINAL TEAMS

Essendon	B	Gardiner	Brittingham	May
	HB	H. Lambert	McConnell	McDonald
	C	C. Lambert	Dale	Collins
	HF	Jones	Snell	Harper
	F	McEwin	Coleman	Reynolds (c)
	Ruck	McClure	Syme	Hutchison
	Reserves	Allanson	Leehane	
	Coach	R. S. Reynolds		
North Melbourne	B	J. Reeves	McCorkell	Kelly
	HB	L. Reeves	Ryan	Jarrard
	C	McKenzie	Dynon	Mogg
	HF	Condon	Jeeves	Marchesi
	F	Robb	Spencer	Brooker
	Ruck	Thornton	Foote (c)	Malone
	Reserves	Lawrence	Hedley	
	Coach	W. Carter		

1951

When Essendon lost to South Melbourne on May 5, 1951, it was the end of their run of sixteen consecutive wins since 1950 and only their second loss in thirty-four games. They slumped somewhat after that defeat, and eventually could finish only third on the ladder, with twelve wins, behind Collingwood (fourteen wins) and Geelong (thirteen wins). Making up the Four was Footscray (fourth) with eleven wins.

Sensation of the season occurred just before the finals when Essendon's trump card, John Coleman, was suspended. Reported in the last home and home game for retaliating when struck by Carlton's Harry Caspar, Coleman was outed for four weeks by the VFL Tribunal as hundreds of fans screamed and hooted outside Harrison House. With Coleman out of the finals, Essendon plunged from favourites to no-hopers for the flag.

Essendon certainly missed Coleman in the first semi-final, although they managed to win. For three quarters, their usual smooth team-work was stifled by the inexperienced Bulldogs, twelve of whom had never before played in a final.

Footscray had three goals on the board before Essendon had scored and their first-quarter burst of six goals one was more than they scored for the rest of the game. They were, in fact, able to add only another two goals four while Essendon, despite haphazard forward work, crept closer and closer. Finally, in the last, Tate's magnificent angle goal gave the Dons the lead for the first time, and they were able to hold Footscray out for the rest of the term to win by eight points. Eighteen-year-old Ted Whitten appeared in his first finals game only due to the intervention of the Prime Minister (Mr. Menzies). Whitten, on National Service, had previously been refused leave for the day of the game.

Collingwood began the second semi-final with a brilliant first-quarter burst of six goals three to Geelong's two goals three before the rot set in. After their initial set-back, Geelong began to utilise their blistering pace and, by moving the ball to the wide open spaces, they ran the Magpies ragged. With Flanagan at centre-half-forward feeding Goninon with deadly precision, Geelong kicked an amazing twenty goals seventeen to Collingwood's four goals seven in the last three quarters. Goninon, with six goals in the last quarter, finished the match with a record-equalling eleven goals.

In the preliminary final, Collingwood surprised when they led Essendon after a fiery first three quarters. The Magpies had won hands down on the wings, and had gained tremendous drive from those positions. Then too, their loose man tactics and Essendon's own inept forward work had the Dons continually struggling.

When Stevens scored Collingwood's tenth goal at the start of the last term, the crowd began to drift away. But suddenly, Essendon men who had struggled all day began to pick up kicks, and when Hutchison goaled and shortly afterwards found K. McDonald for another, the Dons were rejuvenated. More goals followed, before Syme (Essendon), after marking in the pack, scored to make the difference five points. The winning goal came when K. McDonald fell while trying to mark, and Jones picked up and scored full points. Essendon's lucky two-point win put them into the grand final for the sixth successive season.

When some last-minute changes forced Essendon to select a new nineteenth man for the grand final, the job surprisingly went to coach Dick Reynolds, who had retired after the previous season's grand final. It was his 320th and last VFL game and his tenth grand final.

Geelong nearly kicked themselves out of the game in the first half. Starting with a goal to Goninon within a minute of the bounce, the Cats then booted six successive behinds while Essendon, with almost their only forward move, goaled through Hutchison. Norman and Goninon added further goals for Geelong before the first quarter ended.

After some haphazard play to start with, Syme scored Essendon's second goal early in the second quarter. Soon after, the same player added another, whilst Geelong continued to miss. In fact, the Cats added only one goal two for the term, but an improved Essendon booted five goals two and led at half-time.

Geelong's third-quarter burst of five goals three to Essendon's two points, as it turned out, won them the game. Essendon came back strongly, however, but slipped twenty-two points behind again with twenty minutes of the last quarter gone.

At this stage, Reynolds came on, and his presence lifted Essendon. Immediately they came forward, and Reynolds shepherded well for Tate to run in and goal. Seconds later, May plucked the ball from the ruck and added another. Then Hutchison sent the ball to McEwin in front of Bay Five, and McEwin sped off and passed the ball to full-forward where K. McDonald was on his own, a certainty to mark and goal to leave Essendon only five points down. But it was not to be—the anxious Reynolds, rushing in from the pocket, collided with K. McDonald, and Bruce Morrison cleared for Geelong. At the other end, Goninon added a behind and Geelong were able to hold Essendon out for the last few minutes and take out their first premiership since 1937.

The Cats' premiership win completed a clean scoop of the season's top honours—they also had the Brownlow Medallist (Bernie Smith) and top goal-kicker (George Goninon). Collingwood, in 1927 (S. Coventry Brownlow, G. Coventry goal-kicking) and 1929 (A. Collier Brownlow, G. Coventry goal-kicking) is the only other club to achieve this feat.

RESULTS

SEPTEMBER 8 — FIRST SEMI-FINAL

	1st	2nd	3rd	Final	
Essendon	3 . 2	4 . 4	6 . 7	8 . 13	(61)
Footscray	6 . 1	7 . 1	7 . 5	8 . 5	(53)

MCG — Umpire McMurray

Attendance 66,135 — Gate £8,147

BEST —	(Ess)	McConnell, N. McDonald, Dale, Harper, Jones, McEwin, Brittingham, Gardiner
	(Foots)	Bryden, McRae, Donald, Henderson, Scanlon, Gallagher
GOALS —	(Ess)	Tate (2), Gill (2), Harper, McEwin, Snell, Jones
	(Foots)	Collins (2), Laffey (2), Richards, Sutton, Bryden, Linton

SEPTEMBER 15 — SECOND SEMI-FINAL

	1st	2nd	3rd	Final	
Geelong	2 . 3	10 . 6	13 . 14	22 . 20	(152)
Collingwood	6 . 3	7 . 5	9 . 7	10 . 10	(70)

MCG — Umpire Jamieson
Attendance 74,085 — Gate £9,279

BEST —	(Geel)	Turner, Smith, Tate, Fulton, Davis, Goninon, Flanagan, McMaster, Morrow
	(Col)	R. Richards, L. Richards, Davey, W. Twomey, Hamilton, Merrett
GOALS —	(Geel)	Goninon (11), Morrow (3), Pianto (2), Flanagan (2), Tresize (2), Turner, McMaster
	(Col)	R. Richards (3), W. Twomey (2), Purdon (2), Stevens, Davey, M. Twomey

SEPTEMBER 22 — PRELIMINARY FINAL

	1st	2nd	3rd	Final	
Essendon	1 . 2	3 . 3	5 . 7	10 . 10	(70)
Collingwood	1 . 2	7 . 4	9 . 7	10 . 8	(68)

MCG — Umpire McMurray
Attendance 50,414 — Gate £5,662

BEST —	(Ess)	May, Bigelow, N. McDonald, Brittingham, H. Lambert, Dale, C. Lambert, Mann
	(Col)	R. & L. Richards, R. Rose, Lucas, Hamilton, Mann, Hams, Davey, Merrett
GOALS —	(Ess)	Hutchison (2), Tate (2), Syme (2), K. McDonald, McEwin, Jones, Mann
	(Col)	R. Richards (4), L. Richards (2), Davey, W. Twomey, Dunstan, Stevens

SEPTEMBER 29 — GRAND FINAL

Geelong	3 . 8	4 . 10	9 . 13	11 . 15	(81)
Essendon	1 . 0	6 . 2	6 . 4	10 . 10	(70)

MCG — Umpire Jamieson
Attendance 85,795 — Gate £10,587

BEST —	(Geel)	Hyde, Morrison, Smith, Turner, McMaster, Pianto, Tresize
	(Ess)	Gardiner, Mann, N. McDonald, May, Syme, Bigelow
GOALS —	(Geel)	Goninon (4), Davis, Pianto, McMaster, Turner, Flanagan, Morrow, Norman
	(Ess)	K. McDonald (2), Syme (2), Hutchison, May, Snell, Tate, Jones, Payne

GRAND FINAL TEAMS

Geelong	B	B. Smith	Morrison	Stewart
	HB	Middlemiss	Hyde	Worner
	C	Tate	Turner	Fulton
	HF	Renfrey	Flanagan (c)	Davis
	F	McMaster	Goninon	Pianto
	Ruck	Morrow	Norman	Tresize
	Reserves	Hovey	Reed	
	Coach	R. Hickey		
Essendon	B	Gardiner	Brittingham	Bigelow
	HB	H. Lambert	McConnell	N. McDonald
	C	C. Lambert	Dale	Mann
	HF	McEwin	Snell	Jones
	F	Payne	K. McDonald	Tate
	Ruck	May	Syme	Hutchison (c)
	Reserves	Clarke	Reynolds	
	Coach	R. Reynolds		

1952

For the first time since 1946, Essendon missed participating in the grand final. In fact, not only did they miss the grand final, but they also missed the final Four, finishing eighth with only nine wins.

Making up the finalists were Geelong (sixteen wins and a tie), Collingwood (fourteen wins, five losses), Fitzroy (thirteen wins, six losses) with Carlton (eleven wins, six losses, two draws) sneaking into fourth spot by two premiership points from South Melbourne.

A lack-lustre first semi-final saw Carlton, through its failure to kick goals when they were needed, lose the game by a single point in almost the last minute of the match. The Blues did not score their first goal until eighteen minutes into the second term, and at half-time had had one more shot than Fitzroy but trailed by eleven points. Eleven onslaughts right into the goal-square yielded only four behinds at one stage. In the second half, Warburton moved into the centre for the Blues and Ferry went to full-forward. The moves were successful, and Carlton rattled on three quick goals before inaccuracy again set in. Meanwhile, Fitzroy's switch of ruckman Streader to the half-forward flank also proved successful and Fitzroy trailed by only four points at the last change. In a hard-hitting last term, the Maroons regained the lead but Carlton managed to draw level with a minute to go. Then the quick-thinking Fitzroy skipper, Alan Ruthven, broke away from a boundary throw-in to snap the behind that won the game.

At Carlton's celebration dance that night, star forward Keith Warburton suddenly collapsed. He had received a knock in the abdomen early in the game and the injury, which did not become immediately apparent, was to become one of the most serious in League history. After an emergency operation on Sunday morning, Warburton's condition worsened and he was placed on the danger list. Continuous blood transfusions, during which the Carlton star hovered between life and death, eventually saved his life, and Warburton was back in the Carlton side in 1953.

The second semi-final saw Geelong take control in the second half and go on to an easy win. Early, W. Twomey was in brilliant form at full-forward for Collingwood, but they refused to look for him and chance after chance went begging. When Mann had to be replaced at half-time, the writing was on the wall, for Collingwood's two rovers were also having a bad day and the drive from the ruck was thus negligible. Kicking seven goals to two in the third quarter, Geelong sealed the game and they won by fifty-four points, more than double the Magpies' score.

An exciting preliminary final, in which Bob Rose was the outstanding player, saw Collingwood, by virtue of a burst of five goals five to a point in the second term, go on to a nineteen-point win. Fitzroy fought back excellently in the third term to draw to within thirteen points at the last change but the Magpie defence, led by Jack Finck, was able to hold them to three points in the last quarter and that was nowhere near good enough. The Magpies went into their first grand final for twelve years.

Geelong saddled up as the hottest favourites for many years in the grand final. Collingwood missed Lucas and P. Twomey (injured) and brought in Batchelor for his first VFL game. Flanagan won the toss for the Cats, but Collingwood were first into attack, and Merrett, with a nice drop kick, quickly had the first goal on the board. Then it was Geelong's turn, and for most of the quarter they dictated the play. Goninon (two), Davis and Tresize all goaled, Davis' goal being a magnificent drop kick from sixty-five yards out.

Parker got Collingwood's second goal as the second term began, and added another soon after. At this stage, he and Dunstan were Collingwood's only effective forwards. Geelong, not relishing the Magpies' regular doses of vigour, took almost into time-on to score their only goal of the quarter, but still led by twelve points at half-time.

There were some surprise changes to the Magpie line-up after half-time. Finck was full-forward, Mann centre-half-back and Stevens forward pocket/ruck. The changes made no difference, however, for Geelong went straight into attack and Goninon took a one-handed mark and goaled. Parker and Merrett replied for the Magpies, reducing their deficit to only seven points, before Geelong released a brilliant burst of three goals in five minutes. Just before the three-quarter-time break, Davis burnt off three opponents and helped get the ball to McMaster a few yards out for Geelong's sixth of the term, giving them a commanding lead at the last change.

The final thirty minutes saw Collingwood, hopeless up forward, attack constantly for seven successive behinds while Geelong kicked two goals two from four shots. The Magpie full-forward line was slow, lumbering and awkward, and was hopelessly outplayed by Morrison, B. Smith and Sharp. As in the second semi-final, Geelong more than doubled the Magpies' score to convincingly win their second successive flag.

1952

RESULTS

SEPTEMBER 6 — FIRST SEMI-FINAL

	1st	2nd	3rd	Final	
Fitzroy	2 . 1	6 . 3	8 . 5	10 . 9	(69)
Carlton	0 . 5	3 . 10	7 . 15	8 . 20	(68)

MCG — Umpire Jamieson
Attendance 59,970 — Gate £7,199

BEST — (Fitz) Ruthven, Stephen, Goodger, Chanter, Roberts, Gaffney, Broderick, V. Williams
(Carl) English (B.O.G.), Kerr, Hands, Grieve, Conley, Guy, Ferry, Howell, Beasy
GOALS — (Fitz) Ruthven (3), Streader (2), Coates (2), Ongarello, Johnstone, Williams
(Carl) Howell (3), Spencer (2), Ferry, Beasy, Davies

SEPTEMBER 13 — SECOND SEMI-FINAL

	1st	2nd	3rd	Final	
Geelong	2 . 6	5 . 9	12 . 10	14 . 16	(100)
Collingwood	1 . 4	3 . 5	5 . 6	6 . 10	(46)

MCG — Umpire McMurray
Attendance 77,417 — Gate £9,842

BEST — (Geel) McMaster (B.O.G.), Renfrey, Tresize, B. Smith, Morrison, Williams, Sharp, Middlemiss
(Col) P. Twomey, Healey, Tuck, Merrett, M. Twomey, Lucas, Finck, Davey, Mann (till injured)
GOALS — (Geel) McMaster (4), Tresize (3), Goninon (2), Norman (2), Turner, Flanagan, Pianto
(Col) W. Twomey (4), L. Richards, M. Twomey

SEPTEMBER 20 — PRELIMINARY FINAL

	1st	2nd	3rd	Final	
Collingwood	4 . 4	9 . 9	10 . 12	11 . 15	(81)
Fitzroy	4 . 2	4 . 3	9 . 5	9 . 8	(62)

MCG — Umpire Robinson
Attendance 54,046 — Gate £5,928

BEST — (Col) R. Rose (B.O.G.), Finck, Merrett, Healey, Hickey, L. Richards, Parker, Hams
(Fitz) Johnstone, Goodger, Harding, Chanter, Stephen, Gaffney, Roberts
GOALS — (Col) R. Rose (3), W. Twomey (2), L. Richards (2), Hickey, Healey, Mann, Stevens
(Fitz) Ruthven (2), Ongarello (2), Johnstone (2), Gervasoni, Harding, Jarvis

SEPTEMBER 27 — GRAND FINAL

	1st	2nd	3rd	Final	
Geelong	4 . 2	5 . 3	11 . 6	13 . 8	(86)
Collingwood	1 . 1	3 . 3	5 . 3	5 . 10	(40)

MCG — Umpire Jamieson
Attendance 82,890 — Gate £10,220

1952-1953

BEST —	(Geel)	G. Williams (B.O.G.), Tresize, Sharp, Goninon, B. Smith, Morrison, Flanagan, Worner
	(Col)	Merrett, Mann, R. Rose, Tuck, M. Twomey, W. Twomey, Dunstan
GOALS —	(Geel)	Goninon (5), Tresize (4), Davis, McMaster, Flanagan, Worner
	(Col)	Parker (3), Merrett (2)

GRAND FINAL TEAMS

Geelong	B	B. Smith	Morrison	Sharp
	HB	Middlemiss	Hyde	Williams
	C	Worner	Palmer	Fulton
	HF	Turner	Flanagan (c)	Davis
	F	Norman	Goninon	Pianto
	Ruck	McMaster	Renfrey	Tresize
	Reserves	S. Smith	Hovey	
	Coach	R. Hickey		
Collingwood	B	Hams	Batchelor	W. Rose
	HB	Smith	Finck	Tuck
	C	Merrett	W. Twomey	Healey
	HF	Hickey	Dunstan	R. Rose
	F	Parker	Stevens	Mann
	Ruck	M. Twomey	Gooch	L. Richards (c)
	Reserves	Kingston	Aitken	
	Coach	A. Kyne		

1953

Geelong, with thirteen successive wins to start the 1953 season, took their winning streak to twenty-three in a row, a VFL record which is still unbroken. Their winning run was broken at the hands of Collingwood, who went on to become their grand final opponents, but the Cats held first position on the ladder from the first game of the season until the last, winning fifteen of their eighteen games. Collingwood (fourteen wins, four losses) was second, followed by Footscray and Essendon (both thirteen wins).

The Dons, with Coleman obviously unfit due to an attack of the flu, did well to get to within eight points of Footscray at the final siren in the first semi-final. A high westerly wind made ball handling extremely difficult and Footscray did all the attacking early. However, they were off target and, although they had two goals to none within minutes of the start, they managed only one more goal from eight shots before the quarter ended. Essendon's only forward move was topped off by a goal from Coleman who, however, was very much off-colour.

Essendon did most of the attacking in the second term—two goals six to a point—but scoring was remarkably even in the third. It was a battle of defences, as the scores at three-quarter-time indicated—Footscray four goals eleven, Essendon four goals seven. Ollington goaled for Footscray as the last term began. Coleman replied for the Dons, and it was two points the difference. Lifted by Sutton, Footscray bombarded the goal, but could not score. Gill and Monks missed easy shots for the Dons, before Kerr picked up and goaled for Footscray, who then led by eight points, their final winning margin.

In a top-class second semi-final, Geelong's rover Pianto put his team on top early, with four of the Cats' first six goals. Halfway through the second term, Geelong led by six goals two to three goals five but Collingwood came back strongly to bridge the gap and trail by only three points at half-time.

Geelong threw away their winning chance in the third term with seven successive behinds—the turning point came just before three-quarter-time when McMaster's shot hit the post and Tresize also missed. If these shots had been goals and not behinds, Geelong would have had a handy three-quarter-time lead: as it was, they were ahead by only four points, with Collingwood having last use of the wind.

The Magpies moved Mann from the ruck to full-forward, and immediately got moving. The big ruckman kicked two goals himself and helped in a couple of others as Collingwood booted six goals four to Geelong's one goal to win easing up. Bob Rose, beaten early, played excellently in the last term when he was needed and kicked three goals.

Despite kicking seven successive behinds to start the preliminary final against Footscray, Geelong, although missing Middlemiss and Renfrey, fought their way back into the game with four goals in the third term. The wind and rain slowed Footscray up after a bright patch halfway through the third, and they never looked like winning after that. Main feature for Geelong fans was that their side, long suspect against vigour, did not shirk an issue throughout the day. The 1953 Bulldogs, however, had the satisfaction of being the first Footscray team to get past the first semi-final.

As had become usual in recent seasons, thousands of fans were sitting around the boundary line when the Geelong and Collingwood teams ran onto the MCG for the 1953 grand final. Both sides were at almost full strength, although Collingwood had Tuck out. Geelong played Hyde, although his injured leg was not completely healed.

The game began with the Magpies having the majority of the play, but they broke down badly up forward, only one goal—to winger Healey—being on the board from numerous attempts before McMaster equalised for Geelong with half of the first term gone. Tresize immediately handballed to Rayson for another as the Cats showed how it should be done. Play began to get rough as players hurled themselves recklessly into the packs; other players were felled needlessly as both sides put on the pressure. The Magpies goaled towards the end of the term and were slightly ahead at quarter-time.

Collingwood, gaining tremendous drive from winger Healey and half-forward Merrett, forced the ball forward for R. Rose to goal as the second term began. Geelong now proceeded to throw away the game as, aided by a light breeze, they managed only one goal from eight scoring shots and numerous other chances. Collingwood, on the other hand, kicked accurately from not many opportunities, and held a handy half-time lead of nine points.

The third term was the Magpies' best. Batchelor, at full-forward, began to kick goals as the Magpies were provided with many scoring chances through the drive received from the wings and ruck. At centre-half-forward, Waites was leading Hyde a merry dance and it was obvious that Hyde's injured leg was not up to the task of chasing the Collingwood man all over the ground. Originally, the Magpies' tactics had been for Waites to keep moving and have Hyde continually chasing him, more to take the Geelong star out of the play than anything else. But now Waites was starting to pick up kicks as well as run, and the Magpies shrewdly directed several attacks through him. It was noticeable that the Cats were beginning to panic, and the Magpies were able to break through for five vital goals during the term, giving them a twenty-nine point break at the last change.

Geelong, in desperation, resorted to wholesale changes and at last began to get some system into their play. Throwing themselves into the fray, the Cats broke through twice in quick succession to reduce the Collingwood lead to a mere fifteen points. Then came the turning point of the game, as Geelong's nineteenth man, Hovey, missed two sitters from twenty yards out. From the kick-in after the second miss, R. Richards (Collingwood) secured, and found Bob Rose for a Magpie goal. The pressure was relieved, and the Magpies, although desperately pushed in the closing stages, were able to hold on to win the Coronation Year premiership by twelve points.

RESULTS

SEPTEMBER 5 — FIRST SEMI-FINAL

	1st	2nd	3rd	Final	
Footscray	3 . 7	3 . 8	4 . 11	6 . 13	(49)
Essendon	1 . 0	3 . 7	4 . 7	5 . 11	(41)

MCG — Umpire McMurray
Attendance 68,533 — Gate £8,495

BEST — (Foots) Box, Whitten, Ollington, Abbey, Trusler, Sutton
(Ess) Hutchison (B.O.G.), McConnell, Syme, Jones, McDonald, Leek, Bigelow

GOALS — (Foots) Harper (2), Ollington, Trusler, Gilmore, Kerr
(Ess) Hutchison (2), Coleman, Syme, Leek

SEPTEMBER 12 — SECOND SEMI-FINAL

	1st	2nd	3rd	Final	
Collingwood	2 . 3	5 . 7	7 . 8	13 . 12	(90)
Geelong	3 . 1	6 . 4	7 . 12	8 . 12	(60)

MCG — Umpire Barbour
Attendance 70,292 — Gate £8,631

BEST — (Col) Mann, M. Twomey, R. Rose, Healey, W. Twomey, Merrett, L. Richards
(Geel) Pianto (B.O.G.), Renfrey, Morrison, Hyde, Williams, B. Smith, Hovey

GOALS — (Col) R. Rose (4), Mann (3), M. Twomey (2), Batchelor, W. Twomey, L. & R. Richards
(Geel) Pianto (5), Tresize, McMaster, Goninon

1953

SEPTEMBER 19 — PRELIMINARY FINAL

	1st	2nd	3rd	Final	
Geelong	0 . 6	2 . 7	6 . 10	8 . 15	(63)
Footscray	2 . 1	3 . 4	4 . 5	5 . 7	(37)

MCG — Umpire Jamieson
Attendance 58,615 — Gate £6,913

BEST — (Geel) Williams (B.O.G.), Pianto, McMaster, B. Smith, Rayson, Davis, Turner
(Foots) Stevens, Donald, Whitten, McCarthy, Henderson, Trusler
GOALS — (Geel) McMaster (4), Rayson (2), Pianto, Hovey
(Foots) Stevens (2), Trusler (2), Harper

SEPTEMBER 26 — GRAND FINAL

	1st	2nd	3rd	Final	
Collingwood	2 . 4	5 . 6	10 . 10	11 . 11	(77)
Geelong	2 . 2	3 . 9	5 . 11	8 . 17	(65)

MCG — Umpire McMurray
Attendance 89,060 — Gate £11,248

BEST — (Col) Healey (B.O.G.), Mann, R. Richards, R. Rose, Merrett, L. Richards, Waites, Batchelor
(Geel) B. Smith, Williams, Renfrey, Turner, McMaster
GOALS — (Col) Batchelor (4), R. Rose (3), Healey (2), L. Richards, M. Twomey
(Geel) Davis (3), Rayson (2), Hovey, Tresize, McMaster

GRAND FINAL TEAMS

Collingwood	B	Sharp	Finck	Gooch
	HB	Parker	Waller	Kingston
	C	Healey	W. Twomey*	R. Richards
	HF	Merrett	Waites	P. Twomey
	F	L. Richards (c)	Batchelor	M. Twomey
	Ruck	Mann	W. Rose	R. Rose
	Reserves	Weideman	Hams	
	Coach	A. Kyne		
Geelong	B	B. Smith	Morrison	Herbert
	HB	S. Smith	Hyde	Williams
	C	Reed	Turner	Worner
	HF	Rayson	Flanagan (c)	Davis
	F	Swarbrick	Renfrey	Tresize
	Ruck	McMaster	Sharp	Pianto
	Reserves	Hovey	Palmer	
	Coach	R. Hickey		

* Collingwood claimed a record when the three Twomey brothers—Bill, Pat and Mick—all appeared in the grand final side.

1954

For the fourth successive season, Geelong headed the VFL ladder in 1954, with thirteen wins and five losses. The fight for the remaining positions was one of the closest for many years with Footscray and North Melbourne (both eleven wins, one tie) finishing second and third. North became the first team since twelve sides comprised the VFL to reach the final Four with a percentage of less than 100. They actually had a percentage of ninety-nine point five—Carlton in 1957 were to make the finals with the same low figure.

Melbourne made a remarkable jump up from eleventh place the previous season to fill fourth place with eleven wins, closely pressed by Richmond, Essendon and Collingwood, all of whom were a bare game behind.

There was a sensation just after the ball had been bounced in the first semi-final when a Melbourne and a North Melbourne player exchanged blows and both were reported. The incident unsettled Melbourne more than their opponents, and the Demons did not really hit their straps until halfway through the second term when, attacking through Clarke—who was brilliant on the half-forward flank, they briefly hit the front. North hit back swiftly, however, and had a six-point lead at half-time.

For some reason best known to themselves, North began to play the man instead of the ball in the third term. Perhaps they had realised that the game was starting to slip away from them, but at any rate their tactics were amiss and Melbourne smashed through time and time again for five goals in the third and seven in the last quarter to record a convincing victory.

Footscray suffered a set-back prior to the start of the second semi-final when their inspiring captain/coach Charlie Sutton was forced out of the side by injury.

In a nervous opening to the game, Geelong looked good, despite a tricky breeze, but the strong Footscray defence—only 959 points had been scored against it in eighteen home and home games—was equal to the occasion. Towards the end, the tenacious Bulldogs scored three goals against the wind, which was a great effort considering that only one more was kicked at that end for the rest of the day.

When their turn with the wind came, the Bulldogs rushed on four goals six in thirteen minutes before Geelong's backline steadied and was able to hold Footscray out until half-time, at which stage the Bulldogs led by seventeen points. In the third, Footscray kept Geelong on the outer flank, forcing them to attack into a difficult crosswind—as a result, Geelong did not do as well as they should have, only managing to be level at the last change. With the advantage of the wind in the last, the Bulldogs were untroubled to win well, despite an inaccurate four goals nine for the term, and go on to their first ever VFL grand final.

There were several heavy showers in the first half of the following week's preliminary final, but Geelong started well to have two goals on the board before

Melbourne had scored. In fact, it took the Demons until seventeen minutes into the first term to score their first major. As rain poured down in the second, Goninon and Davis goaled. Clarke replied for the Demons, who then added another from a doubtful free, leaving them six points down at half-time.

The unlucky Demons had to replace McMahen (injured) at the interval, but a goal to Laidlaw enabled them to equalise. The pace started to hot up—there had been no rain for forty-five minutes and the ball was fairly dry. Turner goaled for the Cats with a towering sixty-yard punt—Johnson tapped down to Albiston for a Demon answering major. Soon after, Albiston and Johnson added further goals and the Demons had opened up a lead which Geelong were unable to overtake in the last thirty minutes. The Demons thus advanced to the grand final, a remarkable effort considering that they had been second last in 1953 and last in 1951.

Brilliant sunshine bathed the MCG for the grand final. Footscray began smartly in the first term, running rings around the slower Demons to kick six goals three to one goal four. Sutton, back in the side after injury, was the inspiration for the Bulldogs as he continually urged his charges to greater efforts. The Demons were first to goal, after eleven minutes play, but Collins goaled twice in reply for Footscray. Sutton, using weight freely, put Barassi down, and niggled his own opponent, Beckwith, to such an extent that Beckwith was moved away and Melbourne skipper Geoff Collins came down to mind the rugged Bulldog leader. Towards the end of the term, Footscray broke through again for quick goals to Kerr, Stevens and Collins and led by almost five goals at the first change.

The Bulldogs came forward again as the ball was bounced for the start of the second, and a brilliant chain of passes between Ross, Stevens and Kerr landed the ball with Collins, who kicked his fourth for the Bulldogs. Melbourne, starting to show a little system, hit back for goals to Barassi and Spencer as play began to get a little rough. After some see-sawing play, Mithen broke away for another Demon goal but Sutton, from a free, replied almost on the half-time bell for the Bulldogs.

The Bulldog dressing-room generated a tremendous air of confidence during the half-time break, and this confidence was increased by a goal to Stockman as soon as the third term began. A Melbourne error let Sutton in for another, the Bulldog's second in four minutes. Play swung backwards and forwards for the rest of the term, but further goals to Collins and Sutton close to the end of the term made the game safe for the Bulldogs, who had a three-quarter-time lead of over six goals.

The fanatical Bulldogs had no intention of throwing the game away, and kept the pressure well on in a torrid last term that brought them three more goals to the Demon's one and made them exactly double their opponents' score. Jack Collins brought his goals total to seven, equalling the grand final record, and threw away his chance of an eighth when, seconds before the bell, he secured and, seeing Gilmour on his own in the square, popped it over to him. An instant later the siren sounded and Gilmour threw the ball away to join team-mates and deliriously happy fans in celebrating Footscray's first VFL flag.

RESULTS

SEPTEMBER 4 — FIRST SEMI-FINAL

	1st	2nd	3rd	Final	
Melbourne	1 . 4	4 . 7	9 . 11	16 . 14	(110)
North Melbourne	3 . 4	5 . 7	7 . 12	11 . 14	(80)
	MCG		Umpire Barbour		
	Attendance 41,971		Gate £6,019		

BEST —	(Melb)	McGivern, Clarke, Case, Williams, Marquis, Beckwith, Arnold, Barassi
	(N. Melb)	Brady, Marchesi, Lawrence, Templar, Brooker
GOALS —	(Melb)	Clarke (6), Case (3), Albiston (3), McKenzie, Johnson, Collins, Barassi
	(N. Melb)	Templar (5), Aylett (3), Spencer, Grambeau, Brooker

SEPTEMBER 11 — SECOND SEMI-FINAL

	1st	2nd	3rd	Final	
Footscray	3 . 1	7 . 7	7 . 10	11 . 19	(85)
Geelong	4 . 5	4 . 8	7 . 10	8 . 14	(62)

MCG — Umpire Robinson
Attendance 64,686 — Gate £10,287

BEST —	(Foots)	Stevens, Henderson, Whitten, Ross, Reynolds, Box, Collins
	(Geel)	Hovey, B. Smith, Williams, Pianto, Tresize, Sharp, Davis
GOALS —	(Foots)	Collins (4), Kerr (2), Stevens (2), Duffy, Edwards, Gilmour
	(Geel)	Goninon (2), Davis, Palmer, Flanagan, McMahon, Tresize, Sharp

SEPTEMBER 18 — PRELIMINARY FINAL

	1st	2nd	3rd	Final	
Melbourne	1 . 1	3 . 3	7 . 5	10 . 7	(67)
Geelong	2 . 3	4 . 3	5 . 6	7 . 8	(50)

MCG — Umpire Jamieson
Attendance 50,985 — Gate £7,345

BEST —	(Melb)	D. Cordner, Williams, Melville, Arnold, Collins, Beckwith, Case
	(Geel)	Pianto, Tresize, Sharp, Renfrey, Turner, B. Smith
GOALS —	(Melb)	Clarke (3), Albiston (3), Barassi, R. Johnson, Laidlaw, Spencer
	(Geel)	Wiltshire (2), Rayson, Davis, Goninon, Turner, Tresize

SEPTEMBER 25 — GRAND FINAL

	1st	2nd	3rd	Final	
Footscray	6 . 3	8 . 5	12 . 9	15 . 12	(102)
Melbourne	1 . 4	4 . 6	6 . 7	7 . 9	(51)

MCG — Umpire McMurray
Attendance 80,897 — Gate £12,103

BEST —	(Foots)	Kerr, Bryden, Ross, Collins, Whitten, Reynolds, Box
	(Melb)	Cordner, Collins, Barassi, Mithen, McLean, Albiston
GOALS —	(Foots)	Collins (7), Sutton (3), Kerr, Stevens, Duffy, Reynolds, Stockman
	(Melb)	Clarke, Barassi, Spencer, Mithen, McLean, Johnson, Albiston

GRAND FINAL TEAMS

Footscray				
	B	W. Donald	H. Henderson	D. Bryden
	HB	A. Martin	E. Whitten	J. Gallagher
	C	R. McCarthy	D. Ross	D. Reynolds
	HF	R. Duffy	P. Box	R. Stockman
	F	B. Gilmour	J. Collins	C. Sutton (c)
	Ruck	H. Stevens	A. Edwards	J. Kerr
	Reserves	J. Nuttall	A. Abbey	
	Coach	C. Sutton		

1954-1955

Melbourne	B	J. Beckwith	L. Arnold	K. Christie
	HB	D. Williams	N. McMahen	G. Collins (c)
	C	I. McLean	K. Melville	R. Lane
	HF	L. Mithen	G. McGivern	G. Case
	F	K. Albiston	N. Clarke	R. Johnson
	Ruck	D. Cordner	R. Barassi	S. Spencer
	Reserves	F. Adams	B. Dixon	
	Coach	N. Smith		

1955

Melbourne, with ten successive wins to start the season, continued to show their previous year's form, but Footscray slipped, and, although winning twelve games, eventually finished fifth, 0.06 per cent outside the final Four.

The actual fight for the Four and positions therein was extremely exciting. Melbourne (fifteen wins) was on top, followed by Collingwood and Geelong, with fourteen wins each. By dropping the last game against Carlton by six points, the Cats missed the double chance. Fourth team Essendon and fifth team Footscray were both on twelve wins, separated by less than one per cent, the closest margin by which any team had ever missed the Finals. Had Hawthorn got one goal more against Essendon in the last game or North Melbourne one goal less against Footscray, the Bulldogs would have finished fourth.

Injury-hit Geelong surprised Essendon in the first semi-final. The Cats, literally yards too fast for their opponents, got on top after less than fifteen minutes of the first quarter, and never looked back.

They booted four goals before Essendon got their first from a free just before half-time. The Dons, with their trump-cards Hutchison and Gill well held, just could not get into the game until late in the last quarter when Peucker got two goals and Fox three to enable the Dons to draw within eight points of Geelong. The Cats steadied, however, and held their lead until the final siren.

In mud, slush and rain, Melbourne, whose superior fitness told in a torrid last quarter, defeated Collingwood in the second semi-final. The Magpies, captained by Neil Mann after the retirement of Lou Richards on the eve of the finals, put up a good performance, however, and were not disgraced. Considering the low scores, the turning point in the game probably came as early as the second term when the scores were equal, two goals four each.

Collingwood defender Neville Waller was incorrectly penalised for throwing the ball, and Melbourne rover Spencer goaled from the free. On the bounce, Melbourne stormed upfield again for the same player to kick another. This took a lot of the steam out of the Magpies, and thereafter they were a struggling side. Spencer, with five of Melbourne's eight goals for the game, gave a superlative display of accurate goal-kicking with the sodden ball.

Despite the loss of the mercurial W. Twomey for the preliminary final, Collingwood had a good win over Geelong to enable them to have another tilt at Melbourne in the grand final. Mann helped M. Twomey to Collingwood's first goal within thirty seconds of the start, and later added two more from his own boot. The Magpies outplayed the Cats in the first term, and were given even more confidence when Rose rammed home a major from sixty-five yards out in the second. Geelong, however, fought back, wiping off nineteen points in seventeen minutes in the third term before Weideman goaled for Collingwood. In the last the Magpies scored four quick goals early, and although the Cats themselves scored four goals in the last ten minutes—three to O'Connell who had come on as a reserve—they were unable to overtake the Collingwood lead.

The grand final was almost a repeat of the second semi-final, although the day was not as wet. Collingwood were first into attack for a goal and had their second on the board within ten minutes. Melbourne were slow to start but soon began to get on top in the ruck and the two rovers were also beating their opponents. In fact, on the day, the Magpies lost in most of the key positions, notably centre-half-forward and full-forward. Both wingers, from whom the Magpies expected big things, failed to impress.

McMahen struck a telling blow for the Demons early in the first term when he beautifully bumped Rose just as the Collingwood rover disposed of the ball. Weideman goaled from an unwarranted free downfield, but Rose was not the same player afterwards.

The Demons should have sealed the game in the second term, which they dominated, but one goal seven from ten shots told its own tale. Consequently, the Magpies were able to stay within reach of the Melbourne score, and when Smale goaled halfway through the third term and Rose added another almost on the siren, they were only seven points behind.

Immediately the last term began, Jones goaled to reduce the deficit to a single point before the physical strength of Melbourne finally won out. The Demons took complete control from then on—the Magpies did not score again, while Melbourne added four goals three to convincingly win their seventh VFL flag.

The memorable incident of the finals series occurred just before the bell. Adams, Melbourne's nineteenth man, was called onto the field and raced to intercept Collingwood winger, Des Healy, who failed to see him. Both players collided at a fearful pace, were hurtled yards apart and lay unconscious on the turf as play continued. Both were carried off, still unconscious, as fans worked out that Adams' participation in the grand final had lasted about fifteen seconds. This was probably the most sensational crash ever seen on a football field—Healy had his nose broken in five places and his skull fractured, the injuries eventually hastening his retirement. Adams was unconscious for forty-five minutes after the game, but suffered no lasting injuries from the clash. He went on to play another ten years with the Demons.

RESULTS

AUGUST 27 — FIRST SEMI-FINAL

	1st	2nd	3rd	Final	
Geelong	3 . 1	6 . 4	7 . 6	9 . 7	(61)
Essendon	0 . 2	1 . 4	2 . 7	7 . 11	(53)

MCG
Attendance 68,109

Umpire Beitzel
Gate £10,666

BEST —	(Geel)	Tresize, Pianto, O'Neill, Sharp, Renfrey, J. McMahon, Borrack
	(Ess)	McConnell, Heenan, Sewell, Harrington, Bigelow, Carstairs
GOALS —	(Geel)	Tresize (2), Pianto (2), Sutcliffe, Renfrey, McMahon, Rayson, M. Goggin
	(Ess)	Fox (3), Peucker (3), Sewell

SEPTEMBER 3 — SECOND SEMI-FINAL

	1st	2nd	3rd	Final	
Melbourne	2 . 4	4 . 7	7 . 8	8 . 8	(56)
Collingwood	1 . 3	4 . 5	6 . 7	6 . 9	(45)

MCG
Attendance 59,015

Umpire McMurray
Gate £8,960

BEST —	(Melb)	Spencer (B.O.G.), Melville, McLean Williams, McMahen, McGivern
	(Col)	Mann, Sharp, Kingston, Lucas, Waller, Healey, Merrett, Rose
GOALS —	(Melb)	Spencer (5), R. Johnson (2), McKenzie
	(Col)	Mann, Weideman, M. Twomey, Smale, Gooch, Rose

SEPTEMBER 10 — PRELIMINARY FINAL

	1st	2nd	3rd	Final	
Collingwood	5 . 1	8 . 4	10 . 9	14 . 12	(96)
Geelong	3 . 3	5 . 3	9 . 6	13 . 6	(84)

MCG
Attendance 70,430

Umpire Beitzel
Gate £11,246

BEST —	(Col)	Lucas, Mann, Sharp, Kingston, Tuck, Hamilton, R. Richards
	(Geel)	Williams, Hovey, Gazzard, Borrack, Renfrey, Pianto, Cameron
GOALS —	(Col)	Weideman (3), Batchelor (2), Mann (2), M. Twomey (2), Rose (2), R. Richards, Jones, Parker
	(Geel)	O'Connell (3), Pianto (2), Rayson (2), Sutcliffe (2), McMahen (2), M. Goggin, Beardsley

SEPTEMBER 17 — GRAND FINAL

	1st	2nd	3rd	Final	
Melbourne	2 . 3	3 . 10	4 . 13	8 . 16	(64)
Collingwood	2 . 2	2 . 5	4 . 6	5 . 6	(36)

MCG
Attendance 88,053

Umpire Beitzel
Gate £13,731

BEST —	(Melb)	Cordner, Barassi, Melville, McLean, McMahen, Marquis, T. Johnson
	(Col)	Hamilton, Lucas, Mann, Rose, Sharp, Tuck, Healey
GOALS —	(Melb)	Clarke (3), Ridley (3), McKenzie, Laidlaw
	(Col)	Weideman (2), Rose, Smale, Jones

1955-1956

GRAND FINAL TEAMS

Melbourne	B	J. Beckwith	P. Marquis	Trev. Johnson
	HB	D. Williams	G. McGivern	N. McMahen (c)
	C	I. McLean	K. Melville	G. Case
	HF	L. Mithen	C. Laidlaw	R. McKenzie
	F	I. Ridley	N. Clarke	R. Johnson
	Ruck	Denis Cordner	R. Barassi	S. Spencer
	Reserves	F. Adams	T. Gleeson	
	Coach	N. Smith		
Collingwood	B	L. Sharp	J. Hamilton	N. Waller
	HB	R. Kingston	F. Tuck	P. Lucas
	C	T. Merrett	J. Parker	D. Healey
	HF	M. Weideman	K. Smale	W. Jones
	F	R. Rose	K. Batchelor	M. Twomey
	Ruck	N. Mann (c)	A. Gooch	R. Richards
	Reserves	M. Hickey	K. Kupsch	
	Coach	A. Kyne		

1956

The Demons, going from strength to strength, again proved to be the season's top dogs, finishing with sixteen wins to gain first place on the ladder. Collingwood and Geelong (both thirteen wins) were second and third, followed by Footscray (eleven wins) who knocked Carlton out of fourth place with a seventeen-point win over them in the last game. The Blues missed out by two premiership points. A further two points back in sixth place was Essendon.

The Footscray-Geelong first semi-final was a low-scoring but exciting clash. Footscray spent the better part of the second and third terms getting back to level pegging after Geelong had jumped away brilliantly in the first term to kick four goals two to one goal three, and they trailed by only two points at three-quarter-time.

Turning point for the Cats came in the third term when team-mates Davis and Sharp collided heavily, and the Bulldogs raced upfield for a vital goal while both players lay stunned on the ground. To make matters worse, Sharp had to be replaced at three-quarter-time, having broken his jaw, and for the first time the Bulldogs gained control in the ruck, Sharp having previously held sway.

Neither team scored a goal in the last, but the football was tremendously exciting with the scores level for fifteen minutes. Finally, Footscray scored successive behinds from Cross, Reynolds and Rawson to nose ahead by three points before a hurried snap by Rayson (Geelong) bounced over the head of the Bulldog's Ron Porta and through for a behind. A goal would have won the game, so Footscray sneaked home by the narrow margin of two points.

A swirling wind upset both teams in the second semi-final and, after a tremendously even first three quarters, Melbourne went right away at the end to convincingly defeat Collingwood. The Magpies, despite the blanketing of most of their forward line, were able to fight their way to a one-point lead at half-time, and did very well to hold the confident Demons. Especially after a magnificent sixty-five-yard goal by McMahen, playing on from the half-back line, had got the Demons' tails up in the second quarter.

Melbourne had to replace McGivern (injured) at half-time. Sandral came on as a reserve, and the team was re-shuffled. The moves seemed to help—Melbourne began to click, with Sandral coming right into the game on the half-forward flank. Both teams played brilliantly in the third term for five goals each, and Collingwood still clung to their one-point lead at the last change.

There was a ding-dong struggle for the first half of the last term before Ridley and Spencer goaled for Melbourne. Two goals down, the fanatical Magpies attacked for ten minutes but were rewarded with only four points. Just before the bell, a great dash by Ridley landed the ball with Johnson, who goaled to increase Melbourne's winning margin to sixteen points.

Champion full-back Herb Henderson came back to the Footscray preliminary final team after being out for seven weeks, but was surprisingly named on the half-forward flank.

The Magpies began brilliantly with six goals one in the first term, aided by great play at full-forward by Smale. Footscray, on the other hand, struggled and it took them ten minutes to hold their first mark of the game and another seven minutes for Stevens to score first goal. They certainly had all the play in the second term though, and held the Magpies scoreless, but two goals eight for the quarter was match-losing football. (In fact, the Bulldogs kicked almost as poorly in the last quarter, one goal six.)

A point down at half-time, Collingwood made changes. Greve, moved from the backline to second rover, scored a great sixty-yard goal which spurred the team on. Merrett, down in the first half, began to get on top and the Magpies, receiving great drive from his wing, booted five goals four to one goal one for the term and had a big three-quarter-time lead, which they increased in the last, helped by Footscray's inaccuracy. Difference between the two sides was Magpie full-forward Ken Smale, who kicked with deadly accuracy to score eight goals one from nine shots.

Collingwood lined up unchanged for the grand final, whilst Melbourne made only one alteration, replacing the injured McGivern. The ground was in good condition, although there were muddy patches at both centre-half-forward positions. A record crowd of 115,802 crowded into the MCG for the game.

The Magpies were into attack early, and a chain of passes was capped off by a goal to Serong within three minutes of the start. Webb snapped an answering goal for the Demons but Collingwood, making the running, broke through for further goals and twenty minutes into the term, they led three goals three to one goal. But the ominous feature for the Magpies was that Smale—deadly accurate against Footscray—had already missed two fairly easy shots. Right on time-on, Johnson goaled for Melbourne, who then continued to attack until quarter-time but were able to score only three behinds.

The Demons, now on top in the ruck and beginning to take control all around the ground, began the second term with a goal to Webb thirty seconds after the bounce. Mithen was brilliant for Melbourne, and the Demons played through him but were badly off target before Spencer picked up from a ball-up in the goal-square and snapped accurately. Soon after, a Collingwood error let him in for another, and Barassi also added to the mounting Melbourne goal tally. Collingwood's first score of the term came up with time-on about to start—Beckwith dropped the ball and Turner picked up and slammed it through. Play began to roughen up as Spencer, with a glorious drop, answered for Melbourne. Hedt (Collingwood) went down and was carried off—ruckman Kupsch came on and took his place on the wing.

Twenty points down at the interval, the Magpies lined up with a re-cast side for the second half. Again, however, it was Melbourne who did all the attacking. Goals came from Spencer and Johnson before Collingwood belatedly went forward for Smale to kick accurately. Rymer (Collingwood) gave away his second costly free—and Barassi goaled. Moments later, Bob Johnson added another from sixty yards out to give the Demons an unbeatable forty-point lead at the last change.

Further positional alterations failed to help the Magpies. Melbourne, with pace to burn, stormed forward for Spencer to goal twice, the second time after the brilliant Adams had outpaced four Collingwood men to gain possession. Johnson added another, and then Webb, striking a purple patch, scored his third, fourth and fifth in quick succession. When the Magpies did struggle forward, they were off target until W. Twomey goaled from a free after twenty-four minutes. Ridley immediately replied for the Demons, who had proved their right to the 1956 premiership with a great last-quarter burst of seven goals three to Collingwood's one goal six.

RESULTS

AUGUST 25 — FIRST SEMI-FINAL

	1st	2nd	3rd	Final	
Footscray	1 . 3	4 . 6	5 . 8	5 . 13	(43)
Geelong	4 . 2	6 . 2	6 . 4	6 . 5	(41)

MCG — Umpire Nash
Attendance 79,402 — Gate £13,316

BEST — (Foots) Stockman, Porta, Gallagher, Whitten, Kerr, Cross
(Geel) Davis, Smith, Sharp, O'Neill, Pianto, Haygarth

GOALS — (Foots) Cross (4), Collins
(Geel) Wooller (2), O'Connell, Rayson, Bullen, Sutcliffe

SEPTEMBER 1 — SECOND SEMI-FINAL

	1st	2nd	3rd	Final	
Melbourne	1 . 4	3 . 6	8 . 9	11 . 14	(80)
Collingwood	1 . 4	3 . 7	8 . 10	8 . 16	(64)

MCG — Umpire Beitzel
Attendance 91,480 — Gate £15,387

BEST — (Melb) Spencer, R. Johnson, Cordner, Dixon, Barassi, Laidlaw
(Col) Tuck, Weideman, K. Turner, W. Twomey, Gabelich, Kingston

GOALS — (Melb) R. Johnson (3), Spencer (3), McMahen, Barassi, Sandral, Laidlaw, Ridley
(Col) Weideman (3), Mann (2), K. Turner (2), Kupsch

1956

SEPTEMBER 8 — PRELIMINARY FINAL

	1st	2nd	3rd	Final	
Collingwood	6 . 1.	6 . 1	11 . 5	15 . 6	(96)
Footscray	3 . 0	5 . 8	6 . 9	7 . 15	(57)

MCG — Umpire Nash
Attendance 94,104 — Gate £15,987

BEST — (Col) Sullivan, Smale, W. Twomey, Mann, Jones, Tuck
(Foots) Stevens, Whitten, Ross, Reynolds, Gallagher, Rawson

GOALS — (Col) Smale (8), Mann (2), Merrett, Rymer, K. Turner, Greve, Jones
(Foots) Stevens (3), Cross (2), Duffy, Gilmore

SEPTEMBER 15 — GRAND FINAL

	1st	2nd	3rd	Final	
Melbourne	2 . 4	6 . 11	10 . 16	17 . 19	(121)
Collingwood	3 . 3	4 . 3	5 . 6	6 . 12	(48)

MCG — Umpire Nash
Attendance 115,802 (record) — Gate £19,718 (record)

BEST — (Melb) Spencer, Barassi, Adams, Cordner, Beckwith, Melville, Dixon, Mithen, Webb
(Col) Tuck, Serong, Jones, Mann, Weideman, Waller

GOALS — (Melb) Spencer (5), Webb (5), R. Johnson (3), Barassi (3), Ridley
(Col) Smale, Serong, Turner, W. Twomey, Jones, Greve

GRAND FINAL TEAMS

Melbourne	B	J. Beckwith	P. Marquis	Trev. Johnson
	HB	D. Williams	N. McMahen (c)	K. Carroll
	C	B. Dixon	K. Melville	F. Adams
	HF	J. Sandral	C. Laidlaw	L. Mithen
	F	R. Johnson	A. Webb	I. Ridley
	Ruck	Denis Cordner	R. Barassi	S. Spencer
	Reserves	T. Gleeson	R. Lane	
	Coach	N. Smith		
Collingwood	B	L. Sharp	H. Sullivan	N. Waller
	HB	P. Lucas	F. Tuck	R. Kingston
	C	K. Hedt	W. Twomey	T. Merrett
	HF	K. Turner	M. Weideman	W. Serong
	F	N. Mann (c)	K. Smale	R. Greve
	Ruck	R. Gabelich	W. Rymer	W. Jones
	Reserves	J. Hamilton	K. Kupsch	
	Coach	A. E. Kyne		

1957

After one of the most evenly contested seasons for years, Melbourne (twelve wins, five losses and a tie) topped the ladder for the fourth year in succession. The fifty premiership points which put them there, however, was the lowest total since there had been twelve teams in the VFL (Richmond, Essendon and Fitzroy led the list with forty-four points in 1944, but there were only sixteen games that year.)

Further evidence of the evenness of the competition was that Geelong, last, had twenty-two points, and this was the best total by the wooden-spooners during the same period. Only four of the twelve teams had percentages of more than 100—another record low—and Carlton (eleven wins) became only the second team in history to make the finals with a percentage of under 100. They sneaked in with ninety-nine and a half per cent, the same figure as that with which North Melbourne had struggled into the Four in 1954.

Melbourne was the only finalist of 1956 to again make the Four. Most notable newcomer was Hawthorn, making their first such appearance since joining the VFL in 1925. They finished third with eleven wins, a two-point loss to Footscray in the last game costing them second place. Essendon, with a big win over Carlton in the last game, took second place from Hawthorn on percentage. Collingwood and Footscray finished fifth and sixth respectively, six points outside the Four.

Carlton seemed good bets to beat the inexperienced Hawthorn in the first semi-final, despite the Blues' recent poor form; but the fanatical Hawks played brilliantly to boot five goals three to two points in the first quarter. They completely bewildered the Blues by running four rovers, but Carlton's forwards missed three absolute 'sitter' goals during the quarter.

Scoring was even during the second term, although the Blues' inaccuracy was costing them dearly. By half-time, they trailed by almost five goals.

During the break, a tremendous hail-storm hit the MCG, completely saturating the oval. The conditions after half-time made the Hawthorn lead worth twice as much, but Carlton fought back brilliantly despite the sodden ground. With Hawthorn concentrating on holding their lead in the third term, a couple of quick goals by Carlton could have panicked them. And the Blues certainly had chances, but they consistently frittered them away. Despite their blunders, however, they struggled to within seventeen points of Hawthorn halfway through the last quarter before one of their forwards dropped an easy mark in the goal-square. The Hawks were able to clear the ball, and that lucky break gave them time to steady when a goal may have had them in trouble. They were able to go on to win well by twenty-three points.

The confident Melbourne—perhaps they were over-confident—went down to a shock defeat at the hands of Essendon in the second semi-final. After holding the Demons when they were kicking with the wind in the first term, the Dons overwhelmed them in the second with a magnificent burst of nine goals three to two points and led at half-time by forty-eight points.

Positional changes in the second half, which was played in pouring rain, brought Melbourne back into the game, but shocking inaccuracy (four goals ten in the third term) cost them dearly. However, they were able to whittle Essendon's eight-goal lead to a mere ten points with ten minutes to go, but that was the extent of their effort. Essendon was able to steady, and hold on to win by sixteen points. Melbourne had played particularly badly, but it was a measure of their ability that had they not had four posters in their score of eight goals nineteen, they might have won the game.

Hawthorn, in the preliminary final, battled against a strong wind in the first term, and were quite satisfied to hold Melbourne to a three-goal lead. They expected to take control when their turn with the wind came in the second quarter, but such was not the case. Instead, the Demons scored seven goals straight against the wind with a magnificent effort which virtually won them the game, leaving Hawthorn in an impossible position at half-time. Despite many positional changes, the Hawks were unable to make any leeway, and Melbourne eventually almost doubled their score, winning twenty-two goals twelve to eleven goals ten.

It was a different Melbourne side which met Essendon in the grand final, to the side which fumbled its way to defeat in the second semi-final. John Gill's hit out from the opening bounce was intercepted by Mithen, who drove to Barassi for Melbourne's first goal in thirteen seconds. The Demons went right on with the job to snap two more within ten minutes of the start, and six for the term, against the wind. Their method of attack was skilfully planned and executed. The forward pockets were literally hugging the fence, but immediately the chance came, they streamed into goal, using devastating handball. On at least six occasions during the game, the Essendon defenders were drawn out of position to allow Melbourne forwards to run into an open goal. Ridley, too, proved an opportunist around goals, and kicked three off the ground.

Holding a six-goal lead at half-time, the Demons maintained their lead at the final change, and ran away with the game by adding five goals three to five points in the last to win effortlessly by sixty-one points. It was probably the best win of their hat-trick of premierships, as they had to survive a preliminary final and not have the week's rest as in 1955-56. In addition, the Demons had two stars—Beckwith and Adams—carrying injuries which would normally have kept them out for a couple of weeks. Five others—Lord, Marquis, Dixon, Trev. Johnson and Mithen—finished the game with bad injuries, and yet another, Carroll, had to be replaced in the second quarter after tearing a thigh muscle.

RESULTS

SEPTEMBER 1 — FIRST SEMI-FINAL

	1st	2nd	3rd	Final	
Hawthorn	5 . 3	7 . 6	9 . 7	10 . 11	(71)
Carlton	0 . 2	2 . 7	4 . 9	6 . 12	(48)

MCG	Umpire Nash
Attendance 69,455	Gate £22,442

BEST — (Haw) Edwards, Arthur, Falconer, Magennis, M. Young, Cabble
(Carl) Ferry, James, Zeunert, Webster, Comben, Kerr, Hands, Beasy, Nicholls, K. Clarke

GOALS — (Haw) Cabble (3), Arthur (2), M. Young (2), Simmonds (2), Falconer
(Carl) Brereton (2), Hands, Burke, D. Nicholls, Beasy

SEPTEMBER 7 — SECOND SEMI-FINAL

	1st	2nd	3rd	Final	
Essendon	1 . 3	10 . 6	11 . 9	12 . 11	(83)
Melbourne	2 . 4	2 . 6	6 . 16	8 . 19	(67)

MCG	Umpire Nash
Attendance 70,232	Gate £22,464

BEST — (Ess) Pascoe, Gill, Leek, Towner, Mitchell, Clarke
(Melb) McLean, Beckwith, R. Johnson, Barassi, Williams, Case

GOALS — (Ess) Leek (3), Pascoe (3), Birt (2), Booth, Hebbard, Burgess, Fox
(Melb) R. Johnson (2), Tunbridge (2), Fenton-Smith, Case, Webb, Ridley

SEPTEMBER 14 — PRELIMINARY FINAL

	1st	2nd	3rd	Final	
Melbourne	4 . 4	11 . 4	16 . 9	22 . 12	(144)
Hawthorn	1 . 4	3 . 8	9 . 9	11 . 10	(76)

MCG	Umpire Nash
Attendance 74,090	Gate £23,364

BEST — (Melb) Ridley, Williams, Dixon, R. Johnson, Barassi, Wilson
(Haw) Peck, Edwards, Woodley, Simmonds, O'Brien, Hughes

GOALS — (Melb) Webb (4), Adams (3), Tunbridge (3), Case (2), Ridley (2), R. Johnson (2), T. Johnson (2), Barassi (2), Williams, McLean
(Haw) Peck (4), G. Young (2), Arthur, Cabble, O'Brien, Falconer, Simmonds

SEPTEMBER 21 — GRAND FINAL

	1st	2nd	3rd	Final	
Melbourne	6 . 2	9 . 9	12 . 11	17 . 14	(116)
Essendon	2 . 3	4 . 4	7 . 8	7 . 13	(55)

MCG	Umpire Nash
Attendance 100,324	Gate £29,316

BEST — (Melb) Barassi (B.O.G.), R. Johnson, Fenton-Smith, Lord, Williams, Ridley, Dixon, McLean, Webb
(Ess) Clarke, Shearman, Mitchell, Leek, Towner, Birt

GOALS — (Melb) Barassi (5), Ridley (4), Webb (3), R. Johnson (2), Tunbridge (2), Case
(Ess) Gallagher (3), Birt, Gill, Hebbard, Clarke

GRAND FINAL TEAMS

Melbourne	B	J. Beckwith (c)	P. Marquis	R. Fenton-Smith
	HB	K. Carroll	J. Lord	D. Williams
	C	I. McLean	L. Mithen	B. Dixon
	HF	G. Case	Trev. Johnson	G. Tunbridge
	F	I. Ridley	A. Webb	R. Barassi
	Ruck	R. Johnson	C. Wilson	F. Adams
	Reserves	I. Thorogood	P. Brenchley	
	Coach	N. Smith		
Essendon	B	R. Suter	J. Knowles	M. Pascoe
	HB	R. Shearman	J. Gamble	J. Towner
	C	G. Sewell	J. Clarke	R. Burgess
	HF	C. Hebbard	R. Fox	S. Booth
	F	J. Birt	F. Gallagher	G. Leek
	Ruck	J. Gill	H. Mitchell	W. Hutchison (c)
	Reserves	J. Heenan	L. Maloney	
	Coach	R. S. Reynolds		

1958

Melbourne continued on their winning way in 1958, the centenary year of football, finishing on top of the ladder for the fourth year in succession with fifteen wins, three games ahead of second team Collingwood. The Magpies and third team Fitzroy were separated only by percentage, with North Melbourne (eleven wins) sneaking into the Four a game ahead of 1957 runners-up, Essendon. Fitzroy's improvement had been most remarkable, as they had finished second last the previous season.

It was wet for only the second time during the season on the day of the first semi-final. Fitzroy, after kicking three goals in the first ten minutes, failed to make proper use of the wind for the rest of the term, but their backmen did a great job to hold the tenacious North out in the second term.

In the third, Fitzroy winger Aston went down and, while trainers were attending him, North rammed on two goals, helping them to an eighteen-point lead at the last change. Fitzroy, however, fought back splendidly in the last quarter. Aided by a strong southerly breeze which had blown up, and sparked by Abrahams (moved to centre-half-forward) they put on four goals to North's one and looked to have the game won. With only minutes to go there occurred one of those 'incidents' which seem to be talked about for many years afterwards. Aylett (North Melbourne) flattened Williams (Fitzroy) on the centre-wing. Williams, almost unconscious, was given a free kick and helped to his feet to take it. Groggily, he passed to Gale, who marked at centre-half-forward. But Umpire Barbour took the ball from Gale and made Williams take the kick again, as he had not kicked over the mark. The second kick was covered by the North players, and wingman Dwyer's kick found Teasdale, who goaled from sixty yards out to put North ahead by four points. That was the last kick of the day, for the bell rang as the ball was bounced in the centre. Umpire Barbour's decision, whilst technically correct, was blasted by Fitzroy supporters, who protested that their side had been denied the penalty which the free kick was meant to allow.

A top-heavy Collingwood team went down to humiliating defeat at the hands of their 'hoodoo' side, Melbourne, in the second semi-final. The slow-moving Magpies were unable to cope with the pace of the Melbourne men, and they misused the vigour which, if properly applied, may have slowed their opponents down.

The pattern of the play was set early when Melbourne forwards goaled four times in the first term by running into a more or less open goal, and another came when Tunbridge was foolishly manhandled. As they were to do in the grand final, Collingwood had Harrison shadow Barassi all day, but the Demon champion refused to be 'got-in' and turned in a valuable game. Melbourne were untroubled to win by over seven goals—the Magpies in fact scored only four goals for the entire game, and all four came from snaps from the pack.

The Magpies made wholesale changes for the preliminary final, changing every line and including four new men, one of whom was playing his first full game. Surprising North early, Collingwood did all the attacking and after five successive behinds found the target to boot five goals to North's one before the first term ended. North, prepared for Collingwood's vigour, were at a loss to cope when the Magpies, displaying their best form since the memorable Queen's Birthday game against Melbourne in June, concentrated wholly on the ball. The Magpies, seemingly having gained yards of pace in only seven days, had a strong grip on the game by three-quarter-time, after North had kicked a match-losing one goal nine in the second term and had then been unable to stop a Magpie third term onslaught. Big Collingwood ruckman Gabelich, combining brilliantly with Reeves and Sullivan on the last line of defence, disheartened the Northerners when he singlehandedly stopped four attacks with brilliant high marks in the last part of the third quarter. With three goals early in the last, the Magpies sealed the game, and even a last-minute burst of five goals, through Schofield, B. Martyn and Aylett, could not get North any closer than twenty points by the end of the game.

The stage was now set for one of the most memorable grand finals of all time. Melbourne, chasing their fourth successive flag, had Case and Laidlaw unfit and brought in Carroll and Brenchley, the latter for his first game since the second match of the season. Collingwood, endeavouring to stop Melbourne equalling their proud record of four successive premierships*, lined up unchanged, although Tuck (captain) and W. Twomey were still absentees. There was a sensation before the game when the VFL announced that players' numbers would be changed—a local newspaper had violated copyright by printing the numbers. The move caused consternation to players and confusion to spectators.

The game began in wet and sloppy conditions, following heavy rain. It looked as if Melbourne—the hottest favourites for many, many years—were going to have no trouble when they booted five goals one to two goals two in the first term. All the Melbourne stars were firing—Mithen in the centre was dominating, and Barassi and Johnson were well on top in the ruck.

* 1927-8-9-30.

Until this point the game had been rugged, but no more so than any wet day game. But in the second term the crowd began to sense the unbelievable—the Melbourne champions, against the hard-tackling, hard-hitting Magpies, were starting to show definite signs that they did not relish the going. The Collingwood players began to sense it, too, and Weideman and Harrison systematically roughed up the potential Melbourne matchwinners, notably Barassi and Mithen, who seemed to be involved in almost every flare-up. Two goals in two minutes in the teeming rain by rover Bennett sparked the Magpies, and they caught fire and raced to a two-point lead at half-time, something that would have been thought impossible fifty minutes before. The Magpies' matchwinning moves—Fellowes into the ruck, Delanty from wing to centre-half-back and Rose in on the back flank—had improved the lumbering second semi-final side no end.

An explosive third quarter, featuring fights aplenty, saw Melbourne slip out of the game. Too many Melbourne players concentrated on 'evening-up', whilst the Magpies—with Weideman and Harrison the main instigators—shrewdly began the 'incidents' and left the rattled Demons to finish them. Then they themselves concentrated on getting the ball. The Magpies kicked five goals three to two points in the term, and the crowd was stunned when the teams sat down for the final break with the scoreboard, barely visible through the misty rain, showing Collingwood twelve goals nine, Melbourne seven goals six.

That thirty minutes in the third term sealed the result of the 1958 premiership. Although able to score only one behind in the last term, the Magpies, aided by brilliant defence from Sullivan and Reeves, limited the Demons to a mere two goals four, and it was obvious well before the end that the Demons' chance of equalling the coveted Magpie record had gone, perhaps forever. When the siren went with the 100/1 outsiders three goals ahead, the Magpies' supporters exploded in a delirious demonstration of appreciation for the great performance of their side—the Magpies' thirteenth, and probably greatest, premiership victory.

RESULTS

AUGUST 30 — FIRST SEMI-FINAL

	1st	2nd	3rd	Final	
North Melbourne	2 . 2	4 . 6	8 . 8	10 . 10	(70)
Fitzroy	3 . 3	4 . 7	5 . 8	9 . 12	(66)

MCG — Umpire Barbour

Attendance 68,213 — Gate £23,045

BEST — (N. Melb) Brady, Aylett, Eastmure, Doolan, Edwards, Mantello, Teasdale, English

(Fitz) Gale, Vernon, Goodger, Campbell, Aston, McKenzie, Clark, Henderson

GOALS — (N. Melb) Waddington (3), Schofield (2), Aylett (2), Dugdale, McMahon, Teasdale

(Fitz) Abrahams (2), Knight (2), Ongarello, Clark, Weigard, Campbell, Aston

SEPTEMBER 6 — SECOND SEMI-FINAL

	1st	2nd	3rd	Final	
Melbourne	5 . 0	6 . 4	8 . 5	11 . 12	(78)
Collingwood	1 . 0	2 . 4	3 . 8	4 . 9	(33)

		MCG Attendance 77,350	Umpire Nash Gate £24,104
BEST —	(Melb)	Fenton-Smith, McLean, Williams, Beckwith, Mithen, R. Johnson, Ridley	
	(Col)	Turner, Reeves, Serong, Gabelich, Merrett, Sullivan, Smale	
GOALS —	(Melb)	Adams (3), Webb (2), Ridley (2), Barassi (2), R. Johnson, Tunbridge	
	(Col)	Merrett (2), Gabelich, Weideman	

SEPTEMBER 13 — PRELIMINARY FINAL

	1st	2nd	3rd	Final	
Collingwood	5 . 5	6 . 5	11 . 8	14 . 12	(96)
North Melbourne	1 . 1	2 . 10	4 . 11	10 . 16	(76)

MCG — Umpire Barbour
Attendance 77,656 — Gate £25,132

BEST —	(Col)	Reeves, Gabelich, Serong, Sullivan, Turner, Henderson, Gray
	(N. Melb)	Eastmure, Aylett, Brady, Edwards, Dugdale, Doolan, K. Dean (till injured)
GOALS —	(Col)	Brewer (4), Weideman (2), Merrett (2), Serong (2), Smale, Fellowes, Turner, Bennett
	(N. Melb)	Aylett (3), Dugdale (3), Schofield (2), Brady, Waddington

SEPTEMBER 20 — GRAND FINAL

	1st	2nd	3rd	Final	
Collingwood	2 . 2	7 . 6	12 . 9	12 . 10	(82)
Melbourne	5 . 1	7 . 4	7 . 6	9 . 10	(64)

MCG — Umpire Nash
Attendance 97,956 — Gate £25,588

BEST —	(Col)	Merrett, Fellowes, Serong, Reeves, Gabelich, Bennett, Turner, Lucas, Weideman, Harrison
	(Melb)	Beckwith, Williams, R. Johnson, Adams, McLean, Tunbridge, Ridley, Thorogood
GOALS —	(Col)	Weideman (2), Brewer (2), Beers (2), Bennett (2), Merrett (2), M. Twomey, Fellowes
	(Melb)	Barassi (2), Adams (2), Brenchley, R. Johnson, McLean, Ridley, Crompton

GRAND FINAL TEAMS

Collingwood	B	R. Reeves	H. Sullivan	R. Gabelich
	HB	K. Rose	M. Delanty	P. Lucas
	C	B. Gray	J. Henderson	K. Turner
	HF	B. Beers	M. Weideman (c)	W. Serong
	F	M. Twomey	I. Brewer	K. Bennett
	Ruck	G. Fellowes	B. Harrison	T. Merrett
	Reserves	R. Greve	K. Smale	
	Coach	A. Kyne		
Melbourne	B	J. Beckwith (c)	P. Marquis	C. Wilson
	HB	K. Carroll	D. Williams	I. Thorogood
	C	B. Dixon	L. Mithen	I. McLean
	HF	G. Tunbridge	T. Johnson	P. Brenchley
	F	R. Johnson	A. Webb	F. Adams
	Ruck	R. Fenton-Smith	R. Barassi	I. Ridley
	Reserves	N. Crompton	T. Gleeson	
	Coach	N. Smith		

1959

After reaching the dizzy heights of a premiership in 1958, Collingwood stunned the football world by losing their first five games in 1959, the first time such a fate had befallen the previous season's premiers, although South Melbourne (runners-up in 1945) lost the first four games in 1946.

The Magpies, however, staged a magnificent fight-back to win twelve of the remaining thirteen games, and they actually finished in third place, a game ahead of Essendon who, in turn, were half a game ahead of Fitzroy (fifth) and a full game ahead of North (sixth).

Melbourne was again the form team of the season, finishing on top of the ladder with thirteen wins and a draw, but Carlton was the big improver and jumped up the ladder to second place, two points behind the Demons.

The Magpies proved no match for the younger and faster Essendon side in the first semi-final. The Dons, after an even first half, got well on top in the ruck and across the centre-line, while Shelton at centre-half-back had the call over Weideman. The Magpie captain was held kickless in the second and third quarters and, when Collingwood moved him to full-forward, Shelton was moved back with him. Without Weideman's influence, the Magpie forward line struggled, and the Dons were able to break away in the third term to kick six goals two to one goal three. In the last, three Magpie goals in six minutes cut the Essendon lead to eighteen points, but Essendon, well in control, settled down and went on to an easy victory. Collingwood full-back, Harry Sullivan, put up a game performance in this match, taking his place in the side despite a broken toe. He held Ron Evans to six kicks, but the Dons' full-forward got maximum value with five goals from those six kicks.

A fiery second semi-final saw Melbourne annihilate Carlton. In the slippery conditions, Carlton was very hesitant early and fumbled badly, letting Melbourne in time after time through elementary mistakes. The Blues had only one goal on the board at half-time and two at the last change. The Demons had winners everywhere and moved to eleven goals fifteen to two goals twelve midway through the last term before the Blues belatedly put their third and fourth goals on the board. It became obvious very early that the Demons were far superior, and the main interest for the crowd was in watching brawls in the second and last terms. The one in the last was by far the more spectacular, as twenty-eight of the thirty-six players became involved seconds after Case (Melbourne) and Arch (Carlton) swapped blows.

The day of the preliminary final was another wet one. Playing before H.R.H. Princess Alexandra (who met both teams prior to the start), Essendon had four goals four on the board to Carlton's three points halfway through the second quarter. Then, less than thirty minutes later, the Blues were ahead four goals eight to four goals five, mainly through the brilliance of Nicholls in the ruck. Late in the third quarter, however, Peucker and Birt cleverly snapped goals to restore the lead to the Dons. And when Mitchell got two more within three minutes early in the last, it looked as if the Dons were going to run away with the game. But the Blues' defence played brilliantly to hold the Dons out, and two goals to Brereton at the twenty-minute mark reduced the Essendon lead to six points. Carlton could not make further leeway, and when a further Essendon behind was posted to make the difference seven points, Essendon were content to play out time.

The Dons made two changes for the grand final and the confident Demons none. It was the Dons, however, who made the running in the first term. Displaying some of the most blistering pace seen in a grand final since Geelong burnt off the opposition in 1951, the Dons ran wild in the first term, but kicked poorly for three goals five, while the Demons scored only one goal four in reply.

The second term was a different story. Barassi started to elude his 'shadow' for the day (Mitchell) and Jones, well beaten early, eclipsed Fraser. Dixon on the wing began to generate tremendous drive for his side, and with the Demons starting to click, it was a sad blow for the Dons when their tallest ruckman, Sampson, fell heavily when marking and had to be replaced.

The brilliant Barassi, with two fine marks and another snapshot, added three goals in seven minutes just before half-time to give his side a three-point lead, after they had booted seven goals one for the term. Essendon were generally haphazard up forward. VFL top goalkicker Evans was well held, while by contrast Demons' 'decoy' full-forward Rowarth had three goals one from four kicks.

After a strong third term, the Dons again lost the advantage by letting Johnson (twice) and Rowarth in for Melbourne goals only five minutes before three-quarter-time. This gave the Demons a six-point lead and it appeared to be anybody's game. It was not to be, however. Early in the game, the Demons had conserved their big man strength, keeping Lord in the back pocket in the second and third quarters, and giving Johnson only a brief run after half-time. Even Rowarth ran on the ball on occasions to save the strength of the Melbourne rucks. Then, in the last, Fenton-Smith was told to go flat out in the ruck and then go off to be replaced by a fresh reserve in Williams. Johnson and Lord were comparatively fresh, and were able to take the depleted Essendon rucks apart. As a result, the Don's resistance collapsed, and the Demons booted six goals two to one goal two in the last term to easily win their fourth flag in five years. But for their disastrous defeat in 1958, the Demons would have set a new League record of five successive premierships.

RESULTS

SEPTEMBER 5 — FIRST SEMI-FINAL

	1st	2nd	3rd	Final	
Essendon	2 . 5	4 . 9	10 . 11	14 . 16	(100)
Collingwood	1 . 4	4 . 8	5 . 11	8 . 14	(62)

MCG — Umpire Barbour

Attendance 86,198 (record) — Gate £26,984 (record)

BEST —	(Ess)	Shelton, Peucker, Clarke, Leek, Capuano, Birt, Burgess, Hebbard, Fraser
	(Col)	Kingston, Reeves, M. Twomey, Merrett, Gabelich, Serong, Dorman, Henderson
GOALS —	(Ess)	Evans (5), Peucker (4), Clarke (3), Birt, Mitchell
	(Col)	Weideman (2), Brewer (2), Merrett, Beers, Dorman, Harrison

SEPTEMBER 12 — SECOND SEMI-FINAL

	1st	2nd	3rd	Final	
Melbourne	2 . 6	6 . 8	9 . 12	11 . 15	(81)
Carlton	0 . 0	1 . 4	2 . 9	4 . 13	(37)

MCG — Umpire Nash
Attendance 72,822 — Gate £23,878

BEST —	(Melb)	Bob Johnson, Mithen, Beckwith, Jones, Rowarth, Adams, Barassi
	(Carl)	Comben, Brereton, Zeunert, J. Nicholls, Kerr, James
GOALS —	(Melb)	Rowarth (4), Barassi (2), Ridley (2), Bob Johnson, Adams, Mann
	(Carl)	Brereton (2), Barry, Williams

SEPTEMBER 19 — PRELIMINARY FINAL

	1st	2nd	3rd	Final	
Essendon	1 . 4	4 . 5	6 . 8	8 . 9	(57)
Carlton	0 . 1	3 . 7	5 . 8	7 . 8	(50)

MCG — Umpire Barbour
Attendance 65,896 — Gate £25,136

BEST —	(Ess)	Mitchell, Epis, Shelton, Clarke, Burgess, Birt, Capuano
	(Carl)	J. Nicholls, James, Brereton, Gilchrist, Silvagni, Comben, Cox
GOALS —	(Ess)	Mitchell (2), Evans (2), Peucker, Leek, Shaw, Birt
	(Carl)	Brereton (3), Silvagni, Kerr, J. Nicholls, Sankey

SEPTEMBER 26 — GRAND FINAL

	1st	2nd	3rd	Final	
Melbourne	1 . 4	8 . 5	11 . 10	17 . 13	(115)
Essendon	3 . 5	7 . 8	10 . 10	11 . 12	(78)

MCG — Umpire Barbour
Attendance 103,506 — Gate £29,472

BEST —	(Melb)	Barassi (B.O.G.), McLean, Bob Johnson, Dixon, Jones, Beckwith
	(Ess)	Shearman, Birt, Epis, Sewell, Shaw, Clarke
GOALS —	(Melb)	Barassi (4), Rowarth (4), Adams (3), Bob Johnson (3), H. Mann, Tunbridge, Ridley
	(Ess)	Sewell (4), Evans (2), Clarke (2), Shaw (2), Fraser

GRAND FINAL TEAMS

Melbourne	B	J. Beckwith (c)	Tas Johnson	J. Lord
	HB	G. Case	D. Jones	I. Thorogood
	C	I. McLean	L. Mithen	B. Dixon
	HF	G. Tunbridge	C. Laidlaw	H. Mann
	F	R. Barassi	A. Rowarth	I. Ridley
	Ruck	R. Johnson	R. Fenton-Smith	F. Adams
	Reserves	D. Williams	N. Crompton	
	Coach	N. Smith		

Essendon	B	R. Shearman	J. Towner	B. Sampson
	HB	A. Epis	I. Shelton	C. Hebbard
	C	B. Capuano	R. Burgess	A. Murdoch
	HF	K. Peucker	K. Fraser	G. Sewell
	F	J. Birt	R. Evans	D. Shaw
	Ruck	G. Leek	H. Mitchell	J. Clarke (c)
	Reserves	G. Mackie	G. Leydin	
	Coach	R. Reynolds		

1960

Melbourne, who had earlier won eleven successive matches, slipped badly to lose the last three before the finals, but they were still able to finish on top for the seventh season in succession, with fourteen wins and four losses.

Fitzroy, vastly improved, won their last nine games to finish second on percentage, followed by Essendon (thirteen wins) and Collingwood (eleven wins). Unlucky fifth was Hawthorn, nine per cent behind the Magpies. They still had a chance when they beat Geelong in the last game, but Collingwood made certain of their own position by defeating North.

Essendon appeared to be the more accomplished side in the first semi-final, but lost the game. They were let down badly by their forwards.

After an even first quarter, in which both sides sprayed their shots for goal, Essendon, through Clarke, played excellently in the second. Clarke was brilliant in this quarter, kicking one great fifty-five-yard goal and then, when Collingwood hit the front, levelling the scores again with a great angle goal. The Dons went in at half-time leading by a goal, and it looked as if they could go on with it in the third with the wind, if they could score a few goals before the rain, which was obviously on the way, arrived. However, the Magpie defence rose to the occasion, and when later the rain did come, Essendon's lead was nowhere near enough. Nevertheless, the tenacious Dons kept with the Magpies until twenty minutes into the last term when Weideman found Henderson, whose long kick was put through, off by the ground, by O'Dwyer. Essendon had one chance after that to regain the lead, but Hebbard's shot rolled through for a point only. Dorman sealed the game for the Magpies when he marked and goaled from twenty-five yards out.

Fitzroy, whose controversial flick-pass was under criticism about this time, were no match for the Demons in a lack-lustre second semi-final. The 'Roys lacked big men, but their brilliant hand-ball had compensated for this during the season; in this game, however, their hand-balling play-on game fell apart.

The first term started at a tremendous pace, but nearly half the quarter passed before the Demons managed to score the first goal of the game. They carried on with the job, and held a good lead at the first change. Fitzroy's inability to capitalise on first use of the wind suggested that they would be in trouble in the second term and so it proved, with the Demons leading by thirty points at half-time.

The second half was merely a repeat of the first, with Melbourne winning all over the ground. Fitzroy struggled to get into the game, but their forwards, harassed by the close-checking Demon defence, rattled up a disappointing string of behinds. Melbourne continued to move away from their opponents, and had the game well won before the final siren. This was obvious to thousands of fans, who streamed away from the ground long before the end.

The preliminary final was one of the most exciting finals in years. Playing in mud and slush, both Collingwood and Fitzroy showed form capable of tossing Melbourne. The slippery ball helped Fitzroy, as it off-set Collingwood's great aerial advantage, and when the Magpies lost both Serong (broken collarbone) and Dorman (knee ligaments) the Maroons looked certainties. But the dogged Magpies would not concede a thing, and for three quarters there were only a couple of goals in it. When Fitzroy, although well on top in the third, could score only one goal four to one goal one, the Magpies were given their chance. The third quarter all-out effort took a lot out of Fitzroy, and in the last the Magpie rucks overpowered their tired Fitzroy counterparts. From eight points down, the Magpies launched a tremendous assault on goals and were rewarded with a behind to Beers, a goal to O'Dwyer and a behind, pushed through by Harrison, to level the scores after fifteen minutes. Fitzroy went to the lead with behinds to Campbell and Wright, to which Collingwood replied with behinds to Harrison and Beers, again levelling at eight goals ten each. Twenty-five minutes into the term, Beers put the Magpies one point ahead, before Magpie rover Burns picked up a smothered kick and goaled. Fitzroy, in the dying moments, streamed into attack, where Campbell twice got behinds from excellent attempts, leaving the Magpies winners by five points.

Surprise of the team selections for the grand final was Collingwood's recall of veteran Mick Twomey from the Seconds. Barry Harrison, a reserve in the preliminary final, also come into the side. Melbourne lined up unchanged, although they missed Terry Gleeson, who had earlier suffered a broken leg.

Rain Friday night and Saturday raised Magpie hopes of a repeat of the 1958 grand final, but they were to be sadly disappointed. In the first term, the Demons were at their best and Collingwood at their worst. The Magpies did not score, whilst Melbourne impassable on the half-back line and brilliant up forward, booted four goals three, a grand effort in the conditions. Collingwood did not score their first goal until three minutes into the second term and even then it was a piece of luck. Tas Johnson dropped a mark in the goal-square, and Gabelich was able to pick-up and tap it through. The Magpies tried to repeat their 1958 tactics by roughing Melbourne up, but the Demons would not be 'got in'. They showed, too, that they were not going to shirk an issue, and the Magpies were a dejected team at half-time, trailing by almost five goals after having only one scoring shot. The Magpies added another goal in the third term, this also being a bit lucky, as it only just made the distance after Henderson had marked forty yards out. In fact, for the whole day—100 minutes play—the Magpies had only six shots at goal, for two goals two, the lowest grand final score since the formation of the League. The Demons were quite untroubled to win easily by forty-eight points, their fifth flag in six years and easily their most satisfying win of the five.

1960

This win ended Melbourne's golden era, for they missed the grand final for the first time since 1954 the following season. In their seven great seasons, the Demons had played 141 games, won 108 of them and tied two. Whilst their attack did not kick the big scores that the 1939-40-41 sides did, they were certainly the equal, if not the superior, of those sides. From last to first in three seasons was a magnificent effort, but what players the Demons had! Dixon, Bob Johnson, Adams, Barassi, Case, Marquis, Melville, Williams, Laidlaw, Mithen, Ridley and Wilson all joined the club in 1953 or 1954 and what club could fail with recruits of the calibre of these. In later seasons, Trev Johnson, Tas Johnson, Webb, Clarke, Jones, Gleeson, Sandral, Brenchley, Crompton, Fenton-Smith, Lord, Thorogood, Tunbridge, Kenneally, H. Mann, L. Mann, Rowarth, Leahy and Nilsson were recruited, and all played in premiership sides. Other stars of those years included Beckwith, Arnold, Christie, McMahen, Collins, McLean, Lane, McGivern, Albiston, Denis Cordner, Spencer and Carroll.

RESULTS

SEPTEMBER 3 — FIRST SEMI-FINAL

	1st	2nd	3rd	Final	
Collingwood	2 . 7	5 . 9	6 . 12	9 . 12	(66)
Essendon	2 . 6	6 . 9	7 . 13	7 . 15	(57)

MCG — Umpire Irving
Attendance 81,209 — Gate £26,258

BEST — (Col) Gabelich, Willett, Henderson, Rosenbrock, Delanty, K. Turner
(Ess) Burgess (B.O.G.), Clarke, Blew, Leek, Timms, Shearman
GOALS — (Col) Dorman (3), Burns (2), Weideman (2), O'Dwyer, Beers
(Ess) Clarke (3), Dunlop (2), Fraser, Birt

SEPTEMBER 10 — SECOND SEMI-FINAL

	1st	2nd	3rd	Final	
Melbourne	3 . 6	6 . 12	11 . 15	14 . 18	(102)
Fitzroy	1 . 2	2 . 6	2 . 12	4 . 16	(40)

MCG — Umpire Schwab
Attendance 79,796 — Gate £25,143

BEST — (Melb) Mithen (B.O.G.), Ridley, Dixon, H. Mann, Tunbridge, Thorogood
(Fitz) Mackenzie, Gale, Murray, Barclay, Clark
GOALS — (Melb) Adams (3), H. Mann (3), Rowarth (2), Ridley (2), Barassi, Tunbridge, Bob Johnson
(Fitz) Wright (2), Abrahams, Bromage

SEPTEMBER 17 — PRELIMINARY FINAL

	1st	2nd	3rd	Final	
Collingwood	2 . 1	6 . 4	7 . 5	9 . 11	(65)
Fitzroy	2 . 2	7 . 3	8 . 7	8 . 12	(60)

MCG — Umpire Irving
Attendance 65,301 — Gate £25,598

BEST — (Col) Gabelich, Reeves, Turner, Beers, Burns, O'Dwyer
(Fitz) Campbell, Gale, Barclay, McMaster-Smith, Slocum, Aston
GOALS — (Col) Burns (3), Willett (2), Beers, Henderson, Harrison, O'Dwyer
(Fitz) Ongarello (3), Wright (2), Slocum, Gale, Abrahams

1960-1961

SEPTEMBER 24 — GRAND FINAL

	1st	2nd	3rd	Final	
Melbourne	4 . 3	5 . 5	7 . 12	8 . 14	(62)
Collingwood	0 . 0	1 . 0	2 . 0	2 . 2	(14)

MCG — Umpire Irving

Attendance 97,457 — Gate £29,177

BEST —	(Melb)	Lord (B.O.G.), Mithen, L. Mann, Dixon, Bob Johnson, Tunbridge
	(Col)	Burns, K. Rose, Reeves, M. Twomey, Thripp
GOALS —	(Melb)	Bob Johnson (2), Adams (2), H. Mann (2), Tunbridge, Rowarth
	(Col)	Henderson, Gabelich

GRAND FINAL TEAMS

Melbourne	B	J. Beckwith (c)	Tas Johnson	Trev Johnson
	HB	G. Case	J. Lord	I. Thorogood
	C	B. Dixon	L. Mithen	B. Kenneally
	HF	G. Tunbridge	C. Laidlaw	H. Mann
	F	R. Johnson	A. Rowarth	F. Adams
	Ruck	L. Mann	R. Barassi	I. Ridley
	Reserves	B. Leahy	R. Nilsson	
	Coach	N. Smith		
Collingwood	B	R. Reeves	P. Rosenbrock	M. Twomey
	HB	M. Delanty	W. Thripp	K. Rose
	C	B. Gray	J. Henderson	E. Hutchesson
	HF	K. Turner	M. Weideman (c)	B. Beers
	F	G. Fellowes	R. Willett	K. Burns
	Ruck	R. Gabelich	B. Harrison	R. O'Dwyer
	Reserves	I. Brewer	A. Chapman	
	Coach	A. Kyne		

1961

Gathering strength after their unlucky season in 1960, the superbly fit Hawthorn won their last ten home and home games to finish on top of the ladder with fourteen wins, followed by Melbourne (twelve wins and a tie) and St. Kilda and Footscray (both eleven wins).

Fitzroy and Geelong finished fifth and sixth. Fitzroy had a better percentage than Footscray, who only sneaked in the last game by virtue of a good win over Geelong. St. Kilda were lucky, too, their five-point win over North in the last game keeping them in the Four when defeat would have caused them to be replaced by either Fitzroy or Geelong.

This was the first time that Hawthorn had topped the ladder, either in the VFA or VFL, and their success was attributable to coach John Kennedy. Kennedy was convinced that most sides were just not fit enough, so his plan was simply to make Hawthorn super-fit and then, by keeping the ball moving all the time throughout their games, wear the opposition to a standstill. The Hawks were brought to the peak of physical fitness by a gruelling pre-season training schedule, and then, in match-play instructed to keep the ball moving at all times by playing on whenever possible; not kicking out of bounds, which would give opponents a chance to get back their breath; not running with the ball, but kicking as far as possible; and endeavouring to stop every mark, so that the opposition could not dictate terms.

Then, too, the Hawks' desire to win the ball bordered on the fanatical—opponents certainly knew they had been in a football game after meeting Hawthorn.

Although in the end they lost by only nine points, St. Kilda never really looked like winning the first semi-final. They went into the game with full-back Howell obviously unfit (back-pocket Walsh had to kick off) and trailed by four goals at half-time.

The Saints came back strongly, however, with three quick majors at the start of the last term before Whitten marked and brilliantly flick-passed to Bryant for a goal to restore control to the Bulldogs. Again in the last, the Saints drew to within seven points of the lead, but they had no-one to give them the lift to go on and win.

Melbourne brought Collins into the side for his first full game and Leslie for his fourth in the second semi-final, but in an incident-packed game the rugged Hawks proved just too strong. The Demons had four goals two on the board before Hawthorn got their first, from Young, after twenty-three minutes of the first term, and they led seven goals two to three goals one halfway through the second. But then Hawthorn's strength started to tell, and they began to peg the Demons back. Turning point came when Melbourne centre-man Mithen was dropped seventy yards behind the play. After a fiery clash between players, order was restored and Arthur (Hawthorn) goaled from a previously awarded free. Melbourne, angered by the incident, started to give away unnecessary free kicks, and it was Hawthorn who took over. Peck flashed into play with three quick goals and the Melbourne lead was reduced to a single goal at half-time.

Browne lined up at full-forward for Hawthorn as the third term began, and Peck went into the ruck. The move was a success—Browne booted two vital goals, and the Hawks hit the front, although Nilsson (Melbourne) beat three defenders to goal and reduce the Melbourne deficit to a mere three points at three-quarter-time.

The last term was one of the most exciting for years—the Demons made five changes in an endeavour to lift the side, but could not get the goals required. For most of the quarter, only seven points separated the teams, and for the last ten minutes only one point. The Demons had a chance to force a behind to equal the scores in time-on, with the ball only feet from the line, but everyone tried to kick the goal to win the game, and the Hawks were able to force the ball out of bounds. Moments later, Browne marked and goaled to seal the game, after having just previously missed a difficult angle shot. The Hawks scraped in by seven points and entered their first ever grand final.

Footscray brought in B. Ion for his second VFL game in the preliminary final against Melbourne. The Demons were hot favourites, but were never in the race against Ted Whitten's young Bulldogs.

The Demons appeared jaded and never got into the game against Footscray's brilliant handball. They trailed badly at half-time and saw the game slip away in the third quarter. Two minutes after the bounce, Slattery ran into an open goal to score for Footscray, who then put on five more goals without a miss to lead by seven goals at the last change. Slattery goaled twice more within ten minutes of the start of the last, and that was the end of any lingering doubts about the outcome. Melbourne belatedly added four goals late in the quarter, but by then Footscray had relaxed.

The Bulldogs were unchanged for the grand final, whereas Hawthorn made one compulsory change, Cunningham replacing the injured Connell. As the Hawthorn camp had anticipated, the pacier Bulldogs led at half-time. The Hawks, however, were not playing well and only the brilliance of Edwards in the centre kept them in it for the first half.

The Hawks were first into attack for a goal to Law at the two-minute mark of the match, but for most of the first term it was all Footscray, who booted four goals two before Law kicked the Hawks' second almost on the siren.

The second term was Hawthorn's worst, although they somehow held Footscray to only one goal. The Hawks fumbled, crashed into each other, and miskicked for almost the entire thirty minutes. At one stage they kicked five consecutive behinds—including a miss from ten yards out by Peck—and a Footscray goal by McKellar at the twenty-five-minute mark gave the Bulldogs an eight-point lead at half-time.

During the break, coach Kennedy stressed that the Hawks must move the ball faster between the half-back line and the goals, and they were quick to implement these instructions. Peck moved from full-forward to the ruck, and Winneke got on top of Schultz, giving the Hawks control of the centre bounces and boundary throw-ins. Within three minutes of the second half, Hawthorn was in front, and in a great third term they virtually won the flag by kicking six goals six to Footscray's one goal one and it would have been even more had not a shot by Cooper been touched on the line, and another by Edwards hit the post. Only the experience of Whitten kept Footscray in the game in the third term—he kicked their only scores for the quarter.

It was obvious that Hawthorn had run Footscray to a standstill, and when Peck and Mort added goals after nine minutes of the last term, the result of the game was a foregone conclusion. The Hawks were untroubled to win the game—and their first premiership—by forty-three points. Star of the win was centreman Brendan Edwards, who gathered thirty-three kicks in a match-winning display.

RESULTS

SEPTEMBER 2 — FIRST SEMI-FINAL

	1st	2nd	3rd	Final	
Footscray	3 . 3	7 . 7	9 . 11	9 . 15	(69)
St. Kilda	1 . 4	3 . 7	6 . 9	8 . 12	(60)

MCG — Umpire Schwab

Attendance 86,411 (record) — Gate £26,986

BEST —	(Foots)	Spargo, Hobbs, Whitten, Evans, Schultz, Ware, Quarrell, Hoiles, Gardiner
	(St. K)	Morrow, Hodgkin, Oswald, Annand, Guy, K. Roberts, Synman, Rowland, Walsh
GOALS —	(Foots)	Hobbs (3), Whitten (2), Slattery (2), Bryant, Quarrell
	(St. K)	Oswald (2), Guyatt (2), Rowland (2), Young, Morrow

1961

SEPTEMBER 9 — SECOND SEMI-FINAL

	1st	2nd	3rd	Final	
Hawthorn	2 . 1	6 . 4	9 . 8	12 . 8	(80)
Melbourne	5 . 2	7 . 4	9 . 5	11 . 7	(73)

MCG — Umpire Irving
Attendance 87,744 — Gate £25,946

BEST — (Haw) Arthur, Young, Winneke, Mort, Fisher, Peck, Edwards, McPherson, Kaine
(Melb) Lord, Barassi, Roet, Tunbridge, Kenneally, Laidlaw, Leslie, R. Johnson, Mithen

GOALS — (Haw) Peck (4), Browne (2), Young (2), Nalder (2), Arthur, Connell
(Melb) Nilsson (3), Tunbridge (2), Ridley, Rowarth, Collins, Laidlaw, Mann, Barassi

SEPTEMBER 16 — PRELIMINARY FINAL

	1st	2nd	3rd	Final	
Footscray	4 . 3	5 . 4	11 . 6	13 . 7	(85)
Melbourne	0 . 2	2 . 5	4 . 6	8 . 10	(58)

MCG — Umpire Schwab
Attendance 86,118 — Gate £26,483

BEST — (Foots) Schultz, Hoiles, Gardiner, Spargo, Whitten, Evans, Hobbs, B. Ion
(Melb) Kenneally, Trev. Johnson, Dixon, Lord, Adams, Mithen, Barassi, Thorogood

GOALS — (Foots) Slattery (4), Hobbs (3), Whitten (2)' McKellar (2), Spargo, Beamish
(Melb) Mithen (2), Barassi (2), Tunbridge, R. Johnson, Dawson, Lord

SEPTEMBER 23 — GRAND FINAL

	1st	2nd	3rd	Final	
Hawthorn	2 . 2	3 . 9	9 . 15	13 . 16	(94)
Footscray	4 . 2	5 . 5	6 . 6	7 . 9	(51)

MCG — Umpire Schwab
Attendance 107,935 — Gate £29,509

BEST — (Haw) Edwards (B.O.G.), Law, Winneke, Fisher, Mort, Hill, Cunningham, S. Hay, Arthur, Youren
(Foots) Schultz, Evans, Whitten, Hoiles, Quarrell, Ware, Spargo, Lee, B. Ion

GOALS — (Haw) Browne (3), Mort (2), Law (2), Nalder, Peck, Hill, Cunningham, Arthur, Edwards
(Foots) Whitten (3), Quarrell (2), McKellar, Hobbs

GRAND FINAL TEAMS

Hawthorn	B	R. Poole	L. Kaine	G. Cooper
	HB	S. Hay	J. McArthur	C. McPherson
	C	C. Youren	B. Edwards	J. Fisher
	HF	I. Mort	G. Young	M. Browne
	F	J. Cunningham	J. Peck	M. Hill
	Ruck	J. Winneke	G. Arthur (c)	I. Law
	Reserves	P. Hay	R. Nalder	
	Coach	J. Kennedy		

Footscray	B	C. Evans	B. Lee	N. Ware
	HB	J. Jillard	J. Hoiles	B. Ion
	C	I. Bryant	R. Spargo	J. Gardiner
	HF	B. McKellar	G. Ion	J. Quarrell
	F	E. Whitten (c)	J. Slattery	K. Beamish
	Ruck	J. Schültz	C. McDonald	M. Hobbs
	Reserves	Duff	C. Stewart	
	Coach	E. Whitten		

1962

After their great success in 1961, Hawthorn stunned the critics by slipping down the ladder to ninth in 1962, the lowest any premiership team has ever fallen.* Footscray, the other 1961 grand finalist, dropped to fifth. Essendon (sixteen wins, two losses), Geelong (fourteen wins, four losses), Melbourne (fourteen wins, four losses) and Carlton (thirteen wins, five losses) made up the 1962 final Four.

The first semi-final saw Melbourne lead for three quarters even though their star player, Ron Barassi, was badly hampered by a groin injury and Lord was off in the first quarter. But Carlton fought back fanatically and had bridged the gap when Melbourne star Geoff Tunbridge spilled a sitter mark on the half-forward line and was crashed by Carlton's Graeme Anderson. Mithen (Melbourne) grabbed the ball and would almost certainly have put his side in front when Umpire Schwab blew his whistle for a puzzling 'ball-up' decision. Most critics thought the decision should have been play-on or a free kick to either side. Soon after, the siren sounded with Carlton two points ahead. Their come-back had been magnificent, particularly in the last quarter when, spurred by Nicholls and Silvagni, they booted two goals five to the Demons' single behind.

The first half of the second semi-final, which saw Geelong leading Essendon by a point, was one of the best displays seen at the MCG for years. It was a half played at breakneck pace, but the Cats began to slow down in the second half. Missing their young full-forward Doug Wade, they did not have anyone up forward to aim at, and their kicking for goal was atrocious. Had Essendon not kicked equally as poorly, the Cats would have been really slaughtered, as the Dons added seven goals fifteen to one goal four in a dull second half to win easily by forty-six points.

Injury-riddled Geelong, still without Wade, with no rucks to match the big man strength of their opponents, and low on form and confidence, was at long odds the

* See statistics section. It is interesting to note that since 1897, the premier team has missed the following years finals only 25 times; 15 of these occasions have been since the end of World War II.

following week. But the crowd of 82,724 saw the first preliminary final tie in League history.

Geelong, in a great form reversal, had a big lead at half-time, but Carlton, pegging them back slowly, crept to within two points with goals to James and Williams in time-on of the third term. Immediately the last quarter commenced, Carroll snapped a beautiful left-foot goal from the boundary to give Carlton the lead. A few minutes later, Williams goaled for the Blues, but Wooller quickly posted the equaliser for Geelong. Play see-sawed from end to end before Miller goaled for the Cats and, twenty-three minutes into the term, Rice of Geelong was pulled around the neck and goaled from the free to put Geelong six points up. Miller made the difference twelve points with a magnificent angle goal just as time-on began. The tension was tremendous as Gill (Carlton) kicked a behind and Barry (Carlton) received a free in the goal-square to stop a hot Geelong attack. Vinar burst through the pack to score a behind for the Cats with twenty-seven and a half minutes of the quarter gone—it looked impossible for them to lose. Finally, Carlton came back as Carroll handballed to Sankey, who ran some thirty yards without bouncing the ball, and goaled. A tremendous Carlton attack was stopped by Geelong's Roy West, but the Blues were not to be denied, as Cross found Carroll forty yards out and he goaled to level the scores. Finally, with the last kick of the day, James, Carlton's 1961 Brownlow Medallist, who had come on as a reserve and played a great game, had a chance to win the match for his side, but his fifty-five-yard snap shot was off line and went out of bounds near the behind post. So, fittingly, the game was a draw. The third in VFL finals history.

For the replay, Geelong took a gamble and played the injured Wade. They were without their star follower, Polly Farmer, however. Farmer, in his first season with the Cats, had earlier broken down with a cartilage injury. Again, fans needed their heart tablets and tranquillizers, as there was a point separating the teams at half-time and nine points between them at the last change. Then came the action—reminiscent of the previous week's tremendous finish—as the Cats, trailing, hit back with two quick goals by Wade to reduce Carlton's lead to a point. Then brilliant individual efforts in defence by both sides limited scoring to behinds for some time, including Falconer's fourth for the term for Carlton. What was so disheartening for Falconer about his four misses was that he was playing against his old side, Geelong. Finally, the string of behinds was broken when Sutherland (Geelong) marked and booted a glorious goal, giving the Cats a two-point lead with twenty-three minutes of the quarter gone. Cross, coming on as reserve for the Blues, booted a behind, before James whirled out of the pack, steadied, and slammed home the match-winning goal at the twenty-eight-minute mark. The timekeeper's fingers were poised above the siren button when Pomeroy passed to Wooller. The Geelong captain's kick was marked by Wade, thirty-five yards out almost straight in front, and as the crowd of 99,203 roared it looked as if the Cats would steal the game, for Wade had been kicking magnificently and already had six goals one behind on the board. But now came one of the most controversial umpiring decisions of all time. Umpire Irving ran up, took the ball from Wade and gave it to Carlton full-back Peter Barry, who cleared as the siren went. Subsequently, Irving said that the free was given against Wade when he saw him, from the front position as he and Barry jostled, reach back and hold Barry's shorts., the free kick being given for holding the man. It was a courageous decision, but one which was slammed by the majority of critics. However, the fact was that the umpire was in the best position to see what occurred, and paid it as he saw it. But there are still arguments about that decision.

Having been without a match for three weeks, Essendon suffered further setbacks when half-forward Terry Rodgers (injured) was unable to take his place in the grand final side, and top ruckman Geoff Leek turned his ankle in the last minutes of the Thursday night's training and was in doubt until half an hour before the big game. Finally, after pain-killing injections, the giant Don ran out with his team and played a major part in the Essendon win, by keeping the Carlton powerhouse, Nicholls, reasonably quiet.

The Dons began like a whirlwind, kicking six goals five to one goal one in the first term, but Carlton fought back to within thirteen points at half-time. It was the only time they looked dangerous. Essendon, regaining their poise, went to a twenty-point lead at the last change, with Clarke, Birt and Mitchell creating havoc on the forward line. Clarke in particular was in brilliant form, and seemed to be forever on his own. Play see-sawed for the first ten minutes of the last quarter, with plenty of spite creeping in, before Birt goaled, and soon after Johnston took a screamer and sewed up the game with another major to the Dons. Just to make sure, Payne marked and kicked yet another, to give the Dons a thirty-nine-point lead twenty-three minutes into the quarter. Essendon, with the flag in their keeping, had run the Blues off their feet, and relaxed only in the last moments to let Carlton in for a goal to Cross. But there was no doubt that Essendon, on their form in this game and over the entire season, was a worthy premiership winner, probably the best side to take the pennant since Melbourne's great 1955-56-57 sides.

RESULTS

SEPTEMBER 1 — FIRST SEMI-FINAL

	1st	2nd	3rd	Final	
Carlton	2 . 3	6 . 5	9 . 7	11 . 12	(78)
Melbourne	2 . 4	6 . 4	11 . 9	11 . 10	(76)

MCG — Umpire Schwab
Attendance 82,773 — Gate £28,199

BEST — (Carl) Donaldson, Silvagni, Nicholls, Cox, Collis, Bennetti, Buckley, Brereton
(Melb) L. Mann, Dixon, Mithen, Roet, Crompton, H. Mann, Nilsson, Miller, Kenneally

GOALS — (Carl) Donaldson (3), Nicholls (2), Williams (2), Carroll (2), Brereton, Cox
(Melb) Nilsson (4), Mithen (3), Tas. Johnson, Byers, Tunbridge, H. Mann

SEPTEMBER 8 — SECOND SEMI-FINAL

	1st	2nd	3rd	Final	
Essendon	3 . 3	7 . 6	10 . 13	14 . 21	(105)
Geelong	2 . 8	6 . 13	7 . 15	7 . 17	(59)

MCG — Umpire Nunn
Attendance 95,393 (record) — Gate £31,384 (record)

BEST — (Ess) Mitchell, Birt, Fraser, Epis, Leek, Davis, Beissell, Capuano, Rodgers
(Geel) Wooller, Goggin, Rice, A. Lord, West, Sutherland, Callan, O'Neill, Devine

GOALS —	(Ess)	C. Payne (4), Birt (3), Rodgers (2), Fraser (2), Mitchell, Leek, Clarke
	(Geel)	Miller (2), Rice (2), Hamer, Devine, Wooller

SEPTEMBER 15 — PRELIMINARY FINAL

	1st	2nd	3rd	Final	
Geelong	4 . 2	7 . 4	9 . 5	13 . 7	(85)
Carlton	3 . 3	4 . 4	8 . 9	12 . 13	(85)

MCG — Umpire Schwab
Attendance 87,724 — Gate £30,098

BEST —	(Geel)	A. Lord, Goggin, S. Lord, Rice, Brown, Walker, Wooller, O'Neill, Vinar
	(Carl)	Silvagni, Nicholls, Buckley, Lofts, Anderson, Sankey, Cox, Kick, Williams
GOALS —	(Geel)	Wooller (4), Miller (3), Goggin (2), Rice (2), Vinar, Fox
	(Carl)	B. Williams (3), Brereton (2), Sankey (2), Carroll (2), Collins, Nicholls, James

SEPTEMBER 22 — PRELIMINARY FINAL REPLAY

	1st	2nd	3rd	Final	
Carlton	1 . 4	5 . 8	9 . 9	10 . 18	(78)
Geelong	3 . 2	5 . 9	7 . 12	10 . 13	(73)

MCG — Umpire Irving
Attendance 99,203 (record) — Gate £31,982 (record)

BEST —	(Carl)	Nicholls, James, Silvagni, Kick, Cox, Collins, Lofts, Sankey, Crowe
	(Geel)	Callan, Rice, Vinar, Wade, Walker, S. Lord, Wooller, West
GOALS —	(Carl)	James (3), J. Gill (2), Greenwood, Carroll, Sankey, Nicholls, Williams
	(Geel)	Wade (6), Vinar (2), Rice, Sutherland

SEPTEMBER 29 — GRAND FINAL

	1st	2nd	3rd	Final	
Essendon	6 . 5	7 . 7	10 . 10	13 . 12	(90)
Carlton	1 . 1	5 . 6	7 . 8	8 . 10	(58)

MCG — Umpire Irving
Attendance 98,385 — Gate £31,469

BEST —	(Ess)	Clarke, Mitchell, Birt, Leek, Epis, Beissel, Davis, Shaw, Capuano
	(Carl)	Silvagni, Williams, James, Cox, Donaldson, Sankey, Bennetti, Nicholls
GOALS —	(Ess)	Birt (4), Clarke (2), Mitchell (2), C. Payne (2), Leek, Johnston, Timms
	(Carl)	B. Williams (3), Nicholls (2), Cross, Greenwood, Donaldson

GRAND FINAL TEAMS

Essendon	B	D. Shaw	P. Doran	D. McKenzie
	HB	A. Epis	I. Shelton	B. Davis
	C	R. Blew	G. Beissell	B. Capuano
	HF	G. Johnston	K. Fraser	J. Somerville
	F	K. Timms	C. Payne	J. Birt
	Ruck	G. Leek	H. Mitchell	J. Clarke (c)
	Reserves	B. Sampson	G. Gosper	
	Coach	J. Coleman		

Carlton	B	J. Bennetti	P. Barry	M. Sankey
	HB	B. Crowe	W. Lofts	G. Anderson
	C	M. Kick	B. Cox	I. Collins
	HF	J. Gill	J. James	G. Donaldson (c)
	F	K. Greenwood	T. Carroll	P. Falconer
	Ruck	J. Nicholls	S. Silvagni	B. Williams
	Reserves	M. Cross	V. Varlamos	
	Coach	K. Hands		

1963

Essendon, after looking good bets to run up a string of premierships after their 1962 win, surprised by missing the final Four in 1963, but it was only by two point six per cent. In fact, the first five teams staged one of the closest contests for years for the four places. Hawthorn, returning to their 1961 form, and Geelong shared top place with thirteen wins and a draw (against each other), but the Hawks by virtue of a higher percentage took top place. Two premiership points behind them came Melbourne and St. Kilda, each with thirteen wins. The Saints beat Essendon for fourth place only in the last game, by the percentage gained in an enormous win over North.

There was a sensation in the second last game when Melbourne's dynamic skipper Ron Barassi was reported for allegedly striking Richmond's Roger Dean. Barassi still says he was innocent, but his subsequent four-week suspension put him out of the finals series and cost the Demons their chance of taking another flag. It was the first finals series Barassi had missed since 1954. Even without Barassi, the Demons were too good for St. Kilda in the first semi-final, but they really missed him in the preliminary final when, with some typical Barassi determination, they may have won.

The first semi-final was not a great game, but the Demons proved too fast and systematic for three quarters, when they led by five goals. But they slowed to a walk in the last term, and St. Kilda finished all over them, kicking four goals eight to one goal three. Several valuable scoring chances were missed by the Saints including misses by Smith and Roberts in time-on, and this cost them the game, as Melbourne, with a superhuman effort, held on to win by seven points.

Hot favourites Geelong proved superior to Hawthorn in a hard but fair second semi-final. There were few nasty incidents as the Cats and Hawks staged a great battle, particularly in a stirring second term when each side scored five goals. Eight points up at half-time, the Cats saw their lead whittled down to a single point before

Wooller, Farmer and Brown added quick goals to give them a grip on the game. The Hawks again came back strongly in the last term, but Geelong always had an answer, and goals to Wooller and Sharrock kept them in control as the game ended. It must be noted that Hawthorn sadly missed full-forward John Peck, the season's top goal-kicker.

The cut-throat preliminary final saw the Hawks, with plenty of vigour and some of the fiercest tackling seen from them since 1961, battle their way to a win over Melbourne. The Demons played into the hands of the Hawks by failing to open up the play and trying to beat them at their own game. This suited Hawthorn who, winning well in the rucks after Lord (Melbourne) had been injured early, went to the front halfway through the second term and held their lead all day. Melbourne, still without Barassi, suffered a further setback when acting captain Brian Dixon had to drop out on the day of the game, but they staged a great third term come-back to draw within nine points of the lead at three-quarter-time. This lead was further reduced to seven points within three minutes plus time-on to play, but a goal to Olsson and two behinds gave Hawthorn a lead which could not be overtaken, despite Kenneally's impossible angle goal for the Demons with two minutes to go. The Hawks thus moved on to the second grand final appearance in their history.

Hawthorn regained top forward John Peck for the big game, but Geelong were still hot favourites.

However, the Brown and Golds looked the goods in a tremendously fast opening quarter, despite their inaccuracy—three goals six and two misses. Geelong, by way of contrast, had only two shots in the first twenty minutes for two goals.

Inspired by Polly Farmer, Geelong hit back with four goals seven to two goals in the second term, and broke almost even in a do-or-die third term which left them ten points up at the last change.

The crowd, prepared for a tense last term, saw Geelong run the Hawks off their feet. Wade, A. Lord, Hynes and Wooller added goals in nine minutes for the Cats to seal the game. Finally, Hynes and Wooller scored further goals and the Cats had finished on brilliantly to kick six goals six to three points for the term and annex their first flag since 1952.

RESULTS

SEPTEMBER 14 — FIRST SEMI-FINAL

	1st	2nd	3rd	Final	
Melbourne	1 . 4	4 . 11	8 . 15	9 . 17	(71)
St. Kilda	0 . 2	1 . 6	4 . 8	8 . 16	(64)

MCG — Umpire Brophy

Attendance 88,914 (record) — Gate £29,420 (record)

BEST — (Melb) Dixon, Lord, Adams, H. Mann, Leahy, Roet, Kenneally
(St. K) Ditterich, Howell, K. Roberts, Cross, Guyatt, Synman

GOALS — (Melb) Vagg (2), Emselle (2), Kenneally, Rattray, Bourke, Johnson, Mann
(St. K) K. Roberts (3), Smith (2), Wallis, Baldock, Morrow

SEPTEMBER 21 — SECOND SEMI-FINAL

	1st	2nd	3rd	Final	
Geelong	4 . 4	9 . 6	12 . 12	14 . 17	(101)
Hawthorn	2 . 7	7 . 10	8 . 13	11 . 16	(82)

MCG — Umpire Crouch

Attendance 91,471 — Gate £30,626

1963

BEST	— (Geel)	Hynes, Wade, Farmer, Watts, West, Goggin, Yeates
	(Haw)	Coverdale, Arthur, Beck, Olsson, McPherson, Youren, Woodley, Law
GOALS	— (Geel)	Wooller (4), Wade (3), Goggin (2), Hynes, Yeates, Farmer, Sharrock, Brown
	(Haw)	Young (3), Coverdale (3), Mort (2), Arthur, Albiston, Woodley

SEPTEMBER 28 — PRELIMINARY FINAL

	1st	2nd	3rd	Final	
Hawthorn	1 . 4	5 . 9	9 . 9	11 . 11	(77)
Melbourne	2 . 3	3 . 4	8 . 6	10 . 8	(68)

MCG — Umpire Brophy
Attendance 86,586 — Gate £29,243

BEST	— (Haw)	Arthur, Beck, Law, Fisher, Olsson, Woodley, Mort, Young
	(Melb)	Anderson, Crompton, Kenneally, H. Mann, Adams, Rattray, Johnson, Miller, Bourke
GOALS	— (Haw)	Peck (3), Olsson (3), Law (3), Beck, Mort
	(Melb)	Bourke (5), Kenneally (2), Rattray, Groom, Vagg

OCTOBER 5 — GRAND FINAL

	1st	2nd	3rd	Final	
Geelong	3 . 3	7 . 10	9 . 13	15 . 19	(109)
Hawthorn	3 . 6	5 . 6	8 . 9	8 . 12	(60)

MCG — Umpire Crouch
Attendance 101,209 — Gate £31,216

BEST	— (Geel)	Farmer, Devine, Scott, Goggin, Walker, West, Watts, Hynes
	(Haw)	Arthur, Nalder, Coverdale, Mort, Young, Youren, P. Hay, Law, Fisher
GOALS	— (Geel)	Wooller (3), Hynes (3), Yeates (2), Goggin (2), Rice (2), A. Lord (2), Wade
	(Haw)	Peck (3), Woodley, Law, Coverdale, Mort, Fisher

GRAND FINAL TEAMS

Geelong	B	I. Scott	R. West	J. Watts
	HB	S. Lord	P. Walker	J. Devine
	C	H. Routley	A. Lord	J. Brown
	HF	G. Hynes	F. Wooller (c)	J. Sharrock
	F	C. Rice	D. Wade	J. Yeates
	Ruck	G. Farmer	P. Vinar	W. Goggin
	Reserves	K. Goodland	A. Polinelli	
	Coach	R. Davis		
Hawthorn	B	D. Parkin	P. Hay	G. Cooper
	HB	S. Hay	G. Young	C. McPherson
	C	C. Youren	R. Nalder	J. Fisher
	HF	I. Mort	K. Coverdale	G. Arthur (c)
	F	D. Albiston	J. Peck	R. Olsson
	Ruck	K. Beck	A. Woodley	I. Law
	Reserves	K. Connell	P. Lyon	
	Coach	J. Kennedy		

1964

The premiership win by Melbourne in 1964, while being a great win by a very good team, was certainly attended by a good deal of luck. In the second last home and home round, a miraculous goal from the boundary by Hassa Mann in the last moments gave Melbourne a ten goals thirteen to ten goals nine victory over Hawthorn. Had Mann not kicked that goal, Melbourne would not have made the final Four. That win, and a crushing defeat by Footscray in the last game, left them with fifty-six points and gave them top position on the ladder, followed by Collingwood, Essendon, Geelong (all fifty-four points) and Hawthorn (fifty-two). If Hawthorn had beaten Melbourne, they would have finished not fifth but top with fifty-six points. Melbourne would have finished fifth with fifty-two points. That miracle goal was Melbourne's first lucky break—the other, also a goal, was to come in the grand final six weeks later.

Geelong fought their way to a nineteen-point win over Essendon in an action-packed first semi-final. Winning in the air and outpacing Essendon early, the Cats led at half-time, only Essendon's straight kicking—five goals from five shots at one stage—keeping them in it. Heavy rain after half-time helped arouse tempers, and early in the third term there was a 'dust-up' in front of the Press Box. This was followed by another, fifteen minutes later, in front of the Members' Reserve into which the two rival coaches briefly joined. Geelong, however, had a good grip on the game by this time and, despite an Essendon come-back burst in the last term, the Cats finished full of running and won well.

Making their eleventh successive finals appearance, Melbourne crushed Collingwood with a superb display of power football in the second semi-final. Collingwood had two goals two on the board before Melbourne had scored, halfway through the first term. But from then on the Demons swung into top gear and cut the Magpies to pieces. Collingwood did not score their third goal until one minute into the second term, and their fourth until twenty minutes into the third term. While the Magpies struggled, the Demons kicked seventeen goals in the last three quarters, and eventually won by eighty-nine points. It was a shattering blow to the morale of the Magpies but shrewd judges hearkened back to 1958, when the Demons also annihilated the Magpies in the second semi-final, but lost the grand final.

Hot favourites Geelong failed in an exciting preliminary final on the rain-soaked MCG. Play was very even all the way through, even before the rain came. The lead changed six times until ten minutes into the third term when, after a flare-up behind the play, the Magpies grabbed the lead and held it until the finish. The Cats, although suffering a bad blow when A. Lord was carried off in the second term, managed to lead at half-time, but a poor third term gave the Magpies their chance. Both sides scored a goal apiece in the last term, but Geelong threw away valuable chances with misses by Farmer, Routley and Wade (twice) which enabled the Magpies to hang on and win a cliff-hanger by the narrow margin of four points.

In one of the greatest ever finishes to a grand final, Melbourne, again aided by 'Lady Luck', took out their sixth flag in eleven years. Despised under-dogs, Collingwood pleased their host of supporters when they led by two points at half-time, after a low-scoring first half. Immediately the third term commenced, however, Townsend goaled for the Demons. Defences were then on top again and for a further twenty minutes neither side goaled. Then another Melbourne goal—to Bourke—gave them an eleven-point lead at the last change, Collingwood having scored only two points for the term.

Now began a sensational last quarter—after three behinds to Melbourne, Tuddenham goaled to reduce Collingwood's deficit to eight points. Barassi and Kenneally added behinds for the Demons before Gabelich grabbed the ball from a throw-in and goaled for Collingwood with seventeen minutes gone. Then came one of the most exciting moments of any finals match—Tuddenham's pass found Gabelich temporarily unattended on the half-forward flank. Seeing no Melbourne defender near, the seventeen-stone Magpie ruckman began a seventy-yard run to the goals, in the process bouncing the ball four times and very nearly losing it at each bounce. Finally, after a tremendous individual effort, Gabelich slammed the ball through from five yards out and the Magpie fans screamed in delight as their side took the lead with four minutes, plus time-on, to play. Gabelich was entitled to believe that his magnificent effort had won this great game for his side, but Melbourne refused to give in. It seemed as if fortune had finally favoured Collingwood, however, when Melbourne's Hassa Mann marked right in front and managed only a behind, but at the twenty-three-minute mark of the term, Dixon (Melbourne) drove the ball forward, where it came off the hands of the pack to be picked up and booted through for a goal by Melbourne's back-pocket Neil Crompton. Crompton, 100 yards out of position, had followed his rover almost the length of the ground, and his goal, his first of the season, put the Demons ahead by four points. Graham (Collingwood) kicked out of bounds with the crowd at fever-pitch, and then was unlucky not to receive a free kick directly in front. Wise, who had rucked all day, and Bourke, switched from full-forward to the full-back line, made timely saves for Melbourne, who held grimly to their four-point lead as the Magpies attacked with four minutes of time-on gone, but time had run out for Collingwood and the sounding of the siren gave Melbourne their twelfth VFL pennant, only one behind Collingwood's League record of thirteen.

RESULTS

AUGUST 30 — FIRST SEMI-FINAL

	1st	2nd	3rd	Final	
Geelong	1 . 5	6 . 6	9 . 7	12 . 12	(84)
Essendon	4 . 0	5 . 3	7 . 5	10 . 5	(65)

MCG — Umpire Brophy

Attendance 92,231 (record) — Gate £30,512 (record)

BEST — (Geel) A. Lord, Goggin, Farmer, Devine, West, Closter, Vinar, Polinelli
(Ess) Epis, Sampson, Mitchell, Birt, Timms, Shaw, Fraser

GOALS — (Geel) Wade (3), Polinelli (3), Wooller (2), Vinar, Goggin, Farmer, Marshall
(Ess) Sampson (2), Fordham (2), Mitchell (2), Gosper, Birt, Biessell, Fraser

SEPTEMBER 5 — SECOND SEMI-FINAL

	1st	2nd	3rd	Final	
Melbourne	2 . 3	8 . 7	14 . 13	19 . 20	(134)
Collingwood	2 . 2	3 . 6	5 . 8	6 . 9	(45)

MCG — Umpire Crouch
Attendance 93,010 — Gate £30,477

BEST — (Melb) Massey, Dixon, Townsend, Mann, Barassi, Vagg
(Col) Henderson, Gabelich, Wright, Rose, Tuddenham
GOALS — (Melb) Townsend (5), Kenneally (3), Vagg (3), Lord (3), Barassi (2), Mann (2), Bourke
(Col) Tuddenham (2), Waters (2), Rose, Graham

SEPTEMBER 12 — PRELIMINARY FINAL

	1st	2nd	3rd	Final	
Collingwood	2 . 1	4 . 2	6 . 6	7 . 6	(48)
Geelong	2 . 4	4 . 8	4 . 10	5 . 14	(44)

MCG — Umpire Brophy
Attendance 87,091 — Gate £30,885

BEST — (Col) Gabelich, K. Rose, Watt, Henderson, Urquart, Hill
(Geel) Farmer, S. Lord, Marshall, Devine, Goggin, Watts
GOALS — (Col) Graham (3), Norman, Dalton, McLean, Waters
(Geel) Wooller (2), Wade, Sharrock, Yeates

SEPTEMBER 19 — GRAND FINAL

	1st	2nd	3rd	Final	
Melbourne	2 . 6	5 . 7	7 . 10	8 . 16	(64)
Collingwood	2 . 5	5 . 9	5 . 11	8 . 12	(60)

MCG — Umpire Brophy
Attendance 102,469 — Gate £30,939

BEST — (Melb) Adams, Dixon, Tas. Johnson, Wise, H. Mann, Williams, Crompton, Jacobs
(Col) Hill, Steer, Bone, Rose, Potter, Henderson, Reeves, Dalton
GOALS — (Melb) Townsend (3), Lord (2), Mann, Bourke, Crompton
(Col) Waters (2), Gabelich (2), Bone, Steer, Dalton, Tuddenham

GRAND FINAL TEAMS

Melbourne

B	N. Crompton	B. Massey	Tas. Johnson
HB	A. Anderson	B. Roet	F. Davis
C	F. Adams	D. Williams	B. Dixon
HF	B. Kenneally	G. Jacobs	B. Vagg
F	J. Lord	B. Bourke	J. Townsend
Ruck	G. Wise	R. Barassi (c)	H. Mann
Reserves	P. McLean	K. Emselle	
Coach	N. Smith		

Collingwood	B	R. Reeves	E. Potter	T. Steer
	HB	L. Hill	J. Mahon	D. Wright
	C	R. Watt	J. Henderson	A. Chapman
	HF	D. Norman	K. McLean	D. Tuddenham
	F	D. Dalton	I. Graham	T. Waters
	Ruck	R. Gabelich (c)	K. Rose	M. Bone
	Reserves	K. Turner	M. Urquhart	
	Coach	R. Rose		

1965

There was a mass migration of VFL teams to new grounds in 1965. Two moves—Richmond to the MCG and St. Kilda to Moorabbin—were attended by success, but the other, North Melbourne to Coburg, was a failure.

St. Kilda, in fact, became the new glamour team of the League, and they put the performances on the board with fourteen wins and four losses to top the VFL ladder for the first time in their history. Collingwood and Geelong, both with thirteen wins, filed second and third positions, separated by a percentage of only nine per cent. Essendon, twelve wins, easily took fourth place ahead of three other teams on ten wins, including Melbourne who missed the finals for the first time since 1954.

The first semi-final proved to be a one-sided affair. Essendon coach John Coleman sprung a tactical surprise on his Geelong counterpart by switching nine players when the teams lined up, and then switching them back minutes later. The move paid off when Fraser booted a goal within a minute of the start and Fordham added another soon after. It took the Cats twenty-three minutes to score, and the Dons carried on their good early work in the second and third terms to lead by thirty-two points at three-quarter-time. There was still a remote possibility that Geelong could come back, but two quick goals, to Mitchell and Sampson, at the start of the last term dismissed that possibility and the Dons cruised to an easy fifty-two point win as the fans streamed away from the ground a long time before the siren.

One of the most exciting second semi-finals for years saw St. Kilda hold on to beat the luckless Collingwood by one point. Fans were confused at the commencement of the game when some players appeared in altered numbers. This was done at the direction of the VFL when a football publication violated copyrights and printed a list of players' numbers. The same thing, fans recalled, had occurred on the day of the 1958 grand final.

Collingwood got away to an early lead, with full-forward Ian Graham dominant with four first-quarter goals. St. Kilda, however, fought back brilliantly, and despite atrocious kicking for goal, had reduced the margin to five points at half-time. In a brilliant third term, the lead changed seven times as both sides gave great exhibitions of long kicking and high marking in the beautiful playing conditions. It was St. Kilda's quarter, however, and with goals to Howell and Morrow almost on the bell, they went to a lead of twelve points at three-quarter-time. They'd had twelve more scoring shots than Collingwood.

The fans roared as Norman goaled for the Magpies immediately play resumed, this being followed by a behind to Waters and a goal to Graham which gave Collingwood the lead. Waters added another behind and Collingwood's lead was two points. When Henderson goaled with a kick off the ground, it looked as if the Magpies were going to run away with the match. St. Kilda, desperate, would not give in, however, and Howell punted a badly needed goal for them from well out on the half-forward line. Then Baldock's long shot was touched going through, and again only a point separated the two sides before Ditterich snapped a nice goal to put the Saints ahead. Tuddenham flashed into play for a behind for Collingwood with fifteen minutes still to play. Graham added another behind, Howell equalled this for St. Kilda–his sixth behind of the day–and Tully (Collingwood) booted a magnificent drop-kick which bounced through for another behind, all within minutes of each other, and the difference was back to three points. Collingwood were missing vital shots under pressure—Norman's shot was forced through for a behind, then Graham, from deep on the flank, had a chance to win the game, but his shot, too, was off-line. Laurie Hill twice put the Magpies into attack in a desperate finish, but time ran out with the Saints ahead by a point, and sent them marching into their first grand final since 1913.

Collingwood brought in six feet seven inches ruckman Len Thompson for his first VFL game in the preliminary final against Essendon. Thompson played a fine game for the Magpies, but his side was thrashed by the Dons to the tune of fifty-five points. It was still a game to remember, however, because of one incident which occurred ten minutes after the start of play. With the ball forty yards upfield, there was a flare-up on the Essendon half-forward flank and, before the crowd had realised just what had happened, Essendon flanker John Somerville was sprawled unconscious on the turf. A Collingwood backman stood over him and, while few people could have seen the incident, it was obvious that Somerville had not fainted. He was, in fact, rushed straight to hospital and his Collingwood opponent was booed each time he went near the ball for the remainder of the day. Later, he was actually questioned by police, but no charges were laid.

The incident, rather than upset Essendon's game, served only to make them more determined and they threw themselves into the play to such effect that they had the game sewn up by three-quarter-time, with a lead of seven goals. Two early goals in the last term gave Magpies' fans some hope, but this was quickly dashed when Clarke, Fraser and Fordham added quick goals. The Dons had taken over completely and Fordham added his sixth major for them just before the bell. The Dons had sounded a big warning about their premiership prospects in their two finals games, with winning margins of fifty-two and fifty-five points.

Both St. Kilda and Essendon lined up at almost full strength for the grand final, with the exception that Somerville, of course, was unable to take his place in the

Essendon line-up. St. Kilda had Guyatt, Wallis and Oakley all out injured.

Essendon, as they had in their previous two finals games, jumped to the lead early, despite inaccurate kicking, but St. Kilda fought back to draw to within eight points at half-time. Both sides had lost stars through injury—Morrow (ruck) had limped off seventeen minutes into the second quarter for St. Kilda, and Shaw (rover), injured early in the game, was replaced in the second term for Essendon.

A brilliant third term practically won the game for the Dons, as they held St. Kilda to one goal three while booting five goals eight themselves. The Saints edged to within two points before Essendon got away to boot seven behinds in succession, but then Fordham (two), Sampson, Birt and Mitchell all added goals in a brilliant burst of pressure football. St. Kilda even swapped Murray (full-back) with Howell (full-forward) and switched Baldock into the ruck, but all to no avail. With a big three-quarter-time lead, the Dons had only to pace it with the Saints for the final thirty minutes to take out the flag, and this they did, both sides scoring four goals, although St. Kilda finished the game with only seventeen men. Fordham, Don full-forward, capped an excellent finals series with a total of seven goals for the game, an effort which equalled the grand final record. This was the Dons' twelfth League premiership, equalling Melbourne's total, and one behind Collingwood's VFL record of thirteen, and they were the third team to win the premiership from fourth position since the Page System of playing finals was introduced in 1931—Carlton (1945) and Essendon (1949) were the others.

RESULTS

SEPTEMBER 4 — FIRST SEMI-FINAL

	1st	2nd	3rd	Final	
Essendon	3 . 5	8 . 14	10 . 16	14 . 19	(103)
Geelong	2 . 0	4 . 3	6 . 8	7 . 9	(51)

MCG — Umpire Crouch
Attendance 89,833 — Gate £35,493

BEST — (Ess) Fraser, Johnston, Birt, Gosper, Clarke, Sampson, Shaw, Mitchell
(Geel) Goggin, Polinelli, Newman, Devine, Newlands, Marshall

GOALS — (Ess) Fraser (3), Birt (3), Mitchell (3), Shaw (3), Fordham, Sampson
(Geel) Andrews (3), Hynes, Newlands, Brown, Goggin

SEPTEMBER 11 — SECOND SEMI-FINAL

	1st	2nd	3rd	Final	
St. Kilda	2 . 7	6 . 14	11 . 22	13 . 24	(102)
Collingwood	5 . 5	8 . 7	11 . 10	14 . 17	(101)

MCG — Umpire Fisher
Attendance 98,395 (record) — Gate £35,706

BEST — (St. K) Cooper, Morrow, Stewart, Griffiths, Ditterich, Rowland, Kennedy, Read
(Col) Graham, Potter, Waters, Hill, Gray, Norman, Gabelich, Henderson

GOALS — (St. K) Howell (4), Morrow (3), Ditterich (3), Rowland, Kennedy, Smith
(Col) Graham (6), Waters (2), Norman (2), Henderson (2), McKenna (2)

1965

SEPTEMBER 18 — PRELIMINARY FINAL

	1st	2nd	3rd	Final	
Essendon	3 . 6	5 . 9	10 . 10	14 . 13	(97)
Collingwood	1 . 0	3 . 0	4 . 4	6 . 6	(42)

MCG **Umpire Brophy**
Attendance 95,386 **Gate £35,719**

BEST —	(Ess)	Birt, McKenzie, Payne, Fordham, Pryor, Fraser, Johnston, Shelton, Davis, Blew
	(Col)	Gray, Hill, Turner, Tuddenham, Thompson, Mahon, Norman, Rose, Bone
GOALS —	(Ess)	Fordham (6), Fraser (4), Clarke (2), Mitchell, Waite
	(Col)	McKenna (3), Bone, Graham, Gray

SEPTEMBER 25 — GRAND FINAL

	1st	2nd	3rd	Final	
Essendon	2 . 7	5 . 10	10 . 18	14 . 21	(105)
St. Kilda	1 . 6	4 . 8	5 . 11	9 . 16	(70)

MCG **Umpire Crouch**
Attendance 104,846 **Gate £35,225**

BEST —	(Ess)	Sampson, Fordham, Fraser, Gosper, Davis, Birt, Blew, Pryor, McKenzie, Mitchell
	(St. K)	Stewart, Baldock, Cooper, Kennedy, Read, Neale, Rowland, Sierakowski
GOALS —	(Ess)	Fordham (7), Sampson (2), Gosper (2), Fraser, Birt, Mitchell
	(St. K)	Howell (3), Rowland (2), Baldock (2), Smith, K. Roberts

GRAND FINAL TEAMS

Essendon	B	D. Gerlach	G. Brown	C. Payne
	HB	B. Davis	I. Shelton	G. Pryor
	C	A. Epis	J. Clarke	R. Blew
	HF	G. Johnston	K. Fraser (c)	G. Gosper
	F	B. Sampson	E. Fordham	D. Shaw
	Ruck	D. McKenzie	H. Mitchell	J. Birt
	Reserves	B. Waite	K. Egan	
	Coach	J. Coleman		
St. Kilda	B	R. Head	R. Murray	K. Neale
	HB	B. Sierakowski	I. Synman	D. Griffiths
	C	B. McMaster-Smith	I. Stewart	J. Read
	HF	I. Cooper	D. Baldock (c)	D. Kennedy
	F	A. Morrow	V. Howell	R. Smith
	Ruck	C. Ditterich	R. Cross	I. Rowland
	Reserves	R. Morton	K. Roberts	
	Coach	A. Jeans		

1966

The contest for the Four in 1966 was very even between the top five sides, the others being out of the running with many games to go. Richmond, as in 1965, was the one to miss out, finishing fifth after having held top position with four games to play. A loss to Geelong in round sixteen saw them fall from second to fifth, and they never got back, eventually missing out by two premiership points, although they had a better percentage than Essendon (fourth).

Collingwood (fifteen wins, three losses) and St. Kilda (fourteen wins, four losses) were the top sides of the year on home and home results, but Geelong, Essendon and Richmond also had fourteen wins and only percentage decided the final positions.

In a sensational first semi-final, Essendon just scrambled home from a very determined Geelong. Seven goals down at half-time and thirty-three points behind at the last change, the Cats unleashed a terrific burst of power football to draw to within four points of the Bombers in time-on, after throwing away some golden opportunities with five successive behinds. The Cats booted four goals in nine minutes at the beginning of the last term and only a magnificent long goal by Essendon skipper Ken Fraser stopped their run. Fraser's goal and another snapped by John Birt in the last minute were Essendon's only scores of the term, but they were enough to enable the Dons to scrape in by ten points.

The same margin decided the second semi-final between Collingwood and St. Kilda. The Magpies gained a strong grip on the game with a first-quarter burst of five goals two to a point, but St. Kilda, after moving Cooper into the ruck, lifted their game and were two points ahead at half-time. After a fiery start to the third term, when a jostling melee broke out on the St. Kilda half-forward line, both teams gave a wonderful exhibition of pressure football. Both kicked four goals four for the term and St. Kilda still led at the last change. They managed to increase their two-point lead to eighteen early in the last, but Collingwood got goals from Searle (two) and Tuddenham to restore the lead to the Magpies. In a hectic final few minutes the lead see-sawed as Mynott (St. Kilda) goaled, and Tuddenham goaled again—his third in seven minutes and seventh for the match from the forward flank—to make the game safe for Collingwood.

Umpire L. Perkins, when he officiated at the second semi-final, became the first umpire to have charge of a finals game in his first season since P. Ellingsen in 1931.

In the only one-sided game of the finals series, St. Kilda, although held scoreless in the third term, were far too powerful for Essendon. The wet conditions did not bother the Saints, who at one stage had ten goals on the board from eleven scoring shots. The Bombers, on the other hand, were thoroughly at sea in the rain and had scored only three goals nine when the teams changed ends for the last time. A better last-quarter effort netted them four goals, but St. Kilda were untroubled to add five more goals to finish with a remarkably accurate fifteen goals four and go on to the grand final.

Collingwood had probably the two most experienced reserves ever when the teams for the grand final were announced—the 1965 captain (John Henderson) and vice-captain (Trevor Steer) were both on the bench. The Magpies made two alterations to the team which had beaten the Saints in the second semi-final—St. Kilda, except for one reserve, fielded the same team as had defeated Essendon the previous week.

The game began with a high wind blowing up the ground—St. Kilda, aided by this wind, kicked to the Punt Road end and Neale goaled for them after three minutes of play. A minute later, Baldock added another. Then St. Kilda were unable to goal again for the remainder of the term, although Collingwood were not without their troubles, it being eighteen minutes into the term before Gabelich got their first goal. It was almost equal at quarter-time, and there was only a point in it at half-time, Collingwood leading. A bad miss, from five yards out and dead in front by Thompson, just before half-time, ultimately cost the Magpies dearly.

Tuddenham, with a goal in the first minute of the second half, sparked Collingwood, but Baldock, from a free, quickly had the equaliser on the board. That was the pattern of play for the term, with the lead ever changing, but the defences of both sides were generally on top, and clever harassing led to several missed chances—Searle (Collingwood) and Neale (St. Kilda) both missed absolute 'sitters'. The Saints battled to a ten-point lead in the latter stages of the third quarter, before W. Richardson goaled for the Magpies to make the margin four points only at the last change.

The last term was amazing. Collingwood attacked from the bounce and Gabelich missed from right in front. Griffiths (St. Kilda) dashed down the ground brilliantly and his handball to Moran gave the Saints a goal—Neale (two) and Cooper followed with behinds and St. Kilda, after nine minutes, led by thirteen points. Sensations continued as Collingwood's skipper, Tuddenham, booted a tremendous goal. Numerous forward thrusts by both sides were stemmed by some fine defensive work, but Graham (Collingwood) eventually marked and goaled from forty yards out to make the difference one point, St. Kilda ahead. With the crowd in a frenzy, Neale marked in a pack and goaled for the Saints after eighteen minutes of the quarter three minutes later, Henderson found Pitt, and Pitt's magnificent punt replied for the Magpies. Play continued to see-saw before the dynamic Tuddenham with a behind, levelled the scores, with two minutes, plus time-on, to go. Richardson (Collingwood) kicked out of bounds and some desperation football followed, with players literally throwing themselves at the ball. Finally, after two minutes of time-on had ticked away, St. Kilda forward-flanker Breen grabbed the ball from a ball-up and sent a long bouncing kick through for a behind to grab the lead for the Saints. Waters (Collingwood) and Murray (St. Kilda) broke up serious attacks before the bell sounded and the pro-St. Kilda crowd wildly acclaimed the first St. Kilda premiership, a premiership the club had unsuccessfully sought for ninety-three years.

RESULTS

SEPTEMBER 3 — FIRST SEMI-FINAL

	1st	2nd	3rd	Final	
Essendon	6 . 1	10 . 5	13 . 6	15 . 6	(96)
Geelong	3 . 4	3 . 5	7 . 9	12 . 14	(86)

MCG — Umpire Crouch

Attendance 93,765 (record) — Gate $71,646 (record)

BEST — (Ess) Fraser, Clarke, McKenzie, Shaw, Egan, C. Payne, Birt, Pryor, Gerlach
(Geel) Newman, Rosenow, Ryan, Hosking, A. Lord, Closter, Devine, Sharrock, Newland
GOALS — (Ess) Clarke (3), Shaw (3), Birt (2), Fordham (2), Payne (2), Gosper, Fraser, Sommerville
(Geel) Lord (3), Newman (2), Ryan (2), Wade (2), Newland (2) Sharrock

SEPTEMBER 10 — SECOND SEMI-FINAL

	1st	2nd	3rd	Final	
Collingwood	5 . 2	6 . 3	10 . 5	15 . 9	(99)
St. Kilda	0 . 1	6 . 5	10 . 9	13 . 11	(89)

MCG **Umpire Perkins**
Attendance 95,614 **Gate $71,409**

BEST — (Col) Waters, Tuddenham, Wallis, Potter, K. Rose, Patterson, Clark, Montgomery, W. Richardson
(St. K) Murray, Morrow, Cooper, Breen, Smith, Payze, Griffiths, Synman, Oakley
GOALS — (Col) Tuddenham (7), Graham (2), Wallis (2), Searle (2), Richardson, Price
(St. K) Payze (3), Neale (2), Smith (2), Baldock (2), Cooper, Breen, Oakley, Mynott

SEPTEMBER 17 — PRELIMINARY FINAL

	1st	2nd	3rd	Final	
St. Kilda	4 . 1	10 . 2	10 . 2	15 . 4	(94)
Essendon	2 . 4	3 . 4	3 . 9	7 . 10	(52)

MCG **Umpire Crouch**
Attendance 93,453 **Gate $71,455**

BEST — (St. K) Stewart, Morrow, Smith, Murray, Synman, Griffiths, Baldock, Cooper, Head
(Ess) McKenzie, Gosper, Birt, Gerlach, C. Payne, Clarke, Williams
GOALS — (St. K) Neale (4), Davis (3), Morrow (3), Bingley, Cooper, Read, Griffiths, Payze
(Ess) Mitchell (2), Gosper, Williams, Fordham, Noonan, Pryor

SEPTEMBER 24 — GRAND FINAL

	1st	2nd	3rd	Final	
St. Kilda	2 . 5	5 . 6	8 . 9	10 . 14	(74)
Collingwood	2 . 1	5 . 7	7 . 11	10 . 13	(73)

MCG **Umpire Crouch**
Attendance 101,655 **Gate $70,517**

BEST — (St. K) Cooper, Stewart, Sierakowski, Griffiths, Breen, Morrow, Neale, Synman, Mynott, Murray
(Col) Waters, Richardson, Thompson, Patterson, Pitt, Tuddenham, Hill, Gabelich, Montgomery, Tully
GOALS — (St. K) Neale (5), Baldock (2), Griffiths, Cooper, Moran
(Col) Tuddenham (3), Gabelich (2), Richardson (2), Wallis, Pitt, Graham

GRAND FINAL TEAMS

St. Kilda	B	R. Head	R. Murray	B. Sierakowski
	HB	V. Howell	I. Synman	J. Bingley
	C	J. Moran	I. Stewart	J. Read
	HF	I. Cooper	D. Baldock (c)	B. Breen
	F	A. Morrow	K. Neale	A. Davis
	Ruck	B. Mynott	D. Griffiths	R. Smith
	Reserves	T. Payze	K. Billing	
	Coach	A. Jeans		
Collingwood	B	I. Montgomery	P. Boyne	T. Waters
	HB	L. Hill	E. Potter	L. Adamson
	C	P. Paterson	C. Tully	E. Hutchesson
	HF	D. Tuddenham (c)	D. Searle	M. Pitt
	F	R. Gabelich	I. Graham	G. Wallis
	Ruck	L. Thompson	K. Rose	W. Richardson
	Reserves	T. Steer	J. Henderson	
	Coach	R. Rose		

1967

All four 1967 finalists occupied their places in the Four by the end of the fifth round of home and home games, three holding them until the end. St. Kilda was in the unfortunate position of trailing back in fifth position for the last thirteen games of the season, but they had only themselves to blame, for they lost several matches at critical stages of the season when they were within a game of regaining fourth position.

Richmond (fifteen wins, three losses), Carlton (fourteen wins, three losses and a tie), Geelong (thirteen wins, five losses) and Collingwood (twelve wins, six losses) made up the final Four, with the brilliant but unpredictable Cats eliminating the Magpies from the premiership race in an excellent first semi-final.

Geelong, leading by a point after a keenly fought first three quarters, won the game in the opening minutes of the last term with goals from Wade (three), Goggin and Sharrock. The brilliant Wade was the difference between the two sides, kicking eight goals one from ten shots, but Geelong's all-round skill and speed eventually beat Collingwood.

Richmond had a good win over Carlton in the second semi-final, but lost star ruckman Neville Crowe for the grand final. Crowe was suspended after an incident in the third quarter of the match, his first suspension in a ten-year VFL career. Richmond had two goals and Carlton one within three minutes of the start of play, but Richmond, with Hart (full-forward) outplaying an obviously unfit Wes Lofts, had a good lead by half-time and held this advantage at the last change.

Then, in the last term, the Tigers unleashed a brilliant burst of six goals five, sweeping the Carlton defenders aside and going on to a forty-point win, a win which considerably reduced their odds for the premiership. Critics pointed out, too, that the Tigers did not have a single player in their line-up who had previously played in a finals match, making their win even more meritorious.

Geelong, twenty-seven points in arrears at half-time, staged a remarkable recovery in the second half of the preliminary final. Earlier, Carlton had made eight positional changes to their selected side, and 'jumped' Geelong in the first quarter by kicking four goals in eight minutes before the Cats had scored.

The third term was Geelong's best. Holding the Blues to one goal two with the breeze, the Cats, with Wade and Sharrock in everything up forward, booted a match-winning eight goals one for the term and held a handy fourteen-point lead at the last change. Sharrock kicked three goals in the Cats' big scoring third term, and Wade, two. Carlton still had a chance in the last, but were off target, and the accurate Cats were untroubled to hold their lead and advance to the grand final.

In the best grand final for years, Richmond won their first flag since 1943 after a fantastic last quarter during which the scores were level four times.

Conditions were ideal as the Tigers, kicking with the aid of a slight breeze, fought their way to a six-point lead at the first change. Richmond, hottest favourites since Melbourne in 1958, were struggling a little, the Cats' defence being well on top. Barrot, becoming a danger man in the centre for Richmond, was in the van in the second term, and he continually drove the Tigers forward where, despite inaccuracy, they booted five goals to the Cats' four and were sixteen points in front at half-time.

The third term began sensationally—within a minute, Goggin burst out of the pack and goaled for the Cats. Further goals to Andrews and Wade gave the Cats an eight-point lead after seven minutes of the term. After the initial breakthrough, the Richmond defence steadied, and scoring for the rest of the term was almost even, the Tigers having seven more scoring shots than their opponents and leading by two points at the last change.

Now came a grand last quarter. Soon after it began, Bartlett goaled for the Tigers, but Ryan, with a long punt from centre-half-forward, replied for Geelong, and three successive behinds put the Cats a point ahead. The scores were levelled for the second time within minutes before Sharrock goaled for Geelong, but Ronaldson, after a mark in the forward pocket, levelled again with a beautiful drop-kick goal for Richmond. Wade (Geelong) booted a behind and Guinane (Richmond) did likewise—and for the fourth time in twenty-three minutes the scores were equal.

With time-on starting, big Tiger ruckman, Ronaldson, marked on the half-forward flank and drove through a magnificent long distance drop-kick goal which gave the Tigers a six-point lead. Graham (Geelong) scored a behind, but Bartlett made no mistake for the Tigers as he grabbed the ball from a throw-in and kicked their sixteenth goal. Geelong, not giving in, came forward again. Ryan snapped a behind, and a shot by Goggin was marked almost on the line by Swift, Richmond full-back and captain. Almost on the siren, Polinelli's long shot scored a behind for the Cats, but the premiership belonged to Richmond, their first premiership since 1943 and sixth since joining the VFL in 1908. Geelong's Doug Wade, with four goals, took his season's tally to ninety-six, the highest total since John Coleman's ninety-seven for Essendon in 1953. It looked as if the magical 100 goals barrier would soon be broken after a lapse of many years.

1967

RESULTS

SEPTEMBER 2 — FIRST SEMI-FINAL

	1st	2nd	3rd	Final	
Geelong	4 . 5	8 . 7	10 . 10	16 . 12	(108)
Collingwood	4 . 2	8 . 3	10 . 9	11 . 12	(78)

MCG — **Umpire Crouch**
Attendance 91,715 — **Gate $88,253**

BEST — (Geel) Farmer, Goggin, Walker, Rosenow, Marshall, Wade, Closter, Eales
(Col) W. Richardson, Rose, Dunne, Thompson, Tully, Britt, Adamson, Price

GOALS — (Geel) Wade (8), Goggin (3), Andrews (2), Mitchell, Sharrock, Ryan
(Col) Dunne (4), Tuddenham (2), W. Richardson (2), Waters, Britt, Rose

SEPTEMBER 9 — SECOND SEMI-FINAL

	1st	2nd	3rd	Final	
Richmond	5 . 8	10 . 13	14 . 16	20 . 21	(141)
Carlton	3 . 4	7 . 9	11 . 12	14 . 17	(101)

MCG — **Umpire Sheales**
Attendance 99,051 (record) — **Gate $88,160 (record)**

BEST — (Rich) Barrot, Hart, Clay, Dean, Guinane, Burgin
(Carl) Nicholls, Goold, Munari, Barassi, Silvagni, Gallagher

GOALS — (Rich) Hart (6), Patterson (3), Brown (3), Guinane (2), Northey (2), B. Richardson (2), Barrott, Bartlett
(Carl) Nicholls (3), Munari (3), Kekovich (2), Jesaulenko (2), Barassi (2), Silvagni, Gallagher

SEPTEMBER 16 — PRELIMINARY FINAL

	1st	2nd	3rd	Final	
Geelong	1 . 0	6 . 2	14 . 3	17 . 6	(108)
Carlton	5 . 2	10 . 5	11 . 7	11 . 13	(79)

MCG — **Umpire Sheales**
Attendance 95,542 — **Gate $88,178**

BEST — (Geel) Sharrock, Goggin, Farmer, Polinelli, Ryan, Closter, Mitchell, Walker
(Carl) Nicholls, Barassi, Collis, Hall, B. Gill, Goold, Gallagher, Collins

GOALS — (Geel) Wade (5), Sharrock (4), Mitchell (3), Ryan (2), Newland, Polinelli, Andrews
(Carl) Gallagher (3), Jesaulenko (2), Nicholls, Collins, Barassi, Robertson, Auchetti, Stone

SEPTEMBER 23 — GRAND FINAL

	1st	2nd	3rd	Final	
Richmond	4 . 3	9 . 10	12 . 15	16 . 18	(114)
Geelong	3 . 3	7 . 6	13 . 7	15 . 15	(105)

MCG — **Umpire Sheales**
Attendance 109,396 — **Gate $88,256**

BEST — (Rich) Barrot, Brown, Hart, A. Richardson, Dean, M. Perry, B. Richardson, Bartlett
(Geel) Goggin, Sharrock, Polinelli, Farmer, West, Andrews, Newland, Ainsworth

1967-1968

GOALS —	(Rich)	Ronaldson (3), Hart (3), Bartlett (3), Brown (3), Guinane, A. Richardson, B. Richardson, Barrot
	(Geel)	Wade (4), Sharrock (4), Goggin (3), Andrews, Hynes, Eales, Ryan

GRAND FINAL TEAMS

Richmond	B	R. Dean	F. Swift (c)	T. Jewell
	HB	G. Burgin	M. Perry	G. Strang
	C	R. Clay	W. Barrot	F. Bourke
	HF	J. Northey	P. Guinane	B. Richardson
	F	J. Ronaldson	R. Hart	W. Brown
	Ruck	M. Patterson	A. Richardson	K. Bartlett
	Reserves	M. Green.	J. Perry	
	Coach	T. Hafey		
Geelong	B	G. Ainsworth	R. West	G. Rosenow
	HB	D. Marshall	P. Walker	T. Farman
	C	A. Polinelli	W. Closter	K. Newland
	HF	J. Sharrock	G. Andrews	C. Eales
	F	G. Hynes	D. Wade	C. Mitchell
	Ruck	G. Farmer (c)	W. Ryan	W. Goggin
	Reserves	J. Scarlett	R. Graham	
	Coach	P. Pianto		

1968

The 1967 premiers, Richmond, slumped in 1968 and eventually finished fifth, missing the Four by two premiership points, but with a percentage which was much inferior to that of the fourth team, St. Kilda.

Essendon (sixteen wins, three losses and a draw) topped the ladder in 1968, a season in which twenty home and home games were played. Carlton and Geelong (each fifteen wins, five losses) followed, with St. Kilda (fourteen wins, five losses and a draw) next. Hawthorn, despite 125 goals—the first century by any VFL player for sixteen years—from Peter Hudson, could finish only sixth with nine wins and a draw.

St. Kilda held their place in the Four with a great eight-goal victory over Geelong in the last game, and consequently were hot favourites when the same two sides met in the first semi-final seven days later.

However, to the surprise of everyone, the Saints were no match for the rejuvenated

Cats, whose tall ruckmen, Mitchell and Newman, paired together in the first ruck and put St. Kilda's top ruckman, Ditterich, out of the game. The two Geelong ruckmen took twenty-seven marks between them during the day, and Geelong were far too strong in the air for their opponents—in addition, they displayed abundant pace: pace which had been missing just seven days before. Sharrock and Wade were elusive on the forward line and Marshall superb in the centre as the Cats, with five goals in each of the last three quarters, cruised to an effortless forty-three-point win.

Carlton, without captain-coach Ron Barassi who had recently announced his retirement as a player, had a good win over Essendon in the second semi-final. The Blues did it the hard way, coming from behind in the second half despite losing both Jesaulenko and Bennett by half-time. The Dons did not score their first goal until almost time-on in the first term, while Carlton bombarded the goals for five goals eight. Had the Blues' forwards been on target the game would have been settled then and there. The Dons fought back brilliantly with six goals in the second term, the last of which—by Close soon before half-time—gave them the lead at the interval. After the break, however, Carlton's dashing defence, with Goold the leading light, bottled up the Essendon forwards in no uncertain manner and the battling Dons could add only one goal five to their score while Carlton kicked seven goals eight and went on to an effortless six-goal win which put them into the grand final.

A record preliminary final crowd of 103,649 saw a great exhibition of fast open football as Essendon returned to form to defeat Geelong by twenty-four points. The Dons, despite the loss of Fraser and Brown in the last half, held Geelong to only one goal in the final fifty minutes. They wrapped up the game with a third-quarter burst of three goals eight to the Cats' four points. When Geelong drew to within fifteen points halfway through the last term, a goal from Noonan made the match safe.

Essendon, with skipper Ken Fraser and full-back Brown still unfit, recast their side for the grand final and brought in a seventeen-year-old schoolboy—Geoff Blethyn—to fill the full-forward position for his second League game.

The game was spoilt by a strong cross-wind which kept scores low and made kicking and marking difficult. In fact, it was five minutes into the game before the first mark was taken.

The Blues' backs were loose early, and young Blethyn took advantage of this looseness to kick his side's first two goals. Crane and Kekovich replied for Carlton, but it was mainly a quarter in which defences of both sides were on top, despite a lot of fumbling and mistakes.

The second term was the best of the match—Carlton, getting on top, kicked four goals six to the Dons' three straight goals, and held a handy half-time lead of thirteen points.

Hall (concussion) did not return after half-time for Carlton. The swirling wind was still bothering both sides, but Blethyn goaled for the Dons after fifteen minutes to make the difference six points before the Blues went away again when Quirk goaled. The Carlton lead was eleven points at the last change, and the scene was set for a tense last-quarter battle.

The last term started with the same pattern of play that had characterised the previous three quarters, with the ball see-sawing between the respective back-lines. The Blues missed each time they came forward, but increased their lead to fourteen points before Lake, Essendon's reserve, raced in to mark and kick a vital goal. Another Essendon score—a rushed behind—was followed by a spectacular mark and goal by Blethyn which made the difference a single point in Carlton's favour.

The record crowd rocked with excitement as both sides hurled themselves into the fray. From a throw-in, Munari's kick for Carlton was rushed through for a behind —two points the difference. The Dons streaked forward, and Blethyn took a clever mark in the pocket, but his shot from an acute angle went out of bounds. At the other end, Kekovich's long shot also went out. Another attack by the Blues ended with Jones' shot also going out of bounds, before Crosswell snapped a behind, which made the difference three points. This was the final margin as the siren sounded soon after, proclaiming the Blues premiers for 1968—coach Ron Barassi, after playing in six premiership sides, proved his versatitilty by coaching yet another one.

After seventy-two seasons of League football, the 1968 grand final could still produce a 'first'—it was the first time that the losing side in a grand final had scored more goals than the winning side (although Essendon scored three goals less than Melbourne when drawing the 1948 grand final).

RESULTS

SEPTEMBER 7 — FIRST SEMI-FINAL

	1st	2nd	3rd	Final	
Geelong	4 . 4	9 . 7	14 . 10	19 . 13	(127)
St. Kilda	2 . 4	4 . 10	8 . 13	11 . 17	(83)

MCG — Umpire Crouch
Attendance 98,885 (record) — Gate $94,717 (record)

BEST — (Geel) Marshall, Mitchell, Newman, Hosking, Walker, Goggin
(St. K) Bonney, Pascoe, Breen, Smith, Davis, Stewart
GOALS — (Geel) Wade (5), Sharrock (4), Stevens (3), Nankervis (2), Newland, Ryan, Mitchell, Marshall, Gladman
(St. K) Breen (4), Payze (2), Stewart, Smith, Bonney, Trott, O'Donnell

SEPTEMBER 14 — SECOND SEMI-FINAL

	1st	2nd	3rd	Final	
Carlton	5 . 8	6 . 9	11 . 12	13 . 17	(95)
Essendon	1 . 2	7 . 6	7 . 8	8 . 11	(59)

MCG — Umpire Sleeth
Attendance 106,365 (record) — Gate $94,794 (record)

BEST — (Carl) Nicholls, Silvagni, Goold, Hall, Quirk, Jones, Gill, Crane, Crosswell
(Ess) Fordham, Close, Williams, Gerlach, Davis
GOALS — (Carl) Quirk (3), Kekovich (2), Crosswell (2), Nicholls, Wall, Jones, Jesaulenko, Crane, Chandler
(Ess) Noonan (4), Close (2), Gross (2)

SEPTEMBER 21 — PRELIMINARY FINAL

	1st	2nd	3rd	Final	
Essendon	3 . 6	7 . 10	10 . 18	11 . 25	(91)
Geelong	5 . 3	8 . 6	8 . 10	9 . 13	(67)

MCG — Umpire Crouch
Attendance 103,649 (record) — Gate $94,498 (record)

BEST — (Ess) Fletcher, McKenzie, Blew, Payne, Davis, Pryor, Epis, Ellis, Fordham
(Geel) Goggin, Closter, Marshall, Rosenow, Hosking, Ainsworth, Mitchell

Peter McKenna (Collingwood) marks in front of Wes Lofts (Carlton)—finals 1969. *Herald-Sun photo.*

M. Hobbs (Footscray) brilliantly outmarks Trev. Johnson (Melbourne). Whitten (Footscray) runs in at left. Hobbs took this memorable mark in the 1961 preliminary final. *Age photo*

Grand final 1961. Victorious Hawthorn captain, Graham Arthur, holds the Premiership Cup aloft. This was Hawthorn's first-ever premiership.

One of the most famous marks in finals history. Jesaulenko (Carlton) over Jenkin (Collingwood)—Second semi-final 1970. *Herald & Weekly Times photo.*

Crowded centre bounce—the St. Kilda V Hawthorn grand final 1971. Illustrates the congestion that ultimately resulted in the introduction of the centre diamond. *Herald-Sun photo*

The goal that wasn't. Hudson kicks what would have been his 151st goal of the season had it been allowed. Grand final against St. Kilda 1971. *Age photo*

D. McKay (Carlton) marks in the 1972 grand final. Other players (L-R) Hart (Richmond) Doull (Carlton) Balme (Richmond) Hunt (Richmond) and Southby (Carlton). *Herald & Weekly Times photo*

The 1973 Grand final—Bartlett, Richmond's matchwinner, breaks away with the ball. Crane (Carlton) moves in at top right of the picture. Others (L-R) Crosswell (C), Wood (R), Doull (C).

Hart (Richmond) took this mark despite strong Carlton opposition—Grand final 1973.

North Melbourne's first-ever Premiership — 1975. *Herald-Sun Photo.*

Terry Daniher (Essendon) and Laurie Serafini (Fitzroy), 1979. Elimination Final, *Herald-Sun Photo.*

Bill Picken (Collingwood) flies high over Fitzroy's Gerry McCarthy. First semi-final 1979. *Herald-Sun Photo.*

Richmond v. North Melbourne — preliminary final 1975. Neil Balme (Richmond), Mick Nolan and Brent Crosswell (North). *Herald-Sun Photo.*

Collingwood's Peter Moore and Carlton's Mike Fitzpatrick. Grand Final 1979. *Herald-Sun Photo.*

GOALS — (Ess)	Noonan (3), Gosper (2), Fordham (2), Sproule, Payne, Close, Shaw				
(Geel)	Sharrock (3), Wade (3), Closter, Stevens, Ryan				

SEPTEMBER 28 — GRAND FINAL

	1st	2nd	3rd	Final	
Carlton	2 . 2	6 . 8	7 . 9	7 . 14	(56)
Essendon	2 . 1	5 . 1	6 . 4	8 . 5	(53)

MCG — Umpire Crouch

Attendance 116,828 (record) — Gate $94,678 (record)

BEST —	(Carl)	Crane, Nicholls, Robertson, Jesaulenko, Gallagher, Kekovich, Silvagni, Collins
	(Ess)	Gerlach, Williams, Close, Ellis, Gosper, Epis, Fletcher, Pryor, McKenzie
GOALS —	(Carl)	B. Kekovich (4), Crane, Crosswell, Quirk
	(Ess)	Blethyn (4), Sproule, Close, Noonan, B. Lake

GRAND FINAL TEAMS

Carlton	B	I. Collins	W. Lofts	R. Walls
	HB	B. Gill	J. Goold	K. Hall
	C	G. Crane	B. Crosswell	I. Robertson
	HF	A. Jesaulenko	W. Bennett	B. Quirk
	F	D. Munari	B. Kekovich	P. Jones
	Ruck	J. Nicholls (c)	S. Silvagni	A. Gallagher
	Reserves	N. Chandler	P. McLean	
	Coach	R. Barassi		
Essendon	B	D. Gerlach	G. Pryor	N. Evans
	HB	B. Davis	J. Williams	A. Epis
	C	R. Blew	J. Ellis	K. Fletcher
	HF	R. Close	A. Noonan	D. Shaw
	F	P. Sproule	G. Blethyn	E. Fordham
	Ruck	D. McKenzie (c)	C. Payne	G. Gosper
	Reserves	B. Lake	D. Gross	
	Coach	J. Clarke		

1969

Twenty games were played again in 1969 and it was a season of high scores, with all twelve teams kicking more than 1700 points and the top five scoring over 2000. Wade (Geelong) topped the goal-kicking list with 127, followed by Hudson (Hawthorn) 120 and McKenna (Collingwood) ninety-seven, the biggest orgy of goal-scoring by the top full-forwards that the game had ever seen. McKenna's and Wade's efforts helped their sides into the finals, but Hawthorn, despite Hudson's effort, again missed out, although this time it was only on percentage (but a quite considerable percentage —twenty-six per cent).

Collingwood (fifteen wins, five losses) topped the ladder, followed by Carlton (eight point four per cent behind, with the same number of wins), Geelong (thirteen wins, one draw) and Richmond (thirteen wins).

Reaching their peak at just the right time, the brilliant Tigers overwhelmed Geelong in the first semi-final to the tune of a record semi-final score of twenty-five goals seventeen and a record winning margin of 118 points. The Tigers never looked back after a first-term burst of eight goals three, and built up an unbeatable twelve-goal lead by half-time, increasing this to seventeen goals at the last change. The Tigers won all over the ground—they had a damaging centre-line, a dashing defence and match-winners in Moore and Hart up forward. Green, beginning a momentous finals series, dominated the ruck.

Geelong, with a goal on the siren in the third term and four more in the last, made their score only slightly more respectable. Without Wade, who kicked five of their seven goals for the day, the Cats would have struggled to score at all.

After an even struggle up to half-time in the second semi-final, Carlton won the game with a third term burst of six goals two to the Magpies' one goal one. Collingwood, however, staged a dramatic revival to draw to within twelve points in the first fifteen minutes of the last quarter. It took the Blues eighteen minutes to score, but in the remaining time they went berserk to kick five goals one and finish the game well in control and holding a convincing thirty-six-point lead, Collingwood continuing their poor record in finals games on the MCG—since the war they had won only ten out of thirty-two second-round games, for two premierships.

In the preliminary final, however, it appeared for a time that Collingwood had overcome their hoodoo. They led by twenty-five points ten minutes into the second term, before Richmond staged a strong fight-back. The Tigers should have had a big half-time lead, but their three goals ten and several out of bounds for the quarter were costly, and made the scores exactly equal at half-time.

The Tigers slowly got on top in the third term, building up their lead to thirteen points before a deluge of goals came. Barrot, Bartlett and Moore (twice) all goaled as the Tigers tore the Magpie defence apart to boot seven goals two for the term. Moore, returning to full-forward after having been moved for a time, was the dominant figure in the Richmond burst, kicking four goals. The Richmond lead was far too big for the Magpies to overtake, despite a good last term by them, and the Tigers were able to cruise home comfortably by twenty-six points, putting them into their second grand final within three seasons.

Playing their third hard finals game in succession, this time in perfect conditions on a sun-bathed MCG, did not upset the Tigers, who became the fourth side to win the flag from fourth position (Essendon 1949 and 1965 and Carlton 1945).

Both sides lined up at top strength for the match. Richmond, with a goal to Moore within thirty seconds of the first bounce, were away to a good start. Hart kicked their second after eight minutes, but thereafter goals were hard to get, only one more —by Carlton—being scored for the term.

The Tigers gained a good grip on the game with a strong second quarter which netted them four goals to the Blues' one—it took them almost half the quarter to break through the strong Carlton defence, but then they kicked two goals in three minutes. Towards the end of the term Barrot, temporarily switched to full-forward, kicked Richmond's third for the term and almost on the half-time bell further goals were added through Ronaldson (Richmond) and Walls (Carlton), the latter being the Blues' only major of the term.

Both sides made several positional changes at the interval and, although Northey goaled for the Tigers within twenty seconds of the bounce, the rest of the quarter was all Carlton. They came to life when Jackson streaked downfield and goaled on the run. Soon after Gallagher, and then Jackson again, added further goals. The Tigers were starting to become flustered, and the Blues tore into attack again for Nicholls to burst clear of the pack and goal to reduce the Richmond lead to a mere five points. Twenty minutes into the term, Carlton hit the front for the first time when Crosswell beat four Richmond defenders and snapped the Blues' seventh goal. Jesaulenko flashed into play with two shots, the first a goal and the second hitting the post, and it looked as if Carlton were going to run away. However, a goal to Richmond's Moore almost on the siren saw the Tigers trail by only four points at the last change.

The final term was a disappointment for the Blues after their brilliant third-quarter burst—the Tigers slowly got on top and built up a thirteen-point lead by the start of time-on. Then goals to Bond and Bartlett sealed the result of the game. The brilliant Tigers had held Carlton to a mere two points in the last quarter, and won their seventh VFL premiership.

RESULTS

SEPTEMBER 6 — FIRST SEMI-FINAL

	1st	2nd	3rd	Final	
Richmond	8 . 3	14 . 7	20 . 11	25 . 17	(167)
Geelong	2 . 1	2 . 4	3 . 6	7 . 7	(49)

MCG — Umpire Crouch

Attendance 101,233 (record) — Gate $110,267 (record)

BEST —	(Rich)	Green (B.O.G.), Sheedy, Bourke, Barrot, Clay, Bartlett, Hart, Beard, Moore
	(Geel)	Goggin, Ryan, Ainsworth, Stevens, Reid, Wade
GOALS —	(Rich)	Moore (6), Bourke (4), Bartlett (3), Green (2), Brown (2), Northey (2), Barrot, Clay, Hart, Dean, Bowden, Hunt
	(Geel)	Wade (5), Andrews, Ainsworth

SEPTEMBER 13 — SECOND SEMI-FINAL

	1st	2nd	3rd	Final	
Carlton	1 . 4	5 . 8	11 . 10	16 . 11	(107)
Collingwood	2 . 4	5 . 5	6 . 6	10 . 11	(71)

MCG — Umpire Sleeth

Attendance 108,544 (record) — Gate $110,346 (record)

BEST —	(Carl)	Nicholls, Gallagher, Crane, Jackson, Quirk, Walls, Jesaulenko, Lofts
	(Col)	Waters, Tuddenham, Jenkin, Watt, Greening
GOALS —	(Carl)	Jackson (4), Jesaulenko (3), Gallagher (3), Crosswell (2), Walls (2), Jones, Nicholls
	(Col)	McKenna (4), Tully, Tuddenham, Graham, Jenkin, Thompson, Greening

***R. Hart (Rich.), whilst on National Service, played for Richmond in the 1969 grand final, and for Glenelg in the S.A. grand final in the following week. Richmond won—Glenelg lost.**

1969

SEPTEMBER 20 — PRELIMINARY FINAL

	1st	2nd	3rd	Final	
Richmond	3 . 2	6 . 12	13 . 14	15 . 17	(107)
Collingwood	4 . 2	7 . 6	8 . 8	12 . 9	(81)

MCG — Umpire Jolley
Attendance 108,279 — Gate $110,394

BEST — (Rich) Green (B.O.G.), Bartlett, Clay, Dean, Bourke, Strang, Barrot, Beard, Owen, Sheedy
(Col) McKenna, Price, W. Richardson, Potter, O'Callaghan, Wheadon, Thompson

GOALS — (Rich) Moore (4), Bartlett (4), Barrot (2), Dean (2), Ronaldson (2), Hart
(Col) McKenna (6), Farmer (2), Wheadon (2), Tuddenham, Price

SEPTEMBER 27 — GRAND FINAL

	1st	2nd	3rd	Final	
Richmond	2 . 2	6 . 5	8 . 6	12 . 13	(85)
Carlton	1 . 4	2 . 7	8 . 10	8 . 12	(60)

MCG — Umpire Crouch
Attendance 119,165 — Gate $108,675

BEST — (Rich) Green, Bowden, Bartlett, Owen, Burgin, Strang, Dean, Barrot, Northey
(Carl) Quirk (B.O.G.), Crane, Jones, Lofts, Goold, Silvagni, Nicholls

GOALS — (Rich) Barrot (3), Moore (2), Northey (2), Hart, Dean, Ronaldson, Bartlett, Bond
(Carl) Jackson (2), Nicholls (2), Crosswell, Walls, Jesaulenko, Gallagher

GRAND FINAL TEAMS

Richmond	B	K. Sheedy	B. Richardson	C. Beard
	HB	G. Strang	G. Burgin	I. Owen
	C	F. Bourke	W. Barrot	R. Clay
	HF	J. Northey	R. Hart	R. Dean (c)
	F	J. Ronaldson	E. Moore	W. Brown
	Ruck	M. Green	M. Bowden	K. Bartlett
	Reserves	R. Hunt	G. Bond	
	Coach	T. Hafey		
Carlton	B	B. Gill	W. Lofts	V. Waite
	HB	P. Pinnell	J. Goold	K. Hall
	C	G. Crane	I. Robertson	B. Quirk
	HF	B. Crosswell	R. Walls	S. Jackson
	F	P. Jones	A. Jesaulenko	I. Nichol
	Ruck	J. Nicholls (c)	S. Silvagni	A. Gallagher
	Reserves	I. Collins	E. Hopkins	
	Coach	R. Barassi		

1970

In 1970 twenty-two rounds of home and home games were played—an ideal fixture, as it meant that, for the first time, each team played each other team twice.

Collingwood headed the list with eighteen wins in the twenty-two games, with Carlton (sixteen wins) second, followed by St. Kilda and South Melbourne (both fourteen wins). South was making its first appearance in the finals since 1945 and got there despite losing four of the last eight games.

The Swans were the public's favourite for the first semi-final, but the big-man strength of St. Kilda overwhelmed them in the end, after they had put up a great fight in the first half. Despite an opening burst of six goals one by St. Kilda, South came back brilliantly in the second quarter to kick seven goals three and lead by five points at half-time. After that, however, the inexperienced Swans tired, and the Saints slammed on five goals five to one goal two in the third to gain a firm grip on the game. Then a great goal on the run to Mynott and two strong marks by Ditterich within fifteen yards of the goal resulted in three goals to St. Kilda within seven minutes in the last term. This precipitated a burst of eight goals two which ground South into the turf and took St. Kilda's final score to twenty-two goals eleven, fifty-three points more than South's thirteen goals twelve. It was a grand performance by the Saints and made them favourites for the preliminary final.

A record crowd of 112,838 attended the Collingwood-Carlton second semi-final, and saw a torrid last quarter fight-back by the Magpies to take the game.

The early pace was tremendous. Gallagher got first goal for the Blues after five minutes' play, but the Magpies were quick to equalise through Tuddenham. The remainder of the term was goal for goal and, at the end of it, the Magpies led by two points.

The second term was a repetition of the first, with the Magpies still holding a slender lead after a fiery term in which Adamson (Collingwood) and Jackson (Carlton) were both reported.*

Goals to Thompson and McKenna at the start of the third term helped the Magpies race away to a twenty-point lead, the Blues being unable to score even a single point until halfway through the term. Then they came to life, as Hopkins (on as a replacement for the injured Gallagher) found Walls for a goal and then tore in to kick two

* Both players escaped suspension.

more himself to reduce the leeway to eight points. Jesaulenko and Jackson added further goals and the Blues—with a deadly accurate fourteen goals three on the board—held a lead of four points at the last change.

It was a great last quarter—the Magpies finally took the lead when M. Richardson goaled. Thompson and McKenna added further goals before Jesaulenko replied for Carlton. Near the end, McKenna's ninth goal for Collingwood and Jesaulenko's eighth for Carlton did not alter the result, and the Magpies' ten-point win advanced them to the grand final.

The bewildered Saints, displaying none of their first semi-final form, were thrashed by a determined Carlton in the preliminary final. Both sides missed easy chances in the first half, at the end of which the Blues led by two goals, but a devastating third-quarter burst of seven goals four by Carlton sealed the game. The Blues continued on their merry way in the last, eventually winning by sixty-two points, double St. Kilda's score. And the margin would have been greater but for the inaccuracy of Jesaulenko, who kicked four goals ten. In addition, the Blues had lost Goold early in the game, and Quirk later through injury, although St. Kilda were also hampered by an injury to Griffiths.

The stage was set for one of the most remarkable of all grand finals. Conditions were perfect and both sides lined up at almost top strength, only Quirk (Carlton) being an absentee.

The Magpies, kicking against a very slight breeze, shot to a seventeen-point lead before Carlton scored, and at the end of the first term led by twenty-nine points. The defence had held the Blues to a mere three points, but inaccuracy—four goals eight from thirteen shots—was to prove costly to Collingwood later in the game.

The Blues' second term was better, yielding four goals, but Collingwood, in brilliant form, kicked six goals five, Tuddenham's goal almost on the half-time siren giving them what appeared to be an unbeatable forty-four point lead.

Then came a sensational fifty minutes of football which left the record crowd of 121,696 stunned and disbelieving.

Carlton coach Ron Barassi took a gamble at half-time and brought nineteenth man Hopkins into the game. It was a move that had almost a 'fairy-tale' success, for in the space of two minutes Hopkins flashed into play for two goals to give the Blues heart. Soon after, Jackson kicked a great goal from the boundary and Crosswell added the fourth in eight minutes. Carlton players who had not been sighted in the first half were now coming into the game, and the Blues hammered the goals for three more majors, making the total seven in twelve minutes before Thompson goaled for Collingwood to steady the side and put the Magpies ten points ahead. The Magpies managed to hold the Blues for the remainder of the term and still looked safe at the last change, having increased their lead to seventeen points.

The Blues came forward as the last term began, and a hurried snap by Hopkins, five yards out, hit the post. At the other end, Thompson made no mistake for the Magpies, who now led by twenty-one points. Carlton moved Jesaulenko to centre-half-forward and Nicholls to full-forward and immediately Jesaulenko forwarded for Nicholls to receive a free and score a vital goal. Walls' snap was touched on the line before Nicholls goaled again to cut the Magpie lead to eight points. The Blues were playing on consistently, and were using hand-ball at every opportunity, even from the full-back line, and these tactics—risky as they appeared—were paying dividends. The Blues stormed forward again, and Jackson popped the ball over to Hopkins, who kicked his fourth to reduce the Magpies' lead to a point. It was desperate football, with only two minutes, plus time-on, to play. Both defences rose magnificently to the occasion, but the Magpies were obviously leg-weary. Dunne booted a behind for Collingwood, but Carlton came back strongly, and Crosswell marked and goaled to put the Blues ahead amidst scenes of wild excitement. Moments later, Jesaulenko's long snap from centre-half-forward bounced through and the Blues had done the impossible and won a magnificent match by ten points.

RESULTS

SEPTEMBER 5 — FIRST SEMI-FINAL

	1st	2nd	3rd	Final	
St. Kilda	6 . 1	9 . 3	14 . 8	22 . 11	(143)
South Melbourne	2 . 5	9 . 8	10 . 10	13 . 12	(90)

MCG — Umpire Sleeth
Attendance 104,239 (record) — Gate $111,020 (record)

BEST — (St. K) Smith, Colling, Payze, Mynott, Ditterich, Lilley, Manzie, Breen
(S. Melb) Hoffman, Brice, Bedford, Walsh, Murphy, Pitura, Skilton, Haenan, Cook

GOALS — (St. K) Rae (4), Payze (3), Mynott (3), Ditterich (3), Theodore (2), Smith (2), Lawrence (2), Breen (2), McIntosh
(S. Melb) Hoffman (4), Bedford (3), Sudholz (3), Cook (2), Skilton

SEPTEMBER 12 — SECOND SEMI-FINAL

	1st	2nd	3rd	Final	
Collingwood	5 . 2	9 . 7	12 . 11	17 . 16	(118)
Carlton	5 . 0	9 . 2	14 . 3	17 . 6	(108)

MCG — Umpire Crouch
Attendance 112,838 (record) — Gate $110,430

BEST — (Col) Tuddenham, Jenkin, Price, McKenna, Britt, W. Richardson, Waters, O'Callaghan
(Carl) Nicholls, Silvagni, Crane, Hall, McKay, Jesaulenko, Walls, Gill

GOALS — (Col) McKenna (9), Thompson (4), Tuddenham, Waters, Dunne, M. Richardson
(Carl) Jesaulenko (8), Thornley (2), Hopkins (2), Gallagher, Hall Walls, Crosswell, Jackson

SEPTEMBER 19 — PRELIMINARY FINAL

	1st	2nd	3rd	Final	
Carlton	2 . 6	6 . 12	13 . 16	17 . 21	(123)
St. Kilda	1 . 4	4 . 12	6 . 16	7 . 19	(61)

MCG — Umpire Jolley
Attendance 108,215 (record) — Gate $110,436 (record)

BEST — (Carl) Crosswell, Jackson, Nicholls, Gallagher, Jesaulenko, Jones, Robertson, Crane
(St. K) Smith, Breen, Mynott, McIntosh, Trott, Moran, Manzie, Rae

GOALS — (Carl) Jackson (6), Jesaulenko (4), Jones (4), Walls (2), Nicholls
(St. K) McIntosh (2), Breen (2), Lawrence, Mynott, Payze

SEPTEMBER 26 — GRAND FINAL

	1st	2nd	3rd	Final	
Carlton	0 . 3	4 . 5	12 . 5	17 . 9	(111)
Collingwood	4 . 8	10 . 13	13 . 16	14 . 17	(101)

MCG — Umpire Jolley
Attendance 121,696 (record) — Gate $108,713

1970-1971

BEST —	(Carl)	Crosswell, McKay, Silvagni, Robertson, Nicholls, Jackson, Jesaulenko, Walls
	(Col)	Tuddenham, Dunne, M. & W. Richardson, Jenkin, Waters, McKenna, Price
GOALS —	(Carl)	Hopkins (4), Jesaulenko (3), Gallagher (2), Walls (2). Crosswell (2), Nicholls (2), Silvagni, Jackson
	(Col)	McKenna (6), Tuddenham (2), Dunne (2), Thompson (2), Britt, W. Richardson

GRAND FINAL TEAMS

Carlton	B	B. Gill	K. Hall	V. Waite
	HB	J. Goold	D. McKay	B. Mulcair
	C	G. Crane	I. Robertson	P. Pinnell
	HF	B. Crosswell	R. Walls	S. Jackson
	F	P. Jones	A. Jesaulenko	B. Thornley
	Ruck	J. Nicholls (c)	S. Silvagni	A. Gallagher
	Reserves	E. Hopkins	N. Chandler	
	Coach	R. Barassi		
Collingwood	B	C. Tully	J. Clifton	P. Eakins
	HB	D. O'Callaghan	E. Potter	L. Adamson
	C	R. Dean	B. Price	J. Greening
	HF	M. Richardson	L. Thompson	C. Britt
	F	R. Dunne	P. McKenna	W. Richardson
	Ruck	G. Jenkin	T. Waters (c)	D. Tuddenham
	Reserves	R. Heard	R. Watt	
	Coach	R. Rose		

1971

It was almost inevitable that Hawthorn, just by virtue of the overwhelming number of goals being regularly scored by Peter Hudson at full-forward, should sooner or later make the final Four after a run of ill-fortune since 1963. This they finally accomplished in 1971, and in fact finished on top with nineteen wins in twenty-two games. Hudson, with a record-equalling 150 goals for the season, greatly contributed to Hawthorn's total of 2632 points, more than any VFL team had ever scored in a single season.

Second on the ladder was St. Kilda, followed by Richmond. Both teams had sixteen wins. Collingwood (fourth—fourteen wins, one tie) scraped into the Four half-a-game ahead of 1970 premiers Carlton.

The Magpies, after a good fight for three quarters, fell apart in the last term in the first semi-final and lost the game by forty-four points. They had captain W. Richardson and Adamson off injured in the first half, but when Thompson came on as a reserve after half-time he inspired a Magpie fight-back which yielded six goals three in the third term and left them only two points in arrears at the last change. The crowd anticipated an exciting last-quarter struggle, but the Tigers finished full of running. Within five minutes of the start of the last term, they booted three goals two to nil, and eventually kicked seven goals three to three points for the quarter, once more ending the Magpies' chances of taking the premiership.

Hawthorn, well in control for three quarters of the second semi-final, received a fright when St. Kilda fought back brilliantly in the last term. Both sides suffered injuries in the first half—St. Kilda lost O'Dea and Hawthorn lost Knights, injuries which put both players out of the grand final. In the last, St. Kilda suffered further misfortune when their best player, McIntosh, had to go off. He, too, missed the grand final a fortnight later.

The Hawks were thirty-three points ahead at the last change, but St. Kilda hit back hard with goals to Rae, Breen and Bonney early in the last to reduce the deficit to twelve points, but their forwards sprayed other shots which brought behinds when goals were needed. Twenty-three minutes into the term, Lawrence slammed through another St. Kilda goal to leave them only five points behind. Trott had a shot for a behind, then Lawrence, kicking off the ground, hit the post. At the other end, Keddie had a long shot for Hawthorn, which bounced through for a behind. Galt (St. Kilda) raced into an open goal, but his shot was off-line and moments later Payze also missed, the siren sounding with Hawthorn clinging to a two-point lead. It was enough, however, to put them into their third grand final. St. Kilda, with five goals nine for the term, had squandered their chance of victory.

Despite being underdogs, the Saints surprised hot favourites Richmond with a strong victory in the preliminary final, played in the wet. The Saints sealed the game with a burst of five goals three in the third term, in which Davis—left out of the previous week's side—booted three goals. Richmond, with a quick goal to Richardson from the bounce at the start of the last, reduced the leeway to twelve points, but the Saints, full of confidence, fought back excellently, and built their lead to thirty-one points with only minutes to go. A last-minute Richmond goal still left them well behind—it was the first time Richmond had lost a finals match since their long-awaited reappearance in 1967.

Both St. Kilda and Hawthorn, hit by injuries, made changes for the grand final. Light rain was falling as the game began, making the ground slippery. The Hawks, hunting in packs, were first into attack and, after two minutes, Hudson marked wide on the flank and slammed through the first goal of the match—and his 148th of the season. Moments later, Murray (St. Kilda) fell and got up limping—he was obviously in trouble, and was eventually replaced in the second term. To even things up, Hawthorn's Hawken (hamstring injury) limped from the ground minutes later. An even quarter ended with St. Kilda a point behind—Hudson, after a heavy bump, had been very groggy and twice kicked out of bounds for Hawthorn.

Rain was heavier in the second term, marring the game as a spectacle, but the excitement was certainly there. The Saints, although receiving only minimal drive from their big men, did well to keep up with the Hawks in a hard-fought quarter and, in fact, they led at half-time by two points.

Hudson, although still off his game, provided the highlight of the term at the twenty-five-minute mark—from a free kick he calmly booted his 150th goal of the season, to equal Bob Pratt's long-standing record of season 1934.

Day (injured) was replaced by Wilson for Hawthorn at half-time, and Wilson immediately came under notice with some nice play, but the third term was St. Kilda's. They went straight into attack for a goal from Bonney, and kept up a steady attack which resulted in further goals to Bonney, Breen and Smith. At the other end of the ground, Lawrence was brilliant on Hudson, after having moved back on him after Murray had been injured. Time and time again he beat the Hawthorn champion with spendid anticipation, but the Saints were taking no chances and always had a second man on hand to assist Lawrence. Almost on the three-quarter-time siren, Rice snapped the Hawks' first goal of the term, and they trailed by twenty points at the last change.

When the game resumed, Hudson was at centre-half-forward for Hawthorn (Lawrence moved out with him) and Keddie was at full-forward. The pressure was right on as Mathews goaled for Hawthorn, and Keddie followed suit moments later to reduce the deficit to eight points. Hawthorn were now playing with more purpose, and the crowd roared as Crimmins burnt off the opposition for another Hawthorn goal, after only five minutes of the last term. Hudson, who had not had a good day, went down after a marking duel and was again groggy—his ear was badly lacerated, but he helped get the ball downfield where Keddie and Mathews scored behinds to level the scores. It was anybody's game as Wilson found Keddie for another Hawthorn goal—the Hawks were finishing the stronger, in marked contrast to the second semi-final, and a goal to Scott increased their lead to thirteen points. Moore was grand in defence for the Hawks at this stage—he turned several dangerous attacks and for a time he and Lawrence almost played kick-to-kick.

Goals to Keddie (Hawthorn) and Bonney (St. Kilda) followed, before Keddie hand-balled to Hudson in the goal-square for what appeared to be Hudson's 151st goal of the season. But the umpire said no, and Keddie took his kick and goaled to increase Hawthorn's lead to nineteen points. Davis immediately replied for the Saints. Hudson, after marking fifteen yards out, kicked into Lawrence on his mark without scoring, and the Saints rushed forward for Breen to goal, with four minutes of time-on gone. Hawthorn came back, and Hudson, almost on the siren, lost his chance of beating Pratt's record when he raced into an open goal, and kicked out of bounds from thirty yards out. But it made no difference—the siren sounded with the Hawks seven points ahead, their second flag, won with a great last-quarter recovery in which every player had done his part, but Keddie, with four goals, had played the most spectacular role.

RESULTS

SEPTEMBER 4 — FIRST SEMI-FINAL

	1st	2nd	3rd	Final	
Richmond	4 . 4	8 . 8	11 . 10	18 . 13	(121)
Collingwood	4 . 1	5 . 5	11 . 8	11 . 11	(77)

MCG — Umpire Sheales
Attendance 99,771 — Gate $110,233

BEST — (Rich) Sheedy, Bartlett, Hollick, Dean, Stewart, Hart, Bond, Bourke
(Col) Tuddenham, Eakins, M. Richardson, Dunne, McKenna, Jenkin, McKenzie, Rose

GOALS — (Rich) Bartlett (3), Balme (3), Hart (3), Dean (2), Cumming (2), Bond (2), Boyanich, Hollick, McKellar
(Col) McKenna (4), Jenkin (2), Britt, M. Richardson, Rose, Price, Tuddenham

1971

SEPTEMBER 11 — SECOND SEMI-FINAL

	1st	2nd	3rd	Final	
Hawthorn	2 . 7	8 . 12	11 . 16	12 . 18	(90)
St. Kilda	1 . 4	4 . 5	7 . 7	12 . 16	(88)
	MCG		Umpire Deller		
	Attendance 99,822		Gate $110,513		

BEST —	(Haw)	Stevenson, Parkin, Scott, Hudson, Keddie, Moore, Meagher, Day, Hawken
	(St. K)	Breen, Payze, Mynott, Judson, McIntosh, Ditterich, Smith, Besanko
GOALS —	(Haw)	Hudson (7), Martello (3), Keddie, Stevenson
	(St. K)	Breen (4), Payze (2), Lawrence (2), Neale, Galt, Ditterich, Bonney

SEPTEMBER 18 — PRELIMINARY FINAL

	1st	2nd	3rd	Final	
St. Kilda	1 . 2	6 . 7	11 . 10	16 . 12	(108)
Richmond	3 . 2	7 . 2	9 . 4	12 . 6	(78)
	MCG		Umpire Coates		
	Attendance 102,494		Gate $110,156		

BEST —	(St. K)	Trott, Ditterich, Davis, Mynott, Smith, Moran, Neale, Besanko, Payze
	(Rich)	Hart, Bartlett, Dean, Hunt, Green, Clay, Stewart, Bourke
GOALS —	(St. K)	Davis (6), Breen (3), Bonney (2), Theodore (2), Smith, Manzie, Galt
	(Rich)	B. Richardson (5), Hart (2), Cumming (2), Bartlett, Balme, Bourke

SEPTEMBER 25 — GRAND FINAL

	1st	2nd	3rd	Final	
Hawthorn	2 . 2	4 . 4	5 . 7	12 . 10	(82)
St. Kilda	2 . 1	4 . 6	8 . 9	11 . 9	(75)
	MCG		Umpire Sheales		
	Attendance 118,192		Gate $108,762		

BEST —	(Haw)	Scott, Meagher, Moore, Heath, Crimmins, Parkin, Rice
	(St. K)	Smith, Lawrence, Trott, Mynott, Breen, Besanko, Neale, Ditterich
GOALS —	(Haw)	Keddie (4), Hudson (3), Crimmins (2), Rice, Mathews, Scott
	(St. K)	Breen (4), Bonney (2), Theodore, Trott, Manzie, Smith, Davis

GRAND FINAL TEAMS

Hawthorn	B	D. Parkin (c)	K. Moore	L. Hawken
	HB	R. Day	N. Bussell	I. Bremner
	C	L. Rice	G. Angus	D. Meagher
	HF	M. Porter	A. Martello	R. Keddie
	F	K. Heath	P. Hudson	L. Mathews
	Ruck	D. Scott	B. Stevenson	P. Crimmins
	Reserves	R. Wilson	K. Beck	
	Coach	J. Kennedy		

St. Kilda	B	W. Judson	R. Murray	K. Neale
	HB	G. Colling	B. Lawrence	N. Besanko
	C	J. Manzie	G. Elliott	S. Trott
	HF	J. Moran	B. Breen	S. Theodore
	F	C. Ditterich	A. Davis	J. Bonney
	Ruck	B. Mynott	T. Payze	R. Smith (c)
	Reserves	S. Rae	R. Galt	
	Coach	A. Jeans		

1972

There were two notable 'firsts' in 1972—the first final at VFL Park, Waverley, and the introduction of a final Five to replace the final Four system which had been operating since the League began. The new finals system operates as follows:—

First week—elimination and qualifying games (one game at MCG, one at VFL Park).

Elimination match—fifth versus fourth—loser eliminated.

Qualifying match—second versus third for second position. First team—a bye.

Second week—first and second semi-finals (one game at MCG, one at VFL Park).

First semi-final—fourth versus third—loser eliminated.

Second semi-final—second versus first—winner advances to grand final.

The following two games (preliminary final and grand final) are decided as previously.

The battle for the five positions was a tremendously hard-fought one, and positions changed regularly in the last few weeks of the home and home round, with the exception of the top two places, which Carlton and Richmond had tied up with many rounds to go. The third, fourth and fifth teams, in fact, all finished with fourteen wins, Collingwood taking third spot by two extra points gained for a draw. St. Kilda, by beating 1971 premiers Hawthorn in the last game, eliminated the Hawks from the finals and took themselves to fourth position. Essendon, who downed Collingwood the same day, took fifth spot against all predictions that they would not make it. This was a great effort from Essendon, coached by ex-Collingwood captain Des Tuddenham, as they had come from second-last in 1971.

Carlton was the form team of the season, winning eighteen and drawing one of their twenty-two games, two of the three losses being by margins of five and three points respectively. They won their last eight games in succession and finished on top, half a game clear of Richmond whose eighteen wins included their last nine in succession.

1972

Saturday September 9 1972 was a memorable day in the history of the VFL, as it marked the day of the first finals game at VFL Park. In it, St. Kilda had complete control all over the ground for most of the day and eliminated Essendon by fifty-three points. The young Dons matched St. Kilda in the second quarter only, but the pressure was too much and the confident Saints tore them apart in the last half. At the MCG, on the same day, Richmond gave a classical display to thrash a weakened Collingwood team. The Magpies had top VFL goalkicker Peter McKenna unavailable through injury and they certainly missed him. They were well beaten by three-quarter-time, when the Tigers led by over eight goals, and despite a late recovery were unable to make up the leeway.

Still without McKenna, the Magpies made some desperate changes for their first semi-final meeting with St. Kilda, bringing in Cooper for his first full game and another first-gamer in Dunstan to the hot-spot at full-forward. Eakins came in for his third game of the year, and the re-cast team gave St. Kilda a shock, only bad kicking (six goals sixteen to three-quarter-time) letting them down. Both first-gamers played excellently and, had Dunstan kicked accurately, the result would possibly have been reversed. As it was, the Magpies went down gamely by eighteen points.

At VFL Park, Carlton and Richmond played only the fifth finals tie in history. The Tigers were in trouble at half-time, having only one major on the board, but when McMillan replaced Stewart (injured) at the interval, his three goals sparked a Richmond revival which saw them hit the front during time-on. The Blues fought back desperately, however, and a goal to rover Armstrong levelled the scores with seconds to go. At the end, a shot by Jesaulenko from seventy-five yards out failed to make the distance, leaving the scores at eight goals thirteen each.

The Tigers made no mistake in the replay; their confident play shocking Carlton and those fans who expected a near repeat of the previous week's tie. The game was a comparatively low-scoring affair, the Tigers sealing the issue with five goals in the second term to open up a gap that the Blues were unable to overcome. By the time the siren sounded, the confident Tigers were forty-one points ahead and looking certainties for the premiership.

The Blues did nothing to change the minds of the critics when, the following week, they had to struggle to hold off a tenacious St. Kilda in a hard-fought preliminary final. The Saints were hit by injuries but were able to stay with Carlton all day, and in fact trailed by a mere four points with minutes to go before Carlton goals by Kennedy (twentieth man) and Jesaulenko sealed the issue. Jesaulenko, playing at full-forward for the first time in the finals series, kicked a match-winning seven goals.

Richmond was the hottest favourite for many years when the sides lined up for the 1972 grand final. They had beaten Carlton in both home and home games and crushed them in the second semi-final replay and were entitled to favouritism. Both Dean and Hollick were unavailable, but the strength of the side was indicated when they were able to place triple-Browhlow Medallist Ian Stewart on the bench. Carlton had almost their full list to choose from, with the exception of Quirk and Crosswell.

The Tigers lined up for the big game as selected, but Carlton made eight positional changes which, as it turned out, probably won them the game. Most successful was Jones into the first ruck, where he played the game of his life, and Nicholls (a flop in the semi-final replay) to the forward pocket, from which position he proved to be a match-winner. The Blues were first into attack, and Keogh had a goal on the board within two minutes. Richmond struggled forward to equalise, then hit the front as Balme drove through a glorious goal from a long way out. The Blues then hit back in great style, and goals to Nicholls (three) and Jesaulenko (two) helped them to a big lead at quarter-time. Richmond, shocked by Carlton's tremendous first quarter, had more shocks in store in the second. After Morris goaled for the Tigers from the first bounce, Carlton replied with four goals in four minutes. Richmond already were making changes in a vain attempt to stem the flow of goals, but Carlton was playing unbelievable football. Jones, unbeatable in the ruck, and Walls, brilliant up forward, kept the Blues in attack and when the dust settled Carlton had kicked an amazing ten goals two for the quarter, and eighteen goals six for the half to lead by a commanding forty-five points. With half a game remaining, the Blues required only six more goals to equal the record score for a grand final.

Richmond improved slightly at the start of the third term, but almost every goal was met by a quick reply from Carlton. Nevertheless, the Tigers managed to reduce the leeway to thirty-three points before, later in the term, goals to Keogh, Walls, Jackson and Nicholls took Carlton past the grand final record score, and gave them an unbeatable lead.

The last quarter was Richmond's best of the game, as their forward line at last clicked and they rammed on seven goals, three to Sheedy, who had moved from the back pocket to a half-forward flank. Carlton, however, had relaxed slightly, realising they were in no danger of defeat, and when Jesaulenko kicked his seventh to equal the grand final record, the crowd began to leave. Moments before the final siren, Richmond's Hart marked and his kick registered the fiftieth goal of this memorable match. At the end, Carlton was twenty-seven points ahead, and took out the 1972 pennant.

RESULTS

SEPTEMBER 9 — ELIMINATION MATCH

	1st	2nd	3rd	Final	
St. Kilda	5 . 5	11 . 8	15 . 16	18 . 16	(124)
Essendon	2 . 2	8 . 3	8 . 4	10 . 11	(71)

VFL Park — Umpire Deller
Attendance 52,499 — Gate $83,186

BEST — (St. K) A. Davis, Stephens, Trott, Besanko, Judson, Breen, Smith
(Ess) B. Davis, Fletcher, Roberts, Williams, Halley, Parkes, Smith, Wilson

GOALS — (St. K) Stephens (4), Galt (3), Ditterich (2), Davis (2), Lawrence (2), Smith (2), Breen (2), Trott
(Ess) Blethyn (2), Roberts (2), Fields, Parkes, Grinter, Wilson, Tuddenham, Noonan

SEPTEMBER 9 — QUALIFYING MATCH

	1st	2nd	3rd	Final	
Richmond	6 . 3	13 . 6	20 . 11	25 . 14	(164)
Collingwood	5 . 2	8 . 9	12 . 10	18 . 12	(120)

MCG — Umpire Sheales
Attendance 91,900 — Gate $146,574

BEST — (Rich) Bourke, Hart, Bartlett, Richardson, McKellar, Bond, Sproule
(Col) W. Richardson, Wearmouth, Thompson, Atkinson, Price, Clifton

GOALS — (Rich) Hart (6), Sproule (4), Richardson (4), Balme (4), McLean (3), Cumming (2), Hollick, Bartlett
(Col) W. Richardson (4), Atkinson (4), Thompson (4), Jenkin (2), Heard (2), Wearmouth, Dean

1972

SEPTEMBER 16 — FIRST SEMI-FINAL

	1st	2nd	3rd	Final	
St. Kilda	3 . 2	7 . 6	10 . 13	11 . 17	(83)
Collingwood	2 . 7	3 . 10	6 . 16	8 . 17	(65)

MCG **Umpire Sleeth**
Attendance 91,857 **Gate $146,693**

BEST — (St. K) Neale, Trott, Ditterich, Davis, Smith, Theodore, Mynott
(Col) Thompson, Dean, W. Richardson, Cooper, Dunne, Dunstan, Price
GOALS — (St. K) Theodore (2), Mynott (2), Davis (2), Stephens (2), Trott, Colling, Galt
(Col) Gott (2), Dunstan (2), Jenkin (2), W. Richardson, McOrist

SEPTEMBER 16 — SECOND SEMI-FINAL

	1st	2nd	3rd	Final	
Carlton	1 . 1	4 . 7	6 . 10	8 . 13	(61)
Richmond	0 . 3	1 . 8	4 . 9	8 . 13	(61)

VFL Park **Umpire Coates**
Attendance 54,338 **Gate $84,360**

BEST — (Carl) McKay, Southby, Pinnell, Robertson, Armstrong, Jesaulenko, Gallagher
(Rich) Hollick, Bartlett, Hart, Hunt, Clay, McKellar, Sheedy, Bourke, Boyanich
GOALS — (Carl) Jones (2), Gallagher (2), Kennedy, Lukas, Armstrong, McKay
(Rich) McMillan (3), McLean (2), Balme, Bartlett, Richardson

SEPTEMBER 23 — SECOND SEMI-FINAL REPLAY

	1st	2nd	3rd	Final	
Richmond	2 . 5	7 . 8	10 . 14	15 . 20	(110)
Carlton	2 . 2	4 . 6	6 . 10	9 . 15	(69)

MCG **Umpire Deller**
Attendance 92,670 **Gate $131,107**

BEST — (Rich) Clay, Bourke, Walsh, Sproule, Richardson, McKellar, McLean, Bartlett
(Carl) Southby, Doull, Gallagher, Jesaulenko, Keogh, Dickson, McKay, Walls
GOALS — (Rich) McLean (5), Balme (3), Richardson (3), Bartlett (2), Hollick, Bourke
(Carl) Jones (2), Jackson, Keogh, Gallagher, Armstrong, Kennedy, Jesaulenko, McKay

SEPTEMBER 30 — PRELIMINARY FINAL

	1st	2nd	3rd	Final	
Carlton	5 . 3	7 . 7	11 . 11	16 . 13	(109)
St. Kilda	6 . 8	8 . 12	10 . 12	13 . 15	(93)

MCG **Umpire Coates**
Attendance 92,272 **Gate $147,571**

BEST —	(Carl)	Jesaulenko, Southby, Armstrong, Keogh, Jackson, Robertson, O'Connell, Doull
	(St. K)	Trott, Besanko, Elliott, Ditterich, Moran, Manzie, Davis
GOALS —	(Carl)	Jesaulenko (7), Nicholls (3), Jackson (2), Kennedy, Chandler, Jones, McKay
	(St. K)	Corner (3), Lawrence (2), Galt (2), Theodore (2), Ditterich, Manzie, Breen, Stephens

OCTOBER 7 — GRAND FINAL

	1st	2nd	3rd	Final	
Carlton	8 . 4	18 . 6	25 . 9	28 . 9	(177)
Richmond	5 . 4	10 . 9	15 . 15	22 . 18	(150)

MCG — Umpire Deller
Attendance 112,393 — Gate $148,757

BEST —	(Carl)	Walls, Nicholls, Doull, Armstrong, Southby. Jesaulenko, Jones, Keogh, Gallagher, Dickson, Hurst
	(Rich)	Sproule, Bartlett, Morris, Balme, Richardson, Bourke, Sheedy, Hywood
GOALS —	(Carl)	Jesaulenko (7), Walls (6), Nicholls (6), Keogh (3), Jackson (2), Gallagher, Hall, Dickson, Chandler
	(Rich)	Balme (5), Sheedy (3), Richardson (3), Cumming (2), Hart (2), McMillan (2), Stewart, Sproule, Hunt, McLean, Morris

GRAND FINAL TEAMS

Carlton	B	J. O'Connell	G. Southby	D. McKay
	HB	V. Waite	B. Doull	P. Hurst
	C	I. Robertson	B. Armstrong	D. Dickson
	HF	N. Chandler	R. Walls	S. Jackson
	F	J. Nicholls (c)	A. Jesaulenko	T. Keogh
	Ruck	P. Jones	K. Hall	A. Gallagher
	Reserves	A. Lukas	G. Crane	
	Coach	J. Nicholls		
Richmond	B	K. Sheedy	R. Clay	R. Boyanich
	HB	W. Walsh	R. Hunt	S. Hywood
	C	G. Bond	P. Sproule	F. Bourke
	HF	B. Richardson	R. Hart (c)	M. McMillan
	F	N. Balme	R. McLean	D. Cumming
	Ruck	C. McKellar	K. Morris	K. Bartlett
	Reserves	B. Roberts	I. Stewart	
	Coach	T. Hafey		

1973

1973 saw a new rule introduced by the VFL, which resulted in a migration of big-name players to other League teams. The rule in question permitted automatic clearances to be granted to players who had played ten years with a VFL club. As a consequence, North Melbourne was the main beneficiary. Wade (Geelong), Rantall (Sth. Melb.) and Davis (Ess.) all transferred, and in addition the Kangaroos lured ex-Carlton coach Ron Barassi out of retirement. Under Barassi, North had their best season for years, eventually finishing sixth after being right in the race with only two games to go.

Collingwood (nineteen wins, three losses) was the form team of the Home and Home round, followed by Richmond (seventeen wins), Carlton (fifteen wins), Essendon (thirteen) and St. Kilda (twelve). In sixth place, two points out, was North, with Hawthorn a further two points back in seventh spot. During the season, the Hawks great champion, Peter Hudson—side-lined with an injured knee since the first game of 1972—re-appeared for one game and with eight goals against top team Collingwood, showed fans what the Hawks may have done had they had his services for the whole season.

St. Kilda thrashed Essendon in the elimination final at VFL Park, and Carlton convincingly beat Richmond at the MCG.

The game at VFL Park was fairly even until half-time, but then St. Kilda took charge in the ruck and displaying magnificent team-work, added seventeen goals three to six goals eight—including an equal finals record of ten goals one in the last term—to win by sixty-seven points. First year player George Young, on the forward flank, was a focal point in attack for the Saints and notched six goals in a brilliant display.

In the qualifying game, Carlton led Richmond all day to run out winners by twenty points. The Tigers fell down up forward where Hart, despite an injured leg, fought a lone battle. Richmond staged a strong last quarter comeback to draw within nine points, but goals to Nicholls and Walls for Carlton sealed the game.

A VFL Park record crowd of 60,072 people saw the Blues snatch the Second Semi-Final from Collingwood in the last minutes. They began the last quarter two points down, but Collingwood appeared to be finishing on, and with fifteen minutes to go they looked to have the game in their keeping. But Nicholls, who had been quiet all day, goaled twice within minutes to level the scores. Then the suspect Magpie defence cracked and Carlton rammed on three goals without a Collingwood reply to win by twenty points.

Richmond were untroubled to down St. Kilda at the MCG. Despite the closeness of the scores at three-quarter time, the Tigers were always in control and a last quarter burst of six goals three saw them finish well ahead.

The Magpies sprang surprises for the Preliminary Final. McKenna and Price were dropped and the sixteen year old Kink was brought in for his first game. Richmond also named a first-gamer in rover Carter.

1973

For a half, it seemed as though Collingwood had at last thrown off their so-called finals 'jinx'. They led by six goals and were playing brilliant football. But then, in a replica of their 1970 Grand Final debacle, they collapsed and let Richmond come back strongly to win almost on the bell. The Tigers kicked six goals six in the third to be only eight points behind at the last change, and hit the front nineteen minutes into the last term. Collingwood hit back through Atkinson to reduce the Tigers lead to a single point as time on began. The Magpies had several chances to score but the Richmond backline held firm and the Tigers went forward for Bartlett to seal the issue with a snapped goal in the last moments. The Tigers' come-back started from the moment their star centre-half-forward and captain, Royce Hart, took the field after half-time. Hart was considered a risk for a full game, as his badly injured leg had caused him to miss much of 1973, and severely hampered him during the finals. The Tigers named him as a reserve, and brought him on only when things looked grim.

So, for the first time since 1955-56, the same two teams lined up for successive grand finals. Both had their problems with injuries, but Carlton was worse-off. Keogh, injured in the Second Semi, failed to pass a fitness test and was ruled out. Armstrong,their most prolific kick winner, came down with appendicitis also after the same game, and the resultant operation ruled him out. Chandler, another second-semi casualty, was not quite fit but the Blues named him as a reserve. Jesaulenko, after a spell in hospital, was also not 100% fit, and several others in the Carlton line-up were suspect.

Richmond's biggest worries were Hart and Bourke. Both had got through the Preliminary Final, however, and were automatic selections. Bourke's recovery from an injury, which only six weeks before had threatened to finish his career, was remarkable. Morris, side-lined for the earlier finals through injury, was not completely fit, but the Tiger selectors, anxious to have his services, named him as nineteenth man.

To replace their injured men, Carlton surprised by including O'Connell for his first game since July, and Cattogio for his first full game. Richmond, more conservative, replaced Lamb with Hart.

Grand final day was very hot, with a blustery north-west wind making playing conditions less than ideal. Carlton made a number of positional changes to their selected side, the most surprising of which included shifting O'Connell from the back pocket to centre, and Jesaulenko to the half-forward flank.

The game got away to a fiery start and a sensational incident came after three minutes. Carlton's captain, Nicholls, whilst attempting to juggle a mark, was crashed by Richmond's Laurie Fowler, and hit the turf. Revived by trainers, Nicholls goaled from the free, but perhaps the knock affected him, for after that he never managed to get into the game. Sheedy was the shining light for the Tigers in this term, kicking their three goals. The second quarter was all Richmond and produced the best football of the game. Richmond booted eight goals three and Carlton five goals four. But it was a violent quarter of football. Several fights broke out, and fists were very much in evidence. From one of these incidents, a bad break came for the Blues' champion, full-back Geoff Southby. He was concussed, and did not re-appear after half-time. Richmond, with a brilliant burst of four goals in time-on, went to a twenty-six point lead at the long interval.

Mass positional changes by Carlton for the second half failed to bring results, as Richmond, although Bourke and Stewart were limping heavily, went straight into attack. They were rewarded by goals to Hart and Stewart, forcing the Blues, in desperation, to bring on Quirk, their second reserve. Shortly after he appeared, Pinnell went down with severe cramp, and hobbled to the forward pocket—he had been doing well in defence, and thus the Blues suffered yet another misfortune. Down in confidence and form, they faltered and Richmond forged to a six goal lead at the last change.

The come-back, which the Carlton camp had been waiting for, came at the start of the last after Crane was moved to the roving berth. Carlton went forward for two behinds (one a poster) to Walls, before Crane goaled. Walls goaled again and the crowd came to life. Moments later, Crane pushed his opponent out and marked for yet another, reducing the deficit to only eighteen points. Richmond immediately brought Morris on, and he was quickly under notice, but the Blues retained the initiative and attack followed attack; but only behinds, including another poster came. Finally, the rattled Tigers stopped the run, regained control, and had the game fairly well in their keeping before Balme made it a certainty with a goal almost at the end, and Richmond with a thirty point win, had avenged their shock defeat in the corresponding game of 1972. It was the Tigers' eighth League flag, and capped a great day. Earlier they had won premierships with the Reserves, Under Nineteens, and Under Seventeens—a record. Essendon (1950) had previously won pennants in Firsts, Seconds and Thirds.

SEPTEMBER 8 — ELIMINATION MATCH

St. Kilda		4 . 8	7 . 11	14 . 13	24 . 14 (158)
Essendon		3 . 3	7 . 5	8 . 8	13 . 13 (91)
		VFL Park		Umpire Deller	
		Attendance 53,405		Gate $128,651	
BEST —	(St. K)	Young (BOG), Trott, Moran, Davis, Breen, Mynott, Theodore.			
	(Ess)	Wilson, Fields, Smith, Fletcher, Parkes, Hickmott, Close.			
GOALS —	(St. K)	Young (6), Davis (4), Breen (3), Moran (3), Trott (2), Galt (2), Elliott (2), Mynott, Colling			
	(Ess)	Fields (3), Moss (2), Noonan (2), Andrews, Tuddenham, Cassin, Close, Emin, Hickmott			

SEPTEMBER 8 — QUALIFYING MATCH

Carlton		4 . 4	6 . 9	10 . 13	13 . 13 (91)
Richmond		3 . 2	5 . 4	7 . 7	10 . 11 (71)
		MCG		Umpire Robinson	
		Attendance 86,386		Gate $187,702	
BEST —	(Carl)	Southby, Walsh, Nicholls, Pinnell, Armstrong, Walls, Jones Keogh			
	(Rich)	Walsh, Stewart, Bartlett, Hart, Clay, Sheedy, Keane, Green			
GOALS —	(Carl)	Nicholls (4), Davis (3), Walls (3), Armstrong, Walsh, McKay			
	(Rich)	Hart (5), Balme (2), Cumming, Bartlett, Roberts			

SEPTEMBER 15 — FIRST SEMI-FINAL

Richmond		2 . 6	6 . 11	9 . 15	15 . 18 (108)
St. Kilda		1 . 5	3 . 8	8 . 14	9 . 14 (68)
		MCG		Umpire Coates	
		Attendance 86,483		Gate $187,704	
BEST —	(Rich)	Bartlett, Sproule, Stewart, Walsh, Green, Rae, Fowler, Sheedy			
	(St. K)	Neale, Davis, Besanko, Lawrence, Judson, Sarau			
GOALS —	(Rich)	Hart (2), Sproule (2), Bartlett (2), Rae (2), Cumming, Stewart, Dean, Wood, Roberts, Lamb, Green			
	(St. K)	Moran (2), Manzie (2), Mynott, Trott, Davis, Young, Stephens			

SEPTEMBER 15 — SECOND SEMI-FINAL

Carlton	1 . 6	6 . 11	9 . 12	15 . 17 (107)
Collingwood	4 . 8	5 . 9	9 . 14	12 . 15 (87)

VFL Park — Umpire Robinson
Attendance 60,072 — Gate $133,432

BEST — (Carl) Southby, Davis, Armstrong, Crane, Byrne, Walsh, Jones, McKay
(Coll) W. Richardson, Cranage, Bissett, Dean, Wearmouth, Oborne, Price

GOALS — (Carl) Davis (4), McKay (3), Walsh (3), Nicholls (3), Walls, K. Hall
(Coll) Bissett (3), W. Richardson (2), McKenna (2), M. Richardson (2), Wearmouth, Oborne, Heard

SEPTEMBER 22 — PRELIMINARY FINAL

Richmond	2 . 2	4 . 7	10 . 13	15 . 15 (105)
Collingwood	6 . 7	10 . 7	12 . 9	14 . 14 (98)

MCG — Umpire Deller
Attendance 98,652 — Gate $189,159

BEST — (Rich) Keane, Bartlett, Sheedy, Walsh, Balme, Roberts, Stewart, Fowler
(Coll) Dean, Bissett, Jenkin, Thompson, M. Richardson, Cranage, Adamson

GOALS — (Rich) Balme (5), Bartlett (3), Stewart (2), Hart (2), Sproule, Carter, Roberts
(Coll) Thompson (3), Kink (3), Atkinson (3), Heard (2), M. Richardson (2), Holmes

SEPTEMBER 29 — GRAND FINAL

Richmond	3 . 5	11 . 8	15 . 11	16 . 20 (116)
Carlton	2 . 2	7 . 6	9 . 9	12 . 14 (86)

MCG — Umpire Robinson
Attendance 116,956 — Gate $190,487

BEST — (Rich) Bartlett, Sheedy, Green, Sproule, Clay, Hart, Fowler, Bourke, Walsh, Stewart, Hunt
(Carl) Crane, Walls, McKay, K. Hall, Waite, Doull, Pinnell, Jesaulenko

GOALS — (Rich) Stewart (3), Hart (3), Sheedy (3), Balme (2), Walsh, Roberts, Carter, Bartlett, Green
(Carl) K. Hall (2), Crane (2), Dickson (2), Walls (2), McKay (2), Nicholls, Chandler

GRAND FINAL TEAMS

Richmond	B	L. Fowler	R. Clay	R. Hunt
	HB	F. Bourke	R. McGhie	M. Keane
	C	W. Walsh	I. Stewart	B. Wood
	HF	S. Rae	R. Hart (c)	K. Sheedy
	F	N. Carter	N. Balme	M. Green
	Ruck	B. Roberts	P. Sproule	K. Bartlett
	Reserves	K. Morris	C. McKellar	
	Coach	T. Hafey		
Carlton	B	R. Byrne	G. Southby	V. Waite
	HB	K. Hall	B. Doull	P. Pinnell
	C	G. Crane	J. O'Connell	D. Dickson
	HF	D. McKay	R. Walls	A. Jesaulenko
	F	J. Nicholls (c)	C. Davis	V. Cattogio
	Ruck	P. Jones	B. Crosswell	B. Walsh
	Reserves	B. Quirk	N. Chandler	
	Coach	J. Nicholls		

1974

Richmond Football Club could perhaps, when reflecting on season 1974, point to an "all-in" brawl at Windy Hill as the day that they began to win the flag.

The Tigers, rightly or wrongly, were seen as the instigators of a spectacular dust-up just after the half-time siren against Essendon, when, within minutes, players, spectators, and officials were swapping blows. Richmond official, Graeme Richmond, appeared to be singled out by the VFL and the media and the Tigers, angered, vowed to take out the 1974 flag.

Their main threat appeared to be the up and coming North Melbourne, which had made a spectacular rise under the coaching of Ron Barassi the previous season. In 1974, strengthened by the return of Barry Cable from W.A., and with recruits of the calibre of Mal. Blight (S.A.), and Bradley Smith (W.A.), North experienced their best season since 1950 to finish second on the ladder, a game behind Richmond.

Making up the Five were Hawthorn (15 wins, a game behind North), Collingwood (also 15 wins) and Footscray (13 wins), the latter having downed Richmond in the final Home and Home game. Two games out, in 6th place, was Geelong. This was the first time that the three teams admitted in 1925 (Hawthorn, North, Footscray) had made the finals in the same year.

Collingwood, who had been in the doldrums, caused a surprise by winning a final — the Elimination — when they kicked 19.10 to Footscray's miserly 6.19. It was a particularly pleasing win for the Magpies, as Footscray, making their first finals appearance since 1961, was coached by ex-Magpie mentor Bob Rose.

North Melbourne repeated their Round 22 victory over Hawthorn in the Qualifying Final, kicking 7.5 in the last term. The Hawks, hopeless up forward, had compounded their problems by dropping full-forward Moncrieff, then third on the goal-kicking list, and his presence was sadly missed.

The Kangaroos, however, were unable to produce that type of form in the following week's Second Semi-Final against Richmond. Dench, lining up at centre-half back to try and curb Hart, saw the Tiger champion boot an 80 metre goal early in the game, but managed to contain the brilliant Hart for most of the day. However, Dench's stand-in at full-back, Gumbleton, was given the run-around by Richardson, who kicked 5 goals from six kicks as Richmond went on to an easy 21 point victory.

In the First Semi, Collingwood was bundled out of the finals by a revitalised Hawthorn, led by the human tank, Leigh Matthews whose 23 kicks included 7 goals. Martello was a last minute withdrawal, but Moncrieff was back in the side and had a hand in three of the Hawks' seven goals in the first term, which broke the back of the Magpie defence. Hawthorn appeared more desperate than Collingwood and their "win at all costs" attitude proved too much for the Magpies who, under tremendous pressure, made far too many errors to hope to win.

1974

A rain-marred Preliminary Final went North Melbourne's way in an extremely tight finish. The Hawthorn team, already without captain Peter Crimmins, was hit by a mystery infection and lost Knights and Hendrie, two of their match-winners, on the morning of the match. Steele came in for his first full game to take on the unenviable job of minding Greig, but despite their set-backs, the Hawks had first goal on the board within 60 seconds. Three more followed before Schimmelbusch got North's first, but North then added three more in quick succession as they hit their straps in the wet conditions which critics said would not suit their style of play.

Most of the second term saw both teams clashing fiercely and packs developing frequently, but the Hawks, playing desperate football, went in at half time with a nine point lead.

The rain continued to pour down as Wade goaled for North early in the third, and soon after a magnificent passage of play resulted in Peterson getting another to give North the lead for the first time. Just before the term ended, Wade added another and Hawthorn was up against it. In the last, Wade's shot for his 100th goal of the season hit the post, and the Hawks re-bounded, through Scott, to notch their first goal since 19 minutes into the second quarter.

North's lead was cut to five points as the game see-sawed, Hawthorn doing a lot of attacking for no result. Finally, K. Matthews (Haw.) failed to make the distance from 40 metres out with a very heavy ball, and the siren went with North still grimly clinging to their 5 point lead, and advancing to only the second Grand Final in their VFL history. Between them, the two sides had scored nine goals in the first quarter, six more for the remainder of the game.

It was a sign of the times when the sides lined up for the Grand Final and no fewer than nine of the participants had come from other VFL Clubs. Richmond had Sproule (Ess.), Andrews (Geel.), Walsh (S. Melb.), Thorpe and McGhie (Foots.) and North had Wade (Geel.), Rantall (S. Melb.), Davis (Ess.) and Pagan (Carl.).

The pro-North crowd saw Richmond do all the early attacking, but it was North, through a strong Kekovich mark, which had first goal on the board after 8 minutes.

Walsh, freed, replied for the Tigers and Cloke added the second soon after, but the Richmond forwards were spraying the ball everywhere as North exerted tremendous pressure.

Richardson goaled from the angle for the Tigers, and deep into time-on, Wade replied for North, his 100th goal of the season. John Coleman, in 1949, had been the last player to notch his 100th in a Grand Final. With a kick after the siren, Cable also goaled to reduce North's deficit to 6 points at the first change.

A brilliant second term, during which 12 goals were scored, saw Richmond gain a firm grip on the game, only North's accuracy keeping them in it. Hart, dominant, continually put the Tigers into attack, but North, although breaking down across the half-forward line, managed to goal through Davis to level the scores, and another to Wade gave North the lead after seven minutes of the second term. Cable found Wade for another, and North looked to be getting on top, but poor defence let Green in for a goal, and the Tigers then stepped on the throttle, adding two more within minutes to snatch back the lead. North's early drive had waned, and three goals in eleven minutes by Hart gave the Tigers a five goal break, but North hit back with two goals in time-on to go in 20 points down.

Already hard-pressed, the Kangaroos suffered a demoralising set-back when skipper Davis was unable to appear after half-time, and by wasting chances playing around the flanks, they threw away their chances of coming back in the third quarter.

Several fights erupted as Richmond, turning back North's best efforts, held a 19 point lead at the last change.

As the last term began, Richmond unleashed a burst which put the result beyond doubt, Richardson, Sheedy, Hart and Cumming scoring goals. By half-way through the quarter, only a lively brawl was of interest to the spectators, who soon afterwards saw Richardson add another. Greig belatedly replied for North, but Richardson kicked his fourth for the term and the Tigers were content to play out time, even taking match-winner Sheedy from the ground to give Roberts a run. The siren went with Richmond 41 points ahead to take their second successive flag (the first team to do this since Melbourne in 1959-60), having conclusively proved themselves the best side of the season.

RESULTS

SEPTEMBER 7—ELIMINATION FINAL

	1st	2nd	3rd	Final
Collingwood	5 . 6	10 . 6	13 . 9	19 . 10 (124)
Footscray	3 . 1	4 . 11	5 . 11	6 . 19 (55)

VFL Park — Umpire—Robinson
Attendance—57,912 — Gate—$164,424

BEST — (C) Clifford, R. Shaw, W. Richardson, Cranage, Hyde, Thompson, Wearmouth, Dunne.
(F) Dempsey, Abbey, Dell, Gallagher, Huppatz, Sandilands, Parke, Morrison.

GOALS — (C) McKenna (7), W. Richardson (2), Wearmouth (2), Heard (2), Shaw (2), Picken, Gott, Shephard, Atkinson.
(F) Huppatz (2), Parke, Sandilands, Gallagher, Dempsey.

QUALIFYING FINAL

	1st	2nd	3rd	Final
Nth. Melb.	3 . 2	4 . 5	8 . 8	15 . 13 (103)
Hawthorn	1 . 5	4 . 10	6 . 15	8 . 17 (65)

MCG — Umpire—Smith
Attendance—77,519 — Gate—$221,513

BEST — (NM) Davis, Dench, Gumbleton, Kekovich, Greig, Montgomery, Pagan, Feltham, Chisnall.
(H) Hendrie, Knights, L. Matthews, Martello, Scott, Ablett, Douge, Moore.

GOALS — (NM) Kekovich (5), Wade (2), Briedis (2), Cable (2), Burns, Cowton, Feltham, Baker.
(H) K. Matthews (2), Grummisch (2), Martello, Tuck, Scott, Welsh.

SEPTEMBER 14—1st SEMI FINAL

	1st	2nd	3rd	Final
Hawthorn	7 . 5	12 . 7	18 . 11	21 . 12 (138)
Collingwood	2 . 2	7 . 4	12 . 4	13 . 10 (88)

MCG — Umpire—Chapman
Attendance—86,795 — Gate—$226,059

BEST — (H) L. Matthews, Moncrieff, Grummisch, Douge, K. Matthews, Tuck, Knights, Goad.
(C) W. Richardson, Dunne, Shephard, Thompson, Price, Clifford, Shaw, Delahunty.

GOALS — (H) L. Matthews (7), Moncrieff (4), Grummisch (4), Ablett (2), K. Matthews (2), Hendrie, Stevenson.
(C) Shaw (3), Heard (3), McKenna (3), Thompson (2), Wearmouth, Price.

2ND SEMI—FINAL

	1st	2nd	3rd	Final
Richmond	5 . 7	7 . 8	9 . 11	10 . 13 (73)
Nth. Melb.	0 . 0	2 . 8	5 . 11	6 . 16 (52)

VFL Park — Umpire—Robinson
Attendance—57,569 — Gate—$164,652

BEST — (R) Andrews, Morris, Balme, Bartlett, Walsh, Hart, Green, Wood, Thorpe.
(NM) Feltham, Cable, Schimmelbusch, Rantall, Davis, Dench, Burns.
GOALS — (R) Richardson (5), Sproule (2), Hart, Walsh, Bartlett.
(NM) Wade (3), Briedis, Cable, Nolan.

SEPTEMBER 21—PRELIMINARY FINAL

	1st	2nd	3rd	Final
Nth. Melb.	4 . 1	5 . 2	8 . 5	8 . 8 (56)
Hawthorn	5 . 3	6 . 5	6 . 7	7 . 9 (51)

MCG — Umpire—Smith
Attendance—88,262 — Gate—$226,819

BEST — (NM) Davis, Smith, Rantall, Burns, Montgomery, Greig, Pagan, Schimmelbusch.
(H) Ablett, Martello, Stevenson, L. Matthews, Tuck, Rice, Scott, Bremner.
GOALS — (NM) Wade (3), Peterson, Cable, Feltham, Baker, Schimmelbusch.
(H) Ablett (3), Moncrieff, Meagher, Tuck, Martello.

SEPTEMBER 28—GRAND FINAL

	1st	2nd	3rd	Final
Richmond	3 . 8	10 . 11	12 . 17	18 . 20 (128)
Nth. Melb.	3 . 2	8 . 3	11 . 4	13 . 9 (87)

MCG — Umpire—Robinson
Attendance—113,839 — Gate—$224,445 (rec.)

BEST — (R) Sheedy, Hart, Sproule, Morris, Andrews, McGhie, Bartlett, Walsh.
(NM) Greig, Cable, Rantall, Schimmelbusch, Burns, Smith, Baker.
GOALS — (R) Richardson (5), Hart (3), Balme (2), Sheedy (2), Green (2), Cumming, Walsh, Thorpe, Cloke.
(NM) Wade (4), Kekovich (2), Cable (2), Briedis, Peterson, Burns, Davis, Greig.

GRAND FINAL TEAMS

Richmond	B	M. Keane	R. Clay	G. Andrews
	HB	F. Bourke	R. McGhie	K. Morris
	C	B. Wood	D. Thorpe	W. Walsh
	HF	D. Cloke	R. Hart (c)	P. Sproule
	F	N. Balme,	B. Richardson	D. Cumming
	Ruck	M. Green	K. Sheedy	K. Bartlett
	Reserves	C. Clayton	B. Roberts	
	Coach	T. Hafey		

Nth. Melbourne	B	D. Pagan	D. Dench	B. Smith
	HB	J. Rantall	G. Farrant	K. Montgomery
	C	K. Greig	J. Burns	W. Schim-melbusch
	HF	P. Feltham	P. Baker	S. Kekovich
	F	P. Ryan	D. Wade	R. Peterson
	Ruck	B. Gooding-ham	B. Davis (c)	B. Cable
	Reserves	G. Cowton	A. Briedis	
	Coach	R. D. Barassi		

1975

The defeat of North Melbourne in the Grand Final of 1974 meant that the Kangaroos remained the only VFL team to have failed to win a premiership, all other sides having been successful at least once in gaining the coveted pennant. Realising that in 1975 it was almost a now or never situation, the Northerners dedicated themselves to that single aim, and never deviated in their desire and determination throughout the season. Even after losing six of the first nine games, and finally fighting on to finish the Home and Away round in third spot, North was unconcerned by the fact that since the introduction of the Page System of Finals in 1931, no side had taken the premiership from that position.

Hawthorn (17 wins) and Carlton (16 wins — up from 7th position in 1974), were the top dogs over the first round, followed by North (14 wins), Richmond and Collingwood (each winning 13). St. Kilda and Footscray, next best, were well out of the running, 8 premiership points from the "Five".

Richmond, trying for their third successive flag and running into better form at the right end of the season, met Collingwood in the Elimination Final (the first finals match played with a centre "square", instead of the previous centre area diamond which had been introduced in 1973). The enthusiastic Tigers romped away to a 43 point lead mid-way through the second term, but then heavy rain hit VFL Park and as the ground became heavier the younger Magpies came back hard. After trailing by 32 points at half-time, Collingwood reduced the deficit to a mere five points by the 20 minute mark of the last term, and looked capable of going on to win only the sixth of their last 22 finals matches since the 1958 premiership.

But Richmond's Nettlefold coolly goaled to give Richmond breathing space and the hard-pressed Tiger defence pressured the Magpies into six straight behinds in the last ten minutes, allowing Richmond to grimly hang on for a 4 point win.

Carlton, in a slump leading up to the Finals, was no match for North in the Qualifying Final, the Blues much-vaunted aerial strength being overcome by Norths skilful and creative use of handball. With centreman Burns dominating play, North took charge of the game from the start, only Carlton's accuracy keeping them in the game. In the end, the difference was only 20 points in North's favour, but their dominance of the game was hardly reflected on the scoreboard, for Carlton at no stage of the game appeared likely to win.

The day of the 1st and 2nd Semi Finals was a shocker, with rain, wind and mud combining to make the conditions at the MCG the worst seen in 20 years.

A big crowd, however, braved the elements to see Richmond and Carlton clash in the First Semi.

As they had done in the 1973 Finals, the Tigers decided to place the injured Hart on the bench and use him when things got tough. Carlton, slow to the ball early, fought back well in the second term to boot five goals and trail by only 11 points at half-time. But Walls and Jesaulenko failed to fire in the second half, and the Tigers showed much more determination to take out the game by 9 points after a late Carlton fight-back.

At VFL Park, conditions were only slightly better, but the turf was very wet and heavy. Hawthorn made a late change, bringing in Meagher, a noted wet-weather player, and leaving out Jones. Michael Cooke also came in for his first VFL game. Both moves were winning ones, Meagher playing well and Cooke booting 4 goals.

North, despite brilliant passages of hand-ball, was unable to match the tenacity of Hawthorn, which held control in all the key positions and had a star in Knights at centre-half-back. North really never looked a chance but observers noted that Hawthorn had been carried by the dominance of a few stars, and it was obvious that if North could come up with a way to supress these stars, the premiership, despite an 11 point defeat in this game, was still there for the taking.

North, facing up to their third successive finals match, met 1974 Premiers Richmond in the Preliminary Final. It had rained for a solid week, yet VFL Park was in surprisingly good condition for the big clash.

North, little-favoured, sprung the match-winning move of the Finals series by lining Greig up in the centre instead of on his usual wing. Using his pace and great kicking ability, Greig shot holes in the Tiger defence from the opening bounce, and the Tigers were unable to counter him all day.

Jumping Richmond early, North led by 26 points during the third term before the Tigers threw Hart into the fray from the bench. The champion immediately goaled, and Richmond, gaining confidence, came back but the solid North defence, led by Crosswell and Rantall, held firm and in the end the rather tired looking Tigers submitted tamely to a 17 point defeat, ending their hopes of a hat-trick of premierships.

September 27, 1975, will be long remembered at North Melbourne, for it was on that day that all the years of disappointment and frustration ended for the Kangaroos and they ran away with their first League premiership.

Without Melrose (broken thumb), North pulled a last-minute change by relegating Goodingham to the bench and sending Farrant onto the ground at centre-half-back. Hawthorn, taken by surprise, were thus caught with an unbalanced side with too much tall-timber and not enough fleet-footed little men. Crimmins (ill) was much-missed. It was in pace that Hawthorn fell down as it turned out, the North little men being consistently first to the ball and then moving it around in "keepings-off" fashion. Hawthorn also failed to pressure North sufficiently and their usually disciplined play was not apparent this day.

Burns started North off with a 65 metre goal in the first two minutes, but Rowlings replied and play moved quickly up and down the ground before the dangerous Burns marked and kicked his second, followed a few minutes later by a 60 metre punt from the brilliant Crosswell, coming down from the back-line, to put North 12 points up. Crosswell's experience and exuberance were big factors for North, who had gained Crosswell from Carlton in May when the fiery ex-Tasmanian had looked to be "finished".

Hawthorn was struggling, with Rantall minding Matthews closely, even going to the back-pocket on him when Matthews rested, and returning to the back flank when Matthews went onto the ball. North, too fast, held a 12 point lead at the first change, and increased this when Schimmelbusch snapped an "impossible" goal early in the second term to cap off a brilliant passage of play in which ten North players handled the ball without a Hawk touching it.

Hawthorn, forced into making changes, still struggled and when they did get the ball forward, several easy chances were missed before Trott finally put one through on the run from 35 metres out. Moments later, Wade took the ball off the hands of the pack and tapped it through for a North reply. Cooke, kickless, was taken off at the 17 minute mark as Hawthorn forwarded for Ablett to hit the post. Then, from the kick-off, North rebounded for Burns to snap his third, and within two minutes Wade and Burns again scored to give North a 33 point lead. Only the brilliance of Knights kept Hawthorn within touch at this stage, and it was not until late in the quarter that Hawthorn for the first time looked good, adding two late goals to go in at half-time 20 points down.

In the third, play generally see-sawed, but the Hawks suffered a further blow when full-back Moore limped from the field. North, although not easing up, appeared to have more in reserve than Hawthorn at the last change and so it proved in an explosive burst in the last term that sealed the flag.

Neither side goaled for 16 minutes, although Hawthorn had a shocking run of misses. It was not until the 16 minute mark of the quarter that Breidis, who had been quiet, held a strong mark and goaled for North. Within 5 minutes, he added two more, a minute later Schimmelbusch snapped another, and at the 25 and 26 minute marks, Wade and Feltham also scored, North having added six goals in ten minutes to increase their lead from 24 points to 61. This burst, of course, sealed the result, two late Hawthorn goals being answered by his fourth for the term from Briedis, North's 7th in 14 minutes. There was a stunned silence from the Hawthorn camp as the siren sounded with North ahead 19.8 to 9.13, but the scenes of jubilation amongst the North Melbourne supporters was a never-to-be-forgotten sight. It had been a long, long wait, and the fruits of victory were sweet indeed.

RESULTS

SEPTEMBER 6—ELIMINATION FINAL

	1st	2nd	3rd	Final
Richmond	5 . 5	7 . 8	8 . 10	11 . 11 (77)
Collingwood	1 . 1	2 . 6	6 . 7	10 . 13 (73)

VFL Park — Umpire—Smith

Attendance—65,512 — Gate—$214,399

BEST —	(R)	Balme, Sproule, Bartlett, Morris, Nettlefold, Edwards.
	(C)	Shephard, Picken, Moore, W. Richardson, Shaw, Heard.
GOALS —	(R)	Edwards (3), Bartlett (2), Nettlefold (2), Balme, Monteath, Wood, Green.
	(C)	Wearmouth (3), Carman (2), Heard (2), W. Richardson, Atkinson, Moore.

QUALIFYING FINAL

	1st	2nd	3rd	Final
Nth. Melb.	4 . 6	9 . 8	12 . 10	14 . 12 (96)
Carlton	4 . 1	9 . 1	11 . 2	12 . 4 (76)

MCG — Umpire—Henry
Attendance—74,015 — Gate—$233,522

BEST — (NM) Burns, Melrose, Cable, Davis, Dench, Rantall, Gumbleton, Michalczyk (until injured).
(C) Doull, Southby, Maclure, Davis, Ashman, Walls.
GOALS — (NM) Melrose (4), Blight (3), Davis (2), Kekovich, Briedis, Cowton, Cable, Michalczyk.
(C) Walls (4), Keogh (2), McKay (2), Jones (2), Ashman, Austin.

SEPTEMBER 13—FIRST SEMI—FINAL

	1st	2nd	3rd	Final
Richmond	3 . 4	6 . 9	9 . 11	9 . 17 (71)
Carlton	0 . 2	5 . 4	6 . 5	9 . 8 (62)

MCG — Umpire—Sutcliffe
Attendance—76,967 — Gate—$239,453

BEST — (R) Bartlett, Morris, Balme, Bourke, Clay, Carter, Sproule, Sheedy.
(C) Doull, Ashman, McKay, Jackson, Southby, O'Connell.
GOALS — (R) Sproule (3), Roberts, Cloke, Balme, Carter, Monteath, Sheedy.
(C) Ashman (3), Jones (3), Kennedy (2), Jackson.

SECOND SEMI-FINAL

	1st	2nd	3rd	Final
Hawthorn	5 . 2	7 . 4	9 . 8	12 . 10 (82)
Nth. Melb.	2 . 5	5 . 7	8 . 9	10 . 11 (71)

VFL Park — Umpire—Robinson
Attendance—52,076 — Gate—$190,816

BEST — (H) Knights, Jaworskyj, Scott, Trott, Rowlings, Meagher, Tuck.
(NM) Davis, Cable, Schimmelbusch, Rantall, Crosswell, Burns.
GOALS — (H) Cooke (4), Murphy (2), Hendrie (2), Trott, Ablett, L. Matthews, Rowlings.
(NM) Wade (2), Schimmelbusch (2), Davis (2), Briedis, Kekovich, Melrose, Cable.

SEPTEMBER 20—PRELIMINARY FINAL

	1st	2nd	3rd	Final
Nth. Melb.	3 . 5	5 . 6	8 . 11	10 . 16 (76)
Richmond	1 . 5	4 . 7	6 . 9	8 . 11 (59)

VFL Park — Umpire—Smith
Attendance—71,130 — Gate—$216,091

BEST — (NM) Crosswell, Cable, Greig, Rantall, Davis, Burns, Briedis.
(R) Clay, Wood, Walsh, McGhie, Bourke, Keane.
GOALS — (NM) Briedis (3), Feltham (2), Cable, Blight, Davis, Schimmelbusch, Kekovich.
(R) Edwards (4), Walsh, Hart, Wood, Cloke.

SEPTEMBER 27—GRAND FINAL

	1st	2nd	3rd	Final
Nth. Melb.	4 . 2	9 . 2	12 . 6	19 . 8 (122)
Hawthorn	2 . 2	5 . 6	7 . 7	9 . 13 (67)

MCG — Umpire—Smith
Attendance—110,551 — Gate—$308,172 (Rec.)

BEST — (NM) Rantall, Crosswell, Greig, Burns, Dench, Cable, Henshaw, Chisnall, Kekovich.
(H) Knights, Martello, Bremner, Moore, Jaworskyj, Scott.
GOALS — (NM) Briedis (5), Wade (4), Burns (4), Schimmelbusch (2), Blight, Kekovich, Crosswell, Feltham.
(H) Martello (2), Moncrieff (2), Rowlings, K. Matthews, Trott, Meagher, Scott.

GRAND FINAL TEAMS

Nth. Melbourne	B	R. Henshaw	D. Dench	F. Gumbleton
	HB	J. Rantall	G. Farrant	B. Crosswell
	C	P. Feltham	K. Greig	P. Chisnall
	HF	W. Schimmel-busch	A. Briedis	S. Kekovich
	F	B. Cable	D. Wade	M. Blight
	Ruck	M. Nolan	B. Davis (c)	J. Burns
	Reserves	B. Goodingham	G. Cowton	
	Coach	R. D. Barassi		
Hawthorn	B	P. Welsh	K. Moore	M. Moncrieff
	HB	B. Jaworskyj	P. Knights	I. Bremner
	C	S. Trott	K. Matthews	G. Ablett
	HF	J. Hendrie	A. Martello	S. Murphy
	F	B. Rowlings	M. Cooke	B. Jones
	Ruck	D. Scott (c)	M. Tuck	L. Matthews
	Reserves	D. Meagher	L. Rice	
	Coach	J. Kennedy		

1976

As North Melbourne had shown the previous season, a crushing Grand Final defeat provided a stiffening of resolve to make amends and Hawthorn, thrashed in the 1975 Grand Final, certainly was relentless in its quest for the 1976 Flag, but in the Hawks case there was one more tragic reason for their determination. Popular skipper, Peter Crimmins, was gravely ill with cancer and every member of the Hawthorn side had but one aim — win the flag for Peter.

1976

Carlton, with 16 wins and a tie, managed to secure top position on the ladder from Hawthorn, which had 16 wins (but lost their last two before the Finals). Next came North (15 wins).

There was drama aplenty towards the end of the season as Geelong held on to fourth spot despite four losses in five games, whilst Footscray scraped into the Five by virtue of a lucky "after the bell" goal which gave them a 1 point win over Fitzroy, and then a tie against top side Carlton in the last game gave them a half a game advantage over Melbourne, which had its best season since 1964.

The two field umpire system operated for the first time in the 1976 Finals Series and, after initial problems, proved to be a total success.

At VFL Park, Footscray was stunned by the fast-finishing Geelong in a low-standard Elimination Final. There were mistakes galore, but the last 20 minutes of the game provided spectators with plenty of excitement.

At the 13 minute mark of the last term Geelong, which had trailed for most of the day, goaled to make the difference only 2 points. Then, with Footscray still holding on as the clock went into time-on, Geelong's veteran Newman created two opportunities which brought successive goals and the siren sounded with the shocked Bulldogs trailing by 7 points in a match that they had not really looked like losing. Larry Donohue, Geelong's big full-forward, kicked 4 goals to bring his seasons total to 103.

At the MCG, a fanatical Hawthorn side tore North Melbourne apart. An opening bounce all-in brawl was followed by a North goal, but afterwards, with Matthews (7 goals 6 behinds) at his best, Hawthorn was far too strong physically for the injury-hit Kangaroos, and went on to win, easing-up, by 20 points.

North Melbourne made no fewer than four changes, only one of them compulsory, for the First Semi Final. Geelong, by contrast made only two. Then, on a wet and greasy MCG, North sprung another late change, dropping Moore, a big ruckman, from his place on the bench and replacing him with the smaller, faster Feltham. North's big match temperament, their handball skills and dominance of the marking and ruck duels, were too much for Geelong, and although the Cats had at least two chances, in the second and third quarters, to get themselves into a challenging position, they were never quite up to it, their high-markers being greatly disadvantaged by North's running game and by the greasy conditions. Blight (12 marks with a wet ball), Schimmelbusch (6 goals) and Nolan — who kicked the goal that sealed the match — were North's stars, big Nolan playing possibly the best game of his career.

The over-confident Blues suffered a thrashing at the hands of Hawthorn in the Second Semi-Final, despite the fact that at least four Hawks carried injuries into the game. Carlton actually led at half-time, but thereafter the fierce and dedicated Hawks put them out of business, O'Halloran and Bremner doing great work in preventing Jesaulenko and Walls from scoring a single goal, although the two Hawthorn defenders themselves gathered less than ten kicks between them. The move of Martello into the ruck after half-time sparked Hawtorn to their winning break of five goals to two in the third quarter, and the Hawk centerline of G. Ablett, Rowlings and Eade, unbeatable all day, contributed much to the Hawthorn victory. Carlton, by contrast, had many poor players.

Carlton caused an early sensation in the Preliminary Final when Maclure and McConnon, named as 19th and 20th men, took their places in the side in a pre-arranged plan to catch North Melbourne off-guard. The move was successful, but North was able to negate the early disadvantage by strong defence which limited the Blues to only 2.1 in the first quarter. Thereafter, Carlton, although retaining the lead, was subjected to continually applied pressure from North, and early in the last term it became obvious that the Blues' skilful players were running out of steam. Seizing their chance, North hammered home a succession of attacks which resulted in three goals and gave them, at the siren, a one point win and the right to contest their third successive Grand Final. Heroes of the North win were Cable, link-man in their hand-ball game, and remarkable utility Sutton (5 goals).

North Melbourne, without Kekovich (injured) brought in Crosswell and Keenan for the Grand Final. The confident Hawks made no changes.

The game itself turned out to be almost a psychological war, and nerves were evident right from the first bounce when players clustered around the centre instead of going to positions, and Crosswell and Henshaw, named in the side, slipped off the ground to hide amongst the balloons on the boundary whilst Chisnall, named as a reserve, took the field. The "war" continued with Scott and Keenan clashing repeatedly early, but Hawthorn was first away with behinds to Hendrie, Moncrieff (an easy shot running into an open goal) and a snap-shot goal to L. Matthews. Matthews was, however, being closely minded — in a somewhat surprising Barassi move — by North's dashing skipper Greig, who would, perhaps, have been of more value playing his normal attacking game instead of a defensive role. In other ways, too, North went into the game in a defensive frame of mind, with fine attacking players in Blight and Icke playing in defence.

Goad, freed, goaled again for Hawthorn before Cable snapped a remarkable left-foot goal and followed up with a second soon after for North. Minutes later, he suffered a groin injury which hampered him for the remainder of the game. Moncrieff, beating Dench, goaled for Hawthorn, and the elusive Hendrie added another. Melrose and Cowton replied before Moncrieff again outmarked Dench for Hawthorn's fifth.

Moments later, Greig was knocked unconscious in a clash with Matthews, and the Hawk rover had his number taken. Greig was knocked out again later in the match.

Goad began the second term with a goal for Hawthorn, but, after a miss by Blight, Burns replied for North who, although looking slow and making numerous errors, were still able to make the most of their few chances and keep within range on the scoreboard.

Rowlings added another for Hawthorn, Icke replied, and K. Matthews and Scott answered the challenge for the Hawks, who went in at half-time 19 points up. Their lead should have been more — best man afield, Hendrie, had booted 1.6 by then and with a little more accuracy, Hawthorn would have had a six goal lead.

Greig moved onto the wing on Hendrie when the teams came out again, and Sutton was at centre-half-forward. Immediately the moves had some result — North goaled through Icke, and began to get some system into their game, even though mistakes occurred too frequently. Sutton led a good revival, as North, holding the Hawks to 1.6 for the term, booted 3.3 themselves to be only 10 points down at the last change.

North continued to attack for the first ten minutes of the last term, but could not get the break-through they required, attack after attack being repelled by a series of magnificent high marks by Knights. Then, the crisis period eased for the Hawks, as they went forward for a goal to ease the pressure. Now, although there was always a slight chance of a North recovery, the game was to all intents over, as the tenacious Hawks held North out and banged on a goal whenever they themselves went forward. A scrambly last quarter was played out with the result being beyond doubt with ten minutes to go, the Hawks finally winning by 30 points to gain sweet revenge for their defeat in the previous seasons Grand Final.

1976

RESULTS

SEPTEMBER 4—ELIMINATION FINAL

	1st	2nd	3rd	Final
Geelong	4 . 8	6 . 9	9 . 13	14 . 18 (102)
Footscray	3 . 0	9 . 5	12 8	14 . 11 (95)

VFL Park — Umpires—Deller, Sutcliffe
Attendance—50,686 — Gate—$192,841

BEST —	(G)	Hawkins, Sheehan, Higgins, Newman, Turner, I. Nankervis, B. Nankervis.
	(F)	Featherby, Quinlan, Huppatz, Jennings, Stoneham, Blair.
GOALS —	(G)	Donohue (4), Sheehan (2), Cousins (2), Bright (2), Higgins (2), Woolnough, Sarah.
	(F)	Templeton (4), Newland (3), Morrison (2), Quinlan (2), Featherby (2), Dunstan.

QUALIFYING FINAL

	1st	2nd	3rd	Final
Hawthorn	1 . 6	5 . 10	13 . 13	14 . 19 (103)
Nth. Melb.	2 . 3	5 . 6	8 . 7	12 . 11 (83)

MCG — Umpires—Robinson, Smith
Attendance—64,148 — Gate—$274,381

BEST —	(H)	L. Matthews, Hendrie, Rowlings, Scott, Ablett, Knights.
	(NM)	Melrose, Byrne, Icke, Greig, Dench.
GOALS —	(H)	L. Matthews (7), Martello (2), Scott (2), Goad, Hendrie, Moncrieff.
	(NM)	Burns (2), Kekovich (2), Icke (2), Melrose (2), Blight, Dawson, Schimmelbusch, Dench.

SEPTEMBER 11—1ST SEMI FINAL

	1st	2nd	3rd	Final
Nth. Melbourne	4 . 3	7 . 5	9 . 7	14 . 9 (93)
Geelong	0 . 1	3 . 3	6 . 7	8 12 (60)

MCG — Umpires—Smith, Deller
Attendance—71,042 — Gate—$299,281

BEST —	(NM)	Blight, Nolan, Dench, Schimmelbusch, Melrose, Sutton.
	(G)	B. Nankervis, Browne, Bright, Clarke, Turner, Woolnough.
GOALS —	(NM)	Schimmelbusch (6), Crosswell (3), Keenan, Cable, Nolan, Feltham, Blight.
	(G)	Bright (2), Browne (2), Donohue (2), Sheehan, B. Nankervis.

SECOND SEMI-FINAL

	1st	2nd	3rd	Final
Hawthorn	4 . 2	5 . 5	10 . 13	12 . 15 (87)
Carlton	2 . 4	5 . 9	7 . 10	9 . 16 (70)

VFL Park — Umpires—Henry, Dye
Attendance—60,105 — Gate—$237,747

BEST —	(H)	G. Ablett, Rowlings, O'Halloran, L. Matthews, Tuck, Douge, Bremner.
	(C)	McKay, Pinnell, Doull, Austin, Keogh, Armstrong.
GOALS —	(H)	G. Ablett (3), K. Matthews (2), Moncrieff (2), Hendrie (2), Martello, Scott, Rowlings.
	(C)	McKay (4), Fitzpatrick, Keogh, Armstrong, Jones, Pickett.

1976

SEPTEMBER 18—PRELIMINARY FINAL

	1st	2nd	3rd	Final
Nth. Melb.	1 . 0	4 . 2	7 . 7	10 . 7 (67)
Carlton	2 . 1	5 . 5	7 . 9	9 . 12 (66)

VFL Park — Umpires—Robinson, Smith
Attendance—69,234 — Gate—$374,073

BEST — (NM) Cable, Dench, Gumbleton, Blight, Sutton, Greig.
(C) Keogh, Maclure, Byrne, Armstrong, McConnon, Ashman, Southby.
GOALS — (NM) Sutton (5), Blight (2), Dawson, Cowton, Schimmelbusch.
(C) Keogh (2), Ashman (2), Byrne, Walls, Pickett, Jesaulenko, Armstrong.

SEPTEMBER 25—GRAND FINAL

	1st	2nd	3rd	Final
Hawthorn	5 . 9	9 . 12	10 . 18	13 . 22 (100)
Nth. Melb.	4 . 2	7 . 5	10 . 8	10 . 10 (70)

MCG — Umpires—Smith, Deller
Attendance—110,143 — Gate—$564,705 (Rec.)

BEST — (H) Knights, Hendrie, Douge, Rowlings, L. Matthews.
(NM) Dench, Greig, Cable, Icke, Blight.
GOALS — (H) Moncrieff (3), K. Matthews (2), Hendrie (2), Goad (2), L. Matthews, Scott, Rowlings, Martello.
(NM) Cable (2), Icke (2), Burns (2), Cowton, Byrne, Moore, Melrose.

GRAND FINAL TEAMS

Hawthorn	B	B. Douge	K. Moore	B. Jones
	HB	D. O'Halloran	P. Knights	I. Bremner
	C	R. Eade	B. Rowlings	G. Ablett
	HF	K. Matthews	A. Martello	D. Polkinghorne
	F	M. Moncrieff	J. Hendrie	A. Goad
	Ruck	D. Scott (c)	M. Tuck	L. Matthews
	Reserves	L. Rice	P. Murnane	
	Coach	J. Kennedy		
Nth. Melbourne	B	J. Byrne	D. Dench	F. Gumbleton
	HB	D. Sutton	G. Cowton	S. Icke
	C	K. Greig (c)	J. Burns	P. Feltham
	HF	W. Schimmelbusch	T. Moore	M. Blight
	F	G. Melrose	B. Crosswell	P. Keenan
	Ruck	M. Nolan	M. Dawson	B. Cable
	Reserves	P. Chisnall	R. Henshaw	
	Coach	R. D. Barassi		

1977

The performance of North Melbourne in winning the 1977 Premiership was one of the finest team efforts in the long history of the VFL. To win the flag, they had to play five consecutive finals matches and come from 3rd place to do it, equalling their own record, set in 1975, as the only team to become premiers from that position on the ladder.

Despite the wettest Melbourne winter in 40 years, season 1977 was a high-scoring one with ten of the twelve teams scoring in excess of 2,000 points.

Collingwood (18 wins) topped the ladder from Hawthorn (17 wins), North Melbourne (15), Richmond (14½) and improved South Melbourne (whose 13½ wins included a shock win over North in Round 22). Two premiership points away in 6th spot and with a superior percentage to South was Carlton, whose 3 point loss to Richmond and 18 point loss to Footscray in the last two games had cost them dearly.

The performance of Collingwood in heading the ladder was a remarkable one, as the Magpies had finished last the previous season. The coaching of Tom Hafey (ex-Richmond) was the vital factor which enabled the Magpies to equal the record set by Essendon in 1908 in coming from last to a Grand Final.*

Popular South Melbourne, appearing in their first finals series since 1970 and only their second since 1945, was no match for Richmond in the Elimination Final, despite a good battle until half-time. The Tigers, with much more experience in finals, and playing with a lot more determination, outbumped and outmarked the smaller Southerners in a game spoilt by a strong, gusty wind.

Brownlow Medallist Teasdale (South) was well covered by Cloke and the South forward line was kept out of it by the tight Richmond back-line led by Bourke, Sheedy, Keane and Jenkinson, as Richmond went on to win quite easily by 34 points.

Hawthorn, in the Qualifying Final, romped away from North to record their 11th win in their last 13 meetings.

High point of a rather ordinary game was the scoring of his 100th goal, two minutes into the game, by Hawthorn full-forward Peter Hudson. Hudson had returned to the Hawks in 1977 after two years in Tasmania, and showed he had lost none of his old skill.

Hawthorn had very few poor players on the day, kicking 4 goals straight in the second quarter, and 6.3 to 1.3 in the third to seal the game.

North, with three changes to the selected side, sprung a few more before the ball was bounced in the First Semi-Final.

All week, the Richmond camp had let it be known that Balme would take the lumbering North ruckman, Nolan, apart in this game, and it was a shock to the Tiger

* Melbourne, second last in 1953, rose to Runners-up in 1954.

brains-trust when Nolan and Baker suddenly ran to the reserves bench just before the bounce, and Keenan and Sutton came on. Keenan subdued Balme from the start as the Tigers, thrown out of stride by this and the surprise move of Icke from the back-line to centre-half-forward, just could not get their game together. Goal-less in the first term, the Tigers were "gone" at half-time, trailing by over six goals, and the dominance of little North rover, Cable (17 kicks, 18 handballs) made sure that Richmond did not get the chance to come back. Icke (5 goals) was a surprise packet up forward, beating Bourke, one of the Tiger mainstays. With their easy 47 point win, North advanced to their fourth successive Preliminary Final.

A determined team-effort by Collingwood brought them an upset 2 point win over Hawthorn in the Second Semi-Final. Despite finishing on top, Collingwood was suspect due to its poor finals record, but won this game in a pressure finish, the Hawks coming back with goals to Hudson and Hendrie at the 31 and 32 minute mark of the last term after the Magpies, holding a 14 point lead, had relaxed slightly. It was then that Collingwood showed their new-found finals determination and, instead of wilting, fought back and two telling marks by rover Wearmouth, on the half-back line, eased the pressure and helped Collingwood retain their 2 point lead until the siren. The Magpies hand-ball and running-on, plus fine performances by Thompson, who dominated the ruck duels, and Worthington, who blanketed Hudson, were key factors in the Magpies win. The Hawks only spark was when they rattled on 5.3 in a short period after Collingwood's Carman flattened Tuck early in the first term. Carman's subsequent suspension over this incident kept him out of the Grand Final.

North Melbourne again made changes to their line-up, bringing Henshaw and Baker in for the Preliminary Final, and leaving out C. Davis and Jarrott. Nolan, one of the heroes of the 1975 premiership, was left out of the 20. Hawthorn named an unchanged side, but lost Rice (groin) and Welsh (virus) on the day of the game, replacing them with Trott and McCarthy.

The inspiration of Barassi was undoubtedly the main factor which enabled North to overcome the loss of stars such as Greig, Melrose, Burns and Dawson but Hawthorn certainly appeared to have had a lot taken out of them by the previous weeks game.

North's Keenan dominated the ruck early, and Tanner in particular took great advantage, being instrumental in nearly all of North's first-half forward moves. Within the first nine minutes of the match, Cable, Tanner and Briedis had goals on the board and that set the pattern for the day, North playing superb football and Hawthorn, by contrast, putting in their worst game for years.

North sealed the game in the third term, kicking 6.5 to 3 points, the first three goals coming within 2 minutes of the resumption, and went on to win easily by 67 points.

Cable (16 kicks, 22 handballs) was best afield, but North had other stars in Tanner, Dench (who handed out a hiding to Hudson) and Keenan. Baker, who took 11 magnificent marks, should have had a bagful of goals, but poor kicking (2.6 and 2 out of bounds) let him down.

For the first time, the Grand Final was televised live in Victoria in 1977. Despite this fact 108,224 fans attended the match, most of them Collingwood supporters who were sure that, at last, two decades of premiership drought were to end. To make them feel even more confident, North captain Keith Greig was unavailable because of a knee injury.

Both Collingwood and North Melbourne made positional changes before the first bounce, and it was North centre-half-back Dench, named at full-back, who scored first goal of the game when he grabbed the ball on the half back line and scored after a brilliant solo run.

Baker added two more for North to place the Magpie defence under considerable pressure, the elusive Anderson being Collingwood's only goalscorer at this stage.

Another to Baker gave North a 17 point lead at the first change, after a quarter which had been marred by a number of fiery incidents.

Goals to Moore and Kink, and some shocking errors by the North defence, put Collingwood back into the game early in the second quarter. Wearmouth's long runs opened up the Magpie forward line as Collingwood, in their best display of the match so far, kept North goal-less to trail by only 2 points at half-time.

Good as it had been in the second quarter, Collingwood was even better in the third. Beginning with two quick goals to Moore, Collingwood hit the front for the first time, and Crosswell was sent to full-back to pick up the big blonde goalkicker.

The North side was faltering as Shaw and Kink goaled for Collingwood to put them 19 points ahead. North could not find the goals, and despite many chances had put up 11 successive behinds since early in the second quarter. Barham capped off a fine passage of play for Collingwood with a goal which gave them a match-winning 27 point advantage at three-quarter time and it was hard to imagine Collingwood losing from such a position.

Mass changes for North finally paid off when — after Schimmelbusch had kicked their 12th successive behind — Sutton, now at full-forward, goaled. Less than a minute later Baker added another and Briedis missed with a long shot to reduce the deficit to 14 points. The Magpies now began to feel the pressure, which led minutes later to the error of the match when Manassa's handball was intercepted by Dench, now at centre-half-forward for North, and he ran in to boot North's seventh goal, and their third in seven minutes.

Briedis marked strongly for North, but had a long wait to have his shot whilst Gott (Collingwood) was taken from the field on a stretcher. Briedis then booted a behind, for North to trail by only 7 points.

Dench added another behind before Byrne found Baker for a goal at the 14 minute mark, and North after a magnificent fight-back, had levelled the scores!

Fans were screaming as the lead changed through behinds to Dunne and Tanner, but at the 22 minute mark North gained what looked like the winning break when Byrne got a behind and Baker, after a fine mark, goaled to put North 7 points ahead.

Now, with only minutes remaining, Collingwood came back but Moore missed a fairly easy shot, and the resultant behind made it six points the difference.

With 50 seconds to go, Picken came down from the Collingwood back-line and his kick was strongly marked, in a big pack, by Dunne. From 15 metres out, Dunne scored a goal to level the scores and, with Collingwood again moving into attack, the siren went shortly after with the scores still level — the second Grand Final tie in VFL history.

Dual Brownlow Medallist Keith Greig was still an absentee when North lined-up the following week for the re-play of the Grand Final, but the Kangaroos were first away with a behind, to Baker, and a goal, to Cable.

W. Richardson levelled the scores with a goal at the eight minute mark and, with the North defence becoming ragged under pressure, Thompson and Gordon combined to find Manassa, whose goal gave Collingwood the lead.

The dangerous Baker replied for North, and Briedis ran into an open goal for another. Late in the quarter, Blight and Crosswell added further goals but Moore answered after a big mark right on the siren.

North, leading by 13 points, streamed into attack as the second quarter began, but six behinds in six minutes was wasteful football.

Strong play by Icke got the ball to Baker, who goaled, but a bad mistake by Cassin let Collingwood's Wearmouth in for the reply. Briedis, after a 15 metre penalty, goaled for North, and moments later the same player handballed to Tanner for another. When Cassin scored yet again, North held a six goal lead.

Collingwood now fought back strongly — Moore and Dunne (twice) goaled, and the brilliant Barham added a fourth within four minutes during time-on, cutting North's lead to a mere 11 points as the teams went in at half-time.

The third term was the crisis point of the game, with fans wondering if North could halt Collingwood's run. Baker, in the first minute, showed they could with his third goal of the game, but tenacious Collingwood battled back again, and Manassa goaled from a free kick. One minute later, Kink scored with a kick off the ground in the goal square and the Magpies, six goals down at the 20 minute mark of the second quarter, were now 5 points down at the five minute mark of the third.

It was now North fighting for survival, and Briedis eased the pressure slightly when he marked and goaled from the pocket. The ball flashed back and forth for minor scores before Icke sank a magnificent punt kick through from deep out on a forward flank, but Gordon, after a long run, replied for Collingwood. A spate of behinds and a snap goal by Byrne took North to a 22 point lead, and Crosswell and Briedis added further goals to give the Kangaroos a firm grip on the game, which a late goal to Anderson (Collingwood) looked unlikely to shake.

Thirty points up at three-quarter time, North increased their lead further within moments of the opening bounce in the last term when Schimmelbusch, after a brilliant dash, goaled.

Picken, moved to a centre-half-forward, gave Collingwood a lift in attack and the Magpies fought back well with goals to Gordon, Moore and Ireland, the latter a tremendous shot from near the centre. Moore missed a sitter, but made amends soon after and Collingwood, nine minutes into the quarter, trailed by 12 points.

Cable replied for North, only to see Moore kick his fifth and Crosswell was sent from full-forward to full-back to mind the Collingwood champion.

Now North scored telling goals from the boots of Blight and Byrne before Manassa, with a brilliant solo run around the flank, took the ball from the half back line and scored with a beautiful angle shot.

But North was not to be denied, and by holding the Magpies at bay for the next five minutes, they ensured that insufficient time remained for Collingwood to come back.

Deep into time on Barham goaled for Collingwood but Schimmelbusch replied for North with a superb goal as the siren went to herald North's second flag in three years.

RESULTS

SEPTEMBER 3—ELIMINATION FINAL

	1st	2nd	3rd	Final
Richmond	5 . 4	7 . 6	11 . 8	13 . 10 (88)
Sth. Melb.	2 . 3	6 . 7	6 . 10	7 . 12 (54)

VFL Park — Umpires—Deller, Smith
Attendance—63,663 — Gate—$264,238

BEST —	(R)	Bourke, Cloke, Bartlett, Malthouse, Monteath, Sheedy, Edwards.
	(SM)	Round, McLeish, Browning, Morrison, Rantall, O'Neill, Teasdale.
GOALS —	(R)	Dunne (2), Monteath (2), Edwards (2), Cloke (2), Roberts, Noonan, Malthouse, Raines, Bartlett.
	(SM)	Lambert (2), Daniher, Goss, Morrison, Browning, Teasdale.

QUALIFYING FINAL

	1st	2nd	3rd	Final
Hawthorn	4 . 5	8 . 5	14 . 11	19 . 11 (125)
Nth. Melb.	2 . 2	5 . 9	6 . 12	12 . 15 (87)

MCG — Umpires—Sutcliffe, Robinson (Robinson injured—replaced in 2nd qr. by Polites)

Attendance—64,052 — Gate—$291,263

BEST — (H) Scott, L. Matthews, Tuck, Moore, Rice, Hudson.
(NM) Cassin, Icke, Schimmelbusch, Dench, Montgomery, C. Davis.

GOALS — (H) Hudson (6), L. Matthews (4), Hendrie (3), K. Ablett (2), Martello, Paton, Polkinghorne, Knights.
(NM) C. Davis (3), Cassin (2), Cable (2), Crosswell, Briedis, Byrne, Moore, Dench.

SEPTEMBER 10—FIRST SEMI-FINAL

	1st	2nd	3rd	Final
Nth. Melb	3 . 5	7 . 12	10 . 14	16 . 14 (110)
Richmond	0 . 3	2 . 4	4 . 7	9 . 9 (63)

VFL Park — Umpires—Dye, Robinson

Attendance—48,105 — Gate—$202,357

BEST — (NM) Icke, Keenan, Cable, Cowton, Gumbleton, Schimmelbusch.
(R) Sheedy, Bartlett, Wood, Walsh, Balme.

GOALS — (NM) Icke (5), Crosswell (3), Briedis (2), Blight (2), C. Davis, Cassin, Cable, Baker.
(R) Bartlett (4), Laughlin (2), Roberts, Dunne, Walsh.

SECOND SEMI FINAL

	1st	2nd	3rd	Final
Collingwood	4 . 0	7 . 3	11 . 6	17 . 10 (112)
Hawthorn	6 . 5	6 . 8	9 . 13	16 . 14 (110)

MCG — Umpires—Deller, Nash

Attendance—87,421 — Gate—$325,863

BEST — (C) Wearmouth, Thompson, Worthington, R. Shaw, Barham, Manassa.
(H) Tuck, Knights, Hendrie, Scott, Moncrieff, G. Ablett.

GOALS — (C) Carman (4), Moore (4), Kink (2), R. Shaw (2), Gordon, Wearmouth, Barham, W. Richardson, Thompson.
(H) Hudson (4), L. Matthews (3), Moncrieff (2), Tuck (2), Hendrie (2), Eade, G. Ablett, Martello.

SEPTEMBER 17—PRELIMINARY FINAL

	1st	2nd	3rd	Final
Nth. Melb.	4 . 4	7 . 7	13 . 12	16 . 16 (112)
Hawthorn	2 . 3	4 . 9	4 . 12	5 . 13 (43)

VFL Park — Umpires—Smith, Sutcliffe

Attendance—61,242 — Gate—$366,875

BEST — (NM) Cable, Dench, Tanner, Alves, Cowton, Keenan, Briedis, Baker.
(H) Rowlings, Knights, K. Ablett, G. Ablett, Scott.

GOALS — (NM) Cable (3), Briedis (3), Blight (2), Tanner (2), Icke (2), Cassin, Byrne.
(H) L. Matthews (2), Hudson, Tuck, Hendrie.

1977

SEPTEMBER 24—GRAND FINAL

	1st	2nd	3rd	Final
Collingwood	1 . 5	4 . 8	9 . 12	10 . 16 (76)
Nth. Melb.	4 . 4	4 . 10	4 . 15	9 . 22 (76)

MCG **Umpires—Robinson, Sutcliffe**
Attendance—108,224 **Gate—$589,996**

BEST — (C) Magro, Thompson, Picken, W. Richardson, Hyde, Kink, Barham.
(NM) Alves, Schimmelbusch, Dench, Baker, Montgomery, Keenan, Cowton.
GOALS — (C) Moore (4), Kink (2), Shaw, Barham, Anderson, Dunne.
(NM) Baker (6), Dench (2), Sutton.

OCTOBER 1—GRAND FINAL REPLAY

	1st	2nd	3rd	Final
Nth. Melb.	5 . 5	9 . 12	15 . 19	21 . 25 (151)
Collingwood	3 . 4	8 . 7	12 . 7	19 . 10 (124)

MCG **Umpires—Robinson, Sutcliffe**
Attendance—98,366 **Gate—$586,515**

BEST — (NM) Briedis, Blight, Byrne, Cable, Montgomery.
(C) Moore, Thompson, Manassa, Hyde, Wearmouth.
GOALS — (NM) Briedis (5), Baker (3), Byrne (2), Cassin (2), Blight (2), Crosswell (2), Schimmelbusch (2), Tanner, Icke, Cassin.
(C) Moore (5), Manassa (3), Dunne (2), Barham (2), Gordon (2), Anderson, Ireland, W. Richardson, Kink, Wearmouth.

GRAND FINAL TEAMS (RE-PLAY)

Nth. Melbourne	B	R. Henshaw	D. Sutton	F. Gumbleton
	HB	G. Cowton	D. Dench (c)	K. Montgomery
	C	S. Alves	X. Tanner	W. Schimmelbusch
	HF	M. Blight	S. Icke	A. Briedis
	F	B. Crosswell	P. Baker	J. Cassin
	Ruck	P. Keenan	J. Byrne	B. Cable
	Reserves	S. McCann	W. Nettlefold	
	Coach	R. D. Barassi		
Collingwood	B	R. Hyde	K. Worthington	C. Perry
	HB	P. Manassa	W. Picken	A. Ireland
	C	R. Barham	S. Magro	W. Gordon
	HF	G. Anderson	R. Dunne	W. Richardson
	F	R. Shaw	R. Kink	P. Moore
	Ruck	L. Thompson	M. Richardson (c)	R. Wearmouth
	Reserves	G. Bond	G. Betts	
	Coach	T. Hafey		

* D. Gott (Collingwood) played in the first Grand Final but was replaced (due to injury) by C. Perry in the replay.

1978

Season 1978 continued the trend towards higher and higher scores, with no fewer than 153 century scores posted in all games, far exceeding the record of 131 set the previous season. Eighteen of these scores went beyond 150 points, this total also constituting a record, whilst the number of games in which both sides scored more than 100 points was 43, another record. Footscray, although unable to make the finals, had the distinction of booting a VFL record score of 33.15 against St. Kilda in Round 13.

North Melbourne and Hawthorn were the top two teams of the Home and Home round, both winning 16 games but North taking first spot on the ladder by 3.2 percent. Collingwood filled third spot with 15 wins, followed by Carlton (14) and Geelong (12), the latter sneaking in two points ahead of St. Kilda.

The performance of Carlton was noteworthy. The Blues had lost five of their first six matches and were languishing in 11th position before Alex Jesaulenko replaced Ian Stewart (ill-health) as coach. Under Jesaulenko, Carlton made a remarkable revival, winning 13 of their next 16 games, and registering victories over all of the other finalists over the space of nine games. But a thrashing at the hands of St. Kilda in the last game did not auger well for the finals. Hawthorn, also, experienced a slump leading up to the finals, losing two of their last three games and "falling in" in the other, but having a convincing win over premiership favourites, North Melbourne, to their credit in Round 17.

Geelong was hard-hit by injury and suspension as they faced up to Carlton in the Elimination Final. The Cats biggest blow was the loss of big ruckman Manson (suspended), but Jeffreys and Sheehan were also sorely missed. To make matters worse, State wingman Turner was forced out of the side through injury on the morning of the match, and champion David Clarke, injured early, was virtually a passenger for the rest of the game.

Despite these set-backs, Geelong put up a good effort to go down by only 33 points, their shocking inaccuracy preventing them getting even closer. Rover Cousins, with 7 behinds, was a prime offender.

Jesaulenko's match tactics, however, certainly had as much to do with Carlton's win as Geelong's inaccuracy. Ordering Austin to tag prolific kickwinner Bruce Nankervis, Jesaulenko had the satisfaction of seeing Austin keep Nankervis right out of the game and this cut off the main source of supply to big Geelong full-forward, Donohue, who, needing 6 goals for his 100, had to be content with only one. Jones and Maclure dominated the game for Carlton, who were also well served by their fleet-footed smaller brigade.

1978

Hawthorn showed their best form of the season to run away with the Qualifying Final against Collingwood, their winning score of 23.16 being the highest in a Qualifying match since the Tiger's 25.14 in 1972.

The Hawks, regaining their feared aggression and vigour, literally blasted the Magpies aside, and had match-winners all over the ground. In particular, Collingwood had no answer to Scott, Matthews and Moncrieff (whose 8 goals constituted a Qualifying Final goalkicking record).

The form of Thompson for Collingwood was a liability — it appeared as though he may have been carrying an injury, spending most of the match at full-forward. Even the advent of the injured Carman, flung into the fray from the interchange bench at the 27 minute mark of the second quarter, was not sufficient to lift the wilting Magpies, although Carman did well enough to be named as his side's best player!

Traditional rivals Collingwood and Carlton staged a great battle in the First Semi-Final. The form of both sides had been poor the previous week, but the Magpies received a lift when Carman, under a cloud with injury, was declared fit to take his place in the side. Unfortunately, they were then to lose star rover Wearmouth with a thigh injury just before the game.

Jesaulenko himself picked up Carman, but had to relinquish the job to Doull when Carman turned on one of his typical brilliant, but undisciplined displays.

With Picken shutting Carlton's match-winning forward, Maclure, out of the game, the Blues struggled all the first half against Collingwood's bumping and tackling.

A fiery third term saw the Blues fight back with five goals to draw to within 4 points at the last change. During the many skirmishes in the quarter, Kink and Carman of Collingwood were reported for striking, Kink's subsequent two match suspension putting him out of the vital Preliminary Final. Carman, who had been suspended during the previous seasons finals, was luckier this time, being found not guilty by the Tribunal.

The last term promised much, but proved to be an anti-climax. Carlton matched Collingwood for a time, but the Magpies, sparked by three great marks from Carman, turned on the pressure, added three goals in five minutes, and sealed the match.

Another report at VFL Park upset North Melbourne's finals chances. Ruckman Peter Keenan was outed for two weeks for striking and subsequently missed the Grand Final. An additional blow for North was the loss of Crosswell, playing his 23rd final, with a broken arm, which put him, also, out of the remainder of the finals.

Hawthorn's fierceness and pressure did not allow hot favourites North Melbourne to get their normal game flowing, but their own inaccuracy meant they had to struggle to sew up a game that should have been over at half-time. Again, big guns Scott, Matthews, Tuck, Knights and Martello were to the fore for Hawthorn, whilst by contrast North stars such as Brownlow winner Blight (one kick in the first half), Glendinning and Baker were virtually unsighted. With this win, Hawthorn became warm favourites for the Grand Final.

The confident Collingwood bowed out of the 1978 finals series in the Preliminary Final. It was their 30th second-round game since 1958, and their 22nd loss (one other game was drawn).

North's pre-match gamble to leave out Baker on the morning of the match, when rain began to fall, back-fired when the rain cleared before the first bounce, but the Kangaroos gained an early break on the Magpies and never looked like relinquishing it all day. Even when Collingwood drew to within 8 points in the third term, North had plenty in reserve and went away to a 28 point lead early in the last. Then three goals in four minutes put Collingwood back in the match, but once again North answered, and goals to Boyse and McCann sealed the result. The performances of Collingwood stars in Carman (beautifully tagged all day by Greig), Thompson, Moore, M. Richardson, Shaw and Manassa were most disappointing, but veteran Ross Dunne, in his last game, was one of the better players for the Magpies.

Both sides made three changes for the Grand Final, Hawthorn including in their twenty Paton, Dipierdomenico and Goss, and North bringing in Tanner (for only his fifth game of the season) Baker and Cassin.

Scott won the toss for Hawthorn, and within three minutes Moncrieff had twice beaten Glendinning for the mark and had two goals on the board almost before a North player had handled the ball. The Hawks capitalised on their lightning start and, always moving, they ran North ragged in a magnificent opening term to lead by 19 points at the first change. Dipierdomenico, a last minute replacement for O'Halloran (injured) had proved a stumbling block for North, hardly allowing the Kangaroos dangerous half-forward, Briedis, a touch of the ball. Worse, Blight was out of action after the first 10 minutes with a groin injury which later caused him to be replaced.

Early in the second term, North wingman Alves limped off with a leg injury, a sad finish to his 250th VFL game, and it seemed that nothing would go right for the Kangaroos. Then, when even the most ardent North supporters were starting to accept the inevitable, the Roos staged a remarkable comeback. Led by the brilliant Schimmelbusch, who continually speared them into attack, North peppered the goals for Baker to take a series of magnificent high marks from which he booted four goals in twenty minutes to send North in at half time 4 points in front! From looking "gone", North had begun to look like the winners, especially when they added another 8 points in the first four minutes of the third term to go 2 goals up.

Now it was Hawthorn's turn to show their determination. Inspired by Scott, who lifted the whole side when it was in the depths of despair, Matthews turned on the power and in a great effort which gathered him seven kicks for the quarter, the Hawk rover booted three goals and changed the complexion of the game once more. In an awesome display of sheer power, and skill, the Hawks rattled on 7.6 to 3.4 to lead by 22 points at three quarter time, and never looked in any danger in the last, always having enough in reserve to come back after any North challenge. Matthews gathered another 10 kicks for the quarter, and was aided and abetted in his destruction by Knights who, knocked unconscious and sent up forward to recover, promptly kicked two vital goals. The Hawks were untroubled to retain a three goal lead at the final siren, and thus annex their fourth premiership.

RESULTS

SEPTEMBER 9—ELIMINATION FINAL

	1st	2nd	3rd	Final
Carlton	6 . 2	7 . 7	11 . 13	15 . 15 (105)
Geelong	1 . 3	2 . 8	6 . 13	9 . 18 (72)

VFL Park — Umpires—Deller, Nash
Attendance—57,505 — Gate—$297,087

BEST —	(C)	Maclure, Jesaulenko, Cattoggio, Austin, Jones, Doull.
	(G)	Malarkey, Cousins, Sarah, Preston, Card, Neal.
GOALS —	(C)	Cattoggio (3), Keogh (3), Galt (3), Maclure (2), Collins, Doull, Austin, Jones.
	(G)	Sarah (4), Cousins (2), Bright, Newman, Donohue.

QUALIFYING FINAL

	1st	2nd	3rd	Final
Hawthorn	4 . 5	9 . 7	15 . 11	23 . 16 (154)
Collingwood	3 . 1	5 . 6	9 . 11	14 . 14 (98)

MCG — Umpires—Robinson, Smith
Attendance—79,931 — Gate—$404,181

BEST — (H) Matthews, Moncrieff, Scott, Martello, Knights, Russo.
(C) Carman, Moore, Picken, Ireland.
GOALS — (H) Moncrieff (8), Russo (4), Matthews (3), Martello (2), Murnane (2), Scott, Hendrie, Murphy, Walter.
(C) Carman (3), McCormack (2), Wearmouth, M. Richardson, Byrne, Kink, Carlson, A. Shaw, Manassa, Barham, Dunne.

SEPTEMBER 16—FIRST SEMI-FINAL

	1st	2nd	3rd	Final
Collingwood	4 . 3	7 . 8	10 . 10	15 . 18 (108)
Carlton	1 . 2	5 . 7	9 . 12	13 . 15 (93)

MCG — Umpires—Robinson, Sutcliffe
Attendance—91,933 — Gate—$417,546

BEST — (Col) McCormack, Picken, R. Shaw, Carman, Morris, Ireland, Moore, Kink.
(Carl) Towns, Ashman, Doull, Armstrong, Pinnell, Southby, Jones.
GOALS — (Col) R. Shaw (5), Dunne (4), Moore (2), M. Richardson, Morris, Bond, Manassa.
(Carl) Sheldon (3), Galt (3), Maclure (3), Keogh (2), Cattoggio, Ashman.

SECOND SEMI-FINAL

	1st	2nd	3rd	Final
Hawthorn	3 . 7	7 . 11	10 . 13	12 . 15 (87)
Nth. Melb.	0 . 3	4 . 4	7 . 11	10 . 13 (73)

VFL Park — Umpires—Chapman, Deller
Attendance—48,716 — Gate—$245,456

BEST — (H) Matthews, Martello, Knights, Tuck, Murnane, Moore.
(NM) Briedis, Schimmelbusch, Keenan, Sutton, Ramsay, Greig.
GOALS — (H) Moncrieff (4), Martello (2), Tuck (2), Murnane (2), Matthews, Russo.
(NM) Briedis (3), Crosswell (2), Byrne (2), Melrose, Baker, Boyse.

SEPTEMBER 23—PRELIMINARY FINAL

	1st	2nd	3rd	Final
Nth. Melb.	3 . 4	7 . 6	10 . 10	14 . 12 (96)
Collingwood	2 . 1	5 . 3	8 . 8	12 . 12 (84)

VFL Park — Umpires—Robinson, Nash
Attendance—73,354 — Gate—$441,137

BEST — (NM) Greig, Montgomery, Glendinning, Alves, Huppatz, Blight, Boyse.
(C) Morris, Picken, Wearmouth, Dunne, McCormack, Oborne, Stewart.
GOALS — (NM) Briedis (3), Huppatz (2), McCann (2), Boyse (2), Smith (2), Alves, Blight, Schimmelbusch.
(C) R. Shaw (3), Dunne (3), Carman (2), Wearmouth, Morris, Worthington, Moore.

SEPTEMBER 30—GRAND FINAL

	1st	2nd	3rd	Final
Hawthorn	5 . 3	7 . 4	14 . 10	18 . 13 (121)
Nth. Melb.	2 . 2	7 . 8	10 . 12	15 . 13 (103)

MCG — Umpires—Deller, Robinson
Attendance—101,704 — Gate—$691,458 (Rec.)

BEST —	(H)	Dipierdomenico, Matthews, Moore, Wallace, Tuck, Scott, Eade, Ablett.
	(NM)	Baker, Schimmelbusch, Huppatz, Sutton, Henshaw, Glendinning, Nolan, Byrne.
GOALS —	(H)	Moncrieff (4), Matthews (4), Scott (3), Knights (2), Ablett, Martello, Eade, Hendrie, Murnane.
	(NM)	Baker (6), Briedis (2), Huppatz (2), Boyse (2), Smith (2), Melrose.

GRAND FINAL TEAMS

Hawthorn	B	A. deWolde	K. Moore	I. Paton
	HB	R. Eade	P. Knights	D. Polkinghorne
	C	P. Murnane	T. Wallace	G. Ablett
	HF	J. Hendrie	A. Martello	P. Russo
	F	R. Walter	M. Moncrieff	R. Dipier-domenico
	Ruck	D. Scott (c)	M. Tuck	L. Matthews
	Reserves	N. Goss	M. McCarthy	
	Coach	D. Parkin		
Nth. Melbourne	B	R. Henshaw	R. Glendinning	D. Sutton
	HB	G. Cowton	K. Greig (c)	K. Montgomery
	C	W. Schim-melbusch	X. Tanner	S. Alves
	HF	M. Boyse	S. McCann	A. Briedis
	F	J. Byrne	P. Baker	R. Huppatz
	Ruck	M. Nolan	M. Blight	G. Melrose
	Reserves	J. Cassin	D. Smith	
	Coach	R. D. Barassi		

1979

The VFL experienced a boom year in 1979, with attendances topping the three million mark for the second successive season, and a new Home and Away record of 3,096,864 being set.

Records were set on the ground, too. Carlton broke the record for most century scores in a season by recording 22 such totals, and nine of these exceeded 20 goals, breaking a long-standing record set by South Melbourne in 1934.* Fitzroy set a new

* Record now stands at 12 by Essendon 1983 and 1985.

match record with a massive 36.22.238 against St. Kilda, and the 'Lions' 8 twenty goal scores equalled the previous best. And, for the first time since 1951, two matches for premiership points were played in Sydney.

Fitzroy, as indicated above, was the surprise packet of the season, notching 15 wins to finish in fourth place after years in the doldrums. Carlton, with 19 wins, easily topped the ladder, from North Melbourne (17 wins), Collingwood (15) and Essendon (12½ wins) falling into fifth spot by 2 premiership points from Geelong, who blew their chances with defeats in rounds 19 and 20 but thrashed Fitzroy in the last game. Shock of the season was the decline of 1978 premiers Hawthorn, who lost five of their first nine games and eventually finished 7th. However, the Hawks sadly missed Martello, Knights, Matthews and Scott who between them missed over 40 games through injury or suspension.

Fitzroy, in their first finals series since 1960, put Essendon out of the fight with a stunning 81 point win in the cut-throat Elimination Final. The Lions form, after surrendering the double-chance with a loss to Geelong in the last game, was suspect, but no-one would have thought so when Fitzroy booted 4.3 to Essendon's nil in the first 11 minutes of the game. By the end of the term, they had rattled up a first quarter finals record of 9.4 and Essendon never recovered. Despite a free kick tally which ran 29 to 60 against them, Fitzroy went on to win easily with almost every player on top on the day. The star was Wilson, with 17 kicks and 25 handballs. By contrast, Essendon, which badly missed injured quartet Keenan, Van der Haar, Reid and Besanko, and had T. Daniher and Madden both playing with broken bones in the hand, had many "passengers", and was outclassed by Fitzroy's brilliant handball (135 to 74 in Fitzroy's favour).

During the game, Fitzroy full-forward Bob Beecroft kicked 2 goals to take his tally for the season to 85, breaking the club record of 83 set by Jack Moriarty in 1926.

The MCG was slow and heavy and should have suited Collingwood in the Qualifying Final. And so it appeared in the first half, when Collingwood applied great physical pressure on North Melbourne. Within minutes early in the second term, separate clashes saw Cassin and Alves of North flattened, and Magro and Edwards of Collingwood reported. (Magro was suspended for 2 matches, Edwards cleared). The Magpies, despite 17 behinds, held a three goal lead at half-time, with their little men running rings around their North counterparts, and North's prime-movers being right out of the game. But from the 25 minute mark of the second term, there were signs that North was starting to come to life, and the flood-gates burst open in a brilliant third quarter. Dempsey, taking control in the ruck, began to direct a flow of hit-outs to the fleet-footed North little men, and a blue and white avalanche hit the shocked Magpie defence. Even the fine efforts of Picken could not halt North's burst of 10.2 to 1.6 for the term — only the siren could do that, and when it sounded for the end of the quarter, North, had gone from 3 goals down to 6 goals up! The last was a formality for the Kangaroos, who won, easing up, by 39 points.

Craig Davis (who booted 7 straight behinds for Collingwood) was in this match playing in a final for his third side — he had previously featured in finals matches with Carlton and North Melbourne.

The Magpies were boosted by the return of Anderson and Barham for the First Semi-Final against Fitzroy, which had McCarthy out injured. The game was even early, but Fitzroy was well off-target and despite 6 more scoring shots, led by a mere 6 points at half-time. But after the break, the Magpies really exposed Fitzroy's lack of pace and, led by the pacy Barham (who booted 2 goals in 2 minutes), they blasted through the Fitzroy defence to kick 7.6 to 1.4 for the quarter, and have a long lead at three-quarter time. Fitzroy in the last showed glimpses of their best with six goals, but they were outclassed on the day. An interesting Magpie move was that of wingman Anderson to the forward flank after Dreher was injured — Anderson finished the game with 5 goals.

Carlton was rated underdogs in the Second-Semi, partly due to their poor recent finals record (1 win since 1973), and partly due to the thinking that North's experience would be too much. But the Blues surprised in winning well by 38 points, and showed that there was still a place in the game for the little man — Carlton had six or seven of them, in fact, and all were lightning fast, ran long and often, and teamed well with those around them. North fell down up forward — they lost Bryant early, Dempsey at half-time — and Carlton slammed on 7.8 to 2.4 in the third term to take control of the game. The Carlton move of Harmes to the centre was one of the turning points, but perhaps in fairness to North it should be pointed out that beside the two injuries mentioned during the game, they also had Greig, Crosswell, Baker and Byrne unavailable.

It was something of a surprise to see the two sides in the Preliminary Final line-up almost exactly as selected. The Magpies, thrashed by North a fortnight before, showed from the start that they would be a harder nut to crack this time as Anderson eluded three opponents and slammed through their first goal at the two minute mark. Blight put on two goals in four minutes to regain the lead for North, the first of 11 times that the lead would change until near the finish of the third term.

Collingwood's pace and anticipation gave them most of the early breaks, and their finishing-on towards the end of each quarter was noticeable — in fact, eight of Collingwood's goals were scored during time-on, 2 in the first quarter, 2 in the second, three in the third and one in the last.

North, trailing at half-time, made a number of positional changes which brought quick goals to Briedis (2), Melrose and Cassin to take North from an 11 point deficit to an 11 point lead half way through the third quarter. But the Magpies came back with goals from Banks and Kink, and had a purple patch at the 28, 30 and 31 minute marks when Davis, Ohlsen and Brewer kicked truly. The Magpies, with tails up, had the answer to anything North could throw at them in the last, and eventually put the issue beyond doubt with a handball from Kink which gave Morris a goal, and the Magpies were untroubled to win well by 27 points and end North's run of six successive Grand Finals.

Collingwood had many good men on the day, whilst North was kept in the game only by great efforts from Blight and Dempsey (who spent five days in hospital in the week before the game). Greig, who played probably his worst finals game, Dench, Briedis and Crosswell, usually finals stars, were all poor performers. An interesting point is that this match actually caused a change to the whole game of football. Ruckmen Moore and Dempsey continually wrestled each other to the ground at centre-bounces, the whole situation eventually becoming ludicrous when the Umpires apparently decided that as long as neither player punched or kicked, they could do what they liked. The prospect of ruck-play degenerating into wrestling matches caused the VFL to introduce in 1980 a dividing line drawn across the centre circle with opposing ruck-men coming from each side of it. Critics argued that this meant that the side with the tallest ruck-men would win the knock, others replied that it opened out the game as never before. The arguments will no doubt continue.

A huge crowd of 113,545 filled the MCG on Grand Final day, and many millions more watched a direct telecast for the third year in a row.

After 48 hours of steady rain, the turf was muddy with pools of water, and pre-match critics had no doubts that the heavy turf would hamper Carlton's smaller brigade. Both sides made minimal changes, Carlton bringing in Young for the injured Ashman, and Collingwood omitting Dreher in favour of Magro.

The first quarter of the Grand Final was one of the toughest for years. Collingwood did most of the early attacking, with Kink a dominant player. There were plenty of hard clashes, but it was primarily a battle of defences, with Carlton 0.2, Collingwood 0.1 after 12 minutes play. A big blow for Collingwood, however, came when Kink, who had been playing brilliantly, was reported 10 minutes into the match — he subsequently died out of the play and his opponent, Klomp, became one of the Blues stars.

Wearmouth, from a free, scored first goal for Collingwood after 17 minutes, and Ohlsen, also playing well, added another. Fitzpatrick (Carlton) hit the post from 15 yards out, and a couple of other mulled easy shots led fans to think that it just was not going to be Carlton's day.

The Blues' inaccuracy continued in the second term, as Ohlsen found Davis for Collingwood's third goal. In desperation, Jesaulenko moved Harmes to the centre, but then saw Magpie half-back Ireland stream downfield for another Collingwood goal. The Carlton attack was a shambles and the defence poor as Brewer marked and added yet another for Collingwood, who now led by 28 points.

Finally, Fitzpatrick landed the ball forward for Harmes to run in for Carlton's first goal of the match, 19 minutes into the second quarter. Suddenly, Collingwood seemed to stop attacking, and Buckley added a second for Carlton. Moments later, Sheldon's long kick bounced through and Maclure marked and goaled for Carlton's third in 4 minutes! Then, to complete a remarkable recovery, Johnston found Buckley for Carlton's fifth and the Blues hit the front by a point as the half-time siren sounded.

Ohlsen, one of the Magpies prime-movers, did not reappear after half-time, after being heavily downed by Keogh (who was reported for the incident) mid-way through the second term. The Magpies missed his drive, as Maclure took a spectacular mark and goaled for Carlton. Sheldon's long kick was then marked by the limping Jones, who added another amidst scenes of great excitement from the Carlton camp. McCormack was moved to centre half forward for the Magpies, but Carlton was unstoppable, and a hand-ball from Marcou found Francis, who scored a magnificent goal from the boundary.

Sheldon, scouting nicely, and winger Young added two more in quick succession and Carlton, 21 points ahead after booting 5 goals to 2 for the quarter, looked to have the game in their keeping at the last change.

In past years, perhaps Collingwood may not have fought back from this point, but fight-back this side certainly did. Ohlsen, back on, drove forward, where Kink kicked poorly. Picken rose high to take the mark of the match, and drive Collingwood forward where Davis goaled. One minute later, Wearmouth's 60 metre run landed the ball with Carlson, who goaled from 45 metres out. Carlton, recovering, hit back for 2 behinds to increase their lead to 10 points, but Anderson found Kink for another Magpie goal, with 15 minutes gone. Jesaulenko, down in a pack, was carried off as both sides battled out a frenzied finish. Harmes now featured in the play of the match as he won the ball, miskicked, chased it upfield and, diving, hit it back into play just as it was about to cross the boundary line. The ball landed at the feet of Sheldon, who picked up and goaled, giving Carlton a 10 point lead and vital breathing space. Johnston, now in defence, twice saved, and Southby was also strong on the backline as the crisis point of the game was reached with the clock ticking into time-on. Barham

(Collingwood) failed to make the distance and then a mark to McConville was called "play-on" and Edwards picked up and goaled for Collingwood. A moment later, Marcou missed for Carlton, his behind making the difference 5 points, and there the margin remained, the siren sounding moments after with Jezza's Blues taking out the 1979 flag.

The inaugural Norm Smith Medal, for Best Afield in the Grand Final, was awarded to Carlton's Wayne Harmes — many critics, however, voted Blues half-forward Wayne Johnston the best player. Johnston had a unique double out of this game — he had played in Prahran's VFA premiership team the previous season, and now was in a VFL premiership team a season later. It is also worth noting that this match turned out to be the last for Carlton by Alex Jesaulenko and Peter "Percy" Jones.

RESULTS

SEPTEMBER 8—ELIMINATION FINAL

	1st	2nd	3rd	Final
Fitzroy	9 . 4	11 . 9	14 . 17	17 . 22 (124)
Essendon	1 . 3	2 . 4	3 . 8	5 . 13 (43)

VFL Park — Umpires—Sawers, Robinson
Attendance—49,470 — Gate—$273,639

BEST — (F) Wilson, Smith, Alexander, Hansen, McMahon, Irwin, Harris, Higgins.
(E) Madden, Crow, Foulds, Bennett, Taubert.
GOALS — (F) Quinlan (4), Walls (3), Conlan (2), McMahon (2), Beecroft (2), Wilson (2), Richardson, Irwin.
(E) Andrews, T. Daniher, N. Daniher, Fletcher, Robins.

QUALIFYING FINAL

	1st	2nd	3rd	Final
Nth. Melbourne	3 . 2	6 . 5	16 . 7	18 . 13 (121)
Collingwood	4 . 8	7 . 17	8 . 23	9 . 28 (82)

MCG — Umpires—Smith, Deller
Attendance—84,660 — Gate—$482,242

BEST — (NM) Dempsey, Cassin, W. Schimmelbusch, Sutton, Henshaw, Tanner, Boyse, Melrose, Bryant.
(C) Picken, R. Shaw, McCormack, Wearmouth, Kink, Morris, Ohlsen, Carlson.
GOALS — (NM) Cassin (5), Bryant (3), Melrose (3), Boyse (2), Dempsey, Dench, Tanner, Murphy, Easton.
(C) Wearmouth (3), Edwards, Stewart, R. Shaw, Worthington, Kink, Morris.

SEPTEMBER 15—FIRST SEMI FINAL

	1st	2nd	3rd	Final
Collingwood	3 . 5	5 . 7	12 . 13	16 . 20 (116)
Fitzroy	3 . 4	5 . 13	6 . 17	12 . 22 (94)

MCG — Umpires—Smith, Sawers
Attendance—87,139 — Gate—$494,281

BEST — (C) Barham, Morris, Anderson, Picken, McCormack, Kink, R. Shaw.
(F) Wilson, Allan, Conlan, Hansen, Quinlan.
GOALS — (C) Anderson (5), Kink (3), Barham (2), D. Shaw, R. Shaw, Wearmouth, Edwards, Morris, Davis.
(F) Walls (3), Conlan (2), Beecroft (2), Irwin, Quinlan, Mugavin, Harris, Hansen.

SECOND SEMI FINAL

	1st	2nd	3rd	Final
Carlton	1 . 5	4 . 11	11 . 19	15 . 21 (111)
Nth. Melbourne	1 . 2	3 . 3	5 . 7	11 . 7 (73)

VFL Park — Umpires—Chapman, Nash
Attendance—69,142 — Gate—$373,560

BEST — (C) Doull, Harmes, Klomp, Sheldon, Keogh, Buckley, Armstrong.
(NM) Blight, W. Schimmelbusch, Easton, McCann, Alves, Sutton.
GOALS — (C) Sheldon (4), Maclure (3), Brown (3), Fitzpatrick (2), Johnston, Young, McKay.
(NM) Blight (4), Sutton (3), Easton (2), Cassin, Glendinning.

SEPTEMBER 22—PRELIMINARY FINAL

	1st	2nd	3rd	Final
Collingwood	3 . 1	8 . 3	14 . 7	18 . 14 (122)
Nth. Melbourne	2 . 7	5 . 10	11 . 11	13 . 17 (95)

VFL Park — Umpires—Deller, Robinson
Attendance—73,380 — Gate—$469,325

BEST — (C) Picken, Ireland, Byrne, Morris, Worthington, Anderson, Wearmouth, Edwards.
(NM) Blight, Dempsey, W. Schimmelbusch, McCann, Cassin.
GOALS — (C) Anderson (3), Davis (3), Brewer (3), Kink (2), Edwards (2), Wearmouth, D. Shaw, Ohlsen, Banks, Morris.
(NM) Blight (5), Briedis (2), Cassin (2), Crosswell (2), Tanner, Melrose.

SEPTEMBER 29—GRAND FINAL

	1st	2nd	3rd	Final
Carlton	0 . 4	5 . 7	10 . 12	11 . 16 (82)
Collingwood	2 . 2	5 . 6	7 . 9	11 . 11 (77)

MCG — Umpires—Deller, Smith
Attendance—113,545 — Gate—$849,316 (Rec.)

BEST — (Carl) Johnston, Harmes, Doull, Francis, Fitzpatrick, Buckley, Armstrong.
(Coll) Picken, Moore, Morris, Barham, Ohlsen.
GOALS — (Carl) Sheldon (3), Maclure (2), Buckley (2), P. Jones, Harmes, Young, Francis.
(Coll) Davis (4), Edwards, Wearmouth, Kink, Ohlsen, Carlson, Ireland, Brewer.

1979-1980

NORM SMITH MEDAL — W. Harmes (Carlton)

GRAND FINAL TEAMS

Carlton	B	W. Harmes	G. Southby	D. McKay
	HB	R. Klomp	B. Doull	P. McConville
	C	P. Francis	A. Jesau-lenko (c)	M. Young
	HF	T. Keogh	M. Maclure	W. Johnston
	F	M. Fitz-patrick	P. Brown	K. Sheldon
	Ruck	P. Jones	B. Armstrong	J. Buckley
	Int.	R. Austin	A. Marcou	
	Coach	A. Jesaulenko		
Collingwood	B	S. Magro	P. McCormack	K. Worthington
	HB	R. Byrne	W. Picken	A. Ireland
	C	G. Anderson	K. Morris	R. Barham
	HF	R. Kink	A. Edwards	R. Brewer
	F	R. Shaw (c)	C. Davis	D. Shaw
	Ruck	P. Moore	R. Ohlsen	R. Wearmouth
	Int.	L. Carlson	D. Banks	
	Coach	T. Hafey		

1980

A pre-season internal upheaval split the Carlton Football Club into two warring factions early in 1980, and resulted in 1979 premiership coach, Alex Jesaulenko leaving the Blues for St. Kilda. This was a disastrous blow for Carlton, and new coach Peter Jones did a remarkable job to take the trouble-torn Blues into the finals.

The final five was settled in round 21, but even so, the last game still caused a reshuffle in positions when South thrashed Richmond and sent the Tigers tumbling from first to third and allowed Geelong to take top spot on the ladder for the first time since 1954. Geelong and Carlton each had 17 wins, Richmond 16½, (up from 8th in 1979), North Melbourne and Collingwood 14½. Surprise of the season was the slump of Fitzroy which fell from 4th in 1979 to last in 1980. (Surprisingly, however, the Lions scored more "points for" than top team Geelong — the only time this has ever happened in V.F.L. history).

Collingwood had a point to prove when it met North Melbourne in the Elimination Final. North had won the AFC — Escort Cup night Series premiership only a few months before, beating the Magpies with a goal scored after the umpire had failed to hear the final siren. Collingwood vowed revenge, and they certainly had it this day as they knocked North out of the finals series in what was to be Ron Barassi's last day as the Kangaroos coach.

North had appeared the better side early, and looked likely winners when they slammed on three quick goals at the start of the third term to lead by 11 points. But the Magpies regrouped, and slammed on six goals in 21 magnificent minutes, four of them to Carlson, who had been moved to roving after an early injury to Wearmouth. This left the Magpies 11 points up at the last change, but goals to Glendinning and Briedis early in the last snatched the lead back for North.

Then two goals to the previously unsighted Low and one to Davis gave the lead back to Collingwood. Deep into time-on, Wilson got his fourth but Briedis and Icke missed with long shots and North did not get another chance, the siren sounding with Collingwood 8 points ahead. Hero of the match was Collingwood's Moore, with a near perfect game of 22 kicks, 10 marks, and 7 handballs, plus 18 hit-outs.

The Qualifying Final at VFL Park should go down as Kevin Bartlett's match. The little Tiger veteran, now a half-forward after years as a rover, celebrated his record 337th VFL game with a matchwinning display which netted him 22 disposals and 6 goals. The Tigers rattled Carlton with fierce tackling and bumping which kept the Blues from moving into their normal free-flowing game. Tiger small men in Bartlett, Weightman and Wiley roamed unchecked whilst Landy was able to shadow Johnston, hero of the 1979 Grand Final, to the extent that the classy Carlton half-forward was taken off in the third quarter.

The trend of the game most clearly showed in the period from 15 minutes into the second term until 13 minutes into the last, during which time Carlton failed to score a goal while Bartlett, Weightman and Wiley booted 12 between them!

Carlton and Collingwood clashed in a high-class First Semi-Final, the Blues kicking 4 goals in six minutes early in the second term to lead by 2 points at half time. But the Magpies slammed on 6.5 to 2.5 in a dazzling third quarter, and then raced away with six more in the last to win by 50 points in a most polished performance. Collingwood played the old-fashioned "long-game", were totally dedicated, and fully deserved their win.

Top side Geelong was never really in the hunt against Richmond in the Second Semi, their prime movers being cut out of the game by some dogged shadowing by their Tiger counterparts. Peter Welsh, three weeks earlier an interchange for Richmond Reserves, did a particularly effective job against Geelong's Turner, his performance clinching for him a spot in the Tiger's Grand Final team. Tiger little men again dominated the game, as they had done in the Qualifying Final. Weightman and Wiley did well, but the star was again the veteran Bartlett, who booted 8 goals from the half-forward flank, equalling the effort of Lance Collins (Carlton) from that position in the 1945 First Semi.

No VFL team had reached the Grand Final from 5th position since the introduction of the "Five" in 1972, but Tom Hafey's Magpies re-wrote the record books with a fighting win over Geelong in the Preliminary Final. Geelong had the misfortune to lose Malarkey in the first quarter, and Hawkins at three-quarter time, but despite their fighting finish, they never really looked likely winners and never, at any stage of the game, were they ahead on the scoreboard.

A burst of three goals in 2½ minutes during time-on in the third term gave the Magpies a good lead, but the fighting Cats came back strongly in the last, and a goal to Bright made the difference 11 points at the 23 minute mark. Then Bos goaled but a snap by Bruns right at the finish scored only a behind, not the needed goal, and the siren soon after left the Magpies clinging grimly to a 4 point lead. M. Yeates, who had left the field injured in the first quarter of his first VFL game, was a sterling performer for Geelong in this, his second game in League ranks. At the other end of the scale, the

Cats omitted veteran "Sam" Newman for what would have been his 304th, and last, game.

Richmond gained a bonus when injured stars Cloke and Rowlings were declared available for the Grand Final, the first appearances by both in the series. Tempany (ankle) and Scrimshaw were left out. Collingwood included Barham, a late withdrawal from the Preliminary Final, and omitted young Twomey.

The huge crowd of 113,461 which flocked to the M.C.G. to see if Collingwood could break their premiership "hoodoo", saw instead the most one-sided Grand Final in the V.F.L.'s 85 year history.

The Richmond team was cleverly placed to take the maximum advantage from Collingwood's weaknesses and to control their strengths, and this it did to perfection.

A shocking miss by Low four minutes into the game was a sign of things to come for Collingwood, as a minute later Magro made a bad error in defence and Weightman ran in for the Tiger's first goal. Then Richmond suddenly took over almost everywhere on the ground. With Lee, thrashing Moore, providing tremendous drive from the ruck, the Tigers rammed on 6.5 for the quarter with some powerhouse football which Collingwood just could not match. The Magpies only two goals of the term had come from free kicks. The second quarter was more of the same — the Magpies had no answer as Richmond slammed on 5.6 to 2.4 to go in at half-time with a 43 point lead.

The Magpie camp at this stage was looking for a miracle, but it never came as goals to Wiley (2) and Cloke within the first 7 minutes of the third quarter increased the Tiger's lead to a massive 61 points and effectively finished the game as a contest. At three quarter time, the scoreboard showed Richmond 15.17 Collingwood 5.18 and Magpies supporters were already filing from the ground in stunned silence.

A sensational goal to the brilliant Jess sent Richmond away again as the last term began, and no fewer than seven more were run up in easy style during the quarter, one, at the 26 minute mark by Bartlett, receiving a standing ovation. The 339 veteran magnificently wrongfooted Magro, had one bounce, and threaded the ball through from an almost impossible angle to notch his 7th for the day and equal the Grand Final goal-kicking record. When the siren, mercifully for Collingwood, sounded, Richmond had increased their lead to an incredible 81 points in the biggest anti-climax ever seen in a VFL Grand Final.

Bartlett (20 kicks, 7 goals) and Cloke (6 goals) between them kicked more than the entire Collingwood team, and although Richmond did not have a bad player, some had statistics worthy of note — Lee (12 disposals, 32 hit-outs), Raines (19 kicks, 17 handballs), Wiley (26 disposals), Keane (27 disposals), so it went on, with only 2 Tigers having less than 10 disposals in the Richmond total of 326. Collingwood, by contrast, had only 248 disposals, only one player (R. Shaw) having more than 20 compared to Richmond's six.

And as a final indictment of the Magpies struggle on Grand Final day, 1980, it was centre-half-back Picken, moved up forward, who was their main goalscorer with three.

RESULTS

SEPTEMBER 6—ELIMINATION FINAL

	1st	2nd	3rd	Final
Collingwood	2 . 8	5 . 12	11 . 17	14 . 20 (104)
Nth. Melbourne	2 . 2	5 . 5	11 . 6	14 . 12 (96)

MCG — Umpires—Cameron, Robinson
Attendance—82,952 (rec) — Gate—$554,813

BEST — (C) Moore, R. Shaw, Carlson, Magro, McCormack, Davis, Kink.
(NM) Glendinning, Greig, Wright, Dempsey, Briedis
GOALS — (C) Carlson (4), R. Shaw (4), Low (2), Barham, Davis, Kink, Moore.
(NM) Wright (4), Briedis (3), Glendinning (2), Smith, Dempsey, Jarrott, Wilson, Blight.

QUALIFYING FINAL

	1st	2nd	3rd	Final
Richmond	6 . 3	11 . 4	16 . 7	18 . 8 (116)
Carlton	2 . 1	5 . 5	5 . 6	10 . 14 (74)

VFL Park — Umpires—Deller, James
Attendance—59,014 — Gate—$362,759

BEST — (R) Bartlett, Raines, Lee, Wiley, Weightman, Wood, Malthouse, Welsh, Strachan.
(C) Southby, Austin, Klomp, Armstrong, Francis, Marcou.
GOALS — (R) Bartlett (6), Weightman (4), Jess (2), Wiley (2), Roach, Wood, Bourke, Scrimshaw.
(C) Klomp (2), Catoggio (2), Ashman, Marcou, McKay, Harmes, Armstrong, McConville.

SEPTEMBER 13—FIRST SEMI FINAL

	1st	2nd	3rd	Final
Collingwood	5 . 5	10 . 10	16 . 15	22 . 20 (152)
Carlton	4 . 3	11 . 6	13 . 11	15 . 12 (102)

MCG — Umpires—Nash, Smith
Attendance—94,451 — Gate—$558,716

BEST — (Coll) Kink, Picken, Barham, Magro, Ireland, Stewart, Byrne.
(Carl) Fitzpatrick, Southby, McKay, Armstrong, McConville, Marcou.
GOALS — (Coll) Low (4), Barham (4), Kink (3), Stewart (3), Daicos (2), Davis, Young, A. Shaw, R. Shaw, Woolnough, Ireland.
(Carl) McKay (5), Sheldon (3), Buckley (2), Armstrong (2), Johnston, Wells, McConville.

SECOND SEMI FINAL

	1st	2nd	3rd	Final
Richmond	3 . 2	7 . 3	10 . 6	14 . 11 (95)
Geelong	5 . 2	7 . 4	9 . 4	11 . 5 (71)

VFL Park — Umpires—Sawers, Sutcliffe
Attendance—65,303 — Gate—$413,922

BEST — (R) Bartlett, Lee, Wiley, Welsh, Weightman, Dunne, Bourke.
(G) B. Nankervis, Middlemiss, Bright, Malarkey, Taylor, Neal.
GOALS — (R) Bartlett (8), Roach (2), Jess, Monteath, Scrimshaw, Bourke.
(G) Bright (3), Johnston (2), Featherby, Matthews, Clarke, Newman, Bos, B. Nankervis.

SEPTEMBER 20—PRELIMINARY FINAL

	1st	2nd	3rd	Final
Collingwood	3 . 5	6 . 8	12 . 10	13 . 15 (93)
Geelong	2 . 2	5 . 5	9 . 8	13 . 11 (89)

VFL Park — Umpires—Deller, Smith
Attendance—75,526 — Gate—$528,365
(rec—VFL Park Prel)

BEST —	(C)	R. Shaw, Stewart, Byrne, Moore, Wearmouth, McCormack, Woolnough.
	(G)	Turner, Featherby, Clarke, Bruns, Taylor, Yeates.
GOALS —	(C)	Wearmouth (3), R. Shaw (3), C. Davis (3), Young, Stewart, Moore, Daicos.
	(G)	Bruns (3), Clarke (3), Bos (3), Johnston (2), Bright, B. Nankervis.

SEPTEMBER 27—GRAND FINAL

	1st	2nd	3rd	Final
Richmond	6 . 5	11 . 11	15 . 17	23 . 21 (159)
Collingwood	2 . 6	4 . 10	5 . 18	9 . 24 (78)

MCG — Umpires—Deller, Robinson
Attendance—113,461 — Gate—$932,445 (Rec)

BEST —	(R)	Lee, Bartlett, Raines, Wiley, Cloke, Mount, Wood, Keane, Weightman, Jess.
	(C)	Picken, McCormack, R. Shaw, Woolnough, Byrne.
GOALS —	(R)	Bartlett (7), Cloke (6), Wiley (3), Keane (2), Roach (2), Weightman, Jess, Rowlings.
	(C)	Picken (3), R. Shaw, Ohlsen, Wearmouth, Moore.

NORM SMITH MEDAL — K. Bartlett (Richmond)

GRAND FINAL TEAMS

Richmond	B	M. Malthouse	E. Dunne	G. Strachan
	HB	P. Welsh	J. Jess	T. Smith
	C	B. Wood	G. Raines	S. Mount
	HF	K. Bartlett	D. Cloke	M. Keane
	F	F. Bourke	M. Roach	R. Wiley
	Ruck	M. Lee	B. Rowlings	D. Weightman
	Int.	B. Monteath (c)	D. Freame	
	Coach	A. Jewell		
Collingwood	B	S. Magro	P. McCormack	A. Ireland
	HB	K. Morris	W. Picken	R. Byrne
	C	R. Barham	P. Daicos	L. Carlson
	HF	R. Kink	C. Stewart	I. Low
	F	R. Shaw (c)	C. Davis	D. Young
	Ruck	P. Moore	R. Ohlsen	R. Wearmouth
	Int.	A. Shaw	M. Woolnough	
	Coach	T. Hafey		

1981

For the fifth successive season, a new attendance record was set, the 1981 figure being 3,830,231 spectators, who paid receipts of $10,441,541. Two VFL Sunday games were played in 1981, but crowd support was below expectations. Games were also played in Brisbane and Sydney, those in the latter city with the view to moving the South Melbourne club there on a permanent basis in 1982.

The battle for the final five was extremely interesting. Carlton, coached by ex-Hawthorn mentor David Parkin, had a stunning sixty-two point win over 1980 Premiers Richmond in their opening game and, despite an "acclimatisation" period in which the players and Parkin appeared to have difficulties adjusting to different styles of game, the Blues headed the ladder with seventeen wins and five losses, followed by Collingwood (with the same number of wins), Geelong and Essendon (sixteen wins—of which, in Essendon's case, fifteen had been in succession, the largest winning sequence in a season since 1929) and Fitzroy (fourteen wins), whose great last-round victory over Collingwood at Victoria Park gave them the fifth spot and cost Collingwood the top!

Indeed, the final round of the season could well qualify as the most exciting in the history of the VFL, for when if began there were almost twenty variations of the final five possible. Amongst others—Collingwood could have finished 1st, 2nd, or 3rd; both Carlton and Essendon could have finished 1st, 2nd, 3rd or 4th, Geelong 2nd, 3rd or 4th, and three other teams were possibles for 5th spot.

Hawthorn and Richmond both ultimately finished a game out, followed by North Melbourne whose seven year run in the finals series thus ended. Richmond's decline was a surprise—losses to Collingwood and Carlton within the space of the last three games ended their slim hopes.

Another surprise of sorts came in the Qualifying Final when Geelong convincingly accounted for Collingwood. Trailing at one stage in the first term by twenty-seven points, Geelong was put into business by big ruckman-cum-forward pocket John Mossop whose six skyscraping marks in the second term brought him to a personal tally of 5.1 and converted an eighteen point deficit into a fourteen point lead.

Early in the last quarter, Geelong's Bright was felled from behind in a scene evoking memories of the 1965 "Somerville Incident". His replacement, Lunn, immediately came under notice with three quick goals and a late come-back by the Magpies saw them unable to bridge the gap, Mossop's seven goals for the match being the difference between victory and defeat for the Cats.

A magnificent captain's goal by Wilson half-way through the last quarter marked the moment when Fitzroy began to run away with the Elimination Final.

Essendon had just gained the lead when Wilson took the ball from the centre bounce, raced around the member's wing, shrugged off a tackle from the burly Van Der Haar, and hooked a left-foot snap back from the boundary line.

Fitzroy, struggling previously, seemed inspired, and two fine goals from Quinlan, one from sixty metres out, sealed the game for the 'Roys, giving ex-Carlton star

Robert Walls, now coaching underdogs Fitzroy, a surprise win over ex-Richmond champion Kevin Sheedy, whose Bombers had looked world-beaters in running up fifteen successive Home and Away round victories.

Fitzroy's smell of success came to a sudden and disappointing end in the First Semi, when Collingwood held them out to win by a single point, the third such margin in a First Semi-Final this century—and Fitzroy had been involved in all three! It was a match of contrasts. Collingwood, playing superbly led by forty-five points a few minutes after half-time, yet, when time-on began in the last quarter, the 'Roys were ten points in front and looking certainties for the Preliminary Final. Then Brewer (who, incidentally, was cleared by Collingwood the following season) figured in two vital pieces of play, first (at the 28 minute mark) finding Daicos with a pass which led to a fifty metre goal and then kicking a left-foot goal almost over his head from a scrimmage near the goal-line to snatch a two point lead for the Magpies. Murnane (Fitzroy) with a long shot notched a point and Collingwood successfully defended their slender lead for the remaining ninety seconds of play.

McMahon, with four second-half goals (the last two of which gave Fitzroy a seven point lead) was one of the heroes of Fitzroy's revival, but Collingwood, it should be noted, lost captain Moore (hamstring injury) and defender Smith (dislocated shoulder) in the second term and so had only eighteen fit men for the remainder of the game. Finally, it is of interest to note that Fitzroy's entire centre line in this game consisted of players who had begun the season with other clubs—Carlson (Collingwood), Francis (Carlton) and Herbert (Collingwood). On the other hand, Fitzroy's 200-game champion rover Warwick Irwin was appearing in this game (his first finals series in over a decade of VFL football) but he was playing for Collingwood!!

Top side Carlton, benefitting from a week's rest to allow a long injury list to recover, completely eclipsed Geelong in a lack-lustre Second Semi. The Cats suffered heavily early in the game when vital running players in Turner and Bruns were injured, but the Blues skillfully blanketed Geelong's marking strengths up forward where Mossop, the previous week's matchwinner, was almost unsighted. Carlton's much-vaunted little men proved their value, running riot all around the ground, whilst the Blues closely-knit defence turned in one of its finest efforts.

Geelong, after having been strongly fancied for the flag, now found itself up against a desperate Collingwood in a cut-throat Preliminary Final, and, as in 1980, this particular game was as far as the Cats went—it was their sixth successive loss in finals matches since 1976.

The standard of play was not high but it was a tense and exciting clash. Collingwood, without the injured Moore, brought in teenager Noel Lovell for his first game, and selected Cooper, who had appeared on only a few occasions during the year. Cooper, by coincidence, had, like Lovell, played his first senior game in a final, back in 1972.

The Magpies surged away to an early lead but after a clash between Kink (Coll) and Bruns (Geel) in the second quarter, Geelong appeared to be stung into action and slapped on a burst of five goals, the last from Mossop in time-on giving them a half-time lead of two points.

Kink, with two fine goals in the third term, put the Magpies within reach of their opponents, and in the last, after Bruns had goaled to put Geelong eleven points up, Kink's third goal precipitated a burst which resulted in the winning goals coming from Daicos and Davis, the siren sounding with Collingwood marching against all odds into yet another Grand Final, with a winning margin of seven points.

For the club's ninth Grand Final (including the 1977 tie) since its last premiership in 1958, Collingwood regained the services of skipper Moore, and was obviously extremely confident of success, feeling that two good wins over the Blues in the Home and Away round indicated they had Carlton's measure.

Parkin's men regained the services of brilliant rover Ashman (runner-up in the Brownlow Medal) after injury, but suffered a blow when champion full-back Southby had to withdraw from the team ninety minutes before the game. The same injury had kept him out of the Second Semi. Howell replaced him, and Bortolotto was a late inclusion on the interchange bench, displacing Klomp.

A crowd of 112,694 packed the MCG for the match, with millions more watching a direct telecast for the fifth successive year.

In a unique incident, the toss was made by former Grand Final umpire Don Jolley, and as the game began it quickly became apparent that Collingwood's gamble in playing skipper Moore after a hamstring injury may have been a mistake. Moore, a Brownlow Medallist as a ruckman, lined up at full-forward and immediately gave indications that he was "proppy". Carlton, also, had injury worries—Ashman, not his usual self after a knee injury, was off the ground after twenty-two minutes, but his replacement, Marcou, was immediately under notice with his superb pace.

The Magpies bombarded the goals for the first twenty minutes for a dismal score of 1.6, squandering chances which by way of contrast were fully capitalised upon by the Blues who, in their only three forward moves, scored 2.1. The early Collingwood onslaught having failed to bring greater rewards allowed Carlton to trail by only two points at the first change.

The second term was even, but it was obvious that Carlton's magnificent defence was exerting tremendous pressure on Collingwood's key forwards, and that sooner or later either backs or forwards must crack. To date, neither side could really get its game flowing and, although Carlton had nosed a point ahead at half-time, to many in the crowd it seemed an impossibility that Carlton could keep Magpie match winners such as Daicos, Davis, Kink and company as quiet in the last half as they had been in the first.

The opening twelve minutes of the third term seemed to bear out the thoughts of many as Taylor, A. Shaw and R. Shaw goaled (within four minutes), and Williams and Barham added further goals shortly afterwards to turn a Magpie deficit of seven points (Carlton had goaled immediately after the resumption) into a lead of twenty-one points. With rain falling since the interval, this was a tidy break in a low-scoring game and the Magpie fans rocked with delight.

The smiles were even broader when Collingwood stood strong against a desperate Carlton onslaught, and at the twenty-nine minute mark, had managed to retain its twenty-one point break. It seemed now that the long-awaited premiership was almost within Collingwood's grasp—it had only to maintain its lead until the final break, or score just one more goal in that time, and Carlton was broken.

Surely, thought fans, it was impossible to lose from here. But, in the next seven minutes of play, the fate of the premiership was decided. It was not, as had occurred on other occasions, a Collingwood collapse, but more an almost unbelievable lift in the Blues' game. It began with Fitzpatrick, Carlton's inspiring captain, getting the ball to Ashman who made no mistake from fifteen metres out. A minute later Buckley snapped another and Collingwood's twenty-one point lead had shrunk to nine points when the quarter ended seconds later. The burst, when all seemed lost, revitalised the Blues, who crowded around coach Parkin and were obviously revved-up and eager to go. By contrast, an air of gloom appeared to descend on the Magpie camp and players slumped to the ground as coach Hafey moved in to address them.

Sheldon, with a twenty metre left-foot snap after two minutes of the last quarter, maintained Carlton's momentum and further sapped the Magpie's spirit, and three minutes later the dogged Ashman goaled on the run to put Carlton ahead. Four goals in seven minutes of actual play had been the turning point, and from there on it was no contest, as the Blues peppered the goals to score 4.7 to the Magpie's meagre two behinds. Indeed, Collingwood fans were already leaving the ground when McKay marked and goaled from more than sixty metres out to seal the game for Carlton at the twenty-one minute mark.

So, the premiership was Carlton's, a notable triumph for coach David Parkin who had previously won a flag with Hawthorn, and yet another disappointment for Collingwood's Tom Hafey, a legend amongst coaches, whose stint with the Magpies which was to end abruptly in mid-1982. It must have gone close to breaking his heart.

Popular winner of the Smith Medal for best afield was Carlton's champion centre-half-back Bruce Doull, while captain Fitzpatrick must have run him close for the honour. Fitzpatrick, still suffering the after-affects of a broken hand, dominated the rucks and played what old-timers said was one of the greatest captain's games ever seen in a Grand Final. First-year W.A. recruit Ken Hunter, whose eclipse of brilliant Magpie half-forward Daicos was a key factor, was another worthy of note, but the Blues had many workmanlike contributors, whilst Collingwood, by contrast, had few who gave a full 120 minutes. Picken, McCormack, Taylor, Williams and Twomey were notable exceptions.

A unique record came out of this Grand Final when Carlton's Scott Howell appeared in the premiership side. His father, Jack, had previously appeared in a premiership team with Carlton in 1947, and his grandfather, Jack Snr., played in South Melbourne's 1918 premiership side, thus making the first such three-generation combination to achieve the honour of a VFL premiership.

RESULTS

SEPTEMBER 5—ELIMINATION FINAL

	1st	2nd	3rd	Final
Fitzroy	3 . 4	7 . 7	12 . 11	16 . 13 (109)
Essendon	0 . 5	4 . 8	11 . 11	13 . 16 (94)

VFL Park Umpires—Smith, Nash

Attendance—58,598. Gate—$456,951

BEST — (F) Taylor, Alexander, Wilson, Francis, Serafini, Lawrie, Parish.
(E) Foulds, Crow, Andrews, Buhagiar, T. Daniher, Hawker.

GOALS — (F) Quinlan (3), Poynton (2), Carlson (2), Parish (2), Wilson (2), Alexander, Rendell, McMahon, Lewis, Herbert.
(E) Andrews (3), Heard (2), Foulds (2), Schultz (2), T. Daniher, Van Der Haar, Buhagiar, Thomson.

QUALIFYING FINAL

	1st	2nd	3rd	Final
Geelong	2 . 5	8 . 11	14 . 11	16 . 16 (112)
Collingwood	5 . 5	6 . 9	9 . 15	13 . 20 (98)

M.C.G. — Umpires—Robinson, Sawers
Attendance—83,899 — Gate—$642,979

BEST — (G) Mossop, Blake, Reynoldson, Witcombe, Bos, Malarkey, Peake.
(C) Barham, Byrne, Daicos, Smith, Taylor, McCormack, A. Shaw.
GOALS — (G) Mossop (7), Lunn (3), Featherby (2), Reynoldson (2), Witcombe, Bruns.
(Coll) Daicos (4), Barham (2), Williams (2), A. Shaw, Picken, Weideman, Kink, Atkin.

SEPTEMBER 12—FIRST SEMI-FINAL

	1st	2nd	3rd	Final
Collingwood	5 . 6	11 . 13	14 . 15	19 . 19 (133)
Fitzroy	2 . 3	6 . 5	12 . 13	19 . 18 (132)

M.C.G. — Umpires—Cameron, Dye
Attendance—85,133 — Gate—$654,160

BEST — (Coll) Picken, Twomey, Atkin, Barham, Davis, Taylor, Byrne.
(F) McMahon, Serafini, Smith, Alexander, Francis, Wilson, Lawrie.
GOALS — (Coll) Davis (3), Brewer (3), R. Shaw (3), Daicos (3), Barham (2), Irwin, A. Shaw, Worthington, Taylor, Kink.
(F) Rendell (5), McMahon (4), Lawrie (2), Quinlan (2), Murnane (2), Poynton (2), Parish, Wilson.

SECOND SEMI-FINAL

	1st	2nd	3rd	Final
Carlton	1 . 2	5 . 8	10 . 12	16.17 (113)
Geelong	3 . 3	5 . 3	9 . 4	11. 7 (73)

VFL Park — Umpires—Robinson, Sawers
Attendance—66,078 — Gate—$501,319

BEST — (Carl) English, Doull, Sheldon, Fitzpatrick, Maylin, Glascott
(G) Featherby, Peake, Clarke, Hawkins, Malarkey, B. Nankervis.
GOALS — (Carl) Bosustow (3), Harmes (3), Johnston (3), Sheldon (2), Buckley (2), Hunter, Marcou, Glascott.
(G) Mossop (3), Johnston (2), Reynoldson (2), Clarke (2), Jeffreys, Witcombe.

SEPTEMBER 19—PRELIMINARY FINAL

	1st	2nd	3rd	Final
Collingwood	3 . 5	5 . 8	9 . 10	12 . 10 (82)
Geelong	1 . 3	6 . 5	10 . 8	11 . 9 (75)

VFL Park — Umpires—Dye, Cameron
Attendance—69,536 — Gate—$575,784

BEST — (Coll) Cooper, Williams, Picken, Byrne, McCormack, Daicos, Barham.
(G) I. Nankervis, Peake, Bruns, Murrie, Yeates, Malarkey, Featherby.
GOALS — (Coll) Daicos (4), Kink (3), Stewart (2), R. Shaw, Davis, Williams.
(G) Mossop (3), Lunn (3), Bruns (2), Taylor, Blake, Yeates.

SEPTEMBER 26—GRAND FINAL

	1st	2nd	3rd	Final
Carlton	2 . 4	5 . 8	8 . 13	12 . 20 (92)
Collingwood	2 . 6	5 . 7	10 . 10	10 . 12 (72)

M.C.G. Umpires—Robinson, Dye
Attendance—112,964 Gate—$1,042,796
(First million-dollar gate)

BEST — (Carl) Doull (BOG), Fitzpatrick, Hunter, Marcou, Maylin, English, Howell, Harmes, Perovic, Glascott.
(Coll) Picken, Taylor, Williams, McCormack, Kink, Twomey, A. Shaw.

GOALS — (Carl) Ashman (3), Maclure (2), McKay (2), Sheldon (2), Johnston, Harmes, Buckley.
(Coll) Williams (2), Barham (2), A. Shaw, R. Shaw, Stewart, Taylor, Moore, Daicos.

NORM SMITH MEDAL — B. Doull (Carlton)

GRAND FINAL TEAMS

Carlton	B	D. English	S. Howell	V. Perovic
	HB	W. Harmes	B. Doull	K. Hunter
	C	P. Maylin	G. Wells	D. Glascott
	HF	P. Bosustow	M. Maclure	W. Johnston
	F	D. McKay	P. McConville	J. Buckley
	Ruck	M. Fitzpatrick (c)	K. Sheldon	R. Ashman
	Int.	M. Bortolotto	A. Marcou	
	Coach	D. Parkin		
Collingwood	B	R. Byrne	P. McCormack	I. Cooper
	HB	G. Allan	W. Picken	D. Twomey
	C	R. Barham	M. Williams	W. Irwin
	HF	P. Daicos	C. Davis	R. Kink
	F	R. Shaw	R. Brewer	C. Stewart
	Ruck	P. Moore (c)	M. Taylor	A. Shaw
	Int.	S. Atkin	N. Lovell	
	Coach	T. Hafey		

1982

Season 1982 was the driest on record, with only one wet day and that, ironically was Grand Final day.

As a consequence of the weather, a spate of new scoring records was established, including one for century totals—175, beating the previous "high" of 162 in 1979. There were thirty-five scores of 150 points or more (previous best twenty-seven) and twenty-one scores of more than twenty-five goals (previous best thirteen).

However, the talking point of the season was the move of South Melbourne to Sydney, that city becoming the club's home base. The trials and tribulations of the move, one of the most far-reaching in VFL history, need not be related here, other than to record that with the change the name "South Melbourne" disappeared from VFL fixtures, to be replaced by the name "Swans".

The Sydney-based team notched up seven consecutive wins and was well in contention for a finals berth until late in the season, when several costly losses put paid to their chances.

The form sides were again most of the "old reliables" of recent years—Richmond (eighteen wins, four losses) topping the ladder from Hawthon (17/5), Carlton (16/5 and a tie), Essendon (16/6) and Nth. Melbourne (14/8).

Fitzroy, with six successive wins late in the season, made a spirited bid but in the end missed out by a game and a half, followed by the Swans and a much-improved Melbourne. Shock of the season was the poor form of 1981 Runner-Up, Collingwood, whose record for the year showed only four wins (second only to the 1942 "low" of two wins), included eight successive losses, and resulted in the sacking mid-season of the illustrious coach Tom Hafey. Their tenth placing was the lowest ever "next season" slump of a Grand Final Team. Another 1981 finalist in Geelong fell to ninth place in 1982.

For the fifth time in eleven seasons, Essendon bowed out in the Elimination Final, although starting the match as warm favourites against what was seen as a rather ordinary North Melbourne side, now coached by ex-champion rover Barry Cable.

However, all of North's "super-stars" shone, and were well backed up by the lesser lights who had replaced the heroes of their great sides of the 70's. Ruckman Dempsey eclipsed the taller Madden brothers, and Blight—who had played almost all season with a suspect leg—had three goals in the first ten minutes to get North away to a great start. Essendon fought back, levelling the scores early in the last quarter, but two brilliant individual efforts by North captain Schimmelbusch resulted in goals and P. Krakouer sealed the game with a fine running goal at the twenty-four minute mark.

Hawthorn, with six straight goals in the first term, threatened Carlton in the Qualifying Final. The Blues, who at one stage of the season looked likely to miss the Finals, were sluggish early, had lost Southby as a late withdrawal, and missed easy shot after easy shot. Unfortunately for the Hawks, however, they were unable to get the score on the board themselves whilst Cartlon fumbled, and when Harmes (Carlton) broke loose in the third term to boot four incredible goals in eight minutes, Carlton streaked away and were never headed thereafter. The only problems arising out of the game were the subsequent two-game suspension of dynamic forward Wayne Johnson and the one game suspension of Peter Bosustow.

The First Semi was a game of contrasting halves of football, North winning the first, although not building up a good enough lead, and Hawthorn running riot in the second. Matthews, with four goals in the second half, played one of his most valuable games for the Hawks, who received a bonus in the form of five goals from 18-year-old Dermott Brereton, who was a surprise selection for his first VFL game. Both sides lost stars early in the game—Glendinning (N.M.) was off injured within the first six minutes, and Hawthorn lost Knights. Unfortunately for North, they were unable to cover the loss of Glendinning when the pressure was applied in the last half.

Blight's five goals for the match brought his tally for the season to 103, equalling the club record.

According to the score-board, the Second Semi-Final was as good as over by half-time but many would say the match was "no contest" after about fifteen minutes when the Richmond switch of Cloke to full-forward and Roach to centre-half-forward had already devastated the Blues, Cloke having two goals in the first seven minutes.

Richmond's Lee played probably his best game since his memorable display in the 1980 Grand Final, completely eclipsing the Carlton rucks, whilst the Blues' forward line was non-existent and its much-vaunted little brigade, with the exception of Buckley, was completely shut out of the play. Many critics wrote that Carlton had, in fact, stopped trying but this is an unfair criticism. No side ever stops trying; rather it was Richmond's ability to shut down the hand-ball and running game for the Carlton back-line by judicious use of fifteen metre penalties which simply destroyed the Blues' normal style of play and made them look mediocre. Only Hunter, Glascott and Buckley were worthwhile performers on the day.

This morale-sapping defeat put a question mark over Carlton's ability to handle the tough, relentless Hawthorn in the Preliminary Final. However, the intervening week was long enough for Coach David Parkin to build up the players' faith in themselves and their ability, and even when Maclure and Buckley were forced to withdraw from the selected side, it seemed to serve more to strengthen the Blues' determination than sap it.

The game began fiercely, and Austin—assigned to tag Matthews—was floored within the first five minutes. Carlton, learning from the tactics adopted by Richmond the previous week, gave away fifteen metre penalties at every opportunity in its defensive zone, and Hawthorn was not slow to reciprocate. This produced a scrambling first half which brought only five major scores.

Marcou (Carl) swooped in for two quick goals as the second half began, but Goad equalled that effort for the Hawks. Goad also proceeded to pile up three misses from right in front. Fitzpatrick (Carl) was then moved into the ruck, and from that point the Blues began to show more authority, moving away steadily to a lead of seventeen points at three-quarter time, and then virtually sealing the match when Bosustow goaled thirty seconds in the last term. At the siren, the difference was thirty-one points and the unpredictable Blues had given the critics food for thought.

The Tigers were the popular choice as red-hot favourites for the Grand Final, despite the loss of tough backman Malthouse who won the admiration of the football world with a magnificent, but losing, fight to recover from a dislocated shoulder sustained a fortnight before. There was also a cloud over full-forward Taylor, Richmond's leading goal-kicker, who had missed the previous finals matches through injury, but to the relief of Tiger supporters, he was declared fit to play, as also was Jess, who had been out for five weeks.

Carlton had problems of its own—Austin, best afield in the preliminary final, withdrew prior to the match and subsequently saw the game on television from a hospital bed. Southby was also declared unfit. On the credit side Maclure, Buckley and the suspended Johnston were all back.

The Blues, going for back-to-back flags and for the VFL record of fourteen premierships, were revved-up prior to the game and given the message by the coach that they had in the last two seasons never lost a game in which all players worked hard together and never stopped trying. This became their catch-cry for the day. First-year Richmond coach, Francis Bourke, tried to keep his team low-key, attempting to treat the match as just another game.

Twenty-two players ran out with the Carlton team as it entered the arena, Clarke and Marchesani—who were not to play—being given a chance to share some of the glory of Grand Final day. Richmond fans were shocked to see Taylor not on the ground. He was a last minute omission when the Tigers decided that they could not fit both he and Cloke into their forward set-up.

It was a ferocious opening—some critics said the most fiery for twenty years—and late arrivals hardly found their seats before Carlton had two goals on the board in the first seventy seconds! The first came from Johnston who then figured in a marvellous tackle which got the ball to Harmes for a second. Sporadic rain was falling (and continued to fall all day) as brawls erupted all around the ground and fifteen metre penalties—often stretched to fifty metres—flowed thick and fast. Carlton's third goal came up at the five minute mark when Fitzpatrick threw his foot at the ball and Ashman marked right in front.

The clashes continued—Hunter went down from a ferocious, but perfectly fair, bump from Jess and was off the ground for a quarter of an hour.

Richmond, steadying after the initial Carlton onslaught, regained some poise halfway through the term when Bartlett goaled from a free forty-five metres out. Moments later, the veteran of the VFL passed towards Rioli, who successfully converted after a Blues' defender dropped a mark. Soon after Rioli scored again and when Raines ran in for another, the Tigers had taken the lead.

The quarter was almost over, thirty-three minutes having been played, when Carlton's ace full-forward Ditchburn was flattened by a flying boot. He was carried off virtually unconscious and took no further part in the game. Despite this setback, Carlton regained the lead when Johnston goaled from Ditchburn's free kick, right on the siren.

Richmond emulated Carlton's opening burst when the second term began—within eighty seconds, Weightman figured in two brilliant pieces of handball which got the ball to big Cloke who was able to stroll unopposed to the goal line and boot the Tiger's fifth and sixth goals. The elusive Bartlett added another, and Harmes moved onto the dangerous Tiger half-forward. But the Blues' main problem at this stage was the brilliant Rioli, who was providing the Tiger forwards with a constant stream of chances which helped put Richmond eighteen points ahead at the nineteen minute mark. Then the whole complexion of the game changed—Carlton's smaller players began to be more prominent, Bosustow (on in place of Ditchburn) was shining, whilst the return of Hunter to the field had inspired the Blues. When Fitzpatrick began to exert an influence on the game at centre half forward, Carlton looked a different team, and Richmond was held to only two points for the remainder of the quarter. Worse, they lost their fine defender Tempany, whose arm was broken by a flying boot.

At half-time, then, the Tiger lead had been cut to eleven points and many in the crowd predicted that the next half hour would decide the premiership.

And so it proved. Only the appearance of the first Grand Final "streaker"—a female one at that, who displayed her charms to the crowd at the 10 minute mark—threatened to break the Blues' concentration as they hammered the goals in the third term to notch five majors in twenty minutes. Their burst of 5.4 to 0.6 converted an eleven point deficit into a seventeen point lead and gave them a match-winning break—if they were good enough. Vital factors in this term for Carlton included the move of Johnston onto the dangerous Raines in the centre, telling goals by Fitzpatrick (2), Maylin, McClure and Ashman, and the superior speed and superb defence of the Carlton backline, in which Doull held Jess, Perovic had Roach in check, English was in control over the resting rovers, and Bortolotto was putting up a superb performance against Richmond's trump, Cloke.

Another subtle, but telling, factor was the decision of the Carlton brains-trust to resist the tempation to move Harmes (instead of Johnston) into the centre. They preferred instead to leave him to mind Bartlett, who at that stage had notched two goals. The judgement was vindicated when Harmes took a magnificent high mark right on the goal line to turn a hot Tiger attack at the thirty-two minute mark, and proceeded to shut Bartlett out in the vital last term.

Richmond fought back in fine style early in the last, and edged to within five points at the four minute mark after Bartlett goaled after twenty-five seconds and Jess converted from a free thirty metres out.

An amazing save by Doull retained Carlton's slender lead, and the match hung in the balance for seven minutes before Johnston pressured a Richmond defender into a poor clearing kick. Ashman grabbed the ball and handballed to Maclure, who sent the ball on to Bosustow for a vital goal.

For the next thirteen minutes, play see-sawed from end to end with Richmond refusing to give in, and it was only a goal by Marcou almost into time-on which made the game safe for the Blues, and another by McConville (who had done well at full-forward after starting the game on the back-line) which put the final nail in the Tiger's coffin.

A last-minute goal by Rioli for Richmond came too late, and the siren heralded Carlton's premiership, their fourteenth, one ahead of Collingwood's previous VFL record of thirteen. Their "back-to-back" flags were Carlton's first since 1914-15, and the first by any club since Richmond in 1973-74.

SEPTEMBER 4—ELIMINATION FINAL

	1st	2nd	3rd	Final
Nth. Melb.	6 . 3	8. 7	14 10	19 . 14 (128)
Essendon	1 . 3	4.10	10 . 15	16 . 19 (115)

VFL Park — Umpires—Sawers, James
Attendance—50,537 — Gate—$423,339

BEST — (N.M.) Dempsey, Henshaw, Schimmelbusch, Greig, Glendinning, P. Krakouer.
(Ess.) Buhagiar, Copping, Carey, Otway, Hawker, Stoneham
GOALS — (N.M.) Blight (4), P. Krakouer (4), Carman (3), J. Krakouer (2), Kelly, Abernethy, Schimmelbusch, Atkins, McCann, McDonald.
(Ess) T. Daniher (4), Copping (4), Watson (2), Buhagiar (2), Otway, Merrett, S. Madden, Clarke.

QUALIFYING FINAL

	1st	2nd	3rd	Final.
Carlton	3 . 3	7 . 9	18 . 13	25 . 13 (163)
Hawthorn	6 . 0	7 . 4	10 . 7	16 . 9 (105)

M.C.G. — Umpires—Nash, Robinson
Attendance—70,552 — Gate—$642,512

BEST — (Carl) Glascott, Hunter, Harmes, English, Ditchburn, Sheldon.
(Haw.) Loveridge, Paton, Wallace, Mew, Tuck, Russo
GOALS — (Carl) Ditchburn (6), Clarke (4), Harmes (4), Ashman (4), Johnston (3), Maclure.
(Haw) Byrne (4), Buckernara (4), Loveridge (2), Robertson (2), Dipierdomenico, Russo, Kennedy, Tuck.

Hawthorn's Dermott Brereton heads for the turf after North Melbourne's David Dench clears the way for team-mate Wayne Schimmelbusch, 10/9/83. *Photo courtesy The Herald.*

Hawthorn's Leigh Matthews has the prime position in this marking contest during the 1983 grand final against Essendon. *Photo courtesy The Herald.*

Hawthorn's Colin Robertson flies high ahead of Essendon's Simon Madden and Paul Van Der Haar in the 1983 grand final. *Photo courtesy The Herald.*

Collingwood's Ron McKeown spoils Wayne Johnston's attempt to mark, 15/9/84. *Photo courtesy The Herald.*

Jason Dunstall of Hawthorn marks strongly in front of a pack of Footscray opponents, 7/9/85. *Photo courtesy The Herald.*

Hawthorn's Dermott Brereton rises for a mark above Essendon's Mark Harvey, 14/9/85. *Photo courtesy The Herald.*

Essendon's Paul Salmon holds the ball aloft after a strong mark in the 1985 grand final. *Photo courtesy The Herald.*

Michael Tuck (Hawthorn) shows his disappointment as Essendon's Roger Merrett and Tim Watson celebrate their win in the 1985 grand final. *Photo courtesy The Herald.*

Tony Daniher (Sydney Swans) gets his kick away despite a desperate attempt to spoil by Carlton's Stephen Silvagni, 6/9/86. *Photo courtesy The Herald.*

Michael Conlan is congratulated by Fitzroy team-mate Richard Osborne after kicking the winning goal in the 1986 elimination final against Essendon. *Photo courtesy The Herald.*

Hawthorn's Jason Dunstall, watched by Carlton veteran Bruce Doull, juggles the ball during the 1986 grand final. *Photo courtesy The Herald.*

Sydney Swan full-forward Warwick Capper leaps over Chris Langford for this spectacular mark in the qualifying final at VFL Park, 5/9/87. *Photo courtesy The Herald.*

Gary Ayres (top) and his elated Hawthorn team-mates after their 1987 preliminary final win over Melbourne. *Photo courtesy The Herald.*

A determined Tom Alvin (Carlton) sets for a kick in the 1987 grand final against Hawthorn. *Photo courtesy The Herald.*

Melbourne's Jamie Duursma comes down with the ball after outsmarting Stephen Kernahan of Carlton during the 1988 preliminary final at VFL Park. *Photo courtesy The Herald.*

Hawthorn's Gary Ayres, Norm Smith medallist in the 1988 grand final, clears the ball from defence. *Photo courtesy The Herald.*

SEPTEMBER 11—FIRST SEMI-FINAL

	1st	2nd	3rd	Final
Hawthorn	4 . 4	10 . 8	16 . 16	24 . 22 (166)
Nth. Melb.	6 . 2	12 . 2	14 . 4	18 . 6 (114)

M.C.G. Umpires—Sawers, Smith
Attendance—61,729 Gate—$605,386

BEST — (Haw) Ayres, Russo, Goad, Brereton, Matthews, Robertson, Loveridge
(N.M.) Greig, Dempsey, Blight, Atkins, Tanner.

GOALS —(Haw.) Brereton (5), Matthews (4), Byrne (3), Goad (3), Buckenara (3), Geoff Ablett, Tuck, Eade, Robertson, Russo, Loveridge.
(N.M.) Blight (5), Tanner (3), Kelly (2), P. Krakouer (2), Atkins (2), Carman, J. Krakouer, Holt, Schimmelbusch.

SECOND SEMI-FINAL

	1st	2nd	3rd	Final
Richmond	6 . 6	10 . 9	14 . 13	16 . 17 (113)
Carlton	2 . 0	4 . 5	9 . 8	13 . 12 (90)

VFL Park Umpires—James, Cameron
Attendance—65,611 Gate—$541,282

BEST — (Rich) Wood, Rioli, Dunne, Roach, Cloke, Wiley
(Carl) Hunter, Buckley, Glascott, Doull, Sheldon.

GOALS — (Rich) Cloke (5), Bartlett (3), Wood (2), Weightman (2), Roach, Lee, Raines, Welsh.
(Carl) Ditchburn (4), Buckley (2), Maclure (2), Maylin, Klomp, Hunter, Harmes, Glascott.

SEPTEMBER 18—PRELIMINARY FINAL

	1st	2nd	3rd	Final
Carlton	2 . 6	2 . 11	8 . 13	13 . 16 (94)
Hawthorn	1 . 6	3 . 9	5 . 14	8 . 15 (63)

VFL Park Umpires—Nash, Cameron
Attendance—61,307 Gate—$590,874

BEST — (Carl) Austin, Marcou, McConville, English, Perovic, Ashman, Bortolotto, Doull.
(Haw) Russo, Eade, Ayres, Mew, Moore, Buckenara.

GOALS — (Carl) Ditchburn (3), Marcou (3), Clarke (2), Bosustow (2), Ashman (2), Harmes
(Haw) Kennedy (2), Goad (2), Byrne, Matthews, Loveridge, Eade.

SEPTEMBER 25—GRAND FINAL

	1st	2nd	3rd	Final
Carlton	4 . 7	6 . 11	11 . 15	14 . 19 (103)
Richmond	4 . 3	9 . 4	9 . 10	12 . 13 (85)

M.C.G. Umpires—James, Sawers
Attendance—107,537 Gate—$1,166,297

BEST — (Carl) Perovic, Johnston, Fitzpatrick, Marcou, Harmes, Hunter, Doull, English, Ashman
(Rich Rioli, Weightman, Raines, Strachan, Wiley.

GOALS — (Carl) Johnston (2), Fitzpatrick (2), Ashman (2), McConville (2), Harmes, Hunter, Bosustow, Marcou, Maclure, Maylin.
(Rich) Bartlett (3), Cloke (3), Rioli (3), Raines, Jess, Weightman.

NORM SMITH MEDAL — M. Rioli (Richmond)

GRAND FINAL TEAMS

Carlton	B	D. English	M. Bortolott	V. Perovic
	HB	R. Klomp	B. Doull	K. Hunter
	C	W. Harmes	J. Buckley	D. Glascott
	HF	W. Johnston	M. Maclure	P. Bosustow
	F	A. Marcou	R. Ditchburn	P. McConville
	Ruck	M. Fitzpatrick (c)	P. Maylin	R. Ashman
	Int.	W. Jones	K. Sheldon	
	Coach	D. Parkin		
Richmond	B	G. Landy	A. Martello	E. Dunne
	HB	M. Keane	J. Jess	G. Strachan
	C	S. Williams	G. Raines	B. Wood
	HF	K. Bartlett	D. Cloke (c)	M. Rioli
	F	M. Roach	I. Sartori	D. Weightman
	Ruck	M. Lee	R. Wiley	B. Rowlings
	Int.	B. Tempany	P. Welsh	
	Coach	F. Bourke		

1983

There were two major surprises in the battle for the finals in 1983. The first was that Richmond, runner-up in 1982, lost its first five games and eventually finished tenth, resulting in the sacking of the Tigers' favourite son, coach Francis Bourke. Bourke, who certainly experienced the highs and lows as a coach, is one of the few coaches to take his team to a grand final in his first year. His dismissal in his second year represented the shortest span between a grand final appearance and the sack in VFL history, an unwanted record shared by none other than Bourke's predecessor, Tony Jewell, who coached Richmond to a premiership in 1980 and was sacked in 1981.

The second major surprise was the good form of Fitzroy, which, at the half-way mark of the season, climbed to the top of the ladder when it beat top team North Melbourne by an incredible 150 points, surely the most one-sided result ever between teams standing first and second on the ladder. At that stage, Fitzroy looked even money for its first flag since 1944, but developed the staggers with successive losses to the Swans, Carlton and St. Kilda. These proved to be vital games which eventually cost the Lions second place.

North, which showed promise in 1982 when it finished in fourth position, actually grabbed top spot at the end of the home and away round in 1983, finishing a game ahead of Hawthorn, Fitzroy and Essendon, all of which were on fifteen wins and separated only by percentage. Despite this fine performance, critics placed several question marks over North. Their record did include a victory over Carlton (by eighteen goals!), Hawthorn and Essendon (twice), but also showed thrashings at the hands of Fitzroy (150 and forty-five points) and Carlton (thirty-five points).

Hot on the heels of Essendon was Carlton, 1981-82 premiers, which sneaked into fifth spot with thirteen wins, a game ahead of Collingwood and three games ahead of improving Footscray, for which seventh position represented a big advance on their 1982 record of only three victories. Melbourne (nine wins) was next, followed by Geelong, which was undefeated after four rounds and then won only four more for the season.

The Magpies went close to tipping Carlton out in the last few rounds and would have done so had the Blues not lifted their form to down Hawthorn and North in successive weeks, games which few tipped them to win. In the wash-up, Carlton lost the last game to Essendon, but it did not matter as the five had been signed, sealed and delivered the previous week.

There were many stars absent from both sides when Essendon and Carlton met in the cut-throat elimination final. The Dons missed Neil Clarke (medial ligament) and Ron Andrews (hamstring), while the Blues had Bosustow and Bortolotto out suspended, lost Ashman on the morning of the match and Johnston was injured early in the first quarter. Surprisingly, they omitted Jones from the side, leaving little 'tall timber' to match the Dons' array of big men.

Essendon, which had lost the previous five elimination finals it had contested, was well in control throughout the game. Its sustained fierce tackling and dumping took its toll on the strength of the leg-weary Blues after half time. Essendon faltered slightly in the second term when Fitzpatrick threw his weight around and several Dons fell for the old trap of forgetting the ball. However, a third-term blitz of seven goals made the game safe. Despite their impressive win, Essendon expressed displeasure with the umpiring (Carlton forty free-kicks, Essendon twenty-eight), but many suspected this was merely a little gamesmanship by astute Dons' coach, Kevin Sheedy.

At the MCG, a disappointing crowd of just over 58,000 saw an enthralling battle between Hawthorn and Fitzroy. The Lions managed to blanket some of the Hawks' prime-movers, and only strong football by Knights (five first-half goals) together with a burst of four goals in the last eight minutes of the second quarter, gave the struggling Hawks the lead at the last change. Fitzroy, coming home against the wind, looked beaten but Quinlan, striking a purple patch at full-forward, booted three quick goals to put the Lions back in it. Then came the turning point of the game as Nettlefold, who had played magnificently for Fitzroy by blanketing Tuck all day, ran the ball out of bounds in Hawthorn's forward pocket. On most occasions, this piece of defensive play would have been applauded, but umpire James ruled that the action was deliberate and awarded a free kick to Tuck, who converted from the boundary line to put the Hawks ahead by thirteen points. The decision was an extremely controversial one and, after the game, Fitzroy supporters claimed it had cost their side victory. The Lions, to their credit, fought back and Quinlan's fourth and fifth goals of the term actually snatched a four point lead twenty-two minutes into the quarter. However, a free and a goal to Loveridge put Hawthorn back in front. Kennedy (Hawthorn) added a point before the Lions made a last desperate attack. Quinlan managed to get both hands to the ball but was swamped by three opponents and the Hawks rebounded quickly for Matthews to snap a point in the forty seconds remaining. The final siren sounded with the relieved Hawks clinging to a slender four point lead.

Unfortunately for Fitzroy, Quinlan was unable to repeat his eight goal effort when the Lions came up against Essendon in the first semi-final. Full back Weston and the Essendon resting rucks combined excellently to restrict Quinlan, who was hampered by bruised ribs sustained in a heavy clash with Carey fourteen minutes into the match. The Dons were without Wood (injured in the elimination final) but the Lions were probably worse-hit, losing state defenders Serafini (injured at training) and Lawrie, who limped off late in the first quarter and did not return. Nevertheless, Fitzroy's makeshift defence stood firm for three quarters and the Lions were given hope when the veteran McMahon came off the interchange bench and bagged two goals in five minutes to give Fitzroy the lead at half-time. The Lions gradually stretched this into a break of nineteen points twenty-one minutes into the third term. Daniher then booted a magnificent captain's goal for Essendon, Madden quickly added another, and Fitzroy, with its lead suddenly whittled to a mere five points at the last change, faltered. The Dons slipped into top gear, kicked seven goals in the last term and won easily.

For a while in the second semi-final, it looked as though North Melbourne was bound for the grand final. The Northerners ran all over a disjointed Hawthorn in the opening term, keeping the Hawks goal-less but scoring only two themselves in the heavy going. It was not enough. Hawthorn regained its poise midway through the second quarter, North's classy ball-players became bogged down and the result of the match became academic after half-time. Hawthorn won without being severely extended.

Despite this loss, North Melbourne supporters expected their team to prove too strong for Essendon in the preliminary final. North had, after all, finished on top of the ladder, but as the game wore on, it became apparent that a few players were carrying injuries.

Although they were missing Andrews (suspended), the Dons came out breathing fire at the first bounce, running straight and hard at the opposition. Daniher immediately had the first major on the board — Duckworth followed with an amazing goal from the centre, and the Dons, with two goals in two minutes, were off to a dream start.

An all-in brawl had fans roaring, and North, as if to show it would not be intimidated, foolishly gave away a series of free kicks (sixteen to quarter-time). Neagle limped from the ground but the forced change did not cause Essendon a single hiccup. North, although only twenty-one points down at half-time, had really been put out of business by the vigour and tenacity of Essendon's first quarter, which netted them six goals. In the end, the Dons' winning margin was a massive eighty-six points and their consequent grand final appearance represented only the second case of a side reaching that milestone after appearing in the elimination final.

Feeling their team was on a 'roll', Essendon supporters confident of victory congregated in their thousands at the MCG on grand final day. The Dons had regained the services of Wood, who had played in Richmond's 1973-74 premiership teams, but of the others only Clayton and Kink had experienced a grand final before. This, together with the last minute withdrawal of Essendon's Bill Duckworth and the omission of Dons' strongman Ron Andrews, gave Hawthorn supporters plenty of their own confidence.

Knights lined up for his 250th VFL game, but Hawthorn surprised everyone by leaving out regular defender Polkinghorne and proven finals players in Russo, Moore and Moncrieff.

The game began with a sensation when, two minutes after the first bounce, dashing Hawthorn half-forward Buckenara fell in agony as he tried to pivot. He had snapped tendons in his knee and was swiftly removed from the field and taken to hospital. He spent an evening of mixed emotions, far removed from the scene of Hawthorn's premiership celebrations.

The Hawks, despite this setback, did not falter. Judge, also a half-forward flanker, adequately substituted for Buckenara from the interchange bench. Running straight at the ball heedless of any risk to themselves, the Hawthorn team soon sensed that Essendon was 'stepping aside', and this impression was made even more evident when nineteen minutes into the term, Essendon ruck-rover Watson was flattened behind play. Only one Don moved in to support the downed Watson, while the majority were content to observe.

Running in threes, the Hawks bombarded the goals to the tune of 5.6 for the term, and only inaccurate kicking let them down. The Dons, from limited excursions forward, notched three straight goals and, despite everything, were still within twelve points when they goaled four minutes into the second term. At this stage, Hawthorn brought DiPierdomenico onto the ground and he immediately gave the Hawks a further boost with his tough, tear-through play. Equally as important, his tremendous enthusiasm was infectious and lifted Hawthorn. Coincidentally, after their fourth goal early in the second term, Essendon then waited for an unbelievable eighty-two minutes before scoring their fifth. During that time, Hawthorn scored 13.14!

The game, as a contest, was most certainly a 'fizzer' and was virtually over by half-time with Hawthorn fifty-seven points up. Some excitement was generated in the third term when Merrett (Essendon) was reported twice (for striking Wallace and then Matthews) and a streaker made his way onto the ground to relieve the boredom. But the brown and gold 'mean machine' was completely irresistible; by three-quarter time the difference was eighty-seven points, and half way through the last it was a massive 102 points.

Ironic cheers greeted an Essendon goal at the sixteen minute mark of the last quarter and the Dons then showed their only good form of the day by following up with three more in the next six minutes, at a time when Hawthorn, with the flag secure, was coasting. This late burst by the Dons only reduced the final deficit to eighty-three points, when it earlier showed every indication of being over 100. Nevertheless, this eighty-three point difference provided a record winning margin in a grand final and in doing so, gave Hawthorn coach Allan Jeans a little-noticed record of his own. Having previously coached St. Kilda to the 1966 flag by a one point margin, Jeans had now coached sides which had won grand finals by the smallest and the largest margins.

The Hawks, without a single poor player in the entire side, provided the Norm Smith Medallist in utility Colin Robertson. Essendon, on the other hand, broke even in only one or two positions and only Madden, Daniher, Foulds, Neagle, Bradbury, Weston and perhaps Carey, who played the entire second half with a dislocated shoulder, could hold their heads high. Nevertheless, the disastrous defeat in '83 was the springboard from which Essendon coach Kevin Sheedy was to launch successful bids for the 1984 and 1985 flags.

RESULTS

SEPTEMBER 3—ELIMINATION FINAL

	1st	2nd	3rd	Final
Essendon	4 . 3	7 . 5	14 . 5	17 . 12 (114)
Carlton	3 . 3	8 . 4	11 . 7	12 . 9 (81)

VFL Park — Umpires—Robinson, Smith
Attendance—65,881 — Gate—not available

BEST — (Ess) Watson (BOG), Neagle, Hawker, Merrett, Van Der Haar, Madden
(Carl) J. Buckley, Hunter, Sheldon, Montgomery, Doull, Fitzpatrick
GOALS — (Ess) Daniher (4), Van Der Haar (3), Merrett (3), Kink (2), Hawker (2), Buhagiar, Madden, Ezard
(Carl) Hunter (5), J. Buckley (2), Glascott (2), Sheldon, Ditchburn, Montgomery

SEPTEMBER 3—QUALIFYING FINAL

	1st	2nd	3rd	Final
Hawthorn	5 . 4	11 . 8	15 . 10	19 . 13 (127)
Fitzroy	5 . 4	7 . 5	12 . 7	19 . 9 (123)

MCG — Umpires—Nash, James
Attendance—58,288 — Gate—not available

BEST — (Haw) Schwab, Knights, Ayres, Greene, Loveridge, Robertson
(Fitz) Quinlan (BOG), Rendell, Nettlefold, Sidebottom, Harris
GOALS — (Haw) Knights (6), Matthews (3), Judge (2), Tuck (2), Loveridge (2), McCarthy, Byrne, Eade, Schwab
(Fitz) Quinlan (8), Wilson (3), Conlan (2), McMahon (2), Sidebottom (2), Roos, Harris

SEPTEMBER 10—FIRST SEMI FINAL

	1st	2nd	3rd	Final
Essendon	5 . 3	7 . 8	9 . 11	16.13 (109)
Fitzroy	3 . 4	8 . 9	10 . 12	12.14 (86)

MCG — Umpires—Sawers, Smith
Attendance—81,090 — Gate—not available

BEST — (Ess) Daniher, Kink, Weston, Merrett, Neagle, Watson, Williams
(Fitz) Carlson, Harris, Rendell, Wilson, McMahon
GOALS — (Ess) Daniher (5), Buhagiar (3), Kink (2), Madden (2), Dunnell, Merrett, Ezard, Weston
(Fitz) McMahon (3), Quinlan (2), Carlson, Sidebottom, Parish, Wilson, Harris, Clayton, Osborne

SEPTEMBER 10—SECOND SEMI FINAL

	1st	2nd	3rd	Final
Hawthorn	0 . 2	6 . 6	9 . 8	13 . 10 (88)
North Melbourne	2 . 4	3 . 4	5 . 9	6 . 12 (48)

VFL Park — Umpires—James, Bryant
Attendance—41,063 — Gate—not available

BEST — (Haw) Loveridge (BOG), Eade, Greene, Robertson, Wallace, Kennedy, Paton, DiPierdomenico
(NM) Ramsay, Dempsey, Glendinning, Demetriou, Furey, Greig

GOALS —	(Haw)	Matthews (5), McCarthy (4), DiPierdomenico, Buckenara, Loveridge, Kennedy
	(NM)	J. Krakouer, Kelly, Demetriou, Atkins, Schimmelbusch, Hodgeman

SEPTEMBER 17—PRELIMINARY FINAL

	1st	2nd	3rd	Final
Essendon	8 . 2	12 . 5	17 . 10	25 . 14 (164)
North Melbourne	2 . 1	9 . 2	10 . 3	12 . 6 (78)

MCG — **Umpires—Nash, Robinson**
Attendance—63,785 — **Gate—not available**

BEST —	(Ess)	Hawker (BOG), Watson, Ezard, Williams, Van Der Haar, Heard, Merrett, Madden, Carey, Daniher
	(NM)	Abernethy, Hodgeman, Dempsey, Atkins, Fairley, McCann
GOALS —	(Ess)	Watson (5), Merrett (4), Daniher (3), Williams (2), Buhagiar (2), Ezard (2), Van Der Haar (2), Duckworth, Madden, Kink, Bradbury, Hawker
	(NM)	Fairley (4), J. Krakouer (2), Atkins (2), P. Krakouer, Schimmelbusch, Dempsey, Hodgeman

SEPTEMBER 24—GRAND FINAL

	1st	2nd	3rd	Final
Hawthorn	5 . 6	12 . 10	16 . 18	20 . 20 (140)
Essendon	3 . 6	4 . 1	4 . 3	8 . 9 (57)

MCG — **Umpires—Nash, Smith**
Attendance—110,332 — **Gate—not available**

BEST —	(Haw)	Robertson, Kennedy, Greene, Mew, Matthews, Tuck, Wallace, Eade, Ayres, McCarthy
	(Ess)	Madden, Daniher, Foulds, Bradbury, Neagle
GOALS —	(Haw)	Matthews (6), Byrne (3), Loveridge (2), Greene (2), Judge (2), Tuck, Knights, Kennedy, Wallace, O'Halloran
	(Ess)	Daniher (2), Kink, Ezard, Walsh, Copping, Madden, Wood

NORM SMITH MEDAL—C. Robertson (Hawthorn)

GRAND FINAL TEAMS

Hawthorn	B	G. Ayres	C. Mew	D. O'Halloran
	HB	R. Greene	M. McCarthy	J. Kennedy
	C	P. Schwab	T. Wallace	R. Eade
	HF	G. Buckenara	D. Brereton	P. Knights
	F	L. Matthews (c)	M. Byrne	R. Loveridge
	Ruck	I. Paton	M. Tuck	C. Robertson
	Int.	R. DiPierdomenico	K. Judge	
	Coach	A. Jeans		
Essendon	B	S. Heard	P. Weston	S. Carey
	HB	G. Foulds	K. Walsh	P. Bradbury
	C	G. Hawker	M. Neagle	B. Wood
	HF	R. Kink	R. Merrett	A. Ezard
	F	D. Williams	T. Daniher (c)	P. Van Der Haar
	Ruck	S. Madden	T. Watson	A. Buhagiar
	Int.	S. Copping	C. Clayton	
	Coach	K. Sheedy		

1984

Season 1984 was notable for Essendon's first premiership in nineteen years but may be equally well remembered in years to come for one of the most remarkable late season recoveries in the history of VFL football.

The 'Cinderella' in this story was the plucky Fitzroy which had battled for years, chopping and changing its home ground, struggling financially and without a premiership since 1944. Last with only one win after round nine, the Lions then won four games on end, slumped again to lose the next three, and occupied tenth spot after round eighteen. That was better than last, admittedly, but a far cry indeed from a spot in the finals.

However, at the business end of the season, things began to fall apart for a number of teams in contention for a place in the final five. Melbourne, which had been performing well, saw its run come to a sudden halt. In fact it lost six of the last seven games. Sydney Swans also fell in a heap, winning one out of the last six and Geelong and Footscray blew games which would almost certainly have assured them of fifth spot. Fitzroy, meanwhile, bounced back from a sixty-one point thrashing by Essendon in round sixteen with a surprise win over highly-rated Hawthorn, and successive victories over finals contenders Melbourne, Collingwood and Geelong.

This left the Lions playing the bottom two sides in rounds twenty-one and twenty-two, and they easily accounted for North in round twenty-one, to be seventh on forty points. The top ten teams then were:

Essendon	68
Hawthorn	64
Carlton	48
Collingwood	48
Geelong	44
Footscray	44
Fitzroy	40
Melbourne	36
Richmond	36
Swans	36

In the final round, Hawthorn met Geelong, Collingwood met Footscray and Fitzroy met St. Kilda in the matches which had a bearing on which teams made the five. Fitzroy duly did its part by thrashing St. Kilda. Geelong blew it with an eleven goal loss, whilst Footscray, which had convincingly downed Carlton the previous week, lost to Collingwood by forty-three points. When the dust settled, the final five was

Essendon (eighteen wins, four losses), Hawthorn (seventeen wins, five losses), Carlton (thirteen wins, nine losses), Collingwood (thirteen wins, nine losses) and Fitzroy (eleven wins, eleven losses and 102.6%), followed by Geelong (eleven wins, eleven losses and 94.3%), Footscray (eleven wins, eleven losses and 93.8%) and Richmond (ten wins, twelve losses).

The shock of the home and away round was the poor performance of North Melbourne. Top of the ladder in 1983, the Northerners slipped to second-last with only five wins, escaping the wooden spoon by just 6%. North's drop equalled the worst fall by any team, from third spot on the ladder (see Statistics section) but is the worst by any team from top position on the ladder after the home and away round.

The 1984 elimination final made history as the first VFL finals match to take place on a Sunday. Fans appreciated the action and 73,000 of them jammed the MCG for the match. The black and white army, often disappointed in the past, saw Collingwood turn on a top-level performance to end Fitzroy's fairy tale. Many thought Collingwood was in the five only to make up the numbers, but the Magpies gambled on a number of shrewd positional changes. For example, wingman Abernethy played at centre half back on Fitzroy's big forward, Sidebottom and young Ian McMullin was selected for only his second VFL game. All that the Magpies tried came up trumps. Fitzroy, in contrast, missed top performers in Conlan, Serafini, Coleman, Hinchen and Clayton and then lost another star, Barwick, on the morning of the match when he came down with a virus.

Collingwood raced on four goals to nil in the first ten minutes, but Fitzroy fought back. Two goals by Scott when he came off the interchange bench in the second quarter evened up the match. Despite the blanketing of Quinlan up forward, the Lions went in at half-time five points ahead. Magpie coach John Cahill made no fewer than ten positional changes at the break, and the Magpies were rewarded with five goals in the third term. But the dogged Fitzroy stuck with them and at the last change, only inaccuracy saw the Lions behind by a mere four points. At that stage the game was there for the taking by either side but the tremendous work-load on the undermanned Lions affected them. When the quarter began big Magpie ruckman Cloke, who had injured a thumb and been moved to full-forward, kicked two quick goals. Abernethy followed with another and the Magpies lead stretched from four to twenty-two points after only five minutes.

That twenty two point break was enough: the Magpies then streaked away and ten goals for the quarter sealed a fine win. Skipper Williams (six goals from seven kicks) and McMullin (five goals in his first final) were dangerous forwards for Collingwood, while at the other end, Quinlan, who had reached 100 goals for the season the previous week, was well held and failed to score a goal until the twenty minute mark of the third quarter.

The previous day, Hawthorn, missing Kennedy (broken leg), Ayres, Russo, Wallace and Buckenara, met Carlton in the qualifying final. In a high standard game the Hawks steam-rolled the Blues to record a five goal win which was more impressive than the margin indicated. Lanky Hawk ruckman Michael Byrne played on the ball all day and his performance was rewarded by a best afield rating. However, the magic moments of the game were provided by DiPierdomenico whose inspirational play to set up a goal in the first term set the Hawks alight and whose goal of the day in the last brought the house down, and Carlton full-forward Warren Ralph. Recalled to the teams after being dropped in round nineteen, Ralph booted all of his team's five goals to half-time and ended with eight, equalling the qualifying final record.

In addition to his goalkicking, DiPierdomenico provided the sensation of the match when he flattened Carlton half-back 'Curly' Austin in the first term. The Blues appeared stunned and played accordingly as Austin left the field with a fractured cheekbone which ended the finals series for him. Hunter, too, was a casualty, missing most of the game with a thigh injury. Hawthorn's effective tagging of the Blues' little men, particularly in the first half, as well as six goals from Matthews at full-forward and twenty-two kicks and twelve handballs by Greene, told the tale of this match.

Carlton's selection of dynamic Wayne Johnston, out for the previous six weeks with a back injury, was the surprise of the first semi final. It was a calculated gamble by the Blues selectors, as the side already missed Hunter and Austin through injury, but unfortunately for Carlton the move did not come off. Collingwood, on the other hand, dropped pacy winger Barham but then suffered the misfortune of Williams dislocating his shoulder seven minutes into the second term, an injury which put him off the ground for the remainder of the game and out of the finals series. After an even first-half, the Magpies gained a third quarter break, aided by the play of Derek Shaw, who starred after coming off the interchange bench. Collingwood then stretched its lead to an impressive forty-eight points midway through the last quarter. The Blues hit back with several late goals which did not threaten to steal the game, but merely made the defeat look less disastrous on the scoreboard.

The second semi was acclaimed as one of the best finals games for many years. Apart from an opening burst by Hawthorn, it was 'goal for goal' throughout and, in the end, the team that was lucky enough to be in front when the final siren sounded won the game. Continuing the general trend for this finals series, Essendon missed Paul Salmon who had broken down in round thirteen when looking certain to kick 100 goals for the season. They also lost Bradbury and Carey before the game and Wood and Van Der Haar during the course of the match. Kennedy, who had broken a leg in round twenty-one, was a notable absentee for Hawthorn.

A goal by Brereton after the siren put the Hawks ahead by five points at half-time, and another by Matthews right on three-quarter time cut the Essendon lead to a single point. It was Matthews again who broke the deadlock twenty-four minutes into the last term and set up the goal that took the Hawks into the Grand Final. Leading his opponent he gathered the ball, broke a tackle and pushed out a hand pass to Loveridge who slammed the ball through for a goal.

For the next four minutes, Hawthorn fought doggedly to preserve its slender two point lead. Finally, defender Rodney Eade capped off a move set up by Judge, Greene and Robertson to goal on the siren and give Hawthorn victory by eight points.

Collingwood supporters, boosted by the Magpies' impressive form in their previous finals games, were hoping that at last this was their year. Their confidence was dented when Raines withdrew on the morning of the game because of a virus. Only minutes after the start, the Magpies moved swiftly forward where Andrews (cleared that season from Essendon) took a strong mark and goaled. Collingwood's flying start sent their fans wild with glee — but the joy was short-lived. Essendon, with Leon Baker surprisingly lining-up on the half-forward flank rather than in his customary centre position, slipped quickly into gear and T. Daniher, Van Der Haar and Baker himself then tore the Collingwood defence to pieces. The Bombers piled on 8.1. For Collingwood, this was bad enough but the second term was even worse! Essendon this time rammed through 9.4 to Collingwood's 1.2 and went in at half-time with a 17.6 to 3.6 lead.

Despite the loss of the brilliant Van Der Haar, Essendon continued the massacre in the second half. Although the Magpies showed some endeavour for a short period in the third term, they were never in the race and the Dons' final winning margin of 133 points was not only a record for a preliminary final, but the best-ever margin for any final.

As a spectacle many fans rated the game as the worst final of all time, but the truth was that the form of Essendon was simply superlative while the Magpies sorely missed top players in Raines, Williams, Cloke (all injured) and Twomey who left the ground early in the match. When Essendon got on top, Collingwood was left with few experienced players and was unable to halt the charge.

In 1984 the decision to continue to play the grand final at the MCG was good news for fans. The 1983 grand final had been billed as the last at that venue; the VFL wished to play future clashes at VFL Park. Negotiations with the MCG Trustees and the State Government finally resulted in a compromise which satisfied everyone, including the public.

The sensational incidents began even before the first bounce when the team selections became obvious. For the Hawks, Kennedy was still missing through injury and in the final composition of the team the Hawthorn selectors found it necessary to leave out such noted players as Buckenara, Knights, Langford and Polkinghorne. The Dons' brains-trust experienced similar anguish, and Carey, Wood and Buhagiar were missing when the side ran onto the ground.

In a tremendous opening, Matthews had Hawthorn's first goal on the board within 30 seconds and Robertson, utilising his great pace, followed with two more. At this stage, Hawthorn seemed to be blitzing a bewildered Essendon, which had hoped to throw the Hawks off balance by starting with Merrett in the ruck and Madden in the forward pocket. Hawthorn, however, countered by starting with Paton in the ruck and placed lanky Byrne at full-forward. The end result was that Madden, probably the best ruckman in the VFL in 1984, languished up forward during the initial Hawthorn blitz. Coach Kevin Sheedy soon had Madden on the ball, but Essendon continued to struggle, fumbling easy chances and losing possession through silly handball. It was not until Harvey came on from the interchange bench that the Bombers began to infuse some devil into their play. Nevertheless, the first quarter was Hawthorn's, with six goals to two.

Judge, on the run forty metres out, banged through Hawthorn's seventh goal three minutes into the second term and a Matthews' snap ten minutes later extended the Hawks' lead to thirty-two points, the biggest margin of the match. Hawthorn was exerting tremendous pressure on the Essendon backline but, surprisingly, the Dons were handling the ball more only to waste easy chances up forward. Nevertheless, it was with a feeling of some disquiet that the Hawthorn camp regarded the half-time scoreline with the Dons, despite everything, trailing by only twenty-five points and still well in the match.

Essendon came out after half-time and pounded the ball forward for a full ten minutes, only to see the Hawk defence rebound, but in hindsight Hawthorn was, at that stage, starting to run out of legs. There was momentary joy when Matthews steered through another of his miraculous goals but Baker and Duckworth goaled for Essendon, reducing the margin to seventeen points. Now it was Hawthorn's turn to make the errors, shooting several chances out on the full. Finally, Judge found Brereton who marked and goaled, but in the excitement many missed the play of Essendon's Duckworth who, despite giving the pacy Judge twenty metres start, nearly ran him down. It was a supreme effort which, although unsuccessful, seemed to epitomise Essendon's will to win, and to lift those around him.

At the last break, the Essendon camp sensed that Hawthorn was struggling and that knowledge boosted them as the game recommenced. Baker, after only twenty-five seconds, accepted a clever tap down from Van Der Haar and converted. That goal was exactly the start Essendon needed. Moments later, Bradbury followed with another and Weston, who had started the game at full back, just missed. The Dons were now charging forward at every opportunity and the cracks were appearing in the harassed Hawk defence. Thompson took a mark forty metres out and added Essendon's third for the quarter. When Baker, on the run, put Essendon in front a minute later, the grandstands at the MCG erupted. Hawthorn courageously snatched the lead back when Curran, assisted by a fifteen-metre penalty, goaled. Merrett answered, Weston added another and Watson, roaming unchecked, got two more goals. Essendon had scored four goals in four minutes in an effort that broke Hawthorn's spirit.

Into time on, Matthews got his fourth for Hawthorn but Neagle, on the run fifty metres out, popped through the reply two minutes later and it was all but over.

For Essendon, it was the first day flag since 1965, and they became the first team ever to win a day and a night flag in the same season. Their last quarter burst of 9.6 was a record last quarter score in a grand final — until they beat it themselves the following year.

RESULTS

SEPTEMBER 8—QUALIFYING FINAL

	1st	2nd	3rd	Final
Hawthorn	6 . 3	9 . 8	14 . 11	18 . 14 (122)
Carlton	3 . 3	5 . 7	10 . 11	13 . 14 (92)

VFL Park — Umpires—James, Russo
Attendance—55,947 — Gate—not available

BEST — (Haw) Byrne (BOG), DiPierdomenico, Greene, Robertson, Langford, Lester-Smith, Matthews, Loveridge
(Carl) Ralph, Melrum, Murphy, Doull, Maclure, Blackwell

GOALS — (Haw) Matthews (6), Judge (3), DiPierdomenico (2), McCarthy (2), Curran (2), Byrne (2), Langford
(Carl) Ralph (8), Murphy (3), Maclure (2).

SEPTEMBER 9—ELIMINATION FINAL

	1st	2nd	3rd	Final
Collingwood	5 . 2	8 . 4	13 . 8	23 . 15 (153)
Fitzroy	5 . 3	8 . 9	11 . 16	15 . 17 (107)

MCG — Umpires—Nash, Cameron
Attendance—73,994 — Gate—not available

BEST — (Coll) Phillips, A. Shaw, McMullin, Fellowes, Raines, Taylor, Abernethy, McCormack, Williams
(Fitz) Rendell, Pert, Turner, Roos, Lokan, Harris, Burke, R. Osborne, Gotch

GOALS — (Coll) Williams (6), McMullin (5), Richardson (3), Abernethy (2), Cloke (2), Andrews, Banks, Daicos, Millane, N. Shaw
(Fitz) Quinlan (3), Lokan (2), Sidebottom (2), Scott (2), Pert (2), R. Osborne (2), Rendell, Wilson

SEPTEMBER 15—FIRST SEMI FINAL

	1st	2nd	3rd	Final
Collingwood	3 . 4	9 . 8	13 . 12	17 . 16 (118)
Carlton	2 . 2	8 . 4	8 . 6	14 . 9 (93)

VFL Park — **Umpires—Sawers, Smith**
Attendance—70,634 — **Gate—not available**

BEST — (Coll) Abernethy (BOG), Daicos, McKeown, Phillips, Banks, Raines, Millane
(Carl) Doull, Alvin, Murphy, McConville, Dean, Maclure, Jones
GOALS — (Coll) Daicos (7), Richardson (4), McMullin (2), N. Shaw, Williams, Banks, Andrews
(Carl) Dean (3), Ralph (3), Madden (2), Harmes, Maclure, Meldrum, Murphy, Sheldon, Ashman.

SEPTEMBER 16 (SUN)—SECOND SEMI FINAL

	1st	2nd	3rd	Final
Hawthorn	5 . 6	9 . 8	13 . 13	16 . 17 (113)
Essendon	3 . 4	8 . 10	13 . 14	15 . 15 (105)

MCG — **Umpires—Robinson, Russo**
Attendance—76,514 — **Gate—not available**

BEST — (Haw) DiPierdomenico (BOG), Lester-Smith, Schwab, Russo, Robertson, O'Halloran, Mew
(Ess) Watson, Daniher, Walsh, Dunnell, Heard, Foulds, Madden
GOALS — (Haw) DiPierdomenico (4), Judge (3), Matthews (3), Brereton (2), Russo, Wallace, Eade, Loveridge
(Ess) Baker (3), Daniher (2), Madden (2), Watson (2), Neagle (2), Williams, Ezard, Van Der Haar, Weston

SEPTEMBER 22—PRELIMINARY FINAL

	1st	2nd	3rd	Final
Essendon	8 . 1	17 . 6	21 . 6	28 . 6 (174)
Collingwood	2 . 4	3 . 6	4 . 9	5 . 11 (41)

VFL Park — **Umpires—Sawers, Cameron**
Attendance—73,550 — **Gate—not available**

BEST — (Ess) Williams (BOG), Daniher, Baker, Van Der Haar, Clarke, Thompson, Watson, Weston, Heard, Hawker
(Coll) A. Shaw, Banks, Andrews, Millane, Barham
GOALS — (Ess) Baker (6), Van Der Haar (5), Williams (4), Harvey (4), Daniher (3), Watson (2), Clarke, Ezard, Buhagiar, Madden
(Coll) Andrews (3), G. Shaw, A. Shaw

SEPTEMBER 29—GRAND FINAL

	1st	2nd	3rd	Final
Essendon	2 . 4	3 . 11	5 . 15	14 . 21 (105)
Hawthorn	5 . 1	8 . 6	10 . 8	12 . 9 (81)

MCG — **Umpires—James, Sawers.**
Attendance—92,685 — **Gate—not available**

BEST — (Ess) Duckworth, Watson, Harvey, Hawker, Baker, Clarke, Weston, Heard
(Haw) Schwab, Loveridge, Ayres, Mew, Wallace, Matthews

GOALS — (Ess) Baker (4), Duckworth (2), Watson (2), Daniher, Bradbury, Thompson, Merrett, Weston, Neagle
(Haw) Matthews (4), Brereton (2), Robertson (2), Loveridge, Tuck, Judge, Curran

NORM SMITH MEDAL—W. Duckworth (Essendon).

GRAND FINAL TEAMS

Essendon	B	N. Clarke	P. Weston	W. Duckworth
	HB	P. Bradbury	K. Walsh	S. Heard
	C	M. Neagle	L. Baker	G. Foulds
	HF	G. Hawker	P. Van Der Haar	T. Daniher (c)
	F	A. Ezard	R. Merrett	F. Dunnell
	Ruck	S. Madden	T. Watson	D. Williams
	Int.	M. Harvey	M. Thompson	
	Coach	K. Sheedy		
Hawthorn	B	G. Ayres	D. O'Halloran	C. Robertson
	HB	R. Lester-Smith	C. Mew	P. Schwab
	C	R. DiPierdomenico	T. Wallace	P. Russo
	HF	P. Curran	D. Brereton	K. Judge
	F	M. McCarthy	L. Matthews (c)	R. Loveridge
	Ruck	M. Byrne	M. Tuck	R. Greene
	Int.	R. Eade	I. Paton	
	Coach	A. Jeans		

1985

The 1985 season was a particularly high scoring one. Almost weekly one club or another broke its previous record against a particular opponent, or recorded its greatest ever winning margin. The trend of the game in the 1980s often meant that once a team broke away, it was extremely hard to stop. Where five goals in a quarter was once considered excellent, teams now regularly notch nine or ten or more. The higher scoring did not necessarily indicate less upsets — on the contrary, 1985 saw a number of them, the most notable being the last round victory of wooden-spooners St. Kilda over Footscray (second), North Melbourne's fifty-nine point victory over leaders Essendon in round seven, and Richmond's massive score of 188 points to defeat Hawthorn (then second) in round five.

Essendon, shaping as an early premiership favourite, had a dream season, its nineteen wins equalling the VFL record shared by Hawthorn (1971), Collingwood (1973) and Carlton (1979). Its three defeats, however, were heavy ones, at the hands of North (fifty-nine points), Footscray (forty-one points) and Carlton (fifty-two points). Nevertheless, the Bombers striking power was evident in its record of scoring 150 points seven times (equalling the records of North Melbourne 1980, and Richmond 1982) whilst in the return game against North, Essendon had a half-time lead of over 100 points, only the second time in VFL history that such a lead had been obtained at that stage of a game.

Footscray's year was a marvellous one for them and their sixteen wins far surpassed their best-ever effort of thirteen and a draw in 1974. Their second spot on the ladder equalled their best record set in 1954.

Hawthorn, with seventeen century scores (more than any other side in 1985) snatched third place by downing Carlton in round twenty-one. But for a draw against North, the Hawks might have fallen into second spot when Footscray lost to St. Kilda in the last game, for their percentage was far superior to that of the Bulldogs. In the end, however, they were two premiership points behind. On fifteen wins came Carlton, which had struggled early in the season but began a resurgence in round fourteen with a stunning victory over North, followed by its best ever score at Kardinia Park, and then a fortnight later downed Essendon for the first time in eleven meetings. Comfortably fifth was North Melbourne (thirteen wins and a draw) a game and a half ahead of Geelong, which in turn, was two games clear of Collingwood. North's win over Melbourne by a point in round six, and four points in round seventeen, illustrated the importance of winning the close games. In fact North won six and drew one of eight games in which the margin was less than two goals and this proved crucial in staving off Geelong's bid for fifth place. The demise of Fitzroy was a big surprise, given that it was a finalist in 1984. The Lions, ninth with seven wins, had only themselves to blame. They went down twice to wooden-spooners St. Kilda and, in contrast to North, lost all the close ones, by margins of one, four, five, eight, nine and eleven points.

Before the elimination final, Carlton suffered the misfortune of losing both Ashman and Doull through injury, the latter thus missing his first final since 1972. Doull, a veteran of over 300 games, had struggled all season to overcome a knee injury, which had caused him to miss seventeen matches. Speedy rover Marcou came into the side for only his fifth match of the year. North Melbourne's main absentee was rover Jim Krakouer, still with one week of a six match suspension to serve.

At half-time Carlton seemed to have the game well in hand, with a strong thirty-one point lead against rather ineffectual opposition. The turning point came, however, with the move of North's Schimmelbusch — wasted at half back in the first half — onto the ball, where his experience got North moving. A six-goal burst in the third term cut Carlton's lead to seventeen points. It was still anybody's game at the last change, but, surprisingly, Carlton seemed to stop and its early good performers exerted little influence when the pressure was on at the end. North drew away with a burst to snatch a thirteen point lead. A goal to Maclure (Carlton) brought the margin back to seven but from then on it was all North and, with 8.1 in a great last term, they won well by nineteen points, putting Carlton out of the race.

For the qualifying final on the following day, Hawthorn selectors sprang a minor surprise by naming Knights and Judge, who had been declared fit for selection, in their Reserves side. The depth of the team was apparent when the Hawks, in superb touch, thrashed a very disappointing Footscray to the tune of ninety-five points.

It was a game in which everything went wrong for one side and everything right for the other, although there was one jarring note for Hawthorn when it became known that an injury to Tuck had left him in doubt for the Second Semi Final. He was subsequently unable to play.

Footscray hit back hard in the first semi final, showing a complete reversal of its form in the qualifying match. The Bulldogs lost Kellett and Ford through injury in the first quarter but covered admirably, matching North (which had Jim Krakouer back after suspension) goal for goal in an even first-half. A passage of play six minutes into the third term set the scene for Footscray's break-away: winger Daniels, a dismal performer the previous week, desperately smothered a kick off the boot of tough North defender Law, recovered the loose ball and snapped a superb goal on the run. Suddenly Footscray's lead stretched to sixteen points, setting them alight. Just prior to this, Beasley had booted his fifth goal to raise his century for the season amidst scenes of great excitement, and within minutes of Daniels' goal, Beasley and Bamblett each added another. After that, Footscray was never seriously threatened and ran out victors by thirty points.

Essendon's convincing victory in the second semi final made them raging-hot favourite for the flag, but it was only in the second-half that the Dons really established their superiority. Interestingly, this was partially brought about by some radical half-time moves by Sheedy, which had Essendon supporters flabbergasted and some almost ready to lynch the Dons' coach. Walsh, having kept Brereton almost kickless whilst at centre-half-back, went into attack, and two of the Dons' most devastating forwards, Merrett and Van Der Haar, started the second-half on the back-line. Foulds, a good performer in defence, also found himself in attack.

Sheedy's confidence in his players was not misplaced, however, and Walsh and Foulds (three goals) proved to be solid contributors, as did Merrett and Van Der Haar in their unusual roles. Other telling factors were the elusive play of Essendon utility Tim Watson, and the effective work of Thompson eclipsed Wallace in the centre and cut off a tremendous source of drive for the Hawks. The Dons' burst of 7.6 to one point in the third term effectively ended the match as a serious contest.

As expected, the Bulldogs had to omit the injured pair, Kellett and Ford, from their preliminary final side. Hawthorn, attempting to reach its third successive grand final, surprised many by not only leaving out giant ruckman Byrne, but also passing over Buckenara, Abbott, Robertson (the 1983 Norm Smith Medallist) and selecting Tuck, available again after his injury in the qualifying final, for the Reserves team. Judge, omitted since round nineteen, returned, as did Knights, a seasoned finals campaigner.

In the event, it was the appearance of Judge on the field in the second term (when he replaced Matthews) which proved the major difference between the two sides. His elusive play on the forward flank resulted in 4.1 from eight kicks. The Hawks, in fact, struggled for most of the match to shake off a very determined Footscray, which made some bad mistakes at vital times. A grand piece of play by Dunstall mid-way through the second quarter, when his desperate, flying tackle on McPherson enabled Russo to goal, revived temporarily flagging fortunes but the Hawks were still in plenty of trouble at the last change. Coach Jeans then brought Matthews, who had been kept in cotton wool on the interchange bench for almost half a game, back onto the ground. The Hawk skipper, realising that this match may be his last (he had announced that he would retire at the end of the season) threw himself into the fray and came up trumps, booting two match-winning goals and assisting in at least two more. His effort helped to put the Hawks comfortably ahead, after Footscray had slipped away to a nine point lead early in the quarter. The Hawks then went further ahead when Dunstall marked forty metres out and, spotting Judge alone in the goalsquare, hooked the ball to him for another goal.

Footscray, down but not out, refused to give in and reduced the twenty-two point margin to ten before the siren ended an absorbing contest.

Hawthorn, looking desperately for solutions to the problem of combating Essendon's big man strength for the grand final, sprang the selection surprise of the year by bringing in veteran O'Halloran for his first senior game of the year, to mind Salmon. Tuck returned, but Eade, one of the best in the preliminary final, was omitted in the reshuffle. Also out were Buckenara (who then kicked eight goals in the Reserves grand final) and Knights, the latter thus ending a great career in a most disappointing fashion. For Essendon, Neagle (injured) missed at the last moment while Dunnell and Victorian representative Heard were left out.

From the very first bounce, it was obvious that Hawthorn was slightly undermanned. Nevertheless, for the first ten minutes of the grand final they completely unsettled the Dons with all-out aggression, and streaked away to a dream start.

Brereton, given a free kick after forty seconds of play, began an auspicious day with a goal from twenty-five metres out. Attention soon shifted to the outer wing where a minor push and shove developed into an ugly brawl involving all thirty-six players. At least a dozen punches were thrown, but only two reports came out of the incident, which lasted for two minutes. A goal to Harvey (Essendon) was answered by two more to the brilliant Brereton, playing at full-forward rather than his customary centre half-forward spot. Essendon skipper Daniher came down to full-back in an endeavour to curb the Hawk star. At the other end, 206 cm (6ft 9in) Don full-forward Salmon was also in fine form, but was initially off-target until at the fourteen minute-mark a fine mark and goal restored his confidence. Essendon began to regain some composure and four goals in the last ten minutes of the first quarter gave them a nine point lead. They had weathered the best that Hawthorn had to throw at them and now looked to be moving into top gear.

At the start of the second term, Salmon featured in several passages of play, first popping the ball to Harvey in the goal square for Essendon's seventh, but then missing two shots in the space of thirty seconds.

Two goals in three minutes by Brereton mid-way through the quarter got Hawthorn to within six points and the crowd roared as Merrett, on the run, replied for Essendon. Judge snapped truly on the left foot for the Hawks and then Williams did the same for Essendon. Six goals had come in six minutes in a brilliant display of attacking football by both sides. However, the dominance of Madden over the shorter Hawk ruckmen was giving his side first use of the ball at the centre bounces; it seemed only to be a matter of time before the Dons really cut loose. Mid-way through the term, Matthews was rested and, for a while, he and Tuck, with more than 600 games between them, shared the interchange bench. Soon after, Ayres was also replaced. He was just one of a number of Hawks who were struggling.

An absorbing third quarter saw Essendon lay a strong base from which to spring their last-term assault. Watson, always running loose, extended the margin to twenty-nine points with a smart running goal and Salmon added another a few minutes later. The Hawks fought back dourly. Goals to Lester-Smith and Brereton mid-way through the term brought the difference back to eighteen points. A tense battle of the backlines followed before Thompson's left foot snap at the twenty-three minute mark got Essendon on the move again. Three minutes later, the elusive Baker marked and kicked another goal. When the siren sounded for the final break, the MCG had grown very quiet. Most of the crowd sensed that the end was near for Hawthorn.

The final term resulted in a veritable flood of goals for the Dons which crushed the life out of a Hawthorn side that, realistically, had little chance from the start. Merrett's mark and goal at the eight minute mark opened the floodgates and, from that point, there was a goal every three minutes as Essendon jumpers popped up everywhere. Within fifteen minutes, the Bombers led by sixty-seven points. Brereton was still contesting brilliantly for Hawthorn and was rewarded with his seventh and eighth goals late in the term, breaking the record for most goals scored by any player in a grand final. Salmon, Ezard, Williams and Harvey, with a soccer kick right at the finish, piled on four more in four minutes as the Dons responded to Brereton's effort. The siren was a merciful sound for the Hawthorn side which, in an emotional tribute, chaired retiring champion Leigh Matthews from the ground at the end. It was Matthews who provided the most succinct comment on the 1985 Grand Final when, in an after-game interview, he commented, 'It was a bit like fighting a war without weapons'.

Essendon's 11.3 in the last quarter constituted a grand final record and critics were unanimous in declaring the side one of the finest in the history of the VFL. Three, and even four, successive flags were, they said, a distinct possibility for the Dons. On the other hand, it was suggested that Hawthorn's days of glory were over, all of which proves that football is a funny game.

RESULTS

SEPTEMBER 7—ELIMINATION FINAL

	1st	2nd	3rd	Final
North Melbourne	2 . 3	6 . 3	12 . 5	20 . 6 (126)
Carlton	3 . 6	10 . 10	14 . 10	16 . 11 (107)

VFL Park — Umpires—Cameron, Robinson
Attendance—49,126 — Gate—not available

BEST —(NM) Holt, Larkin, Schimmelbusch, Arceri, P. Krakouer, Smith
(Carl) Madden, Maclure, Marcou, Johnston, Hunter, Kourkoumelis

GOALS — (NM) McCann (4), Glendinning (3), Holt (2), Schimmelbusch (2), Demetriou (2), Steele, P. Krakouer, Larkin, McDonald, Dwyer, Jonas, Arceri
(Carl) McConville (3), Maclure (3), Kourkoumelis (2), Harmes (2), Madden, Johnston, Buckley, Murphy, Marcou, McKenzie

SEPTEMBER 8—QUALIFYING FINAL

	1st	2nd	3rd	Final
Hawthorn	6 . 5	11 . 11	15 . 16	22 . 23 (155)
Footscray	2 . 3	3 . 5	6 . 11	8 . 14 (62)

MCG — Umpires—Sawers, Howlett
Attendance—58,000 — Gate—not available

BEST — (Haw) Wallace, Lester-Smith, Morris, Greene, Mew, Handley, Langford, Dunstall
(Foots) Hardie, Bamblett, Hawkins, Wallis, Royal

GOALS — (Haw) Dunstall (5), Byrne (3), Brereton (3), Matthews (2), DiPierdomenico (2), Wallace (2), Handley (2), Russo, Buckenara, Kennedy
(Foots) Bamblett (2), Beasley (2), Edmond, S. McPherson, Royal, Peart

SEPTEMBER 15—FIRST SEMI FINAL

	1st	2nd	3rd	Final
Footscray	3 . 1	9 . 8	14 . 16	19 . 23 (137)
North Melbourne	4 . 3	9 . 5	11 . 9	16 . 11 (107)

		MCG Attendance—56,112	Umpires—James, Robinson Gate—not available
BEST —	(Foots)	Hawkins, Wallis, Royal, Maylin, Foster, B. Cordy, Daniels	
	(NM)	Larkin, Holt, McDonald, J. Krakouer, Steele	
GOALS —	(Foots)	Beasley (7), Royal (5), Daniels (2), Edmond (2), Hawkins, Bamblett, Buhagiar	
	(NM)	J. Krakouer (3), Glendinning (2), Larkin (2), Holt (2), P. Krakouer, McCann, Demetriou, Jonas, Arceri, Spargo, Fairley	

SEPTEMBER 14—SECOND SEMI FINAL

	1st	2nd	3rd	Final
Essendon	4 . 4	4 . 8	11 . 14	14 . 18 (102)
Hawthorn	3 . 2	6 . 2	6 . 3	9 . 8 (62)

		VFL Park Attendance—67,063	Umpires—Cameron, Bryant Gate—not available
BEST —	(Ess)	Watson, Walsh, Thompson, Elshaug, Madden, Baker	
	(Haw)	Mew, Morris, Wallace, Russo, Lester-Smith, Handley	
GOALS —	(Ess)	Foulds (3), Merrett (2), Thompson (2), Baker, Daniher, Ezard, Van Der Haar, Madden, Walsh, Watson	
	(Haw)	Brereton (2), Kennedy (2), Matthews, Buckenara, Morris, Dunstall, Handley	

SEPTEMBER 21—PRELIMINARY FINAL

	1st	2nd	3rd	Final
Hawthorn	3 . 2	7 . 4	10 . 8	16 . 13 (109)
Footscray	4 . 4	6 . 6	10 . 7	15 . 9 (99)

		VFL Park Attendance—55,246	Umpires—James, Sawers Gate—not available
BEST —	(Haw)	Loveridge, Judge, Kennedy, Dunstall, Russo, Lester-Smith, Ayres, Wallace	
	(Foots)	Hardie, Hawkins, Edmond, Bamblett, Royal, Sewell, Beasley, Wallis, Purser	
GOALS —	(Haw)	Judge (4), Dunstall (4), Kennedy (2), Matthews (2), Russo, McCarthy, Brereton, Loveridge	
	(Foots)	Beasley (3), Edmond (2), McLean (2), Sewell (2), Hawkins, Purser, Bamblett, Groenewegen, Royal, Buhagiar	

SEPTEMBER 28—GRAND FINAL

	1st	2nd	3rd	Final
Essendon	6 . 4	11 . 9	15 . 11	26 . 14 (170)
Hawthorn	5 . 1	9 . 3	11 . 5	14 . 8 (92)

		MCG Attendance—100,042	Umpires—Cameron, Robinson Gate—not available
BEST —	(Ess)	Madden, Merrett, Watson, Salmon, Baker, Thompson, Williams	
	(Haw)	Brereton, Lester-Smith, Kennedy, Morris, O'Halloran	
GOALS —	(Ess)	Salmon (6), Merrett (5), Harvey (4), Watson (3), Baker (2), Ezard (2), Williams (2), Thompson, Duckworth	
	(Haw)	Brereton (8), Matthews, McCarthy, Loveridge, Judge, Lester-Smith, DiPierdomenico	

NORM SMITH MEDAL—S. Madden (Essendon)

GRAND FINAL TEAMS

Essendon	B	M. Thompson	P. Weston	W. Duckworth
	HB	G. Hawker	K. Walsh	G. Foulds
	C	B. Wood	T. Watson	N. Clarke
	HF	M. Harvey	R. Merrett	T. Daniher (c)
	F	L. Baker	P. Salmon	P. Van Der Haar
	Ruck	S. Madden	D. Williams	A. Elshaug
	Int.	S. Carey	A. Ezard	
	Coach	K. Sheedy		
Hawthorn	B	G. Ayres	C. Mew	P. Schwab
	HB	R. Morris	R. Lester-Smith	R. Greene
	C	R. DiPiedomenico	T. Wallace	P. Russo
	HB	J. Kennedy	D. Brereton	K. Judge
	F	M. McCarthy	J. Dunstall	L. Matthews (c)
	Ruck	C. Langford	R. Handley	R. Loveridge
	Int.	M. Tuck	D. O'Halloran	
	Coach	A. Jeans		

1986

In 1986 the VFL commissioners decided to reschedule big games at either the MCG or VFL Park, causing the old 'home-ground advantage' to become a relic of the past in many instances. Further innovations included the playing of five Friday night games (North Melbourne participated in all of them) under lights at the MCG for premiership points, and the scheduling of two 'double-header' games at the MCG.

Hawthorn was the outstanding team of the home and away season, suffering only four defeats in the twenty-two rounds (one of them was, however, a massive eighty-seven point loss at the hands of Essendon, their 1985 Grand Final opponent). In round twenty-one the Hawks booted a near record VFL score of 35.15 against Geelong, including an incredible twenty-five goals in the second half, the most prolific fifty minutes in the history of VFL football. The Sydney Swans, recovering well from their poor performance in the previous season's finals series, finished second with sixteen wins, followed by Carlton (fifteen wins, seven losses but with the best percentage (141.9) of all twelve teams). Fitzroy (thirteen wins, nine losses) and Essendon (twelve wins, ten losses) made up the Five, with Collingwood and North, also on twelve wins, missing out on percentage. Footscray, preliminary finalists in 1985, dropped to eighth with only eleven wins.

Essendon's fall to fifth spot (at one stage it looked as if they might even miss fifth) was the big surprise of the season. Before the start of the season the Dons had been widely acclaimed as one of the finest units ever assembled in VFL ranks. Their 'hat-trick' of premierships was the universal tip even before a ball had been kicked.

With few losses to the personnel of 1984-85 and the infusion of a number of exciting recruits, the Dons ran hot and cold throughout the season. Essendon was still magnificent at its best (as in its thrashing of Hawthorn in round eighteen) but simply failed to produce its best often enough.

Fitzroy almost gave fans a repeat of its 1984 performance to reach the finals. A loss to North in round twenty actually dropped the Lions to seventh. North then stumbled against Melbourne in round twenty-one, putting itself out of contention, while, on the same day, the Lions scored an upset win over Essendon. In round twenty-two, the Lions won again, downing the Sydney Swans by ten points. Out at Windy Hill, Essendon went down again in a boil-over to North Melbourne, dropping the Dons to fifth and elevating Fitzroy to fourth.

Collingwood, the only other team with a chance at that stage, won well against St. Kilda. They could only rue their surprise loss to Melbourne at Victoria Park a month before as it was that defeat that cost the Magpies a place in the finals.

Undoubtedly the gutsiest performance of the 1986 finals series was Fitzroy's victory over Essendon in a wet and windy elimination final. The Dons, even though they had lost all but one of their previous six appearances in an elimination final, were hot favourites. Sheer persistence won the game for the Lions.

Fitzroy made a brave selection by leaving out Rendell and Quinlan, both of whom were not fully fit. This left them seemingly undermanned against the tall Essendon rucks. The Lions were fortunate, however, that rain fell throughout the match which negated much of the Dons' marking power. Nevertheless, the sterling effort by Reeves of Fitzroy against the superior height of Madden and Salmon did much to facilitate the Lions' victory. He was able to get the ball to ground at centre bounces where the Fitzroy small brigade, led by B. Harris, outclassed their Essendon opponents. Reeves, incidentally, in this match became the first player since the turn of the century to appear on a VFL ground in knickerbockers, which were specially padded to prevent further injury to a troublesome thigh.

Essendon battled its way to a three point lead at the last change and looked safe, coming home with a strong wind at its back and with heavy rain likely to limit scoring. But the Dons somehow blew it, short passing and overindulging in handball when more direct play probably would have been more productive.

A goal to B. Harris just after the term began gave Fitzroy the lead. It was the boost they needed and the taste of victory that made them fight tooth and nail from that point on. A rushed behind was followed by another to Conlan, but it was only desperate defence by Fitzroy that kept the Dons out for the next five minutes. Finally, Hawker got the goal Essendon wanted, and they then bombarded the goals for behinds to Salmon, two more to Elshaug and another to Merrett who missed a rather easy shot which should have been converted. Fitzroy, though, was exerting extreme pressure and its backline, led by Pert and Roos, and ruckmen, with Keane taking over from Reeves in a sound tactical move by the Lions, were superb. Trailing by only five points, Fitzroy would not give up.

It was yet another saving mark in defence by Roos that led to the winning goal. He quickly handpassed to Harris who ran through the centre and booted long into the forward line, finding Conlan who was unattended. The Fitzroy half-forward, who had been held virtually kickless all day, ran in and, from thirty metres out, steered through the goal that put Fitzroy ahead by a point at the twenty-seven minute mark.

Conlan's goal sealed the game; forty-five seconds later, the siren eliminated Essendon from the 1986 premiership race. Six players were reported in the game.

The Sydney Swans, without injured skipper Dennis Carroll, battled hard in the qualifying final, against a better equipped Carlton side, and, to some extent, made amends for their performance in the corresponding game the year before. The difference lay in the forward strength of the Blues. Kernahan, Meldrum and Hunter kicked thirteen goals between them. In contrast, the Swans main forward, Capper, was well held by the veteran Doull.

The Swans showed their best form in the first fifteen minutes, rattling on 5.1 to 1.1 and causing fan and critic alike to anticipate a boil-over. Carlton, however, came back strongly and went to a long lead before fading badly in the last term. Their only goal came from a lucky mark by Robertson at the twenty-three minute mark, a soccer kick by Evans landing on his chest. The Swans' last quarter effort of 3.6 and three out on the full, was a promising one, and a little more luck may have made the situation much tighter than the final sixteen point margin.

The Swans were warm favourites when they met Fitzroy in the first semi final. The Lions brought back Rendell and Quinlan. For three quarters the Swans justified their favourable rating. Two goals to Daniher halfway through the third team gave the Swans a twenty point lead. Fitzroy had scored only six goals in that time, the last of them fourteen minutes into the previous quarter. B. Harris then came from the interchange bench and his appearance brought a change in fortunes for the Lions. He hooked a kick into the square allowing R. Osborne to soccer through a goal and followed this with a snap goal himself, from close to the boundary line. Fitzroy's game lifted and four goals in eight minutes in pouring rain in the final term snatched back the lead for them, a lead they held until the end. A fine performance by Pert put Capper out of business once again, although the flamboyant Swan forward had one chance at the sixteen minute mark of the last quarter to swing the game around. With Fitzroy eleven points up, Capper was awarded a free kick thirty metres out. However, he foolishly engaged in a pushing match with Pert, and the free was reversed. As a Swans' goal late in the match made the final margin five points, Capper's lack of discipline was a costly lapse.

For Hawthorn, the unfortunate Kennedy missed yet another finals match through injury. They met a weakened Carlton in the Second Semi, the Blues being forced to replace Hunter and Blackwell, both of whom were injured. Hunter, in fact, was considered unlikely for the grand final should the Blues advance that far. The Hawks brought back Eade, after five games in the Reserves. This game was another in which the favourite faltered. The Hawthorn attack, devastating throughout the regular season, was hopeless. Dunstall received a football lesson from Doull and Brereton was also missing. His confidence seemed to disappear when he was reported for striking.

Something seemed to have gone awry with the Hawthorn game-plan. Carlton winger Rhys-Jones was able to roam all day without an opponent, and his thirty-one possessions earned him the critics' unanimous vote as best afield. Carlton advanced to the grand final by virtue of their twenty-eight point win, but the report and subsequent one-match suspension of rover Murphy meant he would not be there on the big day. His chance was to come, in ironic circumstances, twelve months later.

Paul Roos, in doubt through injury almost up to starting time, was a surprise inclusion in the Fitzroy side for the preliminary final. Although obviously not fully fit, Roos' presence on the field was a bonus for the Lions which really had its injury problems strike at the worst possible time. L. Harris, who had missed six weeks with a broken foot, came back into the side to tag Loveridge, but had the misfortune to sustain a suspected broken leg before half the match had passed.

The Hawthorn camp obviously prepared well to throw off the Fitzroy taggers. Jeans' tactic was to run both rovers on the ball at the same time, a move which initially caught the Lions napping. Even so, the Lions got away to an excellent start, leading by twenty points after only eight minutes of play.

Gradually, however, the Hawks clawed their way back into the contest. They had grabbed the lead back by quarter-time, and were never seriously threatened thereafter, keeping the Lions to a mere three goals for the remainder of the game.

Reeves, brought on from the interchange bench in the second term, revived older fans' memories of the Healy-Adams incident in 1955 when he was rammed ferociously by DiPierdomenico and was carried off the ground just sixty seconds after running on to it. Unconscious for thirty minutes, Reeves displayed great courage by actually returning for a period in the second half, by which time injuries had decimated the struggling Lions.

Focal point in attack for Hawthorn was full-forward Dunstall, who in this game showed his best finals' form so far. His brilliant leading and accurate kicking resulted in five goals against a tough opponent in Pert.

The Lions ended the game with at least eight players carrying injuries which would, in all likelihood, have kept them out of the grand final anyway, had Fitzroy won the preliminary final. Harris (broken leg) and Pert (broken ankle) were on crutches, Reeves was concussed, and Rendell (hamstring) and Quinlan (achilles) were barely able to walk. It was a disappointing end to Bernie Quinlan's career, the Fitzroy champion announcing his retirement after 367 games.

Hawthorn received a huge morale boost during the week when it was announced that winger Robert DiPierdomenico was the joint-winner of the Brownlow Medal, the first to be awarded to a Hawthorn player since the club had joined the VFL in 1925*. Supporters took this 'drought-breaker' as a lucky omen. Carlton, meeting Hawthorn for the first time in a grand final, also had a great incentive: the club wanted to see retiring champion Bruce Doull finish his career with a premiership flag.

The Blues made two changes to the successful second semi side, leaving out Murphy (suspended) and Silvagni, and bringing in Blackwell and Hunter after injury. Hawthorn regained the services of Kennedy, and had obviously done a lot of homework to bolster the side which had crashed to Carlton in the second semi. The final line-up showed just how well the Hawthorn camp had ensured that the right man was selected for the opponent, and not necessarily for the position. Most notable instances of this were Ayres on the wing to cover Rhys-Jones, Eade tagging Bradley, Langford to centre-half back and Wallace, although nominally in the centre, playing two and a half quarters at half-back when his opponent, Blackwell, was moved to the forward flank.

Sadly for the 101,861 people at the MCG, the match was something of an anticlimax to the season. Carlton's inability to seriously challenge the Hawks right from the start resulted in another grand final which lacked tension. Hawthorn goaled from its first real forward move, two minutes into the match, after a mark by Dunstall. Meldrum replied for Carlton with a neat goal on the run, but thereafter it was all Hawthorn, their relentless smothering and harassing making it impossible for the Blues to get any fluency into their game.

After twelve minutes, Curran got Hawthorn's second and minutes later a clever tap-on by Dunstall resulted in Brereton charging in for another. Curran's superb pass to Buckenara fifteen metres out brought the third goal in three minutes. Towards the end of the term, Buckenara added another, a somewhat lucky goal which bounced at right angles and went through. Perhaps that shot was an indication that it was to be Hawthorn's day.

Early in the second quarter, Dunstall, who was giving Doull trouble with his fast leading, showed his strength in a one-on-one duel, and snapped accurately over his head for the Hawks' sixth goal.

The brilliant Eade, who not only blanketed Bradley but became a prolific kick-winner himself, found Buckenara alone soon after and the elusive Hawk half-forward scored from a long way out. The Blues recovered some poise mid-way through the term, and goals to Glascott and Rhys-Jones gave them some hope. That hope was quickly dashed when the dangerous Buckenara accepted a handball from Platten and again kicked accurately. Dropped from the previous year's grand final team, Buckenara now had four of the Hawks' first eight goals in a sensational display.

Just before time-on, Meldrum got Carlton's fourth when he took the ball from the hands of the pack and scored from twenty-five metres out, but at the break the Blues looked to be in deep touble. They trailed by twenty-one points, with only 4.11 on the board. Many may have blamed inaccuracy to some degree, but in reality the Carlton score reflected the tremendous harassing and smothering of the Hawks, which meant that nearly every Carlton kick was executed under extreme pressure.

The third quarter has always been regarded as a vital one in football of any standard. During the '80s respected coach David Parkin frequently referred to the third term as the 'premiership quarter', and, in 1986, he was proven correct. A purple patch by Hawk full-forward Dunstall, who had been restricted to three kicks in the second semi, set up the Hawks' victory.

Forty-nine seconds after the bounce, Dunstall beat Doull for pace and snapped accurately. After a fifty-metre goal by Brereton, Dunstall added two more from a long way out and the Hawks, leading now by eight goals, appeared safe even at this stage of the game. With twenty minutes gone, the valiant Meldrum got his third for Carlton, but Ayres quickly replied for Hawthorn, and Russo snapped accurately with his left foot for another. The Blues now appeared to be in total disarray, and spirits sagged further when skipper Maclure and star utility Bradley were relegated to the bench mid-way through the term. Shortly after, Johnston — one of the Blues' star performers in past finals — was taken off with a jarred knee.

Evans notched one of Carlton's infrequent goals late in the term, but Brereton, proving to be a dangerous forward, added his third just before the siren to effectively seal the result of the match.

Both sides went through the motions in a lack-lustre last quarter. The Blues made their score slightly more respectable with a goal to McKenzie and two to the disappointing Kernahan, but the Hawks were never seriously threatened and, although a long goal to Dunstall at the twenty-seven and a half minute mark was their only major score of the term, the end result was never in the slightest doubt. The Hawks coasted to a forty-two point victory.

Hawthorn's Gary Ayres, playing in his fourth premiership side, was a worthy winner of the Norm Smith Medal for his brilliant game on the dangerous Rhys-Jones, who had cut the Hawks to pieces in the second semi-final. There were, however, a number of Hawthorn players who might have taken the award, so even was the team's performance. Carlton, in contrast, found that many of its superstars went missing on the day. It was no doubt a sad final bow for the veteran Doull, himself a member of four premiership teams in his 359-game career, and for skipper Maclure, who, only a month or so later, also retired.

*In April, 1989, the VFL decided to award the Brownlow medal to those players that had previously lost the award on a countback. Under this ruling, Hawthorn's first medallist becomes Col Austen who tied for the award in 1949.

RESULTS

SEPTEMBER 6—ELIMINATION FINAL

	1st	2nd	3rd	Final
Fitzroy	4 . 2	4 . 4	6 . 8	8 . 10 (58)
Essendon	2 . 1	4 . 3	7 . 5	8 . 9 (57)

VFL Park — **Umpires—Cameron, Russo**
Attendance—59,420 — **Gate—not available**

BEST —	(Fitz)	McIvor, Pert, Roos, Thornton, B. Harris, Pekin, Clayton
	(Ess)	Hawker, Thomson, Daniher, Baker, Walsh, Dunnell, Elshaug
GOALS —	(Fitz)	B. Harris (2), Barwick (2), Lawrie, McIvor, Conlan, R. Osborne
	(Ess)	Hawker (2), Duckworth (2), Baker, Van Der Haar, Richardson, S. Clark

SEPTEMBER 7—QUALIFYING FINAL

	1st	2nd	3rd	Final
Carlton	5 . 1	12 . 7	17 . 12	18 . 12 (120)
Sydney Swans	5 . 1	7 . 6	12 . 8	15 . 14 (104)

MCG — **Umpires—Clayton, Robinson**
Attendance—66,016 — **Gate—not available**

BEST —	(Carl)	Kernahan, Dorotich, Hunter, Bradley, Meldrum, Harmes
	(Syd)	Healy, Williams, Bolton, Toohey, Hawke
GOALS —	(Carl)	Kernahan (5), Meldrum (4), Hunter (4), Maclure, Evans, Bradley, Blackwell, Robertson
	(Syd)	Hawke (3), Williams (2), Bayes (2), Healy (2), Capper (2), Daniher, Neagle, Bolton, Wright

SEPTEMBER 14—FIRST SEMI FINAL

	1st	2nd	3rd	Final
Fitzroy	4 . 4	6 . 8	8 . 14	13 . 16 (94)
Sydney Swans	3 . 2	8 . 5	11 . 8	13 . 11 (89)

MCG — **Umpires—Castle, Cameron**
Attendance—65,763 — **Gate—not available**

BEST —	(Fitz)	Lokan, Clayton, Rendell, Pekin, Conlan, R. Osborne
	(Syd)	Neagle, Morwood, Williams, Bayes, Murphy
GOALS —	(Fitz)	Conlan (4), Quinlan (3), R. Osborne (2), McIvor, B. Harris, McGrath, Lokan
	(Syd)	Morwood (4), Capper (2), Bolton (2), Bayes (2), Daniher (2), Wright

SEPTEMBER 13—SECOND SEMI FINAL

	1st	2nd	3rd	Final
Carlton	4 . 4	7 . 9	10 . 12	16 . 16 (112)
Hawthorn	4 . 1	7 . 1	10 . 4	13 . 6 (84)

VFL Park — **Umpires—Sawers, Russo**
Attendance—63,215 — **Gate—not available**

BEST —	(Carl)	Kernahan, Johnston, Rhys-Jones, Murphy, Evans, Motley, Glascott
	(Haw)	Langford, Curran, Loveridge, Platten, Ayres, Wallace, Dear
GOALS —	(Carl)	Evans (5), Maclure (3), Johnston (3), Kernahan (2), Murphy (2), Bradley

	(Haw)	Curran (5), Buckenara (2), DiPiedomenico, Platten, Dear, Judge, Loveridge, Brereton

SEPTEMBER 20—PRELIMINARY FINAL

	1st	2nd	3rd	Final
Hawthorn	5 . 3	8 . 5	13 . 7	16 . 14 (110)
Fitzroy	4 . 4	4 . 9	6 . 10	7 . 12 (54)

VFL Park — **Umpires—Sawers, Castle**
Attendance—68,339 — **Gate—not available**

BEST —	(Haw)	Wallace, Platten, Schwab, Loveridge, Dear, DiPierdomenico, Dunstall
	(Fitz)	Roos, R. Osborne, Lokan, Clayton, Turner
GOALS —	(Haw)	Dunstall (5), Platten (4), Curran (2), Greene (2), Ayres, DiPierdomenico, Buckenara
	(Fitz)	Quinlan (3), Rendell, Conlan, McGrath, R. Osborne

SEPTEMBER 27—GRAND FINAL

	1st	2nd	3rd	Final
Hawthorn	5 . 6	8 . 8	15 . 9	16 . 14 (110)
Carlton	1 . 5	4 . 11	6 .13	9 . 14 (68)

MCG — **Umpires—Cameron, Russo**
Attendance—101,861 — **Gate—not available**

BEST —	(Haw)	Ayres, Buckenara, Eade, Dunstall, Wallace, Tuck, Langford, Russo, Mew
	(Carl)	Madden, Alvin, Glascott, Motley
GOALS —	(Haw)	Dunstall (6), Buckenara (4), Brereton (3), Curran, Russo, Ayres
	(Carl)	Meldrum (3), Kernahan (2), Glascott, McKenzie, Rhys-Jones, Evans

GRAND FINAL TEAMS

Hawthorn	B	P. Russo	C. Mew	P. Abbot
	HB	M. Tuck (c)	C. Langford	P. Schwab
	C	R. DiPierdomenico	T. Wallace	G. Ayres
	HF	G. Buckenara	D. Brereton	J. Platten
	F	P. Curran	J. Dunstall	R. Greene
	Ruck	G. Dear	R. Eade	R. Loveridge
	Int.	R. Morris	J. Kennedy	
	Coach	A. Jeans		
Carlton	B	W. Harmes	B. Doull	P. Dean
	HB	D. English	J. Dorotich	P. Motley
	C	D. Rhys-Jones	W. Blackwell	T. Alvin
	HF	W. Johnston	S. Kernahan	P. Meldrum
	F	B. Evans	M. Maclure (c)	K. Hunter
	Ruck	J. Madden	C. Bradley	D. Glascott
	Int.	W. McKenzie	S. Robertson	
	Coach	R. Walls		

NORM SMITH MEDAL—G. Ayres (Hawthorn)

1987

The ninety-first season of VFL football was one of its most memorable, because it featured an expanded competition with the admission of interstate teams, the Brisbane Bears and West Coast Eagles. This meant that the VFL had teams in Sydney, Brisbane and Perth.

The Bears were forced to put together their team virtually from scratch, recruiting mainly from Victoria and South Australia. The Eagles, on the other hand, had a ready-made recruiting base in Western Australia and, initially, many thought that they would be able to field a team which would prove too strong for the competition. This did not prove to be the case and, although performing well at home, the Eagles found the long air trip to Melbourne difficult and they won only two games away from Perth.

The VFL's Sydney-based team, the Sydney Swans, was the early-season trendsetter, suggesting that it had overcome the deficiencies which caused it to be eliminated in two straight finals' games the previous season. The Swans utilised the small Sydney ground to perfection and booted nine twenty-goal scores for the season, including a VFL record of three successive thirty-goal scores. However, a bad mid-season slump cost the Swans the coveted top spot.

Carlton, runner-up in 1986, sprang a surprise with its appointment of Stephen Kernahan, who had played only twenty-five VFL games, as captain. Kernahan's success in the role revived memories of Carlton's appointment, in similar circumstances, of Ern Henfry in 1947. The Blues, with Kernahan a focal point in attack, steam-rollered their way to top spot with a record eighteen wins and four losses. This left them a game ahead of 1986 premiers Hawthorn, which despite early-season form that was only fair, notched wins over the Blues in both home and away games.

Sydney Swans held third place with fifteen wins, followed by North Melbourne (thirteen wins, one draw) and — making a welcome re-appearance in the finals for the first time since 1964 — Melbourne, with twelve wins.

The composition of the final five went right down to the wire in 1987, and the last home and away round was probably one of the most exciting in the VFL's history. None of the positions on the ladder were finalised before the last round, and three teams — Melbourne, Geelong and Footscray — all had hopes of grabbing fifth position. The Cats, having won only two of their previous five games, made a bold bid when they led Hawthorn all day at Princes Park but the Hawks, with top spot in sight, rallied at the end and turned a nine point deficit with only a few minutes to go into a three point win, ending Geelong's finals' dream. Carlton held top spot only when Kernahan goaled after the siren to give the Blues a four point win over North Melbourne. Out at the Western Oval, Melbourne turned on the pressure after half time and the Demons won through to an emotional fifteen point victory, tipping Footscray and Geelong out and moving into their first finals appearance for twenty-three years.

If Essendon's fall to ninth place was the biggest shock of the year, then Melbourne's rise to the finals was not far behind. Under ex-Swans' coach John Northey, the Demons showed new vigour and took out the night series premiership in fine style. But, by round fifteen they had still lost more games than they had won, although their six victories to that stage was only one short of their total for the whole of 1986. However, successive losses to North and St. Kilda seemed to have ended the Demons' chances. Mathematically, they still had a slim chance, but were dependent upon favourable results in other games and although tremendous motivation was gained through the Demons' wish to give retiring captain Robert Flower his first finals appearance. Realistically it seemed the Demons' hopes were in vain. But dreams sometimes come true, and in this case the Demons ran up six successive wins, including victories over Geelong, the Eagles and Footscray, and the job was done.

The Demons' appearance in the finals gave the series a build-up that was not expected a month before, and their meeting with North in the elimination final created enormous interest. Injured rover Jim Krakouer was a big loss for North, but Melbourne's losses through injury — Lyon and Wilson — looked harder to cover for a team that reputedly lacked depth.

However, the fairy tale continued for Melbourne. Flower, inspired by his first finals' appearance after 270 games, bamboozled the North defence with five match-winning goals. The Demon's pre-match planning was carried out to perfection by a desperate and determined team, which used plenty of physical pressure to overwhelm its opponents. Coach Northey's astute use of the long-kicking game, with less emphasis on handball, paid dividends in this and other games during the year and perhaps heralded a change to the style of game that has been adopted since the early seventies.

The loss of Jonas early in the match upset North's plans, but they were never in the race as Melbourne, rebounding brilliantly and winning in almost every position on the ground, swept on to an amazing 118 point victory, a new record winning margin for an elimination final.

In the qualifying final, the Sydney Swans struggled on the big ground at VFL Park and failed to cover some of the deficiencies that had not been so apparent on their smaller home ground in Sydney. The pre-match withdrawal of Neagle was a massive blow, but this game was another one-sided affair and many Swans' fans believed that the side lacked commitment and had fallen for the old trap of fielding unfit players. Capper played a lone-hand up forward for the Swans and his four goals took his total for the season to 103 — where it remained when a hamstring injury put him out of the First Semi-Final. For Hawthorn, Buckenara, who had tried to leave the club earlier in the season, showed his class and his five goals from the centre won him the critics' vote as best man afield. Brereton (six goals) and Dunstall (five) clearly demonstrated that the Hawks had plenty of firepower up forward.

Melbourne fans (for a time it seemed that everyone in Melbourne *was* a Demon fan) flocked to the MCG for the first semi-final, some convinced, others merely hopeful, of further glory. For Demon coach John Northey, the match represented an opportunity to prove a point to the Swans, whose management had previously sacked him as coach, citing his 'low profile' as one of their reasons.

Undermanned because of the loss of Capper, the Swans again disappointed their fans. For the second week running, Melbourne got the jump on their opponents early in the match and blitzed their way to a big lead at half-time. Staring at their fourth successive finals' defeat in two seasons, the Swans found nothing to stem the onslaught and Melbourne's seven goal burst in the third term set up a seventy-six point win.

Hawthorn, by virtue of its two home and away wins over Carlton, went into the second semi final as slight favourites. After a poor first half, the Blues run of losses against the Hawks looked set to continue and, at one point, they trailed by thirty-three points.

But from the depths of despair, Carlton staged a strong fight back mid-way through the third term, reduced the margin to only nine points at the break, and then over-ran a tiring Hawthorn in the last quarter to record an impressive fifteen point victory. The win not only broke the psychological barrier for Carlton but took them straight into the grand final (and made their win/loss ratio one/eleven in the last twelve meetings between the two teams). Hawthorn, on the other hand, had notably tired in this match and now faced the prospect of meeting a 'pumped-up' Melbourne in the cut-throat preliminary final, without the services of full-forward Dunstall. An ankle injury ended his season when he was within six goals of his century.

Carlton also received a set-back when rover Bernie Evans copped a one-match suspension after the game, and was thus eliminated from grand final selection.

The preliminary final itself was not a memorable spectacle, but it will be remembered for its remarkable finish and for the torture the Melbourne players and coaching panel went through as the game, which they had almost won, slipped away from them.

Melbourne, aided by a change in wind direction at quarter-time, kicked with the benefit of the breeze for the first three quarters of the match, and this certainly helped them as they battled to a clear lead of twenty-two points at half-time. The Hawks, decidedly unimpressive, had won plenty of the ball but Melbourne's pressure, combined with the swirling wind, reduced their effectiveness. There were plenty of physical clashes to set the fans roaring as Flower (Melb), then DiPierdomenico and Mew (Haw) all left the ground after heavy knocks.

A clear change came over the game in the second half, although it was not initially apparent on the scoreboard. Hawthorn, inspired by Greene (brought on from the interchange bench) and Tuck began to get its running game together, breaking the shackles imposed by Melbourne for the first fifty minutes. Nevertheless, when the teams huddled at the last change, the margin in favour of the Demons remained exactly the same as it had been at half-time, but Hawthorn now sensed the mission was not impossible. Several Melbourne players were noticeably sore (Wilson and Jackson were both forced off the ground in the last term) and Hawthorn, for the first time in the match, had the wind at its back.

Both coaches made wholesale changes, the most notable being the move of Brereton, well beaten up forward, to centre-half back where he helped turn the tide for the Hawks.

Hawthorn, through goals to Morris and Kennedy, crept to within nine points before they, too, began to toss away chances, just as Melbourne had done earlier in the game. Paul Dear grabbed two strong marks but missed twice, and Buckenara's shot hit the post.

The pressure was intense as Yeats (Melb) ran into an open goal and missed from thirty metres out. Then the Demons lost another chance when Eishold marked close-in on an angle but slipped as he took his kick from point-blank range and only a behind resulted. Finally, Buckenara ran into an open goal to score for Hawthorn, who then trailed by three points with less than a minute to play. Melbourne persisted, and from the bounce Healy got the ball to Campbell for what should have been the 'sealer' but Campbell, in the clear and only thirty metres out, missed. Tuck's kick-in was marked by Schwab, who handballed to Langford. The big Hawk full-back boomed a kick towards Buckenara, who somehow became entangled with Grinter's legs and went to ground as the umpires whistle sounded for a free kick, fifty metres out from goal.

At that moment, although few on the field or in the crowd heard it, the VFL Park siren sounded. It continued to sound as Demon ruckman Jim Stynes frantically tried to pick up an opponent and in doing so committed the blunder of the season when he cut across Buckenara's mark. The infringement did not put Buckenara off — the Hawk forward said later that he did not even see the incident — but umpire Howlett immediately, and correctly, ruled a fifteen metre penalty. Thus, instead of having a difficult kick from a long way out in a tricky breeze, Buckenara took his kick from just over thirty metres out — and made no mistake. The crowd of 71,298 sat stunned as the delighted Hawthorn team smothered Buckenara — but most eyes were on the bewildered Melbourne players as they walked sadly from the arena, their dreams ended in the most disheartening way.

An interesting point emerged after the match when it became clear that the umpires had not heard the siren: if Buckenara's kick had fallen short, and a Hawthorn player had picked up and goaled, would there have been a protest — or would the crowd have simply rioted?

The preliminary final undoubtedly took its toll on the Hawthorn team. Coach Allan Jeans declared that he had never seen his charges so exhausted. This certainly helped Carlton which was fit and fresh after a week's rest.

When the Carlton team burst onto the ground for the 1987 grand final, no fewer than seven faces were missing from the debacle of the previous year. The lessons had obviously been learned, and delicate changes to the team structure had the overall result of increasing the overall speed and skill of the side. Still remaining to be answered on grand final day, 1987 was the lingering question as to whether the Blues could handle extreme pressure.

With Dunstall, as expected, a scratching from the Hawthorn side, Pritchard took his place, but otherwise the personnel of both sides was as expected. Sartori (injured) and Evans (suspended after the second semi) were the most notable absentees for Carlton. Evans' one match suspension opened the way for Murphy to return to the side. Ironically, the one-match suspension of Murphy in 1986 had caused him to miss the grand final. The surprises, however, came when they lined up and it was seen that Carlton's Dorotich, normally a centre-half-back, was at full-forward, while, surprisingly, Rhys-Jones took Dorotich's spot on Hawthorn dangerman, Brereton. As usual, other tactical moves meant that neither side remotely resembled the positions shown in the *Football Record*.

It was the hottest grand final day since 1961, coincidentally the year of Hawthorn's first VFL flag, and the game itself certainly hotted-up early. Before the ball was even bounced, Johnston drew the umpire's attention to an extra Hawthorn player in the square and instead of the traditional roar for the opening bounce, the roar came as Johnston took a free kick. Hunter, marking from Johnston's kick, just missed, but a minute later Johnston received another free and posted the opening goal. In doubt during the week after injuring his knee at training, Johnston was the inspiration Carlton needed. After four minutes, he was reported for striking Di-Pierdomenico but his first quarter effort had much to do with Carlton asserting itself.

At the twelve minute mark, Johnston added his second and Hunter got another a few minutes later as the Blues stretched their lead to 3.4, to Hawthorn's two meagre behinds.

Somehow, though, Hawthorn came back and in the dying minutes of the term booted four goals — Kennedy (two), Platten and DiPierdomenico — an effort that stunned Carlton. Despite having almost all of the play, Carlton suddenly found itself behind and might well have asked what more it had to do against a side such as Hawthorn.

The early brilliance of Carlton's Hunter had indirectly helped Hawthorn back into the game. Kennedy, Hunter's opponent, was moved up forward and scored two quick goals. Other changes were forced upon the Hawks when Morris went off injured and, four minutes into the second term, a groggy Tuck was also assisted from the ground. Tuck had done an excellent job blanketing Bradley, one of Carlton's prime-movers, and his presence was sorely missed during a danger period for Hawthorn. In addition Brereton was in dismal form, dropping marks, fumbling and running the wrong way.

Nevertheless, the crowd expected Hawthorn to continue in the second term where it had left off in the first and therefore it was a surprise when Carlton's Bradley goaled within a minute of the resumption, followed soon after by a sequence of Hawthorn mistakes which let Dorotich in for another. The game then settled down into a hard slogging affair with neither side able to gain the ascendency. Finally, ten minutes before half-time, Carlton took a risk by resting Madden on the bench after he had run on the ball since the start. Dorotich came into the ruck, and the Blues gained a bonus when, through strong play, he forced the ball forward for Kernahan to goal and the teams went in at half-time with Carlton, having kept Hawthorn goalless during the quarter, leading by eleven points and confident it could break Hawthorn in the third term. The Hawks were obviously tiring in the heat after the exertion of the Preliminary Final.

After two minutes of the second half, however, Curran goaled for Hawthorn — his fifth shot for goal for a reward of 1.3 — reducing the margin to four points. Tuck, back in the fray, was a driving force for Hawthorn and a brilliant piece of play set up a goal for Kennedy. But Carlton seemed to have the answers, and goals to Kernahan, Bradley and Meldrum gave them a comfortable margin. Greg Dear's goal at the nineteen minute mark gave Hawthorn supporters some heart but Bradley replied moments later and it was apparent at the last change that not only did Carlton players look fresher, they *were* fresher. Hawthorn now could only hope that an aggressive opening to the last quarter would lead to a couple of quick goals. Those hopes were not realised. The Blues burst from the centre at the first three bounces for goals to Gleeson, Naley — after a thirty-metre dash — and Kernahan in the first six minutes, stretching the margin to thirty-five points.

When McKenzie added another four minutes later, the game was all but over and Hawthorn's task hopeless. Murphy goaled again for Carlton at the twenty-two minute mark and Hawthorn had only late goals from Pritchard and Collins to show for the quarter. Tension had long been replaced by anticipation in the Carlton camp.

At the siren, the Blues had well and truly answered the doubters and their thirty-three point victory was a just reward for commitment to the team game-plan. For Carlton, which had few poor players, none performed better than Rhys-Jones, long recognised as a 'bad boy', but whose brilliant, disciplined performance completely eclipsed Hawthorn's champion forward Brereton. Rhys-Jones, whose opponent in the 1986 grand final had won the Norm Smith Medal, answered a few critics of his own when he was awarded the 1987 medal.

This match resulted in Carlton extending its premiership record to fifteen, one ahead of Essendon, and it was the ninth grand final umpired by Ian Robinson, who then announced his retirement.

RESULTS

SEPTEMBER 5—QUALIFYING FINAL

	1st	2nd	3rd	Final
Hawthorn	5 . 7	9 . 10	16 . 13	23 . 18 (156)
Sydney Swans	2 . 4	5 . 7	7 . 9	8 . 9 (57)

VFL Park — Umpires—Sawers, Dore
Attendance—47,752 — Gate—not available

BEST — (Haw) DiPierdomenico, Buckenara, Morris, Brereton, Collins
(Syd) Mitchell, Williams, Capper, Bolton, Morwood
GOALS — (Haw) Brereton (6), Buckenara (5), Dunstall (5), Russo (2), DiPierdomenico (2), Kennedy, Tuck, Schwab
(Syd) Capper (4), Mitchell, Bayes, Healy, Wright

SEPTEMBER 6—ELIMINATION FINAL

	1st	2nd	3rd	Final
Melbourne	3 . 6	9 . 11	16 . 16	22 . 26 (158)
North Melbourne	3 . 2	4 . 4	4 . 8	5 . 10 (40)

MCG — Umpires—Robinson, Clayton
Attendance—72,628 — Gate—not available

BEST — (Melb) Flower, Stynes, Yeats, Wight, Jackson, Bailey
(NM) Larkin, Mossop, McCann, Harris, Demetriou
GOALS — (Melb) Flower (5), Williams (3), Dean (3), Campbell (3), Jackson (3), Stynes (2), Richards, Viney, Bailey
(NM) P. Krakouer (2), Hepburn, S. Smith, Steele

SEPTEMBER 13—FIRST SEMI-FINAL

	1st	2nd	3rd	Final
Melbourne	2 . 4	10 . 13	17 . 18	21 . 23 (149)
Sydney Swans	3 . 3	6 . 6	8 . 12	10 . 13 (73)

MCG — Umpires—Cameron, Howlett
Attendance—80,292 — Gate—not available

BEST — (Melb) Stretch (BOG), Lovett, Yeats, Flower, Jackson, Greg Healy, Eishold, Dean, O'Dwyer
(Syd) Gerard Healy, Mitchell, Williams, Bolton, Carter, Browning
GOALS — (Melb) Flower (4), Healy (3), Campbell (3), Yeats (2), Viney (2), Stretch (2), Wilson, Williams, Dean, Stynes, Jackson
(Syd) Healy (2), Carroll (2), Morwood (2), Williams, Scott, Coleman, Wright

SEPTEMBER 12—SECOND SEMI-FINAL

	1st	2nd	3rd	Final
Carlton	1 . 2	2 . 11	6 . 12	11 . 14 (80)
Hawthorn	3 . 2	6 . 2	9 . 3	10 . 5 (65)

VFL Park — Umpires—Clayton, Sawers
Attendance—64,333 — Gate—not available

BEST —	(Carl)	Naley (BOG), Alvin, Silvagni, Hunter, Aitken, Johnston, Madden
	(Haw)	Platten, Tuck, Langford, Kennedy, Ayres, Schwab
GOALS —	(Carl)	Kernahan (3), Evans (2), Johnston, Hunter, Naley, Sartori, Madden, McKenzie
	(Haw)	Dunstall (2), Platten (2), DiPierdomenico, Buckenara, Loveridge, Brereton, Curran, Kennedy

SEPTEMBER 19—PRELIMINARY FINAL

	1st	2nd	3rd	Final	
Hawthorn	1 . 4	3 . 6	7 . 8	11 . 14	(80)
Melbourne	2 . 3	6 . 10	10 . 12	10 . 18	(78)

VFL Park — Umpires—Robinson, Howlett
Attendance—71,298 — Gate—not available

BEST —	(Haw)	Buckenara (BOG), Schwab, Tuck, Russo, Langford, Ayres
	(Melb)	Jackson, Wight, Viney, Hughes, Spalding, Healy, Chiron
GOALS —	(Haw)	Buckenara (5), Jencke, Morris, Brereton, Curran, Kennedy, Pritchard
	(Melb)	Jackson (3), Grinter (2), Wilson (2), Viney, Dean, Stynes

SEPTEMBER 26—GRAND FINAL

	1st	2nd	3rd	Final	
Carlton	3 . 5	6 . 8	10 . 11	15 . 14	(104)
Hawthorn	4 . 2	4 . 9	7 . 13	9 . 17	(71)

MCG — Umpires—Robinson, Sawers
Attendance—92,754 — Gate—not available

BEST —	(Carl)	Rhys-Jones (BOG), Johnston, Alvin, Aitken, Naley, Madden, Hunter, Silvagni
	(Haw)	Langford, DiPierdomenico, G. Dear, Tuck, Collins, Ayres
GOALS —	(Carl)	Kernahan (3), Bradley (3), Johnston (2), Dorotich, Gleeson, Murphy, Hunter, Naley, McKenzie, Meldrum
	(Haw)	Kennedy (3), Curran, Collins, Pritchard, Platten, DiPierdomenico, G. Dear

NORM SMITH MEDAL—D. Rhys-Jones (Carlton)

GRAND FINAL TEAMS

Carlton	B	D. Glascott	S. Silvagni	I. Aitken
	HB	T. Alvin	D. Rhys-Jones	P. Dean
	C	S. Robertson	C. Bradley	M. Kennedy
	HF	R. Dennis	S. Kernahan (c)	K. Hunter
	F	M. Naley	J. Dorotich	P. Meldrum
	Ruck	J. Madden	W. Johnston	F. Murphy
	Int.	A. Gleeson	W. McKenzie	
	Coach	R. Walls		
Hawthorn	B	A. Collins	C. Mew	G. Ayres
	HB	R. Jencke	C. Langford	J. Kennedy
	C	R. DiPierdomenico	M. Tuck (c)	R. Greene
	HF	G. Buckenara	D. Brereton	R. Morris
	F	P. Curran	P. Dear	P. Russo
	Ruck	G. Dear	P. Schwab	J. Platten
	Int.	P. Abbott	D. Pritchard	
	Coach	A. Jeans		

1988

The big shock leading up to the commencement of season 1988 was the serious illness of Hawthorn premiership coach, Allan Jeans. A minor brain haemorrhage forced Jeans to stand down from the coaching position for twelve months, and Hawthorn caused a mild surprise by appointing the club's General Manager, Alan Joyce, to take over the coaching reins. Joyce had captain-coached VFA club Preston to successive flags in 1968-69, and had coached with some success in Western Australia.

The change in coaches, however, seemed to have little effect on Hawthorn, and the club was the pacemaker throughout 1988. It finished comfortably on top of the ladder with nineteen wins and only three defeats, one of those at the hands of Carlton in the round one grand final replay. The Hawks' only other losses were at the hands of Melbourne (whom they convincingly defeated in the return game) and the Sydney Swans.

Collingwood, which climbed from twelfth in 1987, took second spot with fifteen wins, six losses and one tied game. The Magpies showed a development in character which had been missing from so many of its sides since the famous 1958 premiership. The change in attitude was attributed to the coaching of former Hawthorn champion Leigh Matthews.

The Magpies were in the top three for nearly all of the twenty-two rounds, and although they never looked likely to overhaul Hawthorn, they always seemed a step ahead of Carlton, whose fifteen-seven record was good enough for third spot but left fans feeling that the Blues were slightly vulnerable. The most troubling feature of their season, perhaps, was the inability to string together long sequences of wins — they had runs of seven and eight in 1987 — which had characterised their play in their premiership year. Two lots of four in a row was the Blues' best in 1988.

Melbourne eventually gained fifth spot after an amazingly bad run towards the end of the season when, after a 69 point thrashing at the hands of Hawthorn, the Demons lost the next five games on end. This threw the race for fourth and fifth spot into total confusion. After twenty-one rounds, only one game separated fourth (West Coast Eagles) from eighth (Sydney Swans), and the smart money was on Essendon to replace either Melbourne, which had to face Carlton in the last round, or the Eagles, which had to face Footscray at the Western Oval. Indeed, after the Demons caused an upset on the Saturday by downing Carlton to secure a finals' spot, the press speculated that the Footscray versus Eagles game on the Sunday could have the following results. If Footscray won by less than thirty points, the Eagles would take fifth spot or if Footscray won by more than sixty points, then Footscray would go in. Finally, if Footscray won by forty-one to forty-eight points, then

Essendon would go in. In the event, in a low-scoring game, the Eagles triumphed by 7.11 to 3.11 and thus made the finals for the first time.

Of the remainder, Essendon, with a superior percentage to Melbourne but a win less, finished sixth. Their twelve wins gave them the same result as the Swans who disappointed their supporters with poor form late in the season. Footscray (eleven wins) was eighth, followed by an erratic Geelong (ten wins) whose week to week form varied between unbeatable and lamentable.

The West Coast Eagles impressed many Victorian fans with their gutsy performance in the elimination final. For the entire first half, the Eagles outplayed, outbumped and out-thought a disappointing Melbourne. The Eagles continually had first use of the ball and made the Demons look like the side that had won only one of its last six games.

Even with rain lashing the ground for the first part of the opening term, the Demons — noted mud-runners — still did not look to be in the race. O'Dwyer, carrying an injury, became a permanent forward pocket and his opposite number for the Eagles, Keene, was a dominant player. Only Johnson and Stretch kept Melbourne in it for the first half. The Eagles went in at the break with a handy twenty-two point lead.

However, the move of Wight from defence into attack brought results early in the third quarter, the big Demon goaling twice at the eight and ten minute-marks. Then, with Jackson's pace a vital asset, Melbourne slammed on four more in the slippery conditions to grab the lead for the first time. A magnificent fifty-five metre goal from Johnson put them fourteen points up at the last change.

Whether this lead would be enough, with the Eagles having last use of a strong wind, was debatable, particularly when skipper Glendinning cut loose with three successive goals in a 'purple patch' half way through the last quarter. Melbourne, through sheer determination, bounced back and goals to Williams and Lovell snatched back the lead. As the game entered its final minutes, a great fifty metre goal by Hart looked to have sealed the game for the Eagles. But at the thirty minute mark, Spalding marked close to goal for Melbourne. Demon supporters groaned as his shot registered a behind. One minute later, another Melbourne attack saw Williams feed out a brilliant handball to Lyon, whose accurate snap from twenty metres out grabbed back the lead for Melbourne with forty seconds left on the clock. However, the heart-attacks were not over for the meagre crowd of 43,438 (lowest on record for an elimination final). The Eagles broke away from the centre bounce and with the last kick of the day, Wrenstead's running shot from forty metres out veered away for a behind and the Demons were home by two points.

In the qualifying final, Carlton became the first team to register 100 wins over Collingwood. Carlton broke from the centre so quickly, especially in the first half, that often their big marking forwards, Sartori, Kernahan and Dorotich, were given the luxury of being able to contest one out with the Collingwood backs who sorely missed the injured Crosisca. The Magpies left out the tall Fellowes who, in retrospect, may have been a better bet against Carlton's giant ruckman Madden, who was too tall for Manson and Cloke. Madden's dominance at the bounces gave Carlton dynamo Johnston not only continual use of the ball but best-on-ground status as he demolished three opponents: McGuane, Morwood and Brown.

Carlton raced to a thirty-nine point lead at the first change and never looked in any danger, even when Glascott was carried off five minutes into the third quarter. The only minor tremor, perhaps, came when Taylor broke away from Silvagni in the second term to register four goals but the Blues full-back fought back well enough to take the honours on the day.

Millane, the Magpies' most consistent player during the season, was reported and subsequently suspended for three weeks. However, an ankle injury sustained during the game may have made him unavailable for the first semi anyway.

A sensational pre-bounce brawl, in which Melbourne's Stretch was knocked out, marked the opening of the Melbourne versus Collingwood first semi-final.

The Magpies brought in Fellowes, who won well in the ruck duels but lost out to O'Dwyer around the ground where the big red-headed Irishman's marking gave Melbourne much-needed impetus.

Collingwood, trailing by twenty-three points at half-time after a brilliant second term by Melbourne, shuffled the side around. Banks went from centre half-forward to the half-back flank on the brilliant Lyon, Manson went to centre half-forward and Morwood took Spalding at centre half back. These and other moves brought some results. The Magpies trailed by only twelve points at three-quarter time and looked to have a chance.

Melbourne, however, finished the stronger. Newport had tagged Daicos all day and was probably beaten by the Magpie champion, but he had limited Daicos' effectiveness and now featured in two pieces of play which sealed the game for Melbourne. In the first, Newport raced through the centre and booted the ball high up forward where it eluded three Magpie defenders and bounced at right angles for a goal. Then he slipped away to take a pass from Healy and goaled again from fifty metres out. Melbourne, with its thirteen point win, advanced to its second successive preliminary final, whilst the Magpies, publicly castigated by coach Matthews as having 'three or four who took a sideways step' retired to lick their wounds for another year.

Carlton — still missing Gleeson and now with an additional casualty in Glascott — suffered another blow ten minutes into the second semi when their matchwinner, Johnston, was solidly met by Ayres and was carried from the ground with broken ribs. In atrocious conditions, Carlton was struggling and despite first use of a strong wind, was limited to only two goals (both in time-on) in the first term.

The Hawks showed how it should be done with six majors when their turn came to kick with the wind. Ace forwards Dunstall and Brereton were not, this time, the catalysts. It was Kennedy who was dominant, first hitting the post, then threading through a miraculous goal and finding Dunstall for another before seeing his opponent, Aitken, taken off.

In contrast to the week before, Carlton's forward set-up proved too top-heavy for the conditions. Kernahan, Sartori and Dorotich found it difficult to compete for the greasy ball once it hit the ground which it did with monotonous regularity in the shocking conditions.

Kernahan, in addition, found inaccuracy a problem and had four shots, two of them within easy range going out of bounds, before registering his first goal in the third term. The move of Silvagni from full-back to full-forward at half time, however, threatened Hawthorn's dominance for a brief period. He missed a 'sitter' early but gave the Blues a target and, after Murphy soccered one through, Silvagni got another to cut the Hawks' nineteen point lead to a mere six. Kernahan hit the post, but followed with his first goal, and the Blues had hit the front.

However, the comeback was short-lived. Langford moved back onto Silvagni, Mew took Kernahan and the Hawks tightened up to level the scores at the last change. That effectively sealed the game with the knowledge that they were kicking with a strong wind in the final term. And so it proved, with the Hawks twenty-one point victory taking them to their sixth successive grand final.

Carlton, with Johnston out, caused a mild surprise by omitting veteran Buckley from the preliminary final line-up. Melbourne, pumped up, bolted in the first term with six goals to one but Kernahan, smothered by Duursma early, bounced back in the second term with three long goals and the Blues, with 8.3 for the quarter, went in at the long interval with a two point lead.

With the game very evenly poised, it was perhaps a blessing for the Demons when rain poured down midway through the third term just as they had broken away with the benefit of the strong wind.

Melbourne was brilliant in the third quarter with Duursma again well on top of Kernahan and interchange player Flintoff coming on to put Carlton's first-half matchwinner, Naley, right out of business. Spurred by a mammoth goal from Lyon which travelled over seventy metres, the Demons booted seven for the term to have a stranglehold on the game at the last change. Their thirty-nine point lead was going to be almost impossible to pull back in the greasy conditions. Still, the Blues were not without a chance when Kernahan's fourth goal brought them to within nineteen points midway through the last term. Another goal may have made matters interesting, and the Blues did indeed have a chance to score again, but the slippery conditions defeated an intelligent piece of play between Kernahan and Silvagni and the Melbourne defence swept the ball away.

Melbourne's use of a fresh man (interchange player Williams) paid dividends as he contributed a valuable goal against the wind but it was Jackson's second for the term, at the nineteen minute mark, which sealed the result. Given a free kick thirty metres out, his shot appeared to hit the post but was given as a goal, his fifth for the day.

The Carlton comeback petered out and Melbourne's accurate 19.6 gave them a twenty-two point leeway at the final siren, taking them, amidst scenes of incredible emotion, into their first grand final since 1964.

The euphoria, however, dissipated slightly two days later when the Demons' number one ruckman, O'Dwyer, was suspended for a week, putting him out of the big game. This severely affected Melbourne's tactics for the Grand Final, but, more importantly, allowed Hawthorn to play Abbott on the forward line rather than in defence, with devastating results.

Hawthorn's sixth successive grand final (only one behind Melbourne's record seven from 1954-60) was also skipper Michael Tuck's ninth, one behind the record shared jointly by A. Collier, G. Coventry, R.S. Reynolds and W. Hutchinson. It was also the veteran Tuck's 360th VFL game.

Hawthorn lined up virtually as selected with Schwab on Wilson the only real tag. Melbourne, with limited options, sprung a few surprises with Stretch lining up at full-back, Newport tagging Buckenara and Hughes in the ruck. Platten, Hawthorn's dynamic rover, was paid the compliment of having both Melbourne rovers on the ball with him. The move backfired as it left Ayres to virtually roam free across the half-back and centre line.

After two minutes, Schwab, accepting a delightful handpass from Morrissey, opened Hawthorn's scoring with a left foot goal. Stynes contested the bounce for Melbourne, remaining in the ruck for the rest of the day whilst Hughes went back into defence to pick up Abbott. Minutes later, the skies opened and rain poured down in torrents, raising Demon hopes. Hawthorn's Wittman was assisted off with a dislocated elbow at the ten-minute mark and Melbourne immediately scored its first, Williams converting after a pass from Yeats. Both teams had missed easy chances in the slippery conditions and Williams' goal put the Demons a point ahead — the first and only time during the day that they were to be in front.

Brereton, who seemed to be involved in everything, marked strongly in front of

Duursma and goaled from fifty metres out. From the resulting centre-bounce, a furious fight, in which almost every player was involved, saw Buckenara reported.

Brereton added his second goal after marking a long kick by Platten fifteen metres out, and two minutes later, Abbott, aided by a foolish fifty metre penalty, scored again to give Hawthorn an eighteen point lead. Hawthorn's tackling and smothering was tremendous but there was no pressure on Williams in Melbourne's next trip forward as he ran into an open goal and fired from twenty metres out. As if to give an indication that this was not to be Melbourne's day, he missed badly and Hawthorn took a seventeen point advantage into the first break.

Now kicking with the wind, Melbourne got away to a good start in the second term when Healy accepted a chip pass from Grinter and goaled with a long torpedo punt. Rather than signalling a Demon revival, Healy's goal merely served to signal a Hawthorn onslaught.

A lucky free to Dunstall brought the Hawk full-forward his first goal before Brereton brought the crowd to its feet. A poor kick-out by Hughes gave the Hawthorn centre half-forward a difficult free kick hard against the boundary line. A brilliantly executed banana-kick bisected the goals superbly and even die-hard Melbourne supporters began to think that Hawthorn could do no wrong.

Moments later, a brilliant tap-on by Morrissey from the base of the pack was accepted by DiPierdomenico, who goaled on the left foot from a difficult angle. The Hawks were on fire as ruckman Abbott crumbed the ball like a rover off the top of the pack, and ran in to kick another, Hawthorn's fourth in nine minutes.

The most revealing play of the game came soon afterwards when Hawthorn, without ever gaining a clean possession, moved the ball nearly fifty metres goalward through sheer physical force and superb pressure. The Demons seemed to have no answer as wholesale changes had little or no effect. At the nineteen minute mark Dunstall marked a pass from Platten thirty-five metres out and kicked Hawthorn's fifth against a strong wind.

A brilliant smother by Morrissey led to the next goal, when he took the ball almost from the boot of Stretch, and ran in to an open goal to extend the Hawthorn lead to fifty points. Melbourne fumbled three clear chances before the siren sent the teams in with the Hawks forty-nine points up and looking safe.

That was, indeed, how it turned out with the game proving something of a replay of the Hawthorn-Essendon grand final in 1983. Melbourne again managed the first goal of the quarter when play recommenced, but Dunstall scored twice within five minutes, the first after marking alone when clever play by Brereton led the pack under the ball, and the second after a perfectly executed pass from Buckenara. Duursma, clearly outpointed by Brereton, went from the frying-pan into the fire by moving to full-back onto Dunstall as Hughes came out to centre half-back, and the Demons lifted for a short period. Their failure to cap-off promising moves, however, saw them make little impression on the massive Hawthorn lead as Williams hit the post from fifteen metres out. Williams did, at least, kick his second a few minutes later but Hawthorn responded quickly with a goal to Kennedy, the second for the day obtained through the aid of a fifty metre penalty.

Melbourne fought hard but Febey and Johnson missed before Lyon marked strongly and scored his second. Hawthorn, holding all the aces, replied through Abbott one minute later and Melbourne's 'reward' for its best quarter of football for the match was to go into the last term still trailing by fifty-seven points.

As a contest, the game had been over from perhaps as early as quarter-time. Hawthorn ruthlessly crushed any remaining resistance in a superb last term, which opened with a goal to Brereton in the first minute, and ended with Dunstall's sixth and seventh goals in time-on. The Hawks, in fact, kept the foot on the accelerator right to the end, and four of their eight last-quarter goals were scored during the time-on period.

Abbott's long 'bomb' from fifty metres took the margin to eighty-six points, three more than the previous record set in 1983, and, although desperate to avoid such a dubious mention in the record-books, the Demons were disorganised and dispirited as Dunstall stretched the margin to a massive ninety-six points. The final siren, mercifully, ended the slaughter.

Despite a depressed fracture of the cheekbone, Hawk Gary Ayres became the first player to win two Norm Smith medals, but Hawthorn did not have a poor player. Eighteen goals — Dunstall seven, Abbott six, Brereton five — from three forwards trebled the goalscoring by the entire Melbourne team. Comparisons, of course, tend to become meaningless but it is certain that Hawthorn over the period 1982-88 deserves to rank with the greatest teams of all time. During this period, the Hawks finished third, first, second, second, first, second and first, winning 132, drawing one, and losing 43 matches from 176 starts, a record that bears comparison with any of the great teams of the past.

For coach Alan Joyce, it was also an entry in the record books. He resigned shortly after the grand final, handing back the coaching job to Allan Jeans who had recovered from illness. Joyce thus joined Geelong's Charlie Clymo (1931) as one of only two coaches to win a VFL flag at a single attempt.

RESULTS

SEPTEMBER 3—ELIMINATION FINAL

	1st	2nd	3rd	Final
Melbourne	1 . 1	2 . 3	8 . 5	11 . 7 (73)
West Coast Eagles	2 . 4	5 . 7	5 . 9	10 . 11 (71)

VFL Park — Umpires—Cameron, Sheehan
Attendance—43,438 — Gate—not available

BEST — (Melb) Johnson, Stretch, Healy, Spalding, Duursma, Lyon, Lovett, Stynes
(Eagles) Malaxos, Worsfold, Glendinning, Keene, Miles, McKenna, Lockyer
GOALS — (Melb) Jackson (2), Wight (2), Lovell (2), Lyon, Spalding, Healy, Williams, Johnson
(Eagles) Glendinning (5), Lockyer (2), Hart, Langdon, Malaxos

SEPTEMBER 4—QUALIFYING FINAL

	1st	2nd	3rd	Final
Carlton	7 . 3	10 . 8	16 . 9	22 . 13 (145)
Collingwood	1 . 0	9 . 4	12 . 17	16 . 11 (107)

MCG — Umpires—Russo, Carey
Attendance—83,032 — Gate—not available

BEST — (Carl) Johnston, Madden, Sartori, Blackwell, Meldrum, Kennedy, Aitken, Murphy
(Coll) Daicos, Shaw, Morwood, Starcevich, Banks, Millane
GOALS — (Carl) Sartori (5), Dorotich (3), Meldrum (3), Kernahan (3), Murphy (3), Naley (2), Evans, Bradley, Alvin
(Coll) Taylor (4), Starcevich (4), Manson (2), Shaw (2), Daicos (2), Millane, Barwick

SEPTEMBER 11—FIRST SEMI FINAL

	1st	2nd	3rd	Final	
Melbourne	3 . 8	8 . 11	10 . 13	13 . 17	(95)
Collingwood	2 . 5	5 . 6	9 . 7	12 . 10	(82)

MCG — Umpires—Carey, Sheehan
Attendance—87,407 — Gate—not available

BEST — (Melb) O'Dwyer, Lovett, Lovell, Grinter, Yeats, Lyon
(Coll) Daicos, Taylor, Shaw, McGuane, Saunders, Starcevich, Kerrison
GOALS — (Melb) Wight (3), Wilson (2), Lyons (2), Stynes (2), Newport (2), Spalding, O'Dwyer
(Coll) Taylor (6), McGuane (2), McKeown (2), Wright, Ryan

SEPTEMBER 10—SECOND SEMI FINAL

	1st	2nd	3rd	Final	
Hawthorn	0 . 2	6 . 6	6 . 8	9 . 12	(66)
Carlton	2 . 5	3 . 5	6 . 8	6 . 9	(45)

VFL Park — Umpires—Rich, Cameron
Attendance—60,052 — Gate—not available

BEST — (Haw) Platten, G. Dear, Tuck, Buckenara, Ayres, Mew, Collins, Kennedy, Brereton
(Carl) Naley, Blackwell, Bradley, Rhys-Jones, Alvin, Madden
GOALS — (Haw) Brereton (3), Wittman, Buckenara, Dunstall, DiPierdomenico, Kennedy, Greene
(Carl) Naley (2), Silvagni, Dorotich, Murphy, Kernahan

SEPTEMBER 17—PRELIMINARY FINAL

	1st	2nd	3rd	Final	
Melbourne	6 . 3	9 . 4	16 . 5	19 . 6	(120)
Carlton	1 . 3	9 . 6	10 . 8	14 . 14	(98)

VFL Park — Umpires—Castles, Sawers
Attendance—68,516 — Gate—not available

BEST — (Melb) Lyon, Jackson, Johnson, Lovett, Healy, Stynes, Wight, Flintoff, Stretch
(Carl) Bradley, Kernahan, Naley, Gleeson, Madden, Dunlop
GOALS — (Melb) Jackson (5), Wight (4), Lyon (3), Lovell, Williams, Flintoff, O'Dwyer, Wilson, Yeats, Healy
(Carl) Sartori (4), Kernahan (4), Murphy (2), Bradley, Naley, Gleeson, Blackwell

SEPTEMBER 24—GRAND FINAL

	1st	2nd	3rd	Final	
Hawthorn	4 . 4	10 . 9	14 . 16	22 . 20	(152)
Melbourne	1 . 5	2 . 8	5 . 14	6 . 20	(56)

MCG — Umpires—Sheehan, Cameron
Attendance—93,754 — Gate—not available

BEST — (Haw) Ayres, Brereton, Platten, Collins, Abbott, Dunstall, Hall, DiPierdomenico, Morrissey
(Melb) Stynes, Grinter, Lovell, Johnson
GOALS — (Haw) Dunstall (7), Abbott (6), Brereton (5), Schwab, Kennedy, Morrissey, DiPierdomenico
(Melb) Lyon (2), Williams (2), Healy, Johnson

NORM SMITH MEDAL—G. Ayres (Hawthorn)

GRAND FINAL TEAMS

Hawthorn	B	A. Collins	C. Langford	G. Ayres
	HB	S. Maginness	C. Mew	P. Schwab
	C	R. DiPierdomenico	G. Buckenara	A. Hall
	HF	C. Wittman	D. Brereton	P. Abbott
	F	J. Kennedy	J. Dunstall	D. Pritchard
	Ruck	G. Dear	M. Tuck (c)	J. Platten
	Int.	R. Greene	J. Morrissey	
	Coach	A. Joyce		
Melbourne	B	A. Johnson	D. Hughes	R. Grinter
	HB	S. Stretch	J. Duursma	B. Lovett
	C	G. Yeats	B. Wilson	D. Williams
	HF	G. Lyon	E. Spalding	S. Newport
	F	D. Flintoff	S. Wight	R. Jackson
	Ruck	J. Stynes	A. Lovell	G. Healy (c)
	Int.	S. Febey	T. Viney	
	Coach	J. Northey		

APPENDIX

GROUNDS ON WHICH FINALS WERE PLAYED 1897-1988

	Semi Finals	*Prelim. Finals*	*Finals*	*Grand Finals*	*Total*
MCG	166	54	15	76	311
VFL Park	34	14	—	—	48
Princes Oval	9	3	—	3	15
St. Kilda	2	1	2	1	6
Fitzroy	4	—	—	—	4
Sth. Melbourne	3	—	1	—	4
East Melbourne	2	—	1	—	3
Victoria Park	2	—	—	—	2
Essendon	1	—	—	—	1
Corio Oval (Geelong)	1	—	—	—	1

COMPLETE RECORD OF FINALS APPEARANCES 1897-1988

(5th recorded since 1972 only)

	1st	*2nd*	*3rd*	*4th*	*5th*	*Total*
Collingwood	13	23	17	14	1	68
Carlton	15	11	15	14	2	57
Essendon	14	12	6	10	6	48
Geelong	6	4	13	14	1	38
Richmond	10	12	3	7	—	32
Fitzroy	8	5	9	6	1	29
Melbourne	12	4	7	5	—	28
Sth. Melb./Syd. Swans	3	8	6	6	1	24
Hawthorn	7	5	4	—	—	16
Nth. Melbourne	2	4	4	4	2	16
St. Kilda	1	3	5	6	—	15
Footscray	1	1	3	6	2	13
West Coast Eagles	—	—	—	—	1	1
Brisbane Bears	—	—	—	—	—	0

RECORD OF VFL TEAMS WHILST IN VFA 1877-1925

	1st	*2nd*	*3rd*	*4th*	*Total*
Nth. Melbourne	6	8	7	3	24
Footscray	9	5	3	2	19
Geelong	7	3	4	2	16
Sth. Melbourne	5	6	2	2	15
Carlton	2	4	5	2	13
Essendon	4	3	2	2	11
Melbourne	—	4	—	5	9
Richmond	2	3	3	1	9
Fitzroy	1	1	1	3	6
Collingwood	1	1	—	—	2
Hawthorn	—	—	—	1	1
St. Kilda	—	—	—	—	0

COMPLETE RECORD OF GAMES PLAYED IN ALL VFL FINALS

	W	L	Tied	Total	Most Consecutive Wins	Most Consecutive Losses
Collingwood	60	81	3	144	6	7
Carlton	54	59	2	115	8	5
Essendon	53	40	2	95	7	6
Richmond	44	27	1	72	7	3
Geelong	25	39	1	65	4	7
Melbourne	38	23	2	63	6	3
Fitzroy	34	25	—	59	6	4
Sth. Melb./Syd. Swans	18	27	—	45	4	7
Hawthorn	29	16	—	45	5	2
Nth. Melbourne	16	23	1	40	2	4
St. Kilda	11	16	—	27	2	3
Footscray	7	13	—	20	3	6
West Coast Eagles	—	1	—	1	—	1
Brisbane Bears	—	—	—	—	—	—

MOST CONSECUTIVE YEARS . . .

. . . IN FINALS			. . . IN GRAND FINAL	
Carlton	11	1978-88	5	1906-1910
Collingwood	15	1897-1911	6	1925-30
Essendon	6	1946-51, 1981-86	6	1946-51
Fitzroy	9	1898-1906	4	1903-06
Footscray	2	1953-54	1	1954 and 1961
Geelong	8	1962-69	3	1951-53
Hawthorn	7	1982-88	6	1983-88
Melbourne	11	1954-64	7	1954-60
Nth. Melbourne	7	1974-80	5	1974-78
Richmond	9	1927-35	4	1931-34
St. Kilda	4	1970-73	2	1965-66
Swans	6	1909-14	4	1933-36

MOST CONSECUTIVE YEARS . . .

. . . OUT OF FINALS			. . . OUT OF GRAND FINAL	
Carlton	6	1897-1902	12	1950-61
Collingwood	4	1940-44	12	1940-51
Essendon	13	1927-39	16	1925-40
Fitzroy	18	1925-42, 1961-78	44	1945-88
Footscray	13	1925-37	29	1925-53
Geelong	9	1941-49	27	1898-1924
Hawthorn	32	1925-56	36	1925-60
Melbourne	22	1965-86	25	1901-25
Nth. Melbourne	20	1925-44	25	1925-49
Richmond	19	1948-66	22	1945-66
St. Kilda	21	1940-60	51	1914-64
Swans	24	1946-49	43	1946-88

MOST FINALS SERIES WITHOUT WINNING THE PREMIERSHIP

20 Collingwood 1959-88* (total of 47 finals matches)
16 Carlton 1916-36
10 Geelong 1964-81*
9 Fitzroy 1947-86*
9 St. Kilda 1907-65
9 Swans 1934-87*

LONGEST PREMIERSHIP DROUGHTS

Seasons

69 St. Kilda 1897-65
55 Swans 1934-88*
50 Nth. Melbourne 1925-74
44 Fitzroy 1945-88*
36 Hawthorn 1925-60
34 Footscray 1955-88*
30 Collingwood 1959-88*
28 Geelong 1897-1924
25 Melbourne 1901-25
23 Richmond 1944-66
22 Carlton 1916-37
18 Essendon 1966-83

*Sequence may still continue

GREATEST RISES AND FALLS

Greatest Rise from one season to the next —

To Premiers	— Essendon 1946 from 8th 1945
	Hawthorn 1971 from 8th 1970
	Richmond 1980 from 8th 1979
To Runners-Up	— Collingwood 1977 from 12th 1976 (headed ladder in 1977)
	Melbourne 1954 from 11th 1953
	Footscray 1961 from 10th 1960
	Essendon 1908 from 8th (and last) 1907
To 3rd	— Melbourne 1987 from 11th 1986
	Collingwood 1945 from 10th 1944
	Footscray 1953 from 10th 1952
To 4th	— Fitzroy 1981 from 12th 1980
	Footscray 1938 from 11th 1937
	Fitzroy 1958 from 11th 1957
	Geelong 1976 from 11th 1975
	Nth. Melbourne 1985 from 11th 1984
To 5th (Final 5)	— Essendon 1972 from 11th 1971

Greatest Falls from one season to the next —

From Premiers	— Hawthorn 1961 to 9th 1962
	Essendon 1912 to 8th 1913 (out of 10 teams)
	Melbourne 1941 to 8th 1942
From Runners-Up	— Collingwood 1981 to 10th 1982
	Richmond 1982 to 10th 1983
	Sth. Melbourne 1936 to 9th 1937 (last 1938)
	Nth. Melbourne 1950 to 9th 1951
	Collingwood 1960 to 9th 1961
From 3rd	— St. Kilda 1939 to 11th 1940
	Nth. Melbourne 1983 to 11th 1984
	Fitzroy 1986 to 11th 1987
From 4th	— Melbourne 1950 to 12th 1951
	Geelong 1956 to 12th 1957
	Sth. Melbourne 1970 to 12th 1971
	Fitzroy 1979 to 12th 1980
	Footscray 1938 to 11th 1939
	Nth. Melbourne 1954 to 11th 1955
From 5th	— Collingwood 1975 to 12th 1976
	Nth. Melbourne 1987 to 11th 1988

- **UPS AND DOWNS —**
- Footscray 10th in 1950 rose to 4th in 1951, then dropped to 10th in 1952.
- Fitzroy 4th in 1979 dropped to 12th in 1980, then rose to 4th in 1981.

TEAMS REACHING FINALS WITH PERCENTAGE OF UNDER 100

Team	*Year*	%
Collingwood	1908	97.0
Melbourne	1915	99.2
Fitzroy	1916	81.6
Richmond	1916	89.9
Fitzroy	1917	86.4
St. Kilda	1918	92.2
Nth. Melbourne	1954	99.6 (3rd)
Carlton	1957	99.5
Nth. Melbourne	1958	92.7
Collingwood	1975	93.9
Footscray	1976	96.8
Nth. Melbourne	1985	97.9

Note — Only 4 teams competed in 1916, 6 in 1917, 8 in 1918, 9 in 1915 and 10 in 1908.

BROTHERS IN PREMIERSHIP SIDES

J. Dalton Fitzroy 1898; W. Dalton Fitzroy 1898-99
J. Grace Fitzroy 1898-99; M. Grace Fitzroy 1898-99, Carlton 1906-07
T. Collins Essendon 1897, 1901; M. Collins Essendon 1901
A. Leach Collingwood 1902-03; J. Leach Collingwood 1902
E. and G. Lockwood Collingwood 1902-03
L. Barker Fitzroy 1904-05; G. Barker Fitzroy 1905
J. Deas Fitzroy 1899; R. Deas Sth. Melbourne 1909
F. Hiskins Essendon 1901; A. Hiskins Sth. Melbourne 1909*
V. Belcher Sth. Melbourne 1909-18; A. Belcher Essendon 1912
R. F. Daykin Collingwood 1910; P. Daykin Carlton 1914-15**
H. James Richmond 1920-21; W. James Richmond 1920
R. Weatherill Richmond 1920-21; G. Weatherill Richmond 1920
S. Morris Richmond 1920; M. Morris Richmond 1921
C. Pannam Jnr. Collingwood 1917-19; A. Pannam Collingwood 1935-36
S. Coventry Collingwood 1927-28-29-30; G. Coventry 1927-28-29-30-35
A. and H. Collier Collingwood 1927-28-29-30-35-36
F. Murphy Collingwood 1927-28-29-30; L. Murphy Collingwood 1928-29-30
L. and H. Hardiman Geelong 1931-37
L. Metherell Geelong 1931; J. Metherell Geelong 1937
G. Strang Richmond 1932-34; D. Strang Richmond 1932
J. Baggott Richmond 1932-34; R. Baggott Melbourne 1939-40-41
E. Cordner Melbourne 1941; Don Cordner Melbourne 1941-48; Denis Cordner Melbourne 1948-55-56
R. Reynolds Essendon 1942-46-49-50; T. Reynolds Essendon 1942
H. Lambert Essendon 1946-49-50; C. Lambert Essendon 1946-50
M. Twomey Collingwood 1953-58; W. Twomey Collingwood 1953; P. Twomey Collingwood 1953***
R. Rose Collingwood 1953; W. Rose Collingwood 1953; K. Rose Collingwood 1958
L. and R. Richards Collingwood 1953
S. and P. Hay Hawthorn 1961
A. and S. Lord Geelong 1963
G. Cooper Hawthorn 1961; I. Cooper St. Kilda 1966****
B. Kekovich Carlton 1968; S. Kekovich Nth. Melbourne 1975
L. Matthews Hawthorn 1971-76-78-83; K. Matthews Hawthorn 1976
S. Madden Essendon 1984-85; J. Madden Carlton 1987

*Two other brothers — S. Hiskins (Sth. Melbourne 1914) and R. Hiskins (Carlton 1921) played in teams which were runners-up.
**A third brother, A.V. Daykin played in the Essendon 1908 side which was runner-up.
***Three brothers in the same premiership side (1953) is a VFL record.
****Both played in what was their team's first ever premiership.

FATHERS AND SONS IN PREMIERSHIP SIDES

Father	*Son(s)*
C. Pannam Snr. (Collingwood) 1902-03	C. Pannam Jnr. (Collingwood) 1917-19 A. Pannam (Collingwood) 1935-36
W.D. "Son" Thomas (Sth. Melbourne) 1909	L. Thomas (Sth. Melbourne) 1933

J. Howell Snr. (Sth. Melbourne)	J. Howell Jnr. (Carlton)
1918	1947
J. Howell Jnr. (Carlton)	S. Howell (Carlton)*
1947	1982
W. Twomey Snr. (Collingwood)	W. Twomey Jnr. (Collingwood)
1919	1953
	P. Twomey (Collingwood)
	1953
	M. Twomey (Collingwood)
	1953-58
C. May (Essendon)	W. May (Essendon)
1923-24	1949-50
G. Rawle (Essendon)	K. Rawle (Essendon)
1923-24	1946-49
R. Johnson Snr. (Melbourne)	R. Johnson Jnr. (Melbourne)
1926	1955-56-57-59-60
D. Strang (Richmond)	G. Strang (Richmond)
1932	1967-69
R. Emselle (Melbourne)	K. Emselle (Melbourne)
1939-40-41	1964
R. Barassi Snr. (Melbourne)	R. Barassi Jnr. (Melbourne)
1940	1955-56-57-59-60-64
E. Brown (Carlton)	V. Brown (Carlton)
1914-15	1945-47
S. Leehane (Carlton)	E. Leehane (Essendon)
1914	1942-46-49-50
Jack Cassin (Essendon)	John Cassin (Nth. Melbourne)
1946-49	1977
Sergio Silvagni (Carlton)	Stephen Silvagni (Carlton)
1968-70	1987

A father/son combination in J. McMurray Snr. (1921-25-26-27-28) and Jnr. (1948-49-50-53-54) has umpired VFL Grand Finals.

*Only instance of father/son/grandson in VFL Premiership team.

PLAYED IN PREMIERSHIP WITH DIFFERENT TEAMS

E. Drohan	Fitzroy 1898-99	Collingwood 1903
F. Caine	Carlton 1906-07	Essendon 1912
M. Grace	Fitzroy 1898-99	Carlton 1906-07
T. Fitzmaurice	Essendon 1923-24	Geelong 1925
K. Stackpole	Collingwood 1935-36	Fitzroy 1944
B. Diggins	Sth. Melbourne 1933	Carlton 1938
P. McLean	Melbourne 1964	Carlton 1968
J. Carney	Geelong 1931	Carlton 1938
G. Abbott	Geelong 1937	Essendon 1942-46
J. Martin	Essendon 1912	Fitzroy 1913
H. Edmonds	Collingwood 1929-30	Richmond 1934
C. Norris	Collingwood 1910	Fitzroy 1913-16

I. Stewart	St. Kilda 1966	Richmond 1973
B. Crosswell	Carlton 1968-70	Nth. Melbourne 1975-77
D. Wade	Geelong 1963	Nth. Melbourne 1975
B. Davis	Essendon 1962-65	Nth. Melbourne 1975
B. Rowlings	Hawthorn 1976	Richmond 1980
B. Wood	Richmond 1973-74	Essendon 1985

PREMIERSHIP AS CAPTAIN THEN AS NON-PLAYING COACH

Captain	*Coach*
P. Bentley Richmond 1932-34 (Playing Coach in 1934)	Carlton 1945-47
R. Hickey Geelong 1937 (Playing Coach)	Geelong 1951-52
R. Barassi Jnr. Melbourne 1964	Carlton 1968-70 Nth. Melbourne 1975-77
D. Parkin Hawthorn 1971	Hawthorn 1978 Carlton 1981-82

COACHED PREMIERS AND WOODEN SPOONERS

Premiers	*Wooden Spooners*
T. Jewell Richmond 1980	St. Kilda 1983-84 (12th) Richmond 1987 (14th)
N. Smith Melbourne 1955-56-57-59-60-64	Sth. Melbourne 1971 (12th)
R. Barassi Jnr. Carlton 1968-70, Nth. Melbourne 1975-77	Melbourne 1981 (12th)
C. Sutton Footscray 1954	Footscray 1967 (12th)
R. Hickey Geelong 1937-51-52	Geelong 1957-58 (12th)
D. Minogue Richmond 1920-21	Hawthorn 1927 (12th)

COACHED PREMIERSHIP WITH 2 CLUBS

J. Worrall Carlton 1906-07-08	Essendon 1911-12 Fitzroy 1922* (joint coach)
F.V. Hughes Richmond 1932	Melbourne 1939-40-41-48
R. Barassi Jnr. Carlton 1968-70	Nth. Melbourne 1975-77
A. Jeans St. Kilda 1966	Hawthorn 1983-86
D. Parkin Hawthorn 1978	Carlton 1981-82
P. Bentley Richmond 1934	Carlton 1945-47

*Only coach to win flags with 3 clubs.

MOST GRAND FINAL APPEARANCES*

Players

10 A. Collier Coll. 1926-39
G. Coventry Coll. 1920-37
R. Reynolds Ess. 1941-51 (inc. 2 in 1948)
W. Hutchison Ess. 1942-57 (inc. 2 in 1948)
9 H. Collier Coll. 1926-39
M. Tuck Hawthorn 1975-88

Umpires

10 J. Elder 1908-9-10-11-12-13-18-19-20-21
9 **I. Robinson 1973-74-77 (twice)-78-80-81-85-87
7 R. Scott 1929-35
I. Crapp 1898-1902, 1904-05
6 J. McMurray Jnr. 1948 (2)-49-50-53-54

8 R. Barassi Jnr. Melb. 1954-64
F. Adams Melb. 1954-64
J. Titus Rich. 1928-42
B. Crosswell Carl./N.Melb. 1968-77 (inc. 2 in 1977)

5 J. McMurray Snr. 1921, 1925-28
J. Crouch 1963-65-66-68-69
***W. Deller 1972-76-78-79-80

*Note — The deciding game for the premiership, although not necessarily a GRAND FINAL, is included in these totals.
**2 as sole umpire, remainder under 2 umpire system.
***1 as sole umpire, remainder under 2 umpire system.

Coaches

17 J. McHale Collingwood 1913-50
12 R. Reynolds Essendon 1939-60
11 F.V. Hughes Richmond/Melbourne 1927-48
10 T. Hafey Richmond/Collingwood/Geelong/Swans 1966-88

Player and/or Coach

20 J. McHale Collingwood 1903-50
17 R. Barassi Jnr. Melbourne/Carlton/Nth. Melbourne 1953-85
14 F.V. Hughes Richmond/Melbourne 1919-48
14 N. Smith Melbourne/Fitzroy/Sth. Melbourne 1935-72

WINNING COACHES RECORDS

Premier-ships	*Times In Finals*	*Years Coached*	*Coach*	*Team*	*Years*
8	27	38	J.J. McHale	Collingwood	1913-1950
6	12	23	N. Smith	Fitzroy	1949-1951
				Melbourne	1952-1967
				Sth. Melbourne	1969-1972
6	10	18	J. Worrall	Carlton	1902-1909
				Essendon	1911-1915
				Essendon	1917-1920
				Fitzroy (Joint Coach)	1922
5	13	19	F.V. Hughes	Richmond	1927-1932
				Melbourne	1933-1941
				Melbourne	1945-1948
4	14	23	T. Hafey	Richmond	1966-1976
				Collingwood	1977-1982
				Geelong	1983-1985
				Syd. Swans	1986-1988
4	16	22	R.S. Reynolds	Essendon	1939-1960
4	11	20	R. Barassi	Carlton	1965-1971
				Nth. Melbourne	1973-1980
				Melbourne	1981-1985
3	11	22	P. Bentley	Richmond	1934-1940
				Carlton	1941-1955

3	10	17	R. Hickey	Geelong	1932
				Geelong	1936-1940
				Geelong	1949-1959
3	8	18	J. Kennedy	Hawthorn	1960-1963
				Hawthorn	1967-1976
				Nth. Melbourne	1985-1988
3	15	23	A. Jeans	St. Kilda	1961-1976
				Hawthorn	1981-1987
3	8	12	D. Parkin	Hawthorn	1977-1980
				Carlton	1981-1985
				Fitzroy	1986-1988
2	8	20	D.T. Minogue	Richmond	1920-1925
				Hawthorn	1926-1927
				Carlton	1929-1934
				St. Kilda	1935-1936
				Fitzroy	1940-1942
2	7	13	A.E. Kyne	Collingwood	1951-1963
2	5	6	S.Q. Barker	Essendon	1922-1926
				Nth. Melbourne	1927
2	10	12	N. Clark	Carlton	1912
				Carlton	1914-1918
				Richmond	1919
				Carlton	1920-1922
				St. Kilda	1925-1926
2	5	7	P. Parratt	Fitzroy	1913-1916
				Fitzroy	1920-1921
				Carlton	1924
2	4	7	J. Coleman	Essendon	1961-1967
2	6	8	K. Sheedy	Essendon	1981-1988
1	5	8	R. Walls	Fitzroy	1981-1985
				Carlton	1986-1988
1	5	11	J. Dyer	Richmond	1941-1951
1	4	4	J. J. Bissett	Sth. Melbourne	1933-1936
1	4	6	R. Davis	Geelong	1960-1965
1	4	9	C. Sutton	Footscray	1951-1957
				Footscray	1967-1968
1	3	5	F. Hughson	Fitzroy	1943-1947
1	3	6	V. Belcher	Sth. Melbourne	1914-1915
				Fitzroy	1922-1924
				Fitzroy	1926-1927
1	3	3	C. Rankin	Geelong	1925-1927
1	2	2	H. Howson	Sth. Melbourne	1918-1919
1	2	4	A. E. Chadwick	Melbourne	1925-1927
				Hawthorn	1929
1	3	5	C. Ricketts	Sth. Melbourne	1909-1912
				Richmond	1914-1916
1	1	3	B. J. Diggins	Carlton	1938-1940
1	3	3	G. Angus	Collingwood	1909-1911
1	1	1	C. Clymo	Geelong	1931
1	1	1	A. Joyce	Hawthorn	1988
1	3	4	J. Nicholls	Carlton	1972-1975
1	1	5	A. Jesaulenko	Carlton	1978-1979
				St. Kilda	1980-1982

1	1	7	A. Jewell	Richmond	1979-1981
				Richmond	1986-1987
				St. Kilda	1983-1984

MOST FINALS APPEARANCES

(Players)

33	M. Tuck	(Hawthorn)	1972-1988
31	G. Coventry	(Collingwood)	1920-1937
29	W. Schimmelbusch	(Nth. Melbourne)	1973-1987
	B. Doull	(Carlton)	1969-1986
	L. Matthews	(Hawthorn)	1971-1985
28	W. Hutchinson	(Essendon)	1942-1957
27	H. Collier	(Collingwood)	1926-1939
	R.S. Reynolds	(Essendon)	1940-1951
	K. Bartlett	(Richmond)	1965-1983
26	A. Collier	(Collingwood)	1926-1939
25	R. McGregor	(Carlton)	1905-1919
	D. Dench	(Nth. Melbourne)	1974-1983
24	B. Crosswell	(Carlton/Nth. Melbourne)	1968-1980
	R. Eade	(Hawthorn)	1976-1987
23	R. Barassi Jnr.	(Melbourne/Carlton)	1954-1968
	J. Titus	(Richmond)	1927-1942
	J. Dyer	(Richmond)	1931-1947
	F. Bourke	(Richmond)	1967-1980
	J. Nicholls	(Carlton)	1959-1973
	A. Jesaulenko	(Carlton)	1967-1979
	P. Jones	(Carlton)	1967-1979
22	W.H. Lee	(Collingwood)	1906-1922
	F. Adams	(Melbourne)	1954-1964
	R. Kink	(Collingwood/Essendon)	1973-1985
	L. Thompson	(Collingwood)	1965-1978
	G. Cowton	(Nth. Melbourne/Footscray)	1974-1983
	B. Davis	(Essendon/Nth. Melbourne)	1962-1975
	R. Byrne	(Carlton/Collingwood/Geelong)	1973-1982
	M. Blight	(Nth. Melbourne)	1974-1982
	R. DiPierdomenico	(Hawthorn)	1970-1988
21	C. Dibbs	(Collingwood)	1925-1935
	K. Greig	(Nth. Melbourne)	1974-1983
	S. Coventry	(Collingwood)	1925-1934
	H. Lambert	(Essendon)	1940-1951
	W. Picken	(Collingwood/Swans)	1974-1986
	A. Kyne	(Collingwood)	1935-1948
	R. Shaw	(Collingwood)	1974-1981
	M. Maclure	(Carlton)	1974-1986
	C. Mew	(Hawthorn)	1982-1988
	G. Ayres	(Hawthorn)	1978-1988
	D. Brereton	(Hawthorn)	1982-1988
20	R. Clay	(Richmond)	1967-1975
	K. Moore	(Hawthorn)	1971-1984
	P. Moore	(Collingwood/Melbourne)	1974-1987
	G. Southby	(Carlton)	1971-1984
	R. Greene	(Hawthorn)	1978-1988

UMPIRES

39	J. Elder
35	I. Robinson*
23	J. McMurray Snr.
	K. Smith*
20	W. Deller*
19	R. Sawers*
18	R. Scott
17	P. Cameron*
16	J. McMurray Snr.
15	J. Couch
	I. Crapp
14	W. Blackburn
	E. Hawkins
12	N. Nash*
10	A. Nash
	A. Nordern
	G. James*

*Some games umpired under 2-umpire system.

UMPIRED ALL FINALS IN A SEASON

1909-1910-1911-1912-1913	J. Elder
1914	H. Rawle
1917	A. Nordern
1920 and 1922	J. Elder
1925 and 1928	J. McMurray Snr.
1929-1930	R. Scott
1936 and 1938	W. Blackburn
1943-1944	E. Hawkins
1957	A. Nash

Since the introduction of the final five in 1972, two games have been played on the one day, making it impossible to umpire all finals in a series. However, the following umpires have had charge of a game on each day of the finals —

1976	K. Smith
1978	I. Robinson

WINNING CAPTAINS

4 S.A. Coventry (Collingwood) 1927-1930
R.S. Reynolds (Essendon) 1942-46-49-50

LOSING CAPTAINS

4 R.S. Reynolds (Essendon) 1941-43-47-48
(Reynolds, then non-playing coach, made a comeback for the losing 1951 grand final but was not captain on the day.)

MOST GRAND FINALS AS CAPTAIN

9 R.S. Reynolds (Essendon) 1941-1950
(won 4, lost 4, tied 1).
All were as playing coach.

MOST WINS — PLAYER AND/OR COACH

Player	*Coach*	*Total*	
6	4	10	R. Barassi (Melbourne/Carlton/Nth. Melbourne) 1953-1985
4	6	10	N. Smith (Melbourne/Fitzroy/Sth. Melbourne) 1935-1972
1	8	9	J. McHale (Collingwood) 1903-1950
2	5	7	F.V. Hughes (Richmond/Melbourne) 1919-1948

MOST LOSSES

Player

6 R. Kink Collingwood/Essendon 1977-83
(inc. 2 grand finals in 1977)
5 and one tie W. Hutchinson Essendon 1942-1957
5 and one tie R. Reynolds Essendon 1941-1951
(inc. 2 grand finals in 1948)

Coach

9 J. McHale (Collingwood) 1913-1950
7 (and one tie) R. Reynolds (Essendon) 1939-1960

Player and/or Coach

11 J. McHale (Collingwood) 1903-1950

MOST GOALS IN ALL FINALS

112	G. Coventry	(Collingwood)	1920-37
74	J. Titus	(Richmond)	1927-42
71	L. Matthews	(Hawthorn)	1971-84
64	D. Wade	(Geelong/Nth. Melbourne)	1962-75
62	K. Bartlett	(Richmond)	1967-82
62	J. Mueller	(Melbourne)	1936-50
62	W.H. Lee	(Collingwood)	1906-22
55	R. Todd	(Collingwood)	1935-39
53	H. Vallence	(Carlton)	1927-38
51	R.S. Reynolds	(Essendon)	1940-51

MOST GOALS IN ONE FINALS SERIES

23	R. Todd	(Collingwood)	1939
21	K. Bartlett	(Richmond)	1980
20	J. Mueller	(Melbourne)	1948
	H. Vallence	(Carlton)	1932
18	R. Todd	(Collingwood)	1938
	J. Mueller	(Melbourne)	1946

FIRST VFL GAME IN A FINAL

W. Stranger	Collingwood	Semi-Final	1897
C. Campbell	Essendon	Semi-Final	1897
G. Cochrane	Essendon	Semi-Final	1897
D. Ferguson	Essendon	Semi-Final	1897
E.G.S. Greeves	Geelong	Semi-Final	1897
F.M. Sheahan	Melbourne	Semi-Final	1897
J.H. Prout	Essendon	Grand Final	1908
R. Sharp	Richmond	First Semi-Final	1916
M. Beasy	Carlton	Second Semi-Final	1920
W. James	Richmond	Grand Final	1920
G. Rawle	Essendon	Grand Final	1923
C. Chapman	Fitzroy	Second Final	1924
J. Harris	Sth. Melbourne	Third Final	1924
G.H. Miller	Sth. Melbourne	Third Final	1924
F.S. Vine	Melbourne	Grand Final	1926
J. Williamson	Geelong	First Semi-Final (Reserve)	1933
R. Barassi Snr.	Melbourne	First Semi-Final (First full game)	1936
E.J. Tuohill	Geelong	Preliminary Final	1938
S. Silk	Essendon	Preliminary Final (Reserve)	1941
Don Cordner	Melbourne	Second Semi-Final	1941
R. Hay	Richmond	Second Semi-Final	1942
R. Bywater	Sth. Melbourne	First Semi-Final	1942
A. Wilson	Carlton	First Semi-Final (First full game)	1943
R. Jones	Collingwood	Second Semi-Final (First full game)	1946
J. Parker	Collingwood	Preliminary Final (First full game)	1951
K. Batchelor	Collingwood	Grand Final	1952
V. Williams	Fitzroy	First Semi-Final (First full game)	1952
K. Rose	Collingwood	Preliminary Final (First full game)	1958
M. Sankey	Carlton	Preliminary Final (First full game)	1959
M. Collins	Melbourne	Second Semi-Final (First full game)	1961
L. Thompson	Collingwood	Preliminary Final	1965
T. Payze	St. Kilda	Second Semi-Final (Reserve)	1966
G. Dunstan	Collingwood	First Semi-Final	1972
I. Cooper	Collingwood	First Semi-Final (First full game)	1972
I. Corner	St. Kilda	Preliminary Final (First full game)	1972
R. Kink	Collingwood	Preliminary Final (First full game)	1973

N. Carter	Richmond	Preliminary Final (First full game)	1973
V. Cattogio	Carlton	Grand Final (First full game)	1973
K. Steele	Hawthorn	Preliminary Final (First full game)	1974
M. Cooke	Hawthorn	Second Semi-Final	1975
N. Lovell	Collingwood	Preliminary Final	1981
D. Brereton	Hawthorn	First Semi-Final	1982

DETAILS OF FINALS MATCHES

Elimination Final 1972-1988

Equal Highest Score: Melbourne 22.26 (158) v. Nth. Melbourne 5.10 (40), 1987; St. Kilda 24.14 (158) v. Essendon 13.13 (91), 1973.
Lowest Score: Nth. Melbourne 5.10 (50) v. Melbourne 22.26 (158), 1987.
Highest winning margin: 118 points — Melbourne 22.26 (158) v. Nth. Melbourne 5.10 (40), 1987.
Lowest winning margin: 1 point — Fitzroy 8.10 (58) v. Essendon 8.9 (57), 1986.
Highest Aggregate: 260 points — Collingwood 23.15 (153) v. Fitzroy 15.17 (107).
Highest Attendance: 82,952 (1980) Nth. Melbourne v. Collingwood.
Lowest Attendance: 43,438 (1988) Melbourne v. West Coast Eagles.
Best Goalscorers: 7 — P. McKenna (Collingwood), 1974; 6 — G. Young (St. Kilda), 1973, M. Williams (Collingwood), 1984.

Qualifying Final 1972-1988

Highest Score: 25.14 (164) by Richmond v. Collingwood, 18.12 (120), 1972.
Lowest Score: 8.9 (57) by Swans v. Hawthorn, 23.18 (156), 1987.
Lowest winning margin: 4 points — Hawthorn 19.13 (127) v. Fitzroy 19.9 (123), 1983.
Highest winning margin: 99 points — Hawthorn 23.18 (156) v. Swans 8.9 (57), 1987.
Highest Aggregate: 284 points — Richmond 25.14 (164) v. Collingwood 18.12 (120), 1972.
Highest Attendance: 91,000 — Richmond v. Collingwood, 1972.
Lowest Attendance: 47,752 — Hawthorn v. Swans, 1987.
Best Goalscorers: 8 — W. Ralph (Carlton), 1984. M. Moncrieff (Hawthorn), 1978. B. Quinlan (Fitzroy), 1983. 7 — L. Matthews (Hawthorn), 1976. J. Mossop (Geelong), 1981. 6 — L. Matthews (Hawthorn), 1984. K. Bartlett (Richmond), 1980. R. Ditchburn (Carlton), 1982. R. Hart (Richmond), 1972. P. Knights (Hawthorn), 1983.

First Semi-Final 1931-1988

Highest Score: Richmond 25.17 (167) v. Geelong 7.7 (49), 1969.
Lowest Score: Essendon 5.11 (41) v. Footscray 6.13 (49), 1953.
Highest winning margin: 118 points — Richmond 25.17 (167) v. Geelong 1.7 (49), 1969.
Lowest winning margin: 1 point — Collingwood 19.19 (133) v. Fitzroy 19.18 (132), 1981.

Highest Aggregate: 280 points — Hawthorn 24.22 (166) v. North Melbourne 18.6 (114), 1982.
Highest Attendance: 104,239 — St. Kilda v. Sth. Melbourne, 1970.
Lowest Attendance: 1945 — at Carlton — 41,305.
Best Goalscorers: 11 — H. Vallence (Carlton), 1931. 8 — L. Collins (Carlton), 1945; W. Twomey (Collingwood), 1948; D. Wade (Geelong), 1967.

Second Semi-Final 1931-1988

Highest Score: Geelong 22.20 (152) v. Collingwood 10.10 (70), 1951.
Lowest Score: Collingwood 4.9 (33) v. Melbourne 11.12 (78), 1958.
Highest winning margin: 89 points — Melbourne 19.20 (134) v. Collingwood 6.9 (45), 1964.
Lowest winning margin: 1 point — St. Kilda 13.24 (102) v. Collingwood 14.17 (101), 1965.
Highest Aggregate: 242 points — Richmond 20.21 (141) v. Carlton 14.17 (101), 1967.
Highest Attendance: 112,838 — Collingwood v. Carlton, 1970.
Lowest Attendance: 35,934 in 1934.
Drawn Games: Essendon 14.16 drew with Collingwood 13.22. Essendon won play off in 1946. Carlton 8.13 drew with Richmond (VFL Park) 1972. Richmond won replay.
Postponements — August 24, 1918, because of rain. Following week, 35,855 saw Sth. Melbourne 8.10 defeat Carlton 7.11.
Best Goalscorers: 11 — G. Goninon (Geelong), 1951. 9 — P. McKenna (Collingwood), 1970, 8 — J. Metherell (Geelong), 1937, K. Baxter (Carlton), 1938, A. Jesaulenko (Carlton), 1970. K. Bartlett (Richmond), 1980.

Preliminary Final 1931-1987

Highest Score: Essendon 28.6 (174) v. Collingwood 5.11 (41), 1984.
Lowest Score: Footscray 5.7 (37) v. Geelong 8.15 (63), 1953.
Highest winning margin: 133 points — Essendon 28.6 (174) v. Collingwood 5.11 (41), 1984.
Lowest winning margin: 1 point — Nth. Melbourne 10.7 (67) v. Carlton 9.12 (66).
Highest Aggregate: 242 points — Essendon 25.14 (164) v. Nth. Melbourne 12.6 (78), 1983.
Highest Attendance: 108,215 — Carlton v. St. Kilda, 1970.
Lowest Attendance: 1934, when only 34,000 saw match because of bad weather.
Drawn Games: Carlton 12.13 drew with Geelong 13.7 in 1962. Carlton won the play-off but lost Grand Final to Essendon.
Best Goalscorers: 11 — H. Vallence (Carlton), 1932. 11 — R. Todd (Collingwood), 1938 and 1939. 9 — L. White (Sth. Melbourne), 1942; J. Dyer (Richmond), 1944.

Grand Final 1931-1987

Highest Score: Carlton 28.9 (177) v. Richmond, 1972.
Lowest Score: Collingwood 2.2 (14) v. Melbourne, 1960.
Highest Aggregate: 327 points. Carlton 28.9 (177), Richmond 22.18 (150), 1972.

Greatest winning margin: 83 points — Hawthorn 20.20 (140) v. Essendon 8.9 (57), 1983.
Lowest winning margin: 1 point — Carlton 13.8 (86) v. Essendon 11.19 (85), 1947; St. Kilda 10.14 (74) v. Collingwood 10.13 (73), 1966.
Drawn Games: Essendon 7.27 v. Melbourne 10.9, 1948; Collingwood 10.16 v. Nth. Melbourne 9.22, 1977.
Highest Attendance: 121,696 — Carlton v. Collingwood, 1970.
Lowest Attendance: 42,100 in 1943.
Postponements — The 1923 match was postponed one week because the MCG was waterlogged. Essendon 8.15 (63) defeated Fitzroy 6.10 (46).
Best Goalscorers: 8 to D. Brereton (Hawthorn), 1985; 7 each to N. Smith (Melbourne), 1940; R. Harris (Richmond), 1943; T. Reynolds (Essendon), 1943; G. Lane (Essendon), 1946; J. Collins (Footscray), 1954; E. Fordham (Essendon), 1965; A. Jesaulenko (Carlton), 1972; K. Bartlett (Richmond), 1980, J. Dunstall (Hawthorn), 1988.

QUARTER SCORING RECORDS 1879-1987

Elimination Final

1st Qr.	— 9.4	Fitzroy	v. Essendon	1979
2nd Qr.	— 7.3	Carlton	v. Nth. Melbourne	1985
3rd Qr.	— 7.5	Melbourne	v. Nth. Melbourne	1987
4th Qr.	— 10.7	Collingwood	v. Fitzroy	1984

Qualifying Final

1st Qr.	— 7.3	Carlton	v. Collingwood	1988
2nd Qr.	— 8.4	Collingwood	v. Carlton	1988
3rd Qr.	— 11.4	Carlton	v. Hawthorn	1982
4th Qr.	— 8.5	Hawthorn	v. Collingwood	1978

1st Semi Final

1st Qr.	— 8.5	Collingwood	v. Sth. Melbourne	1932
2nd Qr.	— 8.9	Melbourne	v. Swans	1987
3rd Qr.	— 8.4	Fitzroy	v. Geelong	1923
4th Qr.	— 9.7	Carlton	v. Collingwood	1931

2nd Semi Final

1st Qr.	— 7.5	Melbourne	v. Carlton	1941
2nd Qr.	— 9.3	Essendon	v. Melbourne	1957
3rd Qr.	— 8.3	Sth. Melbourne	v. Collingwood	1945
4th Qr.	— 9.6	Geelong	v. Collingwood	1951

Preliminary Final

1st Qr.	— 8.2	Richmond	v. Essendon	1944
		Essendon	v. Nth. Melbourne	1983
2nd Qr.	— 9.5	Essendon	v. Collingwood	1984
3rd Qr.	— 10.7	Carlton	v. Collingwood	1932
4th Qr.	— 8.4	Essendon	v. Nth. Melbourne	1983

Grand Final

1st Qr.	— 8.4	Carlton	v. Richmond	1972
2nd Qr.	— 10.2	Carlton	v. Richmond	1972
3rd Qr.	— 11.8	Essendon	v. Melbourne	1946
4th Qr.	— 11.3	Essendon	v. Hawthorn	1985

Other high scoring quarters —
10.2 in 3rd Nth. Melbourne v. Collingwood Qualifying Final 1979
10.1 in 4th St. Kilda v. Essendon Elimination Final 1972
9.6 in 4th Essendon v. Hawthorn Grand Final 1984

RESERVE GRADE PREMIERSHIPS

1919-20	Collingwood
1921	Essendon
1922	Collingwood
1923-24	Geelong
1925	Collingwood
1926-27-28	Carlton
1929	Richmond
1930	Geelong
1931-32-33-34-35	Melbourne
1936	Footscray
1937-38	Geelong
1939	Melbourne
1940	Collingwood
1941	Essendon
1942-43	St. Kilda
1944	Fitzroy
1945	Footscray
1946	Richmond
1947	Nth. Melbourne
1948	Geelong
1949	Melbourne
1950	Essendon
1951	Carlton
1952	Essendon
1953	Carlton
1945-55	Richmond
1956	Melbourne
1957	Nth. Melbourne
1958-59	Hawthorn
1960	Geelong
1961	St. Kilda
1962	Footscray
1963-64	Geelong
1965	Collingwood
1966	Richmond
1967	Nth. Melbourne
1968	Essendon
1969-70	Melbourne
1971	Richmond

1972	Hawthorn
1973	Richmond
1974	Fitzroy
1975	Geelong
1976	Collingwood
1977	Richmond
1978	Nth. Melbourne
1979	Nth. Melbourne
1980	Geelong
1981	Geelong
1982	Geelong
1983	Essendon
1984	Melbourne
1985	Hawthorn
1986	Carlton
1987	Carlton
1988	Footscray